The Fall of Hong Kong

The Fall of Hong Kong

Britain, China and the Japanese Occupation

Philip Snow

Yale University Press
New Haven and London

The author and publishers gratefully acknowledge the permission granted by A. P. Watt
Ltd on behalf of the National Trust for Places of Historical Interest or Natural Beauty to
reprint lines from Rudyard Kipling's 'The English Flag' and 'The Song of the Cities' and
by the Han Suyin Trust to reprint an extract from *Love is a Many-Splendoured Thing* by
Han Suyin. 'Hong Kong', copyright © 1976 by Edward Mendelson, William Meredith and
Monroe K. Spears, Executors of the Estate of W. H. Auden., from *W. H. Auden: The
Collected Poems* by W. H. Auden is quoted by kind permission of Random House, Inc.
and Faber and Faber.

Photographs are reproduced by permission of the Government of the Hong Kong SAR
from the collection of the Hong Kong Museum of History; the Public Records Office,
Government Records Service Division, Hong Kong; the Imperial War Museum, London;
The Hongkong and Shanghai Banking Corporation Ltd; Heinemann/Harcourt Education
Ltd; FormAsia Books Ltd; Dr Mary Seed; Colonel Oliver Lindsay; and the South China
Morning Post Ltd.

For information about this and other Yale University Press publications, please contact:
U.S. Office: sales.press@yale.edu   yalebooks.com
Europe Office: sales@yaleup.co.uk   www.yaleup.co.uk

Set in Minion by SNP Best-set Typesetter Ltd, Hong Kong
Printed in China through Worldprint

Library of Congress Cataloging-in-Publication Data

Snow, Philip.
    The fall of Hong Kong: Britain, China and the
Japanese occupation / Philip Snow.
        p.   cm.
Includes bibliographical references and index.
    ISBN 0–300–09352–7 (hbk.)
    ISBN 0–300–10373–5 (pbk.)
    1. Hong Kong (China)—History—Siege, 1941.   2. Hong Kong (China)—History—
Transfer of sovereignty from Great Britain, 1997.   I. Title.
DS796.H74 S64   2003
940.53′5125—dc21   2002155540

A catalogue record for this book is available from the British Library.

10 9 8 7 6 5 4 3 2 1

For Amanda

animae dimidium meae

The East Wind roared: 'From the Kuriles, the Bitter Seas, I come,
And me men call the Home-Wind, for I bring the English home.
Look – look well to your shipping! By the breath of my mad typhoon
I swept your close-packed Praya and beached your best at Kowloon!'

Kipling, 'The English Flag'

Contents

Illustrations

Plates

Maps

Acknowledgements

This book took years longer than I had ever anticipated. I am all the more grateful to those institutions and individuals whose support has enabled me to see it through.

The research for the book was made possible by the generous backing of two bodies. The Leverhulme Trust sponsored my original research visit to Hong Kong in 1994–5, plus a short but important side trip to Taiwan. The British Academy arranged for me to complement this by spending ten weeks in Japan in the summer of 1995.

Professor Glen Dudbridge of the University of Oxford and Professor Ralph Smith of the School of Oriental and African Studies, University of London encouraged my project from the start and gave support and advice when I needed it most.

Many archivists and librarians helped my investigations with kindness and efficiency. I remember especially the staff of the Public Record Office at Kew, London; of the Hong Kong Public Record Office, the Hung On-to Memorial Library of Hong Kong University and the Hong Kong Police Archive; of the Museum of Military History in Taipei and the Nationalist Party archives at Yangmingshan; of the Office of the Historian at the State Department in Washington DC and the National Archives of Canada.

Many people shared with me their recollections of wartime events in Hong Kong and of the repercussions of those events in more recent decades. They included, in the United Kingdom, the late Professor Charles Boxer and the late Miss Emily Hahn, Mrs Margaret Watson Sloss and Mrs Mary Goodban; in Hong Kong, Sir Y. K. Kan, Dr Stanley Ho, Mr Y. K. Chan, formerly of Jardine Matheson and Co., Mme Cai Songying, formerly of the East River Column, the late Mr Andrew Choa, Mr Rusy M. Shroff, the Hon. W. S. Lau, Mr Charles Sin, Mr Y. Yanagisawa of the Nishimatsu Corporation, Mr Cyril Kotewall and Mrs Helen Zimmern. For most of them the war years were not pleasant ones to reflect on, and I deeply appreciate the trouble they took to talk to me.

Over the years I have benefited from a wide range of more informal conversations. Dr Steve Tsang and Dr David Faure of the Institute for Chinese Studies at Oxford and Mr S. J. Chan, formerly of the Hong Kong Government, gave me insights into topics ranging from the impact of the Japanese occupation in the New Territories to the post-war British reform drive of 1945–7. Other helpful ideas came from Miss Clare Hollingworth, Sir Jack Cater, the late Lady May Ride, the late Professor Leonard Rayner, Professor Ian Nish of the London School of Economics, Sir Sydney Giffard, former British ambassador to Tokyo, the late Mr Andrew Tu, Mr Dan Waters, Ms Maybo Ching and Mr James Lee.

Dr Graham Healey of the University of Sheffield helped me to acquire a reading knowledge of Japanese, sensibly picking out texts that would contribute to the project. He personally arranged for me to spend a month at International House in Tokyo during my visit in 1995. When the book was nearing completion he checked my translations from Japanese sources and responded swiftly and kindly to constant queries. Without Graham Healey there could have been no Japanese dimension to this book.

My visit to Japan was generously supported by the Japan Society for the Promotion of Science, who handled the arrangements in Tokyo. I received major help from Professor Nakahara Michiko of Waseda University who not only organized a number of valuable meetings but also arranged my acceptance as a Visiting Scholar at her university, enabling me to analyse my findings in a peaceful office. Professor Kobayashi Hideo of Komazawa University, who is probably Japan's leading expert on the war years in Hong Kong, introduced me to the policy debates which took place within the Imperial Army over the fate of the newly conquered colony. Other useful guidelines were provided by Professor Nakajima Mineo and by Professor Shoji Junichiro of the National Institute for Defense Studies. Professor Sanada Iwasuke of the Institute of Developing Economies and Mr Komari Yasuo, former general manager of Mitsui Bussan (Hong Kong) passed on the experiences of this major company and of its long-time representative in the colony, Mr Fujita Ichiro. I was fortunate enough to spend an afternoon with Mr Oda Takeo, the wartime head of the Foreign Affairs Department in occupied Hong Kong, and also had a useful discussion with Mr Okada Akira, former Japanese consul-general in Hong Kong and chairman of the Japan-Hong Kong Society.

My short spell in Taipei was made more productive by the hospitality of Mr Wang Nai-bin and the contacts made for me by Dr and Mrs C. K. Hsu of the Institute of Ethnology, Academia Sinica.

Over the years books and articles of great importance were supplied or recommended to me by Dr Robert Bickers of Bristol University, Professor John Hamilton of Aichi University, Nagoya, Mr Tse Wing-kwong, Mr Joe Carle, Dr

John Weste of Durham University, the Revd and Mrs David Evans, Mrs Bernice Archer, Ms Cheng Sea-ling, Mr Mark Tse and Mr Bob Locking.

My old friend and teacher Mr Tang Tien-chung helped me grapple with the more difficult linguistic points of a wartime Chinese memoir. Ms Louise Cater read a large number of the transcribed Japanese MAGIC documents which I was unable to access for geographical reasons, and Mr Hamamoto Ryoichi of *Yomiuri Shimbun* provided some useful data on post-war Japanese business in Hong Kong.

Valuable introductions and other help were provided by Mrs Olive Mackenzic, Ms Rosemary Yates, Ms Sarah Noble and Mr John Dolfin, by Max and Sophie Ruston of the Voice of America, by Sir John Boyd, former British ambassador to Tokyo and by my sister Lindsay Avebury and my old friends Nicolas Maclean and Robert Lloyd George. Mr Nicholas Bradbury and Mrs Jo Steed gave me shelter at different times from the construction noise that is the nightmare of any writer. And Touchmedia cartographers made the book more accessible by providing a series of maps.

None of the foregoing are responsible in any way for my interpretations but all have my thanks.

With the best will in the world I have no doubt overlooked some major helpers; and to them I can only say that my gratitude has outlasted my memory. But the following I could not forget.

Mrs Maria Ellis typed countless drafts of the chapters and notes with unfailing efficiency. As always her contribution consisted of much more than typing, and her cheerful expressions of interest did much to revive my flagging morale.

My agent Peter Robinson of Curtis Brown and his colleague Sam Copeland were always ready with guidance at difficult times and swift responses to urgent enquiries.

My editor Robert Baldock at Yale University Press was patient, courteous and sensitive throughout the whole gestation of the work. Even at times when he must have despaired of its completion he never permitted himself more than the gentlest of nudges; a forbearance which spared me great strain. In the final months Diana Yeh worked with wonderful accuracy on the copy-editing, and both she and her colleague Sarah Hulbert made helpful suggestions for improving the text. Kevin Brown designed the entire volume and organized the production to meet the demands of a fearsomely tight schedule. I am also grateful for the efforts of Candida Brazil, Kate Pocock and Jacob Lehman.

My friend and former editor Linden Lawson painstakingly worked her way through an early draft and gave crucial advice on the structure, and much needed encouragement. My old friends Rose Heatley of Chatham House and Adam Williams of Jardines read a more advanced draft and improved it with their profound knowledge of Hong Kong and abiding good sense.

Connie Aliban looked after my home and family cheerfully and industriously throughout the making of the book and kept my study in order.

My three young children Renata, Alexander and Isabella withstood gallantly the toll which the book exacted on family life, in the last grim year in particular.

As for my wife Amanda, she bore all and did all. Comforter in the darkest moments, source of wise counsel at doubtful turning-points, calm organizer amid a host of conflicting tasks, she was everything I could ever have asked for. No mere acknowledgement could express all I owe to her in the completion of this book, but the dedication I have made to her tries to say something.

Philip Snow
Hong Kong
February 2003

Note on Romanization

1. Chinese names

The choice is to be inconsistent or bewildering. I have preferred on the whole to use romanizations familiar to the reader, even if this means a slight sacrifice of consistency.

(A) PERSONAL NAMES

With mainland Chinese names I have as a rule followed the *pinyin* system of romanization which is now in general use. I have, however, made exceptions in the cases of certain persons who were prominent in the pre-1949 period, and whose names have long been familiar in an older form. Examples are Sun Yat-sen, Chiang Kai-shek, T. V. Soong, H. H. Kung.

With Hong Kong Chinese names I have used the established Cantonese forms, for example Kwok Chan, Ip Lan-chuen, Ts'o Seen-wan. Every so often, however, I have come across a name in a Chinese source only and have been unable to establish the Cantonese rendering. Under these circumstances I have resorted to *pinyin*. Many Hong Kong Chinese prefer to put their names in the Western order, with the given name first and the family name second, and in these cases I have respected their preference. Examples are Sir Shouson Chow, M. K. Lo, Paul Tsui.

(B) PLACE NAMES

I have used *pinyin* for most mainland Chinese places, but have preferred to retain the traditional forms in the case of Peking, Nanking, Chungking and Canton. Peking presented a special problem in that it was widely known in the Second World War period by the Chinese Nationalist name of Peip'ing (Beiping). I decided that to resurrect this extinct name would be needlessly confusing for the reader. I have, however, preserved one or two names as they appear in contemporary documents, using for instance the Japanese form Dairen for the north-eastern Chinese city of Dalian that was controlled by Japan throughout the wartime years. Places inside Hong Kong territory I have rendered without exception in their familiar Cantonese spellings.

2.   *Japanese names*

Japanese personal names like Chinese ones are properly written with the family name first and the given name second. I have followed this practice throughout the book: thus the first Japanese Governor of wartime Hong Kong appears as Isogai Rensuke rather than Rensuke Isogai.

Glossary

catty (Malay/Javanese)	a weight of 1⅓ lb
comprador (Portuguese)	agent employed by European trading houses to negotiate with Chinese firms
congee (Anglo-Indian)	a thin rice gruel
godown (Anglo-Indian)	warehouse
nullah (Anglo-Indian)	storm drain
praya (Portuguese)	waterfront, embankment
pukka (Anglo-Indian)	genuine, out-and-out
rickshaw (Japanese)	two-wheeled hooded vehicle drawn by a man
sampan (Chinese)	small boat
sepoy (Anglo-Indian)	Indian soldier serving under British command
squeeze	exaction made by Asian official
taipan (Chinese)	big boss; term used for the head of a Western business in Hong Kong or China proper
tiffin (Anglo-Indian)	lunch
typhoon (Chinese)	hurricane
yuan (Chinese)	Chinese dollar

Area occupied by Japanese
forces at the beginning of
December 1941

Key
① SENKAKU
  (Diaoyu)
  ISLANDS (Japan)
② PESCADORE
  ISLANDS (Japan)
③ Xingning
④ MACAO (Port.)
⑤ GUANGZHOU-
  WAN (France)
⑥ HAINAN
  ISLAND

SOVIET UNION

Kurile Islands

Nomonhan

OUTER
MONGOLIA

MANCHURIA

CHAHAR
JEHOL
Peking   KOREA   Tokyo
Tianjin   Yokohama
Yan'an   Dairen   JAPANESE
       Jinan   Port   Osaka EMPIRE
CHINA Taierzhuang Arthur Fukuoka Hiroshima
TIBET SICHUAN   SHANDONG Nagasaki PACIFIC
       PROV. Nanking   PROV.   OCEAN
PUNJAB   Hankou   Shanghai
       Chungking   ZHEJIANG
Amritsar   Yangtze River PROV.
                                    SAIPAN
RAJPUTANA Delhi Changsha Nanxiong ①   ISLAND
NEPAL   Qujiang ③ Xiamen   (Japan)
       Kunming Guilin Canton ② TAIWAN
BRITISH INDIA Wuzhou GUANG- DONG (Formosa)
       GUANGXI PROV. ④ HONG
Calcutta PROV. ⑤ ⑥ KONG
BURMA   (Br.) Subic Bay
       THAILAND FRENCH Manila PHILIPPINE ADMIRALTY
       (SIAM) INDOCHINA   ISLANDS ISLANDS
       Bangkok   South   (US)
                      China   NORTH   NEW
              Sea   BORNEO   GUINEA
       Trincomalee   (Br.)
Kandy CEYLON   MALAYA SARAWAK
Panadura (Br.) (Br.) Singapore
                       (Br.)

DUTCH EAST INDIES   AUSTRALIA

1. East Asia, 1941

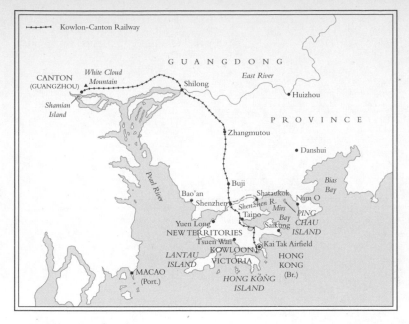

2. Hong Kong and environs, 1941

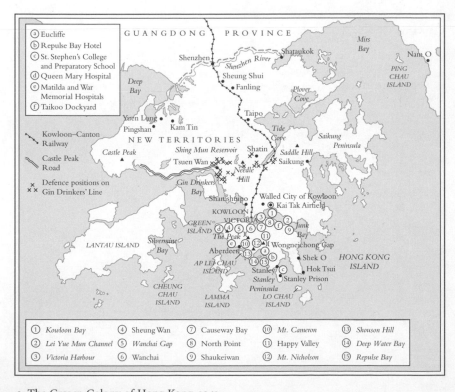

3. The Crown Colony of Hong Kong, 1941

4. City of Victoria, 1941
© Crown Copyright 1939–45/MOD

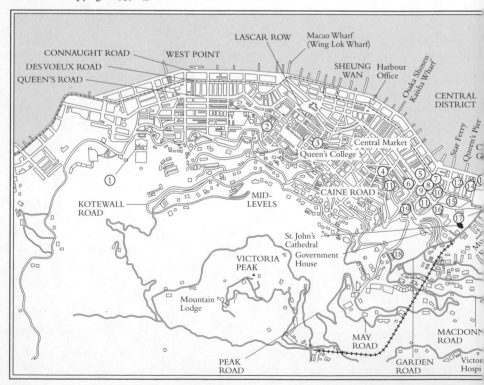

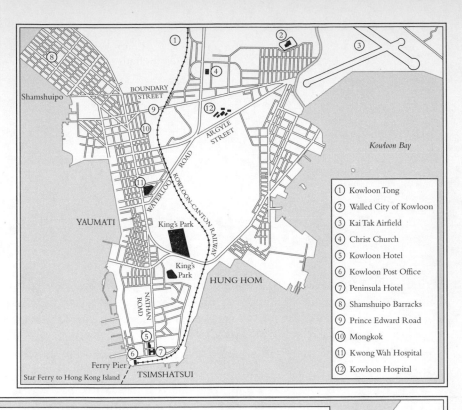
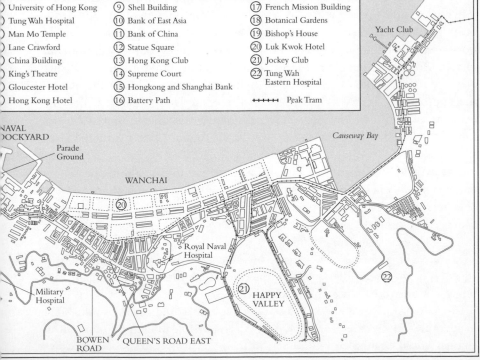

Introduction

At midnight on 30 June 1997 the trading colony of Hong Kong was restored to China after just over one hundred and fifty years of British rule. With the return of Macao, the small Portuguese settlement on the other side of the Pearl River delta that followed as an afterthought two years later, the handover of Hong Kong put an end to the last remains of five centuries of European over-lordship in Asia.

British Hong Kong had been a long time dying. It had lasted over a generation longer than Britain's other possessions on the continent – fifty years longer than India, forty years longer than Malaya. And its demise had not been heralded, as theirs were, by dramatic events, Gandhi's campaign of non-violence or the Emergency in the Malayan jungles, but by a humdrum question of land tenure. In 1898 the colony had acquired a hinterland, the New Territories, under the terms of a ninety-nine year lease; and it was the approaching expiry of the lease on this hinterland, without which the original core of the colony was no longer remotely sustainable, that in the end forced the British to sign the colony over in the Anglo-Chinese Joint Declaration of 1984.

The extinction of British rule in Hong Kong had thus in a sense been prepared at the very height of Victorian grandeur. But the outcome had not always been seen as inevitable. Doubts had been raised in Whitehall about the colony's prospects without the New Territories as early as the 1920s. But this had not stopped bold officials from making suggestions of ways in which the hinterland might be grafted on to the core of the colony on a permanent basis. It was only at the end of the 1950s that the celebrated phrase began to gain currency – 'A borrowed place on borrowed time'.[1]

From an historian's angle this raised the question, could any clear watershed be identified in the case of Hong Kong? Was it possible to define a moment of change (social, political, economic) at which the British grip slipped irretrievably – a twist in events after which the colony's long-term fate was both certain, and seen to be certain? The history of Hong Kong in the twentieth century did not, at first glance, lend itself to such pinpointing. The dominant pattern seemed to be one of uneventful money-making, punctuated by the occasional outbreak of strikes or riots.

There had indeed been a phase when the British lost control of Hong Kong altogether. In December 1941 the colony had been wrenched from British hands by the Imperial Japanese Army, who proceeded to manage it for their own purposes for almost four years. But conventional wisdom insisted that this episode, while dramatic, did not ultimately matter very much. In August 1945 the British had returned and had taken up the threads where they had left off four years earlier; and life had carried on pretty much as before. Major developments, it was asserted, took place only in the late 1940s and early 1950s, when the colony acquired a whole new population in flight from war and revolution on the Chinese mainland. It was then that Hong Kong plunged into the industrial take-off which made it the gleaming metropolis we know today. Any changes which might have taken place as a result of the Second World War were buried beneath this post-war avalanche.

The impact of the huge events of the post-war decade could scarcely be questioned. Yet they did not quite seem to represent the whole truth. Scattered here and there in the conventional chorus were one or two gently discordant voices. One authority suggested that the 'British Mandarinate', whatever that might mean, had come to an end in the war and had not been replaced.[2] Another referred to the pre-war and post-war parts of the Hong Kong story – 'so very unalike'.[3] It seemed possible at least that something had happened in those wartime years, between Britain and China, between the British and the Chinese inside the colony, which would repay closer scrutiny. But all this led into the murky waters of wartime occupation.

For most of the sixty years that have now elapsed since the end of the Second World War accounts of life in the territories occupied by the Axis have been painted in simple colours. Brutality and terror; collaboration and resistance; joyous liberation followed by the well-deserved punishment of the wicked and the reward of the brave. In many ways such portrayals are both natural and altogether right. Treachery and heroism, hideous cruelty and unspeakable suffering were all in evidence, and any account that attempts to look beyond these phenomena risks seeming to belittle them. Recent scholarship has none the less begun to demonstrate that the truth was more complex, and that in between these extremes of experience much else went on which has been overlooked. In the Loire valley of France, for example, we now know that the conquering German forces behaved fairly well to begin with, and that the first year of the conquest was characterized by a process of negotiation with local prefects and mayors. The savagery came later, when the war had begun to turn against Germany and control had shifted from the harsh but correct German military government to the Gestapo whose sole object was repression. Local notables did play ball with the Germans, but not in the main out of any appetite for treason: what had happened was rather that the pressures of conquest had narrowed their loyalties, and the desire to take care of their families, towns and regions had come to eclipse any broad sense of national duty. Social life went on vigorously, in forms ranging from charitable endeavours to sports, theatre-going and religious processions, and resistance only took place on the fringe. Liberation was marked by a high degree of administrative continuity. Concerned above all to avert social turmoil, the incoming Free French authorities preferred to leave established local leaders in their place. Dignitaries who had worked with the Germans were on the whole let off lightly, while punishments were reserved for the small fry; and a comforting legend was woven that everyone, with a few very minor exceptions, had been resisters at heart. Much of the picture, in other words, was not so much black and white as shades of grey.[4]

Similar patterns have also begun to emerge from studies and memoirs of the Japanese occupation of parts of East Asia. In newly conquered Shanghai leading Chinese industrialists are said to have sought first and foremost to keep their businesses running. They did not wish to have any more contact with the invaders than was strictly essential, but they were prepared to strike deals providing for their factories to start up again under Japanese auspices. Some of them tried to balance this by sending family members to invest in Chinese Nationalist enterprises in the unoccupied western half of China.[5] In Singapore Mr Lee Kuan Yew, then a young man of eighteen, enrolled in a Japanese language course. Later on he set up as a broker on the black market. The Japanese, he recalls, seemed likely to remain in charge for some years; armed resistance was out of the question; the overriding priority was to survive.[6]

In East Asia, however, the day-to-day expedients of occupation were overlaid by a further complexity. The fact was that many of the territories the Japanese conquered were places already under alien rule. The Japanese claimed to be freeing these places from European tyranny, and it seems clear that their claim met with fairly widespread acceptance at the start. In several parts of the region Indian traders and Indian auxiliary troops in the British service are known to have been fired by the Japanese gospel.[7] Other groups, the Malays or Burmese, seem at least to have been prepared to accept the Japanese in place of the British as an alternative set of patrons. The Chinese on the whole had a different perspective. For several years Japan had been engaged in a naked attempt to subjugate their country that could in no way be prettified by talk of freedom. Yet for the Chinese too, in areas long dominated by Europeans such as the foreign settlements in Shanghai, a deep-seated aversion to Western supremacy is said to have 'complicated the choices of patriots'.[8]

The Japanese as it turned out took a remarkably short time to make themselves loathed by their fellow Asians. Within a few months they had perpetrated all the same sins as the Europeans before them. They commandeered the clubs and mansions and set themselves up as an arrogant, exclusive caste. They peddled opium and fortified their control at the grass roots through corrupt dealings with local criminal networks.[9] And on top of that they repressed any threat to their power with a viciousness rulers which the European had never displayed. But they had none the less by the very fact of their conquest dealt a mortal blow to the prestige of the whites. After the great rolling-back of European power in the region which took place in 1941–2 it was impossible for the local populations to look on their former masters with the same eyes. The new outlook became visible from the moment Japan was defeated in 1945. In Indochina and the East Indies local partisans took up arms to resist the return of the French and the Dutch. In Malaya the guerrillas who had fought the Japanese in the war returned to the jungle to drive out the British. In China, where the European powers had been driven to court the goodwill of their wartime Chinese Nationalist allies by signing away their rights in the old 'treaty ports', the Nationalists who recovered those ports from the Japanese took swift action to show the expatriates that it was they, from now on, who would have the last word.[10]

Occupation by and large means stagnation. The Germans who pulled out of France in the wake of the Normandy landings not only left nothing constructive: they left nothing different. The social discourse which picked up in France in 1944–5 appears to have been much the same as the one which broke off in 1940.[11] In East Asia, however, it seems inescapable that the Japanese conquests, for all the misery they inflicted, had a dynamic effect. The Japanese left behind them societies that were brutalized, desolated – but irreversibly changed.

It was hard to believe that Hong Kong could be an exception to this general East Asian picture. But perhaps because it has been the last place in the region to emerge from formal European tutelage, Hong Kong has also been the last to move beyond the conventional presentation of the war as a self-contained episode, simple, crowned by victory and without any legacy for the future.

The approaches to wartime Hong Kong which have been adopted up to now can be classified into three groups. The first of these approaches is that of the British. Memoirs and histories written by them have explored with admirable thoroughness the European side of the experience: the defence of the colony against the Japanese onslaught in 1941 and the heroic resistance put up by individual Allied units and men, the stoic endurance displayed by the British and other Westerners during nearly four years of harsh captivity in the military and civilian internment camps, the daring escapes, the brave underground work and the savage Japanese reprisals. What they have not done, in any great detail, is examine the fate of the Hong Kong Chinese (98 per cent of the whole population) and the colony's other Asian communities. At most they have devoted a chapter or two out of twelve or fifteen to the lives of the uninterned population in town. And they have made little or no use of Chinese, let alone Japanese, language sources.

The second approach is that of the wealthy Anglicized elite who dominated local Asian society before, during and after the war. Their contribution has been one of profound silence, sustained now for almost six decades. This silence has been a pity insofar as it has obscured not only those aspects of their wartime record that might be thought worthy of criticism but also the genuinely public-spirited side to their role. Of the two memoirs which can be traced to elite families only one describes life in the occupied urban areas in any fullness: the second, by a lady who spent the war alongside the British in the civilian internment camp, broadly follows the British account.[12]

The third approach is to be found in the Chinese-language tradition. This consists partly of memoirs by mainland Chinese journalists and celebrities who left the colony in the early months of the Japanese takeover, and partly of a series of popular histories that have begun to appear in more recent years. These Chinese sources in many ways offer an illuminating corrective to the English-language works. They reveal, for example, the gulf that existed between the wartime circumstances of the Asian elite and those of the Chinese populace: as the caption to a photograph shown at a war exhibition in Hong Kong's City Hall in 1995 phrased the contrast, 'While the rich were pouring money into horse-racing the poor were starving and trembling on the streets'. And they disclose the unspeakable cruelties inflicted on the Chinese populace by the Japanese forces – cruelties far worse in both scale and severity than those endured by most of the British in Hong Kong, grim though the ordeal of the latter undoubtedly was. Yet the Chinese accounts also have their limitations. They tend to overlook the real dilemmas and pressures faced by the local Asian leaders (accounts by the mainlanders are especially scant of charity in this regard). And while emphasizing, quite rightly, the vile misdemeanours committed by many of the Japanese officers and troops they are apt to portray all of the Japanese as uniformly fiendish, ignoring the humanity that was shown by some individuals and the occasional efforts made by the occupation regime to pursue a relatively moderate or constructive line of policy. In this respect it is often the British, with their sense of the challenges facing a fellow imperial power, who come up with a more balanced assessment.

This book represents an attempt to move forward a little by offering a rounded picture of wartime Hong Kong from the viewpoint of all the communities – not just the British but also the Chinese and the various Asian minority groups. Even the Japanese, to the extent that some documents recently published in Japan have made it possible to explore the dissensions among them. The book is not primarily an exercise in praise or blame. Farsighted reformers, courageous partisans, noble altruists all leave a mark on the record. Blinkered troglodytes, venal informers, sadistic torturers are all abundantly present, and their crimes and follies speak for themselves. But the centre ground is occupied, as in most human events, by the day-to-day people – British officials seeking to follow what they perceived as their imperial duty, Chinese and Eurasian businessmen struggling to maintain their position while at the same time doing what they could for the public, humbler Chinese citizens endeavouring to scratch a living in the teeth of famine, Japanese officers trying grumpily to fend off local protests while fulfilling the dictates of their war machine. What the book does uncover, however, is a process of steady, remorseless change in the social, political and economic spheres, from British lordliness, confidence, aloofness to uncertainty, dependence and an altogether weakened position vis-à-vis both the China that loomed outside the colony and the Chinese population within it. It is the story, in microcosm, of the decline and fall of European power in Asia. On a more positive note it also bears out, to a point, the contention of Aeschylus that wisdom comes through suffering. In the upheaval and hardship of the occupation the British and their Asian subjects were thrown together as never before and began, often for the first time, to look at each other with a measure of sympathy. This change was not total, or altogether enduring, but it was enough to make a difference. And to demonstrate that even out of the darkest human experience some good may emerge.

CHAPTER ONE

A Late Victorian Hill

Pre-war Hong Kong: the British and their subjects

One September evening at the beginning of the 1930s the novelist Stella Benson was entertained by the Governor, Sir William Peel, at Government House in Hong Kong. 'After dinner', she confided to her diary, 'Lady Peel talked to me a long time in a flurried way about white ants.'[1] Ninety years after its annexation from the enfeebled Manchu dynasty, this British trading colony off the coast of south China was a soporific place. Ultra-modern in the late nineteenth century, when it was celebrated for its early acquisition of electric lighting and trams, it remained one of the principal business centres in the Far East and one of the top half-dozen ports in the world. But it had, none the less, been eclipsed by the glittering rise of Shanghai, the great Chinese city up the coast to the north, where Jardine Matheson, doyen of the renowned Hong Kong trading houses, had moved their head office. In 1931 the British invested around £130 m in Shanghai, compared with a mere £35 m in Hong Kong. While majestic piles arose on the Shanghai waterfront, the city of Victoria on Hong Kong Island had almost no buildings of more than four storeys, apart from the grand new headquarters of the Hongkong and Shanghai Bank, completed in 1935 with an Art Deco interior under the prodding of the Bank's general manager, Sir Vandeleur Grayburn, and duly referred to by the British colonists as 'Grayburn's Folly'.[2] On the other side of the harbour the broad, tree-lined avenue built in the early years of the century by Governor Nathan ('Nathan's Folly') ran through the middle of Victoria's sister city of Kowloon, which was little more at this period than a quiet residential suburb dotted with market gardens. Beyond Kowloon the New Territories, the rural hinterland which the British had acquired from the Manchus on a ninety-nine-year lease in 1898, were still haunted by bandits and the occasional tiger.

Hong Kong ranked among the less distinguished postings for officers of the British Colonial Service. One contemporary referred to it as 'the dumping

ground for the duds'.[3] There was so little to do there that even such dignitaries as the Governor and his right-hand man, the Colonial Secretary,
spent large amounts of their time attending to trivial matters which might
have been left to their juniors. But for both the officials and the merchants
who constituted the bulk of the expatriate population, Hong Kong was a place
where the clubbable could enjoy a very pleasant, and very British, existence.
There was polo and golf and tennis and racing at Happy Valley and diving
from launches by moonlight in secluded bays. Governor Peel rode to hounds
with the Fanling Hunt, splashing through the rice paddies in pursuit of the
civet cat.[4] For the ladies there were fetes and bazaars and a dogs' home and
'bridge luncheons' that continued for seven hours. On Twelfth Night, 1930,
the community gathered at the recently opened Peninsula Hotel in Kowloon
for a St George's Ball at which nostalgic declamations were made from
Wordsworth while the Somerset Light Infantry played 'The Roast Beef of Old
England' and a company of Beefeaters stood by in full regalia. To an acid out-
sider like Stella Benson, an associate of the Bloomsbury Group, Hong Kong
was the acme of provincial philistinism, where life revolved around sport and
gossip and the ladies displayed their 'cultchah' by sending a servant down to
the library with a chit instructing the librarian, 'Please give bearer two books'.
In short, 'an island of tenth-rate men married to eleventh-rate women'.[5]
But the majority of the British who lived in Hong Kong appear to have seen
little reason for changing their lifestyle. It was, remarked an official of the
Colonial Office in London in 1934, 'the most self-satisfied of all the colonies,
except Malaya'.[6]

Everyone did their best, seemingly, to look down upon anyone different. The
officials were scathing about the expatriate merchants, whom they regarded as
uncouth Scotsmen. They had little more use for the rest of the British professional classes. One Governor remarked of Sir Henry Polluck, a veteran lawyer,
'He is rather exceptionally stupid, but he is an honest, straightforward gentleman whom I have always found eminently reasonable when matters have
been fully explained to him.'[7] The merchants and other professionals took an
equally scornful view of the officials, whom they considered to be fresh-faced
tinkerers with a minimal grasp of local realities.[8] Officials and merchants combined in despising the seedy expatriate policemen who came from the wrong
sort of background and were to be found drinking *samshu*, a Chinese rice spirit,
in Upper and Lower Lascar Rows.[9] And all the British exhibited disdain for the
various lesser breeds who shared the colony with them, jumpers on the bandwagon of Empire, the sprinkling of Eurasians and Portuguese, Parsees and
Sindhis, Jews and Armenians, Frenchmen and other disreputable Europeans.
They even appear to have taken a somewhat lofty attitude towards the 500-
odd Americans. Sir Vandeleur Grayburn of the Hongkong and Shanghai Bank
is said to have commented, 'There is only one American in the Bank and that

is one too many.'[10] But in particular they looked down upon the 98 per cent of the population who happened to be Chinese.

They looked down upon them in a very literal sense. The most senior British officials and the leading merchants, the *taipans*, made their homes on the Peak, the cool heights overlooking Victoria, while the Chinese masses congregated below. Residence on the Peak was debarred to Chinese by the Peak District Reservation Ordinance of 1904, which provided that no Asiatic could rent property there, and by the Peak District (Residence) Ordinance of 1918 which, less explicit but more comprehensive, laid down that all applications to live there should be approved by the British authorities.[11] No Chinese could so much as visit the Peak unless they had been invited or were delivering goods. Those invited to visit could take the Peak Tram, the spectacular cable car which led up to the heights, provided they had no objection to using a separate waiting room; but labourers delivering goods had to climb up on foot. And except when delivering goods, no Chinese whatever were permitted to ascend beyond a certain point on the Peak Road.

Numerous other measures, partly legislated and partly informal, kept the Chinese population below and apart. No Chinese could belong to the Hong Kong Club or the Royal Hong Kong Yacht Club or the Hong Kong Golf Club at Fanling.[12] The Matilda Hospital, completed in 1916, was whites-only; so were the Botanical Gardens; so were some of the lounges at the Hong Kong Hotel. On the Star Ferry, crossing the harbour, no Chinese could travel in the first-class section, or any Europeans in the second and third. At one period when the ferries were scarce and overcrowded, a correspondent proposed to the *China Mail* that 'European ladies ought to be given the first chance of getting a seat and the Chinese allowed on afterwards, if there is room'.[13]

There was, naturally, no thought of according the Chinese any kind of political representation. Hong Kong was a classic Crown Colony in which the Governor wielded supreme power, qualified only by the need to report to the Colonial Office in London. He had a cabinet, the Executive Council, but did not need to take their advice; he had a parliament, the Legislative Council, but the members were unelected and over half of them were officials obliged to vote as he saw fit. The only elected personnel in the administration were two members of the ten-strong Sanitary Board. Even the British expatriates were thus allowed only the smallest chance to make their voices heard in the formulation of policies; and the Chinese were effectively denied even that. The franchise for electing the two members of the Sanitary Board was restricted to jurors, which for practical purposes meant people literate in English, ruling out all but a tiny minority of the Chinese.

In 1894–6, and again in 1916–23, expatriate groups had badgered the Colonial Office for 'constitutional reform' in the shape of elections to the Legislative Council, with a franchise designed to convert Hong Kong into a self-governing democracy. But the democracy they had in mind was for Europeans only. And in any case the Colonial Office said no. In a high-minded sort of way they felt it would not be fair to permit a few hundred transient British merchants to exercise unlimited power over the Chinese majority.[14] A few steps ahead, as they usually were, of expatriate thinking, they could also see the result would be lethal. Any right of election conceded to the European residents would have to be granted to the Chinese as well; and that would be the end of British Hong Kong.[15]

Debarred from any share in the making of government policies, the Chinese were also excluded from almost any significant role in carrying policies out. The Cadets, the elite who obtained all the senior jobs in the civil service, were recruited entirely in Britain from persons 'of pure European descent'; and even the lowlier posts in many government departments were filled by Europeans.[16]

The same pattern prevailed in the economic sphere. The British broadly occupied the commanding heights of the Hong Kong economy. They owned the chief trading houses and the three banks authorized to issue currency and the major insurance firms.[17] In addition they owned the colony's handful of heavy industrial undertakings (three large shipbuilding companies, the Taikoo Sugar Refinery and the Green Island Cement Works); and they ran the tramways and gas works and other public utilities.[18] They also operated a number of leading department stores such as Lane Crawford and Whiteaway, Laidlaw and Co. British business interests had a mouthpiece in the form of the Hong Kong General Chamber of Commerce, but no Chinese company was admitted to this. No Chinese could aspire to as much as a clerical job in the Hongkong and Shanghai Bank. Some other British firms did employ junior Chinese staff, but such staff were kept well in their place. In 1924 the manager of the Lane Crawford department store circularized his employees,

> The first customer to arrive in a department should be served by the No. 1 of that department. Subsequent customers should be served by the European assistants until all are engaged, when Chinese and other Asiatics will be brought forward to serve.[19]

British supremacy was not, however, quite as all-encompassing as it appeared at first glance. Here after all were a few thousand Europeans scattered thinly among half a million Chinese. With the exception of the Cadets, who received special language training, very few of the British, even after thirty years in the colony, spoke more than a few words of Cantonese, the local Chinese dialect. Most were limited to communicating with servants and rickshaw pullers in the horrors of pidgin English. Total control of Chinese life was impossible under these circumstances, and the British made no attempt to achieve it. From the mid-nineteenth century onwards the government increasingly left it to the Chinese community to handle their own internal

policing, adjudication, social welfare and medical care through an assortment
of institutions they had developed themselves – the neighbourhood associations (*kaifongs*) and the Man Mo Temple Committee, the Tung Wah Hospital
and the District Watch Force.[20] By the 1920s the government's management of
the Chinese in Victoria and Kowloon was largely confined to a monthly dialogue between a solitary British official, the Secretary for Chinese Affairs, and
the fifteen members of the District Watch Committee – a body which, originally formed to supervise the operations of the District Watch Force, the
private Chinese police, had assumed representative powers within the community sufficiently broad to earn it the wry expatriate nickname 'the Chinese
Executive Council of Hong Kong'.[21] British control of the countryside was still
more vestigial. The British dealt solely with the village headmen: as one District Officer put it, 'We just accepted the natural leaders we found.'[22] There was
no one in charge of agriculture,[23] and the peasants were left to struggle along
at the subsistence level (or sometimes below it). In a sense, then, the British
presided over Hong Kong as all-powerful rulers; in another sense they barely
ran it at all. And pushing forward within the framework of their own self-
contained world the Chinese were starting in various ways to pose a steadily
growing challenge to British hegemony.

In seizing Hong Kong for themselves the British had also created an
admirable environment for Chinese merchants, who could pursue their calling
in the comfort of an orderly city, protected by laws and free from the harassment and extortion they had endured at the hands of officials in mainland
China. Within little more than a generation the results were beginning to show.
By the mid-1870s it had been discovered that Chinese firms rather than the
great British trading houses were handling the bulk of the entrepot trade
through which the colony made its living. By 1881 it had further emerged that
seventeen of the twenty highest ratepayers in the colony were Chinese, and
that the Chinese contributed over 90 per cent of the colony's revenue.[24] (This
was one of the factors which helped to persuade the Colonial Office that they
could not fairly accede to the expatriates' calls for a whites-only franchise.)
Half a century later Chinese business interests were visibly eating into the old
British-dominated sectors of the Hong Kong economy. Powerful Chinese-
funded banks had begun to make their appearance, for example the Bank of
East Asia, which was founded in 1918 and operated out of one of the few office
blocks to compete in stature with 'Grayburn's Folly'.[25] China Underwriters,
launched in 1924, had joined the ranks of the British insurance firms, and the
China Merchandise Emporium had risen up to compete with Lane Crawford.
The public utilities which the British ran had Chinese shareholders, and so
did the British-owned Green Island Cement Works: in 1924 a Chinese
businessman, Li Tse-fong, one of the founders of the Bank of East Asia, was
propelled on to the board of Green Island by a shareholders' revolt. Chinese

entrepreneurs were displaying their ability to tackle heavy engineering projects: in 1912 Ho Kai and Au Tak formed a partnership to fill in the north end of Kowloon Bay, where the reclaimed land was in 1928 developed as Kai Tak Airport. And in the meantime the Chinese were making their own a newly emerging sector – light industry. In 1914 Jardine Matheson had given up on climatic grounds an attempt to operate a 55,000-spindle cotton mill, and the machinery had been moved to Shanghai. By the 1920s, however, new textile factories were appearing; and these factories were run by Chinese. Other Chinese manufacturers were engaged in the production of electric torches and rubber shoes. It is reckoned that up to 3,000 Chinese-owned light industrial plants may have been active in Hong Kong before 1930. Most of these would undoubtedly have been tiny workshops, but the impact they made is suggested by the government census of 1931, which revealed that no less than 24 per cent of the labour force in this trading entrepot were employed in industrial occupations.[26] In the following years of world-wide depression the footwear plants in particular were exporting their goods so successfully that the home government in London became alarmed for the welfare of British domestic producers and twice came close to imposing quotas on Hong Kong shoes.

This diffuse business energy gave rise to a growing number of Chinese magnates whose wealth was at least as great as that of their British counterparts. The Hong Kong General Chamber of Commerce had no place for them, so they grouped together in their own Hong Kong Chinese General Chamber of Commerce. They could not join the British clubs, so they set up other clubs in the West Point district of Victoria which were intended for Chinese alone. They could not make their homes on the Peak, so they vied with the British by erecting mansions of dazzling opulence in other parts of Hong Kong Island. The millionaire Eu Tong-sen put up three Gothic castles called Euston, Eucliffe and Sirmio and filled them, a touch impudently, with statues of naked European nymphs.

A more direct challenge to British control was the political one posed by the rise of nationalism on the Chinese mainland. Even in the days of the Manchus, who ceded the colony in the first place, the British were never left in any doubt of China's displeasure at the loss of Hong Kong. In 1857, instigated apparently by officials in the neighbouring Chinese city of Canton, a Hong Kong baker named Cheong Ah Lum had attempted to poison the entire British community by putting arsenic in their bread: a piece of the poisoned bread was preserved for decades in a cabinet in the office of the Chief Justice, a kind of collective *memento mori*.[27] In 1911 the alien Manchu dynasty which had ruled China for almost three centuries was swept away in the revolution inspired by the Chinese Nationalist movement of Sun Yat-sen. The Chinese Nationalist drive to rid China of foreign control had obvious implications for Britain as well, and the effect in Hong Kong was immediate. Europeans were attacked on the streets, bomb-making factories were discovered and the Governor, Sir Frederick Lugard, felt compelled to curb the disorder by authorizing extensive use of the cat o'nine tails and marching his troops through the streets with fixed bayonets. The following year an attempt was made by a young Chinese to shoot Lugard's successor, Sir Henry May, as he was being conveyed by sedan-chair from the Victoria waterfront to his inauguration at the City Hall. May subsequently reported that the assailant in this Sarajevo-like episode was a man of 'weak intellect' who had nursed a long-standing personal grudge against him. But the assailant himself made it clear to the magistrate that he had been incensed by a recent British ordinance prohibiting the use of new copper coins from Canton, which was functioning (as it would do on and off for the next fifteen years) as the principal Nationalist base in a divided China. His landlady wrote to a friend that her lodger had fired a shot at the new Governor 'and most unfortunately missed him'.[28]

After a decade of relative calm the turmoil resumed with a vengeance at the start of the 1920s, when the colony found itself launched abruptly on a roller-coaster of strikes. Major trouble began in 1922, after the trading firms Butterfield and Swire and Jardine Matheson refused a demand by the Chinese seamen in their employment for a 30 to 40 per cent increase in their wages.[29] At the call of the newly established Chinese Seamen's Union, the crews walked out – and were followed by the electricians, the fitters, the boiler-makers, the barbers, the office boys and the printers, the tram conductors and drivers, the waiters in the tea-houses, the servants and cooks on the Peak and the entire Chinese staff at Government House. The stated motives for the strike were economic ones; but the context was anti-British, and the strikers received support, funds and shelter from the Nationalist regime in Canton.

Worse followed in 1925. This time the motive was overtly political. News had spread of the shooting by the British authorities in the leased enclaves on the mainland of demonstrators protesting against the continued foreign domination of China. Nine protesters had been shot dead by British police in the International Settlement at Shanghai, and a further fifty-two by a Royal Navy contingent defending the entrance to the British concession on Shamian Island in Canton. The Hong Kong Chinese struck back with one of the longest campaigns in industrial history. A hundred thousand Chinese workers, a fifth of the population, walked out of Hong Kong altogether. In the atmosphere of a ghost town, bereft of their labour force, British lawyers hauled the ice, British bankers delivered the mail, British matrons did their own ironing, and 'elegant European ladies in white frilly aprons' became waitresses in the fashionable Cafe Wiseman. Many other expatriates packed the steamships for home. Hong Kong, whose name in Chinese means Fragrant Harbour, became a Stinking Harbour as the buckets of nightsoil sat uncollected; while the Governor, Sir Reginald Stubbs, who was now referred to by the population as 'Shit-tubs', bestrode the chaos declaring that anyone disturbing the peace of the colony would 'be treated, as is the way with the English, justly but sternly'.[30] The second, and more devastating, step was a total boycott of British goods which lasted for fifteen months. The number of ships entering the harbour fell by 60 per cent; the transshipment trade in rice, silk and textiles was pronounced 'literally dead'; the colony's trading firms were said to have lost HK$500 m; in short Hong Kong was threatened with strangulation. Once again the upheaval was backed by mainland Chinese political forces. Chiang Kai-shek, who had just succeeded Sun Yat-sen as leader of the Chinese Nationalists, noted approvingly that 'British power in the Orient had passed its peak'.[31] The dominant role in this campaign was, however, played not by the Nationalists but by their still more radical junior partners, the four-year-old Chinese Communist Party. Chairman Mao's future rival Liu Shaoqi and other leading Communists ran the Strike Committee which orchestrated the campaign from Canton. Representatives of the Committee presented the Hong Kong authorities with a series of demands which included the election of Chinese members to the Legislative Council, equal treatment for Chinese and Europeans and freedom for Chinese residents to live on the Peak. The *South China Morning Post* reported this petition under the headline 'LABOURERS' EXTRAORDINARY ATTITUDE'.

Against the background of this rising challenge the attitude of the British to their Chinese subjects was one of distrust and unease. The expatriates looked to the Chinese population to keep them in the style to which they were accustomed; but they could never feel quite sure that the Chinese would do it dependably. The Lane Crawford circular of 1924 prescribed:

> The No. 1 in each department should, whenever possible, make a point of speaking to the customers being served by Asiatic salesmen, in order to ensure that such customers are receiving, or have received, the attention and satisfaction to which they are entitled.[32]

The authorities nursed the same lurking doubts. Chinese recruits to the police force were required to pay HK$50 as a bond for good behaviour. And as the political challenge intensified, one or two of the leading officials were moved to give expression to their deepest fears. In a moment of gloom in 1922, Governor Stubbs wondered aloud to the Colonial Office just how long the Chinese would continue to tolerate British rule in Hong Kong. Their basic attitude to their British overlords, he had no doubt, was one of dislike. All the British could count on was a 'passive acquiescence' which might turn at any time into 'more or less active opposition'.[33]

To neutralize the dangers the British devoted some effort to fostering the emergence of a trustworthy local elite. By as early as the 1860s the government had begun to concern itself with the education of local Chinese boys. The private missionary schools which had served the authorities up till then as a source of Chinese interpreters and other low-grade assistants were superseded by the creation of a new Central School, later known as Queen's College; and the best and brightest products of this official establishment were sent on to Britain to round off their education there. This approach was given a new impetus by the arrival in 1907 of Governor Lugard, best known for his record of empire-building in Nigeria. In spite of the draconian regime he inflicted on Hong Kong in response to the Nationalist revolution on the mainland, Lugard was an enlightened figure, and his wife, Flora Shaw, a former *Times* journalist, was if anything more so: the chief disagreement between them revolved around the question of whether (as Lady Lugard suspected) the Chinese were actually superior to the Europeans in industry and intelligence, or whether (as her husband preferred to suppose) they occupied a middle range well above the worst Europeans but not quite on the level of the best ones. Chivvied by his wife, bitterly opposed by expatriate traders afraid 'that if we educate the Chinaman, he may become a serious rival', Lugard pushed through in 1910 the inauguration of a University of Hong Kong which he visualized as developing into 'the Oxford and Cambridge of the Far East'.[34] This educational drive soon produced a new species of Anglicized Chinese, often born in Hong Kong, English-speaking and endowed with a smattering of Western ideas that distinguished them from the bulk of the Chinese population who surged in and out of the colony from the mainland. The British co-opted these men, made them Justices of the Peace, sometimes even knights, and appointed them to the two seats which in the last two decades of the nineteenth century were created for Chinese on the Legislative Council. The overt attitude to them was one of approval. Sir Boshan Wei Yuk, who sat on the Legislative Council for twenty-one years in the course of which he said virtually nothing, was described by an admiring British biographer as 'a prince of good fellows'.[35]

Under the surface the British were never in fact entirely sure of the loyalty of these Anglicized Chinese. In 1914 Governor May felt obliged, very affably, very discreetly, to eject the first and grandest of all of them, Ho Kai, the begetter of Kai Tak Airport, from the Legislative Council seat which he had occupied for a full quarter-century. In spite of his lifelong residence in Hong Kong, his munificent endowments of schools and hospitals, there was just a little too much evidence that Sir Kai, as he had been dubbed, had a foot in the Nationalist camp. He was even suspected of having links with an anti-British newspaper which the Nationalists were publishing in Canton. May allowed (a little ruefully, one imagines, in the light of his hair-raising inauguration two years earlier) that Sir Kai's surviving colleague on the Council, Wei Yuk, retained 'as much of my confidence as it is safe to repose in any Chinese'.[36]

In the years after 1911 the Anglicized Chinese were, none the less, natural allies of the British for an obvious reason. Wealthy businessmen, they were, like their British counterparts, extremely conservative, easily alarmed by the social radicalism that the Nationalist revolution had brought in its wake. One example was Shouson Chow. Born in Hong Kong in 1862, he spent his early career on the mainland, where he held a number of posts in the Foreign Ministry of the declining Manchu regime. After 1911, he withdrew to the colony and devoted himself to business, becoming Chairman of the Board of (among other concerns) the Bank of East Asia. He spoke out against the attempts that were made in the early 1920s to rid Hong Kong of such traditional Chinese customs as the use of child labour in factories and the system by which young girls were sold by poor families to work as unpaid servants in better-off homes.[37] In the crisis of 1925 he declared, in the slightly stilted English which these products of the colonial schools were apt to employ, 'We do not want Bolshevism or Communism. . . . What we want are peace and good order, and the right to follow our callings without let or hindrance.'[38] But the British still found it advisable to cast their net a little wider, to take in one of the colony's most important minority groups.

Back in the 1850s one of the colony's early Governors, Sir John Bowring, hymn-writer and polyglot, had delivered himself of an ominous warning. 'A large population of children of native mothers by foreigners of all classes', he observed, 'is beginning to ripen into a dangerous element out of the dunghill of neglect.'[39] Bowring had reckoned without the shrewdness of the Chinese mothers, many of whom were quick to see the advantages of sending the sons they had borne to European traders to establishments like the Central School. By the turn of the century these Eurasians, as they were called, were beginning to make an impact. Many worked in a humble capacity. For some mysterious reason it was considered appropriate that lighthouses should be manned by Eurasians. Eurasians obtained solid, plodding jobs as clerks in the government offices and in the great British trading firms (the same jobs that the British were typically unwilling to entrust to the local Chinese.)[40] But a talented few also managed to win posts as compradors, the agents who were employed by British firms to conduct the dealings with Chinese businesses for which the British themselves lacked the cultural and linguistic equipment, and who in the process were often able to amass, quite legitimately, prodigious fortunes on their own account. The most celebrated case was Robert Ho Tung. Son of a Dutch (or possibly Belgian) merchant by a Chinese mother, he was sent to the Central School, where he performed spectacularly; and in 1882, at the age of just twenty, he became the chief comprador to Jardine Matheson. By the time he was thirty he had become Hong Kong's first millionaire on the strength of some lucrative interventions in the sugar trade with the Philippines and the Dutch East Indies; and for decades he remained far and away the richest man in the colony, a plutocrat whose wealth was suspected to place him in the Carnegie or Rockefeller bracket. In the earliest years most Eurasians were inclined to assimilate with the Chinese majority. Robert Ho Tung himself conformed to this traditional pattern: he wore Chinese dress, and we are told that 'only his sparkling blue eyes betrayed his Eurasian origin'.[41] When his eldest daughter was born in 1897, however, he named her Victoria Jubilee. By around that date the most successful Eurasians had begun to diverge from their fellows at the clerks' desks and to form themselves into a tightly knit, intermarrying clique. They turned their faces away from the rise of Chinese nationalism, and identified with the British to whose social status they aspired.

The general attitude of the British to the Eurasians was scarcely benign. The interracial liaisons which, as Bowring's remarks indicate, had been common enough in the early years of the colony met with bristling antipathy from the British memsahibs who began to arrive in the late nineteenth century and who regarded svelte Cantonese girls as a potential threat to themselves and their daughters. Association with a Chinese girl was a sure bar to advancement in either the civil service or the big trading firms. In 1918 a certain Dr Woodman applied to the Colonial Office for a promotional transfer. It emerged that his social position was 'not as good as it might be' because he had taken a Chinese wife, and the official dealing with his request was instructed to 'reply discouragingly'.[42] Relationships with local women had come to be viewed as a sordid pursuit of low-grade whites such as soldiers and policemen, and it followed that any offspring of such relationships were themselves to be seen as disreputable. Rank and file Eurasian employees in the expatriate firms may have been trusted somewhat more than the Chinese were, but the difference was only one of degree: at the Hongkong and Shanghai Bank printed slips bore the message, 'NOT VALID UNLESS SIGNED BY A MEMBER OF THE EUROPEAN STAFF'.[43]

Yet the most dazzlingly successful Eurasians were hard to keep down. In 1906 Robert Ho Tung took advantage of a loophole in the new Peak District Reservation Ordinance, which debarred Asiatics from *renting* a property on the Peak but had nothing to say about *purchase*, and bought three bungalows in the holy of holies.[44] And in the aftermath of the Nationalist revolution, British officials began to appreciate that the leading Eurasians might prove to be even more promising allies than the Anglicized Chinese. 'The true citizens of Hong Kong', as they were sometimes described,[45] had all the attractions of the Anglicized Chinese without that disturbing alternative focus of allegiance: as one old Hong Kong hand with a Chinese wife has observed, 'not many Eurasians were moved by the passions that sweep China'.[46] So in their case, too, approval began to drip down. In 1915 Robert Ho Tung was awarded a knighthood. Three years later Governor May honoured with his presence the grand Eurasian society wedding of Victoria Jubilee Ho Tung to the brilliant tennis-playing lawyer, M. K. Lo. And from the same period Eurasians began to occupy on a near-permanent basis one of the two seats which were reserved for Chinese on the Legislative Council – converted by this sleight of hand into *de facto* heads of the Chinese community.

Beginning in 1923 the occupant of this Eurasian seat was a certain Robert Kotewall. While his mother was Chinese, he wasn't, in the strictest sense, a Eurasian at all, since his father was not European but Parsee. His career, however, fitted admirably into the classic Eurasian mould. Born in 1880, educated at Queen's College, he advanced straight from school to a post in the government service and rose up doggedly from one clerical job to another until in 1916 the British awarded him the post of Chief Clerk in the Colonial Secretariat – an office that had never previously been filled by a non-European. Resigning soon afterwards to embark on a business venture, he was formally thanked by the government for his 'efficient and trustworthy services'.[47] Like other leading Eurasians he made a certain amount of money, although his main business activity seems to have been a curiously humble one: he occupied himself with the import and export of gramophones. Unlike other leading Eurasians he had a marked intellectual bent. He is variously said to have been a 'fine Chinese scholar' and to have published bad translations of Chinese poetry.[48] In 1921 he composed a play called *The Maid of the Hills* which he had adapted from an old Chinese drama, and the following year he produced it in honour of the visiting Prince of Wales.

Known in Chinese as the 'gentry-merchants' (let us call them the gentry),[49] this little elite of Anglicized Chinese and Eurasians came to play a key intermediary role. Appropriately, they tended to live in the Mid-Levels, the area halfway between the British on the Peak and the mass of Chinese in the city below. In the name of the Chinese community they served as interlocutors of the British Secretary for Chinese Affairs, changing places incessantly on the District Watch Committee and its ten sister bodies. And in the crises of the 1920s they came into their own. In 1922 Sir Robert Ho Tung mediated a settlement of the seamen's strike: he deployed his huge fortune to guarantee the payment of half the wages the seamen had lost through their walk-out, and persuaded Jardines and Swires to grant wage increases of the order of 15 to 20 per cent. In the 1925–6 strike and boycott the whole corps of gentry went into action. A taciturn bigwig named Ts'o Seen-wan distinguished himself by organizing a special constabulary to keep watch in the streets against the danger of arson. But the decisive interventions were those of Robert Kotewall and Shouson Chow. Kotewall convinced the assembled ranks of the Executive and Legislative Councils to recommend to the Secretary of State for the Colonies in London that he should arrange for a special loan of HK$30 m to keep local businesses going until normal trading could resume – a triumph of eloquence which went down in the colony's history as the 'million-dollar speech' and earned for its author among the Chinese merchant community the nickname of Silver Tongue.[50] And both Kotewall and Chow were involved in a range of what the British discreetly referred to as 'other services' aimed directly at crushing the strike. They publicized the Bolshevik nature of the campaign through a newspaper called the *Gong Shang Ribao* (Industrial and Commercial Daily), and paid a team of street orators HK$60 a month to harangue the Chinese population against joining it. They set up the Labour Protection Bureau, a force of 150 heavies whose function was to intimidate anyone trying to threaten those employees who stayed at their jobs. 'Though it is necessary', Kotewall observed, 'that our agents for this dangerous work should act for us in a clean way, they should not be required to furnish proof of having worn kid gloves from their youth up.'[51] Finally the two men took part in an attempt to eradicate the trouble at its mainland source. They persuaded the Tung Wah Hospital Committee to raise HK$50,000 to pay for a minor warlord named Wei Bangping to lead a *coup d'état* against the Nationalist–Communist regime in Canton. The *coup* attempt failed dismally; but its collapse made no difference to the gratitude which the British authorities felt for the exertions of Kotewall and Chow. The Colonial Secretary, Claud Severn, wrote to them praising the 'invaluable service' which they had rendered 'in the face of great difficulty and danger'. In the course of the next two years Chow received a knighthood, and Kotewall became a Companion of the Order of St Michael and St George.[52]

Still more pro-British zeal was displayed by the offspring of the gentry who had started to take up places at Lugard's new University of Hong Kong. In the crisis of 1925–6 they were said to have performed additional unaccustomed work, and to have 'behaved admirably' despite fierce political pressure.[53]

The British also called in help, of a more mundane kind, from two of the colony's other ethnic minorities. Rather marked trust was placed in the Portuguese, whose forbears had moved to Hong Kong in the early days of the settlement from Macao, Portugal's colony on the other side of the Pearl River delta. Most of these Portuguese were in fact a variety of Eurasians, of part-Portuguese and part-Chinese ancestry. Like the Eurasians of British and other northern European stock, they looked on Hong Kong as their home, and their patterns of employment were roughly similar. A small number of them made it into the merchant or professional classes, while others gave steady service as clerks in the Hongkong and Shanghai Bank and the other expatriate firms.[54] In the upheavals of 1922 and 1925–6 they were felt to have 'played their part loyally', helping out in the absence of the Chinese labour force in domains ranging from the cross-harbour ferries to the kitchens of the Repulse Bay Hotel.[55] A Portuguese unit was added to the Hong Kong Volunteer Defence Corps, the colonial militia which had until then been effectively an all-British outfit. Another was created as part of the Police Reserve which evolved out of the special constabulary founded by Ts'o Seen-wan.[56]

Considerable use was also made of the Indians. Hong Kong at this period was thought of as a far-flung extension of Britain's Indian empire. It had been taken with sepoy troops, and had flourished for decades as a receiving station for Indian opium. Its expatriate residents ate *tiffin* at midday and stored their merchandise in *godowns* and drained away their rainwater through *nullahs*; and the ladies did their light shopping at Kayamally's dry goods emporium and similar enterprises run by the small but prosperous band of Sindhi and Parsee merchants. It was, then, only natural that Sikhs and Punjabi Muslims should be shipped in to serve as auxiliaries in the colony's police force. These Indian policemen were brought in over decades in numbers that often approached those of the Chinese police, who for security reasons were never allowed to constitute more than 50 per cent of the total.[57] After the 1911 revolution they were deployed along the border with mainland China and (unlike their Chinese colleagues) were issued with revolvers. In spite of these arrangements the Indian policemen were not viewed with the same trust as the Portuguese reservists. During the First World War there were worries that the Muslim contingent might be sympathetic to Ottoman Turkey; grave doubts were entertained of the Sikhs in the aftermath of the Amritsar massacre of 1919. An extra 200 Indian police were none the less recruited in response to the great strike and boycott of 1925–6. Their deployment avoided the peril of relying exclusively on Chinese police to control a mob of Chinese strikers. The risk of collusion was minimal, since the Chinese public both feared and detested the Indian constables.[58] In using Indians to hold the line in Hong Kong the British were applying in all of its simple elegance their classic principle of 'divide and rule'.

With the help of these various local confederates, British Hong Kong had weathered the storm of the mid-1920s. The great strike and boycott had faded away without destroying the colony, and without securing for the strikers the slightest concession in response to the political demands they had made. In the following few years the British took steps to prevent the resurgence of any mainland-inspired Chinese political activity. From 1925 onwards the Chinese press in Hong Kong was subject to censorship, and in 1927 the authorities suppressed a dozen of the principal Chinese trade unions. Particular efforts were made to forestall any further annoyances from the Chinese Communist Party. Two of the banned unions, the General Labour Union of Hong Kong and the Chinese Seamen's Union, were well known for their Communist leanings. A special Anti-Communist Squad in the police devoted itself to the hunting down of Communist Party members: one stray activist captured at the end of 1929 was the father of a future prime minister of Communist China, Li Peng. By 1935 the police felt able to report contentedly that the colony was 'entirely free from organized Communism'.[59]

Much of the crackdown on Communists was carried out in teamwork with the Nationalist adherents of Chiang Kai-shek. The British in Hong Kong had been quick to seize the opportunity presented by the rift which opened up on the mainland in 1927 between the Nationalists and their Communist allies. Approaches were made to Canton, which was now in the hands of Nationalist-affiliated military chiefs of a violently anti-Communist disposition. One of the early go-betweens for the British authorities was the indefatigable Kotewall: another was Dr Li Shu-fan, an Anglicized Chinese member of the gentry who had served the Nationalists briefly after the 1911 revolution as China's first Minister of Health but had since retreated to his native Hong Kong, where he ran a private hospital with a cheerful appetite for profit and indulged his passion for hunting and shooting at weekends.[60] Thanks to the efforts of these envoys and others like them cooperation between Hong Kong and Canton was restored, and indeed became intimate. Li Peng's father was handed over by the Hong Kong police to the Canton authorities, who promptly executed him.[61]

The Nationalists themselves remained a potential nuisance. After 1926–7, when Chiang Kai-shek had led his armies out of Canton and crushed the northern warlords, they had constituted the government of a unified China, with its capital at Nanking. This new Nationalist government issued statements calling in general terms for the abrogation of the 'unequal treaties' which their Manchu predecessors had signed with the European powers from 1842 onwards, and in the first instance of the agreements leasing territory to the European powers which the Manchus had made in the final years of the nineteenth century. These agreements, of course, included the 1898 Convention of Peking which had granted Britain its ninety-nine-year lease on the New Territories. In 1933–7 the Nationalist Foreign Ministry sent a series of notes and cables to the Hong Kong government asserting their authority over the Walled City of Kowloon, an enclave within the New Territories which the Manchu authorities had retained for China under the terms of the 1898 Convention, only to have the British evict their officials on security grounds the following year. The British were proposing to demolish the tenements in this rather squalid area, and to drive out the residents with a view to creating a public park – and the Nationalists accordingly sprang to the residents' defence.[62]

But the Nationalists' bark was worse than their bite. The fight they put up against the demolition plans never went beyond the level of ritual protest; and they never put forward an explicit or formal claim to the New Territories as a whole.[63] They were too much in need of the funds that Britain was making available to them for road and railway projects (funds which included £8 m worth of hard-currency loans from the Hongkong and Shanghai Bank), and too weak to be able to contemplate a head-on collision with a major European power. Their control of large parts of China was strictly theoretical: the military chiefs in Canton, for example, while professing allegiance to Nanking, enjoyed *de facto* independence throughout the first half of the 1930s. In the light of these circumstances the British for their part saw no reason for making any concession whatever to Nationalist sentiment where the New Territories were concerned.[64] Their demolition of the Walled City went ahead regardless of Nationalist protest, and by the end of the decade was largely complete. And any suggestion of looking again at the terms of the leasehold of 1898 was dismissed out of hand.[65] By the late 1920s Whitehall had already reached the conclusion that the New Territories were strategically and economically an indispensable part of the colony, and that if they were to be returned to China, Hong Kong Island and Kowloon would have to go too. Far from wanting to cut the lease short, Sir Cecil Clementi, who served as Governor in the years that immediately followed the great strike and boycott, strongly favoured taking advantage of the Nationalist government's weakness to cement the New Territories permanently to the rest of Hong Kong. In December 1935, some years after his retirement from the Governor's post, Clementi declared in a speech to the Royal Empire Society in London, 'It behoves us to offer, and the sooner the better, terms on which the Chinese can honourably agree to the cession of the New Territories in perpetuity to Great Britain'; and a plan for buying the freehold from the Nationalists was proposed by the British Treasury as late as 1939.[66] (If this plan had been implemented, the deadline of 1997 would of course have ceased to hang over the colony. One can only speculate whether, under such conditions, the present regime in Peking would have liquidated the colony a great deal sooner – or whether they might just have allowed it to continue, world without end.)

The British authorities in Hong Kong had none the less been badly shaken by the 1920s upheavals. For several years after the end of the great strike and boycott a consensus seems to have prevailed that some reform of the colony's social, political and economic arrangements would have to be made. The driving force for reform was, precisely, Sir Cecil Clementi, a translator of Cantonese love songs whose reputation as a Sinologist did not entirely re-commend him to the expatriate rank and file. (Rumour had it that Sir Cecil was in the habit of slipping out of Government House late at night dressed in mandarin robes to visit his favourite Chinese brothel.) Clementi was dismayed at the extent to which the British and Chinese inhabitants of Hong Kong led separate lives, neither community 'having any real comprehension of the mode of life or ways of thought of the other'.[67] He went so far as to make the icon-oclastic suggestion that the Hong Kong Club should be abolished and replaced by a multiracial establishment. Nothing came of that, but a few attempts were undoubtedly made to narrow the social gulf between the communities. In 1926 Chinese were admitted for the first time to membership of the Jockey Club. Some of the rules governing Chinese access to the Peak Tram were apparently lifted, and by the mid-1930s it was permissible for Chinese to climb the whole way up the Peak Road. Robert Kotewall, as befitted his intermediate status, was prominent in a number of these bridge-building exercises. He initiated a monthly Anglo-Chinese tiffin party; he helped to establish a Hong Kong branch of the Rotary Club; in conjunction with Bella Southorn, wife of the

Colonial Secretary, he organized a Women's International Club where Chinese and expatriate ladies could meet for lunch. By 1936 a Chinese visitor was able to comment that the colony's Europeans were 'just beginning' to mix with the Chinese on a social basis, and an expatriate officer of the Hongkong and Shanghai Bank recalled how around that time one of his colleagues 'started to get to know the Chinese, which had never been done by anybody before'.[68]

Clementi also tried to expand the role which the Chinese played in the formal machinery of government. In 1926 he took the dramatic step of appointing a Chinese to serve as a member of the Executive Council, his choice for this privilege falling on the newly decorated Sir Shouson Chow;[69] and three years later he raised the number of Chinese seats on the Legislative Council from two to three. A further hopeful-sounding step followed in 1936, when the Sanitary Board with its modest elected component was replaced by an Urban Council, whose name suggested an eventual shift to a broadly based municipal administration. Some thought also began to be given to increasing the access of Chinese to minor posts in the colony's civil service. Sir Andrew Caldecott, Governor from 1935 to 1937, was a leading advocate of this process of 'localization': in particular he backed a scheme under which about fifty Chinese 'of good education and culture' would be introduced into the police force at the rank of sub-inspector as replacements for Europeans.[70]

Finally the British began to display a new concern for improving the welfare of the impoverished Chinese masses. In 1927 Clementi presided over the setting-up of an Agricultural Association with a view to encouraging the peasants of the neglected New Territories to experiment with new types of crop. The employment of child labour in the colony's factories was largely eliminated. A Building Ordinance passed in 1935 provided for improvements in the lighting, ventilation and hygiene of Chinese tenements.

The trouble was it was all far too slow. The sense of urgency which had impelled Clementi to action was lost as the British recovered their confidence and the threat from the mainland began to recede. Life began to settle into the tranquil rhythms that Stella Benson observed in the autumn of 1930; and the reform campaign petered out in half-measures or ran aground on shoals of expatriate apathy.

The social *rapprochement* between the British and Chinese communities was partial at best. Chinese could belong to the Jockey Club, but continued to be barred from the Club's prestigious committee. British businessmen were beginning to lunch with their Chinese counterparts, but no British families thought of asking Chinese to informal parties; and the efforts the government made to promote inter-communal mingling were apt to be painfully artificial. Stella Benson remarked in her diary on the 'parish tea atmosphere' of an at-home which Bella Southorn gave in August 1931 for a mixed company of 'Peakites' and Chinese.[71] Not all the blame for the social gulf can attach to the

British. The Chinese themselves displayed little inclination to mix, and their women still lived in something resembling purdah.[72] But the fact remains that, once the flutter of concern in the late 1920s had subsided, the structures and attitudes of the mini-apartheid that the British had built in the colony re-emerged very much as they had been before. People were so *rude* to the Chinese, a British survivor remembers. Not so much the top merchants, but especially middle-ranking personnel like inspectors of police. It was still a society in which a sixty-year-old Chinese waiter in an expatriate club could be summoned with a cry of 'Boy!'[73]

One of the seeming advances in the political sphere turned out to be purely cosmetic. The Urban Council was just the same as the Sanitary Board it replaced, an advisory body concerned with public health matters; and its sole democratic feature remained the election of just two members out of a slightly expanded total of thirteen. The plans to increase opportunities for the Chinese in the civil service were thwarted for the most part by local British resistance. Caldecott's drive to substitute Chinese officials for Europeans in junior posts, which had originated as a cost-cutting measure insofar as the Chinese could be paid lower salaries, was regarded in expatriate circles as bizarre.[74] Some heads of department were reluctant to take on Chinese staff, and the British contingent in the police force maintained that Chinese sub-inspectors would never make satisfactory substitutes for European chargeroom officers.[75]

The attempts to enhance the welfare of the Chinese population were even more torpid. An Economic Commission which sat in 1936 advised that any legislation for the improvement of working conditions in Hong Kong should be 'cautious and not over-ambitious, lest it defeat itself'. An expatriate chronicler writing at the end of the decade admitted that the Agricultural Association in the New Territories had 'probably never been heard of' outside one or two villages, but praised it as an example of 'the gradual development brought about by British administration'.[76] Most expressive, perhaps, of the whole sleepy mood of the 1930s was the government's attitude to the opium issue. Ever since the first years of the century the Hong Kong authorities had found themselves faced with demands to abolish the opium traffic which had been the reason for the colony's establishment and the basis for its early wealth. The Nationalists on the mainland had made some attempt (more, admittedly, in theory than practice) to put an end to their people's degrading dependence on opium. Calls to close down the traffic had come from global bodies like the League of Nations and the International Labour Organization, and increasingly from the United States. But the Colonial Office had dragged its feet. In 1914 the old system under which the sale of the colony's opium stocks was farmed out every three years to a private company had been replaced by a government monopoly. The idea was that the government would phase out opium consumption by gradually raising prices and reducing the amount of the drug put on sale. But the monopoly had proved to be a rather tidy revenue earner. At the end of the First World War it had provided almost 50 per cent of the government's total income, and it continued to yield around 10 per cent in the early 1930s. None of the Governors (not even the enlightened Clementi) could see any need to accelerate the stamping out of the traffic. Opium smoking, they felt, was an ingrained and not specially reprehensible aspect of Chinese life. Total suppression of opium, the Hong Kong authorities explained to the International Labour Organization in 1935, could only lead to 'unrest and resistance' in the working class.[77]

Yet beneath the stodgy surface of the society the pressures for change continued to mount. For the first time the basic assumptions of British supremacy were being challenged from the British side. Mavericks like Stella Benson were arriving and bringing with them the doubts about aspects of Britain's imperial mission that had begun to permeate thinking society in Britain itself in the aftermath of the First World War. And as the decade wore on a few of these mavericks were beginning to side actively with the Asian populace. One example was C. M. Faure, a Royal Navy commander stationed in Canton who had resigned from the service in 1928. According to one account he had played a part in the Navy's suppression of Chinese demonstrators at Shamian three years earlier; and if this account is correct it seems possible that the experience may have produced a reaction in him against the cruder manifestations of British power. In the 1930s he made his way to Hong Kong, where he 'went native', as his fellow expatriates put it, living among the Chinese in the Wanchai district and advising members of the banned leftist unions in their collisions with the colony's government.[78] Something of the same championship of the Asian underdog was apparent in the work of a young lawyer by the name of Frank Loseby. In 1931 Loseby took up the case of a Vietnamese who had been caught by the Hong Kong police in their anti-Communist dragnet. The authorities in French Indochina were anxious to secure the extradition of this troublemaker, Nguyen Ai Quoc, who would one day become better known by the name Ho Chi Minh, and officials in Hong Kong were disposed to comply. Asking Ho as few questions as possible on the grounds that 'all revolutionaries have their secrets', Loseby obtained for him first release, then a twelve-month stay of deportation. When the twelve months were up, at the end of 1932, Loseby booked Ho on to a steamer bound for Singapore in the guise of a servant to a police officer named F. W. Shaftain. Soon after the ship had sailed Ho presented himself to the astonished Shaftain, who was treated to lucid expositions of Marx and forced to admit that the Vietnamese was 'a captivating, I might almost say lovable character'.[79]

Better known than either of these two figures was Ronald Hall, a clergyman who at the end of 1932 took up office as the new Bishop of Hong Kong and South China. Offspring of a long line of clerics (one of his ancestors had been a close friend of the chaplain to Oliver Cromwell), Bishop Hall had lived for a year among the Chinese in Shanghai in the 1920s, and had learned to perceive them as 'a great group of human beings going through a remarkable period of growth'. He arrived in the colony straight from a parish in the slums of depression-era Newcastle, and rapidly caused a stir with his asceticism and his burning compassion for the less privileged. On one occasion he ordered coffee and rolls at the Hong Kong Hotel in place of a meal on the grounds that 'no one should spend all this on food'. He had no time for the expatriate assumptions of British superiority. 'Foreigners', he said tersely, 'have exercised too much authority over the years. If ever there should be a difference of opinion between a European and a Chinese, I shall back the Chinese.' He resigned from the Hong Kong Club when he found that he was not allowed to take a Chinese friend there. Unwilling to serve as nothing more than 'the senior chaplain to the British community', he broke precedent by appointing a Chinese Assistant Bishop and allowing Chinese to use the main entrance at Bishop's House.[80] This turbulent priest was regarded by his compatriots with a mixture of suspicion and the indulgence reserved for the cranky.[81]

The maverick element within the British community was vocal, but very small. More significant, possibly, were the hints of disquiet in the mainstream, the 'little protest' made by a young Cadet named David MacDougall, who felt sufficiently ill at ease with the trappings of British supremacy that he declined to acquire a uniform or a sword.[82]

More significant still were the stirrings among the non-Europeans. For the first time resentment of British rule was becoming detectable in the ranks of the gentry. Wealthy Anglicized Chinese and Eurasians were embittered to find, when they returned to Hong Kong polished by the best education Britain could offer, that whatever their qualifications and whatever their talents there was a level in the local professions above which they would never be permitted to climb. The scales would be tilted against them: if they set up as lawyers, for example, they knew they would have a struggle to win their cases because their British opposite numbers would always be able to hobnob with the British judges in the seclusion of the Hong Kong Club.[83] In the mid-1930s M. K. Lo, the Eurasian lawyer who had married the eldest Ho Tung daughter, Victoria, abruptly emerged as a vociferous champion of non-European rights. Succeeding to Kotewall's seat on the Legislative Council, he worried away at any sign of discrimination, bombarding the government with more questions than the rest of the Council put together. He persuaded them to try the experiment of employing Chinese nurses in the hospitals; and in August 1936 he pressed unsuccessfully for the abolition of the one-sided censorship which had been imposed ten years earlier on the Chinese press. It is difficult to be sure how far Lo was acting as the spokesman for a unanimous gentry opinion. The gentry, like the British, were divided among themselves. The Chinese were disdainful of the Eurasian 'half-castes': Sir Shouson Chow is said to have enjoyed ribbing Sir Robert Ho Tung by describing himself as the only living knight of pure Chinese descent.[84] Some Chinese also viewed the Eurasians as suspect, maintaining that they frequently went and tattled to the British bosses.[85] It would seem none the less that the motion Lo brought in the Legislative Council against the censorship of the Chinese press enjoyed fairly widespread support. A Chinese biographer of the leading gentry described it as a service to the community for which Lo's name would always be remembered; and the general outcry against Ts'o Seen-wan, Lo's colleague on the Legislative Council who had defended the British controls on the grounds that the Chinese press were less likely than the English-language press to behave responsibly, is thought to have been a factor in Ts'o's resignation from the Council the following year.[86]

Here and there some unhappiness was also to be found among the younger gentry generation. Sir Robert Ho Tung's daughter Jean had never forgotten her childhood on the Peak, the occasions when the expatriate children had suddenly refused to play hopscotch with her and her siblings 'because we were Chinese'.[87] Man Wah Leung, who entered the Arts Faculty of Hong Kong University in September 1936, recorded her 'deep disappointment' at the apparent lack of interest among the teaching staff in the students' progress and intellectual concerns and at the stifling atmosphere. 'The meeting of minds and the clash of opinions were unknown', she complained, 'chiefly because a British colonial university, especially that of Hong Kong, did not encourage criticism or dissent'.[88]

Finally there continued to be certain signs of disgruntlement among the wider Chinese public, if anyone had thought to pay them attention. In June 1934 the police reported that five expatriate children playing near the lower terminus of the Peak Tram had been thrown by a 'crazed Chinaman' into a nullah.[89] In May 1936 a Chinese resident named Lau Ti summed up his opinion of the colony in an article which many years later got published on the mainland:

> The division in this society is clear-cut. The people who get served live on the Peak, and the menials who do the serving work on the waterfront or at the foot of the mountain, where they writhe like maggots.[90]

Contemplating the future from the gloomy depths of the strike year of 1922, Governor Stubbs had expected the colony to survive for another twenty years 'at the most'.[91] After that, he believed, British rule in Hong Kong would succumb finally to the deep-seated antipathy of the Chinese subject population. As a short-term forecast Stubbs's guess proved to be uncannily accurate. At the end of the 1930s the colony was to be confronted abruptly by the most lethal menace in its history. This menace, however, arose from an altogether different quarter.

The shadow of Japan

In the early morning of 4 February 1862, a vessel bearing envoys of the decayed Tokugawa shogunate of Japan slipped into Hong Kong harbour. The envoys were bound for Europe, one of the first few Japanese missions to visit the Western world since the country had been forced out of more than two centuries of isolation by the United States naval flotilla of Commodore Matthew Perry just nine years before. Hong Kong had been Perry's last port of call before he arrived in Edo Bay in 1853: it was the first port of call for the Japanese now. The seventy samurai warriors on board the vessel stared attentively at the three great British warships which lay at anchor in the harbour. Each warship, they counted, had three decks, and each deck had seventeen gun-holes. Even the civil official in attendance, a certain Fukuzawa Yukichi, busied himself with totting up the numbers of British warships, gunboats and merchantmen. The conclusion the mission arrived at was that Hong Kong was a centre for European aggression against their country.[92]

After the Tokugawa regime was overthrown in 1868 and replaced by the revived Japan of the Meiji period, the anxiety the Japanese felt about Hong Kong as the nearest European naval base to their islands seemed if anything to intensify. An army officer was assigned to Hong Kong as Japan's first consul in 1874 – the same year, a later Japanese account noted portentously, in which the then Foreign Minister, General Saigo Takamori, first conceived the idea of eliminating the threat from the European colonial powers through a military drive to the South.[93] Fortunately for the British the dominant idea of the early Meiji period was not to attack the Europeans directly but to absorb from them the institutions and technology that would enable Japan to play in their league. When the rapidly modernized Meiji army and navy struck out for the first time in 1894–5, the target was not Hong Kong or any other European colony but Manchu China; and the goal was to carve out for Japan an empire similar to that of the colonial powers themselves.

The British in Hong Kong for their part showed little immediate sign of perceiving a threat from the Japanese. Encouraged by Perry's example,[94] they viewed Japan chiefly as a promising outlet for the colony's trade. In 1870 the Lane Crawford partnership, one of the most dynamic British ventures in the young colony, set up in the city of Yokohama the first Western tailor's establishment to supply the Japanese market; and a considerable part of Japan's foreign trade in the early Meiji period was financed by loans from the Hongkong and Shanghai Bank.[95] Imports from Japan began to find favour among the expatriates, including the quintessential Japanese conveyance of the time, the rickshaw; and the Japanese yen became such a common medium of exchange that by 1880 both the British and Chinese communities were petitioning the government to make it legal tender.

Against this placid background Governors of the colony started to spend occasional summers in the coolness of Japanese mountain resorts – and Japanese visitors to Hong Kong found a ready welcome. Cadets of Japan's new navy arrived in the colony to study on British warships; Japanese warships paid courtesy calls; and princes and ministers of the Meiji government heading for Europe in search of knowledge stopped off in Hong Kong on the way. The Hong Kong authorities played host to these Japanese callers with cheerful insouciance. In 1886, for example, the garrison commander, Major-General W. G. Cameron, took the Meiji government's Minister of Agriculture and Commerce, who was also a general, on a tour of the colony's gun emplacements, stressing 'repeatedly' that these were a military secret which he was disclosing for the first time.[96] Eight years later the sudden display of Japan's newfound military potential came as a shock. As Japan trounced the Manchu navy in the Yellow Sea, and stormed Port Arthur, and went on to annex the island of Taiwan, apprehension was briefly rife among the expatriates that the Japanese might take advantage of their spectacular victory to launch an attack on Hong Kong. But Japan's intentions towards the colony still appeared to be entirely amicable. In the same year in which the Japanese went to war with Manchu China the colony was ravaged by an outbreak of bubonic plague. The Meiji government dispatched a physician called Kitazato Shibasaburo to investigate the epidemic. The doctor politely declined a British offer of funding, worked non-stop for two days analysing the blood and lymph vessels of a stream of plague victims who were brought to his quarters by local labourers, watched his assistant succumb to infection – and succeeded, at the end of it all, in identifying the bacillus which had for centuries inflicted on Asia and Europe the horrors of the Black Death.[97]

In 1902 Britain concluded an alliance with Japan designed to safeguard British interests in the Far East against any possible expansion by Tsarist Russia. This alliance dispelled any lingering fears of a Japanese peril, and for the next twenty years the British in Hong Kong regarded Japan with high favour. When the Japanese in 1904–5 came to blows with the Russians – their first conflict with a European adversary – everyone cheered the astonishing triumph of Britain's plucky little Oriental partner. When Japan cast its lot with Britain and the other Allies in the First World War the Japanese Navy was actually given the task of protecting Hong Kong from a hypothetical German attack in order to relieve the pressure on British resources (a Japanese naval patrol was deployed for the same purpose in the Mediterranean); and in the victory celebrations of 1919 the effigy of a samurai warrior was displayed side by side with other appropriate Allied symbols outside one of the Hong Kong stores. All of this British approval encouraged the steady growth of a Japanese trading community. By 1921 Hong Kong contained a population of just over 1,500 Japanese. Many of them were petty traders, ship's chandlers and druggists and dealers in watches and books; but they also included representatives of such major concerns as Mitsui Bussan (an offshoot of the great Mitsui trading house) and the Yokohama Specie Bank. They had their own club, their own temple, their own hospital, their own hotels, their own primary school and their own newspaper, the *Honkon Nippo*.

In spite of the approval the British bestowed on their country in the abstract, these Japanese still encountered the same social barriers as the rest of the Asiatic population. The careful recasting of the Peak District Reservation Ordinance into the Peak District (Residence) Ordinance of 1918 is said to have been undertaken in part to permit the expatriates to keep the Japanese off the Peak without violating the egalitarian terms of the Anglo-Japanese Alliance. But the better-off Japanese were allowed none the less to edge their way some distance up the colony's great social pyramid, making their homes in the lower part of the Mid-Levels, as far as MacDonnell Road. There they rubbed shoulders with the Anglicized Chinese and Eurasian gentry; and a number of business ties between the Japanese and the gentry were formed at an early date. At least two of the gentry who founded the Bank of East Asia in 1918 had longstanding business connections with Japan. The Chinese tycoon Fung Pingshan had made his fortune by pioneering the import of Japanese farming produce and seafood, and the Eurasian Kan Tong-po had worked, like his father before him, for the Yokohama Specie Bank.[98]

From the end of the First World War strategists in London began to regard Japan with a certain unease. The war had engendered a surge in Japan's naval power, dramatized by its acquisition of a large number of German-ruled islands in the western Pacific. Some action was felt to be needed to restrain the Japanese advance. In 1921–2 the Washington armament conference was convened by the Western powers with a view to creating a secure post-war order in the Pacific region. The alliance between Britain and Japan was discreetly liquidated, subsumed in a broader trilateral understanding between Britain, Japan and the United States. The wartime naval partnership was replaced by a calibrated balance of forces in which Britain, the United States and Japan were to maintain fleets in the Pacific in the ratio 5:5:3. The effect of the treaties concluded in Washington was not altogether reassuring. Japan, weakest power overall, was left with a clear naval dominance in the western Pacific, and Hong Kong in particular was left vulnerable insofar as it fell within a zone where the three signatory powers had guaranteed that none of them would construct any new defensive fortifications. In Hong Kong itself, however, the British authorities were too preoccupied with the immediate unrest in the Chinese community to pay much attention to a hypothetical threat from Japan. There are signs that the Japanese may have taken some advantage of this. Both the Japanese business world and the Navy were sympathetic to Foreign Minister Saigo's old idea of expansion to the South; and in the course of the 1920s both these two groups appear to have stepped up their activities in the colony. The entourage who accompanied Crown Prince Hirohito when he stopped in Hong Kong at the start of a world tour in March 1921 are said to have noticed that the local authorities were not watching them with any particular vigilance – and their visit was followed by a spate of commercial and industrial espionage. During the great strike and boycott of 1925–6 Japanese business interests in Hong Kong took the opportunity to secure from the government fishing rights for themselves in the colony's waters. In the early 1920s a murky figure, Count Otani Kozui, who flitted about regions of interest to Japan in the shifting guises of priest, archaeologist and plantation owner, was deployed in the colony with instructions to lay the groundwork for a general surveillance of the activities of the European powers in South-east Asia; and subsequent agents who were assigned to South-east Asia by the Navy headquarters in Tokyo almost without exception went first to Hong Kong.[99]

Fortunately for the British, however, the main target of the Japanese drive for empire continued to be China. The extent of Japan's ambitions on the Chinese mainland had been revealed in 1915, when, under cover of the First World War, the Japanese government had served on Yuan Shikai, President of the new Republic of China in Peking, Twenty-one Demands which ranged from an extension of territorial rights Japan had already secured in parts of Manchuria, in the north-east, and of the eastern province of Shandong to an effective overlordship of the country's entire economy and administration. Expansion into China was particularly favoured by the Army, the stronger and more aggressive of Japan's two armed services. For most of the 1920s the Army were held in check as Japan passed through a phase of apparent evolution from oligarchic towards parliamentary government and of relative mildness in its dealings abroad: by the end of the decade, however, they were restless for action and impatient to shake off the constraints of civilian rule. In 1928 they gave the Chinese a foretaste of things to come. Part of the Sixth Division who were stationed in Shandong under the command of an officer called Sakai Takashi came into conflict with a unit of Chiang Kai-shek's Chinese Nationalist troops who had recently arrived at the city of Jinan in the course of Chiang's great advance from Canton to the north. Sakai's forces seized Jinan and proceeded to slaughter approximately 6,000 Chinese troops and civilians. A Nationalist official who had been deputed to act as the formal negotiator with the Japanese stationed in the province was relieved of his eyes, ears, nose and tongue before being murdered with seventeen of his staff.[100] Three years later, in September 1931, a clique of three Japanese colonels staged the 'Chinese' bomb attack on a section of the Japanese-owned South Manchurian Railway, which gave the Army the excuse they had been waiting for to occupy the whole of Manchuria.[101] The first great mouthful of China had been bitten away.

In Hong Kong British rulers and Chinese subjects reacted to these developments in strikingly different ways. The mass of the colony's Chinese seem to have identified passionately with the fate of the motherland. In 1915 the community added their voice to the chorus of protest which rang out around China at the news of the Twenty-one Demands; and they also supported the demonstrations that broke out in Peking four years later when Japan's wartime gains in southern Manchuria and Shandong were ratified by the Allies in the peace settlement at Versailles.[102] In 1930 a Japanese writer on his way through the colony stepped into a public lavatory on a street corner and was mortified to discover that the walls (as sure a gauge, perhaps, of grass-roots opinion as any) were covered in Chinese graffiti denouncing Japan.[103] And in September 1931 the tranquillity of Sir William Peel's governorship was abruptly shattered when the populace responded to a call from the Nationalist regime in Nanking for all Chinese to observe a Day of Humiliation at the loss of Manchuria. For six days the colony was convulsed by the worst outbreak of rioting since the Nationalist revolution twenty years before. Windows of Japanese shops were smashed, and the goods inside them were looted and burned. Japanese ships were stoned at the waterfront, and empty boxes of fish alleged to be of Japanese origin were thrown into the harbour in a sort of latter-day Boston Tea Party. Fifty Japanese homes were wrecked. Angry crowds gathered outside the Japanese Club and the Tokyo Hotel. Isolated Japanese were chased and attacked, and six members of the family of a Japanese gardener were murdered at an outlying villa.[104]

The British community by contrast appeared unperturbed by Japan's assault on the Chinese mainland. In 1915 the expatriates are said to have shrugged off the furore surrounding the Twenty-one Demands as 'a purely Oriental affair'.[105] In 1931 the garrison troops were called out to quell the disturbances; and the sympathies of the Hong Kong authorities were unmistakably with the victimized citizens of the fellow imperial power. Governor Peel expressed in the Legislative Council his 'most intense horror' at the 'disgraceful acts' which had been committed against the Japanese residents. Swift arrangements, he declared, had been made to concentrate the Japanese in places of safety: there had been 'some inevitable overcrowding and discomfort at first', but this had 'been overcome'. Nothing was said about the Japanese military thrust which had provoked the disturbances, except that the Chinese had rioted in response to what Peel said sniffily 'has been usually described as a day of humiliation'.[106] So far as Peel and his colleagues were concerned it was the great strike and boycott all over again, an upheaval engineered by the Chinese Communists and subversive of law and order in general.[107] As in the great strike and boycott the British were able to call on a certain amount of support from the gentry. The gentry undoubtedly shared in the public distress at the rape of Manchuria. The *Gong Shang Ribao* newspaper, which had passed into the ownership of Sir Robert Ho Tung (and which the authorities did not dare to suppress for that reason), took a consistently anti-Japanese line. But the gentry's indignation at Japan was apparently outweighed by their dread of public disorder. 'Responsible Chinese', Peel reported to the Colonial Office, 'greatly resent the action of the rioters and are assisting the government'.[108]

All things said and done, Japan's advance in Manchuria was a long way from British Hong Kong. But the trouble was edging closer. In July 1937, after years of local clashes between the Japanese and Nationalist troops in north China, Japan plunged into an all-out invasion of the Chinese interior. A China Expeditionary Force was formed, and began to advance down the Yangtze valley. First Shanghai fell, and then Nanking, the Nationalist capital, in a victory celebrated by the Japanese troops with the massacre of an estimated 300,000 Chinese civilians and the rape of perhaps 50,000 Chinese women. After that it was south China's turn. In October 1938 Major-General Tanaka Hisakazu landed his 21st Army at Bias Bay, on the coast of Guangdong province, a short distance to the north-east of the New Territories. Tanaka's objective was not Hong Kong but Canton, which he duly captured after a nine-day campaign. But the war had arrived at the colony's gates. Had, indeed, swept through them, as the Hong Kong population was swelled by the influx of more than half a million mainland refugees.

The effect was to throw the contrast between the perspectives of the British and Chinese communities into even sharper relief. Hong Kong now became a principal centre of the Chinese resistance to Japan. As the Japanese captured the mainland ports and Chiang Kai-shek's government retreated to Chungking in the south-western province of Sichuan, the colony started to serve the beleaguered Nationalists as a lifeline to the outside world. Up until early 1939, around 60 to 70 per cent of the war materials reaching the Nationalists from overseas came in through Hong Kong, at first on the railway which ran from Kowloon to Canton and later, after the fall of Canton when the Japanese cut the railway route, on innumerable junks. With a view to speeding up these supplies the Nationalists moved back on to the Hong Kong stage, pouring into the colony in large numbers and bringing with them an entire administrative infrastructure. By 1939 a total of thirty-two Nationalist government organs were operating in Hong Kong on what the British Foreign Office described as an 'official and semi-official' basis. They included the Ministries of Finance, Railways and Communications, a Government Purchasing Commission and a Natural Resources Commission of the Bureau of Foreign Trade, a National Salvation Bonds and Flotation Committee and a Central Trust Bureau.[109] The Bank of China, directed by the father of the architect I. M. Pei, printed hundreds of millions of Chinese yuan to replenish Chiang Kai-shek's coffers. Most important of all, almost certainly, was an obscure-sounding body called the South-west Transportation Company, which not only played the leading role in arms procurement but also served as a cover for an elaborate intelligence network. This network was supervised by some of Chiang's toughest henchmen, notably Wu Tiecheng, a former Nationalist police chief and mayor of Shanghai, and Du Yuesheng ('Big-eared Du'), kingpin of the Shanghai underworld, who was wearing the innocuous hat of vice-president of the Chinese Red Cross. Officers of the network monitored the activities of the Japanese forces in occupied regions of south China, while simultaneously keeping an eye on the Communists and other potential opponents through an agent they had positioned among the Chinese employees of the British Special Branch. Finally several of the chief figures in the Nationalist regime, such as Mme Chiang Kai-shek, her brother T. V. Soong, then serving as Chairman of the All-China Economic Commission, and her brother-in-law H. H. Kung, China's topmost financier, treated the colony as a kind of offshore shelter where they retreated for weeks or occasionally months at a time. The journalist Lady Drummond Hay declared with only a touch of exaggeration that British Hong Kong had become 'the capital of China'.[110]

The Communists also were back on the scene, harnessed to their Nationalist rivals under the uneasy agreement which the two parties had reached at the end of 1936 to join forces against Japan.[111] Like their rivals the Communists busied themselves with procuring war supplies. In January 1938 Liao Chengzhi, a leading Cantonese official of their Party, set up on the premises of a wholesale tea business at 18, Queen's Road Central an office whose function was to act as a purchasing agency for the Communist Eighth Route and New Fourth Armies.[112] Like their rivals the Communists kept watch on the movements of the Japanese forces with the help of no less than three different intelligence outfits, streamlined from the middle of 1939 by two agents who had been transferred for that purpose from Mao's headquarters in the north-western stronghold of Yan'an.[113] In addition the Communists drew on their traditional strength in the Hong Kong labour movement. The Communist-leaning trade unions which the British had banned ten years earlier stirred back into life: the Chinese Seamen's Union, for example, concealed its identity by adopting the somewhat flimsy pseudonym of the Hong Kong Seamen's Union and set about raising funds for the resistance and instituting a boycott of Japanese goods. One of the principal organizers of the Seamen's Union was a Chinese brought up in Australia by the name of Zeng Sheng. He began to recruit local volunteers to cross over to Guangdong province and lay the foundations for a guerrilla movement behind the Japanese lines. Relief supplies for this fledgling guerrilla force were mobilized through the exertions of Mme Sun Yat-sen, the left-leaning widow of the founder of the Nationalist Party and elder sister of Mme Chiang Kai-shek. In June 1938 Mme Sun had set up in Hong Kong a China Defence League devoted to channelling money and medicines to the Chinese armies resisting Japan, and more especially to the Communist ones. She was said to be 'sending charcoal in snowy weather'.[114]

Other categories of mainland Chinese in Hong Kong made their own contributions to the war effort. Industrialists from Shanghai and the other occupied cities of the interior withdrew to the colony and set up there new factories designed to meet the needs of the Nationalist forces. These factories included iron and steel works and a number of plants which made overtly war-related equipment such as gas masks, metal helmets and military radios. Writers and journalists arrived intent on striking a blow in the form of anti-Japanese propaganda. Some of them worked for Nationalist propaganda organs. The Nationalist Central News Agency ran an office in the colony, and most of the principal newspapers of the Nationalist Party and government were published there.[115] But most of the prominent Chinese writers of this period were left-of-centre or Communist-inclined personalities at odds with the Nationalist government; and it was they who played the leading role. The first of them moved in from the mainland following Japan's seizure of the intellectual capital, Shanghai, in 1937. Hundreds more followed four years later, when the Nationalist regime were beginning to resume their harassment of their Communist allies: Hong Kong was a natural bolt-hole, and the Communist leader Zhou Enlai gave instructions that it should be used as a base for disseminating his Party's perspective on the Sino-Japanese conflict to South-east Asia and the West.[116] The effect was that while the British expatriates played polo and rugger, the colony became a headquarters for very nearly everyone who was anyone in the Chinese literary world. Among the more celebrated of these intellectual immigrants were the novelist Mao Dun and the Shanghai journalist Qiao Guanhua, who would serve nearly forty years later as Communist China's Foreign Minister at the tail-end of the Cultural Revolution. They launched a whole series of journals and literary supplements, and the Symbolist poet Dai Wangshu devoted himself to translating a Spanish work entitled *Lullabies of the War of Resistance*.

The British were caught between a rock and a hard place. The authorities did not want to run the political risk of enraging the Chinese public by suppressing all manifestations of resistance activity. In addition they felt a good deal of sympathy for Nationalist China's efforts to stand up to Japan: this was not 1931. Sir Geoffry Northcote, who had succeeded Sir Andrew Caldecott as Governor shortly after the outbreak of full-scale war, wrote to the Colonial Office that while he wished to avoid giving the Japanese any 'legitimate ground for complaint' against his administration he was on the other hand 'anxious to do nothing which would hamper the Chinese authorities in the defence of their own country'.[117] At the same time Hong Kong was supposed to be a neutral zone in the conflict: neutrality was formally proclaimed in September

1938, and the overriding priority of the home government in London was to stop Britain getting dragged into a war with Japan at precisely the same time it found itself confronted in Europe by the double menace of Hitler and Mussolini. The officials in Hong Kong were also perturbed by the general resurgence in their domain of mainland-linked political activism, and especially by the new stirrings of the Chinese Communist Party. While the war had diverted the energies of political agitators from undermining the government to opposing Japan, this respite, the officials considered, might only be temporary. 'The communistic element was there', they observed, in the Hong Kong Seamen's Union, 'although kept in the background for the moment'.[118] There was still, it appears, a sense in which a threat to the Japanese was regarded as a threat to the British too.

The result was a nervous compromise. The authorities certainly turned a blind eye to a great many aspects of the resistance campaign. The Nationalist chiefs were allowed to move in and out of the colony, and Mme Chiang Kai-shek became the first non-European since 1918 to be granted permission to live on the Peak.[119] The 'official and semi-official' Nationalist government organs pursued their work unmolested, and the Nationalist Party, which was officially banned, operated out of the second floor of the Shell Building, its presence an open secret. The Communists were a harder mouthful to swallow, but the obvious diplomatic objection to their reappearance in the colony had been removed by the pact they made with the Nationalist government in 1936; and Liao Chengzhi was permitted to open his office following a personal representation made by Zhou Enlai to the British ambassador in Chungking. The two gas mask factories were reported by Northcote to the Colonial Office, but no action seems to have been taken against them; and the Chinese community were quietly given the chance of supplying strategic goods to the mainland in oblique ways that avoided infringing the colony's formal neutrality. No one, for example, was allowed to supply petrol to unoccupied China in bulk. But petrol could still be retailed to local Chinese motorists – who drove it to a central depot, where it was poured into five-gallon tins, which were packed into small wooden boxes and taken to a border beach to await transportation to the interior.

These marks of indulgence, however, were abundantly offset by curbs. British favour to the Nationalists stopped short of countenancing any activity which might be construed as directly provocative to Japan. As early as November 1937 the Cabinet in London decided to veto a request by some foreign firms to assemble military aircraft in Hong Kong for export to the Nationalist regime. Restrictions on arms supplies were gradually tightened as Japanese pressure on the British government mounted, and in January 1939 all direct transportation of arms and ammunition from the colony to the mainland was banned. The following autumn Dai Li, the grand spymaster at the apex of Chiang Kai-shek's intelligence organization, was arrested by the British police on his arrival at Kai Tak airport. He had just enough time before the police reached him to swap the suitcase he was carrying, which contained his revolver and a sheaf of incriminating documents, for a second bag in which he kept a set of instruments for treating an inflammation of the nose. In May 1940 David Kung, son of H. H. Kung the financier, was expelled from the colony for attempting to operate an illegal radio station;[120] and in early 1941, when a contingent of Nationalist troops crossed the border into the New Territories to get away from the pursuing Japanese, the troops were disarmed and interned.

Equally stringent measures were taken to rein in the Communists and their sympathizers. In 1938 the Seamen's Union was suppressed once again; and any possible trouble from leftist elements was pre-empted by a Sedition Ordinance which empowered the authorities to punish or deport anyone who might 'raise discontent or disaffection against either the Hong Kong or British government'.[121] Despite (or perhaps because of) her great prestige Mme Sun Yat-sen was refused permission to broadcast over the colony's radio station an appeal to the American public to boycott trade with Japan and to American companies to stop supplying the Japanese with the scrap iron they used to make shells. In August 1939 the censorship regulations of 1925 were revamped. All Chinese publications now had to be registered with the authorities. Mainland journalists began to find themselves summoned to tense meetings with R. A. C. North, the Secretary for Chinese Affairs, who would issue them with lists of expressions their papers were not to use in referring to the Japanese. Taboo phrases included 'enemy', 'dwarf pirates', 'dwarf slaves', 'dwarf barbarians', 'shrimp barbarians', 'island barbarians', 'Eastern slaves', 'Japanese pirates', 'savage pirates', 'savage Japanese', 'bestial acts', 'bestial nature', 'bestial troops', 'bandits', 'shameless burning and looting', 'rape', 'plunder' and 'butchery'.[122] Correspondence between Hong Kong and the Chinese mainland was also made subject to censorship. The poet Dai Wangshu was hauled in for interrogation for having received anti-Japanese propaganda from the interior.

A number of the expatriates were outraged at this policy of equivocation. The war on the mainland had brought to Hong Kong a new wave of British progressives determined to alleviate the suffering of the refugees in the colony and to do what they could for the mainland resistance. Prominent among them was Selwyn Selwyn-Clarke, who arrived in 1938 to take up the post of Director of Medical Services. A high-minded Victorian liberal, he had maintained from his childhood an unswerving belief in the brotherhood of man. He coaxed Governor Northcote to accompany him on a night-time walk among the thousands of refugees sleeping out on the streets in order to secure the Governor's backing for the establishment of a number of refugee camps. The Director's wife Hilda, a redhead with an 'electrifying' presence who had stood for Parliament in Britain as a candidate of the Labour Party, assumed the role of Honorary Secretary to Mme Sun Yat-sen's China Defence League, and busied herself with the shipment of medicines and funds.[123] Margaret Watson, a graduate of the London School of Economics, came out in 1939 and ministered to the refugees as the colony's first almoner, or medical social worker responsible for nutrition and hygiene. By the end of the year she had trained four Chinese social workers to help in her efforts.[124]

Attached to this activist circle were a couple of gadfly American journalists. One of them, Emily Hahn, had come down from Shanghai, where she had written a column supportive of the mainland resistance called 'Candid Comment'. Busy researching a biography of Mme Sun and the two other famous Soong sisters, she mixed easily in Chinese company and also managed to advertise her unorthodox outlook in certain peripheral ways. She gave birth to a child by Major Charles Boxer, the (married) head of British army intelligence, and announced the event in the colony's press with the notice, 'To Major Boxer and Miss Hahn, a daughter'. And she made a habit of roaming the Hong Kong streets in the company of a pet gibbon.[125] A second, more steely reporter was Agnes Smedley, who arrived in the colony in the summer of 1940 after a long and admiring stint with the Chinese Red Army. She held political meetings, gave lectures and arranged funds and medical treatment for Xiao Hong, a girl novelist from Manchuria who was dying of tuberculosis.

In circumscribing the role Hong Kong played in the Chinese resistance, the government none the less mirrored the attitudes of the bulk of the British trading community. Typical Peakites had no time for the exertions of the expatriate radical set. They did not approve of 'Septic Selwyn' and 'Red Hilda', and they thought Agnes Smedley should be locked up.[126] They did not want help to be given to the mainland refugees for fear of encouraging an influx of millions more. And they had no great feeling for the Chinese cause. Some of them viewed the Japanese invasion of China as quite a useful antidote to the upsurge of nationalism there. Many others hoped that Japan would arrive at a non-aggression arrangement with Britain in a sort of riposte to the Nazi–Soviet pact.[127] Above all they wanted business as usual. They wanted to leave the Orientals to fight each other while they carried on making money and pursuing the pleasant round of swimming and racing and dinner at the Parisian Grill. Passing through the colony in February 1938 on his way to observe the fighting in China, the poet W. H. Auden commented on the ludicrous detachment with which his hosts on the Peak went about their daily routine:

> A bugle on this Late Victorian hill
> Puts out the soldier's light; off-stage, a war
> Thuds like the slamming of a distant door.
> Each has his comic role in life to fill
> Though Life be neither comic nor a game.[128]

The Janus-like posture of the government also seems to have been quite acceptable from the point of view of the gentry. The gentry undoubtedly made handsome gestures of support for the mainland resistance. In 1936, even before the all-out fighting had started, Sir Robert Ho Tung donated a military aircraft as a fiftieth birthday present for Chiang Kai-shek; and when the fighting did start, his son, Major Robbie Ho Shai-lai, served as a staff officer with the Nationalist command. Sir Shouson Chow sat on the committee which had been set up to promote the sale of Nationalist government bonds, and M. K. Lo chaired another committee which busied itself with raising money for mainland relief work. But the gentry also had a good deal to gain from the colony's continued neutrality. The conflict on the mainland had given a tremendous fillip to the Hong Kong economy. With the mainland ports occupied, around half of China's entire foreign trade had begun to pass through the colony; and the millions of dollars invested by refugee mainland tycoons had produced a dramatic growth in the colony's Chinese-owned light industrial sector. By 1940 it is thought that the colony may have possessed as many as 7,500 factories, still mostly but by no means entirely tiny; and Prince Edward Road in Kowloon hummed to the sound of textile looms.[129] In the shadow of war Hong Kong boomed, with a rapidly growing export surplus and the supremacy it had lost to Shanghai at the turn of the century for the moment regained – and the impetus behind the boom was coming from the Chinese and not from the British side. Neutrality also permitted the gentry, like the expatriates, to continue enjoying an agreeable lifestyle. In 1938 Dr Li Shu-fan, for example, went off to shoot elephant in French Indochina: two years later he was in Canada bagging moose. The British for their part relied on the gentry to help them manage the mainlanders' outpouring of patriotic zeal. Any mainlander wishing to register a journal for publication had first to find a member of the gentry to act as their sponsor. The gentry were felt to be restrained enough in their own resistance activity to merit exemption when the postal censorship was introduced.

The British authorities considered that their approach to the Chinese cause was one of 'benevolent neutrality'.[130] The mainland activists and their local supporters took a different view. In their eyes the British were feeling their way to a 'Far Eastern Munich'.[131] Dai Li, the grand spymaster, is said to have been sufficiently livid as a result of the two-day detention in a police-cell which followed his arrest at Kai Tak that he never wanted to set foot in Hong Kong again: we are told that from then on he 'especially hated the British and praised the Americans'.[132] The measures the government took to stifle attacks on Japan in the Chinese press were widely resented – all the more so in view of the discrimination that already underlay the government's censorship rules. One veteran mainland diplomat pointed out that the muzzling of Chinese reportage was not only unfair but ridiculous, in that items of war news which had been excised from the Chinese press by the government censors had a tendency to appear anyhow – in the uncensored English papers.[133] Once they had managed to track down a sponsor among the gentry (not always an easy process), any mainlanders wishing to bring out an anti-Japanese publication then had to bamboozle the censors by choosing an innocuous title such as *Hua Shang Bao* (Chinese Commercial Daily).[134] The exasperation all this caused was reinforced by a certain outrage at the way in which British and gentry alike were enjoying the soft life – were fiddling while China burned.

In spite of the refugees, to a great extent even in spite of the outbreak of war in Europe, the colony coasted into the 1940s with its serenity unimpaired. The golf-balls clacked. The cafés and dance-halls were crowded. Visitors flying in by night from the blacked-out cities of the mainland were astounded at the glitter of lights below. Even Xia Yan, a journalist hand-picked by Zhou Enlai to take charge of the left-wing propaganda drive, conceded that the colony seemed like an Arcadia. But how long could Arcadia last? As far back as 1936 a mainland Chinese politician with contacts in Tokyo had prophesied to Emily Hahn, the American journalist, over a peaceful lunch on the terrace of the Repulse Bay Hotel that the British were in for 'a rude awakening'.[135]

The Japanese plan an invasion

In that same year, 1936, the Japanese Chief of Staff, Prince Kanin, presented Emperor Hirohito with a defence plan in which Britain was formally listed, for the first time, as a potential enemy country. The Emperor raised an eyebrow. His visit to Britain in the course of his world tour in 1921 had left him imbued with a certain amount of Anglophilia; and there were still some circles in Japan in favour of a return to the palmy days of the Anglo-Japanese Alliance. Kanin explained that the listing of Britain as a possible foe was necessary 'in order to provide for an emergency', citing among other reasons the recent British refortification of Hong Kong and Singapore.[136] This shift in strategic thinking seemed vindicated the following year when Japan embarked on its all-out invasion of China. For all its official straining after neutrality, Hong Kong became a thorn in the Japanese flesh. Some authorities have suggested that the volume of arms supplies which reached the Chinese Nationalists through the colony was not, in fact, very large in absolute terms.[137] But in June 1940, when the railway link from Kowloon to Canton had been severed, when Japanese aircraft were carrying out incessant bombings of suspect Hong Kong junks, when maximum diplomatic pressure had been exerted on the British government and the colony's share of China's military imports had shrunk to 20 per cent, General Staff Headquarters in Tokyo still estimated that Hong Kong was channelling munitions to the interior at the rate of 6,000 tons a month.[138] If Hong

Kong could be seized it was clear that the defeat of Chiang Kai-shek might be brought significantly closer.

The Japanese Army were by this stage acutely frustrated with the colossal and endless China war. Some of their leaders were still intent on an outright military victory: many others however were looking for a way to bring the war to a victorious end without the trouble of fighting. At the end of 1938 they had won over a segment of the Chinese Nationalists under Chiang Kai-shek's long-standing rival Wang Jingwei and had moulded it into a puppet regime. But Wang's willingness to cooperate was uncertain, and his group had been ineffective in attracting wider support. By the autumn of 1939 elements in the Army, associated ironically with Ishiwara Kanji, one of the three colonels who staged the original bombing incident in Manchuria, had begun to favour extracting Japan from the war through a deal with Chiang himself. As a neutral enclave frequented by several leading members of the Nationalist government Hong Kong was an obvious place in which to put out feelers; and in November the headquarters of the China Expeditionary Force embarked on a gambit that became known as Operation Kiri. Secret peace talks were initiated in the colony with a Nationalist team headed by Song Ziliang, an obscure younger brother of Mme Chiang Kai-shek who was currently serving as director of the South-west Transportation Company. By July 1940 the talks had bogged down. The Japanese envoys had failed to win any substantial concessions from the Nationalist side, and were indeed in some doubt as to whether their chief interlocutor was really Song Ziliang, or a Nationalist agent posing as Song Ziliang who had been given the special mission of leading them up the garden path.[139] Many of the Army top brass, however, continued to believe that Hong Kong might be the key to a settlement. If the colony could be taken, they reasoned, Chiang might be induced to recognize the futility of relying on help from the outside and might see the advantages of coming to terms.[140]

In the meantime events in Europe were beginning to open up altogether new vistas. In June 1940, with France and the Netherlands subdued by the Nazi blitzkrieg and Britain under siege, the European colonies in South-east Asia had been left headless. The chance seemed at last to have come to realize General Saigo's old dream of a thrust to the South that would put an end to European power in the region. Such a thrust would also enable Japan to secure access to the wealth of the former European colonies by merging them into a great, Japanese-managed empire – the 'Co-Prosperity Sphere'. Hong Kong in this context lacked the vast natural resources of territories like Malaya and the Dutch East Indies. But to a poor country such as Japan still was, Hong Kong too appeared a choice morsel with its huge concentration of Chinese and Western capital. One Japanese merchant in the colony remarked that he felt as though he were 'looking into a well-to-do man's charming garden through a hedge'.[141] The mood in Tokyo was expectant, and the watchword (a mocking echo of a fatuous comment which the British Prime Minister Chamberlain had made about Hitler on the eve of the blitzkrieg) was 'Don't miss the bus!'[142]

Virtually from the moment that Britain was marked down as a potential enemy by Prince Kanin, the Army began to make preparations for an eventual attack on Hong Kong. The first step was intelligence gathering. Major Arisue Yadoru, a strategist who had been serving as an assistant military attaché at the Japanese embassy in London, was transferred to the Military Operations Section of General Staff Headquarters and given the task of collecting information about the defences of Hong Kong and Singapore. Japanese historians observe in an apologetic tone that on account of the Army's embroilment in the China war the collection of data on Hong Kong took place only 'gradually';[143] but the intelligence drive can scarcely be faulted for slackness. Most of the principal branches of the Army's Special Service Organization, the Tokumu Kikan, were active in Hong Kong, and the numbers of agents are reckoned to have run into hundreds. Hong Kong as a neutral zone was wide open to visitors from Japan as well as from Nationalist China; and Japanese passed in and out in a constant stream. By May 1937 staff of the 'China Development Company', a Canton-based subsidiary of the South Manchurian Railway which was endowed with a constitution of spectacular vagueness and received its expenses direct from the Army Ministry in Tokyo, were making repeated 'business trips' to the colony and laying the groundwork for much of the subsequent espionage.[144] A Colonel Suzuki Takuji arrived in the colony on a secondment 'to study English': he made no discernible progress, but instead assumed overall control of the local spy network.[145] Japanese 'tourists' pressed in to photograph the beautiful dockyards and to hunt and fish in the neighbourhood of gun emplacements and military roads.[146] Other visitors included trainee diplomats, journalists, medical missions and teams of 'economic investigators', and even a troop of elderly Boy Scouts.[147]

In addition the Army were able to call on the services of local Japanese who had been in the colony so long as to become part of the landscape. A Mr Yamashita who had worked since 1929 as the barber in the Hong Kong Hotel cut the hair of leading British officials from the Governor downwards and asked superfluous questions about the comings and goings of ships. At Nagasaki Joe's, a popular Japanese bar in the Wanchai district, a pint of beer cost ten cents less than anywhere else in town; and the girls made a beeline for British naval ratings.[148] Officials employed by the local Japanese institutions began to develop a new urge to seek out British friends. One of the chancellors from the Japanese consulate explained that he was an aristocrat and a Cambridge man who had been banished from Japan because of his pro-British leanings, and a monolingual chief priest at the Japanese temple professed to be a Shakespearean scholar.[149]

Finally, just in case Japanese might be unduly conspicuous, some use was made of auxiliaries in the form of intelligence agents recruited in Japan's long-established Chinese colony of Taiwan. From as early as 1932 immigrants from Taiwan had been moving into Hong Kong and finding work there as shopkeepers, farmers and fishermen. These 300-odd newcomers spoke a different form of Chinese to the Cantonese dialect prevalent in Hong Kong; but this does not seem to have hindered their ability to blend in. The British authorities made no distinction between them and the rest of the Chinese population, and did not require them to declare on arrival in the colony their status as Japanese nationals. By 1937 a contingent of these Taiwanese were quietly setting up small farms at selected points in the New Territories, where the Japanese Army arranged for them to be provided with radio transmitting sets.[150]

Within two or three years the industry of this legion of spooks was producing all the data Japan could desire. In August 1939 General Staff Headquarters were able to distribute to their troops a map of the Defence Installations in the Vicinity of Hong Kong. The scale of the map was 1: 25,000.[151] It has been conjectured that no target in the entire history of warfare was ever spied out with such thoroughness as Hong Kong in the run-up to the Japanese attack.[152]

From the end of 1939 the intelligence drive began to be supplemented by an equally massive programme of covert operations. Ultimate control of this programme was exercised by the Eighth Section of General Staff Headquarters, which was in charge of the Army's propaganda and subversion work.[153] The officer immediately responsible, however, was Major Okada Yoshimasa, who had been transferred from the Eighth Section to the intelligence and subversion staff of the China Expeditionary Force. Okada was the founder of an agency which was to play the leading role in Japan's penetration of British Hong Kong. It changed names several times, but eventually came to be known as the Asia Development Organization or Koa Kikan. One of its principal tasks was to pave the way for Japan's attack on the colony by mobilizing the non-European majority population to undermine British rule from within.[154]

Okada's team accordingly set about recruiting local adherents. One method they used was propaganda. Since November 1938, when the Japanese premier Prince Konoye had unveiled his concept of a New Order in East Asia, Japan had been seeking to offer itself as the champion of all the Asian peoples in a grand crusade against Britain and the other European imperial powers. Okada's men began to disseminate anti-British publications in Hong Kong under cover of a body called the Canton Toyo Culture Research Office. Their efforts were aided by the old Japanese community paper, the *Honkon Nippo*, which now appeared in both a Chinese and an English edition.[155] But the Koa Kikan were not disposed to rely solely on their powers of conversion to build

up the full-scale fifth column they had in mind. Their principal target groups
were to be the Triad societies, the Chinese mafia who operated in many parts
of south China. These Triad networks abounded in the colony, and were reckoned to have not less than 60,000 members in Hong Kong Island alone.[156] The
Triads did, as it happens, nurse certain grievances against the British, who had
tried somewhat ineffectually to curb their activities; but the essential point was
that they could be bought. Hired Triad gangsters had already played a useful
part in the Japanese capture of Canton in October 1938.

In January 1940 Okada dispatched to Hong Kong a subordinate named
Sakata Seisho, a China hand who had studied in Peking in the 1920s and had
subsequently worked for the 'China Development Company'. Basing himself
at the Hong Kong Hotel under the Chinese alias of Tian Cheng, Sakata proceeded to make contacts among Triad members who ranged from seamen to
the hotel's attendant population of cooks, rickshaw pullers and 'boys'. Huge
sums, we are told, were distributed to the main Triad gangs. With the help of
the Triad bosses Sakata organized two underground squads whose assignment
was to foment anti-British disturbances on Hong Kong Island and in Kowloon.
These squads were known respectively as the Heaven Group and the Help
Group, after the Chinese saying 'Success comes with Heaven's help'; and in due
course revolvers and hand grenades were issued to them. Before Sakata could
proceed any further his Japanese-accented Mandarin gave him away, and on
12 May he was arrested and imprisoned by the Hong Kong police. This however
was a mere hiccup: within two weeks Sakata had escaped, with the help of his
Triad connections, and had slipped across the Pearl River delta to Macao.[157]
Ever since the 21st Army arrived in Canton in October 1938, the Japanese had
had their eye on the Portuguese colony as a place where the level of vigilance
against them was low and their influence potent. (The dentist who headed
their local community had the run of the Governor's mansion.)[158] In Macao
Sakata enlisted the aid of Fung Yung, a leader of the powerful Wo Shing Wo
Triad whom the British had deported from Hong Kong with his followers the
previous year. At least 1,000 of the Wo Shing Wo's total membership of 5,000
were purchased for Japanese service, and Fung was instructed to infiltrate them
back to Hong Kong with the task of engaging in arson and other disruptions
when the critical moment arose.[159]

The idea was that these various anti-British disorders inside the colony
would evoke an immediate response from outside in the form of a Chinese
army of liberation. The Koa Kikan had set up for this purpose two entire divisions of mafiosi comprising between 10,000 and 20,000 men. Recruited this
time from a different set of secret societies in the northern province of Henan,
and placed under the leadership of a certain Xie Wenda, this irregular force
hovered on the edge of the Pearl River delta between Canton and Macao with
a fleet of 200 junks. In April 1940 a portion of the force slipped across the delta

to the county of Bao'an, on the north-western border of the New Territories, and busied themselves with seizing the petrol supplies that continued to be smuggled out of the colony for the benefit of Chiang Kai-shek. In early October, it was reckoned, the time would be ripe for them to cross the border and strike at Kowloon.[160]

In the meantime the Army themselves were getting ready, slowly but steadily, for the regular military thrust. On 14 December 1939 the Imperial sanction was given to a hypothetical Hong Kong Operation, to be carried out by the Army with naval support. Captain Sejima Ryuzo was given the task of researching the Operation, and in July 1940 he came to Hong Kong in person and carried out a full-scale feasibility study. Sejima recommended that the invasion force should begin by securing possession of the New Territories and Kowloon. The next stage was more difficult. Sejima had a healthy respect for the British defences, and he tended to feel that a naval blockade was to be preferred as a means of subduing Hong Kong Island to a hazardous attempt at landing troops. If a landing had to be made (and he conceded that a naval blockade might well prove ineffective), then the troops should be set down on the south shore of the Island rather than made to run the risk of a frontal assault from Kowloon.[161] Sejima's views on this point, however, were overruled following a report from Triad informants that the British had recently conducted a military exercise in which a direct attack had been staged on the north shore – and the landing had proved a success.[162] Throughout the euphoric summer of 1940 the 21st Army were ready to move.[163] In September the invasion was shelved (along with the projected advance by Xie Wenda's mafiosi), partly because it now seemed clear that Britain was not yet about to collapse and partly because the Japanese were busy with the occupation of the northern part of French Indochina.[164] From the end of the year, however, the 21st Army were getting intensively trained for a stealthy ninja-type onslaught upon the British positions in the New Territories. Amid the judiciously chosen terrain of White Cloud Mountain near Canton they scrambled up rope ladders and wriggled between mock-ups of the British fortifications. In particular they practised night fighting, a technique Japanese troops had perfected during the war with Russia in 1904–5, wearing dark glasses during the daytime to simulate a continuous nocturnal environment. A swimming squad also got trained to negotiate any mines that the British might have laid to obstruct the crossing of Hong Kong harbour. On 2 July 1941, with a possible northern threat from the Soviet Union taken care of by Germany, an Imperial conference in Tokyo took the essential decisions that committed the Japanese forces to striking south. The 21st Army was reorganized into a new force of 39,700 men; and this new 23rd Army was placed under the ominous leadership of Lieutenant-General Sakai Takashi, who had presided over the storming of Jinan in 1928. Sakai reached his post in Canton in the second week of November, and was promptly issued with orders to prepare to invade the colony. By December artillery intended for the invasion is said to have been ready and waiting in Hong Kong territory, camouflaged in the bunkers of the Japanese golf course at Shatin and hidden inside the godowns of Japanese companies on the Kowloon wharves.[165]

'An outpost to be held for as long as possible'

In a series of assessments carried out in the course of 1937–8, the Chiefs of Staff in London had arrived at the bleak conclusion that Hong Kong was indefensible. The colony, they advised, was an outpost, important but scarcely vital. If attacked by Japan it should be held for as long as possible; but no attempt should be made to strengthen its garrison or to reinforce its defences. By the summer of 1940 Lord Ismay, the Chief of the Imperial General Staff, even favoured reducing the garrison to cut down on the casualties they would suffer in a hopeless attempt to fight the Japanese off. The military authorities in Hong Kong responded to the Japanese danger in an appropriately passive way. From October 1938, when Canton fell, all work was abandoned on the miniature Maginot Line which the garrison had been constructing across the New Territories from Gin Drinkers' Bay to Tide Cove. Up on the border British police officers socialized with the forward units of the 21st Army, and Major Charles Boxer, the head of British army intelligence who was also a distinguished Japan scholar, organized beer parties and baseball matches in an effort to keep them sweet. The authorities were of course well aware of the extent of Japanese infiltration. How could they not be? Some of the Japanese agents had been almost comically obvious, like the man who was caught sitting in a boat near the harbour fortifications with a camera attached to his fishing rod.[166] But for fear of provoking Tokyo, crackdowns on Japanese spies were infrequent and cautious: three months of deliberation took place, for example, before the ringleader, Colonel Suzuki, was finally requested to clear out of the colony in December 1940.[167] The fatalistic approach of the Chiefs of Staff also seems to have commended itself to the leading officials in the Hong Kong government. Selwyn-Clarke, the liberal-minded Director of Medical Services, felt on humanitarian grounds that the colony ought not to put up any resistance whatever. Governor Northcote himself is said to have proposed (unsuccessfully) to the British War Cabinet that Hong Kong should be declared an open city and the Japanese forces allowed to march in.[168]

From the end of 1940 the strategic orthodoxy which had ruled out any serious defence of Hong Kong began to be challenged unexpectedly by a new, bullish school of thought. In February 1941 Air Marshal Sir Robert Brooke-Popham, the newly appointed British Commander-in-Chief in the Far East, recommended to London that the colony both could and should be reinforced.

Churchill growled. The British Prime Minister was certain that if Japan invaded there was 'not the slightest chance of holding Hong Kong or relieving it'.[169] Eight months later, however, Churchill accepted an identical recommendation which had been made through the Chiefs of Staff by the retiring commander of the Hong Kong garrison, Major-General A. E. Grasett. The Chiefs of Staff had argued on Grasett's behalf that a change of policy was warranted by the general improvement of Britain's position in the Far East, citing the recent strengthening of British defences in Malaya and 'a certain weakness' which they had detected in the behaviour of Japan.[170] A more compelling reason for Churchill's uncharacteristic reversal was the attitude of the United States. Ever since the end of 1940 the Chiefs of Staff had been engaged in consultations with their United States counterparts about the common Japanese threat in the Pacific; and from at least April 1941 the American service chiefs had been urging the reinforcement of Hong Kong. The Americans reckoned that, along with their own domain of the Philippines, Hong Kong might perform a valuable service in containing or delaying a Japanese attack.[171] For Churchill, preoccupied that autumn with the urgent need to enlist the United States as an ally in the world conflict, reinforcing Hong Kong had suddenly assumed a symbolic importance. It would display solidarity with the Americans, who had just sent fresh troops to the Philippines; and it would impress the Americans with Britain's 'growing strength'.[172] A new orthodoxy had emerged that (in Selwyn-Clarke's neat phrase) Hong Kong 'could not be held but must be defended'.[173]

Charge of affairs on the spot had now been assumed by a new Governor, Sir Mark Young, an austere and awe-inspiring figure of an almost Churchillian toughness who arrived at his post in September 1941.[174] Young was assisted by a new garrison commander, Major-General C. M. Maltby, an Indian Army stalwart with a face like 'the mellowed red brick of an Elizabethan country house' who is said to have feared little but the presence of garlic in his curry and who maintained that the colony might even be turned into a base for attacking the Japanese forces in mainland China.[175] Together these two men did their best to prepare Hong Kong for a gallant stand. Some of the lesser officials had their private misgivings, but they carried out their instructions. The Gin Drinkers' Line was restored and reassigned its original function of holding up the Japanese invaders in the New Territories; and Hong Kong Island was prepared for a siege. Large stocks of tinned beef were accumulated for the benefit of the military. Mainly thanks to the efforts of Selwyn-Clarke, rather vigorous measures were also adopted to cater for the general public. A network of depots was organized in the urban areas where rice could be sold to the populace at a subsidized rate. Around the countryside reinforced concrete food stores were built and provisioned with rice, soya beans and groundnut oil; and dispersal zones complete with kitchens, running water and sanitation were set up to house any civilians who could be persuaded to move out of range of the expected Japanese bombers. In mid-November the reinforcements which had been recommended by Grasett arrived in the form of two battalions from Canada (Grasett had been a Canadian). The plan was to ensure that the colony could hold out for ninety days – until the United States fleet could arrive from Pearl Harbor.[176]

Unfortunately the public were not in any mood to slot into the role of heroic defenders that had been assigned them. The expatriates, to begin with, were in a state of semi-revolt. In June 1940, alarmed at the threat of invasion by both the regular Japanese forces and the mafiosi of Xie Wenda, the authorities had abruptly ordered the evacuation of all British women and children to Australia. As summer turned to autumn, however, and the expected crisis failed to develop, the evacuation seemed in expatriate eyes to have been an exercise in futility. To make matters worse it was found that the scheme had not been inflicted on all of the British alike. A minority of women, frantic to stay with their husbands, had managed to get themselves made exempt from the evacuation order, transmuted miraculously into nurses, stenographers and other 'essential personnel'; and a conspicuous number of these women turned out to have been the wives and daughters of high-ranking officials like the Commissioner of Police. The result was a furious hullabaloo from the ordinary British men who had not had the clout to keep their families with them. Four hundred of these men organized themselves into a noisy pressure group called the Bachelor Husbands. In a reminder of the old antipathy between the colony's officials and businessmen, the group received the support of the Hong Kong General Chamber of Commerce. Through the whole of the next year the Bachelor Husbands held mass meetings and fired off petitions to the Colonial Office demanding that the evacuation order be overturned. Some of them talked of downing tools and staging demonstrations at Government House. (Their wives joined the chorus from Australia: one woman wrote to Churchill informing him that 'a little Nazi colony' had taken shape in Hong Kong.)[177]

The discredit the government had brought on themselves in expatriate eyes through this episode was increased by the outbreak of two epic scandals. In the winter of 1940–1 a department which had been set up for the first time in the colony's history to control immigration was found to be operating in a state of virtual chaos, with 'irregularities' taking place on all sides as its agents blithely dispensed unauthorized residence permits. The following summer it emerged that an urgent programme which had been launched for the construction of air-raid shelters had spawned a whole mass of disreputable contracts. The official in charge of the programme, Wing Commander A. H. S. Steele-Perkins, the Director of Air Raid Precautions (ARP), was suspected of having been coaxed by his Chinese girlfriend, Mimi Lau, into letting her company supply the shelters with pre-cast concrete breeze blocks which failed to match up to specifications (and were subsequently known as Mimi Laus).

Two successive commissions of inquiry had to be instituted to deal with these embarrassments, and the belief became widespread among the expatriates that the entire government apparatus was riddled with graft. In September the outgoing Governor Northcote set off for home with 'a nasty taste in my mouth'.[178]

The gentry still seemed outwardly to be as dependable as ever. They were still headed by the same two stalwarts who had rescued the British in the crisis of the mid-1920s – Sir Shouson Chow, now rising eighty but in the words of a Chinese chronicler still 'vigorous and kind',[179] and Sir Robert Kotewall, who had succeeded to Chow's seat on the Executive Council in 1936 and had received his knighthood two years later. In January 1941 these two veterans appeared at the broadcasting station to deliver addresses marking the centenary of British rule in Hong Kong. Chow praised the 'sound and just administration' of the British and the security which it offered to trade, investment and industry. 'No less productive of good', Kotewall added, 'has been the relationship between Government and people'; and he drew attention to 'the practice of consulting responsible Chinese opinion before a decision is made'.[180] This forelock-tugging, however, was not a sure guide to the gentry's opinions. The growing danger of war had in fact tended to aggravate a good many of the discontents that had festered in gentry circles over the past several years. In 1939 M. K. Lo, champion of the non-European underdog, had taken exception to the reported provisions of a Compulsory Service Ordinance which had been passed as war loomed in Europe to mobilize all British nationals in the colony for military duties. Those mobilized had included an appreciable number of Eurasians, many of whom held British passports – but rumour had it that the Europeans were to be accorded higher rates of pay.[181] The following year the government's evacuation order hit the Eurasian gentry every bit as hard as it did the stampeding Bachelor Husbands – for the opposite reason. Many leading Eurasian families could see, more clearly than their expatriate counterparts, that a Japanese invasion was inevitable. Their women wanted to leave, and they assumed that as holders of British passports they were entitled to do so. But the evacuation was restricted to persons of 'pure' British descent. The government in Canberra had signalled that only 'pure' British would be welcome in their Dominion under the White Australia policy of the day. The position, however, was not relayed in time to prevent some Eurasian women from leaving on the evacuation ship alongside the 'pures'; and these women duly found themselves weeded out in the course of a stopover at Manila by two energetic British memsahibs. Back in Hong Kong M. K. Lo condemned the 'disgraceful discrimination';[182] and the distress was by no means limited to him. The ban on 'impures' had also upset the usually docile Portuguese merchant and professional families, many of whom also held British passports. Their spokesman, Leo d'Almada e Castro, warned the Legislative Council that the government had 'placed an appreciable strain on the loyalty of a large section of the community'.[183] Further indignation was aroused after applications for the post of Assistant Director of Immigration were found to have been restricted to 'pure' Europeans. Under the surface Emily Hahn detected 'a strong anti-British feeling' among the Asian upper classes.[184]

Ordinary Chinese, too, were starting to show their impatience with British privilege as Britain came more and more obviously under threat in the outside world. After the outbreak of war in Europe in 1939 some hairdressers refused to climb up the Peak any longer to give the expatriate ladies their shampoos and sets. Feeding an ice-cream to one of her gibbons in a side-street in the company of a British official, Emily Hahn drew an angry crowd. 'It's not nice to buy an ice cream for a monkey. The money you rich people have spent on that ice cream is probably as much as my wages for a day'.[185] One Chinese source estimated that fully 30 per cent of the population were aggrieved at the British for their authoritarian rule and their lack of interest in consulting with anyone but the gentry.[186] There was certainly some disgust among the Chinese as well as among the expatriate public at the mounting evidence of government sleaze. Phyllis Harrop, an enterprising Manchester girl who had been seconded to the police force by the Secretariat for Chinese Affairs, observed looking back on the second half of 1941, 'Feeling against us has been running high for some months now, and the ARP scandal did nothing to help.'[187]

Even more ominously there had begun to appear certain pockets of unmistakable sympathy for Japan. The Japanese had combined their call to arms against the European overlords with a firm stand against revolution in traditional Asian societies; and this formula seems to have won them a number of adherents among the propertied Asians of Hong Kong. Opposition to the Europeans appealed, for example, to a manager of the Bank of Communications named Lau Tit-shing. A graduate of the Law School of Tokyo Imperial University, Lau had returned to the colony impressed with the need to fight the White Peril. To promote this objective he took up office as president of an association of Hong Kong Chinese who had studied, as he had, at universities in Japan.[188] Chan Lim-pak was more interested in the social plank of the Japanese manifesto. This ultra-conservative member of the gentry, who had made a huge fortune as a comprador of the Hongkong and Shanghai Bank, first gave evidence of his political outlook in 1924, when he served the British (in exactly the same way as Kotewall and Chow were to do a year later) by organizing an armed attempt to overthrow the Nationalist regime in Canton. Employed in Canton by the Bank in the late 1920s, Chan developed a friendly relationship with Wang Jingwei, the future puppet, and also with a military attaché at the Japanese consulate called Isogai Rensuke; and in the following years he seems to have reached the conclusion that a Japanese conquest of China, including Hong Kong, offered the best protection for traditional Chinese society against the twin evils of Nationalism and Communism. He was the counterpart of those members of the contemporary French upper classes who adopted the motto '*Mieux Hitler que Blum*'.[189]

Further down the society scattered support for Japan was also to be found among those Asian minority groups whom the British liked to use as buffers between themselves and the mass of the Chinese population. Occupying as they did a sort of social limbo, accepted by neither the British nor the Chinese, these lonely communities made rather obvious targets for Japan's pan-Asiatic evangelism. One or two of the humbler Eurasians had gravitated towards the Japanese from an early date. Joseph Richards, for instance, had been working as an 'adviser' to the Japanese consulate since 1932. He declared that he had received very little consideration from the British, in spite of the fact that his father had been a British consul – whereas the Japanese appreciated his services.[190] A small-time wheeler-dealer named Joseph Carroll was linked to Japan through his mother, who had grown up in Yokohama. In 1939 he had helped the Japanese consulate to buy a new office building conveniently situated overlooking the Naval Dockyard. He expressed his astonishment at the general prejudice against Japanese goods and helped Japanese firms to obtain strategic metals such as tungsten and manganese.[191] A small knot of eight to ten journalists were in the habit of voicing pro-Japanese views. Their backgrounds were varied (some were actually British, of a seedy variety); but the majority were Eurasians.[192]

Disaffected already thanks to the aloof attitude of the local European masters, the Indian community had one powerful extra reason for finding virtue in Japan. Many of these 7,000-odd Indians were absorbed in their homeland's struggle for independence from the British Raj.[193] Indians opposed to the Raj had found sponsors in Tokyo as far back as the time of the First World War;[194] and as the Imperial Japanese Army began to rear up for a strike at the European empires in Asia it seemed to some Hong Kong Indians to hold out hope of national freedom. Particular excitement was fermenting among the Sikh police, some of whom had set up a local branch of the secret Indian Independence League. By December 1940 Sikh policemen involved with the League had begun to defect from the colony to Japanese-occupied Canton: news of their arrival was sent by the 21st Army to the Eighth Section of General Staff Headquarters in Tokyo, and three of them were forwarded to Bangkok to establish ties on behalf of the Japanese military with the League's other branches in South-east Asia.[195] The following year reports began to spread through the colony that the Sikh troops in the Hong Kong and Singapore Royal Artillery were plotting a mutiny. The cause of the trouble, like that of the original Indian Mutiny in 1857, was a religious one; the Sikhs claimed that the British were affronting their creed by compelling them to wear steel helmets instead of their traditional turbans; but the authorities had no doubt that Japanese propaganda had been at work. In the course of the year British experts had to be called in from India both to 'sort out' the Sikh contingent in the police force and to preempt the 'Tin Hat Mutiny' of the garrison troops. Major Boxer, the army intelligence chief, confided to Emily Hahn his opinion that when the 'maddened populace' finally turned on their European masters the Sikhs might well be in the lead.[196]

The Hong Kong Chinese masses were, understandably, less impressed by the gospel from Tokyo. Many of them, after all, had come to the colony precisely in order to get away from the Imperial troops who were devastating their country. Even here, however, certain enclaves were in cahoots with Japan. After Wang Jingwei deserted the Nationalists at the end of 1938, his partisans used Hong Kong as their initial headquarters; and a significant Wang faction emerged. This Wang faction published their own newspaper, the *Nan Hua Ribao* (South China Daily), and ran their own underground network.[197] Their ranks were augmented by the arrival of several hundred supporters, some partially armed, who had slipped into the colony alongside the mainland refugees.[198] By mid-1940 the British authorities had come to view the Wang faction as a potential source of revolt.

Added to these, finally, were the Triad gangsters and other low-life figures whose allegiance had been bought by the Koa Kikan. Typical recruits included George Wong, who managed a garage in Nathan Road, and Howard Tore, the proprietor of the Capital Ballroom in West Point, who welcomed all comers with an invariable opening gambit of 'Call me Howard'. A certain Millie Chun led a ring of girl spies who collected information for the Japanese from unsuspecting British Cadets and bank staff. In some of these cases the basic inducement of cash may have been reinforced by certain political or personal inclinations. George Wong is said to have liked watching films of Nazi rallies, and Call Me Howard had possibly been embittered by racial slights he experienced during a visit to Britain as a boy.[199]

By 1941 these assorted surrogates of Japan were visibly gnawing at the foundations of British power. During the spring and summer disturbances took place in the dockyards where the Royal Navy's warships were being built. Fitters and riveters walked out citing various minor grievances against the European foremen. The authorities were sure that either the Japanese or the Wang Jingwei faction had instigated the trouble.[200] In early October more than a hundred members of the Wo Shing Wo Triad were arrested at a meeting they had organized to decide how best to support a Japanese invasion.[201] During a series of air-raid drills which were held in the autumn unknown hands in a number of districts took advantage of the black-out to scatter anti-British leaflets around the streets.[202]

Faced with this general restlessness the British authorities understandably felt that their task was to keep up public morale and to guard against the worsening threat of subversion. In pursuing these goals they unfortunately cut themselves off more than ever from the colony's other social groups. To keep up morale they fed the expatriates a diet of remorseless optimism which wholly failed to convey the gravity of the Japanese danger or to prepare them for the prospect of a desperate siege. Military spokesmen propagated the dogma (first heard, and distrusted, by Rudyard Kipling on a visit to the colony in 1889) that Hong Kong was an 'impregnable fortress'. Cheerful newsreels described how the Peak was 'bristling with guns like the quills on a porcupine's back'.[203] Military intelligence was not always made fully available even to the most senior British businessmen, and they too were apt to be given the most optimistic possible spin on events. As late as the beginning of December 1941, when the 23rd Army was known to be stirring on the other side of the border, Young and Maltby combined to assure Sir Vandeleur Grayburn of the Hongkong and Shanghai Bank that if the Japanese made any trouble a naval force would be sent to the rescue from Singapore 'and everything would be hunky-dory'.[204]

For fear of subversion the government judged it best to rely as little as possible on the non-Europeans. Minimal information was shared with the gentry. On a shooting expedition near Junk Bay with his old friend Walter Scott, the Assistant Commissioner of Police, Dr Li Shu-fan was startled to witness the arrival of the Canadian reinforcements, about which he had heard not a murmur. The Assistant Commissioner, who had been in the know, was 'apologetic'.[205] Minimal effort was made to draw on local Asian manpower to supplement the garrison troops. Some training was administered to the Eurasian and Portuguese reservists who formed part of the Hong Kong Volunteer Defence Corps. But almost no steps were taken to mobilize the far larger numbers of Hong Kong Chinese. Controversy had raged for years round the question of whether local Chinese could safely be admitted to the Corps. A solitary Chinese company had been formed in 1937; but the experiment was not taken any further, and British resistance remained obdurate three years later in spite of the fact that the vast majority of the Hong Kong Chinese population were hostile to Japan. A letter sent by the War Office to the Colonial Office in London in August 1941 spelled out the official attitude:

> From the point of view of defence it would be no exaggeration to say that all Chinamen in Hong Kong would be open to suspicion of anti-British intentions should they be present in a siege of Hong Kong as part of a beleaguered populace. We feel that their reactions would immediately turn to the side which appeared likely to be the probable winner. The world situation and other such things we feel are unlikely to influence the transient loyalty of a Chinaman.[206]

As the war preparations intensified during the autumn the authorities were no longer able to be entirely fussy. In October Maltby embarked on an attempt to win permission from the War Office to recruit for the regular forces a single machine-gun battalion of British-officered Chinese. But the recruitment of Chinese seems to have been perceived very much as a last resort. A number of Chinese, we are told, 'had to be' enlisted in the First Regiment of the Hong Kong and Singapore Royal Artillery because the unit was much below strength. In November the government approached leading firms in the hope of obtaining 'responsible Hong Kong Chinese' who might be engaged as junior officers in the Civil Defence Services.[207]

For different reasons the British were equally reluctant to take help from mainland China. From the moment the Japanese threat to Hong Kong had begun to grow obvious the Nationalist regime in Chungking had been only too delighted to hold out a hand.[208] In 1939 Chiang Kai-shek had twice offered to take part in the defence of the colony. He was even prepared to send Hong Kong a defence force in the form of 200,000 Nationalist troops. The government in London declined. The risk of provoking Japan outweighed all other considerations.[209] In July 1940, with the Japanese and mafiosi poised to attack the New Territories, General Grasett was explicitly ordered not to get involved in any negotiations with Chiang. The following month Chiang made a fresh overture. He suggested the setting up of an armed Hong Kong Chinese volunteer force which would fight the Japanese side by side with the Nationalist armies in south China. London again said no.[210]

Some partnership was accepted in the restricted field of intelligence. In August 1940 Grasett sent Major Boxer to Chungking to improve Hong Kong's knowledge of the movements of the Japanese forces. With Chungking's blessing the British established a network of wireless telegraphy stations in parts of south China adjoining the colony to give warning of possible Japanese air raids. And in Hong Kong itself a close link was developed with Chan Chak, a Nationalist admiral raised in the colony who hobbles on to the stage like a kind of Chinese Long John Silver with a wooden leg and a prominent, pugnacious jaw. Shortly after Canton fell in 1938 this picturesque figure had been sent to Hong Kong by Chiang Kai-shek to take charge of the Nationalist underground there. Ostensibly a stock-broker, he had begun working quietly with the British police and intelligence services; and by 1940 he was helping to plug the gaps in British security in a fairly big way. Under Chan Chak's supervision steps were taken to counteract the manœuvres of the Koa Kikan. A Nationalist trade union official was brought into the colony to steady the seamen; and Zhang Zilian, a leader of the Triad network in Shanghai who had been coopted by Big-eared Du, was assigned to combat Japanese influence on the Hong Kong Triads.[211]

Over the following year, as the British rethought their fatalistic attitude to the defence of Hong Kong, it began to seem possible that this intelligence teamwork might after all blossom into an outright military alliance. In January

1941 Major-General L. E. Dennys was dispatched by Sir Robert Brooke-Popham to serve as military attaché to the British embassy in Chungking, in a first step towards the anticipated establishment of a wartime Military Mission. After some months of exploratory discussions Dennys agreed in a series of talks held in July and August with a group of Chiang's military chiefs that when (not if) the 23rd Army invaded Hong Kong the Nationalist forces would create a diversion by launching attacks on the Japanese rear. If the invasion were conducted by means of a blockade and bombing rather than a head-on assault the Nationalists would ease the pressure by breaking through the Japanese lines in one chosen sector in order to send in food supplies and at the same time evacuate the civilian residents.[212]

These advances, however, were less than they seemed. The British were not prepared to commit themselves to any joint action with China until the Japanese actually attacked them. They were also mistrustful of Chiang's motives for wanting to rescue Hong Kong.[213] It is striking that Dennys at no point suggested in his talks with Chiang's generals that a Nationalist army should actually march on the colony to raise the hypothetical Japanese siege. The agreements with the Nationalists were at least partly concluded to please Chiang and to encourage him in his war of resistance – which was, after all, tying down immense numbers of Japanese troops. By the beginning of December, as the 23rd Army stirred on the border, the British at last showed signs of coming round to the view that there might be a case for accepting some full-blooded Nationalist aid. Zheng Jiemin, a top-ranking staff officer from army headquarters in Chungking, arrived in the colony to visit Young and Maltby and to inspect the British defences.[214] Colonel S. K. Yee, who was stationed in the colony as second-in-command to Admiral Chan Chak, later claimed to have made in this first week of December a secret agreement with the British authorities under which he would take command of a Nationalist division to help defend Hong Kong.[215] But by then it was well past the eleventh hour.

The Communists too were willing to offer their help, and for a few weeks in the autumn of 1941 it looked as though the British were keen to enlist them. In late October and mid-November British military representatives held two rounds of exploratory talks with Liao Chengzhi at the Communist Party office in Queen's Road Central. The talks focused mainly on some Communist partisans known to be operating in Hainan, a large island 250 miles to the southwest of the colony which Japan had occupied almost three years before. The British suggested that these partisans might blow up the airfields on the island to prevent the Japanese using them to launch bombing raids on Hong Kong. Possibly because of the sheer remoteness of this Communist force such a project seemed harmless, and the British are actually said to have shipped a consignment of dynamite to Guangzhouwan (Fort Bayard), a French-held enclave on the mainland near Hainan, where the partisans picked it up.[216]

More directly relevant to the colony's prospects, however, was the Communist guerrilla band which had been taking shape behind the Japanese lines in Guangdong province, and which was now concentrated around the East River. By the autumn of 1941 these East River guerrillas were easily the most active Chinese resistance formation in the neighbourhood of Hong Kong. As the 23rd Army began to mass near the colony in the first few days of December the British military were moved to contact the Communists once again to discuss what support the guerrillas might be able to give them in the event of a Japanese attack. A third round of negotiations duly took place at Liao Chengzhi's office. The British were represented by a major from Maltby's headquarters, while Liao was joined by a political commissar attached to the guerrillas, a man named Lin Ping. Liao and Lin asked the British to supply the guerrillas with weaponry; and like the Nationalists they wanted the British to mobilize the mass of the Hong Kong Chinese. In return the guerrillas would do their bit to pin down the Japanese invasion force. The British response to begin with appeared highly positive. Maltby's delegate invited the guerrillas to set up a liaison group in the colony, and agreed to supply them with light and heavy machine-guns and other arms and ammunition enough to equip a contingent of 2,000 to 3,000 men. Matters had reached the point where the guerrillas had actually sent an envoy to sign an agreement and take delivery of the arms – when the British recoiled. They would, they now conveyed, only go ahead with the deal on certain drastic conditions. They would need to send instructors to the guerrilla headquarters to oversee the use of the weapons; and they would not allow the guerrillas to enter the New Territories and fight the Japanese on Hong Kong soil. The Communist representatives found these conditions unpalatable, and the talks fizzled out.[217] It is possible that the deal had been aborted by continuing optimism on the part of Maltby. British records indicate that the General had received by 3 December two independent reports from the Chinese interior that 10,000 to 20,000 Japanese troops were heading for the border, but had preferred to believe his own, more cheerful intelligence sources.[218] Why rush to call in auxiliaries if the threat was not grave? Chinese accounts, however, suggest – and the Chinese provide the only detailed accounts of this episode – that the obstruction had been caused by Governor Young. The likelihood seems to be that the suspicion of the Chinese Communist Party which had pervaded the thinking of British officials in Hong Kong ever since the strikes of the 1920s had simply proved too strong to be overcome. Liao and Lin had thrown in with their military requests a demand for democratic reform in the colony; and perhaps this had come as an unwelcome reminder of the pressures the Communists had tried to exert on the government at the time of the great strike and boycott campaign.

From the first months of 1941 a wide range of observers had been predicting the end. In April Ernest Hemingway had passed through the colony on his way home from a tour of the south China war zone. With the eye of a seasoned observer of warfare he foresaw that the isolated British garrison would die 'trapped like rats'.[219] Setting off for the United States a few weeks later his compatriot Agnes Smedley offered a slightly different insight. She had stayed in the colony longer and had formed some impression of the mood of the populace. In her judgement Hong Kong would fall 'like a rotten fruit'.[220] Among the Chinese masses a verse was going the rounds about the centenary of British rule. Translated roughly it ran:

> The fish will return to the ocean;
> The dog will have had his day;
> The hundred years are over
> And the glory will fade away.[221]

'Please buy, Missy,' one Chinese shopkeeper urged an expatriate lady, 'the Japanese soon come.'[222] Some of the mainland Chinese who had taken shelter in the colony still believed that they would be safe under the protection of the British flag. But there was no consensus on this; and by the end of November the steamers were packed each day with wealthy Chinese residents clearing off to Macao and other points on the coast.[223] On 2 December Sir Robert Ho Tung celebrated his diamond wedding. It was the largest private function ever held in the celebrated restaurant of the Hong Kong Hotel which was known to expatriates by the mysterious sobriquet of The Gripps. Governor Young attended, and so did General Maltby; and the band played the Wedding March as the Governor locked arms with Sir Robert and his lady and escorted them to the dais. Two days later Sir Robert left for Macao. It was given out variously that the venerable tycoon was convalescing after the party; that he was returning the courtesy of the Portuguese governor, who had also been present; and that he was 'settling some philanthropic matters'.[224] The truth was that he had received a friendly tip-off from the Japanese consul, Kimura Shiroshichi.[225]

The expatriates alone were phlegmatic. The more astute of them guessed that an invasion would come at some point, but they did not know when. Most of the others were lulled by the government's reassurances, and convinced that Japan would never dare to assail the Empire.[226] On Saturday 6 December the social round was as busy as ever. The Happy Valley racecourse was crowded. A football match took place between the Middlesex Regiment and South China Athletic, and a fete was held in the grounds of Christ Church on Waterloo Road. There was a sound of revelry by night at the Peninsula Hotel, where a charity ball had been organized to raise money for the war in Europe. The orchestra had just struck up 'The Best Things in Life are Free' – when the merrymaking was suddenly brought to a halt by an urgent summons to all navy and merchant navy men to report to their ships. The following morning

Maltby and his staff filed grimly out of their pews at St John's Cathedral in the middle of Church Parade, and the reservists enrolled in the Hong Kong Volunteer Defence Corps were called to their units. Yet the bullish mood which had dominated British military thinking throughout the autumn was still not completely deflated; for someone found time that last Sunday to file an intelligence report to the War Office that the Japanese were 'distinctly nervous of being attacked'.[227]

CHAPTER TWO

The Debacle

The Japanese cross the border

'Japanese planes over Kowloon City and Kai Tak Airfield; our planes flattened.'[1]
So ran a British official's bleak record of the events which took place at 8.20
a.m. on 8 December 1941. Within five minutes the Takatsuki Aviation Squadron
of the 23rd Army had surprised and eliminated the colony's token air force of
two flying boats and three elderly torpedo bombers. With similar ease, a little
uncomfortable at the lack of resistance,[2] infantry units of the 23rd Army's
38th Division began to cross the Shenzhen River into the New Territories. The
British command on the border had not been caught napping, but Maltby and
his staff had no defence in mind for the border area apart from dynamiting a
few bridges and roads and fighting a few delaying actions. They had pinned
their hopes on containing the Japanese onslaught further south, in the forts
and tunnels of the newly refurbished Gin Drinkers' Line.

On paper the contending forces were not so ill-matched. The total British
garrison in Hong Kong amounted to almost 12,000 men – a figure which compared quite respectably with the initial Japanese attacking strength of 15,000.[3]
If the British had no air force (after the first five minutes), and a fleet which
amounted, in one dismissive summary, to 'a few naval launches',[4] they did at
least possess an impressive artillery arm: their guns had a much longer range
than those of the Japanese. But the advantage the invaders enjoyed in the mainland portion of the colony was more substantial than these data might suggest.
Most of the British troops were concentrated on Hong Kong Island, the all-
important 'fortress' where the principal resistance was supposed to take place.
In spite of his last-minute burst of faith in the Gin Drinkers' Line, Maltby had
felt unable to spare more than a meagre 3,000 men to hold this defence works.[5]
The British were also inhibited by a traditional and still widespread conviction that any major assault on the colony would come from the sea. ('Yet guard,
and *landward*', Kipling had pleaded in a poem inspired by his visit to Hong

Kong in 1889.)[6] Twenty-nine of the colony's heavy guns were positioned on the south of the Island, pointing out to the open ocean and useless for tactical infantry support. And the Japanese were better equipped with mobile artillery.

An even more fundamental difference lay in the quality of the troops. The garrison was a motley assemblage of British and Indian units and the newly arrived reinforcements from Canada. Language difficulties were encountered with both the Indian troops and the Canadians, many of whom were French-speakers from Quebec. The two British units were soft from years of garrison duty: the 2nd Battalion of the Royal Scots had been stationed in the colony since 1936, and the 1st Battalion of the Middlesex Regiment since 1937. The Royal Scots, who guarded the key central section of the Gin Drinkers' Line known as the Shingmun Redoubt, had also been ravaged both physically and psychologically by the effects of malaria. The Canadians were half-trained recruits. The Japanese invaders, in contrast, were homogeneous and hardened by years of warfare in the Chinese interior. Most of the British were blissfully unaware that the Japanese might have an edge over them. From Maltby down-wards they had allowed themselves to be lulled by reports that the enemy soldiers were second-raters, good only for fighting the rag-tag Chinese. Notions prevailed that the Japanese suffered from poor eyesight which pre-vented them from fighting effectively after dark; that they were unimaginative and incapable of deviating from a pre-arranged plan.

As the 38th Division pushed southward into the New Territories, the true nature of the contest began to emerge. It was Scott versus Amundsen. The British wore heavy knapsacks and clumped about in stockinged feet and hobnailed boots of a pattern unchanged since the time of the Boer War. One Japanese major remarked that he and his men 'could hear the British moving in the dark three miles off'.[7] The Japanese loped along lightly equipped in silent, rubber-soled footwear. The British followed the roads, while the Japanese struck out across open country, camouflaging themselves by inserting twigs and grass in the stitches of their uniforms. In a very short while the myths of Japanese ineffectiveness had been blown to the winds. 'The lesson of today', reported Maltby's headquarters gloomily in the early hours of 9 December, 'is that the enemy can operate strongly on a moonlit night.'[8] On the afternoon of the same day, the 228th Regiment of Colonel Doi Teihichi arrived with unex-pected rapidity at Needle Hill, a point immediately to the north-east of the Shingmun Redoubt. ('Trouble with fighting the Japanese', observed the *South China Morning Post*, 'is that the blighters don't seem to have tiffin.')[9] Spotting 'something like white clothes being dried', Doi deduced that the Royal Scots were unprepared and vulnerable to attack.[10] The Shingmun Redoubt had in fact been assigned as an objective to a different Japanese regiment; but Doi attacked and took it that night, ignoring, in true Nelson style, two subsequent orders to abandon his position. The Gin Drinkers' Line had proved no more effective than its prototype, the Maginot Line in France. The centrepiece of the British defence in the New Territories, which had been expected to hold for a week, had been knocked out in less than forty-eight hours.

Revolt in Kowloon

This however was only half of the trouble the British faced on the Kowloon side. The other half came from the local population. The British authorities had made little attempt to keep the non-European public abreast of the war. Almost no one except the army and police were aware at the outset that the Japanese had invaded, and most of the Kowloon populace thought that the Takatsuki Aviation Squadron's descent on Kai Tak airfield was just another air-raid practice. No immediate announcement was made on the radio, and it was 2.30 p.m. on that first day before Governor Young proclaimed formally that a state of war existed with Japan.[11] In the meantime, again without any immediate announcement, the British had abruptly curtailed communications between Kowloon and Hong Kong Island. Almost all Europeans and 'as many Portuguese as possible' were evacuated from Kowloon, but the Chinese inhabitants, apart from a handful employed by the military, were forbidden to cross the harbour without special permits.[12] The authorities had concluded, naturally enough from a military angle, that the chances of keeping order and maintaining a food supply on the Island would be minimal if they were obliged to contend with an additional torrent of refugees from Kowloon. For the Chinese in Kowloon, however, this decision had grave implications of an economic kind. It spelt unemployment for office workers who had commuted from Kowloon to their jobs in Victoria, and destitution for merchants who had kept their money and valuables in the Victoria banks.[13] To make matters worse the government's arrangements for feeding the public in Kowloon had broken down hopelessly. Food depots were scarce; minor officials were riding around in cars which should have been used to distribute food; rice merchants intent on profiteering were shutting up shop. A British police officer noted that his Asiatic colleagues were lucky if they got rice once a day.[14] The result of all this, not surprisingly, was panic; a panic which intensified as rumours of British setbacks began to filter back from the front line.[15]

In the light of the government's attitude most of the Chinese public tended to deduce that the war was a British affair that had nothing to do with them. Even those who had been assigned bit parts in the war effort felt no compelling need to rally to the British cause. Faced with this crisis, their instinct was to run. Already on the first morning Chinese doctors and orderlies who had been detailed to staff a relief hospital at the Peninsula Hotel failed to report for their duties;[16] and by 9 December the British in Kowloon had begun to experience a haemorrhage of ancillary workers from almost every branch of the civil and military establishment. The ground staff at Kai Tak airfield had vanished. The drivers employed by the army and police were melting away on account of the lack of food. No Chinese constables were to be seen on their beats in the districts of Shamshuipo and Hung Hom. The streets were littered with helmets discarded by air-raid wardens, and armbands belonging to a Chinese sapper and a Chinese driver of the Royal Army Medical Corps were found abandoned in a dustbin.[17]

In the meantime the British troops at the front had begun to find their operations impeded by acts of deliberate sabotage. On 8 December, within minutes of the outbreak of war, a large tub of soapy water was thoughtfully poured on to a charging engine and wireless batteries used by the signals corps at the British headquarters on the border. At 9 a.m. on 9 December – twelve hours before Colonel Doi sprang his assault – the Royal Scots officer in charge of the Shingmun Redoubt reported that 'Japanese in civilian clothing' had spent the night cutting his barbed wire and telephone lines.[18] The fifth column which had been so painstakingly nurtured by the Japanese Army's subversion team was showing its hand. Triad members and Wang Jingwei partisans began to guide the invaders along the precipitous mountain paths of the New Territories; friendly directions enabled a Japanese contingent to land from the sea and overwhelm an inadequate force that was guarding the western end of the British defence line at Castle Peak. Army drivers who left their posts (not all the desertions were spontaneous) disabled their lorries by smashing the engines or swiping the carburettors and left the vehicles abandoned at the roadside. This ploy largely paralysed the ability of the British command to distribute supplies to their men.

Finally the fifth columnists set to work inciting open rebellion in the British rear. From the very first day of the war they were active in the refugee camps where tens of thousands of vagrants were waiting for erratic hand-outs of rice. 'Hooligans' at a camp in the village of Kam Tin stole all the available rice and beheaded the European superintendent.[19] By 11 December a full-scale insurrection was in progress. Shortly before noon that day the British police came under fire in the neighbourhood of the Police Training School, on the inner frontier which ran between the New Territories and urban Kowloon. The trouble was once again ascribed to 'Japanese in plain clothes'; but a British sub-inspector of police observed that 'he did not think the Japanese were the attackers'.[20] At different points in Kowloon British police cars and ambulances had to battle their way through crowds of hundreds or even thousands of armed and hostile Chinese.[21] The crowds shot and stabbed, burned and rioted and above all they plundered: witnesses spoke of gangs emptying the contents of shops into lorries as though moving house, of 'the roar of the looting in Nathan Road'.[22] And this was no random epidemic of burglary, but a carefully organized operation designed to maximize the chaos. The looters had been deployed by the largest Triad faction, the Wing On Lok. They wore white identity armbands and issued safe conducts, when it pleased them, to favoured Chinese citizens. They proclaimed their political allegiance by yelling 'Victory! Victory!' (a slogan which earned them the nickname of the Victory Fellows),[23] and described themselves as members of the Koa Kikan. Towards evening the Rising Sun flag of Japan was suddenly hoisted on the roof of the Peninsula Hotel, the highest point in Kowloon; and continuous sniping began from the hotel's upper floors. Some Canadian troops who had been stationed at the north-eastern approach to the city are said to have taken fright and laid down their arms, believing themselves to be caught in a Japanese pincer movement. But no Japanese forces had at this stage so much as set foot in Kowloon.[24]

By noon on 11 December Maltby had reached the reluctant decision to pull his troops out of the mainland part of the colony that night. It was not before time. The Chinese launch crews who were supposed to evacuate the British forces across the harbour had begun to take part in the general walk-out. Most of the boat hands deserted during the night under cover of darkness, and the few who remained the next day had to be kept under guard to prevent them following suit.[25] The Star Ferry pier in Kowloon was a scene of chaos, with police firing shots in the air to discourage the exodus of desperate crowds of cursing, screaming Chinese. 'Some compulsion' had to be used on the Indian constables assigned to this duty,[26] and most of the Asiatic police seized the opportunity to make their own getaway on the first ferry that went. In the early hours of 12 December the 2/14 Punjabis, an Indian regiment who had been left to cover the retreat of the rest of the British forces, were withdrawn on the final Star Ferry. The Japanese still had not entered Kowloon (they would not be seen till the evening); but the ferry transporting this last Allied unit set off in a hail of bullets, strafed with captured British machine-guns by a Triad contingent who had installed themselves in the Kowloon Post Office.[27]

Stemming the tide: British and Nationalists on Hong Kong Island

For several days it had looked as though an identical disintegration was about to take place on Hong Kong Island. From 10 December the Island had been subject to shelling and bombing from the Japanese on the other side of the harbour. Once again the overriding concern of the Chinese work-force was to ensure their own survival and that of their families. On 11 December the Island's tram and bus drivers went on strike on the grounds that a number of their colleagues had been killed by the Japanese shelling. They only agreed to return to work on the following day after their employers had undertaken that medical care would be provided for any future staff who were injured and compensation would be paid to the families of anyone killed.[28] The stretcher-bearers and cooks in the hospitals made themselves scarce, and the lorry drivers employed by the essential services were 'openly restive'. The Europeans even found themselves forsaken by the auxiliaries most essential to their day-to-day comfort: Emily Hahn's cook, Ah King, reported that he was the only houseboy still at work on the Peak.[29]

Fifth columnists were active all over Victoria. Once again they provided direct help to the Japanese forces. With strips of white cloth, mirrors, flashlights and wireless transmitters they signalled across the harbour to the Japanese artillery units, enabling them to direct fire of uncanny precision on to the British gun emplacements and pillboxes. And once again they exerted themselves to undermine social order and stir up the population to revolt. They put sand in the government rice rations, and paraffin in the water buckets which were kept at the police stations for use against fire. As Japanese planes approached to bomb the Island, air-raid sirens would unexpectedly sound the 'all clear'. Small change disappeared mysteriously from circulation, making the British unable to pay lorry drivers and labourers who received their wages by the day.[30]

The potential for trouble was greatly increased by the abrupt British exit from Kowloon and the New Territories. The Chinese on the Island were bitterly critical of the British authorities for failing to inform the Kowloon population of their decision to withdraw. Chinese merchants in Victoria had now been deprived of access to large quantities of goods which they stored in the Kowloon warehouses: many other Chinese found themselves cut off from relatives and friends in Kowloon.[31] It was also apparent that if the fighting continued the Chinese in Kowloon would soon be exposed to shelling from the British on the Hong Kong side.[32]

In response to the growing danger of unrest the authorities reached for their time-honoured instruments of social control. In traditional style they invoked the aid of the gentry.[33] Sir Robert Kotewall was made director of a new Office for the Superintendence of the Chinese, and he and the other gentry leaders issued statements appealing to the Chinese community to support the war. The Special Branch of the police were deployed under the command of F. W. Shaftain, the officer who had ten years earlier been treated to political homilies by Ho Chi Minh. On the morning the war began they embarked on a round-up of the eighty-odd Japanese civilians still in the colony. In the course of the next few days they also hauled in an assortment of Japanese sympathizers and Wang Jingwei partisans, notably Chan Lim-pak, the extreme right-wing businessman, who was interned for having 'spread pacifist rumours' and incited the masses to revolt.[34] By 11 December they had arrested some 260 saboteurs and signallers, and 'drastic action', as the police records euphemistically phrased it, had been taken against twenty of the most important ones.[35] (Shaftain put it more bluntly: 'I took upon myself the responsibility of having them shot.')[36] As the British retreated across the harbour all available police from Kowloon were directed to reinforce the efforts of Shaftain's team. The plan was that the police should now devote all their efforts to suppressing the 'internal enemy', leaving the military free to handle the Japanese.[37]

But the old methods were plainly inadequate. The gentry were nowhere near numerous or cohesive enough to deal with a security threat of this magnitude. (Some of them are reported to have gone to ground in the air-raid shelters for the duration of the war.)[38] The police round-up wasn't efficient: a good many of the Japanese and their supporters had escaped before the search teams reached their doors. And as often as not the police themselves were part of the problem. The entire 'C' contingent of the police force, that is, the section recruited from the local Chinese population, is said to have been a nest of fifth columnists. The several hundred Chinese employed as detectives were 'very shaky' from the first day.[39] When the British pulled out of Kowloon this Chinese detective force became 'definitely hostile', and threatened to stir up the Triads against the government to bring the fighting to an end.[40]

There was nothing for it but to call on outside assistance. Only one organization on Hong Kong Island had both the will and the infrastructure to prevent the British from succumbing to a second stab in the back. Step by step the authorities were compelled to upgrade their wary teamwork with the emissaries of the Chinese Nationalist Party.

Already on the first day of the invasion discussions took place with the Nationalist chief, the one-legged Admiral Chan Chak. Arrangements were apparently made straight away to tighten the cooperation between the Nationalists and the British police force: by 9 December Phyllis Harrop, the Manchester girl who had been seconded to the police force, was describing herself as 'attached to the Chinese secret police'.[41] On 10 December the one-legged Admiral called a meeting of all the various Nationalist government organs which had been active in the colony. He relayed a number of requests that he had received from the Hong Kong authorities, and directed his followers to keep order on the Island and help the British to hold out. The different Nationalist organs were amalgamated into a Temporary Joint Liaison Office of All Chinese Organizations in Hong Kong which amounted, in effect, to a shadow government. It included a secretariat and eight other groups responsible for army and police matters, foreign relations, intelligence, propaganda, transport, food supply, finance and general affairs. Shortly after this meeting a British deputation consisting of David MacDougall, the head of the Information Bureau (representing Governor Young), Major Boxer (representing the army), R. A. C. North from the Secretariat of Chinese Affairs and a

police delegate called at the illicit Nationalist headquarters in the Shell Building, and provision was made for a daily exchange of intelligence.[42]

Possibly there was still at this stage an element of polite consultation on the
British side, and a sense in which the Nationalists were pressing ahead by
themselves with their own enthusiastic agenda. On 11 December, however, as
Maltby's forces pulled out of Kowloon, the internal threat to the British position on Hong Kong Island took a critical turn. At 7 p.m. Shaftain received
information that the Triads on the Island had laid plans for an uprising timed
to take place at 3 a.m. on 13 December. The uprising was to entail nothing less
than the massacre of the entire European population.[43]

The logical answer to the Triads was money; and Shaftain contrived in the
space of an hour to raise a sum of HK\$20,000 with the help of his superior,
the Commissioner of Police. But the British still had to get through, urgently,
to the Triad bosses – and only one well-disposed organization on the Island
had the necessary links. 'In desperation' Shaftain got in touch with the
Admiral's right-hand man, Colonel S. K. Yee.[44]

Yee and the Admiral promptly enlisted the help of Zhang Zilian, the Triad
chieftain from Shanghai whom they had already been using for months to
combat Japanese influence among the Triads. Zhang approached some of the
local Triad bosses, and these lords of the underworld duly appeared at Chan
Chak's office for an emergency meeting with the chiefs of the British police.
This relatively calm negotiation was followed by a second round of talks at
the British police headquarters during which Shaftain and his colleagues
grew increasingly angry. It seems possible that Zhang's contacts were (as they
claimed) merely mediators whose function was to serve as a bridge to the real
conspirators: certainly no breakthrough was made until 200 'sub-heads' had
been collected by bus and delivered to a conference in the dining-room of the
Cecil Hotel. At this point it emerged that the plotters might after all be
amenable to a cash settlement. (Perhaps that is all they had had in mind from
the outset; though the day's events in Kowloon suggest that a Triad uprising
was entirely on the cards.) The difficulty was that the sum demanded was very
much larger than the HK\$20,000 which Shaftain had managed to raise.
Shaftain was understandably leery at the prospect of having to inform Sir Mark
Young that the government of Hong Kong was being subjected to a protection
racket. The situation was saved by Zhang Zilian, who agreed to pay the local
Triads the necessary sum from his own vast resources in return for a British
promise of repayment after the war. By just before 6 a.m. on 12 December the
deal had been struck. The massacre had been averted. The Triad 'sub-heads'
were content, and left peacefully, helping themselves to a small advance in the
form of the Cecil Hotel's silver plate.[45]

In the meantime the Nationalists were preparing to deal with the rest of the
fifth column by more forcible means. On the night of 11 December Chan Chak

ordered the immediate mobilization of a squad of 2,000 vigilantes. These vigilantes were to be recruited from amenable gangs and given the task of suppressing pro-Japanese saboteurs in return for a daily food allowance of HK$2.
They were to operate under the innocuous name of the Loyal and Righteous
Charitable Association. On 12 December a headquarters was set up for the
squad in Happy Valley, and the Island was divided for counter-subversion
purposes into a western, a central and an eastern district. Zhang Zilian took
command at the headquarters, with a staff composed wholly of mainlanders
rather than Hong Kong Chinese. By 14 December the ranks of the Loyal and
Righteous had swollen to 15,000: the one-legged Admiral and Zhang Zilian
offered the services of 1,000 of these men to the Special Branch, and the British
not only accepted but asked for 400 more. Over the following days the Nationalist vigilantes captured a total of 500 to 600 Wang Jingwei partisans.[46] At
least 400 of these subversives were liquidated by the Loyal and Righteous
themselves. Others were dispatched with a shot in the back of the neck by the
British police in a cul-de-sac running between the Gloucester Hotel and Lane
Crawford's department store which became known as Blood Alley. The one-
legged Admiral assumed energetic overall charge of the counter-insurgency.
One evening he personally hurled a hand grenade to eliminate a fifth colum-
nist who was flashing a signal light.

Chan Chak's shadow government went into action in a number of other
ways. The Admiral issued repeated statements through both the press and the
radio urging the Chinese community to rally to the defence of Hong Kong.
The main thrust of his argument was that in defending Hong Kong they would
fight not for Britain but for China. The propaganda group supported his
efforts by maintaining a flow of Nationalist newspapers which called on the
general public to maintain law and order and on retailers to keep prices down.
They also distributed leaflets on behalf of the British to the tens of thousands
of citizens in the air-raid shelters, refuting defeatist rumours that had been circulated there by members of the fifth column. The transport group mustered
about 1,500 drivers to take the place of the ones who had fled from the army
and police force and help Maltby's staff with the movement of arms and
ammunition. The food supply group mobilized 600 teachers and students to
help the British run their network of food kitchens and centres for the sale of
subsidized rice.[47] Representatives of the Guangdong branch of the Bank of
China, who sat on the finance group, agreed to let the British authorities
'borrow' several million of their newly issued five-yuan notes. The Hongkong
and Shanghai Bank overprinted these notes, converting them into bills of
HK$1, and put them into circulation as a device for relieving the dangerous
shortage of small change.[48]

These initiatives stopped the rot. In the days that followed the crisis of 11
December sabotage and signalling still went on, but at a much reduced level.

There was no panic, no rioting, no appreciable looting.[49] It seems clear that Chan Chak and his shadow government had forestalled a repetition on Hong Kong Island of the internal revolt which engulfed the British in Kowloon. The British themselves acknowledged the extent of the Nationalist contribution. Already by 12 December Phyllis Harrop was noting in her diary that 'the Chungking men had done wonderful work'. The following day she recorded that the Nationalist vigilantes were operating effectively and that the 'disorderly element' on the Island was being 'kept well under control'.[50] David MacDougall, the information chief, summed up that if the Nationalists had not deployed their organized influence in support of the British authorities 'internal order could almost certainly not have been maintained for more than a few days'. He added that the internal situation could not have stood another twenty-four hours of the small-change shortage.[51] The British discovered in passing that they rather admired the one-legged Admiral. He was believed (incorrectly) to have served as a midshipman in the Royal Navy during the First World War and (again incorrectly) to have lost his leg on the Yangtze in the heat of a naval battle.[52]

None of this of course altered the unpleasant reality of the Japanese advance. The rout in the New Territories had come as a devastating blow to the British in their island 'fortress'. When news was received on 10 December of the almost instantaneous fall of the Shingmun Redoubt, one officer at the military headquarters reported that he had 'never seen General Maltby more shocked or angry'.[53] Two days later morale among the troops reached a nadir after their headlong retreat from the mainland part of the colony. Backbiting set in, as different units endeavoured to blame each other for the collapse.[54] The civilians were equally shattered. On the night of 12 December the tension among the expatriates in the lounge of the Hong Kong Hotel 'hit you in the face like a wet cloth the moment you entered'.[55] To make matters worse the British on Hong Kong Island had now become conscious that the naval forces which they had expected to come to their rescue were not going to materialize. The United States fleet at Pearl Harbor had been destroyed on the first morning, even before the Japanese warplanes swooped down on Kai Tak. On the following day Japanese torpedo bombers had cornered and sunk the *Prince of Wales* and *Repulse*, the two battleships which had just arrived in Far Eastern waters to spearhead the British naval contingent at Singapore.

Once again, however, the Chinese Nationalists stepped into the breach. On the first morning of the invasion, the one-legged Admiral Chan Chak had called on Maltby in the company of Zheng Jiemin, the visiting representative of the Nationalist general staff. Talks took place about military cooperation and war plans; and shortly afterwards Zheng set off by air for Chungking with an officer from Maltby's headquarters.[56] The time had now come for the Nationalists to fulfil the agreement which they had made with Major-General

Dennys the previous summer and contribute to the defence of Hong Kong by deploying their forces to harass the Japanese invaders in the rear. On 9 December Chiang Kai-shek directed that a relief force should be sent to the colony under the leadership of General Yu Hanmou, the commander of his Seventh War Zone, an area which included Guangdong province; and on 13 December Chan Chak received cables from Guangdong advising him that Nationalist troops were indeed on the move. On the previous day, he was told, the vanguard of the relief force, an independent unit of divisional strength, had pushed south as far as Zhangmutou, on the Kowloon–Canton railway, a few stops away from the border town of Shenzhen. The bulk of the force, consisting of three further divisions, was expected to catch up in three or four days, after which Yu would launch an immediate attack. The Admiral promptly conveyed this information to Maltby. Maltby was sure the reports were exaggerated, and that effective Nationalist intervention would be impossible before January:[57] in this hour of despair, however, Chan Chak's message came as a propaganda godsend. The news was deliberately spread that a rescue force was, after all, on its way to the colony – in the form of an army of mainland Chinese.[58]

From the moment the 23rd Army took over Kowloon their objective was to secure Hong Kong Island through a British surrender and spare themselves the trouble of an assault. Early on the morning of 13 December, a small launch slipped quietly out from the Kowloon waterfront across the tense harbour. The launch bore three Japanese officers under a white cloth banner inscribed with the words PEACE MISSION. In the bows, as a kind of additional insurance, sat two European women who had been stranded on the Kowloon side. Once arrived at Queen's Pier in Victoria the three officers handed over a 'letter of advice' from Lieutenant-General Sakai enjoining Governor Young to come to immediate terms. A second 'peace mission' was sent with a similar message on 17 December. In the meantime the Japanese deployed both stick and carrot in an effort to undermine the garrison's will to resist. The bombardment was intensified. Hong Kong Island was now being shelled and bombed virtually around the clock. At night Japanese propaganda squads trundled loudspeakers on to the Kowloon wharves and did their best to make the defenders nostalgic by serenading them with recordings of winsome numbers like 'Way Down Upon the Swanee River' and 'Home Sweet Home'.

In the light of the British performance over the previous days such tactics might have been expected to have some effect. In fact they proved useless. Governor Young replied to the first 'peace mission' that he 'utterly rejected the advice of the Japanese Army', and Major Boxer, the Japan expert, who bore Young's reply to the 'mission', elaborated it in the language of Japanese military honour: 'We have not yet completely discharged our duty of loyalty to the King-Emperor.'[59] When the second deputation arrived Young coupled his rebuff with a warning that any further 'peace envoys' would be shot out of hand.[60] Young was doing no more than implement the long-standing plans for the Island to hold out against a Japanese siege; but eyewitness accounts make it clear that there had been simultaneously an abrupt turnaround in British morale. Within twenty-four hours of the panic on 12 December nerves on Hong Kong Island had 'settled down again'.[61] The garrison troops were said to have been in excellent spirits, while the civilians 'went stolidly but not too grimly about their jobs'.[62] A woman named Gwen Priestwood who worked as a volunteer driver for the government's food supply organization steered her lorry coolly through the thick of the shelling. The expatriate ladies who were employed as senior secretaries in the government offices discharged their regular duties with calm and efficiency. The principal factor behind this dramatic recovery was undoubtedly the news of the Nationalist relief force. In spite of the shelling and bombing and the British lack of aircraft and shortage of men and guns there was always, Gwen Priestwood assured herself on 13 December, 'that Chinese army, eighty miles away over the hills, battling to retake Kowloon'.[63] 'We are heartened', an officer in the Royal Artillery observed in his diary on 15 December, 'by a report that a Chinese army, 100,000 strong, is fighting towards us.'[64] 'We have been told', noted Phyllis Harrop two days later, 'that Chinese troops are on their way down from Chungking.'[65]

This new British doggedness didn't unfortunately translate into any practical ability to hold off the expected attack. The garrison troops were strung out thinly around the perimeter of Hong Kong Island, since no one could be certain where the Japanese assault force would land. Maltby's staff were initially inclined to think that the landing would be made on the south side of the Island. Even when it became apparent that the 23rd Army were preparing for a frontal assault British intelligence still got it wrong. Maltby expected the blow to fall on the north-western shore, where the population was densest; but in fact the Japanese were aiming at the north-*east*. On the night of 17 December the essential preparations were made by a young officer Lieutenant Masujima Zenpei. With a team of three other expert swimmers, one of whom had won a silver medal for swimming at the 1932 Olympic Games, Masujima struck out across the harbour and reconnoitred a number of possible landing sites. Using their rifles which they had brought along (and had kept well clear of the water), Masujima and his men proceeded to disable the British searchlights and the mines which the British had laid to prevent a landing taking place.[66] On the night of 18 December 7,500 troops of the 38th Division packed into every rowing-boat, raft, rubber dinghy and junk they could muster (a sort of Dunkirk in reverse), crept across the harbour and made their landfall in the districts of North Point and Shaukeiwan.

Once again the defenders were outclassed both in tactics and in man-for-man calibre. In the aftermath of their landing the 38th Division made no immediate attempt to battle their way along the shoreline into the heart of Victoria. Instead they pushed out across the middle of the Island through the high country to the east of the Peak. Their idea was to cut the Island into two halves, after which they would turn and mop up the defending troops in each isolated pocket. The British had already divided the garrison into a Western and an Eastern Brigade. On 19 December General Maltby acceded (against his own better judgement) to a request from Brigadier Cedric Wallis, who commanded the Eastern Brigade, that he should be allowed to regroup his troops further south, in the area of the Stanley peninsula. The result was that the Eastern Brigade lost touch with its Western counterpart – which of course did the invaders' work for them. On the following day the redoubtable Colonel Doi, as usual ahead of the other Japanese units, captured the strategic summit of Mount Nicholson; and by 21 December the bisection of the Island was largely complete. The Japanese maintained their new positions with their accustomed resource and ferocity, throwing stones to ward off an Allied counter-attack when they ran out of hand grenades. The chief defending force in the interior of the Island consisted of the two newly arrived Canadian regiments, the Royal Rifles of Canada and the Winnipeg Grenadiers. The unfortunate Canadians had not received any training whatever for hill fighting, and they even had problems telling the difference between Chinese and Japanese. They were nervous and confused, and within hours of the Japanese landing it was becoming apparent that they would not be capable of any real fight.[67]

As the days went by, too, the Japanese began more and more to enjoy the advantage of numbers. Unlike the British they could draw on reserves of fresh troops: the 38th Division represented no more than about a third of the total strength of the 23rd Army. The initial, quite modest landing force of 7,500 swelled in the course of the following week to at least 20,000. The British, by contrast, were obliged to make do with their original units – and those units were anything but fresh. None of them had enjoyed any rest since the start of the fighting. David MacDougall watched a contingent of Royal Scots coming back from a position in the hills. 'They were asleep on their feet: deep lines of exhaustion on their faces, rifles clutched stiffly in rigid hands, they were led in like children.'[68]

Behind the lines the underpinnings of the British resistance were being rapidly knocked away. In the run-up to the landings Japanese bombers had assailed the various oil storage installations on the Island: fires from the burning tanks, a British police officer recorded poetically, 'blazed in anguish throughout the war, like three great wounds in the black body of night'.[69] By 21 December the Island's electricity and gas supplies had been cut off, and by 23 December the principal reservoirs were in Japanese hands.[70] And in the midst of all this the civil defence arrangements were gradually falling apart. Every department, Phyllis Harrop lamented, seemed to be working against the others.[71] The British undoubtedly did make genuine efforts to meet the needs of the civilian populace. Over 100,000 free meals were served each day from the communal food kitchens; and the air-raid tunnels which had been the cause of such scandal provided shelter to a quarter of a million citizens.[72] But the food was still failing to get through to the points where it was needed most urgently. Cartloads of starvation victims were seen in the slums of the Wanchai district, the soles of their feet white from anaemia.[73] The air-raid shelters were never used to the full because the authorities had not drilled people to go there.[74] An administrator from French Equatorial Africa who had chanced to arrive in Hong Kong on leave the week before the invasion provided a bleak corrective to the rosiness of some of the official British reports. He judged that while the fire, ambulance and rescue and demolition services all continued to function competently throughout the attack, the food rationing and air-raid precaution systems were 'inefficient beyond description'.[75]

Finally there was still no sign of the promised Nationalist relief force. On 21 December the British military attaché in Chungking relayed a message from Chiang Kai-shek that his troops would not be able to get to Hong Kong for at least another ten days.

Maltby and his staff appear to have had no doubt from the start that the Island was doomed. Already on 18 December, in the first hours of the Japanese landing, MacDougall the information chief was privately notified that the military situation was hopeless and surrender was only a matter of time.[76] Similar messages were conveyed to Governor Young. On 21 December Maltby advised Young that the garrison would soon find themselves reduced to defending a small pocket in the centre of Victoria, leaving the bulk of the population at the mercy of the Japanese. The implication was clear, and Young apparently felt that he had no choice but to act on it. He sent a cable to the Admiralty in London passing on Maltby's comments and requesting permission to ask for terms.[77]

This however was not the idea in London at all. Churchill had, as he later acknowledged, no illusions about the colony's imminent fate 'under the overwhelming impact of Japanese power'.[78] But, 'saved and thankful' after the news that Japan's attack on Pearl Harbor had finally brought the United States into the war, the British Prime Minister was looking at the overall picture. *Hong Kong could not be held but must be defended.* By persisting with their defence the garrison would buy time for Malaya and the other British possessions in South-east Asia; and their example might even discourage the Japanese armies which had invaded those larger territories.[79] On 12 December, as the siege of Hong Kong Island began, Churchill issued a characteristically ringing instruction to Young and his people. 'You guard a vital link long famous in world civilization between the Far East and Europe . . . Every day of your resistance brings nearer our certain victory.'[80] 'There must be no thought of surrender', he added on 21 December. 'Every part of the Island must be fought over and the enemy resisted with the utmost stubbornness. Every day that you are able to maintain your resistance you help the Allied cause all over the world.'[81] On receiving Young's cable (which had crossed with Churchill's second clarion call), the Admiralty merely repeated the Prime Minister's exhortation to resist to the end.[82]

The Governor duly persevered, a study in anguish and gallantry, under pressure from his own military to end what they viewed as a pointless slaughter, yet straining each day to carry out Churchill's instructions and in his own words 'to add another twenty four hours to the credit of the account'.[83] On the night of 22 December his private secretary observed him playing Chopin in the rat-infested Government House as he brooded on the prospect of being the first man to surrender a British colony since Cornwallis at Yorktown. By daytime, however, he was greeting his staff with a determined display of jauntiness: 'No evening haste, no morning flap, Whatever can have happened to the Jap?'[84]

The morale of the garrison which had revived so dramatically in the previous week saw them through the immediate shock of the Japanese landing. Here and there, in the following days, the British defenders fought back with a stubbornness which has earned them an honoured place in the war histories. One celebrated stand was made by a sub-section of the Hong Kong Volunteer Defence Corps, a band of expatriates aged between fifty-five and seventy who had been organized on the eve of the war by Colonel A. W. Hughes of the Union Insurance Company and were known to the British community as the Hughesiliers (or still more irreverently as the Methuseliers). On 18 to 19 December these elderly gentlemen defended the power station at North Point against steel-helmeted troops of the Japanese 230th Regiment for a full eighteen hours. And from 20 to 23 December, in the south of the Island, a contingent of stragglers commanded by Major Robert Templer of the 8th Coast Artillery Regiment staged an equally valiant defence of the Repulse Bay Hotel. As the days passed, however, it seems clear that the sense of hopelessness in the high command was beginning to spread through the rank and file. By 21 December, Maltby noted in a later dispatch, the morale of the troops had been seriously affected by a feeling that it was futile to continue the resistance with inadequate equipment, insufficient support in the form of mobile artillery and no support whatever from the air. Senior British observers described the garrison as fighting 'in a half-hearted manner','according to the style of Dunkirk without attaining its standard'.[85] Among the expatriate public the demand had once again been voiced that Hong Kong should be declared an open city. Unlike Churchill the British inhabitants of Hong Kong Island were not, for the most part, preoccupied with the overall picture. Some of them did however perceive that they were pawns being sacrificed in a larger strategic game

('Every day of *your* resistance brings nearer *our* final victory'); and they didn't entirely like it.[86]

The authorities were still able to evoke a degree of support from the Island's non-Europeans. This support came most noticeably from the various Anglicized enclaves which the British had created over the decades by accident or design. The gentry continued to profess their allegiance. On 23 December, 'eyebrows sprouting as belligerently as ever', the aged Sir Shouson Chow gripped MacDougall's arm in Pedder Street and asked him, with a gesture towards the Kowloon side of the harbour, 'Do you think that we cannot beat those damned monkeys over there?'[87] Students from Hong Kong University did their best to control the crowds who milled in the Central Market awaiting the distribution of subsidized rice.[88] The Eurasians, the only community who had no other home, stood their ground against the invaders with conspicuous bravery: many of them were killed fighting in the Hong Kong Volunteer Defence Corps, and the 5th Battalion, an all-Eurasian unit, was wiped out.[89] Most of the ordinary Hong Kong Chinese had little faith by now in the ability of the British to protect them. But they were galvanized, even more than the British had been, by the news of the Nationalist relief force. A rumour spread that the Nationalist vanguard had been sighted through binoculars from the tops of the tallest blocks in Victoria advancing on Kowloon with their White Sun flags.[90] (One is reminded of the Russian reinforcements who were supposed in the First World War to have landed in Scotland 'with snow on their boots'.) And this hope of deliverance seems in turn to have generated an urge in some quarters to help the British hold out. Chinese women in Victoria took wounded soldiers into their houses. Prostitutes in the Wanchai district tried to encourage the Royal Scots with offerings of green tea, aspirins and razor blades.

Japanese propaganda, however, was hard at work. Leaflets dropped from the air urged the Asiatic populace to rise up and kill their white masters and 'deflate the bloated figure of John Bull'.[91] Much of this propaganda was aimed at the Indian auxiliary forces; and there seems little doubt that it had some effect. The Sikh contingent of the police are said to have been 'sullen and uncooperative' and at one point 'nearly mutinous'.[92] On 16 December, two days before the Japanese landing, the entire Sikh constabulary at Shaukeiwan absconded from their police station and fled to the hills. In the days that followed the landing a number of Indian prison warders and medical orderlies began to fraternize with the Japanese civilians who had been interned in Stanley gaol.[93] By 22 December the morale of the Indian garrison troops had become 'very problematic'. Armed deserters from the Rajput regiment had abandoned their units and taken refuge in the air-raid shelters.[94] To a certain extent these defections can be viewed as a natural consequence of fear and fatigue. The Punjabis and Rajputs between them had borne the brunt of the invasion. They had been the first troops to engage the invaders in the New Territories; the last to be evacuated across the harbour; the first to confront the Japanese landing force on the beaches of Hong Kong Island. The Rajputs had sustained more severe total damage than any other regiment: one of their units, the C Company, had lost all their officers and 65 per cent of their men. But it would also appear that the defections were encouraged in some cases by Japan's pan-Asiatic gospel. On 23 and 24 December small groups of thirty to forty Indian soldiers gave themselves up to the invaders bearing Japanese leaflets in their hands.[95]

The Hong Kong Chinese showed no perceptible interest in the Japanese efforts to win them over. But as the days passed and the Nationalist relief force still failed to arrive, their morale too disintegrated fast. More and more of the ancillary staff employed in the British civil and military services deserted their posts. No one was even prepared any longer to work the Peak Tram. On 19 December, when word got round that the Japanese had landed on the Island, nearly all the remaining lorry drivers went off with their vehicles. On 20 December the last Chinese naval ratings abandoned the military patrol vessels of the colony's little naval force. They were disenchanted with their round-the-clock work and meagre rations, and had also resented an order which had been issued to them a few days earlier to shell fellow-Chinese on board a collection of suspect junks. Their British commander wrote plaintively that they had 'stayed longer than any other Chinese'.[96] Law and order were finally crumbling, and by 23 December the Chinese public were no longer awed by the police. One British constable on a motorbike briefly succeeded in scaring away a crowd of looters by firing his pistol into the air; but the crowd closed in again as soon as he had moved on.[97]

Only one section of the public remained unequivocally determined to keep up the fight. On 18 December, the night the Japanese landed, Admiral Chan Chak decided in consultation with Zhang Zilian and the other local Nationalist bosses that the time had now come when the Loyal and Righteous vigilantes should be sent into action as front-line troops. The following morning, at the regular meeting which was held at the Nationalist headquarters to exchange intelligence with representatives of the British Army and police, Chan Chak offered the garrison the services of an initial contingent of 1,000 trained men, and requested that the British military headquarters should issue them with arms and ammunition. On 20 December the one-legged Admiral repeated his offer. On 22 December he ordered the formation of a 200-man desperado squad who were to advance in three brigades to assist the exhausted British forces defending Mount Cameron, and once again pressed Maltby's headquarters for arms.[98]

The Admiral's efforts were complemented by the demarche of a group of refugee mainland Chinese intellectuals headed by the distinguished left-of-centre political philosopher Liang Shuming. On Christmas Eve Liang and his colleagues called on R. A. C. North, the Secretary of Chinese Affairs, and presented him with a set of carefully drafted proposals for speeding up the arrival of Nationalist help from outside. A message, they urged, should be dispatched to Chiang Kai-shek asking him to send down his air force. In the meantime some emissaries should be smuggled out of the Island under cover of darkness to link up with General Yu Hanmou's relief army, which was believed to have got as far as the town of Danshui. Five thousand Nationalist troops could then be infiltrated through the Japanese lines in civilian clothes and put ashore on the Island, again under cover of darkness, as a first step towards raising the siege.[99]

The British in Hong Kong had been compelled to depend on Nationalist backing to an extent unimaginable before the war. After their wireless communications broke down at an early stage in the fighting they had even been forced to use the Nationalist wireless network for all their important military messages.[100] But these latest suggestions of help were ones that could only be contemplated with considerable sucking of teeth. Like all other colonial governments in South-east Asia, the Hong Kong authorities had taken care to retain a monopoly of modern weapons. Not even the Police Reserve, whom they had trained themselves, had up to this point been entrusted with guns; and yet here were the Nationalists asking for weapons with which to equip an irregular army of their own. Someone, we are told, at Maltby's headquarters 'had visions of ruffians and Triad members dashing around in civilian clothes tossing grenades everywhere'.[101] In addition the authorities still seem to have harboured a certain ambivalence about the actual idea of being rescued. From 20 December they themselves were working out plans under which a party of British officers and leading Nationalists should slip out to the mainland and try to establish contact by wireless with General Yu Hanmou's advancing troops. This scenario, however, presupposed that the British would retain the initiative. And the idea was still to accelerate General Yu's attack on the Japanese rear – a rather different matter from receiving the Nationalist vanguard in the heart of Victoria.

So the response was equivocal. On 19 December the British authorities accepted in principle Chan Chak's initial offer of trained reinforcements, but made it clear that they were unwilling to part with any arms. The next day they continued to stall, expressing their conviction that they were still capable of defending Hong Kong by themselves. On 22 December they agreed to supply the Loyal and Righteous desperadoes with two hand grenades and one pistol per man. But still the arms were not delivered. It was nightfall on Christmas Eve before Maltby's headquarters finally provided the Admiral with twenty boxes of hand grenades and seventy-five machine-guns; and even then they got back in touch with second thoughts, asking him to postpone handing the weapons out to his men.[102] North received Liang Shuming and his deputation with patience – and scepticism. He doubted that Chungking would be able to send any planes. He thought it unlikely that the authorities could find the arms to equip the proposed Nationalist infiltrators. And he believed that the advent of 5,000 Nationalist soldiers in mufti would 'cause major problems for order in Hong Kong'.[103]

By the time they at last got their weapons the one-legged Admiral and his lieutenants had come to the reluctant conclusion that the battle was lost and they were going to have to 'prepare to cope with a drastic change'.[104] Liang Shuming and his fellow enthusiasts, however, persisted with their proposals for another twenty-four hours. They were assisted in their campaign by Elsie Fairfax Cholmondeley, a young British lady of fur coats and independent means who was currently acting as a liaison officer for MacDougall's Information Bureau, but who also happened to be a member of the expatriate radical set. (She had worked on a Chinese journal advocating agrarian reform, and was a friend of Agnes Smedley.)[105] At 2 p.m. on Christmas afternoon this British champion of the Asiatics escorted Liang and his group to the China Building for a final appeal to the senior Asiatic employed by the British – Sir Robert Kotewall, who had become for the moment North's nominal superior in his wartime capacity as Superintendent of the Chinese. Kotewall heard the group out, and even agreed to send Chiang Kai-shek a cable on Liang's behalf urging that immediate reinforcements should be sent to Hong Kong. At the end of the meeting, however, he permitted himself an ironic sigh: 'Ever since the war started we've wasted an awful lot of time, and to do all this now . . . it's simply too late, too late!'[106]

The British give in

By Christmas Eve Hong Kong was 'a sea of fire'. The Japanese regiments assigned to mop up the western half of the Island had pushed their way into the urban area as far as the Wanchai district. One Canadian officer wrote that 'half the world around us seemed dead or dying'.[107] Sanitation had broken down, and every building stank. General Maltby once again advised Young to surrender; but still Young held out.[108] Maltby's recommendations however were now being reinforced by increasing pressure from the British civilians. The memsahibs had started to demand that the misery should be brought to an end.[109] In the course of the siege which took place at the Repulse Bay Hotel on 20 to 23 December the British civilian inmates of the establishment had elected a three-man committee to run their affairs. This committee continued to function even after the hotel had fallen into Japanese hands; and as Christmas Eve drew to a close two of its members, A. L. Shields, a Legislative Councillor, and Major C. M. Manners, set out for the British lines in the hope of persuading Young to order a ceasefire. Shields and Manners had, of course, been prompted to make this attempt by their Japanese captors; but they had also judged independently that any further British resistance was futile in view of the remorseless influx of fresh Japanese troops, artillery and equipment, which they had observed as their captors marched them across the Island.[110] Early on Christmas morning the two envoys arrived in Victoria and were escorted to Government House, where a meeting of Young's Defence Council was immediately summoned. The 23rd Army meanwhile suspended their air and artillery bombardment of the city for three hours in order to give the defenders time to reflect. All of the senior officials who attended Young's meeting are said to have shared the views of Shields and Manners. The Governor looked 'very sad and worried'[111] – but once again he refused to give in. The meeting concluded (almost in Churchill's own words) that there could be 'no talk of surrender';[112] and by noon, when the bombardment resumed with unprecedented ferocity, Young had repositioned his mask of jaunty defiance. One of Maltby's aides-de-camp who had just emerged from the military headquarters was astonished to see the Governor strolling towards him, in the thick of the shelling,

> in a beautifully cut, light-weight grey suit, grey Homburg hat and highly polished shoes. He was unconcernedly swinging a Malacca walking stick. . . . He smiled and said 'Hallo, MacGregor! Lovely day, isn't it?'[113]

Young sauntered into the headquarters and repeated to Maltby his belief that, as a matter of principle, the defenders should fight to the last man. By 3.15 p.m., however, Maltby had had enough. The fighting had virtually reached his headquarters. He informed Young by telephone that 'effective military resistance was no longer possible'.[114] After one more round of consultations Young at last issued orders to Maltby and the commodore in charge of the naval squadron to bring the fighting to a halt. Two officers were sent to convey the news of his decision to the nearest Japanese outpost. The Governor had exerted himself to carry out Churchill's instructions in the teeth of both the prevailing local opinion and the immediate military logic. Perhaps he can hardly be blamed if, in the words of an eyewitness, he 'sat in a corner of the drawing-room and literally retched'.[115]

At around 6.30 that evening Young and Maltby set off through the lines and gave themselves up to the local Japanese commander in Wanchai; and from there they were carried by motor boat across the harbour to the headquarters which Lieutenant-General Sakai had established in the Peninsula Hotel in Kowloon. In a candle-lit lounge ('History is made at night!' exulted a Japanese officer), Young signed a document of unconditional surrender. One British observer reported that Sakai 'had a stubborn face' and appeared 'very sure of himself'; but another maintained that the Japanese conqueror felt for Young and treated him with 'the greatest courtesy and kindness'.[116]

The colony had been expected to hold out for ninety days: it had managed eighteen.[117]

The flight of the Admiral

The immediate effect of the surrender was to push the defeated British and the Chinese Nationalists still closer together. As soon as he learned of Young's decision to halt the resistance the one-legged Admiral announced to Maltby's headquarters that he and his aides proposed to make an attempt to break out of the colony before the door clanged shut. He asked whether the British had any naval vessels he could borrow to get off the Island, and whether any of their officers would care to accompany him. The British fell in with Chan Chak's proposal. They had come to a kind of gentleman's understanding with Chiang Kai-shek that they would ensure the escape of the Admiral and his lieutenant, Colonel Yee, both of whom had a Japanese price on their heads; and there was some concern (a concern which would probably not have been uppermost before the invasion) that Chiang must not be allowed to lose his confidence in Britain.[118] In addition, as we have seen, a group of British officers had already been making plans to break out to the mainland in the hope of establishing contact with the relief force of General Yu Hanmou.[119] Maltby's headquarters accordingly agreed to make the colony's remaining naval force of five motor torpedo boats available for the proposed break-out; and arrangements were made for the Admiral, Yee and their party, accompanied by a dozen senior British officers, to rendezvous with this squadron on the south side of the Island at the fishing village of Aberdeen.

There now followed a getaway worthy of a sequence in a James Bond film. The party arrived at the rendezvous some time after 5 p.m. to discover that the motor torpedo boats had already left.[120] (Wires had been crossed, in the disorder of that last afternoon, with the naval authorities, in whose eyes it was 'unheard of for a commander to prejudice the safety of his ships to save two Chinese, however distinguished'.)[121] The group promptly commandeered a small motor launch and set off from Aberdeen under a barrage of Japanese machine-gun fire. With the launch sinking under them the passengers sprang into the water: the Admiral, his left wrist shattered by a machine-gun bullet, unstrapped his wooden leg and was borne through the sea on the back of one of his aides. The party swam to the neighbouring island of Ap Lei Chau, where for two and a half hours, under continual sniping, they 'dodged like water-rats from rock to rock' or lay passively waiting for the Japanese to come out in a boat and 'pick us off the rocks like winkles'.[122] Luckily the naval squadron had now received orders to wait. At around 10 p.m. the fugitives spotted a solitary motor torpedo boat still lurking in the vicinity. Several of them swam out to make contact: the party were hauled on board and the injured Admiral was plied with cocoa and rum.

The British considered themselves to be rescuing Chan Chak: Chan Chak, however, had no doubt that *he* was rescuing *them*,[123] and from this point onwards he had good grounds for that attitude. Only he had the local knowledge and contacts that would enable the party to proceed into the Chinese interior. Maltby's headquarters had tacitly admitted their dependence by placing the naval squadron under Chan Chak's command;[124] and from the moment he hobbled on board the motor torpedo boat there was no question who was in charge. Perching the peaked cap of the senior British naval officer, Lieutenant-Commander Gandy, at a rakish angle on his head, the Admiral straight away ordered the squadron to race for the island of Ping Chau in Mirs Bay, on the north-eastern fringe of the colony, where he said that they would obtain 'valuable information'.[125] At Ping Chau he consulted with the local headman, and was advised to move on to the nearby mainland village of Nam O. At Nam O he discovered a band of anti-Japanese partisans and enlisted their cooperation. He directed them to remove all the arms and wireless sets from the motor torpedo boats (which he then had sunk); and he assigned to their leader, a certain Leung Wing-yuen, the task of guiding the expedition inland through the Japanese lines. The party struck into the mountains on the evening of Boxing Day, and on 29 December Chan Chak and his following of sixty-two British officers and men emerged unscathed at the first major Nationalist stronghold in Guangdong province, the town of Huizhou.

And there at last they encountered the soldiers of General Yu Hanmou's elusive relief force – 'columns and columns of them'.[126] The relief force had not been a fiction, as many of the British had by this time come to believe. It had been on its way. Chinese memoirs confirm that Yu's vanguard, the 9th Independent Brigade, had indeed got as far as the town of Zhangmutou. The Brigade had been under orders to head straight for Kowloon, and one regiment had actually clashed with a Japanese garrison as far south as Buji, the last stop on the railway line before Shenzhen and the border. The main force, consisting of the 151st, 153rd and 186th divisions of the 63rd Army, had by Christmas arrived at Huizhou and had been preparing to launch attacks on the Japanese at other points in the neighbourhood. Morale had been high, and the troops were even said to have used up all their Nationalist currency in the expectation that they would soon be dealing in Hong Kong dollars.[127]

But the Japanese had been keenly aware of the Nationalist advance. On 13 December Emperor Hirohito himself had been moved to enquire of his Chief of Staff, General Sugiyama Hajime, whether there was any risk that Nationalist units might interfere with the attack on Hong Kong. Sugiyama had replied that there was such a risk, but it could be handled;[128] and indeed from the outset of the invasion every effort had been made to protect the

23rd Army's rear. Sakai as the army commander had taken extensive precautions. The Takatsuki Aviation Unit (the same squadron that had knocked out the British air force at Kai Tak in the first five minutes) conducted repeated bombings of the nearest Nationalist airfields at Guilin and Nanxiong to prevent any Chinese intervention in the skies. On the ground the 23rd Army's defences in the Canton area had been strengthened, and a regimental group called the Araki Detachment had been posted on guard about forty miles to the north-east of the colony.[129] And in the meantime, from the middle of December onwards, a different Japanese force, the 11th Army, was moving into position for a huge new offensive against Changsha, the Nationalist-held capital of south-central China, in an operation designed in large part to forestall any serious Nationalist reinforcement of Hong Kong.[130]

The result had been that the Nationalists, who were supposed to pin down the rear of Sakai's invading army, got pinned down themselves. It seems clear that in spite of their reported elan Yu's relief force made no significant progress after the vanguard arrived at Zhangmutou on 12 December. The bulk of the vanguard went no further south; and such attacks as were launched by other contingents against the 23rd Army were no better than fleabites. On 15 December Nationalist patrols were driven off by the Japanese in a handful of skirmishes at Danshui and other places, and on 20 December three Nationalist bombers staged an ineffectual raid on the Japanese positions in Kowloon.[131] Chinese sources explain that because of the Japanese pressure on Changsha only weak and ill-armed units could be made available to help out the British. These various units had to be assembled from far-flung districts, and some of them were weighed down by their baggage and artillery: communications in rural Guangdong were primitive, and movement was slow.[132] Despite having a degree of personal incentive to get through to Hong Kong (his wife was stranded in the colony), General Yu himself showed no inclination to hurry. His initial plan was to mount a counter-offensive against Kowloon early in the New Year.[133] Possibly he was one of those commanders who are cautious to the point of immobility, like McClellan in the American Civil War.[134] But he also appears to have had some difficulty believing that the British garrison were on the verge of collapse. After receiving a series of emergency wireless messages from the colony he brought forward his timetable slightly: by Christmas the vanguard had been instructed to enter Kowloon before New Year's Day.[135] But the British, as it turned out, could not even keep going that long.

In the last resort the alliance between the British and the Nationalists had failed in its declared objective of saving Hong Kong, and this failure sowed the seeds of disenchantment on both sides. As the war continued a view began to gain ground in British official circles that the Nationalists had never made any serious effort to disrupt the Japanese rear. Chiang Kai-shek and his generals, it was suggested, had been quite content to let the colony fall to the Japanese: with the British removed from the scene the way would be clear for the Nationalist forces to march in at an opportune moment and claim Hong Kong as their 'legitimate prize'.[136] The Nationalists for their part found themselves speculating why the British had been unable to sustain their resistance for even another few days. Not long after the great escape in the motor torpedo boats a piquant story began to go the rounds in Nationalist circles. It was ascribed to no less a person than Chan Chak, who in turn was said to have heard it from the British officers he had led from Hong Kong to Huizhou. The story went that at some point in the last desperate hours of the siege Governor Young had put a telephone call through to Churchill insisting that he could still hold out with the help of the Admiral and the approaching Nationalist relief force. Churchill however had counselled Young to give up on the grounds that if the British surrendered the colony to Japan they could get it back in due course: if they allowed themselves to be rescued by a Chinese army they would lose it for ever.[137]

Whatever the truth behind these conjectures it is clear that the Nationalists had no further stomach for fighting the Japanese troops in the Hong Kong area after the British defence had collapsed. As soon as word came through of Young's surrender General Yu issued orders to his units to abandon their operations and to pull back northwards to their original bases – which is where they were headed when the escape party ran into them at Huizhou on 30 December.[138] The officials who had formed part of the huge pre-war Nationalist infrastructure in the colony and had later joined in Chan Chak's shadow government were intent, like the Admiral himself, on getting out of Hong Kong as fast as they could. The Admiral set up two offices to take in these fugitives, one at Huizhou and the other at Qujiang, in the north of Guangdong province, and issued instructions that all personnel were to 'wait until work could be allotted to them'.[139]

As the Nationalists crept off the stage the spotlight slowly began to shift to their allies and rivals – the Chinese Communist Party. On the very first day of the fighting two small contingents of the East River guerrilla band had slipped across the border into the New Territories, close on the heels of the Japanese invasion force. These guerrillas immediately set about picking up an assortment of arms, ammunition and other supplies which the British and Indian troops at the border had abandoned in the course of their hasty retreat to the Gin Drinkers' Line. The flurry of Communist activity seems to have caught the eye of the British authorities, and one further attempt was made to explore the possibility of joint operations against the Japanese. On 12 or 13 December talks were held at the Hong Kong Hotel between Franklin Gimson, who had arrived (with spectacular timing) on the day before the invasion to take up the post of Colonial Secretary, and a Communist deputation consisting of Liao Chengzhi, the local Party boss, Qiao Guanhua, the future Foreign Minister, and the journalist Xia Yan. The Communists said once again that they were prepared to work with the British provided the British could issue them with arms. Gimson is said to have made cooperative noises; but the talks got no further, once again blocked apparently by the opposition of Governor Young. It was never made clear whether Young had objected to the supply of munitions to the Chinese in general, or the Communists in particular. The Communists were inclined to share the view of their Nationalist rivals that the British had judged it more politic to lose Hong Kong temporarily to the Japanese invaders than to be rescued by Chinese troops.[140]

They pressed on regardless. Like the Nationalists they were preoccupied with escape plans: Liao Chengzhi had called on the guerrillas to help him evacuate the galaxy of left-wing writers and artists who had been taking shelter in the colony since the start of the Sino-Japanese war. Unlike the Nationalists they were also digging in for a long-term resistance campaign. By 15 December the East River guerrillas were beginning to make an appreciable nuisance of themselves in the Japanese rear. The officers of the 38th Division, newly arrived in Kowloon and straining their energies towards the imminent landing on Hong Kong Island, reported that night in a state of some agitation that the summit of Saddle Hill behind them had burned 'in the form of a headband' for a period of two hours.[141] The following day the guerrillas staged a raid on the border towns of Shenzhen and Shataukok;[142] and there are signs that by the time the colony fell they were beginning to lay the foundations for an efficient underground network in the colony's hinterland. For if the British officers who escaped from Hong Kong on Christmas night were dependent on the guidance of Admiral Chan Chak, Chan Chak (though he was reluctant to admit it) was equally dependent on Communist help. The partisans who escorted the escape party from the coast through the Japanese lines to the safety of Huizhou were a company of the East River guerrillas.[143] The British observed the role played by these guerrillas with surprise – and appreciation. David MacDougall the information chief, who took part in the break-out, recalled that the guerrilla leader Leung Wing-yuen 'arranged everything; he arranged boats, he arranged places to hide during the day, and food. He was absolutely wonderful.'[144] By the end of December these scattered Communist groups represented the only flicker of active resistance to Japanese rule in Hong Kong.

A season of anarchy: Hong Kong in the hands of the 23rd Army

In the meantime the colony sank into chaos.

In Victoria, as in Kowloon two weeks earlier, the British collapse was followed by a strange interregnum of almost twenty-four hours. Chinese sources maintain that this was the pay-off the 23rd Army had agreed with the Triads in return for their contribution to sabotaging the British defence.[145] Right through Christmas night, at all events, and the whole of Boxing Day morning, the victorious Japanese forces remained at a standstill while the Triads rampaged. The European houses on the Peak were picked clean: Phyllis Harrop, the former police aide, who returned to her flat some days later, 'had never seen anything like the completeness of the looting'.[146] In the Chinese quarters bands of gangsters advanced from house to house demanding protection money. The Day of the Triads ran its course in an orgy of pillage punctuated by episodes of rape and arson and murder; and fresh fighting broke out in the ravaged city as a Cantonese gang battled over the spoils with a rival gang hailing from the adjacent coastal province of Fujian.[147] By the afternoon, when the first Japanese army lorries rolled down Queen's Road Central and the first Japanese sentries were deployed at the intersections, quite a few members of both the British and Chinese communities seem to have viewed the advent of the conquerors with a degree of relief.[148] But the Japanese forces brought more of the same.

At an Imperial conference which took place in Tokyo on 5 November, a month before the great southward offensive, instructions had been issued that the forces dispatched to the South should behave themselves well. The campaign was to be an historic one, for the liberation of the downtrodden peoples of Asia: the eyes of the world would be watching, and the excesses committed by the Japanese soldiers on the Chinese mainland should not be repeated. The essence of these instructions appears to have been conveyed to the chiefs of the 23rd Army, and from them to the regimental officers. Major-General Sano, the commander of the 38th Division, is said to have ordered his regiments to treat any British and other Allied prisoners they might take in Hong Kong with humanity and justice. A particular effort was to be made to spare the Indian auxiliaries who had been obliged to fight on the British side.[149] And to highlight still further the pan-Asiatic ideals of the expedition, all due concern was to be shown for the lives and possessions of the mass of Chinese civilians. What is not quite so clear is how far these fine, chivalrous precepts were passed down by the officers to the rank and file. It was one thing to urge moderation on the relatively educated officer caste; quite another to implant it in the line troops, who were for the most part ignorant, xenophobic and brutalized by a training intended to turn them into mindless fighting machines.

Some chivalry was undoubtedly in evidence during the take-over of the New Territories and Kowloon. A number of expatriates who had elected to stay or been stranded in the mainland part of the colony after Maltby withdrew his troops testified that the incoming Japanese forces had treated them with the utmost correctness.[150] Officers of the 38th Division are said to have been polite, pleasant and 'even respectful' to a team of British doctors whom they found still at work in the Kowloon Hospital.[151] And at the same time a studied attempt was made to show favour to the Chinese civilian populace. A 'reassurance proclamation' signed by Lieutenant-General Sakai which was posted up in the Kowloon streets on the first morning of the conquest declared, 'WE PROTECT CHINESE PROPERTY. THE WAR IN HONG KONG IS A WAR AGAINST THE WHITES.'[152]

Japanese officers similarly took the line that their quarrel was only with the British. While the British in the Kowloon Hospital were kept under guard, the remaining Chinese staff were left free to move about as they pleased.[153] The conduct of the rank and file was patchier. Several reports speak of cases of looting and rape and murder committed against Chinese residents, particularly in the outlying villages.[154] But some of the soldiers at any rate seem to have lived up to the standards prescribed by the army command. One mainland Chinese journalist who witnessed the arrival of the first Imperial troops in the Nathan Road area recorded that 'they were all very amiable and polite'.[155]

The shelling and bombing of Hong Kong Island which gathered pace in the following days was also conducted with a significant degree of restraint. The bombardment was aimed at military targets and government buildings. No incendiary bombs were used, and some care was taken to avoid hitting downtown Victoria.[156] Even on 17 December, when an 'intimidatory shelling' of Victoria was ordered as part of the second attempt to induce Young to surrender, the Japanese gunners were under instructions to avoid private houses and to bring only tanks and mortars (rather than heavy artillery) to bear on the populous districts near the waterfront.[157] The results were not of course as tidy as this might suggest: several of the larger hospitals got hit, for example. But most of the Allied accounts of the siege concur that these strikes on hospitals were an accident, and that the Japanese fire had been directed at anti-aircraft guns which the British had stationed in the vicinity.[158]

Up to this point, however, the tempers of Sakai's troops had been kept sweet by their effortless progress. Pleasantly surprised by the rapid fall of Kowloon, they had taken it for granted that the rest of the campaign would be a walkover. Major Boxer's assertion that 'We have not yet completely discharged our duty of loyalty to the King-Emperor' had been interpreted as implying that the British refusal to give in straight away was a matter of face-saving, and that the garrison would come to terms the moment a Japanese landing had been effected on Hong Kong Island.[159] Instead the assault force which landed on 18 December met unexpected resistance and sustained (if weakening) mauling from the British artillery. The result was that an ominous gap began to open up between Japanese theory and Japanese practice. As the maddened troops fought their way across the Island it seemed as though any notion they might have had of treating Allied prisoners in a civilized manner had been thrown to the winds. On the night of the landing the troops overran a first-aid post on the outskirts of Shaukeiwan: they seized ten unresisting British officers and privates of the Royal Army Medical Corps and eight wounded Canadian soldiers, lined them up by a storm drain and 'amid shouts of laughter' stabbed them in the back with bayonets, or cut off their heads.[160] On 23 December fifty-three British and Canadian prisoners who had been captured in the neighbourhood of the Repulse Bay Hotel were tied up with ropes and put to death on the nearby coast, just outside the Chinese millionaire's Gothic folly of Eucliffe. Some of them had their arms sliced off; some were decapitated; others were bayoneted, or shot over the cliff.[161] On the morning of Christmas Day, fifty-six wounded soldiers, mostly Canadians, who had been receiving treatment in an emergency hospital at St Stephen's College on the Stanley peninsula were slaughtered in their beds. The bayonets went right through the bodies into the mattresses, and the gutters 'literally ran with blood'.[162] Later that day, finally, in the grounds of the Victoria Hospital, thirty more British captives were bayoneted and burned with petrol. A Japanese corporal remarked that 'they cried like a lot of pigs'.[163]

Several European women were also victimized in the frenzy. Four British nurses were raped by the Japanese troops at a temporary hospital which had been set up on the Happy Valley racecourse, and three others were raped and murdered in the hospital at St Stephen's College.[164]

No greater tenderness was shown to the non-Europeans. The troops of the landing force seem to have assumed that all Asiatics employed by the British military would rally to them; and they treated as traitors a number who unaccountably failed to do so. A contingent of Indian soldiers were machine-gunned in the back of a lorry. Three Chinese stretcher-bearers of the St John's Ambulance Brigade were hacked to pieces alongside the British medical team in the massacre at Shaukeiwan, and ten others who had been stationed in the Wongneichong Gap in the heart of the Island were captured and killed at the end of the fighting in that sector without any thought for the Red Cross armbands they wore. Few of the troops now remembered that they were supposed to go easy on the ordinary Chinese population. At North Point on 20 December a captured Canadian of the Winnipeg Grenadiers saw Chinese civilians being tortured and executed and their bodies thrown into the harbour.[165]

Discipline had in other words broken down in a very big way, in the final week of the fighting. And it wasn't only the troops who had strayed from their script. Few of the officers seem to have made any notable effort to hold the men back, and one or two were even prodding them to commit their excesses. Colonel Tanaka Ryozaburo, for instance, the officer in charge of the 229th Regiment, which had been assigned to overrun the eastern part of the Island, is said to have issued orders that all prisoners of war should be killed – in apparent defiance of the orders received from the army commanders.[166] By the end of the siege it would seem that the commanders had themselves been inflamed into disregarding the policy of restraint which had been agreed on in Tokyo. In the early afternoon of Christmas Day, as part of the final drive to force Young to surrender, the War Memorial Hospital and the Matilda Hospital were both shelled in what one senior British observer construed as a 'definite and purposive change of attitude'.[167] The campaign of nobility and liberation had ended up as a horror.

And the horror went on. On 28 December Lieutenant-General Sakai and Major-General Sano led a march of 2,000 troops through the centre of Victoria to commemorate this most spectacular Japanese triumph over a European power since the defeat of Tsarist Russia in 1905; and at the end of the march, in accordance with Army traditions, the conquering force were indulged with a three-day 'holiday'. Country boys, for the most part, from a still backward nation, the troops helped themselves greedily to all the material comforts Hong Kong had to offer. They grabbed cars or motor bikes and careered around the streets on precarious joy-rides. Like the Triads, they plundered, but with a narrower focus: they were especially keen to lay their hands on up-market Western consumer goods. Several soldiers were seen sporting half-a-dozen Rolex watches, right up to the elbow; and one sentry deployed near the Peak was even observed to be wearing an elegant lady's mink coat. When they had finished with looting they drank and caroused. And when they were well primed with liquor they set off round the houses to take whatever liberties they pleased with the local civilians.

At this juncture however an interesting distinction began to make itself felt. In the three days which elapsed between the British surrender and the start of the sack the 23rd Army officers had apparently reimposed some discipline *in respect of the treatment of Europeans*. Steps were taken to punish some of the men who had been involved in the recent atrocities against European victims: one senior Japanese officer is said to have ordered the immediate execution of the nine soldiers who took part in the rape of the British nurses in Happy Valley.[168] These measures plainly had the intended effect. No further British or Canadian prisoners were slaughtered in the course of the sack, and few if any British women appear to have been molested. Margaret Watson the almoner recalled how a diminutive Japanese soldier who marched into her house contented himself with playing Mozart amiably on her gramophone.[169] Efforts were made to redress one or two offences that were committed against members of the expatriate public. Another Japanese soldier went at the height of the sack to a jeweller's shop to buy a replacement for a watch which had been pilfered from a passing expatriate by one of his fellows.

No such curbs were however imposed on the handling of the ordinary Hong Kong Chinese. Over 10,000 Chinese women, from the early teens to the sixties, are reckoned to have been raped or gang-raped by the Japanese conquerors during the sack of Hong Kong.[170] And for the Chinese, unlike the Europeans, the killings went on. A band of troops who broke into a house in Happy Valley discovered a plump and prosperous Buddhist sitting unclad in an armchair whirling a prayer disc in the confidence that his religion would save him from harm. The sight of his naked paunch aroused a sadistic instinct, and the troops sliced him open with their bayonets in a kind of enforced hara-kiri.[171] Looked at coldly the sack was not, in fact, a major affair compared with the 'holidays' the Imperial Army had enjoyed in some of the cities of the Chinese interior. The killings ran into the hundreds rather than the tens of thousands. But it was none the less, in the phrase of one British eyewitness, 'a taste of Nanking'.[172]

In other words it would seem that the 23rd Army had lost sight, by this stage, of the very pan-Asiatic ideals on which their campaign was supposed to be based. Any harsh treatment should in theory have been meted out (if at all) to the overthrown British rulers. But in spite of their proclaimed goal of ending British supremacy the Japanese chiefs still craved, to an almost pathetic extent, the esteem of their fellow imperial power.[173] Sakai and his colleagues are said to have gone to great pains to insist to their British counterparts that they had fought in a civilized manner; and their conduct during the sack suggests a continuing effort to make the same point. They wanted, said Emily Hahn, 'to show these snooty British that they could be gentlemen too'.[174] Any gentleness ought to have been bestowed above all on the Hong Kong Chinese whom the Imperial forces had come to release from bondage. But in spite of their grand design to liberate Asia and replace European rule with 'universal brotherhood', the Japanese tended to look on their fellow Asiatics *de haut en bas*. 'Although we say "universal brotherhood"', a Navy think tank in Tokyo had ruefully acknowledged the previous summer, 'it probably means that we are equal to the Caucasians, but to the peoples of Asia we act as their leader.'[175] In the particular case of China the Japanese forces had been engaged in a brutal war of subjugation for over ten years. Sakai, conqueror of Jinan, had been in the forefront of that war; so had his officers; and so had his rank and file troops who had learned in the course of it to perceive the Chinese masses as less than human. And it would seem that in the heat of triumph the habits of a decade were hard to break.

The results of the sack, then, were diametrically opposite to those which the conquerors should in principle have hoped to achieve. Quite a number of the British found the 23rd Army's conduct 'obliging' and courteous. One British police officer, Superintendent W. P. Thompson, went so far as to comment in a report dispatched some months afterwards to the Colonial Office in London on the 'most admirable restraint' which had been exhibited by the Japanese high command. He had the 'highest praise for the orderly manner in which the Japanese set about the occupation of the city'.[176] Looking back twenty years later many British survivors remained unexpectedly reluctant to subscribe to a general condemnation of the Japanese record in the first few days of the take-over.[177]

The Chinese, by contrast, were left in a condition of abject terror. During the three-day rampage they had huddled in their apartments while the 23rd

Army made merry. By night, we are told, as the drunk, lustful soldiers came hammering at the street doors, the roof tiles cracked beneath the scrabbling feet of the women who rushed up and down on the housetops in a desperate effort to get away. Householders endeavoured to protect their womenfolk through a primitive form of joint self-defence, banging gongs, drums and wash-basins in the hope that sheer noise would frighten the marauders off.[178] On New Year's Eve, when the 'holiday' came to an end, the Chinese population began to creep back on the streets; but the fear was in no way diminished. In Queen's Road Central the crowds

> pressed together to one side of the thoroughfare. . . . Everyone had a panic-stricken appearance. When they passed a Japanese soldier not a single person would look him in the eye; by the same token not a single person would fail to cast a furtive look over his body.[179]

Women skulked out of sight of the troops and wore dingy black as a form of protective colouring: to reduce their attractions still further they hunched their backs, daubed their faces with mud and wore sanitary pads irrespective of the time of the month. On 2 January 1942 the shopkeepers put up notices announcing their own three-day holiday – ostensibly to mark the New Year but in practice to avoid having to open again and expose themselves to the attentions of the Japanese looters. Little by little, in the following weeks, the Chinese shops in downtown Victoria started to reopen for business – but 'only through grilles'.[180]

As the 'holiday' drew to a close the 23rd Army chiefs finally set about implementing a set of Guidelines which had been issued for their benefit by General Staff Headquarters in Tokyo at the start of the invasion three weeks earlier. The Guidelines had advised them that their first task was to be 'the restoration of order'. After that they were to impose a 'strong military rule' in the newly occupied colony until the authorities in Tokyo had decided upon a more permanent form of administration.[181] On 29 December, consequently, Lieutenant-General Sakai closed down his combat headquarters in the Peninsula Hotel and replaced it with a Military Government Office – the Gunseicho, to give it its Japanese name. The Gunseicho was organized, rather neatly, into five departments, for general, civil, economic, judicial and maritime affairs. These departments were mostly placed under the care of the appropriate member of the 23rd Army bureaucracy: thus the Economics Department was headed by the Army's chief accountant and the Judicial Department was assigned to the officer in charge of the Army's legal section. By 10 January 1942 Sakai and his staff were reporting contentedly to their colleagues in the China Expeditionary Force that they were 'in the process of carrying forward all preparations relating to the introduction of military rule'.[182] Once again, however, a gulf is apparent between the proclaimed Army policy and the reality on the streets of Hong Kong. On 21 January Sa Kongliao, a mainland Chinese journalist who had been stranded in the colony by the invasion, remarked in his diary that in spite of the imposition of military rule 'the disorder in the society had not only not been alleviated but was evidently growing still more profound'.[183] Chaos still raged; and it would continue to rage unabated throughout the eight weeks in which the Gunseicho remained in charge.

Part of the trouble continued to stem from the locals. The lawlessness of the Triads and other local criminals that had engulfed Kowloon and Victoria in the aftermath of the British collapse hadn't simply died out when the Japanese forces arrived on the scene. On 11 January Sa Kongliao watched a procession of local people helping themselves to the furniture in the Northcote College of Education, 'each person taking one item, just like a column of ants transporting food'. Queen's Road Central became 'like a country fair', as hawker stalls sprang up to retail the mounds of goods looted from the European houses on the Peak.[184] Muggings by local ruffians took place in broad daylight: citizens were held up at gunpoint in the downtown areas and sent home in their shirts. And strategically placed Triad thugs levied money from residents approaching the turn-off which led to the Peak, or going for water to their neighbourhood wells. The same anarchy reigned in many parts of the New Territories, which had fallen prey to a dozen gangs of rural brigands.[185]

Some observers conjectured that the Gunseicho were deliberately abetting this turmoil. A few weeks of disorder, the 23rd Army chiefs were supposed to have calculated, would have the effect of persuading the bulk of the colony's citizens of the joys of submitting to Japanese rule.[186] This theory, however, seems needlessly Machiavellian. The fact was that the Japanese simply lacked the manpower to establish effective control. The Army presence, which may have amounted to 40,000 men at the time of the British surrender,[187] dwindled fast during January, as more and more troops were shunted off to other theatres of war; and by the end of the month no more than 3,000 to 4,000 Japanese soldiers remained in the colony.[188] Most of these soldiers were concentrated in the two cities. In the countryside Japanese efforts were restricted to holding the principal roads and the line of the Kowloon – Canton railway and a handful of market towns.[189]

To compensate for their weakness the Army chiefs made a series of *ad hoc* alliances with such local forces as seemed to be in a position to help them keep order. Amazingly (or perhaps not so amazingly, given what we have noticed of their ambivalent feelings towards the beaten enemy) they even, in a limited way, had recourse to the British. Already in the first few hours after the British surrender the European section of the police force had been directed to stand by in the Gloucester Hotel and get ready to help their Japanese conquerors restore calm to Victoria; and several patrols of British policemen had actually been deployed on the streets. These operations had had to be quickly cut short after a British police squad got set upon by a Japanese unit which had not been made privy to the arrangement. But British constables were still being used to stand guard outside the Japanese consulate building right up to the end of January.[190]

A more significant accommodation was reached with the Triads. Principal violators of order, the Triads were also, paradoxically, the great last-ditch source of order at this time of universal confusion when all other structures had broken down. In exchange for protection money paid by local house-holders they were organizing a network of vigilante groups that went by the name of Street Guards; and these Street Guards were making the sole percep-tible effort in the urban neighbourhoods to keep down petty crime. They erected bamboo barricades at the ends of the side-streets which could be closed at night to fend off would-be burglars. They captured small-time looters and pickpockets, hung placards round their necks and tied them to posts for the edification of passers-by.[191] The Gunseicho had little choice, for the moment, but to accept and encourage these poachers turned gamekeepers. To keep peace in the neighbourhoods they sought the help of a number of Triad leaders – as well as Zhang Zilian, the Shanghai Triad boss who had rescued the British the previous month.[192] They arranged for the Street Guards to be registered, and dispatched a senior officer to inspect one of their headquarters in the Wanchai district. And they established a permanent link with the Triads in the form of a lieutenant by the name of Miyahisa Denichiro, who had grown up in Taiwan, spoke two Chinese dialects, and even made use of a Chinese alias – Li Zhiting. In return for their services, however, the Triads as usual exacted a price. The story goes that at some point in the early days of the take-over Miyahisa was approached by a certain Lam Moon, a Red Pole or high-ranking officer of the Fook Yee Hing Triad, who was eager to win permission for his organization to operate a chain of gambling dens. Miyahisa gave quiet consent, and about ten establishments were duly set up in Sheung Wan towards the western end of Hong Kong Island. Similar approaches were then made to Miyahisa by the bosses of a series of envious rival gangs, and once again consent was forthcoming.[193] The result, for a time, was to turn much of urban Hong Kong into a massive casino. In every convenient spot, from Queen's Road to the dingiest side-streets, the Triad chieftains set up gambling joints. Gam-bling tables blocked the path of the traffic, and sounds of laughter and cursing drifted across from the fan-tan games. Makeshift gambling booths on the pavements appealed to the horde of uprooted, aimless citizens to COME IN AND MAKE MONEY, and punters emerged with bloodshot eyes from their round-the-clock sessions. And at each booth or table, as proof of the Gunseicho's blessing, the Triad bosses displayed the names of their long-banned outfits and hoisted the Rising Sun flag.[194]

In the countryside, similarly, the Gunseicho were obliged to entrust much of the policing to the Chinese partisans of the puppet Wang Jingwei regime.

Groups of these partisans had been left behind to take charge a month earlier when the 23rd Army moved into Kowloon. Several accounts from the early weeks of 1942 testify to the presence of Wang Jingwei policemen equipped with white armbands and sticks, to the clashes which broke out in the Saikung district between the Wang Jingwei units and the rural brigands.[195] One Parsee merchant who got out of Hong Kong at the end of January stated flatly that the New Territories were controlled at this period by 'Wang Jingwei henchmen'.[196]

The Gunseicho supplemented the efforts of these auxiliaries with their own more drastic crime-busting techniques. One Chinese source remarked tersely how in order to put a stop to the crime wave the 23rd Army 'chopped off a few hundred heads a day for some time after their entry';[197] and a similar picture was given by a number of British eyewitnesses. On New Year's Day 1942 Phyllis Harrop walked past a former playing field piled high with the corpses of Chinese who had been bayoneted or shot – 'supposed looters, we were told'.[198] Gordon King, the dean of the Faculty of Medicine at Hong Kong University, reported seeing six Chinese looters being lined up against the wall in Ice House Street and 'beaten to death one after the other by Japanese soldiers with heavy bamboo poles'.[199] Thanks to such measures the Gunseicho slowly began to get the upper hand in the battle against local lawlessness. But the remedy had proved to be rather strikingly worse than the disease.

Local lawlessness was not in any case the sole reason for the continuing chaos. A large part of the turmoil can be put down to the deliberate action of the Army leaders themselves. The conquest had disclosed to them, to their delight, that the colony was jam-packed with warehouses. In Kowloon alone they could count, stretching into the distance for over two kilometres, six times the number of godowns that lined the road between Tokyo and Yokohama. And beyond the godowns they could see the abundance of well-stocked offices and affluent private mansions that dotted this richest city they had so far encountered in their stampede across China. The result was that even as they took steps to deter the Chinese public from looting the Gunseicho were embarking on their own operation to pick Hong Kong clean. The 'holiday' was barely over before they were sending the troops out again on fresh rounds of pillage – this time pillage of a systematic and purposeful kind. 'Dirty and shabby and grinning and busy',[200] the Army detachments advanced through Kowloon and Victoria, clearing buildings of their inhabitants and slapping seals on the doors which proclaimed them to be Army property from that moment on.

Much of this organized plundering was carried out in the service of the Japanese war effort. Premier Tojo Hideki himself is said to have issued instructions from Tokyo that the colony was to be scoured for useful British goods.[201] Around 107,000 lb out of a total of 127,000 lb of rice which the

British had stockpiled in the fond expectation of sustaining the populace through a ninety-day siege were set aside for shipment to the Japanese mother-land and the various war zones.[202] Twenty thousand private cars and buses were heaped up on the Cricket Ground, to be cannibalized or dispatched to the fronts. 'Quantities of iron gates' were observed being hauled down from the gutted European homes on the Peak, to be sent to Japan and melted down for scrap metal;[203] and the ears of Tojo were reportedly gladdened by news of the find in one godown of several thousand strips of radium, which could be used to make luminous compasses and time-pieces for military aircraft.[204] But the hunt was on also for luxury items. The Army officers just as much as their men were intent on raking in Kodak cameras, Johnny Walker whisky, Omega wristwatches, Parker fountain pens – all of those Western treats which the Japanese coveted but which they had not yet learned to produce for themselves. Some of the treats were consumed locally by the garrison, while others were forwarded at the urgent request of the Army high-ups in Tokyo. As the scouring progressed merchant ships 'loaded down with loot' could be seen lined up all the way from the wharves to Green Island at the harbour mouth.[205]

The Gunseicho also contributed to the chaos through their persisting inabil-ity or lack of determination to rein in their troops. After the 'holiday' ended they had, it is true, got the men to refrain from the most flagrant acts of individual looting.[206] But that didn't mean that the 23rd Army had been transformed overnight into a disciplined force. On the contrary, the crack-down on local lawlessness seems to have been interpreted by many of the soldiers as a licence to carry on with the random brutalizing of the ordinary Hong Kong Chinese. In Wanchai, for example, a young Chinese man is said to have strayed one day into a neighbourhood that had been earmarked by the troops as a military zone. A sentry promptly dashed up and ran the intruder through the chest with his bayonet.[207] On 27 January, a full four weeks after the end of the sack, Phyllis Harrop set off on a walk along the corpse-littered waterfront:

> Further down the road I saw a Chinaman being beaten up with a heavy bamboo pole by a couple of Japanese sentries. Past the Harbour Office I saw an old woman being dragged along by her hair. Another younger woman I saw being pushed down into a pool of water and sat upon. Further down an old man was also being used as a seat.
>
> When we reached Wing Lok wharf two men were thrown into the harbour, and another being beaten was screaming his head off. He soon followed the other two into the water. . . .[208]

A final ingredient in the confusion was the inability of the 23rd Army to form a cohesive regime. Far from being in undisputed command of the newly won colony, the Army found themselves jostling for position with other branches of the Imperial forces. In the first place they had to contend with their traditional rivals – the Navy. On 20 November a general agreement had been reached between the Army and Navy headquarters in Tokyo for a division of authority in the soon to be conquered South. Hong Kong had been placed fundamentally in the Army's domain; but a subsidiary pact providing for some naval role had been made locally between the 23rd Army and the Navy's force off the coast of south China, the 2nd China Expeditionary Fleet. The Navy had played their part in the invasion by blockading the colony's offshore waters. They had failed to take part in the first 'peace mission' to browbeat Young into surrender, but had insisted on being represented – with separate and equal status – on the second.[209] Now, with the colony captured, they wanted their place recognized – and their share of the loot. Within days of the take-over, we are told, friction had arisen over the division of booty between the Army men in their patched, shabby uniforms and the Navy in their smart, grass-green serge. To avoid still more turbulence the Army had little choice but to accommodate the Navy's pretensions. The pre-war pact was duly implemented. A naval commander named Honda Katsukuma was seconded to the Gunseicho as head of the Maritime Department, and a division of turf was arrived at between the two rival services. Kowloon and the western half of Hong Kong Island were placed in the Army's charge; but the Navy received as their sector the entire eastern half of the Island as far as the Naval Dockyard and Garden Road.[210]

A second, more sinister challenge to the Army's preeminence came from the Kempeitai – the Japanese military police. The Kempeitai occupied themselves with a range of activities which went well beyond the arresting of drunken privates on leave. Their task was to ferret out subversion, regardless of whether the threat came from troops or civilians, from compatriots or foreigners, from inside or outside Japan. Nominally subordinate to the Army, they operated for all practical purposes as a law unto themselves. The invasion force had included a squad of Kempeitai officers under the leadership of Colonel Noma Kennosuke. Noma had started off taking his orders from the field commander, Major-General Sano; but by the time the invasion force landed on Hong Kong Island he had already begun to go his own way. By Christmas Eve he had set up a Kempeitai headquarters at the Cuttlefish Commercial Bookshop in North Point. (He would later claim credit for authorizing, on his own initiative, the dispatch of Shields and Manners through the British lines to urge the case for surrender on Governor Young.) By Boxing Day he and his team had become detached altogether from the command of the 23rd Army,[211] and in the following weeks they rapidly gained the upper hand in the local battle for clout and spoils. Observers described how the Army or Navy would drive the inhabitants from a building only to be evicted in their turn by the more potent gendarmes; how the Army would order one thing and the Navy another, while the Kempeitai would countermand both.[212]

While the colony languished, torn this way and that by its various local and Japanese predators, the power centres in Tokyo were waging their own battle over its longer-term fate. The Navy apparently made the first move. Their aims are unrecorded, but it seems possible that in spite of the basic assignment of Hong Kong to the Army which had been made in November they still had some hopes of securing control of this first-rate port. Japanese sources at all events speak of 'agitation by the Navy', of a 'cut and thrust' which took place between the headquarters of the two services as to which of them should have jurisdiction over the newly won colony.[213] In Hong Kong itself in these first weeks of 1942 competent observers appear to have judged it by no means a foregone conclusion that the Army would come out on top. On 18 January a Japanese civilian official employed by the Gunseicho predicted that the Army and some of the Kempeitai were going to leave and that 'shortly the whole colony would be run by the Navy Department'.[214]

In reality the Navy stood little serious chance. The bulk of their forces were far away seizing islands from the Allies in the Pacific: their position in China waters was strong enough to support a claim for representation in the colony, but no more than that. Hong Kong would inevitably remain first and foremost an Army possession. What the Navy's *démarche* did, however, was to trigger in Tokyo a 'sudden debate' among the Army general staff.[215]

The decision to strike out at the Europeans and Americans had given rise to a tension between two Army coteries which have been labelled the 'China faction' and the 'Southern faction'. The China faction, as their name suggests, drew their backing especially from the China Expeditionary Force and its off-shoots – including the 23rd Army. Their priority was to bring Japan's long drawn-out conflict on the Chinese mainland to a painless and satisfactory end. The Southern faction consisted of those generals who were organizing the Army's assault on Malaya, Burma, the Dutch East Indies and the other European-ruled territories of South-east Asia. Their concern was to bring into play all resources which might add to the momentum of their onrushing legions. And Hong Kong, lying at once on the coast of China and on the fringe of the European empires in South-east Asia, formed a natural bone of con-tention between the two groups. The China faction were anxious that the 23rd Army should stay in charge of the colony. They had hopes that they might be able to use Hong Kong as a base for 'political schemes' designed, like the failed Operation Kiri of 1940, to subvert Chiang Kai-shek's regime in Chungking and induce Chiang to drop his resistance to the Japanese subjugation of China. The Southern faction's objective was to prise Hong Kong away from the grip of the 23rd Army and turn it into a centre of transport and supply, a logisti-cal stepping-stone for the grand advance to the South.[216]

The arguments deployed by the two rival factions were summarized in a report on the Hong Kong controversy which was submitted by Chief of Staff Sugiyama to Premier Tojo on 10 January. The China faction held out for the standard arrangement under which newly occupied territories were administered by the local Japanese forces. They suggested that the colony might be ruled by a 'defence commander' responsible to the 23rd Army's headquarters in Canton. Alternatively the 23rd Army's commander-in-chief, Sakai, could serve simultaneously as the colony's Governor. The Southern faction however proposed that in Hong Kong's case a break should be made with the standard procedure. Instead they recommended the highly unusual expedient of direct rule. Hong Kong, they urged, should be placed in the hands of a Governor directly appointed by and responsible to Imperial Headquarters in Tokyo. Such an innovation would be justified by the fact that Hong Kong 'differed somewhat in character' from the general run of territories which the Army had occupied on the Chinese mainland. It would also, they added deftly, be consistent with the intention that had already been formed at Imperial Headquarters to preserve the separation of Hong Kong from the mainland and annex it as an integral part of Japan.[217]

The upshot was that the Southern faction prevailed.[218] On 19 January the first Japanese Governor of Hong Kong was presented by Tojo to Emperor Hirohito in the Phoenix Hall of the Imperial Palace. Announcing the appointment in the Diet on 21 January, Tojo explained that because Hong Kong had for years been used by the British as a base for 'creating disturbances' in East Asia, the Empire had decided to secure it as a 'bulwark' for the region's defence.[219] On 1 February the new Governor set off, as a Japanese war history aesthetically puts it, 'from a Tokyo adorned with the year's first snow',[220] and two weeks later he arrived in the colony. On 20 February the Gunseicho was dissolved. The blue armbands of the 23rd Army were replaced by the yellow ones of a newly created Governor's Office, and the Governor formally took up his duties as the direct representative of the Supreme Command. After eight weeks of turmoil Japanese rule in the colony had at last been established on a more or less stable basis.

CHAPTER THREE

The World Turned Upside Down

Yazaki, Isogai and the case for benevolence

Roman sources inform us that the reign of Caligula started off with an encouraging display of moderation, mercy and largesse. A similar exhibition of seeming benevolence marked the opening months of Japanese rule in Hong Kong. Rather surprisingly, the main impetus behind this exhibition was given by the interim leadership of the Gunseicho. The Gunseicho presided indeed over eight weeks of the most savage chaos. Yet for a whole range of reasons they wished to conciliate certain elements at least in the local society; and with that aim in view they were trying, amidst all the chaos, to grope their way back towards the neglected pan-Asiatic ideal.

The military chiefs who ran the Gunseicho were adherents, as we have seen, of the China faction in the Army. Preoccupied with the quest for a political short-cut to victory in the war on the Chinese mainland, they were eager to win the cooperation of any residents of Hong Kong who might be of some help. Foremost representative of the China faction in the colony during the opening weeks of 1942 was a major-general named Yazaki Kanju. Yazaki was the intelligence chief of the 23rd Army. After the takeover he was appointed head of both the General and the Civil Affairs departments of the Gunseicho, and he seems to have been the brains behind the interim military regime. He is said to have been a disciple of Ishiwara Kanji, the colonel who after fomenting Japan's attack on Manchuria in 1931 had turned into one of the leading advocates of a deal with Generalissimo Chiang Kai-shek.[1] In February 1942 Yazaki set out his ideas for a policy of conciliation in a memorandum entitled 'A Personal View of the Policies to be Applied in Ruling Hong Kong'.

Yazaki's dominance was abruptly curtailed some days later when the Gunseicho was displaced by the new Governor appointed from Tokyo. But the conciliatory approach which he had recommended was carried on, to a certain extent, by the successor regime for much of the next year. There are certain obvious reasons for this continuity. The defeat of the China faction which led to the changeover had in fact been qualified by a significant degree of compromise. While required to answer for most of his actions directly to Tokyo, the new Governor had been placed at the orders of the China Expeditionary Force in respect of defence, logistics, intelligence gathering and all other matters relating to the furtherance of the war in south China.[2] And the individual chosen to fill the Governor's post was a general who had spent a large portion of his Army service on Chinese soil.

We first caught a glimpse of Isogai Rensuke in the late 1920s, when he was serving as Japanese military attaché in Canton and hobnobbing with Wang Jingwei, the future chief puppet, and with the ultra-conservative Hong Kong Chinese businessman Chan Lim-pak. On the outbreak of the Sino-Japanese war ten years later Isogai was brought back for fresh Chinese duties, with not altogether impressive results. He was assigned first of all the command of the 10th Division of the 2nd Army in north China – where in March 1938 he spectacularly lost the Second Battle of Taierzhuang. Twenty thousand Japanese troops were killed in the worst defeat which had ever been suffered by the Imperial Army. Isogai then became Chief of Staff of the Kwantung Army in Manchuria, only to preside over a still more calamitous setback when the Kwantung Army was routed by Soviet and Mongolian forces in a clash which erupted at Nomonhan on the border of Outer Mongolia in August 1939.[3] Following Nomonhan, Isogai was retired from active service, and by 1942 he was to all outward appearances a thoroughly unpromising candidate for further promotion. He is said to have landed the job in Hong Kong principally because he was an old crony of Premier Tojo's: he had passed out from the Military Academy the year before Tojo and had joined, with Tojo, the Army clique known as the Isseki-kai.[4] Isogai had however retained from the earlier stages of his somewhat inglorious career a certain reputation as a China Hand, and in particular as an expert on the political affairs of the southern Chinese provinces. There was even a rumour that he had once been on friendly terms with Sun Yat-sen.[5] On the cultural side he is said to have been a gifted practitioner of Chinese calligraphy. We are told that on one occasion he 'surprised his subordinates by writing three sublime Chinese characters meaning *The Sword Which Liberates Lives*'.[6] On a personal level he was apparently quite a mild figure by the standards of the Imperial Army. A widower predeceased by his two daughters, he was already advanced in years by the time he arrived in the colony, and thus, in the words of one otherwise hostile Chinese historian, 'had good self-control'.[7] Following his arrival in Hong Kong the ageing Governor moved into the abandoned house of a European overlooking Repulse Bay. His adjutant records that he spent his spare time working on his calligraphy and walking in the garden in his slippers to listen to the croaking of the bullfrogs.

No private papers have yet been released which might allow us a detailed insight into Isogai's outlook. We cannot tell whether Isogai studied Yazaki's memorandum, or indeed whether any significant contact took place between the incoming Governor and his predecessor.[8] But Isogai's public utterances do correspond in a number of ways to the China faction positions put forward by Yazaki. Taking their comments together, and combining them with the observations of some lower-ranking officials, we can reconstruct the case which appears to have presented itself to the Japanese rulers in the early months of their conquest for the winning of certain select hearts and minds.

Both Yazaki and Isogai looked on Hong Kong as an outstandingly promising arena in which to develop 'political schemes'. In the first place they hoped to work on the large number of leading mainland politicians who had used the colony as a haven in the early years of the Sino-Japanese war. Not all of these politicians had managed to get out of Hong Kong before the British surrendered. It seemed possible that some of them might be persuaded to help the Japanese undermine the resistance of Chiang Kai-shek's government, either by announcing their defection to the puppet regime of Wang Jingwei or by acting as go-betweens in Japan's secret efforts to coax the Generalissimo into coming to terms. Some political mileage might also be made out of the local gentry, products as they were both of China and of the European colonial world. There were grounds for supposing that these local leaders, accustomed as they were to foreign domination, might adjust themselves to the Japanese conquest with a somewhat better grace than their counterparts in China proper. 'Seeing that the local people have hitherto been under British rule', Yazaki remarked confidently in his memorandum, 'they are not going to put up direct resistance to Japan.'[9] At best there might even be a legacy of anti-European feeling which would translate into active goodwill for the Japanese. Isogai aimed to turn Hong Kong into a 'model district' of China exhibiting the harmonious partnership which would come about in the future when all the Chinese were prepared to accept Japan's hegemony. 'Because of its ideal geographical position', he observed some months into his governorship, the colony was 'the most suitable place for a movement to work for better understanding between China and Japan'.[10]

This political vista in turn conjured up an economic one. Yazaki argued that the Japanese military should use Hong Kong to get access to the wealth of the southern Chinese provinces, in the same way that they were using Dairen as the key to Manchuria and Shanghai as the key to the Yangtze valley. If the railway line from Kowloon to Canton could be brought back into service and a new line constructed from Canton to the Yangtze port of Hankou, iron and coal, copper, manganese, tungsten, antimony and other strategic minerals could all be extracted from the interior of south China and shipped out through Hong Kong to supply Japan's wartime industries. To achieve this however help would once again need to be sought from the Hong Kong gentry, with their large resources of money and know-how. A string of joint ventures should be set up with Hong Kong Chinese interests, including a new Bank of Commerce and Industry to provide finance capital and a shipping firm to replace the Taikoo Steamship Company of the old British trading house Butterfield and Swire.[11] Isogai seemingly sympathized with this concept of integrating Hong Kong economically with the Chinese hinterland. In a first policy statement delivered from Tokyo on 21 January 1942 he predicted that the colony would 'rapidly take its place as the heart of south China'.[12]

Other groups in the colony might have a part to play in the new war against Britain and the United States. In particular they might help to facilitate the Army's conquest of the European empires in South-east Asia and beyond. Hong Kong had been one of the historic springboards for the southward expansion of the Overseas Chinese trading communities, and quite a few Chinese entrepreneurs in Hong Kong had their bases in Singapore or Malaya or the Dutch East Indies or other points to the South. Sensitively handled they might help to reconcile their relatives or business partners in those territories to the new reality of Japanese rule.[13] Above all interest focused on the Hong Kong Indians, several of whom had already shown such conspicuous signs of sympathy for Japan. In late 1941, a few weeks before the grand thrust to the South, the Imperial General Staff and Foreign Ministry in Tokyo had concluded an agreement with Rash Behari Bose, an exiled revolutionary from India who was acting as the Tokyo representative of the Indian Independence League. The agreement provided that any Indians living in those regions of South-east Asia about to be occupied by Japan were not to be treated as enemy subjects, and that an Indian National Army was to be recruited from Indian auxiliary troops who were caught there fighting for the British, with a view to attempting, in due course, an assault on the British Raj. As a part of this strategy the Army Staff Headquarters in newly occupied Hong Kong were assigned the special task of conducting 'operations directed at the Indians'.[14]

Finally the new rulers had to find some way of overcoming the immediate predicament of Hong Kong itself. Looting and banditry were only part of the problem. The colony lay prostrate in the absence of any firm order. The streets were a mess of corpses and shell-holes and severed telephone lines, and the harbour was clogged with the sunken hulks of two hundred vessels. The water, electricity and other public services which had been cut off in the course of the invasion were not yet restored. The food shortage, grave enough in the weeks of the fighting, was becoming acute: the outbreak of war had disrupted the colony's usual rice supply from South-east Asia, and such stocks as remained (once the Army had shipped out the bulk of the British reserves for their own purposes) were being doled out haphazardly at a handful of depots to frantic, jostling crowds. And normal commerce and industry had ground to a standstill. The Japanese were themselves all too keenly aware of the crisis. Colonel Noma and his colleagues in the Kempeitai agreed that public order in these first weeks of 1942 was 'in very bad shape'.[15] An official from the Ministry of Finance in Tokyo who arrived in Hong Kong on 15 January for a five-day tour of inspection was aghast at the 'suffocation' of business, and saw no hope for a revival of economic life in the colony until order had been restored.[16]

It was clear at the same time that the Japanese couldn't put things to rights on their own. The administrative skills they had shown in the first few weeks of the conquest had scarcely been outstanding: one local Japanese resident who had been coopted to help out in the Civil Affairs Department of the Gunseicho commented sadly on the 23rd Army's performance, 'Look what they have done to *my* Hong Kong'.[17] The new rulers faced a number of basic obstacles. They knew appreciably less than the British had done of Hong Kong Chinese customs, and they were only slightly better equipped than the British from the linguistic point of view. One of the most common sights of the conquest was that of the Imperial troops scrawling on their own palms and wrists as they tried to make themselves understood in the characters which are common to both the Chinese and Japanese scripts.[18] Added to this was the ongoing problem of limited numbers. A report by the Ministry of Finance which was published in April placed the blame for the chaos squarely on 'the shortage of managerial staff'. Colonel Noma considered his force of 150 officers and NCOs 'extremely insufficient' for the task of keeping order in view of the size of the local population.[19] Little prospect existed that the shortfall of manpower could be replenished from the Japanese homeland: Yazaki observed presciently that Japan would be in ever greater need of its human resources as the war went on.[20]

Some attempt had been made by the conquerors to redress these deficiencies by bringing in contingents from their older Asian dominions. Large numbers of Taiwanese were given influential posts as interpreter–secretaries. Koreans were used as soldiers and grooms for the cavalry horses, and northern Chinese were imported to serve as policemen, leading to a short-lived florescence of the Mandarin dialect. But none of these auxiliaries were very much more useful from the cultural (or linguistic) standpoint than the Japanese were themselves.

Serious help had therefore to be sought from the gentry in their role as the traditional leaders of the Chinese community. With this object in mind the new Governor's Office established by Isogai formulated a doctrine of 'using Chinese to govern Chinese'.[21] Help equally would be called for from some lowlier Cantonese who could act as interpreters, and from the Indians and Eurasians who had occupied so many of the humbler pre-war policing and clerical posts. Even though they had been debarred by the British from holding any responsible posts in the old civil service these locals were still, in the main, more sophisticated than their Japanese counterparts;[22] and above all they knew their way round.

The task for the Japanese, then, was to win the support of these various target groups and to mould them into a pliant local elite. And that entailed some attempt at constructive government. Possibly with a backward glance at the horrors of the sack six weeks earlier Yazaki drew attention in his memorandum to the shameful fate of the Mongols

> who conquered a vast empire but failed to give profound thought to their administration . . . Not only did they leave no trace, but they brought about the ruin of the very land from which they had sprung.[23]

The aim in Hong Kong, he suggested, should be to avoid relying on repression and instead to secure the 'cheerful cooperation' of the native inhabitants. On the one hand the conquerors should do their best to preserve, where appropriate, the more positive features of the British legacy. Care should be taken to keep up the liberal economic policies which had enabled the old colonial government to attract 'influential Chinese' to invest in Hong Kong, and to maintain in particular the pre-war British tolerance of free movement and trade. An endeavour should also be made to reassure investors by following the established forms of local administration: 'at the least it will be important to avoid causing any precipitate change in their lives'.[24] At the same time the new regime should take care not to give local residents the impression that they had merely exchanged the domination of Britain for that of Japan. Measures should be introduced to restrict the arrival of immigrants from the Japanese homeland who might compete with the businesses of local citizens and capture their jobs. Local people should not be force-fed, as those in Taiwan and Korea had been, with the language and customs of their new Japanese rulers, but should be left to become 'imbued gradually with the culture of the Empire'.[25]

The same conclusion, in general terms, seems to have been drawn by the incoming proconsul from Tokyo. In his first policy statement Isogai proclaimed that in the absence of his two lost daughters he would 'regard the Hong Kong Chinese as my most beloved children'. This somewhat saccharine pledge was accompanied by the hard-headed rider that 'unless we give them more than the British did it will be difficult to expect ideal governing'.[26]

Elevating the Asians: the Japanese choose an elite

As the upshot of these various calculations the new Japanese rulers launched themselves into their short-lived parade of reform. Their measures were both piecemeal and highly erratic. Emily Hahn, looking on from the sidelines, observed wryly how the Imperial Army officers 'dropped old ideas and picked up new ones with the enthusiasm of caged monkeys over a bunch of bananas'.[27] But the campaign was consistent at least in its central objective – to topple the old British colonial hierarchy and set up instead a New Order based on the pan-Asiatic ideal and inspired by the guiding principle that the first shall be last, and the last shall be first.

It began with a general propaganda barrage. One of the first moves the conquerors made following the British surrender was to reactivate the various newspapers which the local Japanese community had published in the colony on the eve of the war. Prominent among these papers was the English-language *Hong Kong News*, which now became the new regime's leading vehicle for appealing to the English-speaking Asians, from the Anglicized Chinese and Eurasian gentry to the ordinary Eurasians and Indians. In a series of articles published in January and February 1942 the *Hong Kong News* set about laying open the whole range of grievances which had festered under British rule. One polemic, for instance, devoted itself to exposing the pre-war denial of career opportunities to the non-Europeans. In both government and business organizations, it noted,

> callow British youths just out of school and half-witted Englishmen were often placed in charge of departments over the heads of Asiatics who, perhaps, had spent nearly half their lives in those very same departments and who, therefore, knew their work inside out.[28]

A second piece entitled 'The Question of Colour – British Snobbery that Destroyed an Empire' looked back on the aversion which the overthrown rulers had displayed towards social mixing. Some attempt, the writer conceded, had been made in recent years to achieve a degree of *rapprochement* between the communities: none the less 'social intercourse between Chinese and Europeans was rare where it was not artificial'.[29] Only the year before a young British member of the Cadet Service had been reprimanded by the Committee of the Royal Hong Kong Yacht Club for taking to the Yacht Club Ball 'a highly respectable Chinese girl, daughter of a leading Chinese family'. The writer went on to point out the very special taboo which had attached to miscegenation:

> Members of the Colonial Administrative Service who showed any familiarity with the Chinese found their progress hampered; and any hint of matrimony with a Chinese or Eurasian girl resulted in the young enthusiast being sent Home. Even in the lower ranks of the Government service, European dockworkers, Police inspectors, sanitary officers and the like who married Chinese and Portuguese girls invariably thereby put a seal on their advancement.[30]

Another article described how British arrogance and exclusiveness had been brought to the fore in the course of the recent invasion:

Pompous officials exerted their authority needlessly, and many of the better class Chinese were stopped from entering centres where food and other commodities were available because they seemed to be for Europeans only.[31]

The *Hong Kong News* promised that 'the new outlook arising from the New Order Japan is seeking to create will not tolerate the return of the "Boy, whisky soda" era'.[32]

This press offensive was reinforced by a series of vivid symbolic gestures. The statue of Queen Victoria which had sat gazing out over the Victoria waterfront was hauled down from its pedestal and shipped off to Japan, like the rest of the colony's metal fittings, to be melted down into scrap. Shipped off with it were the whole array of British effigies which had stood in attendance on the Queen-Empress round the fringes of Statue Square – Edward VII and Queen Alexandra; George V and the Duke of Connaught; Sir Arthur Kennedy, a nineteenth-century Governor, and Sir Thomas Jackson, the founder of the Hongkong and Shanghai Bank. To round off this dismantling of colonial grandeur the conquerors uprooted and made away with the arrogant pair of bronze lions which had guarded the Bank's portals. The apartheid-type barriers which the British had used to prevent Asian access to areas like the Peak were removed, and the innermost sanctums of expatriate life were thrown open to the subject communities. Steps were taken to organize a new Jockey Club whose committee would be composed, for the first time, of wealthy non-Europeans. Labourers in cotton pyjamas, newly flush with loot, were encouraged to take their families for lunch at the Hong Kong Hotel, and boat people from the harbour were directed to the other great hotel, the Peninsula – where, unfamiliar with chair seats, they squatted on the restaurant chairs in the posture they normally assumed on the decks of their sampans when eating at sea.[33] In some places the old pre-war rules of discrimination were neatly reversed: provision was made, for example, that from now on a whites-only lift in the Watson's Building should be made available for the exclusive use of Asiatics.[34] Intimations were given that the wealth amassed by the colonial rulers would now be placed at the disposal of all. A party of troops who had marched into the British-owned Tramways Company hacked open a safe, then called over the company's watchmen and workers and invited them to 'Take whatever you want.'[35]

To exalt local culture the conquerors introduced a programme of Asianization. A ban was imposed on the use of spoken and written English (except in the *Hong Kong News*), and a drive was launched to dismantle all English shop signs and advertisement hoardings. Places with English names were encouraged to adopt Chinese substitutes: so the King's Theatre became the Yu Lok

Theatre and Jimmy's Kitchen, a popular restaurant, was converted into the Sai Mun Café. Personal names of the local Chinese were no longer to be written in Western fashion, with the surname last, but put back into their traditional Chinese order. On his arrival in February Governor Isogai proclaimed the replacement of selfish Western materialism by the 'spiritual values' of the Orient – the Kingly Way which had been bequeathed by Confucius to the peoples of both China and Japan. Education was from now on to be based on 'traditional Asian morality'. In place of indecorous Western pastimes such as ballroom dancing, citizens were invited to rediscover traditional entertainments like listening to singsong girls and attending performances of Cantonese opera.[36]

Finally the authorities publicized their resolve to wipe out that great evil which had underpinned Hong Kong's founding and rise to prosperity and which the British had been so slow to eradicate – the consumption of opium. In late March Isogai announced the introduction of an Opium Suppression Policy. All secret opium divans were to be 'cleaned up' and steps taken to control the opium traffic. Over the following months a register was compiled of the colony's opium addicts, with a view to ensuring that these addicts should receive their fix only through designated sales outlets, at a high price and in quantities that were to be reduced year by year. By late July the *Hong Kong News* was declaring triumphantly, 'Already the dark fumes of drugs are gone'.[37]

All of these innovations, and others with less potential appeal, were set out for the scrutiny of the public in a startling exhibition of 'open government'. As if to emphasize the opaqueness of the pre-war British administration, the conquerors made a point of explaining each policy they adopted in painstaking detail through a system of regular press conferences. Isogai talked to the local media at the start of each month, and between times press interviews were accorded by the heads of the various government departments and even by Colonel Noma of the Kempeitai.[38]

To the background of these stirring new departures the Japanese set to work on recruiting the different target groups. The chief instrument they brought to bear on this task in the opening phase of the occupation was the Koa Kikan – the same Army intelligence unit that had played the key role in Japan's penetration of pre-war Hong Kong. The head of the Koa Kikan, Lieutenant-Colonel Okada Yoshimasa, had arrived in the colony with the invasion force. On 16 December he set up his office in the Peninsula Hotel, moving across the harbour to the Hong Kong Hotel two weeks later after the final British defeat. With a core staff of just nine officers Okada's unit came to enjoy, in the following weeks, considerable authority and freedom of action: the entire two-month interlude of the Gunseicho is even referred to by one source as the 'Koa Kikan period'.[39] The brief of the Koa Kikan was to secure the collaboration of 'important people'.[40] Following Isogai's arrival the Koa Kikan faded into the

background; but their assignment was taken over, with considerable per-
tinacity, by the new Governor himself.

Top of the agenda in the early weeks were the eminent mainlanders who
had been stranded in Hong Kong when the colony fell. Okada and his team
had arrived with a list of mainland personalities whom they classified under
a range of different headings. Some of these, labelled 'Communist-leaning' or
'strongly pro-Nationalist', were clearly unsuitable targets for Japanese recruitment; but others were designated more hopefully 'neutral' or 'third party'
or 'pro-Japanese'.[41] Here perhaps were the surrogates to deploy in the grand
political drive to subvert Chiang Kai-shek. Interesting possibilities included a
couple of ex-Foreign Ministers, W. W. Yen and Eugene Chen. Yen had spent
years in the Nationalist service; but he had also served previously in some of
the warlord regimes that had held power in north China before the Nationalists took over the country in 1927. Chen had belonged in the late 1920s to a
breakaway faction of the Nationalist movement which had been led by Japan's
future puppet, Wang Jingwei. The Koa Kikan put him in their 'neutral' cate-
gory. Yen, Chen and an assortment of fellow celebrities were duly rounded up
in the days after the takeover, and accorded what the Koa Kikan described as
'preferential treatment'.[42] Seventeen of them were interned in all comfort at
the unit's headquarters, the Hong Kong Hotel, while their families were fed
and protected; and another seventeen were detained in their homes. In some
cases this club-class imprisonment lasted for up to three months, but no
strong-arm tactics seem to have been used. Instead Okada and his staff focused
on persuading their captives, with every lure and argument they could muster,
to fall in with the China faction's designs. Both Yen and Chen are said to have
been invited to join Wang Jingwei's puppet government, Yen as Foreign
Minister and Chen in another ministerial post.[43]

Isogai built on these efforts by making full use of his much-touted sensitivity to Chinese culture. Frequently, we are told, he would summon mainland
men of letters to his residence to engage them in rarefied conversation about
the arts. Special patronage was bestowed on one eminent scholar renowned
for his skill at the Governor's favourite pastime of calligraphy. Isogai had
decided to set up an Oriental tea-house at the upper terminus of the Peak
Tram, and he thought that it would be romantic to call this establishment the
Pavilion for Thinking of Clouds. He invited the scholar to write out the three
appropriate Chinese characters and get them carved into a tree-trunk on the
site. In return he presented the scholar with six large bags of white rice – a
valuable reward in a hungry town.[44] Against this background of pottering
dilettantism the Governor was exploring every possible avenue to a peace
settlement with Chiang Kai-shek. Much of his interest was focused on an
elderly warlord named Xu Chongzhi, who had been prominent among the
mainlanders detained by the Koa Kikan in the Hong Kong Hotel. Xu, as it

happened, had received his formal training as a soldier in Japan, where he had sat in Isogai's class at the Military Academy. He had then, in the early 1920s, gone home to serve as commander of the Nationalist forces in Guangdong province – and the particular beauty was that as such he had been for a period Chiang Kai-shek's immediate boss. While offering Xu the inducement of a top post in the Wang Jingwei regime (probably that of head of the regime's Military Affairs Commission), Isogai is said to have urged him to go to Chungking on Japan's behalf and impress the advantages of a peace deal on his former subordinate, Chiang.[45]

Next in line for recruitment were the local gentry. On a paper appended to their list of mainland VIPs the Koa Kikan had recorded the names of a number of 'well-known Hong Kong Chinese managerial personnel of British nationality'. These too were sought out within days of the takeover with a view to extracting from them a commitment 'to cooperate in the future partnership between China and Japan'.[46] Sir Robert Kotewall and the lawyer M. K. Lo were picked up on 27 December and handed over to Okada; and a series of other leading gentry figures were delivered to the Hong Kong Hotel in the course of the following week.[47] Sir Robert Ho Tung was known to have gone away to Macao, but the Koa Kikan had hopes of retrieving him with the help of some agents they maintained in the Portuguese enclave.[48] If anything the gentry were handled with even more forbearance than the mainland politicians. A Work Report compiled by the Koa Kikan in mid-February noted that the organization had 'imprisoned several of their representatives for a day before allowing them to retire to their homes'. Other sources suggest that the period of detention may have been longer, but it seems in no instance to have lasted for more than three days to a week. Once again the preferred technique was persuasion. Gentry members were questioned about their contacts in Chungking and invited to 'have a change of heart'. Some of the gentry are also said to have been coaxed to come out in favour of Chinese submission on the mainland with the prospect of 'generous' rewards.[49]

At the same time the gentry were asked to apply their 'managerial' talents to the day-to-day business of running Hong Kong.[50] By 5 January 1942 the Koa Kikan are said to have asked seventy or eighty of the most prominent personages in Hong Kong society to 'step forward and help in the restoration of order'.[51] Three days later the entire body of gentry – 137 former Justices of the Peace and other civic notables – were informed that they were to be treated to lunch at the Peninsula Hotel by the chief of the victorious Imperial forces, Lieutenant-General Sakai. At the lunch, which took place on 10 January (a 'sumptuous' banquet accompanied by 'excellent wine'), Sakai inveighed against the rule of the British, observing indulgently that 'you gentlemen happened to form a part of it'. He hoped that the gentry would 'recognize the change that had come', and would, as the 'influential and wealthy element of the population', do all in their power to get the colony moving again. In particular he asked them to form a 'local assistance committee' to handle the food shortage and to encourage the public to maintain order, clean up their neighbourhoods and return to their jobs.[52] Further appeals were made over the next few days for gentry assistance with the critical problem of importing and distributing food. At some point in mid-January a Gunseicho deputation called at the house of Peter H. Sin, an Anglicized Chinese lawyer who had run a street policing unit for the British during the invasion. The Gunseicho officials asked Sin to devise a rice rationing scheme to replace the chaotic 'first come first served' arrangement which prevailed at the sales depots.[53]

These appeals were backed up by a general Gunseicho attempt to redress gentry grievances. The excesses of the sack had prompted a burst of complaints from leading residents about the molestation of 'family women'. 'Many meetings' are said to have been held at the 23rd Army's headquarters to discuss the rape epidemic, and as the weeks passed a number of counter-measures began to unfold.[54] Lieutenant-General Sakai lent his support to the local efforts at joint self-defence, issuing an order that as soon as the sound of gongs reached their ears the Kempeitai should send out a squad to arrest any soldiers who had broken into a private home.[55] From as early as the first day of the sack Colonel Eguchi, the 23rd Army's chief medical officer, was making plans to avert any further violations of 'family women' through the establishment of military brothels, and over the following month the Gunseicho began looking for appropriate, non-family women to staff them. Posters appeared on the streets advertising for 'comfort women', some hundreds of whom were recruited both locally and in the countryside of Guangdong province, and a total of 1,700 Japanese prostitutes were brought in from Canton.

Action was also taken to shield the gentry from the wave of organized raiding and expropriation that followed the sack. The more prominent citizens had official notices stuck on their doors forbidding the soldiers to enter their houses; and these edicts were reinforced by the on-the-spot interventions of Japanese officers. Colonel Eguchi, for instance, was asked by the Gunseicho to take care of his fellow medic, Dr Li Shu-fan, who had been identified as a 'Number One man'. He called on Li, promised him full protection and undertook in particular to make sure that no awkward questions were asked about the huge array of rifles and other weapons which the pleasure-loving physician had amassed in his years as a big game hunter. Most of the gentry appear to have escaped the indignity of being turfed out of their homes. One squad of troops were successfully dissuaded from taking over a house in Caine Road which was occupied by a younger brother of Sir Robert Ho Tung: the Ho Tung family were also allowed to retain possession of part of Idlewild, Sir Robert's principal mansion in the Mid-Levels.[56] On 16 January 1942 Yazaki's Civil Affairs Department put the process of expropriation into partial reverse with a decree stipulating that civilian residences should be returned to their owners. A number of the leading men of property were permitted for good measure to hold on to their private cars.[57]

Isogai followed up the conciliatory moves of the Gunseicho weeks with his usual exhibition of charm. We are told that the Governor made it his practice to call in leading members of the gentry for wining and dining and heart-to-heart talks. He didn't discuss the war on the mainland or ask his guests to do anything specific for the Imperial Army; but he 'assumed the air of being extremely concerned for their lives'.[58]

Much the same sort of tactics were brought to bear on a rather special member of the Hong Kong plutocracy named Aw Boon-haw. Aw was an Overseas Chinese magnate based in Singapore who had made his fortune by marketing a hugely popular ointment called Tiger Balm. So prodigiously rich that he claimed not to know his exact worth, the 'Tiger Balm King' now controlled an immense pharmaceutical and newspaper empire that stretched across the length of South-east Asia; and for this reason he caught the eye of the conquerors as a key potential ally in the Southern offensive. Hauled in by the Koa Kikan with the rest of the gentry Aw too was treated with a high degree of courtesy. 'Not subjected to any personal harshness, or deprived of the luxuries he had come to regard as his due', he was released after a few weeks of hotel confinement to his Hong Kong mansion, where a chauffeur was available to drive him every day to and from his office.[59] After Singapore fell to the Japanese forces in mid-February Isogai started putting together a plan to establish a puppet regime there consisting of Aw and a number of his associates who had been captured in Hong Kong. (Such a regime, the Governor hoped, could be used incidentally as yet another channel to Chiang Kai-shek.)[60]

Side by side with these gambits a drive was launched to win over the intermediate layers of Asian society. The most conspicuous effort was aimed at the Indians. By early 1942 the Punjabi and Rajput troops who had fallen into Japanese hands after Young surrendered had been segregated from their British counterparts and were being courted with 'intense propaganda'.[61] Japanese spokesmen suggested that in the course of the recent fighting the British had put the Punjabis and Rajputs in the front line while their own soldiers hid in the hills, and that after the fighting was over, the corpses of Indian troops had been left to lie unattended while the British collected their dead. In the meantime 'negotiations' began with the Indian section of the old colonial police force; and all possible steps were taken to cultivate both the police and the rest of the Indian civilians. Disdained by every other group in the pre-war years, these lonely immigrants now suddenly found themselves catapulted to the status of 'most favoured race'.[62] Japanese sentries were ordered to wave any *Indujin* through the ubiquitous roadblocks and allow them to move freely about the streets. In the anarchic first weeks, as starvation threatened the populace, special measures were introduced to make sure that the Indians at least would get food. On 8 January the Gunseicho's Commissioner of Police addressed a mass meeting of the Indian community and arranged for a list to be drawn up of their members so that rations could be allotted to them; and from the first week of February every Indian family duly received a free monthly issue of 7 lb of flour, some salt and some cooking oil. Indian residents were also given the privilege of buying rice and firewood at the lowest rates; and instead of having to line up at the sales depots in huge queues, as the Chinese were doing, they were simply permitted to collect their supplies at the local mosque. The Indians were assigned a Japanese patron saint in the form of Lieutenant-Colonel Endo Ekichi, an aristocratic intelligence officer with an engaging manner and a smattering of Hindustani. Endo took a 'keen and paternal interest' in their welfare, and at the same time did his best to stir up anti-British feeling among them.[63] In late September an Indian Affairs Inquiry Office was opened in Pedder Street under Endo's supervision. One of its functions was to help local Indians get themselves jobs: another was 'to give greater opportunity for the Indians in Hong Kong to cooperate in the war'.[64]

Similar if rather less spectacular moves were made to attract the Eurasians, the obvious candidates to fill the local clerical and secretarial posts. The Eurasian community were allowed, like the Indians, to enjoy certain privileges in their access to food supplies.[65] Like the Indians too they received at least one Japanese guardian angel in the form of a Kempeitai officer, Nakazawa Chikanori, known to some of his local contacts as Chick. Chick is reported to have set himself a deadline of a month to win over a pair of Eurasian sisters, Irene Fincher and Phyllis Bliss. Both of them had been born into the Gittins family, a prominent Eurasian clan, and both had held worthy jobs in local trading and shipping firms. Chick entertained the two sisters to beer and tinned pineapple and endeavoured to stir up in them a sense of pride in their Chinese blood and indignation at the sins of the British. He played on the resentment which the Eurasians of Hong Kong had felt when their women were denied the chance to get out of the colony with the British memsahibs in the 1940 evacuation scheme. In addition he made full use of the fact that both the two sisters had lost their husbands during the recent campaign. It was obvious, he declared, that the British authorities had put the Eurasian units of the Hong Kong Volunteer Defence Corps in the front line in order to save the white troops.[66]

Finally the conquerors did what they could to coopt a judicious selection of middle-ranking Chinese. Efforts were made, for example, to find recruits among a handful of Overseas Chinese from Australia. Australia had been earmarked as an eventual target for the Southern advance, and the Army chiefs were keen to engage Chinese who could serve them as guides and agitators in the Australian cities. Most of the Chinese, however, were sought out for their potential value to the local administration. By the first days of 1942 'negotiations' were under way with the Chinese section of the police force on the same lines as those with their Indian counterparts. On 7 January a summons was issued to all Hong Kong Chinese who had studied at universities in Japan and who might, therefore, be in a position to help the conquerors overcome the daunting language barrier. These returned students were asked to report to the Hong Kong Hotel to register with the Koa Kikan. On the following day, after their registration, they were ferried across the harbour for a welcoming banquet at the Peninsula.[67] The urgency of the linguistic need is perhaps underlined by the fact that this jamboree for interpreters was laid on a full forty-eight hours before the gentry had theirs.

These attempts to win over the local middle classes redoubled with Isogai's arrival in February. Former Asian members of the civil service were encouraged to take jobs in the newly established Governor's Office with the offer of salaries higher than anything the British had paid.[68]

There is, of course, no question but that the velvet glove concealed a mailed fist. The Guidelines adopted by the 23rd Army at the outset of the invasion had provided for 'the immediate suppression of hostile influences' as soon as the colony fell into Japanese hands. This meant in practice that the mainlanders designated by the Koa Kikan as 'Communist-leaning' or 'strongly pro-Nationalist' – all of those mainland diehards who had been using Hong Kong as a base from which to pursue the War of Resistance against Japan – were to be hunted down and imprisoned or liquidated. The apparently amiable Yazaki Kanju, who expressed such concern that Hong Kong should be governed with moderation, was in overall charge of the trawl, and the task of effecting it was assigned to the counter-subversion squads of the Kempeitai.[69] One of the first acts of the Kempeitai on Hong Kong Island was to search out and slaughter a team of a dozen officials from the Nationalist Ministry of Communications who had been employed handling the transport of strategic goods and materials to the mainland out of a house in Blue Pool Road. Various remnant leftists and hard-core Nationalists were being bundled off into prison even as the 'neutral' and 'third-party' VIPs from the mainland and the local gentry leaders were brought in for their sessions of civilized persuasion at the Hong Kong Hotel.[70]

And even with these more promising subjects an element of implicit compulsion was always there. The 'neutral' and 'third-party' mainlanders and the gentry were picked up in the first instance by the Kempeitai before being handed over to the silkier attentions of the Koa Kikan. During their confinement in the final days of the old year they were put through a long series of cross-examinations, carried out sometimes in seclusion, sometimes in the silent presence of their captive colleagues. Some accounts maintain that no pressures were applied to them more forceful than 'the veiled threat of continued detention'; but others speak of hints of unpleasant consequences and reminders that Lieutenant-General Sakai could be 'very stern if he is disobeyed'.[71] The Koa Kikan themselves commented in their Work Report that they 'caused' the gentry to assemble together and 'made them swear' to contribute to the future Sino-Japanese partnership. On their release from detention the gentry leaders were sent home under 'joint and several guarantees of responsibility'.[72] When the banquet for the gentry at the Peninsula Hotel was organized in the second week of January no invitations were issued and acceptance was seemingly taken for granted: the guest list was actually published in advance in the newly revived local press.

Much the same quiet arm-twisting may be detected in the approach to the middle classes. On New Year's Day 1942 Yazaki's Civil Affairs Department decreed that all government officials (apart from the British) were to return to their posts. The Hong Kong Chinese alumni of Japanese universities were obliged, as we saw, to present themselves to the Koa Kikan to be earmarked for employment before being forwarded to their welcoming feast. We may also observe in this context that the food shortage, though genuine, was being used by the conquerors as a means of control. By cornering what little remained of the food supply, the conquerors had secured a potent weapon for forcing people to get back to work.[73]

It is also apparent that the Japanese charm offensive was aimed overwhelmingly at the well-connected, well-heeled upper tiers of society. In recommending soft treatment of the native inhabitants, Yazaki's memorandum referred to 'influential Chinese', to those citizens who had attained 'a high cultural level' and 'a high standard of living'.[74] Persons of more modest background were of interest providing they had acquired a modicum of education and skills; but even here the main focus was on minority groups like the Eurasians and Indians who had served the British in an intermediary role. Apart from the picturesque gestures to labourers and boat people (gestures which, we may suspect, were most likely intended to capture the imagination of the designated elite), little sign can be made out of any effort to cultivate the impoverished mass of the Hong Kong Chinese.

Yet in spite of all this it would seem that Yazaki and Isogai and their associates did enough in these first few months to make a significant impact. By the end of the winter the new regime was clearly felt to have emerged from the initial barbarities of the sack. Several observers reported that the Japanese were pursuing a generally moderate policy in the occupied colony; that they were 'making a real attempt to promote the goodwill of the people' and 'seemed to be trying to please the Chinese in Hong Kong'.[75] Mainland Chinese in particular were struck by the contrast with their own past experience of Japanese conduct. One Nationalist assistant of Admiral Chan Chak who escaped from the colony shortly after the takeover declared to a British newspaper in early February that the Chinese civilians in Hong Kong had been 'unusually well treated by the Japanese'.[76]

The gentry acquiesce

The lunch which Lieutenant-General Sakai held for the gentry in the Rose Room of the Peninsula Hotel on 10 January 1942 was attended by 133 of the 137 original invitees. Top of the guest list were the two veterans, Sir Robert Kotewall and Sir Shouson Chow, now relieved of their British titles in the interests of Asianization and referred to in the official media as Mr Lo Kuk-wo and Mr Chow Shou-son. Each in turn got up to respond to Sakai's address. Kotewall began his remarks by expressing his appreciation 'that the Japanese Army had avoided harming the people of Hong Kong or destroying the city'. He noted that the object of Imperial Japan was 'to release the races of East Asia'. With regard to Sakai's appeal for help in reviving the colony he undertook that he and his colleagues would 'put out all our strength in Hong Kong to cooperate with the Japanese Army authorities'. They were indeed 'very fortunate' to have been 'placed under the instruction' of Sakai and his senior officers. 'We thank the Emperor of Japan', he wound up, 'and *banzai* ["may he live for ever"]!' Chow 'agreed heartily' with everything that Kotewall had said. He had been, he observed, a long time in the colony, and he believed that the Hong Kong Chinese fully understood the need for cooperation between Japan and China that General Sakai had 'so kindly' proclaimed. '*Banzai!*' he too finished.[77] Three days later Kotewall and Chow were appointed respectively chairman and vice-chairman of a nine-man Rehabilitation Advisory Committee. The remaining members were all conspicuous figures in the local gentry and big business world. Some of them had occupied the seats set aside for Chinese in the pre-war Legislative Council, and most had served in addition on the District Watch Committee and the other associated bodies which managed the Chinese community's internal affairs. They included M. K. Lo (now Asianized as Lo Man-kam); Li Koon-chun the rice merchant and his younger brother Li Tse-fong, the managing director of the Bank of East Asia; Tung Chung-wei, the proprietor of the Dao Heng Bank who was currently serving as chairman of the Hong Kong Chinese General Chamber of Commerce; and Li Chung-po, the chairman-elect of the Tung Wah Hospital Group.[78]

On 25 February Kotewall and Chow presided again at a ceremony which was held at the King's Theatre to celebrate the arrival of Governor Isogai.[79] Most of the same local leaders appeared as had appeared five months earlier at the same stately venue to welcome Governor Young. Kotewall declared on behalf of the Chinese community that the one and a half million people of Hong Kong 'shared in the reflection of the glory of the Imperial Army' and thus 'enjoyed the benefits' of the New Order of Co-Prosperity in East Asia. 'What greater happiness', he asked, 'could there be?' Commenting on Isogai's donation of rice to the public, he likened the act to 'the gesture of a father towards his children'. 'We all know', added Chow, 'that Your Excellency has been long in China. You fully understand our customs and have always entertained the utmost affection for the Chinese people . . . We are thankful that you have come to govern this place, and we are extremely glad to await your instructions.'[80] On 30 March the Rehabilitation Advisory Committee was replaced on Isogai's orders by two more permanent bodies, a Chinese Representative Council with four members and a Chinese Cooperative Council with twenty-two. Kotewall was made chairman of the first, and Chow of the second.[81] The two Chinese Councils, as they became known, were joined by all the remaining participants in the old Rehabilitation Advisory Committee, and the Cooperative Council included a further accretion of leading businessmen. Among the more notable were Tang Shiu-kin, the manager of the Tang Tin Fuk Bank and vice-chairman of the China Bus Company; Kwok Chan, the chief comprador of the Banque de l'Indochine and vice-chairman of the Hong Kong Chinese General Chamber of Commerce; and Ip Lan-chuen, the chairman of the United Chinese Industrialists Association.[82]

Absent from the gentry line-up were two prominent members of the pre-war Legislative Council, Ts'o Seen-wan and T. N. Chau. Pleading illness or other excuses they had dodged the grand public functions and had slipped away respectively to the mainland and the shelter of neutral Macao.[83] With these two exceptions every Anglicized Chinese and Eurasian grandee who had loomed large in public life in the days of the British came forward, it seems, in response to the Japanese call.

No single motive is adequate to account for the near-unanimity of the gentry's behaviour. One explanation which later emerged was that the gentry leaders had been given a kind of imprimatur by their old British chiefs. On New Year's Day 1942 Kotewall and Chow, by their own account, were approached in the China Building by a trio of former British officials – R. A. C. North, the pre-war Secretary for Chinese Affairs, J. D. Fraser, the Secretary for Defence, and Sir Greville Alabaster, the Attorney General. North and his colleagues asked their one-time protégés to work with the new Japanese rulers as a way of safeguarding the interests of the Chinese community. There are no grounds for questioning the existence of this imprimatur, which was later confirmed by the surviving officials on the British side.[84] What is less clear is the degree of cooperation it authorized. It seems doubtful, for instance, that North and his colleagues envisaged the warm expression of gratitude to the Imperial Army or the triumphant calls of '*Banzai!*'

The takeover was clearly received with real enthusiasm by one or two of the gentry and business leaders. Newly released from internment the merchant

Chan Lim-pak lost no time in offering his services to the invaders and in renewing his pre-war connection with Governor Isogai. He is said to have put forward the idea of establishing the two Chinese Councils and even to have provided the Governor with a name list of possible members.[85] The banker Lau Tit-shing, who like Chan had exhibited open support for Japan in the pre-war years, now surpassed himself with his aggressive endorsements of the Japanese war effort. After Singapore fell he proposed that the Japanese and the other peoples of Asia should join forces to wipe out the British land bases in regions like Burma and Tibet (*sic*). 'We must fight there', he urged, 'with the ferocity of animals.'[86] Both of these two hard-core partisans were chosen by Isogai to join Kotewall on the Chinese Representative Council, the more senior and prestigious of the new consultative bodies. If Kotewall and Chow had been cast as the colony's Pétains, these two were the Hong Kong Lavals.

These two men were without any question extremists. None of the rest of the gentry (including Kotewall and Chow) gave evidence in their conduct and statements of a disposition to work actively for the Japanese cause. But nor, on the other hand, did they show any outward unwillingness to accept the New Order. In some cases it looks as though the anti-colonial bile which observers detected among the non-European upper classes of pre-war Hong Kong may have translated into a certain *schadenfreude* at the British come-uppance – and, correspondingly, into a certain gratification at the new regime's initial reforms. Something of this attitude seems to have been manifested by Ho Kom-tong, a younger brother of Sir Robert Ho Tung who had served the British as a sort of master of ceremonies, organizing the grand public festivities which were held successively to mark King George V's Silver Jubilee and the coronation of King George VI. Following the takeover he was picked out by the conquerors to serve as the first Chinese chairman of the Jockey Club. He was reported to have remarked to a friend that for the best part of twenty years he had been trying ineffectually to get Chinese accepted on the Club's committee: now he in his turn would ensure that no British person was ever admitted to the Club.[87] In April 1942 he officiated at the first races to be held by the Club after its reorganization, declaring ebulliently that all had been done to ensure the success of the day and that 'everything now depended on Jupiter Pluvius'.[88] Dr Li Shu-fan later recalled having been impressed to begin with by Isogai's proclamation of an Opium Suppression Policy.[89]

Further evidence of this mood may be found in the conduct of the gentry-owned Chinese press. The *Wah Kiu Yat Po* (Overseas Chinese Daily), one of the principal Chinese-language newspapers, was back in production the day after the British surrender, and two more of the four leading Chinese papers had joined it by 3 January. One mainland Chinese reader observed that the editors of these papers were 'doing their merciless utmost to find fault with all kinds of shortcomings in the former British administration'. The mainlander interpreted this behaviour as a reaction to the censorship of the Hong Kong Chinese media which the British had imposed for the past sixteen years. Local editors, he deduced, were seizing the chance which the Japanese conquest offered to vent 'their accumulated rage'.[90]

One partial, and at first glance rather startling, exception to the general acquiescence was M. K. Lo. Many observers had taken it for granted that Lo, the long-standing scourge of British injustice, would be more zealous than anyone in his embrace of the new regime.[91] But Lo had always been something of an independent spirit, and in his case it seems the habit of independence was hard to shake off. He took his seat successively on the Rehabilitation Advisory Committee and the Chinese Cooperative Council, but by all accounts made little effort to disguise his reluctance to hold any public office and his aversion to everything Japanese.[92] He was said to have registered his displeasure at sitting on the Cooperative Council by making no contribution to the Council's proceedings; and some minutes of the Council's sessions which have survived do indeed confirm that this irrepressible point-scorer of the pre-war legislature maintained a silence as eloquent as that of the dog in the night-time.[93] Asked on one occasion by the Japanese military chiefs what the Army could do to improve its relations with the Chinese community he broke his silence for long enough to comment that it would help, for a start, if the troops would desist from urinating in public places.[94]

Fear was, of course, a big factor. Leading figures were haunted by the thought of what might happen to themselves and their families if they failed to cooperate. Even M. K. Lo was described by one British onlooker as having been 'weak and frightened'.[95] In theory the gentry might have been expected to follow the example of their two colleagues who called in sick and slipped off to Macao or the mainland. But it was easier said than done. Kotewall and most of the others were watched very closely. Movement was severely restricted: some of the magnates, for instance, weren't allowed to sleep away from their mansions without the knowledge of the Kempeitai.

Mixed in with the fear was a fairly large dose of pragmatism. Most of the gentry and business chiefs had little chance to form a clear picture of the events taking place in Kowloon or the New Territories, let alone in the wider world.[96] No one could be sure how the war would turn out. It was possible that the British would one day recover the colony, and some leaders may have thought it wise to insure themselves against such a scenario. Certainly Kotewall and Chow (unlike Lau Tit-shing) appear to have been rather careful to avoid denouncing the British explicitly in their public statements, confining themselves instead to vague references to 'century-old aggression' and 'the returning dawn'.[97] But as the fall of Hong Kong was followed by the still more spectacular fall of Singapore, and the newspapers celebrated Japan's triumphant assault upon one European possession after another, it seemed much more likely that British rule had been extinguished for ever, and that Japan would remain in control of the colony for a long time to come.[98] And under these circumstances there were ample reasons for the gentry to strike the best deal they could manage with the Japanese.

They wanted to hold on to the status they had won, in some cases quite recently, as the chief figures of local Chinese society. This status had accrued to them in large measure as a result of the appointments they had been given to the councils and committees of the old colonial government; and one obvious way to preserve it was to accept similar appointments from the successor regime. One Japanese official who took up his post in Hong Kong in these early months recalled the gravitational movement of leading citizens drawn to 'whoever was in authority'.[99] They wanted, as they had always done, to maintain social order. Faced with the upsurge of violence by local criminals which had gripped the colony in the aftermath of the takeover, they were naturally inclined to a certain extent to look on the Japanese troops as restorers of calm. Li Shu-fan later confessed that he had nurtured in the early days of the occupation a 'naïve' faith in the Kempeitai as an elite force that would protect life and property.[100]

They wanted, perhaps most of all, to revive their own businesses. Within days of the conquest the leading merchants had started, of their own volition, to turn to the new regime for its help in restoring a normal business environment. On New Year's Eve 1941 – a full week before Sakai issued his lunch invitation – a first petition was submitted to the Gunseicho by Tung Chung-wei and the Hong Kong Chinese General Chamber of Commerce. The petitioners sought the repeal of a ban which the Gunseicho had imposed, ostensibly to hold back inflation, on the acceptance of any large banknotes above the value of HK$10. This currency measure, they noted, had thrown the markets into confusion and crippled any prospects for the resumption of large-scale trade.[101] Two weeks later the Chamber went on to draw the Gunseicho's attention to another pressing financial need. If business were to recover, they urged, the authorities must arrange for an adequate money supply by allowing customers to draw on their deposits in the various British and Allied banks which had been sealed off by the Imperial forces. In the meantime leading firms were also beginning to put out feelers to ascertain if the Gunseicho would let them get going again. By 20 January 1942 the four major Hong Kong Chinese department stores, Wing On, Sincere, Sun and the China Merchandise Emporium, were said to be 'making preparations to resume business'. They had notified the authorities of the quantities and value of their stocks and had 'sought permission' to open their doors.[102] On 27 January the Hong Kong Chinese Chamber sent in a range of proposals to Yazaki's Civil Affairs Department which included the reopening of the local banks. By the following day one of the main Hong Kong Chinese industrial enterprises, the Nanyang Tobacco Company, had 'asked the authorities for permission to reopen'.[103]

Similar eagerness to resume operations was displayed by those gentry members who had followed professional callings. Following Isogai's arrival the solicitors and barristers began in their turn to stir back into life. On 1 March they were reported to have clubbed together into an Association of Chinese Lawyers of Hong Kong and petitioned the Governor's Office for authorization to take up their practices.[104]

Some of the gentry may also have wanted to seize the new chances for business that presented themselves with the change of regime. In February Yazaki remarked in his policy memorandum on the 'enthusiasm' which had been shown by both Tung Chung-wei and Kwok Chan of the Hong Kong Chinese Chamber for his idea of combining Japanese and local Chinese capital in a new, jointly owned Bank of Commerce and Industry: he believed that if shares could be widely distributed to businessmen and industrialists in the Hong Kong market the bank would be 'absolutely certain' of general support.[105] Some intriguing advertisements appeared in the following weeks in the columns of the *Hong Kong News*. On 12 March, for example, a notice read

> Chinese Gentleman desires Japanese partner for an enterprising transportation and import business. Advertiser owns ships.[106]

On 7 April 'a gentleman of good position and financial standing, with private office, long experience and intimate connection with local business' sought a 'Japanese gentleman as partner for developing and operating business projects'.[107]

Lastly they wanted to do what they could for the public. This was not quite the paradox it appears. Mixed in with all their go-getting the Hong Kong gentry had always had a strong tradition of helping out the less fortunate. Businessmen who had made good were expected to give of their plenty to those in need. And at this time of crisis the gentry felt at once, without having to wait for the prompting of North and the other British officials, that they were duty-bound to engage the new regime in a dialogue with a view to relieving the general hardship. In the petition they lodged on New Year's Eve 1941 the Hong Kong Chinese Chamber appealed to the Gunseicho to restore public utilities. Representations were also made to the authorities to improve public safety through such measures as giving help to the locally assembled Street Guards. On 13 January 1942 the newly constituted Rehabilitation Advisory Committee submitted proposals to the Gunseicho for the restoration of 'peace and security', and three days later Kotewall and his colleagues called on Sakai to discuss ways in which the general anarchy might be brought to an end.[108] In some of these areas (notably the restoration of order), the interests of the public coincided rather obviously with those of the gentry themselves; but there were also occasions on which a clear-cut concern was displayed for the less privileged. In late January, for example, when most of the public utilities had been brought back into service, both the Rehabilitation Advisory Committee and the Hong Kong Chinese Chamber were peppering the Gunseicho with appeals to reverse the sharp increases which it had imposed in the water and electricity rates. On 18 March, in the same way, when public transport was once again functioning, Kotewall and his colleagues petitioned Governor Isogai's new Communications Department to reduce a hike which had just been announced in the tram fares.[109] In particular efforts were made to respond to the Japanese call for help in resolving the problem of food supply. Li Koonchun the rice merchant and his fellow-traders established a special task force to examine possible ways of resuming the import of rice into Hong Kong from places like Thailand and Annam, and by 23 January they had already presented two suggestions to the Rehabilitation Advisory Committee. Peter H. Sin the lawyer decided despite some misgivings to accede to the request the Gunseicho had made to him to work out a scheme for rice rationing. Somebody, he declared later, who 'knew the ropes of this town' had to take charge, or 'the people would have starved even worse than they do'.[110]

Keen as they were to endear themselves to their chosen protégés, the Japanese went a fair way towards meeting the gentry's demands. Trouble was taken especially to accommodate the petitions relating to business. On 11 January 1942, in response to the currency protests, the Gunseicho announced that large banknotes of denominations ranging from HK\$50 to HK\$1,000 would be circulated again. In the following weeks they arranged for the Hongkong and Shanghai Bank and a number of other British and Allied banking houses to open up for short periods so that limited withdrawals could be made.[111] And in the meantime the green light began to be given to a whole series of local business enterprises. Early in February the Bank of East Asia resumed operations, accompanied by eight other Hong Kong Chinese banks.[112] Wing On, Sincere, Sun and the China Merchandise Emporium duly received the permission they asked for, and by early March all four stores were in business again. Nodded through in the space of two days, the Nanyang Tobacco Company was gearing itself to restart production by the end of January, and in May it was followed by a second industrial concern, the Fook Hing Oil Refinery Company. Quite on what basis these companies were singled out for approval can only be guessed at. It seems likely the Japanese wished to show favour to some gentry members with whom they had had business dealings already in the pre-war years. The families controlling the Bank of East Asia had, as we have seen, a history of contacts with Japan going back many decades.[113] There would also seem to have been a certain correlation between the ownership of these favoured firms and the leadership of the new advisory bodies. Sir Shouson Chow, for example, was (as he had been for the past twenty years) chairman of the board of directors of the Bank of East Asia. Li Koon-chun the rice merchant, who had been appointed Chow's deputy on the Chinese Cooperative Council, was a fellow director of the Bank, and his younger brother Li Tse-fong, who became the fourth member of the more select Representative Council, was the Bank's long-time manager. Chow, Li Tse-fong and the local Laval, Chan Lim-pak, were all directors of the China Merchandise Emporium, and Chan Lim-pak was the owner of both the Nanyang Tobacco Company and the Fook Hing Oil Refinery Company.

By the summer of 1942, at any rate, a large part of the gentry appear to have been benefiting commercially from Japanese favour. More and more local businesses were stirring back into life. In the first half of July, for example, nineteen Chinese insurance firms were reopened, and close on 200 Chinese factories were stated to have put in applications to start up again.[114] For the following six months reports from the colony testify to a general bullishness in big business circles. 'Prominent Chinese merchants' whose companies dealt in foodstuffs and other imported necessities were quoted as declaring that they had been having 'a good and profitable year'. 'Wealthy Chinese' were said to have begun to invest their funds in 'safe enterprises'. Shares in Wing On, Sincere and the other department stores were observed to have gone up 'considerably', together with shares in many Chinese-managed commercial concerns.[115] Quite a lot of new money had also been ploughed into real estate: property prices had collapsed in the aftermath of the take-over, and a 'roaring land boom' was reported as many businessmen jumped at the obvious opportunities for speculation.[116] Some of these rosy accounts emanate from official Japanese sources, and might on those grounds be regarded as suspect. On 12 January 1943, however, the overall picture was confirmed in a letter from one Kan Yuet-keung to a correspondent in California. Sent out by a circuitous route through the mainland and London, the letter was subsequently intercepted by the British wartime censorship. The writer Kan Yuet-keung would seem to be identical with a young lawyer of that name, the son of Kan Tong-po, one of the founders and the chief manager-for-life of the Bank of East Asia. The letter reads:

> As to the conditions regarding the bank, compared with when you left Hong Kong things are brighter: some money is being deposited every day, thus showing public confidence. Banks with Chinese capital will soon be free with regard to the paying out of money. Chinese business is now showing good results. The value of shares is rapidly rising. A share originally worth $10 has now risen to $25. 'East Asia' shares that were originally worth $100 have now risen to $140 and more. Property generally in Hong Kong is rapidly improving in value (like bamboo shoots after rain). In Central district it has risen to double the value . . . At present joint stock land company business is increasing daily.[117]

Some official encouragement also seems to have been given to those local entrepreneurs who aspired to take Japanese business partners. On 11 November 1942 the *Hong Kong News* reported the establishment three weeks earlier of a Hong Kong Trust Company, a joint Hong Kong Chinese–Japanese venture with a capital of HK$1m. In January 1943 a group of Hong Kong Chinese merchants were said to be joining forces with Japanese interests with a view to opening a big soy factory in the district of Mongkok in Kowloon.

To a certain extent the new rulers also showed themselves willing to accept the gentry's more public-spirited representations. On 2 February 1942 the Gunseicho announced that in the light of the complaints received from Chinese community leaders, the charges for water and electricity would be reduced. Kotewall confirmed the next day that the reduction had largely been achieved through the efforts of the Rehabilitation Advisory Committee.[118] The appeal over tram fares was less successful: the Communications Department insisted that the fare increases were necessary to prevent congestion on the trams. But the Japanese chiefs do seem to have complied with the gentry's request to put a stop to the crime wave. On 14 March Kotewall announced that there had lately been a general reimposition of order, a development for which the public had much to thank the authorities – 'though personally', he smiled, 'I may say I contributed a little towards this result'.[119]

All these gains were, however, secured at a price. To extract what they wanted from the new regime the gentry had to be prepared to allow themselves to be used in some measure for the purposes of Japanese propaganda. In the middle of March the elusive Sir Robert Ho Tung unexpectedly reappeared from Macao. The great plutocrat was rumoured to have lost HK$16m as a result of the war.[120] He was said to have been particularly worried about the fate of his current account balance of HK$1,100,000 with the Hongkong and Shanghai Bank; and he seems to have been lured back to Hong Kong by the new access to British and Allied bank accounts which had been agreed by the conquerors. (One later description of the visit explains that he returned for the humble purpose of 'withdrawing money from the bank for household expenditure'.)[121] In return for this privilege, though, Sir Robert clearly felt that he had to make one or two formal nods to the new dispensation. On 28 March he paid a courtesy call on Governor Isogai, and at the end of the meeting he gave an interview to a team of local reporters. He expressed his desire to help the authorities build up the New Hong Kong, and undertook to contribute to the establishment of Japan's projected Greater East Asia Co-Prosperity Sphere. The aged tycoon was far too canny to allow himself to be drawn into an outright endorsement of the Japanese conquest. Pressed for his views on the war, he declared that as he had devoted his whole life to business he wasn't qualified to give an opinion; and he brought the interview to a bland close by asking the journalists how he looked and basking in the inevitable compliments about his health.[122] He declined to take a seat on the Rehabilitation Advisory Committee, and by early May he was back in Macao. Some further necessity, however, drove him across to Hong Kong once again in the course of the summer; and once again he appears to have danced to a certain extent to the Japanese tune. He is said to have delivered a speech in praise of Japan, and it is possible that he may also have found it expedient to make a token invest-ment in the occupation regime. On 8 June he was referred to by the *Hong Kong News* as the 'chief organiser' of a Tai Tung Publishing Company which was being set up to produce pictorial magazines with titles like *New East Asia*.[123]

Specifically the gentry were obliged to lend themselves to the efforts of the Japanese Army chiefs to wear down the will to resist on the Chinese mainland. Time and again they were mobilized to appeal to the Nationalist Chinese lead-ership to come to terms. At the welcoming lunch in the Peninsula Hotel Kotewall declared that he and his colleagues were 'in full agreement that there should be peace between Japan and China' and 'would do all they could to further' that object; and Chow hoped that 'from now on Japan and China would join hands more and more'.[124] At a rally convened in July to mark the fifth anniversary of the start of the Sino-Japanese conflict, Li Tse-fong of the Bank of East Asia moved a resolution urging Chiang Kai-shek's government to lay down its arms. Kotewall once again added his contribution, pointing out in a broadcast delivered that evening that the war was 'more like a family quarrel between two brothers due to a momentary loss of temper'.[125] As one descendant recalls, there were 'certain statements you had to make'.[126]

Few of the gentry appear to have been perturbed by the need to come up with these statements. With the British removed their allegiance showed little sign of shifting, as might have been expected, to the beleaguered rulers of Nationalist China. On the contrary, the slight inhibition that most of them seem to have felt when it came to repudiating the British was noticeably absent where Chungking was concerned. Even M. K. Lo joined his colleagues in appending his name to a cable which was sent out on 26 January pledging the support of the Hong Kong Chinese community for Wang Jingwei and the puppet regime in Nanking.[127] Of the top leaders only one or two of the pure-blooded Chinese, as opposed to the Eurasians, were visibly distressed by the need to take a public stand incompatible with the Nationalist war effort. Chow, the one-time main-land diplomat, is said to have cut 'a pathetic figure, attempting repeatedly to communicate to the Chungking government his entreaty that they withhold judgement on him'. Peter H. Sin the lawyer looked 'thin and pale' and 'fidgeted with the pencils on his desk' as he sought to rebut the suggestion that his deci-sion to help the Gunseicho out with the rice rationing had discredited him in the eyes of Chungking.[128] But they went on playing ball, just the same.

The gentry compromise policy was followed in most respects by Aw Boon-haw, the Overseas Chinese magnate from Singapore. The Tiger Balm

King agreed to set up a company called the Kok Sui Kai to make 'token imports' of rice from South-east Asia, most of it for the benefit of the Imperial forces. In addition to this he agreed to permit the newspaper he published in Hong Kong, the *Xing Dao Ribao* (Star Isle Daily), to be used as a vehicle for Japanese propaganda. The title was changed to *Xiang Dao Ribao* (Fragrant Isle Daily), since all of Aw's newspaper titles contained the word 'star', and he wished, as he later explained, to avoid sullying the purity of the original logo. Aw was also named, with Sir Robert Ho Tung, as a 'chief organiser' of the new Tai Tung Publishing Company. In return for these gestures he was allowed to continue running the Tiger Balm business and raking in the profits from his newspaper.[129]

The gentry's approach contrasted rather sharply, however, with the attitude of the mainland Chinese VIPs who had been the prime targets of the conquerors' initial recruitment drive. With striking unanimity the captured mainland dignitaries refused to take part in Japan's political game. The veteran diplomat W. W. Yen protested to Sakai about his detention by the Koa Kikan, arguing that it was against international law for such treatment to be meted out to a man over sixty. We are told that he tried at one point to put an end to himself by swallowing disinfectant. Eugene Chen declined to say a word to the Japanese media and was led away mute to Shanghai. The most that the Japanese ever extracted from him was a statement in August deploring the British arrest of Mahatma Gandhi. Neither Yen nor Chen would accept the offers which were made to them of top-level posts in the Wang Jingwei regime.[130] Xu Chongzhi the old warlord was forced to deliver a radio broadcast informing the Hong Kong public about the kindness which had been shown him by the Imperial forces; but at the end of the broadcast, before anyone could stop him, he slipped in a disclaimer, 'That's the end of the statement I have been given to read.' Subsequently he turned down all the attempts of his old classmate Isogai to recruit him for Japan's 'peace diplomacy'.[131]

Preoccupied as they were with the larger issue of saving the Chinese motherland, unconcerned with Hong Kong now that it no longer had the value of a bolt-hole, the mainland contingent inevitably viewed the conduct of the local gentry as unheroic, to say the least. The journalist Sa Kongliao commented on reports of the lunch at the Peninsula Hotel that Kotewall had delivered an 'extremely toadying speech'. Sa was struck to observe that at this time when all leading mainlanders were frantically trying to get out of the colony the local upper classes seemed happy to stay.[132] Within a few weeks the gentry of Hong Kong had begun to acquire an unsavoury reputation in much of unoccupied China. One mainland woman who came to the colony in early 1942 in the hope of retrieving her valuables from the bank wondered whether some local friends of hers would be found among 'the collaborators one heard about in the interior'; and the Chungking authorities are said to have ruled that any Hong Kong Chinese official who left for Free China after more than a month had elapsed from the time of the British surrender would be liable to arrest and execution as a Japanese agent.[133]

Mainland observers came up with a number of different theories to account for the conduct of the Hong Kong grandees. Some ascribed it to the effects of a colonial education, which had produced Chinese lacking in an appropriate sense of national pride. Others blamed the poor treatment of the local elite by the British administration, which had left them feeling that they had little or nothing to lose from the change of regime. Still others spoke harshly of 'mercenaries'.[134] Each of these theories, arguably, hit on part of the truth; but none of them seems to have captured the essence of the Anglicized Chinese and Eurasian gentry of Hong Kong. The fact was that in spite of the sizeable business empires which some of them had built up on the mainland and in South-east Asia, the Hong Kong gentry were for better or worse parochial people. One report based on conditions in autumn 1942 noted that they 'did not take any interest in the general war or even in the war in China'.[135] Their concerns were focused on the small coastal enclave where they had been raised and lived and had founded their fortunes. They did have their loyalty; but their loyalty, in the final analysis, was to Hong Kong, and Hong Kong alone.

Back to normal: the response of the middle classes

Much the same acquiescence in the new regime was displayed in the middle ranks of society. Large numbers of Asians who had occupied the more junior posts in the British-run civil service came back to their jobs in response to the Gunseicho's call. By 5 January 1942 the only remaining obstacle to the return of the Asian police was a 'dispute over conditions', and two weeks later some 2,000 Chinese policemen were seen on the beat. Of these 75 to 80 per cent were said to be members of the old colonial police force. Eighty-five per cent of the pre-war fire brigade returned to their duties, and so did about 75 per cent of the old government's clerical staff.[136]

Back to life too crept a growing number of small businesses. In the first weeks operations were largely confined to enterprises such as small restaurants and barber's shops which had little by way of fixed assets and didn't, consequently, have to worry too much about looting. By the spring however a general revival of trade was becoming apparent, and by the middle of 1942, 23,812 shops were said to have put in applications for permission to start up again.[137]

In some cases this compliant stance was infused, as the gentry's had been, by a certain relish at the turn of events. Rather marked satisfaction was reported, for instance, among the colony's Indians whom the new regime had been courting with such intensity. Like their counterparts in South-east Asia many Indians in Hong Kong had been roused to a pitch of excitement by the possibility that the overthrow of the British in their neighbourhood might turn out to be a curtain-raiser to the collapse of the Raj. After the British surrender the banned Indian Independence League came out into the open and, with the Gunseicho's encouragement, took charge of the community's affairs. On 26 January 1942, which had been designated as Indian Independence Day, 'several thousands' of Indians are said to have packed Statue Square to hear speeches by the League's local chiefs, M. R. Malik and Sehil Khan. 'We all know full well', thundered Malik, 'that British rule in India has been nothing but robbery, jobbery and snobbery.'[138] Over the following months the *Hong Kong News* recorded a succession of similar rallies, which were said on some occasions to have been attended by 'the whole' or 'practically the whole' Indian resident population of some 5,500.[139]

More thrilling possibly even than this for the Hong Kong Indians was the abrupt elevation in their social status. Indians who frequented the Watson's Building were said to have taken 'great joy' in the fact that the Europeans were now made to walk up the staircase, while they used the lifts.[140] One Indian spokesman observed after the reception which was held for Isogai at the King's Theatre in February, 'This is the first time in the history of Hong Kong that the Indian community have been invited to welcome the new Governor.'[141] At some point in the same weeks a merchant named Saleh sent his relations in India a letter describing conditions in the colony which was picked up, in due course, by the British censors. Saleh commented cheerfully on the practical benefits which had flowed from the Japanese upending of the colony's ethnic hierarchy:

> By the Grace of God we are quite well. Blessed is God's name that we Indians as an exception get, at reasonable prices, eatables such as rice, flour, grain, ghee etc. We are passing reasonably comfortable days buying vegetables etc. in the markets.[142]

Certain sections of the Indian community seem to have come forward with particular zeal. Fired by the chance to pay the British out, at long last, for the Amritsar Massacre, the Sikhs were reported to be widely ready to serve the new masters; while the merchants of the Sindhi Association 'lost no time in protesting their filial bonds with the Japanese'. To some witnesses it seemed as though almost the entire community had welcomed the occupation. Phyllis Harrop consoled herself in early January with the thought that there were 'still a few loyal Indians about who have refused to join the New Order.'[143]

A measure of quiet satisfaction at the British debacle was also reported among some Eurasians. In response to the claim made by Chick Nakazawa of the Kempeitai that Eurasian volunteers had been used by the British as cannon-fodder during the recent campaign, Irene Fincher of the Gittins clan commented, 'The English have always treated us like that, in peacetime too.'[144]

More positively enthused was a well-known Eurasian jockey named Victor Vander Needa. Needa had served gallantly throughout the invasion with the Hong Kong Volunteer Defence Corps, and had distinguished himself by collecting ammunition under fire during the siege of the Repulse Bay Hotel. But he had not forgotten the expatriate jokes that had been made at his expense in pre-war days at the Happy Valley races; and it also happened that his Asian forbears had hailed (rather unusually) not from China but from Japan. Now he was said to have been roused to 'a state of trembling hope and even occasional exaltation' by the rediscovery of his Japanese blood.[145]

The anti-British backlash among the minority groups found its most coherent expression in the colony's one surviving English-language newspaper. The *Hong Kong News*, as we have seen, was a Japanese propaganda organ, published and financed from pre-war times by Japanese interests. But who actually wrote the articles, with their chiselled, immaculate, ever so slightly pompous English, replete with redundant synonyms ('ways and means', 'to assist and help', 'business premises or offices') and a wealth of inside information? The answer is, an assortment of Indians, Eurasians and Eurasians of partly Indian stock. One frequent byline, for instance, was that of Douglas Jansz, a journalist from Ceylon. Son of the principal of St John's College, Panadura, he had been educated at the University of London before striking out into the newspaper world. He was said to have been a fervent member of the Hong Kong branch of the Indian Independence League. Other contributors included D. O. Silver, M. R. Abbas and S. A. Ramjahn.

These early outbursts, however, should not be allowed to have more than their due share of weight. In the first place there was still a certain amount of residual loyalty to the overthrown British. Even among the Indians, as Phyllis Harrop's comment makes clear, people still hesitated to cast off their British allegiance; and this hesitation was probably more extensive than may have appeared at first sight. A maximum of 400 of the 1,530 Indian POWs captured in Hong Kong are believed to have broken their oaths to the British Crown and volunteered for the Indian National Army which was being formed under Japanese sponsorship.[146] The defection of the Indian civilians, though dramatic, was also far from universal. Two other sub-groups, the Parsees and the Punjabi Muslims, are said to have been unwilling, in the main, to forsake their colonial ties. Not even the *Hong Kong News* gives a figure for total membership of the local branch of the Indian Independence League higher than 1,500. One Parsee merchant who lived through the takeover estimates that perhaps a quarter to a third of the colony's Indian residents were disposed to sympathize with the Japanese cause.[147]

In the second place, quiet pleasure at the humbling of the British didn't necessarily imply rapture at the prospect of Japanese rule. Many of the Eurasians, for instance, had been raised on Western lines, and from their point of view the abrupt imposition of pan-Asiatic culture was as alien as it would have been to a European. Irene Fincher and her sister complained that they were unable to read the new Chinese street and shop signs which had been substituted for English ones as part of the Asianization campaign. The same applied, *a fortiori*, to the Portuguese. In the first months of 1942 several thousands of Portuguese voted with their feet, boarding ferries to neutral Macao in response to an invitation which had been extended to them by the government there to return to their colony of origin.

For a good many people the missing incentive was supplied, once again, by coercion and fear. Backstage pressures no doubt helped to swell the crowds at the Indian rallies, not to mention the fact that the Indian Independence League controlled the issue of rations.[148] In March 1942 the new administration formed by Governor Isogai ordered shops to reopen, and the revival of trade which was reported soon after seems likely to have taken place in large measure in obedience to this decree.

And at the same time, for these average individuals of moderate income, life had to go on. For the petty functionaries who returned to their posts a government job represented one of the few ways in which a citizen could be sure of a 'rice bowl'. Plenty of small-time merchants appear to have needed no prompting from the Japanese to reopen their doors. The Indian silk shops in downtown Victoria, for example, sought leave to start up again virtually at the outset of the take-over, and were back in business by the beginning of February.[149] The same pragmatic instinct was shared by many Eurasians, and also by those Portuguese who chose not to clear off to Macao. A Portuguese woman by the name of Maria Augusta Leigh appealed to the Gunseicho for permission to reopen a beauty parlour which she had set up in the Peninsula Hotel. 'I asked it back . . . it was mine before the war. That was my shop and I wanted to take back what I could.'[150]

Whatever precisely their frame of mind it seems clear that large numbers of these middle-drawer Asians were seeking, like the gentry, to make the most of the new opportunities. The conquest was followed by what one observer described as an 'odd little boom in brokerage'.[151] Several hundreds of Eurasians and Portuguese managed to recreate their traditional intermediary role by setting themselves up as 'brokers' to traffic between the conquerors on the one hand and the Hong Kong Chinese population on the other. Some of these brokers specialized in meeting the needs of the Japanese forces for scrap metals and other strategic materials. They paid local people to scrabble in the asphalt of the streets for small iron nails, slivers of copper and similar items which they then resold to government firms set up by the Japanese. Needa the jockey, for instance, was said to have turned himself into a 'flourishing merchant'. He employed lots of men to rake in quantities of iron, bronze and aluminium for the benefit of the Imperial Navy.[152] Working on the same lines was Joseph

Carroll, the Eurasian businessman whom we met briefly trading with Japanese companies in the pre-war years. He collected materials ranging from tungsten to grease for ball-bearings and passed them on to a firm called Hing Cheong Hong, which in turn forwarded them to the Navy authorities. Other brokers devoted themselves to satisfying the personal needs and appetites of the new masters. They bought up immense quantities of medicine, tinned foods and luxury goods and resold them at high prices to the Japanese military. Joseph Richards, the Eurasian malcontent who had worked for Japan's consulate in the colony during the 1930s, was one example of this type of entrepreneur. Richards began his career as a broker by trafficking in cameras, watches and radios; later on he switched to supplying the Japanese officers with wine and brandy, whisky and gin. Indians also took a hand in the brokerage game. One Sindhi family, the Harilelas, who would later go on to construct an immense clothing and property empire in post-war Hong Kong, made their living at this time by selling local goods to the Japanese Army. In return they took rice, which they retailed to the hungry Chinese.[153]

The Harilela example shows that the brokerage boom enabled some vital goods to flow down to the desperate masses. But there seems to be no doubt that many brokers contrived at the same time to do themselves pretty well. By March 1943 some of the less successful Indians were grumbling in the *Hong Kong News* that the war had made many members of their community 'enormously rich'.[154] For the first eighteen months or so after the conquest the brokerage business was palpably humming. In June 1943 the *Hong Kong News* reported that many restaurants, cafés and similar enterprises had decided not to permit the use of telephones by brokers 'to discourage the practice of negotiating over the telephone'.[155]

Some of the small Chinese traders also managed to accumulate quite hefty profits in the midst of general want. Pawnbroking establishments enjoyed a sudden heyday (more than thirty of them had reopened by September 1942), and most kinds of firms engaged in what we should now call recycling appear to have been doing well. Furniture dealers, for instance, were said to have done good business throughout 1942, buying up old articles and restoring them to look like new ones; and second-hand clothes dealers in the Wanchai district reported good profits for the year. Dyeing enterprises were busy, as people poured in to have their clothes darkened – whether for reasons of economy or to dodge the attentions of the Japanese troops. Quite a number of traders went in for freight business, transporting second-hand clothes, medicines and cooking oil to Macao and the mainland and bringing grain back in return. It was a brisk time for coffin merchants, and about sixty of them were observed to be functioning.

And where adequate profits couldn't be realised out of regular business they could still be induced artificially. The occupation had rapidly turned Hong

Kong into an anthill of hoarding, speculation and black marketeering. The pages of the *Hong Kong News* were full of diatribes aimed at 'the mischievous machinations of unscrupulous profiteers'.[156] Traders were said to be resorting to every possible gambit to eke out their limited stocks of food and firewood, clothing and medicine, tobacco and soap, and to force up the prices of such necessities. These complaints in the Japanese-sponsored media were echoed, if anything with still greater force, in a series of accounts published subsequently by the Allied side. One post-war writer, apparently drawing on the experiences of the Eurasians, Portuguese and other minorities, recalled of the colony's Chinese shopkeepers,

> They profiteered, they cornered commodities, they adulterated anything and everything – poured small stones into the rice, sand into the bran, water into the sugar. Every trick to add to the weight was used – as though faked scales were not enough.
>
> Some had no scruple in adding lime to wheat flour, or ground glass to granulated sugar. Soya bean powder was sold as full cream milk powder, a thin layer of the genuine powder being scattered over the surface to defeat olfactory test. Canned milk was carefully drained out, the tins filled with mud and sealed again. Soap held so much water that in drying it almost disappeared. Boxes of matches bearing well known brands were half filled up with headless sticks. Reels of cotton proved to be mostly wood. 'Genuine brandy' was largely cold tea . . .
>
> The whole business of retailing fell into disrepute, and not a few people vowed that after the war they would never patronise a Chinese shop again.[157]

Here undoubtedly were a good many hard-pressed Chinese citizens, desperate as their neighbours and using all the assets at their disposal to keep themselves going. But it is also apparent that the ill wind of the conquest had blown a fair number of resourceful if unpopular individuals a deal of good.

Delegation of functions: the local underpinnings of Japanese rule

Hamstrung as they were by their ignorance of the language and customs of the colony and their shortage of manpower, the Japanese carried on delegating a fairly wide range of responsibilities to the local inhabitants. At the top of the social tree the two Chinese Councils were given the task of serving as intermediaries between the conquerors and the mass of the public. The Cooperative Council collected the reactions and grumbles of the different sections of the citizenry and passed them up to the Representative Council, which conferred with Governor Isogai and his department chiefs on a regular basis.

Isogai and his colleagues in turn briefed the Representative Council on their latest decrees, and the leading members of both the two Councils did their best to explain these decrees to the public through a system of press conferences which they held (like the Japanese department chiefs) two or three times a month. Retrospective accounts written after the war were inclined to portray the two Chinese Councils as mere rubber-stamp bodies; and they certainly had no part in the taking of any major decisions. But their advisory functions, in the earlier stages at least, may not have been negligible. A survey of the colony which was produced by the new regime's Information Department for the benefit of readers in Japan observed that because 'the overwhelming majority' of the inhabitants of Hong Kong were of Chinese origin, it was 'certainly not the case that their opinion is ignored'.[158] Some of the gentry leaders who sat on the two Chinese Councils were assigned simultaneously to a specialist advisory role. In February 1942, for instance, the Laval figure Lau Tit-shing was placed at the head of a newly organized Chinese Bankers' Association. We are told that the conquerors reckoned the Hong Kong Chinese bankers could 'give them valuable help in the execution of various economic policies'.[159]

The Japanese also tended to cede to the two Chinese Councils and the gentry as a whole certain spheres of activity in which they had no disposition to get involved. One of these spheres was rent management. In the months after Isogai's accession to office the two Councils were put to work regulating the squabbles which had arisen between local landlords and tenants following the collapse of the property market.[160] Ichiki Yoshiyuki, an official who had taken over as chief of the reorganized Civil Affairs Department, declared flatly in August 1942 that the government had 'no intention whatever' of fixing the rents. Any disputes should be settled by the landlords and tenants themselves, and if they were unable to reach an agreement the matter should be referred to the Representative Council for a definitive ruling.[161] A second, more extensive sphere of official disinterest was that of relief work. From the outset the conquerors showed themselves anxious to offload such work on to the Tung Wah and Kwong Wah hospitals and similar gentry-run bodies which had traditionally busied themselves with the care of the destitute. The Gunseicho gave notice that while the 23rd Army were temporarily issuing the poor with rice and gruel the latter were 'very numerous', and 'it was hoped that charitable organizations would hasten to extend their activities'. In the same spirit Isogai advised the Representative Council that any scheme for relieving local unemployment should be worked out by 'the people themselves'.[162]

Equally noticeable was the delegation of functions to the petty civil servants and clerical personnel. Throughout the central government the Japanese lost no time in invoking the skills of their newly acquired Asian subjects. Reports reaching British intelligence in the spring of 1942 pointed out that while Japanese bureaucrats had occupied the more senior positions in the new

Governor's Office created by Isogai, 'all others' were held by the Hong Kong Chinese.[163] Not all of these jobs were entirely menial: one Chinese is known to have been employed, for example, as director of the Department of Postal Affairs. It is also apparent that the local job-holders included many new recruits as well as pre-war civil servants returned to their posts. Quite a number of prestigious new appointments were dispensed to the Hong Kong Chinese alumni of Japanese universities who had assembled in the first fortnight of the takeover at the summons of the Koa Kikan. One former clerk who happened to be a Japanese speaker was reported at the end of February to have been installed, 'splendidly prosperous', as interpreter in the main Kempeitai office on the Victoria waterfront.[164]

The same trend asserted itself (if anything, still more strongly) in the local government sphere. The delegation of functions at a local level had its origins in the middle of January when the Gunseicho placed the overall problem of food supply in the hands of the lawyer Peter H. Sin. In a few days Sin came up with a workable answer. The entire population, he proposed, should be registered household by household, and each household should be issued with a rice ration card. Hong Kong Island and Kowloon should be divided into districts, and each district should operate a rice rationing station from which card-carrying citizens could collect their supplies. The Gunseicho not merely accepted Sin's scheme but assigned him the leading role in its implementation – earning him from the Chinese public the appreciative sobriquet of 'the Mayor of Hong Kong'.[165]

Building on the framework envisaged by Sin the authorities proceeded to set up, between January and July 1942, a whole network of District Bureaux – twelve for Hong Kong Island and six for Kowloon. In addition to the basic tasks of household registration and rice rationing, the Bureaux were assigned a wide range of responsibilities in their jurisdictions, including health and welfare, the drawing-up of an annual budget and the determination of the rights and duties of the local inhabitants. But their most striking feature was their composition. Starting with the 'Mayor of Hong Kong', who was placed in charge of the Bureau for the Central District of Victoria, all the Bureau chiefs, their deputies and the twenty-odd members of their staffs were local Chinese. Each Bureau was advised by a District Assembly consisting of between five and ten Chinese householders.[166] As if to emphasize their importance the Bureau chiefs were granted the privilege of direct access to the Governor's Office. For the time being they were obliged to rely on direct financial aid from the central government, but it was envisaged that they would be made self-supporting at a later stage.

The process didn't stop there. On 9 February 1942 the *Hong Kong News* reported that 131 ward leaders had been elected in the Central District. The paper predicted that 2,000 ward leaders would in due course be elected to represent wards throughout the twelve districts of Hong Kong Island. A ward was supposed to comprise thirty households, and the system in theory conferred a degree of authority on local citizens down at the very grass roots. By September the constituencies had been redesigned, and no more mention was made of elections; but the drive to organize grass-roots representation was still going on. Street committees were being set up to represent the householders, and an initial 777 residents of Hong Kong Island had been designated as leaders of the individual streets. By February 1943 there were said to be a total of 1,366 street chiefs on Hong Kong Island, and 1,462 in Kowloon.[167]

A similar devolution took place in the countryside. In the absence of any effective Japanese control during the early weeks of the takeover, authority in the New Territories had been assumed in a haphazard fashion by the village elders and the leading traders who ran the chambers of commerce in the market towns. Uneducated and even more ignorant than the urban gentry of the events taking place in the outside world, these rural leaders for the most part acquiesced without difficulty in Japanese rule. The Japanese accordingly confirmed their authority, and in some ways enlarged it. The village elders were organized into self-governing committees, and the chambers of commerce were recognized as components of a newly formed network of ten rural District Bureaux. Like their counterparts in the cities these rural bodies had as one of their principal functions the task of allotting the rice rations. They were also expected to act as purchasing agents for the Japanese troops in the neighbourhood, and to provide labour for local construction schemes.[168]

Some attempt had initially been made to cut down Japanese dependence on local backing in the critical arena of public order. Already by late January 1942 the Gunseicho had been getting annoyed by the Triad dominance reflected in the ubiquitous gambling dens, and a decree had been issued against public gambling. Further bans were proclaimed after Isogai took up office, and mahjong, the adored Chinese gambling game, was thrown in (somewhat strangely) with the decadent Western pastimes to be stamped out in the name of 'Asian morality'. At the end of April the Governor's Office announced that the time had now come to disband the Street Guard vigilante squads which the Triads had been running for the benefit of local residents. These squads, the announcement observed, had undoubtedly helped to keep peace in the neighbourhoods, but had also included some 'undesirable elements'. Now order had been restored they could safely be replaced by regular forces.[169]

The Triad gangsters, however, played too important a role in the back streets to be got rid of lightly. The April statement in effect admitted as much, concluding rather lamely that if residents still considered Street Guards to be necessary they could 'apply to the Governor's Office for their recognition'; and three weeks later the people of the Shamshuipo district in Kowloon were indeed said to have organized their 'own group of watchmen'.[170] By September the conquerors were themselves once again reaching out willy-nilly for Triad support. In that month they decided to go ahead with a plan to convert a large section of Wanchai into a red-light district as part of their programme for channelling the lusts of the soldiery. Triad gangs were sent out to evict the inhabitants – and to bear the brunt of whatever odium the evictions might entail.[171]

And in the meantime the regular forces with which Isogai and his colleagues proposed to replace their embarrassing Triad allies were themselves being heavily supplemented by local recruits. By the early summer of 1942, as more and more units of the Japanese garrison were moved out of the colony for active service in South-east Asia and the Pacific, widespread use was being made of those POWs from the Punjabi and Rajput regiments who had thrown in their lot with Japan. Between two and three hundred Indian soldiers were said to have been installed in the Murray Barracks in the heart of Victoria. They received infantry training, and could be seen coming out periodically to practise bayonet charges on the former Hong Kong Cricket Ground. (We are told that their Japanese sergeant-majors 'led them shouting wildly across the pitch'.)[172] At one point in July the presence of the POWs was sufficiently striking to give some observers the impression that the colony was actually being 'garrisoned by Indian troops'.[173]

It was the same with the counter-subversion establishment. As the weeks passed the Kempeitai found it steadily harder to carry out their assignment of tracking down mainland Chinese celebrities. More and more wanted persons were slipping out of the colony or melting into the general populace. A new body was consequently formed out of the Hong Kong Chinese detectives who had been employed by the British Special Branch; and by the middle of February the abler of these sleuths were said to be getting 'activated in all quarters'.[174] In addition a motley assortment of local citizens reckoned to number anything from 1,300 to 4,000 were attached as agents to the Kempeitai and the garrison or worked for them as freelance informers. They included the scattering of low-life characters who had helped the Japanese before and during the invasion – George Wong, Call Me Howard, Millie Chun and her ring of girl spies. George Wong in particular came to loom increasingly large among the murkier underpinnings of Japanese rule. Starting out as a driver for the Political Section of the Koa Kikan, he was hired as one of the garrison's picked Chinese secret agents before winding up as the Kempeitai's chief local tough.[175]

In the interests of putting an end to the general turmoil the Kempeitai had also taken over from the Civil Affairs Department the management of the colony's routine policing work. For the successful performance of their policing functions, however, Colonel Noma's small outfit of 150 officers and NCOs were compelled to rely heavily on the services of a far larger number of local civilian police. Some of these policemen were re-enlisted members of the old pre-war force, but a great many others were new recruits whom the Kempeitai turned out regularly at their 'very active' police training school. Noma later recalled having had something like 2,300 to 2,400 local policemen at his disposal, both Chinese and Indian. The importance attached to these Kensa, as the Japanese called them, is suggested by a report that they were the only local employees of the new regime who got paid in cash.[176]

The objective in all of this delegation was not, of course, for Japan to surrender control of the colony. On the contrary, the Japanese were doing all in their power to exert control as intensively as conditions allowed. In creating new Chinese-run bodies, for instance, they took care to provide against any danger that those bodies might evolve into genuine centres of power. Some recourse was apparently had to the classic British tactic of 'divide and rule': thus the District Bureaux are said to have been established in part to offset the potential influence of the Rehabilitation Advisory Committee that preceded the two Chinese Councils. Supervisory structures were at the same time put in place to keep within drastic limits such freedom of action as the new Chinese bodies in theory enjoyed. In April 1942, for example, Isogai and his colleagues introduced a still further layer of local government in the form of three Area Bureaux which were set up respectively in Hong Kong Island, Kowloon and the New Territories.[177] These Area Bureaux were headed by Japanese officials;[178] and there seems little doubt that they were meant to act as a check on the Chinese-run District Bureaux. They were given authority over the District Bureaux in all major fields of activity (including education, health and the rice supply), and their Japanese chiefs went on tours of the District Bureaux to make sure that the latter were functioning as intended. It was the Area rather than the District Bureau chiefs who picked out local householders to sit on the District Assemblies. It was the Area Bureaux which appointed 'responsible citizens' to serve as street leaders, and which had the job of organizing the street committees.

In any case we should note that the new Chinese bodies were themselves set up primarily as control mechanisms. The two Chinese Councils were used first and foremost as a kind of megaphone through which the orders emanating from the Governor's Office could be dinned into the general public. The District Bureaux were essentially an attempt to reproduce in Hong Kong the minute supervision of daily life which had been exercised in the towns and countryside of Japan since the mid-1920s. Their main tasks were to keep track through the household registration process of the identities, numbers and whereabouts of all citizens, and 'to make all the people cooperate fully with the authorities'.[179] The street and village committees were designed to extend Japan's grip to the grass roots by enforcing the old and draconian East Asian principles of mutual policing and collective responsibility.[180] The major function of the street chiefs and the village representatives was to spy on their neighbours and to report any suspicious activity to the District Bureaux and the Kempeitai.

The same quest to maintain and expand control may be detected in the new regime's approach to recruiting local employees. In particular the deployment of Indians in the garrison and the police force reveals the 'divide and rule' tactic in all its beauty. Like the British before them the Japanese clearly felt that the Indians were more to be trusted than the Chinese majority – a faith which they demonstrated, again like the British, by issuing guns to the Indian members of the police force but not the Chinese. It seems likely that the Japanese also banked on exploiting the latent antagonism between the Indian and Chinese communities; and certainly if they did they were not disappointed. The Sikh constables returned to their former jobs in the police force eager to get their own back for the years of ostracism they had undergone at the hands of their Chinese neighbours. They flogged Chinese malefactors and took a lascivious pleasure in body-searching the Chinese women who passed through the check-points the conquerors had set up at the Star Ferry piers. The Chinese for their part struck back by lodging furious protests through the medium of the Cooperative Council at the way the Sikh constables were 'pawing' their wives.[181]

Yet in spite of all this the widespread Japanese delegation of functions in practice permitted many local Asians to play an increased public role by comparison with pre-war days. True to their strong tradition of social duty the gentry took up with some vigour the invitation the conquerors had issued to them to extend their charitable work. Their major opening came in the summer of 1942, when the Japanese were requesting contributions from leading citizens to an 'East Asia Construction Fund' – in part as a kind of loyalty test. Kotewall proposed, seemingly on his own initiative, that the HK\$160,000 or so which had been raised for this fund should be used to alleviate hunger in the colony. Isogai graciously acceded to this suggestion. The Construction Fund monies were converted into a government grant, and the two Chinese Councils were instructed to manage the grant and more generally 'to take full charge of plans to give relief to the poorer people of Hong Kong'. The two Councils responded by forming a body known as the General Association of Chinese Charities (GACC) – the first central welfare agency in the colony's history. The GACC's brief was to distribute the grant among the various individual charities, and to coordinate future efforts to raise money for charitable purposes from the colony's rich. Kotewall was elected to serve as the chairman, and the Bank of East Asia was appointed to look after the kitty.[182] In early 1943 the GACC embarked on the first in a series of major fundraising drives. The local business chiefs were reported to be turning their pockets out on a considerable scale: among the more prominent donors were Li Tse-fong, the manager of the Bank of East Asia and Ho Kom-tong, the master of ceremonies. Richer than any of his local counterparts Aw Boon-haw, the Tiger Balm King from Singapore, made the most handsome contribution of all, fortifying both the GACC and the individual charities that had been brought under its umbrella with cash injections of up to HK$125,000. As well as trying to meet the basic need for food the GACC launched an appeal for cotton padded jackets to see the poor through the winter; while the member charities stepped up their attempts to provide free medical treatment to the poorest residents and to take orphaned children off the streets.

The gentry also picked up the buck which the Japanese passed them in other major areas of public hardship. In response to Isogai's admonitions the Cooperative Council prepared their own scheme for unemployment relief which was forwarded through the Representative Council to the Governor's Office. And a sustained endeavour was made to respond to the glaring deficiencies in education – always a sector of paramount importance for the Chinese. In January 1943 a meeting of the Cooperative Council decided that the wealthy families in the colony should be asked to contribute funds to enable children from poorer backgrounds to obtain a schooling. An Education Sub-Committee of the two Chinese Councils was formed to supervise the process, and a portion of the GACC's grant was assigned to support the endowment of free places in primary and secondary schools. By September about 1,000 pupils in selected schools had benefited from the scholarship programme.[183] During the pre-war years there had been a handful of free schools operated by charities, but no kind of scholarship system had existed to give poorer children a foothold in the regular teaching establishments. In this sense the gentry's educational thrust represented a real innovation in spite of the modest numbers involved; and it was indeed described by one post-war British historian as 'a significant social welfare project'.[184]

For the humbler officials, too, the effect of the Japanese tendency to delegate was to confer a measure of new opportunity and prestige. Whatever their motives the conquerors undoubtedly brought more Chinese into the central administration of the colony than the British had ever done; and those Chinese were undoubtedly given many posts that would in pre-war days have gone to Europeans. Still more of an opening was provided at the local level. In creating the District Bureaux the Japanese had endowed the colony with a whole new infrastructure of local government. Pre-war Hong Kong had had districts, but these had been primarily geographical expressions, and the British had never tried to maintain any regular district offices, let alone offices run by Chinese.[185] Whatever their motives the conquerors had also been responsible for a certain advance in the area of popular representation. No district assemblies had existed under the British in either Hong Kong Island or Kowloon; and in the villages, as we have seen, the British had been content to deal with one or two headmen rather than encouraging the formation of any kind of a local committee. Even the talk of elections at ward level, propagandist in purpose though it undoubtedly was, marked a contrast with pre-war Hong Kong, where the only elected officials had been the two lonely members of the Urban Council. There is some evidence to suggest that the Hong Kong public were by and large fairly comfortable with the schoolmasters, village storekeepers and other obscure worthies who were picked out to serve as their local chiefs. It was, we are told, widely recognized that the staff of the District Bureaux were in a difficult position, and they were not generally viewed as collaborators.[186] The Bureau staff for their part continued to maintain in post-war testimonials that their Bureaux were 'organizations for the people', and that 'therefore we had the closest connection with the population'.[187]

The British dethroned

The logic of Japanese propaganda dictated that the vanquished British should be dethroned for the whole population to see. From the moment Sakai accepted the British surrender a systematic attempt was made to inflict the maximum possible humiliation on the 10,000-odd British and Canadian soldiers who had fallen into Japanese hands. Some of the Allied captives were forced to bow to Hong Kong Chinese citizens, while others were directed to clear up the refuse which had accumulated in the colony's streets. On 30 December 1941 the Allied POWs were marched into internment in Kowloon along roads lined with hundreds of Chinese spectators. The procession was headed by General Maltby, who had been compelled to pick up his own haversack and suitcase and tramp through the city along with the rest of his men. The captive soldiers eventually reached a barracks in the Shamshuipo district which the pre-war government had put up to confine stray contingents of Chinese Nationalists; and there, in the words of one officer, they were 'let loose just like a flock of sheep being driven into new fields'.[188] Some days later the officers were detached from the rank and file and moved out to a separate camp in Argyle Street, where they were subjected to regular indignities at the hands of the Japanese guards. On one occasion Maltby is said to have been beaten for turning out at a roll-call with dirty fingernails.

As with the troops, so with the civilians. In the first hours of the conquest a range of techniques were adopted to advertise the downfall of the British expatriates. Groups of them were driven around town in lorries 'for the delectation of the Chinese', or were made to pull rickshaws with Chinese and Indians in the passenger seats.[189] After that for them too the next step was imprisonment. Their leader, Governor Young, was shut up straight away in an upper room of the Peninsula Hotel, where he remained in isolation throughout the following weeks. Subsequently he was flown off to a series of captivities outside the colony, fetching up in September 1942 at a camp in Taiwan where he was put to work herding goats. The rest of the expatriates enjoyed a few strange days of limbo while the 23rd Army dealt with more urgent matters. Finally, however, on 5 January 1942 they received an abrupt summons to report to the conquerors on the parade ground of the Murray Barracks in Victoria. Civil servants and businessmen plodded in through the drizzle lugging their hastily assembled belongings, and even in some cases resorting to Chinese carrying-poles. In 'a sight seldom seen in the Colony', as the *Hong Kong News* gleefully described it, memsahibs arrived wearing slacks instead of their usual dresses and humping their babies along on their backs in the Chinese fashion.[190]

Some of the leading British had appealed to the conquerors through the person of the Chief Justice, Sir Atholl MacGregor, for the right to be interned in the familiar surroundings of the Peak. But that wasn't the idea at all. The European lords of creation were to be brought down both physically and symbolically to the level of ordinary mortals.[191] The roughly 2,500 British and other Allied nationals who had gathered at the parade ground were ushered down to the waterfront and packed into a row of seedy Chinese boarding houses – the Luk Kwok, the Sun Wah, the Lok Toi Hong – that had previously doubled as brothels; and there, chewing raw rice, they began to experience the transition from expatriate comfort to the life of an Oriental gaol. Once again every opportunity was taken to drive home the message that the ethnic tables had been turned. One expatriate lady recorded that the conquerors 'allowed the Chinese to charge any price they wished for the things they sold to us'.[192] On 22 January, after just under three weeks in these 'black holes of Hong Kong',[193] the bulk of the inmates were shipped round to the south coast of the Island and installed in a permanent compound which the Japanese had created on the Stanley peninsula from the outbuildings of the old colonial prison and the dormitories of St Stephen's Preparatory School.

The humbling of the expatriates was brought to an artistic climax in the arrangements imposed at the new Stanley camp. Accommodation consisted of a series of unfurnished rooms, each of which was expected to house eight or nine people. The worst quarters went to the 'Peakites', the former glitterati who now found themselves relegated to premises occupied until recently by the Indian warders of Stanley gaol. Internees were obliged to perform all their own manual labour. Elderly expatriates, eminent in their professions, began to be seen hauling bricks or pounding away with a Chinese rice grinder. Food took the form of a skimpy allowance of rice and other local victuals: one Japanese official later claimed to have been instructed by no less a personage than Premier Tojo that the European internees in Hong Kong should be denied access to high-quality foodstuffs and should be issued only with such rations as might be sufficient to keep them alive.[194] And the whole spectacle was

enacted in front of an audience drawn from the colony's former subject communities. Most of the guards in Stanley were Sikhs who had served in the old
Hong Kong Police Force, and for the first two months of internment the actual
command of the camp was assigned to a one-time Chinese member of the
Police Reserve named Cheng Kwok-leung. In March Superintendent Cheng
was replaced by a couple of Japanese civilian administrators; but this move too
seemed designed to rub a certain amount of salt in the British wounds. For
one of the Japanese who now came forward to oversee the direction of Stanley
was a figure well known to expatriates from the pre-war years. He was Mr
Yamashita, the barber who had asked them questions about the movements of
warships as he cut their hair in the Hong Kong Hotel.

From one angle the British in Hong Kong appear to have got off more lightly
than their compatriots in some of the other camps the Imperial Army were
establishing up and down South-east Asia. The keynote of their treatment
was humiliation rather than brutality for the sake of it.[195] And the brutality
that did occur was interspersed with the flashes of sympathy some Japanese
went on manifesting for their British opponents. Even in the POW camps,
where conditions were grimmest and beatings were often inflicted for minor
infringements of the rules, the behaviour of the administration was mixed.
The commandant-in-chief, Colonel Tokunaga Isao, was said to have been
'gross, cruel and sadistic', while one of the sub-commandants in charge of the
Shamshuipo camp was remembered as being 'a good man from every point of
view'.[196] Life was made wretched by a powerful and vicious interpreter, Inouye
Kanao, known to the prisoners as Slap Happy, who took his revenge for an
unhappy childhood as an immigrant in British Columbia by lashing out with
his fists or his belt buckle at every available European. But Slap Happy was
offset by a second interpreter named Watanabe Kiyoshi, a gentle little Lutheran
minister who was made physically sick by his colleague's excesses. 'Miserably
incapable' of beating prisoners even when ordered to do so, Watanabe told one
designated victim 'I think it will be better if we are friends', and advised him
to pretend that he had been beaten by groaning suitably for the benefit of
Colonel Tokunaga.[197] In Stanley the clear preference of the Japanese overseers
was to leave the expatriate internees to their own devices. For the first
eighteen months no personal injuries are said to have been inflicted by Japanese within the camp boundaries, and such interventions as were made by the
overseers were largely benign. One inmate reported that Yamashita the barber
and his associate, a former shipping clerk called Nakazawa, 'have appeared to
take a genuine interest in the welfare of internees and have been most helpful
in small ways'.[198]

Even so the impact of the overall Japanese policy of studied humiliation was
traumatic enough. In the space of a few weeks both the POWs and the Stanley
internees were reduced to a famished condition in which food, or the lack of

it, came to constitute 'three quarters of our conversation and as large a proportion of our dreams'.[199] The meagre camp rations were made even harder
to bear by the fact that most Europeans in Hong Kong at this period were
unaccustomed to Asian food. Professor Gordon King of the University medical
faculty reported 'that many of the denizens of the camps were 'unable to eat a
continuous diet of rice in sufficient quantity to maintain their body weight'.[200]
One of the captives expressed his opinion of the rice diet by inviting his room-
mates to consult the New Testament at Hebrews 13:8 ('Jesus Christ, the same
yesterday, today and forever'); others struggled with meals enlivened by
'a lettuce leaf floating in a putrid yellow liquid' or by 'tiny lumps of stringy
buffalo or horse meat with the occasional boiled Chinese cabbage leaf'.[201]
Inmates suffered equally from the contemptuous withholding of medical supplies. The POW camps were racked by epidemics of wound sepsis, dysentery
and diphtheria, and POWs and civilians alike started to contract deficiency
diseases such as pellagra and beri-beri. For the civilians in Stanley these hardships were given an added sting by the contrast with the privileged social status
they had enjoyed in the pre-war years. One appalled diarist noted that the 300
cubic feet allotted to each internee was the amount of air space usually made
available to 'Chinese coolies in Chinese boarding houses'.[202] Not all of the
captive expatriates found it easy to adjust to the absence of servants. Some of
them were reluctant at first to dig sewers, in spite of the dreadful risk of infection, because they felt that so lowly a task ought by rights to be performed by
the local Chinese. Faced with this ghastly reversal of fortune many new arrivals
in Stanley are said to have taken refuge in a kind of demoralized nostalgia.
They played bridge, reminisced about the furniture in their houses and assured
themselves that their life in the camp was only a passing nightmare and that
their pre-war status and comforts would soon be restored. Rumour insisted
that Churchill had promised to deliver the colony 'in the spring', 'within three
months', 'by March 17'.[203] But in the meantime the combined shock of the
defeat and internment were undermining the entire pre-war edifice of British
supremacy in Hong Kong.

In the first place the calamity had subverted the rigid framework of relations among the British themselves. Within a few hours of the surrender the
beaten garrison troops were suffused with a wave of contempt for their own
commanders which in some cases brought them to the verge of mutiny. A
private in the Middlesex Regiment recalled that by Boxing Day

> discipline had vanished. We encountered our superiors only when it was
> unavoidable; they had lost the respect and authority conferred by rank and
> uniform. We scrounged, looted and stole. . . .[204]

The disgust soon encompassed not merely the military command but the whole
of the pre-war Hong Kong establishment. As the POWs settled into their new

existence in Shamshuipo some of them chanted their scorn for the Bachelor Husbands and other feckless expatriates they had been asked to defend:

> On the fruits of sweating coolies' toil
> They lived their complacent lives,
>   And on the eve of battle
>   We still heard them prattle
> 'Why don't they send us back our wives?'[205]

The civilian backlash was even more drastic. The former officials of the colonial government were thrown into Stanley side by side with the business panjandrums; and both of these rival elites found themselves obliged to share the congestion, the dismal food and the drudgery with the despised lower orders of policemen and salesmen and clerks. Social standing now counted for less than physical stamina and the resourcefulness necessary to procure additional food supplies. Some of the pillars of the pre-war community started to break down under the strain and shame of internment, while humbler men and women displayed unexpected strengths.[206] Under these conditions a surge of disdain for the old pecking order began to make its way from the bottom of society up. The lower orders jeered at the business chiefs from the Peak who had lost all their money and been compelled to move into the squalor of the Warders' Quarters:

> Rock-a-bye, Taipan, on the Peak's top.
> While your bluff holds, the fortress won't drop;
> But when your bluff's called, the fortress will fall
> And down will come Taipan, vested interests and all![207]

And both business chiefs and lower orders rounded in unison on the old colonial government, which they considered to be primarily responsible for the recent debacle. All the old pre-war scandals were aired; all the old grievances were raked up with a vengeance. Why had the colony not been declared an open city? Why had the government been so unprepared and so short-sighted in their response to the threatened invasion? And why, when the invasion came, had so many senior officials deserted their posts or 'stayed permanently in their funk-holes'?[208] On 24 January, two days after the main contingent of internees had moved into Stanley, Kenneth Uttley, a government doctor, remarked in his diary

> There is a very strong anti-Government feeling in the camp. I had some foul remarks thrown at me when I went round. . . . The people feel that they have been let down by the extremely bad leadership we have had since the war began. They harbour a resentment against the Government for this . . .[209]

The effects were immediate. On the same day that Uttley made his glum observations the British in Stanley broke dramatically with the authoritarian habits of colonial rule by electing a temporary committee to run their affairs. One representative was elected to the committee from each of the blocks of buildings in which the inmates were housed. And with the exception of the Commissioner of Police (who was put forward, amid some grumbling, by the block set aside for the Police Force), not a single official of the old colonial government was voted to power. Instead the expatriates chose for their new Committee of Management the senior executives of Jardine Matheson and Butterfield and Swire, of Shell and ICI and the British–American Tobacco Company. On 8 February the camp went on to elect a more permanent British Communal Council chaired by a certain L. R. Nielsen, an entrepreneur from New Zealand with mining interests in the United States. Camp politics were 'all the rage'; and the business leaders for their part were said to have commented that 'they had at last got Government where they wanted it to be'.[210]

This mini-revolution among the British in Stanley was naturally a source of annoyance to the leading government figures, who are said to have 'strongly resented their lack of position in the camp'.[211] In particular it presented a challenge to Franklin Gimson, the newly arrived Colonial Secretary who following Young's disappearance into the Peninsula Hotel had become the most senior British official in Hong Kong. Arriving in Stanley on 11 March, some weeks after the bulk of the camp population, Gimson promptly declared himself the representative of King George VI and the home government in London and called on the internees to accept his command. This lunge for authority, however, as Gimson himself acknowledged, was 'not welcomed universally'. On 28 March he was obliged to accept a sort of constitutional settlement in the form of a memorandum limiting his powers and assigning to him a somewhat ill-defined position as partner of Chairman Nielsen. Gimson didn't approve of Nielsen, whom he regarded as having 'a reputation of doubtful integrity'. Nor did he believe that the government of a colony (even one circumscribed by barbed wire) should be placed in the hands of a randomly elected committee. But he could see well enough that in the mood then prevailing any administration composed solely of unelected officials would have 'added to the opposition at times freely expressed to the detriment of efficiency'.[212] And for the moment his authority hung by a thread.

A second, more far-reaching result of the cataclysm was to topple the British from their position of dominance over the colony's other ethnic groups. In a small way this process could be observed even in the relations between the British and their American cousins. The 2,325 British civilian internees had been relegated to Stanley along with a smaller contingent of some 350 Americans.[213] From the outset it was evident that the Americans were getting a better deal. This may well have been part of an overall Japanese policy to show favour to American non-combatants: the military leaders in Tokyo were still hoping in early 1942 that they could coax the United States to pull out of the war and leave Japan in possession of the territories it had wrested from Britain and the other European powers in South-east Asia. At the same time it is also clear that the Americans (who arrived in the camp first) were vastly better prepared than the British majority to make the most of the new situation. Cohesive where the British were divided, self-confident where the British were demoralized, they plunged into vigorous talks with their captors and rapidly secured for themselves all the best accommodation, most of the available furniture and a supply of prized commodities such as vegetables and tomato ketchup. Their success soon provoked an upsurge of the anti-American feeling which had never been far from the surface among the British of pre-war Hong Kong. A verse went the rounds:

> Yankee Doodle came to Camp
> Sitting on a lorry,
> Grabbed the best of everything
> And never said 'I'm sorry'.[214]

In the meantime the Americans had been electing their own representatives as if to the manner born; and it would seem that in spite of the communal friction they played a significant part in promoting the democratic ferment which had broken out in the British blocks. Uttley the government doctor complained in his diary of the 'universal influence' exerted by the chief American spokesman, a rich and resourceful executive by the name of Bill Hunt. One British memoir describes Hunt as having been the *de facto* leader of the internees during the opening weeks of the occupation, with Nielsen as his 'assistant'.[215]

Still more conspicuous was the shift in the social balance between the British captives and the non-Europeans. The POWs being marched to internment were shown that they could no longer count on the automatic respect of the Asian population. Some of the Chinese spectators are said to have jeered 'You British are no use!'[216] and a number of villagers on the south side of Hong Kong Island even threw stones. The British civilians sent into Stanley found themselves suddenly exposed to the caprices of those Hong Kong Chinese and Indians whom the conquerors had set in authority over them, and who seem to begin with to have treated them with a good deal more ruthlessness than the conquerors themselves. Cheng Kwok-leung, the Camp Superintendent, was remembered by one British policeman as 'a pukka bastard in every respect'. His chief contribution was to establish a camp shop in which he sold the internees extra supplies at a level of 'squeeze' so extortionate that he put himself out of business.[217] The Sikh guards who patrolled the camp were more directly unpleasant, and a number of them are said to have chastised internees by the standard Japanese method of slapping their faces. At the same time the captive British were impelled by the critical shortage of food, medicines and other necessities to cast themselves in the unfamiliar role of suppliants seeking the charity of their former Asian subjects in town. 'In desperation' Walter Scott, the Assistant Commissioner of Police, sent Dr Li Shu-fan a cheque for HK$500 which he hoped might be cashed at the Hongkong and Shanghai Bank. J. D. Fraser, the former Defence Secretary, appealed to Li for tobacco and medicines; and the doctor began to receive begging letters from expatriates he had scarcely met.

Not all of the British were put in the camps. In one more indication of the strange respect many of them still felt for their defeated imperial rivals, the Japanese chose to keep back in town (for a while, anyway) certain people whose knowledge and skills they expected to need. Gimson, for example, was retained with a number of his staff for the first few weeks to help out with such tasks as compiling name lists of the POWs and internees and more generally to provide a measure of continuity till the new regime's Civil Affairs Department got into its stride. A handful of British engineers were kept on at the telephone exchange, the gas works and the electricity plants, to repair the war damage and get those various installations in service again. In the last week of January, when the bulk of the British civilians were shipped off to Stanley, a group of some sixty bankers – senior personnel of the Hongkong and Shanghai Bank, the Chartered Bank and similar institutions – were left behind at the Sun Wah Hotel. Every day for the next several months they were let out in the morning and marched through the streets to their offices, where the conquerors had some residual work for them. A decision had been taken that all pre-war debtors should go to the banking halls to clear their overdrafts, and the bankers were needed to administer the repayments.[218]

One or two of the more resourceful of these hived-off British detected in the new regime's patent inadequacies a chance of retaining some influence over events. Gimson is said to have tried to persuade the Japanese Army bosses to keep on the entire pre-war corps of British administrators.[219] A more successful initiative was taken by Selwyn-Clarke, the high-minded maverick who had been attached to the old government as Director of Medical Services. Selwyn-Clarke saw no reason to abandon his mission to the Hong Kong public merely because a new set of rulers had taken power. As early as Boxing Day he had called on the senior officers of the 23rd Army at the headquarters they were organizing in the Hongkong and Shanghai Bank and had badgered them to restore the water supply and provide some basic sanitary facilities. Within a short while he had won a respectful hearing, in part through the sheer altruistic force of his personality and in part because of his obvious lack of interest in any distinction of nation or race. He secured most importantly the endorsement of the 23rd Army's chief medical officer, Colonel Eguchi. In the late 1930s Eguchi had visited Hong Kong, ostensibly on a medical errand: his visit may well have had more to do with intelligence gathering than medicine, but Selwyn-Clarke alone of the colony's officials had received him with courtesy, and Eguchi had not forgotten. With the help of Eguchi Selwyn-Clarke went on to achieve his first breakthrough, convincing the Gunseicho to intern the bulk of the British civilians in the relatively healthful surroundings of the Stanley peninsula. Selwyn-Clarke did not, however, have the slightest intention of going into internment himself. His task, as he saw it, was to serve the medical needs of the whole population – not only the British but also the general mass of Chinese and Indians, Eurasians and Portuguese. 'The nature of my duties', he wrote afterwards, 'made my choice as straightforward and as binding as the Hippocratic Oath.'[220] Eguchi accordingly obtained the official blessing of the captive Governor Young for the Director of Medical Services to continue performing his functions ('a thoughtful step', the Director observed, 'for an enemy officer to take'); and some weeks later a second well-disposed colonel persuaded the new Governor Isogai to retain in addition the services of a team of British doctors who had been employed on Selwyn-Clarke's staff.[221] The Japanese seem to have adopted towards Selwyn-Clarke's Health Department something of the same prickly attitude displayed to Western aid donors by Third World governments in recent decades. They kept a few of their own men in the Health Department office for appearances' sake, and satisfied their own pride by referring to the British as 'advisers'.[222] Only one fleeting mention of the Health Department was ever made in that organ of pan-Asiatic evangelism, the *Hong Kong News*.[223] Yet as the months passed there were signs that the Japanese were in practice paying quite a bit of attention to what Selwyn-Clarke and his team had to say.

The conquerors had divided the non-Chinese population of the colony into two categories. On the one side were the British, Americans and other enemy aliens who were in principle destined for internment. On the other side were the 'third nationals', a broad group which included not merely the Eurasians, Portuguese and Indians but also an assortment of Europeans from the neutral and Axis states. This distinction, however, wasn't watertight, and a number of quick-witted British managed to avoid internment on their own initiative, either by making a plausible claim to 'third national' citizenship or by getting themselves 'guaranteed out' of Stanley by neutral friends.[224] One such tearaway was Phyllis Harrop, the former policewoman, whom we have already glimpsed wandering around Victoria in the latter half of January 1942. She had got herself classified as a German on the strength of her connection with a German baron to whom she had been fleetingly married eight years before. The motives of the camp-dodgers varied considerably. Phyllis Harrop was chiefly anxious to preserve her freedom of movement in order to escape from the colony and continue her service to the Allied cause. Other stray British appear to have been more concerned with promoting their own private interests. A government official named Kennedy-Skipton who returned to his desk proclaiming himself to be Irish was believed to have been intent on looking after his family and his two Asian concubines. And there was one open shift of allegiance. A

certain Arthur Grover who worked as a butcher on the Dairy Farm is said to
have gone flat out to embrace the conquest and the chance for enrichment it
brought. Transformed magically into a White Russian, he roamed around town
with bands of Kempeitai looters, raiding houses and introducing himself with
a 'nasty, smirking face' as 'the chief of the local Gestapo'.[225]

A more curious case altogether was that of C. M. Faure, the retired naval
commander turned champion of the underdog whom we last met in the late
1930s defending the legal rights of left-wing Chinese trade unionists against
the colonial authorities. Now he suddenly re-emerged at the head of the
Eurasian and Indian propaganda team on the *Hong Kong News*. Much of his
energy seemed to be channelled into a special column he contributed every
Sunday under the heading, 'Is Anything New?'. Faure was a man of vast if
eccentric erudition, and the aim of his column was to demonstrate the vaguely
pan-Asiatic hypothesis that various branches of ancient Greek scientific and
mathematical learning had been derived from Egypt, India and points further
east. Week after week bemused readers were treated to Faure on Pythagoras,
Faure on Neo-Platonism, Faure on the history of calculations of *pi*. Seldom,
one might imagine, could an enthusiast have had in a more literal sense a
captive audience. But there was more to Faure than met the eye.[226]

In some ways the position of these uninterned British residents was fairly
tolerable. Every European still at large in Kowloon and Victoria was allotted a
monthly flour ration of 7lb – the same quantity as had been set aside for the
privileged Indians.[227] And the Japanese civilian officials who had been assigned
to watch over the stray Europeans mostly treated them with every consideration. Kimura Shiroshichi, the former consul, who stayed on in the colony
during the early weeks of the takeover, was remembered by one expatriate
widow as having been 'extraordinarily kind'. He even undertook to ensure the
safe delivery of a letter she had written requesting money from the British consulate in Macao. 'We should never have fought you', he lamented, 'we admire
you, we did not want to fight you.'[228] Much the same attitude was adopted by
Oda Takeo, a handsome and engaging young diplomat who was brought in
after the consulate closed to take charge of the Europeans in the colony as head
of a newly created Foreign Affairs Department. A member of the consulate's
staff during the pre-war years, he had been greatly shocked by the changed
circumstances of his British contacts, and was said to have been moved to tears,
on a visit to Stanley, by the sight of a taipan named Bagram who had been
reduced to wearing an apron and peeling onions. He supplied one or two of the
expatriates still in town with loans out of his own pocket, and commiserated
with them about the unpleasant behaviour of the 'so-tiresome Kempeitai'.[229]

Some of the uninterned British were able to participate along with their
fellow-Europeans in a kind of ghostly continuation of pre-war social life,
as the 'third nationals' tried to keep themselves going by opening cafés,

restaurants and night-clubs. By late January 1942 daily tea dances had resumed at the Lido Dance Hall ('Mr Tuazon and his Swing Boys Will Entertain You'), and the Balalaika Restaurant was offering floor shows in the Kowloon Hotel. Frau Angelika Steinschneider of the Vienna State Opera advertised singing lessons, and a 'distinctly Viennese atmosphere' was reported from Nathan Road.[230] The conquerors tolerated these lingering manifestations of Western glitziness, and even joined in. A White Russian named George Goncharoff was employed teaching ballroom dancing to many prominent Japanese. Emily Hahn, the madcap American journalist, who had managed to get herself declared Chinese on the strength of her 'marriage' to a Chinese poet with whom she had had an affair in Shanghai, drank whisky with Oda at The Gripps and felt free to drop in casually on his successor, Hattori, at the former Japanese consular flat. Small wonder, perhaps, that some of these floating expatriates reckoned Japan's rule in Hong Kong to be 'very mild'.[231]

But these minor indulgences couldn't disguise the clear evidence that the British colonial world had collapsed. 'The look of the streets', wrote one lady, 'is indescribable, they are filled with people, all natives of one sort or other, all brown and yellow faces. You rarely see a European . . .'[232] All the neat ethnic barriers of the pre-war decades had dissolved in the new mixture of chaos and deliberate Asianization. With the bulk of their maids and 'boys' put to flight by the conquest the surviving memsahibs were forced to squeeze in among the crowds in Queen's Road Central and buy their own groceries from the proliferating hawker stalls. People of all ethnic origins squatted wherever they could find a roof. Emily Hahn returned one night to her flat in the Mid-Levels to discover that it had been taken over by a family of refugee Eurasians – the Gittinses from Kowloon.

Flour rations notwithstanding, the British and their fellow-Europeans around town were engaged every bit as much as the internees in a constant battle to keep themselves fed. Sir Vandeleur Grayburn of the Hongkong and Shanghai Bank was reported to be looking 'as gaunt and grey as a timber wolf'.[233] And in town as in Stanley the quest for food left the struggling Europeans no choice but to call on the help of the lesser breeds. The bankers found themselves in the novel position of seeking loans from their Chinese and Indian customers. Other expatriates were compelled to offer their jewellery for sale through the Eurasian and Portuguese brokers. Those memsahibs who still had a servant or two found themselves relying as never before on the servants' ability to ferret out the next meal.

In the early stages of the occupation, however, it was far from obvious how much help the Asian communities would be willing to give. On the night of the British surrender Phyllis Harrop, huddled with a crowd of fellow-expatriates in the Gloucester Hotel, had witnessed the emergence of a new attitude among the Hong Kong Chinese:

The hotel boys are showing their uneasiness and during dinner several refused to work and serve meals. There was almost a fight at one table when one of the boys told a woman, if she wanted any food, she could get it herself. It was her own fault; she had been most unpleasant to the boys from time to time, and they don't forget it.[234]

By 3 January 1942 there were 'marked signs of anti-British feeling among the Chinese people': when the food supplies left behind by the old government ran out, Phyllis Harrop predicted, the Chinese would 'definitely turn against us'.[235] The removal of most of the expatriates two days later did nothing to lessen the mood of antagonism towards those who remained. In the smart shops on Queen's Road Central for the next few months 'anyone who appeared to be a foreigner could expect nothing but rudeness'.[236] European passengers on the trams had their tickets thrown at them.

The smaller Asian communities too took it out on the Westerners with varying degrees of vehemence. In the Gloucester Hotel three nights after the conquest drunken Sikh police, their uniforms cast aside, raced around in their turbans and red underpants swearing and spitting at any of the British who came within range. As news spread of the rounding-up of the British civilians, Irene Fincher and Phyllis Bliss, the two Eurasian sisters from the Gittins family, permitted themselves a comment of gentle smugness to their involuntary hostess, Emily Hahn. When the evacuation scheme had been introduced by the British in 1940, they noted, only *pure* Englishwomen had been given the chance to get out of the colony – 'and now only *pure* Englishwomen are being interned'.[237]

Even the handful of local people who had stuck with Western employers out of a residual loyalty behaved in a different way from before. 'Boss in the house' ever since the surrender, Emily Hahn's cook, Ah King, went about his tasks with a new assertiveness, breaking into her conversations with visitors and supplying her with unsolicited advice. Reprimanded on one occasion he 'grinned broadly': before the conquest, she observed, he 'had never grinned like that'.[238] Underlying all these changes of manner was the blinding revelation of British defeat. The secret of empire was out – that the white man wasn't invincible. Phyllis Harrop summed up gloomily, 'We have lost a dreadful amount of face and prestige over the fall of Hong Kong, and we shall never regain what we have lost.'[239]

Britain versus the Allies

Dislodged from their high estate by Japan for as long as the war might last, the British were also confronted by a major threat from their own side to their prospects of ever ruling in Hong Kong again. The shock of the British defeat which had overturned the old structure of ethnic relations inside Hong Kong had been felt just as strongly on the mainland, among Britain's new Chinese Nationalist allies. On a personal level the fall of the colony came as a heavy blow to the many leading Nationalists who had in the previous years entrusted their money, their wives and their mistresses to the imagined security of British Hong Kong. On a political level the news of the disaster gave rise to a spate of recriminations. Why, in the run-up to the invasion, had the British declined to accept (until it was too late) the repeated Nationalist offers of military help? Why, when the invasion began, had they failed to make use of their vast reserve of Hong Kong Chinese manpower? Why, in a word, had they not been prepared to *trust* the Chinese?[240] As the fall of Hong Kong was followed in February 1942 by the still more devastating loss of Singapore, the Nationalist attitude to the British began to be characterized by a growing contempt. On 19 April Mme Chiang Kai-shek gave voice to this new perception in a stinging article which appeared in the *New York Times*. 'During the last three months', she declared, 'the Chinese people have watched with amazement the spectacle of Western armies surrendering because, it was explained, of Japan's superior might.'[241] Contemplating the British debacle the Nationalists could scarcely avoid being overcome by an upsurge of pride in their own martial prowess. For the last four years, after all, Nationalist China had held out, alone, in the face of a full-blooded Japanese onslaught without having felt the need to surrender. The contrast in performance appeared to the Nationalists to dictate some adjustment in the world pecking order. If the defeated British were reckoned to be a world power, why not the undefeated Chinese?

Was there any reason, the Nationalists began to demand, why their armies should not in due course be able to expel the Japanese from Hong Kong by themselves, without British aid? And once they had done so was there any reason why they should allow the British to get Hong Kong back? The fall of the colony had provoked a new outburst of the antipathy which the Nationalists had always felt towards British colonial rule. In the summer of 1942 Tommy Lee, a political fixer with top-level connections in the Nationalist hierarchy,[242] presented the British embassy in Chungking with a memorandum appraising Britain's whole record of rule in Hong Kong. Westernized and on close terms with some of the embassy staff, Lee was politely remorseless in his dissection of the old colonial order – the high-handedness of the British administration, the ubiquitous barriers to Chinese advancement, the comforts enjoyed by the white elite against a background of Chinese squalor and misery. 'It must be admitted', he observed, 'that non-Europeans were treated most shabbily.' Even the Japanese conquest didn't appear to have put a complete end to expatriate arrogance. Lee had got word that some of the British internees in the colony had complained of the episodes in which the Japanese military had forced them to pull Chinese and Indians in rickshaws. 'It is', he suggested, 'legitimate to protest against being made to pull rickshaws, but very bad form to object to the nationality of the passengers.'[243] We may catch in Lee's comments a hint of the impact Japan had made even on its opponents in Nationalist China through its successful assault on the European colonial powers. Many Chinese on the mainland were said to have been impressed in spite of themselves by the lightning victories of their fellow Asians. And the new truculence evident in the Chungking regime's manner towards the British was attributed in part to the influence of Japan's doctrine of 'Asia for the Asiatics'.[244]

In this climate the Nationalist leaders were emboldened to go down a road along which neither they nor any preceding regime on the mainland had felt able to venture before. They embarked on a formal diplomatic campaign to induce Britain to relinquish its rights in Hong Kong. The British themselves had provided the opportunity. Anxious to remove the remaining irritants in relations with their new Chinese allies, they were planning to engage Chungking in negotiations for the abolition of the remaining leases and extra-territorial rights which the British Empire had enjoyed within China. In May 1942 the Chungking authorities duly greeted the news of these plans with a public proposal that the agenda should also include the termination of Britain's lease on Hong Kong's New Territories. The proposal said nothing about the rest of the colony, which had been ceded to Britain in perpetuity; but the Nationalists were as aware as the British that if the New Territories were returned to the mainland Hong Kong Island and Kowloon would almost inescapably have to be given up too. As it happened 29 August was the centenary of the Treaty of Nanking under which Hong Kong Island had been signed away to the British Crown; and Chiang Kai-shek's government seized upon the occasion to call publicly for the abrogation of *all* the old 'unequal treaties'.[245] In October the extra-territoriality negotiations began in Chungking. To begin with the talks were confined to the subject of the British leases in China proper; but on 13 November the Nationalists raised the stakes by submitting an outright demand that Britain should also discuss the New Territories with a view to handing them over as soon as the war with Japan had been brought to a victorious end.

The Nationalist campaign was reinforced by the vigorous backing of Britain's key wartime ally, the United States. The United States had entered the Pacific conflict in a strongly anti-colonial mood. Many senior officials in the Roosevelt administration were inclined to blame the British defeat in the Far East on Britain's colonial policies. The American public reckoned that they should be going to war with Japan for a nobler objective than merely to enable the Europeans to restore their shattered empires in South-east Asia, and demands had begun to be voiced for a Pacific Charter which would guarantee to the subject peoples of Asia the same future rights that the

Atlantic Charter had promised a few months earlier to the peoples of Nazi-occupied Europe. A representative of the Foreign Office in London reported from Washington in May 1942 that 'the British Empire has been entirely written off by American opinion'.[246] Natural enough in the light of history (after all, the United States had once been a British colony too), this anti-colonial outlook was accompanied by a great surge of sympathy for the embattled Chinese. In the course of a conference hosted at Mont Tremblant, Canada, by the United States Institute for Pacific Relations, one British participant noted that 'it was improper to mention China without slightly moist eyes and an all but breaking voice'.[247] The Americans were, consequently, emphatic that Britain should relinquish its claim to Hong Kong. Even before the Japanese onslaught the Roosevelt administration had contemplated using their lend-lease agreement with Britain as a lever for getting the British to hand their colony back to the Chinese motherland. Now, with America in the war and Hong Kong in the hands of the Japanese, the prospects for leverage seemed appreciably greater. President Roosevelt, who harboured a strong personal wish to redress the 'unequal treaties', ebulliently informed his son Elliott, 'We are going to be able to bring pressure on the British to fall in line with *our* way of thinking.'[248]

Faced with this diplomatic bombardment the British authorities in London came close to throwing in the sponge. There seemed little point in antagonizing two major allies for the sake of a second-rate outpost of empire. The Foreign Office, whose task it was to conduct the talks in Chungking, were largely in favour of retroceding the colony. In the summer of 1942 Ashley Clarke, the head of the Far Eastern Department, urged on his opposite numbers in the Colonial Office the desirability of giving up Hong Kong as a 'non-essential' and 'cutting off the arm to preserve the body'.[249] In a second submission dated 20 November, when the Chungking negotiations were well under way, Ashley Clarke even went beyond the official position of the Nationalists. Not only, he urged, should the British agree to discuss the New Territories: they should get down to the heart of the matter by raising the future of Hong Kong as a whole. The Colonial Office were in less of a hurry to write Hong Kong off; but they too had been thrown heavily on the defensive. On 18 August they put forward a policy paper drafted in large part by David MacDougall, the information chief who had escaped from Hong Kong when the colony fell. MacDougall and his assistants suggested conceding that after the war 'the British government would not regard the maintenance of British sovereignty over the Colony as beyond the scope of discussion'.[250] After all, they observed in a passage laced with the faintest tang of sour grapes, Hong Kong's value would decline year by year as the lease on the New Territories approached its expiry, and the importance of Hong Kong's economy would be undermined by the onerous restrictions and taxes which the post-war mainland government could be expected to impose. On 30 December, after attending the conference at Mont Tremblant, MacDougall expressed the glum view that

> As no other nation (not even the Dutch) betrays the slightest sign of supporting an attempt [by Britain] to retain Hong Kong for any purpose whatsoever, I think we ought to remember that we are likely to get better terms as regards an interest in the colony if, sooner rather than later, we tell the Chinese that the place is theirs.[251]

Even Churchill was less than dogged. At a time when, in his own famous phrase, Britain stood 'subservient to the friendly strength of the United States',[252] he appears to have felt that there was no scope for resisting the overwhelming thrust of American sentiment. In a conversation with Wellington Koo, the Chinese Nationalist ambassador to London, he is said to have agreed reluctantly that Hong Kong would have to be returned to China after the war. The retrocession should, however, take place in an orderly way, and the incoming rulers should be prepared to take on all the appropriate obligations of the old colonial government, from the pension system to the upkeep of public properties.[253]

For the moment the British decided to cover their retreat. On 22 November Anthony Eden, the Foreign Secretary, overruled Ashley Clarke's suggestion that Britain should offer to discuss with the Nationalists the return of the whole of Hong Kong. The Nationalists, he decreed, should be told in response to their recent demand for negotiations that Britain was willing to discuss the New Territories: any such discussions, however, should take place after the war, and the British would not be prepared to commit themselves to curtailing the lease on the New Territories in the course of the current talks in Chungking. The adoption of this stance unfortunately caused a crisis, for the 'face' of Chiang Kai-shek and his colleagues was now on the line. Both T. V. Soong, the Nationalist Foreign Minister, and Ambassador Koo, who had come back from London to join in the talks, intimated that their side had now gone too far to draw back. They warned that Chiang might well refuse to endorse the proposed goodwill treaty abolishing British privileges in China unless the New Territories formed part of the deal. The British had made up their minds to adhere to their stance even if it meant jeopardizing the treaty: the prospect of a breakdown of negotiations was, none the less, one that they could only contemplate with the utmost alarm. The Americans had been pressing ahead with a separate treaty renouncing their own special rights inside China, and were getting ready to sign it on New Year's Day. If the British were late in signing their treaty, or failed to sign it altogether, the contrast would do Britain's already tarnished image on the Chinese mainland no good at all. The British negotiators tried to placate their Nationalist counterparts by sketching out the content of the hypothetical post-war discussions about the New Territories. If the Chinese government wished, they declared, Britain would in that context be ready to reconsider the terms of the lease. On Christmas Day, however, Foreign Minister Soong expressed his suspicion of the formula 'terms of the lease', which he saw (understandably) as a British attempt to wriggle out of making any substantive promise; and two days later the Nationalist authorities confirmed that they would not sign the treaty unless Britain made a clear statement of its intention to restore the New Territories to Chinese rule. The British decided to drop the offending words 'terms of', but felt unable to make any further concession. On 28 December, with matters now at an impasse, Eden obtained the permission of Churchill and the War Cabinet to issue a last-ditch appeal for American support.

Which way the United States would have jumped will never be certain,[254] for on New Year's Eve the Nationalists unexpectedly shelved their campaign. They would sign the treaty as it was. Their last-minute climbdown appears to have been the result of a judicious intervention by Wellington Koo. The ambassador had advised Chiang Kai-shek, in effect, that half a loaf was better than no bread. If the Nationalists were to scuttle the treaty on account of the New Territories they would, he observed, miss the chance to win back all of the leased enclaves the British were willing to surrender in China proper. The collapse of the British treaty might well have a negative impact both on the United States (whose treaty, if signed, would still need to be ratified by Congress) and on a number of lesser Allied powers that were lining up to conclude agreements of their own. Wartime Allied unity would be impaired, and the Nationalists would forfeit in addition the British good offices which, in Koo's view, they would need to resolve certain difficulties with the Soviet Union. Chiang was also persuaded to give way by a private reflection which he jotted down in his diary that New Year's Eve. When the time came, he predicted, it would be the Nationalists rather than the British who would retake Hong Kong from the Japanese forces; and under those circumstances, even if they 'played tricks', the British would have little hope of preventing the colony's reabsorption by China.[255] For possession would be nine points of the law.

On 11 January 1943, then, after a short interval necessary for preparing the documents, the treaty was finally signed without any British commitment regarding Hong Kong. The American treaty, which had been held back to avoid any danger of odious comparisons, was signed the same day. At first glance it would seem that the British had emerged easy winners from the six-week confrontation. But in a note attached to the British treaty the Nationalist government reserved their right to bring up the issue of the New Territories again 'at a later date'; and in an answering note the British agreed that the Nationalists would be free to do so 'when victory was won'.[256] The fact was that the British had given a massive amount of ground. From asserting, as they had done in the pre-war years, that the New Territories were an internal concern of Hong Kong and no business of China's, they had come round to acknowledging that the lease and its future were a legitimate matter for the Chinese government to bring up with them. From expressing vague willingness, as they had done at the start of the stand-off, to discuss the New Territories at a future time of their choosing, they had come round to conceding to Nationalist China the right to take a fresh look at the leasing arrangements as soon as it pleased at the end of the war. And behind these shifts of attitude were further signs of Whitehall's wavering resolution to get back the colony. In his desperation to break the deadlock in the talks Sir Horace Seymour, the British ambassador in Chungking, is said privately to have insisted to Koo 'that Hong Kong would surely be returned, but only after a practical plan had been negotiated and agreed upon'.[257] Irrespective of how long the Japanese managed to hold Hong Kong, the defeat of the British had already made one thing certain. The colony's future had now been placed firmly on the international agenda; and there it would stay.

CHAPTER FOUR

The Japanese Miss Their Chance

Isogai, Arisue and the triumph of the jackboot

The reform measures which had been launched with such fanfare at the start of the occupation took no more than twelve to eighteen months to run into the sands. The outcome was only to be expected. The struggle in the Imperial Army over Hong Kong's future had been won, after all, not by the China faction, with its interest in winding up Japan's conflict on the Chinese mainland, but by the Southern faction, with its overriding eagerness to pursue the Pacific War. True, the new Governor Isogai represented a nod to the China faction, with his record of service in the campaigns on the mainland and his attempts to make overtures to Chungking. But Isogai was a Janus-like figure. Some of his attitudes seemed to reflect the concerns of the Gunseicho leaders he had been sent to replace, but at other times he spoke unmistakably for the Southern faction whose victory had produced his appointment. And Isogai was in any case offset by the Chief of Staff who had been sent out with him from Tokyo, Colonel Arisue Yadoru. We have already met Arisue in his role as director of the intelligence-gathering effort which the Japanese brought to bear on Hong Kong in the late 1930s. Previously deployed as a military attaché at the Japanese embassies in London and Washington, Arisue had thus spent the bulk of his recent career sizing up Japan's designated Anglo-Saxon opponents, and was naturally more disposed than the Governor to subscribe to the Southern faction's priority of knocking them out.[1] The Chief of Staff had direct charge of all the departments in the newly established Governor's Office, and was empowered to take decisions on all routine matters without reference to his boss. One department head later recalled that it was Arisue, not Isogai, whose 'words carried weight'.[2]

The coming of the new leaders was bound to entail, in due course, the effective abandonment of the Gunseicho's bid to win local support. From the point of view of the China faction Hong Kong had been a promising part of China, with a distinctive colonial background which they might hope to exploit for political ends. From the point of view of the Southern faction Hong Kong was politically an unpromising part of South-east Asia. The Chinese who constituted the overwhelming majority of its people were unlikely to share in the sympathy for Japan's Southern war aims which was being widely expressed among the colonized populations of Burma, Malaya and the Dutch East Indies, or to play any part in furthering them. Only the Indian community might perhaps have some small contribution to make to the drive to the South. As the new long-term government got its bearings the emphasis switched more and more to a Southern faction agenda characterized by indifference to local wishes and needs.

It was clear in the first place that the main idea would from now on be militarization. 'The principal aim now', Isogai stressed on assuming office, 'is to prosecute the war to a successful conclusion. There are many plans for Hong Kong, but that belongs to the future.'[3] Over the following months the familiar landmarks of the pre-war colony were transformed as Hong Kong became an armed camp. The Peak was fortified and bristled with look-out posts. Anti-aircraft guns were installed on the roofs of the Peninsula and Gloucester Hotels. Troops drilled every morning in the Botanical Gardens and the Fanling Golf Club, and St John's Cathedral was turned into a stable for cavalry horses. As the Japanese conquests spread further the colony also started to play the role which the Southern faction had envisaged for it as a logistical relay post. Troops passed through on their way to the fronts in South-east Asia and the Pacific, or came back on sick leave to sample the colony's version of 'rest and recreation'. In September 1942 work began under Arisue's direction on a construction project designed to expand Kai Tak airfield into one of the largest airports in the world. Twenty thousand Chinese villagers were cleared out of their homes in the neighbourhood to enable the work to take place. And as if to remind Hong Kong of its part in the broader world conflict the garrison's progress was monitored intermittently by Japan's allies through the approving descent of a German or Italian military mission.[4]

The institutional framework for running the colony was set up in accordance with this general picture. Yazaki of the Gunseicho had advised in his policy outline that an attempt should be made to reassure the local elite by maintaining the pre-war forms of administration. But the interim junta to which Yazaki had belonged was replaced not by a civilian government but by a regular military regime. The Governor's Office established by Isogai and Arisue was in the last resort nothing more than a military headquarters similar in its nature to any number of others organized by the Imperial Army in occupied Asia. While a number of nominally civilian departments – of Foreign Affairs, Civil Affairs, Transportation and so forth – were created within it the mild-mannered Japanese officials who ran them had no voice in the decision-making process, and none of them dared to express any kind of dissent at the twice-weekly meetings to which they were summoned to pick up their instructions from the top brass.[5] On the day Isogai assumed office, 20 February 1942, a military tribunal was set up to replace the old British judiciary. The new Governor threatened 'severe punishment' for anyone caught disobeying official decrees, and such threats were appended routinely to subsequent edicts.

Yazaki had urged adherence to the British rulers' traditional policy of allowing free movement into and out of Hong Kong. But the new long-term rulers were more concerned with security. Complex rules were imposed to control entry into the colony, and anyone wishing to leave had to apply for an exit permit which might take as much as three weeks to obtain. Even inside the colony all migration was scrutinized. People wishing to move house were required (on pain of 'severe punishment') to report the move both to the District Bureaux in charge of their old and new neighbourhoods, and to the local branches of the Kempeitai; and the change in their whereabouts was recorded on boards which were hung up outside every building to indicate the names of the occupants. Actual physical progress around town was impeded by checkpoints and barriers. When the Governor swept from one place to another, or a senior officer passed through on a tour of inspection, or some secret troop manœuvre was being conducted, all traffic in the affected districts was brought to a halt. Pedestrians were expected to 'freeze' where they stood till the cortège had passed, and were sometimes obliged to remain in that 'frozen' posture for anything up to eight hours.

Yazaki had recommended that the conquerors should follow the British example of allowing free trade. But the new long-term rulers, while in principle keen to revive economic life in the colony, preferred to opt for a *dirigiste* approach. The resumption of business was made, as we have observed, strictly subject to official approval. An inquiry was launched to determine which of the 1,027 companies registered with the pre-war government were hostile to Japan. Some 250 of these registered companies were eventually authorized to resume operations; but their scope for manœuvre was hemmed in by a ban on the holding of meetings which made it effectively impossible for them to hold an AGM.[6] As a further control measure each line of business was placed under the management of a syndicate whose function it was to collect taxes and disseminate the instructions of the regime. Finally every stage in the regular trading process was tied down with bureaucracy. In March 1942 Isogai introduced controls on the transportation and sale of virtually all types of goods. Traders wishing to export had to obtain special permission from the Finance Department of the Governor's Office, and any imports had to be reported within five days of their arrival in Hong Kong.[7] Five months later Arisue announced that similar restrictions would be imposed on the output of the newly reviving factories. Arisue explained that free trade was considered unsuitable to the needs of a wartime economy.[8]

'The first use of Hong Kong', declared the official Domei news agency in a statement announcing Isogai's appointment as Governor, 'is as a centre of supplies for the troops.'[9] The Southern faction's agenda implied new and vigorous efforts to strip the colony of every conceivable form of wealth. Under the new long-term leadership the bouts of organized looting which had been set in motion by the Gunseicho became institutionalized. Procurement firms were established to furnish the Imperial forces with the scrap metals and other strategic materials that were being amassed by the industrious brokers. A Godowns Decree ratified the 23rd Army's initial confiscation of the local ware-houses, all of which with their contents were now formally classified as 'enemy property'. The contents of the warehouses, however, were not limited to the rice and the other foodstuffs which had been stored up by the British in antic-ipation of a siege. Many of the godowns had been rented out to Chinese and other Asian merchants, and the goods stored in them represented the stock of many local companies as well as the private assets of individual members of the gentry.

Scrap metals and foodstuffs were not, of course, the only kinds of wealth that Hong Kong had to offer the Japanese war effort. One of the top priorities of Isogai and his team was to corner the money. The first step in this process had been the initial takeover of the British note-issuing banks. At the start of the conquest the 23rd Army troops had marched into the banks and had grabbed all the holdings of Hong Kong dollars they could find in the bank vaults. The second step, as we saw, was to summon all citizens owing debts from before the invasion to the banking halls, where they were expected to pay off their debts under the supervision of Sir Vandeleur Grayburn and his captive colleagues. All the hard currency raked in as a result of this action (some HK$22m were reckoned to be circulating at the time of the British surrender) was used by the regime to pay for their war preparations and general admin-istrative costs. Not content with their efforts to round up the dollars already issued the Governor's Office also hit on an inspired method of generating a fresh supply. A search of the bank vaults had revealed, side by side with the ready cash, a huge stock of additional notes, most of them in large denomi-nations of HK$500 or HK$1,000. This was money which the bankers had not yet got round to validating in the cumbrous fashion of the period, when each individual note had to be signed by hand, but which at the same time they hadn't got round to incinerating before the Japanese forces moved in. In the spring of 1942 the unfortunate Grayburn and his colleagues were accordingly put to work signing these notes – unbacked, unlawful, distinguishable only by their serial numbers from the genuine ones validated before the surrender. Over the following years some HK$65.5m of these 'duress notes', as the bankers called them, were released on to the Asian market as the result of this massive scam.[10]

In the meantime the authorities were trying to wean the public on to a different currency altogether. Within two weeks of their capture of Hong Kong the 23rd Army had set to work introducing the 'military yen'. Isogai and his entourage took up the cause of the military yen and advanced it with still greater vigour. The introduction of military yen was a traditional measure which had been adopted by conquering Japanese troops in the regions they occupied ever since the defeat of Tsarist Russia in 1904–5. It was also one more form of organized pillage. The military yen had no more inherent value than the bogus 'duress notes'. The notes were unbacked; they were marked with no serial numbers; and the quantity in circulation was never disclosed. Their deployment facilitated the gouging of resources out of the colony in two distinct ways. In the first place it afforded another means of inducing the locals to part with their holdings of Hong Kong dollars. Citizens were encouraged to trade in the old currency for the new one, at first at a rate of HK$2 : M¥1 and then from July 1942, when the Hong Kong dollar was 'devalued' by Isogai, at a greedier rate of HK$4 : M¥1. With the help of this Monopoly money the Imperial forces could also requisition any supplies they needed from the colony and could acquire land and property from individual citizens – in effect, free of charge.

Finally an attempt was made to extract any wealth that remained after these depredations through a fiscal blitz. In 1942–3 the Governor's Office imposed a whole series of taxes on this polity where the tax burden had always been light. A tax was slapped on annual business profits in excess of M¥5,000. Other taxes were levied on houses and properties, food and liquor, entertainment and vehicles, and the onslaught was supplemented with a stamp duty and a barrage of registration and licensing fees. Most of these taxes were steep (the business profits tax, for example, was charged at a sliding rate of up to 30 per cent), and a stipulation was added that all of them would be subject to upward revision.[11] In this context the Governor executed a striking retreat from the posture of liberation that had been in evidence at the start of his rule. At a press conference in January 1943 he announced that in view of the numbers of addicts in the colony an abrupt suppression of opium smoking would after all be 'difficult to carry out'. Instead the authorities had decided to 'suppress opium by taxing it'.[12] Like the British they planned to create an official monopoly by establishing an Opium Sale Syndicate to manage the traffic. Any private holdings of opium had to be sold to the Syndicate by the end of the following month, and the Syndicate would then take charge of retailing the drug to registered smokers at a suitably prohibitive price. In theory the quantities channelled through the Syndicate were to be reduced year by year, but in practice the signs are that the Governor's Office milked the craving for opium for all it was worth. Large consignments of the drug are said to have been specially brought into Hong Kong by the Army from regions of north China such as Chahar and Jehol.

As a military base Hong Kong couldn't be allowed to support a larger population than it could readily feed. Already under the Gunseicho plans had been laid to trim down the existing population of 1.6m to a more manageable 500,000,[13] and the drive to achieve this objective became one of the central features of Isogai's policy. In particular the government had no intention of feeding the 800,000 refugees from the mainland whom the British had allowed to drift into the colony in the years leading up to the war. Such people didn't even have wealth to provide for the war chest, and every effort had accordingly to be made to rid Hong Kong of these 'useless rice buckets'.[14] For the first year of Isogai's reign the methods employed were comparatively gentle, and the idea was to coax the 'rice buckets' into clearing out of the colony of their own accord. A Repatriation Committee was given the task of directing the return of the refugees to their mainland villages. Three different routes were opened up for the refugees to follow into the interior of Guangdong province and points further north, and help in the form of transport and protection from bandits was sought from the various residents' groups which had been organized in the colony by immigrants from the same mainland province or district. But the process didn't advance as rapidly as the Governor's Office had hoped, in part because many of the 'rice buckets' preferred to take their chance in Hong Kong rather than to risk starvation in the Guangdong countryside, and in part too because of the sheer complexity of the exit procedures the Japanese themselves had imposed.[15] By the first months of 1943 the population was still hovering round the million mark, and the authorities were starting to drum their fingers. In March a new Repatriation Scheme was unveiled. Derelicts would be given free passage to their places of origin, but they had to be out of the colony by the end of April. After that deadline, it was indicated, 'drastic measures' might have to be introduced.[16]

The Southern faction's victory also implied that Hong Kong was to be well and truly transformed into part of Japan. Rather than being appended, on the lines proposed by the China faction, to the jurisdiction of the 23rd Army command in Canton, the colony as we saw had been formally annexed as a Conquered Territory of the Japanese Empire. There had in fact been yet another conceivable option, and that was to hand Hong Kong back to China by making it over to the puppet mainland regime of Wang Jingwei. So far as can be ascertained this option was never considered for a moment by either of the two Army factions involved in the Hong Kong debate.[17] Expectations, however, appear to have been raised in some Hong Kong Chinese circles by the uncertainties of the Gunseicho weeks; and Isogai on his arrival moved swiftly to douse them. At a press conference given on the day he took office in

1942, the new Governor was asked by a local journalist 'whether there was any question of the administration of Hong Kong being handed over to the Nanking government in future, on the same lines as Philippines for the Filipinos'. Isogai replied 'laughingly' that 'so far as he understood Hong Kong was not part of China', observing in this connection that the colony had been under British rule for the previous hundred years.[18] The annexation was also justified, like everything else, as a matter of wartime necessity. Isogai proclaimed that Hong Kong 'had tremendous value as far as military operations were concerned, and was to be kept for such purpose'.[19]

In the weeks after Isogai's arrival such trends as might have seemed to point to the Wang Jingwei option were deftly reversed. Those Wang Jingwei supporters who had been so active during both the invasion and the Gunseicho period were elbowed into the wings. Nothing more was now heard of the Wang partisans in the New Territories. Cheng Kwok-leung, the Chinese commandant of Stanley internment camp, who is known to have been a Wang adherent, was replaced as we noticed by two Japanese.[20] The possibility of giving up Hong Kong to Wang Jingwei lingered on for a while in the minds of some officials in the Japanese Foreign Ministry. At the end of 1942 Wang went to Tokyo to negotiate an agreement committing his regime to line up with Japan in the broader Pacific conflict by declaring war on Britain and the United States. The negotiations took place at exactly the same time as the two Allied powers were preparing the treaties relinquishing their privileges on the Chinese mainland to the rival government of Chiang Kai-shek. In spite (or because) of Wang's puppet status the Foreign Ministry team assigned to draft the agreement believed that Japan would be wise to reward his regime for its entry into the war with concessions to Chinese irredentist feeling at least as handsome as those which the Allies were making to Chiang; and one logical area for concession was clearly Hong Kong. Suggestions put forward ranged from an undertaking to guarantee China's sovereignty over the New Territories to a deal under which the whole of Hong Kong would be handed back in exchange for acceptance by Wang of Japan's long-term domination of Hainan, the large and strategically crucial island close to Vietnam.[21] But the Army, not the Foreign Ministry, held the power in Tokyo; and the Army had no intention of committing themselves to the return of Hong Kong in whole or in part – at least till the war had been won.

In the meantime Hong Kong started to be converted with all speed from a British colony into a Japanese one. For all their high-flown rhetoric of liberation the new Governor and his colleagues took over without any sign of embarrassment the former British role of political overlords. The new overlordship was symbolized at the outset by a proconsular rescript which Isogai issued on his arrival in February 1942. Carved on a stone tablet this proclamation was enshrined in the empty throne which had served as a frame for the dismantled statue of Queen Victoria. The new long-term rulers moved smoothly into the principal seats of the overthrown British power. The former Government House with its ants and rats was rebuilt for Isogai's future use by a firm from Osaka who adorned it in Japanese style by adding a pagoda-like structure to the roof, and the Governor's Office was installed in the Art Deco splendour of the Hongkong and Shanghai Bank.

Japanese domination was also proclaimed in the economic sphere by the steadily growing insistence on the use of military yen. Yazaki had advocated retaining the old colonial currency as another way of reassuring the local business chiefs;[22] and for the first eighteen months of the conquest the Hong Kong dollar was indeed allowed to continue in circulation. Isogai and his colleagues however were determined to ensure that the military yen attained a position of total supremacy. Quite apart from its use as a sponge for soaking up local assets the Army scrip was an instrument in Japan's grand design for converting East Asia from a European to a Japanese economic bloc through the creation of a yen-based Co-Prosperity Sphere. The 'devaluation' of the Hong Kong dollar in July 1942 was, in this context, a first step towards driving the old British money out of the market. All taxes and other government payments had from now on to be made in military yen. From the start of the following year successive indications were given that the 'sound' military yen was soon to displace the old currency in which the population 'no longer had any faith',[23] and in June 1943 the Hong Kong dollar was banned.

Like the British before them Isogai and his team made sure to get a grip on the key sectors of the Hong Kong economy. The Governor's Office took charge at the outset of all those strategic enterprises which the British had owned in the pre-war years – public utilities such as the water, gas and electricity works, public transport concerns like the tram and bus companies and certain other heavy industrial plants.[24] The authorities also took over a number of other British undertakings of a profitable if less crucial character such as the Hong Kong Brewery and the Hong Kong Ice Factory in Causeway Bay.

At the same time the long-term leadership started to foster the emergence of a Japanese business elite who would take the place of the British taipans. New prestige now descended on the sprinkling of Japanese firms which had lurked in the colony since the late nineteenth century, and in particular on the local branches of the great trading conglomerates of Mitsui and Mitsubishi. These trading houses were called upon to play their part in the drive to the South by providing the Governor's Office with data on the strategic resources not only of Hong Kong, but also of the whole surrounding region of southern China and Vietnam.[25] In return they were granted high favour, and their managers are said to have been in attendance on Isogai 'all day long'.[26] The degree of their prominence may be inferred from a rumour which filtered out of the colony in October 1942 that all official posts were to be filled by the staff of Mitsui and that Hong Kong would shortly receive a 'Mitsui Governor'.[27] A key role in financial affairs was assigned to two Japanese banks which had operated in the pre-war colony, the Yokohama Specie Bank and the Bank of Taiwan. These two institutions replaced the Hongkong and Shanghai Bank and the other two British banks which had been responsible for issuing the colony's banknotes. They churned out the supplies of military yen and received all the taxes which were paid in that currency. In addition they presided over the liquidation of the various Allied banks.

As the months passed the government also made room for growing numbers of other Japanese companies which flocked into the colony on the heels of the Imperial troops. In June 1942 just over 1,350 Japanese civilians were recorded as living in Hong Kong: they included 560 employees of Japanese firms and their women and children. Six months later the Japanese civilian population had swollen to 4,000, and the total appears to have climbed to as much as 10,000 by 1944.[28] In admitting these settlers the long-term leadership flew, once again, in the face of Yazaki, who had wished to protect the jobs and businesses of local citizens by restricting the influx of immigrants from Japan. Isogai with his relative sensitivity to local feeling is indeed said to have made some attempt to keep the settler tide within bounds: we are told that he even sent a number of Japanese immigrants back to their homeland. But Isogai's efforts failed to command the support of his military colleagues, many of whom are said to have derided the Governor for having 'gone native'.[29]

In the course of 1942 the authorities parcelled out to this emerging plutocracy a wide range of the less strategic British concerns. Some were bestowed on the older generation of Japanese businesses, and others were presented to the new wave of carpet-baggers. The Gloucester Hotel, for example, was made over to the Matsubaras, a family who had operated a lodging house in Hong Kong since the turn of the century; while Lane Crawford's department store was reopened with fanfare by Matsuzakaya, a newly arrived company from the city of Fukuoka in southern Japan.[30] By the following year the Governor's Office was ready to part with some factories and other enterprises of a more central importance.[31] In July 1943 the management of the water, gas and electricity works was transferred into private Japanese hands.

This Japanese carve-up of the Hong Kong economy did not take place solely at the expense of the British. In the first months of Isogai's reign the Governor's Office also appropriated the bulk of the light industrial enterprises – rubber and textile factories, wooden boat-yards and sawmills – which had been set up by Chinese businessmen during the past two decades. Some of these enterprises were bought outright in exchange for a dollop of military yen. In other cases the owners were forced to take Japanese partners, and to accept a new system of 'guided management'.[32] The new Japanese business elite were accorded permission to operate well in advance of most local firms, and before long it was clear they were getting opportunities which had been withheld from the Chinese and other Asian communities. In July 1942 the Governor's Office proclaimed the establishment of a Hong Kong Commercial Federation. This chamber of commerce consisted exclusively of ninety-two leading Japanese business houses. The member firms were empowered to supervise all the trade that took place between Hong Kong and the ports in its immediate neighbourhood; and only they had the right to engage in long-distance trading beyond the south China coast.[33]

In keeping with these arrangements the Japanese in Hong Kong also started to take on an aura of social supremacy. During the first year of Isogai's governorship their superior status was underscored by a number of special privileges. Members of the armed forces and administrators employed in the Governor's Office were entitled to free public transport. Japanese residents were uniformly exempt from the martial law that ground down the rest of the citizens; and while in theory they depended for their food, like everyone else, on the rice ration scheme, observers guessed that their rations were 'probably augmented in one way or another'.[34] By the spring of 1943 this new privileged caste were beginning, like the British in earlier years, to entrench themselves with a range of elite institutions. A Residents' Association, the Yamato-kai, was set up 'to promote closer relations' among the Japanese settlers.[35] Various other fraternities and interest groups were established, sometimes moving straight into a vacuum left by the British: thus the Hong Kong Cricket Club was converted into a Japanese sports club. And the Japanese National School of pre-war years was revived for the benefit of settler children. As the process of settlement gathered pace the new rulers increasingly tended to forget their supposed role as liberators and to fend off the Chinese masses with apartheid-type barriers similar to the ones they themselves had torn down. Kowloon Tong, a suburb which the British had built in the 1930s as a 'garden city' for Europeans only, was taken over as an exclusive residential area for high-ranking Japanese officers and businessmen. The Queen Mary Hospital and the red-light district of Wanchai were reserved for the sole use of Japanese soldiers in need of 'rest and recreation'.[36] Elegant Japanese dining out at the Hong Kong Hotel were annoyed by the sight of the Chinese labourers who had been allowed in there in the first flush of anti-colonial fervour, and the Tea Rooms in the newly renamed Matsubara Hotel put up Japanese signs to discourage the Chinese public from going in.[37]

Finally work began on endowing Hong Kong with a new Japanese personality suited to its annexed status. Yazaki had stressed the need to avoid unsettling local residents with a breakneck imposition of Japanese culture like that which the Empire had attempted in its other conquered provinces of Taiwan and Korea. The new leaders, however, embarked on a programme of Nipponization far more drastic than anything inflicted on either of these earlier acquisitions. Urgent efforts were made, in the first place, to inculcate the Japanese language. Japanese was designated the basic medium of instruction in Hong Kong's schools, and fifty-two schools were founded to teach it exclusively. Special Japanese tuition was organized for teachers, doctors and other adult professionals. A Committee for Japanese Language Testing was set up to assess the proficiency of Chinese and other Asians employed in the Governor's Office, and a Committee for Japanese Language Examinations kept track of the progress made by the population at large. This campaign rapidly overshadowed the sporadic attempts which had been made during the Gunscicho period to elevate the language of the Chinese majority. The Japanese language, not the Chinese, was appointed in the place of English as the colony's lingua franca. For every place name that got turned from English into Chinese in the spirit of Asianization a dozen got turned into Japanese. Major thoroughfares which had borne the names of British monarchs or governors were restyled in honour of Japanese emperors: Queen's Road in Victoria thus became Meiji-dori (Meiji Road), and Des Voeux Road, named after a Governor of the late nineteenth century, became Showa-dori, a reference to Showa, Enlightened Harmony, the title used in Japan for the reign of the Emperor Hirohito.[38] The Peninsula Hotel became the Toa, from the Japanese term for East Asia, and the popular Café Wiseman was renamed the Fuji Café. The Chinese language was not merely bypassed, but in some cases even effaced. One or two Chinese place names were discarded in favour of Japanese substitutes: the Hung Hom district in Kowloon, for example, was turned into the Yamashita district.

The same trend was apparent in the wider sphere of traditions and customs. In May 1943 the authorities proudly announced the establishment of the Toa Gakuin (East Asia Academy) – an institute of higher learning at which local Asians destined for employment in the government, business and teaching sectors were to be imbued with a knowledge of Japanese 'morality, customs and social habits'. The curriculum even included courses in judo and Japanese fencing.[39] No similar drive, however, was launched to promote any high-level study of the Chinese legacy. In the early weeks of the conquest there had been some talk of reopening the University of Hong Kong with a pan-Asiatic syllabus that would be designed to include a Chinese component. But by the following year this project had been quietly dropped. Instead plans were made for dispatching a handful of Hong Kong Chinese to receive a university training in Japan.[40]

Vigorous steps were taken to graft on to Hong Kong the succession of public ceremonies which punctuated the Japanese year. All the festivals held in Japan to express adoration for the Emperor Hirohito and the Imperial forces were introduced to the colony, and local citizens were expected to play a full part in them. In April, on the Emperor's birthday, Kotewall and Chow and their colleagues on the two Chinese Councils were ushered to the Murray Parade

Ground and required to bow reverently to the north-north-east in the approximate direction of the Imperial Palace in Tokyo; and at the time of the Yasukuni Shrine Festival which was held to commemorate the Japanese war dead all Hong Kong residents wherever they happened to be were obliged to stand up and observe a minute's silence as a mark of respect. Moves were made to enforce the observance of Kigensetsu (Empire Day), of Kannamesai, the harvest festival, and of the festival that was held to mark the demise of Japan's founding Emperor Jimmu. But no such emphasis was placed on the red-letter days in the Chinese calendar. In February 1943 Isogai remarked at a press conference that he realised some older people still had a desire to celebrate the Chinese New Year: he hoped, however, that this celebration would be dropped, and 'the sooner the better'.[41] The Christian calendar which had been in use under the British was superseded not by the calendar of the Chinese Republic but by the Japanese system of reckoning the years from the start of the current Emperor's reign.

The very landscape began to be Nipponized, finally, through the preparation of a number of grandiose monuments. On a spur of Mount Cameron overlooking the Wanchai district Arisue directed the start of work on a huge war memorial designed both to honour the souls of the Japanese troops who had died in the fight for the colony and to celebrate the arrival of Japanese power. A samurai sword was embedded in the foundations, and the ground-breaking ceremony was solemnized by a bevy of Shinto priests dressed in white. Members of the gentry were called upon to display their conversion to Japanese values by joining Arisue on the committee in charge of the war memorial project and donating the necessary funds. Various other edifices were put up to commemorate the recent conquest,[42] and the public were expected to treat them with appropriate awe. Citizens in the Causeway Bay area were even made to bow to a cemetery housing the remains of some Japanese cavalry horses which had fallen to British shellfire during the landing on Hong Kong Island.[43] To the north of Kowloon stood a monument to the last emperor of the Song dynasty, a boy sovereign who had taken refuge there by jumping into the sea when the Mongols overran southern China in 1279. The Chinese had venerated this historical landmark to the extent that in 1860 they made its preservation their sole condition for ceding the Kowloon peninsula to the British crown. But the monument got in the way of the grand new military airport Arisue and his fellow officers were planning at Kai Tak. The Japanese had it dynamited.[44]

Military rule and annexation might have been semi-tolerable if Isogai had at least managed to deliver a streamlined regime. But the rule of the Japanese in Hong Kong continued to be bedevilled, as it had been from the start, by a basic lack of cohesion. Isogai was for most purposes little more than a figure-head. He had no troops under his personal command. He enjoyed scant respect among the local Army officers on account of his dismal record as a general, and was rumoured to be on consistently bad terms with both the Army and Navy chiefs. He was consequently in no position to impose his will either on the Army garrison or on the other armed services.[45] And under his ineffectual leadership the old jockeying for position between the Army and the other services went on as before.

Some attempt was initially made to rein in the Navy. In May 1942 the new Governor signed in his capacity as the ranking Army officer in the Conquered Territory an agreement with his naval counterpart, the Commander-in-Chief of the Second China Expeditionary Fleet. The agreement set out to resolve any lingering question of whether the Army or Navy was to have charge of the colony. The Army's preeminent role was indicated quite clearly. The Navy were required to hand over to Isogai most of the installations which they had appropriated on Hong Kong Island, and a naval staff officer was to be attached to the Governor's Office to 'receive the orders' of Arisue in the latter's capacity as the Army Chief of Staff. But the agreement still left the Navy a share of both assets and clout. They still kept control of a number of facilities in the eastern half of the Island, from a new Harbour Office which had been created in the former Yacht Club to the Tung Wah Eastern Hospital and the Hong Kong Hotel. They had the task of constructing a naval base to defend the approaches to the colony, and the Commander-in-Chief was to be informed by the Governor's Office of all decrees with a bearing on his sphere of operations.[46] And continued friction with the Army was guaranteed by the fact that the Army were running the warehouse system while the Navy had use of the shipbuilding yards.[47]

As for the Kempeitai, no one even tried to restrict their prerogatives. By the time Isogai reached Hong Kong the dreaded gendarmerie, as we saw, had expanded beyond their proper domain of counter-subversion and taken control of the regular police force, in the process creating an empire unmatched by the Kempeitai branches in any other Japanese-occupied zone. Under Isogai they went from strength to strength. On paper their chief, Colonel Noma, was a mere section head in the Army establishment, but in practice his authority was at least on a par with that of Chief of Staff Arisue. The Governor viewed him indulgently (Isogai and Noma went back a long way), and seldom ventured to interfere with the details of his activities. Noma himself agreed subsequently that the Kempeitai 'held strong power' in Hong Kong.[48]

This lack of strong central government opened the way to an orgy of private greed. Each of the three rival services was out to milk Hong Kong for its own enrichment, over and above what it could extract for the purposes of the war effort. The Army, for example, sold off large amounts of the goods confiscated from the godowns to Mitsui and the other Japanese trading houses. Army

officers slipped across the Pearl River to neutral Macao, where the Hong Kong
dollar was still generally accepted, and spent wads of the 'duress notes' extorted
from the captive British bankers on gambling and shopping sprees. Naval officers and ratings brought bags of rice up from Indochina and sold them on the
black market. And the Kempeitai waxed fat on the narcotics trade. A Kempeitai
officer was said to have taken over the running of the Nanyang Tobacco
Company, the firm owned by Chan Lim-pak, the Laval-like cheerleader of the
New Order. Disregarding the pious noises put out by the Governor's Office,
which warned of 'severe treatment' for anyone caught taking heroin pills, the
Kempeitai also set up their own depot for the sale of heroin – with fairly striking results. A report which leaked out of the colony in June 1942 observed that
this new drug 'was much cheaper than tobacco and was becoming popular'.[49]

Some individual officers even set out to line their own pockets in ways
that ran clean contrary to the government's interests. Chick Nakazawa, the
Kempeitai agent, built himself up a lucrative sideline selling off supplies of
government oil.[50] Racketeers of this kind mostly ploughed their gains into real
estate: they bought property under assumed names and avoided depositing
funds in the banks, where they might run the risk of detection.

Every so often the Governor's Office made an attempt to crack down on the
cowboys. Nakazawa was ultimately shunted out of the colony to run a chain
of night-clubs in Canton.[51] In May 1943 a decree was issued ordering all
persons engaged in a deal for the purchase of property worth more than
M¥ 20,000 to apply for official permission, so that a check could be made to
find out how the Japanese buyer had come by his money. But the Governor's
Office itself was awash with shenanigans. The individual bureaucrats whose
task it was to farm out the old British-owned enterprises to Japanese businesses
were rewarded by their chosen managers with large payments that ought to
have gone to the Finance Department; and officials at every level accepted bribes.
Isogai, at the apex of the pyramid, appears to have been far from squeaky clean.
He is said personally to have placed the Taikoo Sugar Refinery in the hands of
a crony named Matsumoto, a member of the Japanese Upper House who was
later expelled in disgrace.[52] In addition he made over the running of the government's new Opium Sale Syndicate to his former classmate Xu Chongzhi,
the elderly warlord from the Chinese mainland. Xu, who had declined to act
as Isogai's envoy to Chungking, was quite happy to get his fingers into this
juicy monopoly (evidence incidentally that the refusal of mainlanders in Hong
Kong to collaborate in a political sense didn't necessarily rule out commercial
hanky-panky); and the Governor was reported to have taken a cut of the proceeds.[53] The Japanese rulers of Hong Kong, as a British observer later commented, were 'a queer mixture of official rectitude and unofficial corruption'.[54]

The feebleness at the centre also left scope for the exercise of unchecked
brutality. Just as the government's policy of abasing the British was apt to be

eroded in practice by the sneaking respect which many Japanese went on feeling for the beaten whites, so the official goal of exalting the Asians, of making Hong Kong a laboratory for Sino-Japanese friendship, was sabotaged daily by the contempt and indifference with which most of the Imperial military viewed the Chinese. While the Navy are said to have shown a degree of restraint,[55] a large portion of the other two services clearly felt no compunction in treating the Chinese masses like serfs. Numerous accounts testify to the manhandling of ordinary Chinese residents by the Army rank and file. Sentries at checkpoints routinely slapped passers-by whom they felt had insulted the Army's honour by wearing dark glasses, or forgetting to take their hats off, or failing to bow to the Horses' Cemetery in Causeway Bay. And roving squads of troops continued to subject Chinese households to periodic displays of gratuitous violence. On one occasion a squad stopped a man in the act of leaving his home and demanded that he sweep the street. The man demurred, pleading that he was on the way to fetch medical help for his wife, who had gone into labour. The soldiers decided that seeing was believing. They burst into the bedroom of the mother-to-be and, excited apparently by the glimpse of her birth pangs, rampaged around, yelling and kicking the bed and jabbing in every direction with their bayonets. In the end the husband was forced to buy their departure by giving them a large wad of banknotes and a pair of gold rings. Another squad pushed their way into a house to be met by an elderly servant who told them that he had been left there by the owners to guard the door. Roaring with laughter, the troops nailed up the old janitor to the door by his fingers and thumbs so that he could 'guard it forever'.[56]

The Army officers seem if anything to have taken an even more savage attitude to the ordinary Chinese than their men. Chief of Staff Arisue, for instance, is said by a former Japanese colleague to have been 'well known for his stern decisions'.[57] Confronted one morning in March 1942 with a group of villagers in the New Territories who were suspected of taking part in subversive activity, he had them shot on the spot without troubling to wait for any kind of judicial procedure. Colonel Eguchi, the medical chief, who behaved with such chivalry to Selwyn-Clarke and the other British doctors, was also reported to have been 'no Sunday school teacher' in his dealings with the Chinese.[58] This appears to have been a slight understatement. At a dinner party the Colonel gave at his house he is said to have grown annoyed with the cook, who had served the meal late or otherwise failed to give satisfaction. He hauled up the unfortunate man, browbeat him for thirty minutes and finally beheaded him with his sword. A Portuguese lady who viewed the scene from the house opposite 'had to go to bed for a week'.[59]

More sinister, because more systematic, was the brutality employed by the Kempeitai. Noma and his lieutenants had no time whatever for the notion that Hong Kong was in some way different from the rest of China, or more likely to be receptive to Japanese rule. They saw only a population that was overwhelmingly Chinese, and therefore hostile.[60] And in the light of this judgement they reckoned themselves under no obligation to be squeamish in their policing methods. In May 1942 they were given the task of enforcing the crackdown on gambling which the regime had launched as part of its short-lived effort to clip the wings of the Triads. They set about this assignment with some inventiveness. Sometimes they simply contented themselves with propelling gamblers from their homes and making them kneel by the road-side for 'the amusement of other pedestrians'. On one occasion, however, catching a party deep in a game of mah-jong, they grabbed the players and forced them to swallow the tiles one by one until they choked to death.[61] Lorries filled with 'dangerous elements' trundled regularly to King's Park in Kowloon, which the Kempeitai had designated as their execution ground. The escorts were often observed to be carrying two buckets of water, 'probably to wash their swords'.[62]

In spite of these barbarities it must be allowed that the government headed by Isogai did have certain positive sides. By the end of 1942, for example, reports indicate that the wave of local gangsterism which had swept through the colony during the Gunseicho period had been suppressed. Crime had become minimal because no one dared to commit it. In this case it seems evident that the remedy was a good deal worse than the disease. But there was also some progress of a less equivocal kind.

In their overriding concern to promote the welfare of the garrison the new long-term rulers displayed something close to a mania for the preservation of public health. Four days after Isogai took up his duties the Governor's Office announced the establishment of an Anti-Epidemic Bureau. The Bureau deployed twenty-seven squads which fanned out through the districts every spring and autumn and enforced the cleaning of each street and house. 'Total war' was waged against flies. Citizens handing over two ounces of 'dry flies' – flies which they had caught live, rather than dredging them out of rubbish dumps – were rewarded with a free *catty* of rice.[63] Similar drives were launched to exterminate mosquitoes and rats, and to deter the Chinese from their habit of spitting.[64] In an effort to upgrade the quality of the colony's drinking water the regime built two water maturing tanks at Castle Peak and Tsuen Wan in the New Territories – a scheme which the British had talked about in a vague way for years.[65] Last and most important, the authorities made the public submit, for the first time in the colony's history, to a series of mass inocula-tion campaigns against smallpox and cholera.

The background to this health campaign was probably rather more com-plicated than appears at first glance. Behind the official exertions it may, for example, be possible to detect the hidden hand of Selwyn-Clarke and his team of uninterned British doctors. According to one source the redoubtable Director of Medical Services took the opportunity provided by the conquest to initiate a programme of mass compulsory cholera inoculations which the pre-war colonial government had been unwilling to let him pursue. The crackdown on mosquitoes has been ascribed, in the same way, to Dr J. B. Mackie, the pre-war government's malariologist.[66] The Japanese contribution seems to have been entwined (yet again) with the feverish quest to rake in local currency. The public were obliged to pay for their compulsory jabs at the rate of HK50¢ for a smallpox vaccination and HK$1 for a cholera shot. The Army health chiefs are said to have worked up a 'squeeze' of their own which entailed holding back travellers setting out from Hong Kong on suspicion of carrying cholera, and releasing them only on payment of sums which could run to as much as several hundred dollars. But whatever the background it seems clear that the health campaign did achieve some important objectives. No serious smallpox or cholera epidemic was reported from Hong Kong during the occupation apart from a couple of cholera outbreaks in 1942–3; and those outbreaks were by common consent very minor compared with the ones that had raged in the pre-war years.[67]

The regime's plans for the colony also led for a while to a limited amount of economic advance. As a military base in conditions of all-out war Hong Kong was expected to strive for the maximum possible degree of self-sufficiency. One way in which it could do this was by turning itself into 'a supply depot for industrial production'.[68] Manufactured goods could be exported to the South in exchange for foodstuffs and key raw materials; and local produce could take the place of a wide range of inessential imports. Isogai and his colleagues accordingly made an attempt to sustain the pre-war upsurge in the colony's light industrial sector. By March 1943 around 800 factories had been brought back into service, including the bulk of the existing textile mills. A large number of rubber footwear plants were set up under Japanese guidance: they recycled old tyres and processed the occasional shipments of raw rubber which arrived in the colony from Indochina and Malaya. And soap-making became a significant industry for the first time.[69]

With the same aim in mind a robust operation was launched to exploit the food-producing potential of the New Territories. A race-track on which the British had diverted themselves at Fanling was taken over and used for rice-growing experiments, and rice began to be planted in virtually every available square inch of arable land. The New Territories Agricultural Association which the British had fostered so sleepily in the dozen years before the invasion was revived with a view to increasing the output of fruit and vegetables. Model farms were created to alert local peasants to the latest methods of cultivation, and in August 1943 an Agricultural Training Institute opened its doors at Fanling.

Above all steps were taken to promote the development of fisheries – always Japan's strongest suit. Several Japanese fishing firms had established themselves in the colony since the mid-1920s, and others had moved in after the conquest in the wake of the Imperial Navy. These firms were soon trawling for fish for Hong Kong's consumption as far afield as Vietnam. In the meantime they set to work galvanizing the local fishing communities. They dispensed fishing tackle and fitted the local wooden fishing junks with engines torn out of commandeered British cars; and they also endeavoured to pass on to the still primitive operators of Shaukeiwan and Cheung Chau their own more sophisticated fishing techniques. By December 1942 around 18,000 Hong Kong Chinese fishermen were reported to be receiving instruction from the Amakusa Marine Products Industrial Company. Finally moves were made to streamline the colony's haphazard fish marketing system. Hong Kong fishermen found themselves organized into one of eight new district syndicates. Rather than handing over a catch to be sold by a local middleman, as they had done in the past, they delivered it to their syndicate, which in turn passed it on to be auctioned at a newly established Central Wholesale Market. The idea was that the fishermen would obtain their food and equipment from the syndicate at a subsidized rate, while the proceeds from the auction would be deposited for their benefit in a government bank.[70] This new system (like all the regime's economic initiatives) in practice worked first and foremost to the benefit of the Japanese troops. Most of the proceeds in fact ended up with the military, and so did some 70 per cent of the catch. None the less local experts agreed that the system was an efficient one, and that it had the potential, if properly managed, for transforming the lives of Hong Kong's fisherfolk.[71]

But while all this was happening the war had gone sour for Japan. By the last months of 1942 the Allied powers were beginning to recover from the shock of the early Japanese triumphs. United States forces had started to push back across the Pacific, and American aircraft and submarines were picking off merchant ships in the waters of the Co-Prosperity Sphere at a rate which climbed rapidly to almost one ship a day. For a time the Imperial government hoped to stanch this haemorrhage by exploiting Hong Kong's potential as a shipbuilding centre. The colony's shipyards would be put to work turning out auxiliary merchant vessels for the use of both Hong Kong itself and the entire Southern Region. In January 1943 the first such vessel rolled off the slipways, and the media claimed that Hong Kong would be able to produce another one every three days. But the colony proved unable to sustain this momentum. In the following months, to judge from official announcements, just five more auxiliary ships were produced.

The result was that much of the progress which had been made in the direction of public health and economic autarky was cancelled out by the slow strangulation of the colony's overseas trade. The fight against malaria began to be lost, for example, because no shipping could be provided to bring in anti-malarial drugs from Japan.[72] As fewer and fewer raw materials made their way to Hong Kong from the South the output of the factories grew increasingly shoddy. Rubber soles cracked up or split in two, 'leather' shoes turned out to be made of paper, and pairs of socks failed to stand up to a single washing.[73] And in spite of the effort to maximize local food production the mass hunger of the Gunseicho period began to creep back as United States bombers and submarines started sinking the freighters which had brought occasional shipments of rice to the colony from Indochina and Siam. By the end of 1942 the food situation was dangerous; by the middle of 1943 it was desperate. People with bloated faces dragged themselves about on swollen feet, and the corpses of some 300 famine victims were found on the pavements each morning and hauled off in carts. Few holds were now barred in the struggle to keep alive. The head of a dog was put out for sale in a market, and one man was seen carefully peeling the fur off a rat. Some of the corpses lying on the pavements had their buttocks and thighs suggestively lopped off, and rumour insisted that the meat which bubbled in the woks of the roadside hawkers might well be human flesh.[74]

Under these dire conditions the Governor's Office became more determined than ever to ensure that the colony's meagre resources were kept back for the troops. Vicious action was taken against any locals who tried to infringe this monopoly. In January 1943 a Kempeitai squad were observed setting two Alsatians upon a group of ten Hong Kong Chinese women who had been caught trying to collect grass for fuel. 'Huge lumps of flesh were torn from their bodies, and then they were allowed to go.'[75] By July the regime's early efforts to persuade vagrants to clear out of Hong Kong of their own accord had got visibly nowhere. The deadline had been extended three times, and ignored three times; and the approach now switched to all-out deportation. Once again the mechanics were left to Noma and his men. The Kempeitai drove around in special trucks looking for people in shabby clothing and snatching them off the streets 'like fowl'.[76] Most of the derelicts rounded up in this fashion were packed first of all into a transit camp in the North Point district. After that they were put aboard motorized junks and dropped off, at the rate of around 2,000 a week, on the plague-ridden coast of Guangdong or on one of the barren and uninhabited islands on the fringe of the colony, to fend for themselves. Local fishermen didn't dare to go near Lo Chau island off the Stanley peninsula:

> On this island it was said people ate each other and it was very noisy there
> . . . The people there were calling for help and there was another island in
> front of that island, but the water was running very fast and they could not
> reach the other island by swimming. They shouted for help and it could be

heard by the village of Hok Tsui which was in front of the island because of the east wind.[77]

The elite drop away

As the months passed the early disposition the gentry had shown to accept the New Order began to give way to a process of creeping disenchantment.[78] The social status which they had enjoyed at the start of the takeover was undermined by the onset of Nipponization and the imposition of a Japanese ruling caste. Kotewall and Chow are said to have been treated by the authorities increasingly 'in a cavalier manner', and some of their colleagues encountered behaviour a good deal more demeaning than that. At one banquet the government staged for the local community leaders a Japanese officer, irked by some minor solecism, walked across to a prominent table and gave one of the most conspicuous guests a resounding slap. 'Every Chinese there', wrote Dr Li Shu-fan who was present, 'felt that blow as though it had been dealt to him personally.'[79]

Even the few zealous acolytes of Japan seem to have been aware of a certain diminution in their prestige. One of the only members of the Wang Jingwei faction to have retained a major role after the first few weeks of the takeover was a journalist named Kong Kai-tung. Editor-in-chief of the Wang Jingwei publication, the *Nan Hua Ribao*, Kong was also a leading official of the Wang regime's Ministry of Propaganda. After Isogai's arrival he continued to edit his paper, and he was also assigned a seat on the Chinese Cooperative Council. The new Governor however is said to have ignored Kong consistently, paying him just the minimum attention required to exhibit a scrap of respect for the puppet regime in Nanking. Kong not surprisingly resented this attitude; and he may also have been aggrieved by the fact that Hong Kong hadn't been handed over to the puppet Chinese government. Isogai grumbled that Kong only recognized 'Chairman Wang', and felt no loyalty to the Imperial Japanese Army.[80]

At a more tangible level the gentry began to perceive that they weren't going to recover the whole of their pre-war wealth. In spite of repeated requests they were unable to persuade the Governor's Office to release their goods from the confiscated godowns. At one point in July 1942 Isogai made the gesture of publishing a 'godown schedule' under which certain warehouses would be opened up to the public. Many others, however, continued to be sealed off; and the following April the authorities coolly announced their intention of buying up all the contents. Compensation on some basis so far undetermined would be paid to the owners at some indefinite date.[81] In addition it seems to have grown distressingly obvious that the liquidation of Britain's share in the Hong Kong economy wasn't about to entail any significant increase in the gentry's slice of the pie. At a colloquium of leading citizens which the Japanese media organized in December 1942 to discuss Hong Kong's Future Role in East Asia Li Chung-po, a member of the Chinese Cooperative Council, took the opportunity to slip in a discreet but unmistakable protest. 'What we should like to ask the Japanese', he declared, 'is that they be kind enough to offer us considerable shares of business without monopolising the larger businesses.'[82]

Any opening the regime did allow to develop was liable to prove a mirage. In April 1943, for example, a scrap of encouragement seemed to be offered to the gentry in the professional sphere. One year after their first petition to the Governor's Office the Association of Chinese Lawyers of Hong Kong were finally given permission to stage an inaugural ceremony. Prominent among them was Peter H. Sin, the 'Mayor of Hong Kong', who hoped to revert to his pre-war legal practice after his year-long service as chairman of the Central District Bureau. But what kind of law could be practised under a military regime? The chief of the General Affairs Department in the Governor's Office reminded Sin and his fellow solicitors that their function could only be to 'assist in the proper administration of martial law' insofar as this impinged on civil matters.[83]

At the same time any wealth which the gentry managed to keep or build up in spite of these various obstacles threatened to make them vulnerable to the gangster-like elements in the regime. In every corner they noted a disquieting tendency of the Japanese forces to home in on the well-heeled. Travelling businessmen, for example, made an obvious target for the cholera check which the Army health chiefs had imposed on all persons leaving the colony as a pretext for raking in extra dollars. Dr Li Shu-fan, who observed the check with professional interest, was 'astonished at the high incidence of cholera carrying among people of means'.[84] The Kempeitai took advantage of the deportation campaign which was launched against vagrants in July 1943 to detain, for good measure, a number of richer people whom they then threatened to cast out of Hong Kong with the rabble unless a ransom was paid. Some of the gentry appear to have been quite amenable to the removal of vagrants to their mainland villages, particularly so long as peaceful persuasion was the method used. Li Tse-fong of the Bank of East Asia was quoted as observing that as soon as the 'beggars and destitutes' had been cleared off the streets the appearance of the city would be 'improved considerably'.[85] The arrest of 'respectable citizens' was another matter.

Minutes survive of a number of the routine weekly meetings which were held by the Chinese Cooperative Council during the summer of 1943. Right through the summer, these minutes disclose, the gentry who sat on the Council were formulating a series of appeals to be submitted to the regime. Many of these appeals seem to have focused on the issues of especially acute concern from their point of view. They continued to press for the release of goods from the godowns. They moved that the government should be asked to allow time for inquiries which might prevent the deportation of persons of substance as the result of 'mistaken arrests'. At the same time, in keeping with the public-spirited streak in their make-up, they called on the Japanese masters to take certain larger steps needed to lessen the suffering of the population at large – to increase the rice ration, bring down the soaring price of rice and improve the distribution of such staple commodities as firewood, cooking oil and salt.[86] All of these entreaties were handed upwards, in the approved fashion, to Kotewall and his three colleagues on the Representative Council; and Kotewall and his colleagues then pursued them at their regular audiences with Governor Isogai. But Kotewall and the others no longer retained their early ability to wangle concessions out of the Japanese. Isogai's responses amounted to little more than a peevish reiteration of the celebrated British refrain of the period, '*Don't you know there's a war on?*' No, he couldn't permit the release of large stocks from the godowns because they would quickly be used up by businessmen intent on pursuing their own selfish aims. Yes, he knew that the deportations were being conducted most stringently, and that abuses had been committed; but the victims of those abuses just had to be sacrificed in the interests of the majority. No, he couldn't increase the rice ration, and the price of rice wouldn't necessarily fall if he did. The current price was in any case excessively low, and the government had incurred a huge loss by maintaining it. Distribution was basically a question of petrol. The Governor's Office were trying to find ways of shipping more petrol into the colony, but for the moment there was nothing to be done.[87]

These rebuffs incidentally helped to bring the gentry abreast for the first time of the course of events in the outside world. By the summer of 1943 a whole range of clues were combining to indicate that the war was not going exactly as the Japanese might have desired. Quite a lot of the truth could be figured out in the first place from the conquerors' own publications. Absorbed in their conflict with the Americans in the Pacific, the Japanese made oddly little attempt to suppress news of Allied successes in theatres in which they themselves weren't involved. Their media placidly carried reports of the setbacks endured by their German partners on the Russian front and of the Anglo-American landings in Italy. At the end of July the *Hong Kong News* announced the resignation of Mussolini ('the biggest political development in the history of the current war'), and six weeks later it referred in passing to Italy's unconditional surrender.[88] The Pacific war, certainly, was presented in terms of an unbroken succession of Japanese triumphs; but even in that context the press seemed unable to avoid letting slip an occasional indication that all was not well. Early in June Hong Kong readers were called upon to lament the demise of Admiral Yamamoto, the mastermind of Pearl Harbor, who had been shot down by United States aircraft over New Guinea; and in October it turned out that disaster had also befallen one of the leading lights in the local regime. Arisue, the Chief of Staff, who had been transferred out of the colony at the end of the previous year to serve as a staff officer in the fight against the Americans, was declared to have been killed in action at an unspecified point on the Southern front. These official disclosures were amply supplemented in letters received by European neutrals from their countries of origin, in gossip brought in by visitors from Macao and in the short-wave radio broadcasts put out by the Allies. The possession of short-wave receivers was banned in the colony on pain of savage reprisals; but numerous members of the gentry listened in none the less to the Allied broadcasts in attics, in basements and under blankets.[89] Most tangible evidence that the tide had turned came in the form of United States bombing fleets. A first tentative air raid had been launched on the Imperial garrison in Hong Kong as early as October 1942: serious punishment started at the end of July 1943 with a three-day attack aimed at the dockyards and the Kempeitai headquarters. These portents evoked a swift response in Hong Kong business circles. Mussolini's dismissal was greeted with a fall of up to 50 per cent in the value of the military yen.[90] The July air raids were construed as a sign that the Japanese presence in Hong Kong might not after all be indefinite; and as Emily Hahn put it caustically, 'the appeasers began to look worried'.[91]

Whatever precisely the factors in their calculations, before the end of this watershed summer the first of the gentry had started to make themselves scarce. At the end of July local society was shaken by the disappearance of the affable doctor, Li Shu-fan. For some months Li had been hosting lavish parties, frequenting racecourses and dance halls and in general doing his best to convey the impression that he positively revelled in the New Order. In the meantime he quietly laid his plans for escape. He packed up his belongings and bribed some amenable Japanese soldiers to smuggle them out of the colony in an Imperial Army truck. Early one morning he crept out of his house dressed up as a fisherman and slipped off on a pre-arranged sampan round the headlands of the New Territories to the Chinese-held zone of Mirs Bay. In the following months several of the notables who remained in the colony began to show signs of placing a certain amount of daylight between themselves and the regime. On Christmas Day 1943 Sir Robert Kotewall was called upon to deliver a radio broadcast in honour of the second anniversary of the Japanese conquest. The Chairman of the Chinese Representatives discoursed at some length on the progress Hong Kong had achieved under Isogai – but he took as his benchmark the chaos of the Gunseicho weeks rather than the preceding decades of British rule. 'It is my opinion', he concluded, 'that in celebrating this second anniversary we should not simply eulogize the achievements of the Government: that is only a narrow view of the celebration'.[92] A still more ambiguous note was struck by Aw Boon-haw, the Tiger Balm magnate from Singapore. At a rally commemorating the overthrow of the British the Tiger Balm King 'expressed deep sympathy with the reconstruction of Hong Kong and *said he knew how terrible it was to be under the rule of the invaders.* [my italics]'[93]

Mounting discomfort could also now be detected in swathes of the colony's middle class. By 1943 there were signs of a widespread unhappiness with the soaring prices – a trend that was blamed at least partly on the imposition of the military yen. In early June one of the journalists at Isogai's monthly press conference pointed out to the Governor that since the recent ban on the use of the Hong Kong dollar the cost of virtually all goods had rocketed upwards. Many people were suspicious that the new currency wasn't in fact worth what the authorities claimed. At another press conference held later the same month Nakanishi, the chief of the Finance Department, was forced to defend the military yen, explaining that they were backed by the home government in Tokyo, that they were 'placed on the same basis as banknotes' and that the Governor's Office were keeping a record of the notes issued 'to prevent any inflationary tendency'.[94] The uncontrolled surge in prices hit particularly hard at the local Asians employed in government service. Civil servants were now said to be complaining incessantly that the salaries they received were no longer keeping pace with the high cost of living. At the end of June 1943 staff of the various District Bureaux on Hong Kong Island petitioned the head of their Area Bureau for an increase in salary and extra rice rations.

Small businessmen had their own range of frustrations with military rule. Traders complained that the efforts they made to set any business in motion were strangled in a mass of red tape; that the eggs and vegetables which they tried to bring into the colony had gone off by the time they completed the paperwork necessary to import any goods. Many of them grumbled, too, about the new business profits tax, pointing out that the government levied any amount they saw fit rather than assessing the tax in a uniform way on the basis of the profits reported by each firm. By the first half of 1943 the optimism that had buoyed up many merchants during the previous year had perceptibly faded. Pawnbrokers were said to be finding conditions increasingly difficult. Furniture dealers were reported to be having a 'quiet time': all their remade furniture had been sold, and nobody could afford the cost of any new articles.[95]

Discontent now appears to have been rife among the Eurasian minority whom the Japanese had relied on to fill many of the humbler posts in the Governor's Office. An editorial which appeared in the *Hong Kong News* in May 1943 criticized the Eurasians for their lack of desire to cooperate either with the other communities or with the government. They were said to have been using their current freedoms and privileges for their own selfish ends and against the ideals for which Tokyo was working.[96] Brokers like Richards and Carroll continued their lucrative occupations but were observed, like the gentry, to be getting 'worried' by evidence of the changing course of the war.[97]

With singular genius the regime had even succeeded in provoking the disaffection of their most supportive minority group. The rift which developed between the Japanese and the Indians may well have had its beginnings (like the original alliance between them) in events taking place a good way from Hong Kong. In December 1942, after months of increasing mutual distrust, the Imperial Army in Singapore dismissed and arrested Mohan Singh, a one-time captain in the British Indian forces whom they had chosen to serve as commander of the Indian National Army being organized to march on the Raj. The dismissal was sharply opposed by the Indian Independence League: the Japanese struck back with a purge of the League's leaders in Singapore and Malaya, and the ill feeling is said to have had repercussions in far-flung parts of South-east Asia.[98] That same December, at all events, the Governor's Office in Hong Kong suddenly started cutting back on the privileges which had been conferred on the local Indians at the start of the occupation. The generous flour ration of 7 lb a month which the Indians had enjoyed was abruptly suspended. Exempt the whole year from the travel restrictions which hobbled everyone else in the colony, Indians were now only permitted to leave Hong Kong if they had first obtained the approval of the Kempeitai; and a number found to have embarked without proper passes were removed from a Japanese ship. A detachment of Sikh police in Caine Road who had been indulged with free electricity were unexpectedly given a bill, and in general the attitude of the Japanese to the Indians was said to have changed for the worse.[99] The Indian reaction was predictably bitter. An Indian trader who left for his homeland that December deplored the paralysis of local business and the 'propaganda deception' being practised by the Japanese media.[100] By March 1943 there had been a sharp drop in the subscriptions received by the local branch of the League, and by September 'considerable friction' could be observed between Japanese patrons and Indian protégés. Even the rich Sindhi merchants who had rejoiced in the takeover were said to be fleeing the colony 'simply because they found the Japanese harder taskmasters than the hated British'.[101]

The attitude of the ordinary Hong Kong Chinese to their Japanese masters had never been in any serious doubt. In the words of one survivor, 'the hatred was immeasurable'.[102] Many people who managed to avoid the attentions of the Kempeitai death squads seethed none the less at the daily round of humiliations. Much anger was aroused, for example, by a ruling that all visitors to government buildings should first wash their hands in a basin of antiseptic: the arrangement no doubt made good sense in the context of the regime's drive for hygiene, but it was widely perceived as implying that the Chinese were dirty. Still more keenly resented were the continual slappings. An airport cleaner named Lee Lap recalled of the Japanese decades later, 'They made me feel low, very low'.[103] By the last months of 1942 a senior Japanese official who had been installed in the Matsubara Hotel was complaining that he had to order Western dishes rather than Chinese ones for fear that the Chinese chefs might poison his food (Europeans on the staff were apparently free from suspicion) and that he didn't dare sit in his room with the windows open to the street.[104] The increasing brutality which the Imperial forces displayed as the war began to turn against them discouraged any attempt to pursue normal life, and by the middle of 1943 most of the Chinese public were said to have sunk back into the mood of fear and withdrawal which had followed the British surrender.[105]

Nothing much could at any time have been expected by the conquerors from the mass of Chinese shop assistants and waiters, factory hands and stevedores, hawkers and vagabonds. Many of them, after all, had poured in to Hong Kong precisely in order to get away from the Imperial Army. Like the Nazis who marched in to 'liberate' the Ukraine from the Soviet Union the Japanese had none the less started with the advantage of taking over a society already under alien rule. They had had scope for appealing to some restive enclaves within that society, and they had indeed enjoyed to begin with, as Li Shu-fan put it, a few 'iotas of goodwill'.[106] With more tact and more discipline they might have built on those foundations sufficiently to leave behind them some positive memories. But like the Nazis they missed their chance.

Hong Kong resistance – and British dependence

Hong Kong wasn't natural terrain for resistance. The colony was after all, a small place, and most people were packed into two cities which offered effectively nowhere for a partisan to go to ground. But there was ample scope for passive obstruction. Past masters for decades at dodging British regulations that they considered intrusive, the Hong Kong Chinese and their fellow Asians soon found ways of circumventing the stream of edicts put out by the Governor's Office. Many people, for instance, ignored the deadlines the regime had imposed for applying for business and residence permits, with the result that these deadlines had to be constantly and somewhat ridiculously postponed. Numerous citizens failed to file their returns for the business profits tax and other new-fangled levies, and as the months passed the authorities found it increasingly hard to collect the tax revenue. Thousands of residents, frightened by the cholera vaccinations, managed to avoid having them by the simple device of procuring a vaccination certificate from some industrious go-between. (One entrepreneur who had made it his business to peddle these documents to his fellow citizens is said to have dropped dead after subjecting himself to nineteen cholera shots in a single day.) The vagrants, as we saw, turned a deaf ear for months to the government's repeated exhortations to clear out of the colony, and a number who did get ejected promptly found local sponsors and wriggled back in.

Using the same techniques of evasion and apathy the Asian public succeeded in frustrating a good deal of the overall Japanese design for Hong Kong. After the vogue of the early weeks fewer and fewer people bestirred themselves to assimilate the colony's new lingua franca. Chinese staff in the Governor's Office neglected to turn up for their Japanese language classes, and three quarters of one batch of schoolteachers who had been packed off for training in Japanese proved unable to pass their exams. In the end the authorities had to accept the continuing use of Cantonese for day-to-day purposes simply because all communication would have broken down without it.[107] Almost no one exerted themselves to receive the prescribed introduction to Japanese values. Schools decamped to the mainland rather than submit to the new curriculum designed to instil adulation for Japan and the Emperor, and residents mostly boycotted the ones that remained. The Education Department tried frantically to keep up attendance through measures which ranged from encouraging the gentry's endowment of scholarships to interleaving the textbooks with lottery tickets; but to no apparent avail. In early 1943, six months after the first schools had been given official permission to start up again, only 3,200 pupils were going to school compared with 110,000 before the invasion.[108] A majority of businesses remained closed despite all of the government's attempts to get them to reopen,[109] and those that had resumed operations increasingly looked for pretexts to avoid having dealings with the new ruling caste. Staff of the Wing On department store were often seen refusing to sell goods to Japanese on the grounds that they had 'no such goods in stock';[110] and many humbler firms took part in the same quiet embargo. The widow of one bricklayer in the Eastern District of Hong Kong Island recalled subsequently that her husband had declined to undertake construction work for the Kempeitai and 'only did Chinese business'.[111] In some cases the general noncooperation appears to have shaded into a deliberate sabotage of the Japanese war effort. Labourers assigned to the dockyards to repair Japanese battleships loafed on the job; and they also took the chance, when they saw it, to damage tools and machinery and to make away with construction materials.[112]

And in spite of the obstacles an assortment of organized resistance movements contrived to take shape. By the last months of 1942 the Chinese Nationalist Party had reconstituted 'a sort of underground' out of a handful of activists who had stayed behind when the bulk of their colleagues pulled out of Hong Kong in the wake of the one-legged Admiral Chan Chak.[113] Agents in various guises were scattered across Kowloon and Victoria. One hung around the Ginza Tea-house which had opened in the Tsimshatsui district of Kowloon for the entertainment of Japanese officers. Two got jobs in the No. 1 Work

Department of the Imperial Navy, where they monitored the construction and repair of Japanese warships, and another bold pair even managed to infiltrate Kempeitai posts by getting themselves taken on as civilian police. Information collected by these agents was transmitted to Nationalist bases in the interior from a wireless station run by a certain Sun Bonian. (Nominally manager of the Shanghai Canned Foods Company, this supposed businessman was in fact a Nationalist of distinguished credentials, insofar as he was a nephew by marriage of one of the chief Party barons, Chen Lifu.)[114] But the Nationalist *maquis* never seems to have been very formidable. Japanese surveillance was keen, and the Kempeitai frequently intercepted both the agents' communications with the interior and the funds they received from there. Many of their activities were pretty minor: one agent, for instance, was charged with the task of smuggling out of the colony a surveying instrument and some spare parts for military radios. Another confided to his sister that he was planning to clear out of Hong Kong because there was 'nothing for him to do'.[115]

The Chinese Communists were a different story. We last met the East River guerrillas creeping across the border from Guangdong province in the aftermath of the British collapse. Their approach was to concentrate on embedding themselves in the mountains of the rural New Territories – the one part of the colony which did hold some promise for an active resistance campaign – and on filling the political vacuum which had developed there in the absence of any major deployment of Japanese troops. One ethnic consideration worked in their favour. Many of the guerrillas belonged to a Chinese sub-group, the Hakka, who formed a minority in the overwhelmingly Cantonese population of Hong Kong as a whole but who were, as it happened, widely represented in the peasant villages of the New Territories – in particular in the isolated peninsula of Saikung, in the north-east of the colony, where the guerrillas were able to win the allegiance of one of the main clans, the Li. In addition the guerrillas bid for the support of the villagers in classic Maoist style. They put paid to the dozen or so bandit gangs which had preyed on the countryside since the British withdrawal, and began to address the longer-term problems of this dirt-poor region by setting up night schools and literacy classes. And against this backdrop of good works they started to preach to the villagers the importance of standing up to the Japanese.[116] The results were substantial. Most of the local headmen had acquiesced, as we saw earlier, in the Japanese conquest; but a generation gap rapidly opened up in the villages as growing numbers of young men and women turned their backs on their elders and joined up with the East River bands.[117] Without for the time being making any explicit avowal of their Communist loyalties, the guerrillas were also able to build up their following at the expense of the rival Nationalist faction. (The Nationalists also ran a few partisan groups in the countryside, but the members of these formations were mostly ex-bandits and signally failed to impress the villagers, who referred to them as 'chickens with parasites'.)[118] On 1 February 1942, at a meeting held in their power base of Saikung, the assorted East River contingents which had infiltrated the colony merged themselves into a new, special unit, the Hong Kong and Kowloon Independent Brigade. With a strength that built up only gradually from a dozen or so to a few hundred, the Brigade never ventured to take on the Japanese in a frontal engagement; but they managed to make a significant pest of themselves all the same. By late March they exerted effective control of large parts of the New Territories and the colony's outer islands. Even in market towns like Yuen Long and Taipo the writ of the Japanese ran only in the daytime, and the Army units and Kempeitai stations were under continual threat of guerrilla attack. The guerrillas were also embarking on raids calculated to sever the Japanese lines of communication. Robin Hood-type celebrity began to attach to a number of the Brigade leaders, notably Tsoi Kwok-leung, the commander-in-chief, a consumptive individual said to have been involved in a number of minor pre-war businesses in Hong Kong and the mainland port of Xiamen, and 'Blackie' Lau, a swarthy peasant who made his name as a crack shot and master of disguise. By 1943 the guerrillas had started to inflict a succession of telling blows on the Japanese forces. In early June they blew up a railway bridge at Shenzhen on the border. A troop train had been crossing, and the Japanese Army passengers died by the score.[119]

Finally there were the British. The driving force in their case was an officer of Australian origin, Colonel Lindsay Ride. Formerly a professor of physiology and dean of the medical faculty at the University of Hong Kong, Ride had served during the invasion as Commander of the Hong Kong Field Ambulance and had then, following the surrender, been consigned with the rest of the beaten British troops to the Shamshuipo prison camp. Ride was a man of boundless energy coupled with a burning loyalty to the British imperial cause. 'If our Colonies were populated with Rides', the information chief MacDougall wrote of him, 'we would run an Empire which would be the marvel of the age.'[120] Like de Gaulle Ride was not inclined to consider the war lost on the basis of just one defeat: he was also imbued with a de Gaulle-like disdain for the weaknesses of more ordinary mortals. 'In Shamshuipo', he remarked, contemplating his fellow POWs in early January 1942, 'there is not enough of the fighting spirit in evidence; the inevitable seems to have been accepted.'[121] During these first few days of internment the security measures enforced by the Japanese at Shamshuipo were visibly lax (yet another reflection of the near-anarchy of the Gunseicho period). The wire around the camp was tattered, and the guarding erratic. Ride resolved to escape and fight on. On the night of 9 January he slipped under the wire in the company of two like-minded officers, and eight days later he emerged on to Chinese-held soil in Guangdong. Just a month after that he was in Chungking, pressing the British

Military Mission in the Nationalist capital to back a scheme he had worked out for a special army unit to be set up in southern China. The main tasks of the unit would be to smuggle badly needed supplies to the British POWs left behind in Hong Kong; to keep them abreast of events in the outside world; to urge them to try to escape in their turn; and to help any of them who elected to do so. By 6 March Ride was back in Guangdong working on the formation of this British Army Aid Group (BAAG). A headquarters was organized in the town of Qujiang, in the north of the province, and in June an advance base was added at Huizhou in the south – the same place where the first party of fleeing British officers had arrived with Admiral Chan Chak immediately after the fall of the colony. By the autumn, in keeping with their emblem of a scarlet pimpernel, the BAAG had helped to spirit a further twenty-nine British and Allied servicemen from the Hong Kong camps. In the meantime they started to develop an intelligence network to gather data on the activities of the Japanese forces and on conditions in both the colony and its immediate neighbourhood.[122]

The BAAG's efforts were supplemented in various ways by the handful of British civilians who had been allowed to remain at large inside Hong Kong. Selwyn-Clarke, the relentlessly dedicated physician who had badgered the Japanese into letting him continue in his pre-war post as Director of Medical Services, used the cover of his routine duties to organize an underground of his own. He and his staff secretly set about procuring a whole range of desperately needed medical items – drugs and surgical instruments, vitamin biscuits and powdered milk – and smuggling them both to the inmates of the POW camps and to the Allied civilians interned in Stanley. Sometimes they also slipped in wads of money with which POWs and internees could bribe the camp guards to secure them additional food. The relations between the BAAG and this little medical network, two outfits each headed by an iron-willed personality, were wary, to say the least. Selwyn-Clarke took the line that his role had to be confined to relief operations. If he allowed himself to become entangled with the BAAG's attempts to encourage escapes from the POW camps he would merely give the regime a pretext for curtailing his endeavours to care for the British captives – not to mention the mass of the non-European population. Consequently, 'the less I knew about other people's secrets the better it would be for all of us'.[123] Ride for his part was incapable of understanding the outlook of this humanist who was willing to carry on working under the auspices of the Japanese enemy, adamant that the Japanese too had their pockets of decency and intent on coopting the services of those occasional good men in the interests of the public as a whole. In Ride's view Selwyn-Clarke was 'clever, cunning, crooked and unscrupulous to a degree . . . [he was] doing this work to save his own skin and be saved the discomfort of the concentration camp'; and he arranged for a dossier to be compiled on the activities of this 'Japanese helper'.[124] Still, the BAAG did once or twice bring themselves to send medical supplies into the colony for Selwyn-Clarke's use. The British bankers also took part in the relief drive. In the midst of their enforced toil in the banking halls manufacturing cash for the benefit of the Japanese forces Grayburn and his colleagues quietly secreted a hoard of some HK\$2 m which they started to smuggle out either to Selwyn-Clarke or directly to the camps in instalments of up to HK\$10,000 a time. Unobtrusive support also seems to have been given the POWs and internees by C. M. Faure, the ex-naval commander, left-wing crusader and polymath who had emerged unexpectedly after the conquest as editor of the Japanese-sponsored *Hong Kong News*. As an organ of Japanese propaganda the *Hong Kong News* was circulated without restriction in all the camps. Faure is said at great risk to himself to have quietly subverted his own publication, lacing it with half-truths, subtle hints and accounts of Japanese victories so absurdly exaggerated that the camp inmates reading it would have little trouble in guessing the actual trend of the war.[125]

A third branch of the British resistance was to be found in Macao. By the beginning of 1942 this small, baroque colony of neutral Portugal lay deep in the Japanese shadow. Japanese bombers flew overhead daily. Japanese Army and Navy officers strutted about in full uniform. Vast amounts of behind-the-scenes power were exercised by the Japanese consul and by Colonel Sawa, the local Kempeitai chief. Dominant for some thousands of miles in every direction, the Japanese forces kept a stranglehold on the colony's imports: they refused, when the mood took them, to allow shipments of oil to be brought in from Indochina, and cut off the rice supply for two weeks at a time. Yet in spite of some pressure from Wang Jingwei partisans who were keen that Japan should live up to its pledges of 'Asia for the Asiatics' by putting an end to this last European toehold on the coast of south China,[126] the Japanese never brought themselves to deliver the *coup de grâce*. One reason is said to have been pressure from Japan's German partners, who insisted that no action should be taken which might risk propelling Portugal into the war on the Allied side. It has also been suggested that Tokyo was concerned at the possible impact which the seizure of a Portuguese territory might have on the treatment of the sizeable Japanese minority living in Portuguese-speaking Brazil.[127] In any event Macao was allowed to retain its formal neutrality; and it continued to harbour a British consulate headed by a man named John Reeves. Within a few weeks of the fall of Hong Kong a trickle of British civilian refugees had begun to turn up in Macao: first to arrive was Phyllis Harrop, the former police official, who made her escape from Hong Kong in late January with the help of her spurious German identity papers. Reeves provided these refugees with hospitality, and before long had started to involve himself actively in assisting their onward progress through the Japanese lines into Free China, where they would once again be able to do their bit for the Allied cause. The consulate also began to provide a back-up service to the two other centres of British resistance. The BAAG appointed a member of Reeves's staff, Mrs Joy Wilson, as their official representative, and used Macao as the route for all their business in Hong Kong not directly related to the POWs. Selwyn-Clarke used the consulate as the conduit for messages which he sent out imploring the International Red Cross to press the Japanese government for the right to establish a presence in conquered Hong Kong.

All of the consulate's work had to be carried out in the swirling intrigue of this East Asian Casablanca. Japanese agents assigned to keep track of the other side's movements had bought themselves clusters of well-chosen houses (one lane near the airfield was known to the British as Axis Alley) and infested the larger hotels. Reeves reported that when he went for a drink at the Hotel Riviera

> [Japanese] Naval Intelligence head phoned upstairs for two extra men; their Gendarmerie chief did the same and so did one other of theirs who sent for men from outside. Some of my own people heard a buzz and mobilized themselves quietly. Then there was a general loosening of guns in holsters but when six Nips, at least pretending to be tight, sat down at the next table I quickly walked out; there was no point in letting them provoke a row. But I assure you my hand was on my gun . . .[128]

While the Portuguese Governor, a naval commander called Gabriel de Teixeira, showed the British conspicuous sympathy, many of his entourage had inclinations more natural to Lisbon's Fascist regime. They injected reports on their way to the Governor's desk with material calculated to damage Reeves, and in general did all they could to embarrass the consulate and the British community.[129] The consulate was also viewed with ill will by a number of local civilians. One British report spoke darkly of Gus de Ross, 'the bad hat of Macao', who was said to have forced Reeves to abandon the planned surreptitious dispatch of an Allied contingent into Free China by passing the word to the Japanese consul.[130] And lastly Reeves had to contend with the presence of Japanese agents among his own staff. An affable soul, Reeves was sometimes the despair of the Allied underground workers who passed through the Portuguese colony. One visitor who made contact with him sighed that there was 'no hope of him moderating his voice so that the whole staff cannot hear'.[131] But he none the less managed to turn his consulate into both a haven for Allied agents of several varieties and a useful intelligence organization in its own right. By 1944 he was declaring with characteristic ebullience that he had sources in Hong Kong at every conceivable social level.[132]

As the local backlash against Japanese rule intensified, the different Asian currents of resistance began gradually to intermingle with the British stream.

Asians in occupied Kowloon and Victoria started to show a new sympathy for the overthrown British masters, coming forward with all manner of material help for the POWs and internees. Chinese girls who had gone out with British soldiers trudged off weekly bearing food parcels for their imprisoned boyfriends in Shamshuipo. Kenneth Uttley, the government doctor, received a blue pullover which he assumed had been sent by his wife, 'but it turned out to be from Dr Yu'.[133] Prosperous Chinese, Eurasian and Indian merchants responded to the appeals of the captive British officials and taipans, sending them packages of food and medicine and funds. Portuguese clerks who had been employed in the great trading houses kept routine business going on behalf of their interned British bosses – and kept watch on the Japanese managers who had taken their place. The non-Europeans also bestowed a variety of unexpected – and dangerous – kindnesses on the handful of British still at large around town. Chinese and Indian clients who came to the Hongkong and Shanghai Bank to pay off their overdrafts slipped tins of food and other items to the bankers who had been dispatched there to supervise them. After dark Sik-nin Chau, a well-known Chinese private doctor (his uncle was no less a figure than Sir Shouson Chow), crept furtively into the Sun Wah Hotel where the bankers were quartered and provided them with consultations and treatment free of charge.[134]

In the same way local Asians began to contribute increasing help to the organized British resistance movements. Already by the summer of 1942 a succession of young Chinese and Eurasians and Portuguese had made their way out of the colony and joined up with the BAAG. These recruits were, in essence, the same body of Westernized, English-speaking young people who had stood firm six months earlier in the darkest hours of the Japanese attack. Many of them were students and graduates of Hong Kong University: quite a few had indeed sat at Ride's feet in the Physiology Department.[135] Others had served in the Hong Kong Volunteer Defence Corps and in the Police Reserve. A fair number were children of gentry families – an indication that something of a generation gap may have prevailed in urban Hong Kong as well as in the countryside.[136] In the occupied city Chinese and Indian merchants donated a total of HK$1 m to Selwyn-Clarke's network, and the local clients who came in to the Hongkong and Shanghai Bank unobtrusively left envelopes stuffed with thousands of dollars for Grayburn and his colleagues to pass on to Selwyn-Clarke or the camps. Asian residents fleeing from Hong Kong to Macao linked up with Reeves and the consulate, and took jobs in the newly created Chinese and Indian sections of the consulate's staff.

The result was that the British came to depend even more massively than they had done already on the services of the non-Europeans. And the organized British resistance was every bit as dependent as the POWs, or the internees, or the individual British in town. The BAAG's efforts, for instance,

were underpinned by the skill and devotion of a series of young Anglicized
Hong Kong Chinese of high calibre who became their key aides. Ride and his
party were only able to make their initial escape from the Shamshuipo prison
camp thanks to Francis Lee, a thin, shy, bespectacled young man who had
worked as a clerk in Ride's Physiology Department before enlisting in the Hong
Kong Volunteer Defence Corps. When the Japanese struck he had got himself
placed under Ride once again in the Hong Kong Field Ambulance, and when
the colony fell he had gone into Shamshuipo alongside the captive British
troops with the conscious intention of helping in any break-out that his old
employer might wish to attempt. As soon as the party had got through the
wire and out into the New Territories Lee's role became crucial: he talked to
the villagers in their own language, picked up food and information and
steered Ride and his fellow officers along mountain tracks and away from the
pockets of known sympathizers of Wang Jingwei. In April 1942 it was once
again Francis Lee who laid the groundwork for the BAAG's activities by establishing contacts inside Hong Kong and setting up channels of communication
between Hong Kong and the BAAG's proposed advance base at Huizhou.[137]
The pivotal job at Huizhou was assigned two months later to Paul Tsui, a Hong
Kong University graduate of some brilliance. He was employed as a secretary,
adviser and interpreter, with the particular function of selecting and training
recruits. David Loie, an Overseas Chinese from New Zealand who had held a
command in the Police Reserve and was said to have been filled with an
'intense loyalty' to the British cause, had emerged by the end of the year as the
mastermind of the BAAG's rapidly expanding intelligence network inside
Hong Kong. Hong Kong Chinese also formed the essential component of the
BAAG's rank and file. Only they (for obvious physical reasons) could slip in
and out of the colony without attracting the notice of the Japanese border
guards. Only they could blend in with the mass of the public and gather news
of local conditions and Japanese troop movements under the very noses of the
Kempeitai. By October 1942 the BAAG had succeeded in winning over a
number of the Chinese lorry drivers who had the job of delivering stores to
the camps. They became the chief couriers, using their regular visits to convey
secret messages from the BAAG to the POWs and transmit the replies. Other
Chinese smuggled notes from the BAAG to parties of POWs whom the
Japanese were using as labourers on their project for the extension of Kai Tak
airfield.

Much the same sort of dependence became the norm in the other centres
of British activity. In the occupied city the relief operation launched by the
Director of Medical Services was carried out through the efforts of a small
legion of steadfast Chinese and Eurasian volunteers. T. J. Hua, the doctor in
charge of the Kwong Wah Hospital in Kowloon, hived off quantities of food,
soap and vitamins for Selwyn-Clarke to supply to the POW camps; and a

Eurasian chemist named Arthur Rowan 'scouted around' for drugs needed by sick British and Allied officers who had been transferred from the camps to the Military Hospital in Bowen Road.[138] In Macao the true linchpin of British resistance was a Chinese known as Phoenix. In his day-to-day life he was Y. C. Liang, a young businessman who worked as comprador for the local firm of Wong Tai. Under this cover he served as the chief local agent for the BAAG. It was Phoenix who organized the escape routes on which Reeves dispatched Allied workers from Macao to Free China, and which served as the arteries for the BAAG's intelligence work. Some of Phoenix's exploits were mildly spectacular. On one occasion he brought about the deliberate flooding of some bank vaults where he knew vital radio valves to be stored. Handymen in his pay were called in to pump out the water – and took the opportunity to secure the valves.

In addition to all this the British found themselves profoundly beholden to both of the two mainland Chinese factions. To get going at all the BAAG needed to have the support of the Nationalists, for no British military enterprise could be launched on Chinese-held territory without the consent of the Nationalist regime. In April 1942, consequently, the British ambassador and the head of the British Military Mission in Chungking had approached Chiang Kai-shek for his agreement in principle to the establishment of Ride's organization. Mme Chiang Kai-shek, who sat in on the meeting, is said to have played a decisive role in securing her husband's permission, urging him, 'You *must* do something to help those poor prisoners. I know they are having a horrible time.'[139] Further negotiations were needed to win the approval of the independent-minded Nationalist military chiefs in south China for the setting-up of the specific BAAG bases at Qujiang and Huizhou.[140] In a more positive fashion the Nationalists contributed to a number of the British rescue and intelligence operations – particularly in Macao, where they seem to have run a more effective underground than they did in Hong Kong. Nationalist agents arranged Phyllis Harrop's escape from Macao to Free China.[141] The Nationalists also helped to stem the Japanese infiltration of Reeves's consulate by conducting a quarterly check-up on the domestic staff.

More significant still was the role played by the Chinese Communists of the East River. The East River guerrillas alone could ensure, through their dominance in the New Territories, that British soldiers escaping from the Kowloon POW camps got safely through the Japanese lines and into the Chinese-held areas to the north of Hong Kong. They had shown their potential at the very outset by intervening decisively in Ride's successful break-out from Shamshuipo. Valuable as Francis Lee proved to be, he could in the end have achieved very little if he hadn't managed, on the fourth night of the break-out, to deliver Ride's party into the safekeeping of Tsoi Kwok-leung and his band. The guerrillas provided the party with food and shelter and escorted them night by night, in a series of furtive sampan journeys and scrambles along mountain trails, all the rest of the way to the Guangdong border. Almost every one of the twenty-nine British and Allied POWs who escaped from the camps in the following months at the BAAG's instigation were tended and escorted in the same way by the newly created Hong Kong and Kowloon Independent Brigade.[142] The guerrillas also shepherded an assortment of British and Allied civilians whom the BAAG started to winkle out of the occupied city as the Japanese tightened their grip on the camps.[143] In October 1942, for instance, a guerrilla team led by a former cook at the Peninsula Hotel took part in the rescue of T. J. J. Fenwick and J. A. D. Morrison, two of the stranded executives of the Hongkong and Shanghai Bank. The East River guerrillas furthered the BAAG's operations in a number of other ways. They helped the BAAG set up liaison posts to facilitate contact between the Huizhou advance base and the agents deployed in Kowloon and Victoria. They permitted themselves to be used as a sort of post office for a stream of letters which Ride sent to General Maltby, the commander of the interned British troops. By their own account they even 'guided the BAAG in the techniques of secret work and prosecuting the underground struggle'.[144] Ride himself later commented that without the assistance of the East River guerrillas the BAAG would have been unable to function at all.[145]

In the light of this widespread support the British began to exhibit a new appreciation of their Asian subjects. Ride observed in his diary during the break-out of January 1942 that he had discussed future plans with his old clerk Francis Lee, 'and the more I see of him, the more I admire him'.[146] Selwyn-Clarke praised the 'wonderfully inspiring conduct' of the various Asians who had helped his relief work in spite of the treatment accorded to them by a 'none too generous' colonial government, and the bankers commented on the succour which they had received from the locals: 'They played very well, the Chinese.'[147] Above all glowing tributes were paid by the British escapers to the Communist escorts who saw them through the New Territories. Morrison of the Hongkong and Shanghai Bank recorded of his rescue in October 1942,

> I cannot speak too highly of these guerrillas. The care they took and their kindness will always be remembered by me with the deepest gratitude. As we proceeded on our journey we met people who disapproved of them because their politics were different from the regime in Chungking and classified them as Reds, but I shall always remember them as hardy, brave and kind men.[148]

Joint resistance also started to breed between the British and their Asian helpers a new camaraderie unimaginable in the pre-war years. Some of the warmest rapports appear, once again, to have been those struck up between the contingents of British who made their escape across the New Territories and the East River guerrillas who served as their guides. Early in 1942, on the eve of the Chinese New Year, a guerrilla band treated a party of fleeing British POWs to a feast of goose and rice wine; and one of the British officers sang to the guerrillas round the camp fire. 'We found that many of our tunes were patriotic songs to them: *The British Grenadiers* and the *Eton Boating Song* were especially popular . . .'[149] But the taboos were dissolving wherever the British and their former subjects were propelled into partnership. For the first time, it was said, British and Asians were able to intermarry without losing face in their own ethnic groups.[150] One of the leading lights in the BAAG, Major Ronald Holmes, married a Eurasian girl named Marjorie Fisher; and a number of other cross-racial pairings took place at the BAAG headquarters in southern China.[151]

In February 1943 the Kempeitai began to strike back, with efficiency and in every direction. Early that month they caught a British internee in the act of smuggling M¥4,000 into Stanley, on his return from an exeat which he had been granted for medical treatment in town. It was the beginning of the end for the local British resistance. Two weeks later Grayburn was arrested with one of his fellow-bankers and charged with supplying the money. The trail soon led on to Selwyn-Clarke and the doctors, and in early May the Director of Medical Services was picked up and consigned to a Kempeitai cell.[152] Next came the turn of the BAAG. Ride's organization had already been for some months the target of a counter-intelligence drive, directed by Lieutenant-Colonel Endo, the Indian expert, and carried out with the help of a number of bogus Indian adherents to the Allied cause. By the end of the month the Kempeitai were ready to move in. Their first step was to seize David Loie, the brains behind the BAAG's espionage work in Kowloon and Victoria. In the middle of June they began to detain the Chinese lorry drivers who brought the BAAG's messages to the POW camps. Confessions prised from the drivers helped them to track down a succession of POWs who had been communicating with the BAAG by means of hidden radio sets. At the end of the month they began to detain members of a similar network of internees in Stanley, and by mid-July the BAAG's infrastructure inside the colony was effectively smashed. A still heavier blow had in the meantime been dealt to the somewhat feeble Chinese Nationalist underground. Sun Bonian and twenty-six of his fellow agents were arrested in the course of a one-day sweep on 19 April. Most of the other Nationalists were mopped up through a neat mathematical procedure: each captured agent was assured that if he disclosed the names of *two* of his confederates he would go unpunished. Only the East River guerrillas, in their mountain hideouts, remained unscathed.

Retribution was now meted out to the British offenders. Since the fall of the colony the British had generally been handled with forbearance; but this time the kid gloves were off. For his role in the smuggling of cash to the internees

Sir Vandeleur Grayburn was sentenced to three months' hard labour in Stanley gaol. Offered half a handful of rice every day, denied medical care, he was reported in late August to have been found dead of cardiac failure brought on by beri-beri. Emily Hahn wrote incredulously that 'the most powerful financier in the Far East, chief of the biggest bank, had died of starvation'.[153] Selwyn-Clarke, whom a fair number of his fellow countrymen had suspected of Japanese sympathies, was accused by the Kempeitai of being the head of British espionage in Hong Kong. He was beaten, hung up from beams and subjected to the Kempeitai's speciality torture – the notorious process in which the inquisitors forced water through the victim's mouth and nostrils until he was bloated and then sat or stamped on his stomach until it deflated in a gush of water and blood. On 29 October a van set out from Stanley gaol containing J. D. Fraser, the former Defence Secretary, Walter Scott, the Assistant Commissioner of Police, and five other internees who had been caught in possession of illicit radio sets. It was said that a hand was stretched out in a wave and a voice called 'Goodbye, boys' as the van swept past a group of internee children who were playing beside the main road. The seven men were beheaded on Stanley beach.[154] On 18 December three POWs who had been convicted of the same offence were dispatched by a firing squad on the colony's other top beach, at Shek O.

Similar forms of punishment were visited on the various non-European activists. On the last day of May David Loie was ushered on to the verandah of the old Supreme Court where the Kempeitai had set up their torture cubicles. Rather than risk betraying his fellow agents he dashed to the balcony and leaped to his death. Twenty-six other Asians who had worked for the BAAG or been in touch with them were driven out to Stanley beach and beheaded that autumn – a Eurasian, an Indian and twenty-four Chinese. One of the Chinese was kicked into his grave 'crying piteously' as the lifeblood continued to pour from his half-severed neck.[155] Of the twenty-seven Chinese Nationalists who were rounded up on 19 April at least twenty-six were subjected to torture. Eighteen of them are said to have died of their injuries before they could be brought to the execution ground: the remainder, including their leader Sun Bonian, were put to death on Stanley beach on 4 October.

Looked at from a clinical angle the British had got off fairly lightly compared with the other ethnic groups. Around thirty of them – POWs, internees, doctors and bankers – were detained in the course of the Kempeitai crackdown of 1943. Torture was used very seldom against British suspects except where there was strong evidence of espionage, and some of the Japanese seem even then to have been quite inhibited about its infliction: one Japanese serving as an interpreter for the Kempeitai was said to have 'appeared very pale and frightened' when the water treatment was administered to a British POW.[156] Neither Grayburn nor Selwyn-Clarke was executed, though sentence of death was on one occasion pronounced on the latter; and the total number of British execution victims amounted to ten. In the meantime some hundreds of Chinese and other Asians both inside and outside the resistance were hauled in for questioning.[157] Torture was routinely deployed to extract their confessions, the water treatment accompanied by a whole ghastly repertoire of electric shocks, thumb-hanging, pulling of finger-nails, singeing of the nipples or genitals and slashing with bamboo swords. Death sentences were not generally imposed in the absence of a confession (the regime liked to make a point of observing certain formal procedures); but as fast as confessions could be obtained the heads kept rolling. Some hundreds of Chinese at least would appear to have been beheaded in the course of the following months.[158] 'It is time we executed some more,' a Japanese captain is quoted as saying; 'my sword arm will get out of practice.'[159] On top of all this the luckless Asian residents became prey to protection rackets. Local Kempeitai henchmen like George Wong and Call Me Howard picked people up independently and demanded money or sex from them or their relatives in return for keeping them out of the Kempeitai's hands. Some of the British themselves were aware of the contrast. Kenneth Uttley, the government doctor, recorded that the Europeans hadn't been tortured on the scale he had expected: 'it is the Chinese (and the loyal Chinese especially) who have been through the mill'.[160]

Even making allowance for these differences, the fact remains that the ordeal was a shared one. British and Asians were flung side by side for months at a time into packed, lightless, reeking and cockroach-ridden cells, and were tortured within earshot if not sight of each other. And on the afternoon of 29 October the seven condemned British internees and the twenty-six Asians who had helped the BAAG were driven out to the beach together to meet the same end.[161] The British victims are said to have derived comfort from a pep talk administered before they set off to their decapitation by the doomed Indian, Captain M. A. Ansari, who urged on them that everyone had to die some time and that death for a noble ideal was to be preferred to the ravages of a wasting disease. By the end of this dreadful year the new camaraderie had been sealed in blood.

Thoughts turn to Britain: nostalgia with qualifications

Whatever the faults of the British had been as colonial rulers it was clear that the Japanese who replaced them were infinitely worse. By the summer of 1943 some Europeans in town were reporting a widespread nostalgia among the Chinese they encountered for the old British days.[162] The *Hong Kong News* complained of a tendency among the Eurasians to remember only the 'meagre benefits' they had derived from the British and to forget all about the exploitation and prejudice.[163] Even the Indians were said to have begun casting affectionate backward glances. In an effort to stop the collapse in support for the Indian Independence League the Japanese (so one anecdote went) summoned the whole of the Indian community and scolded them for their lack of cooperation. Indian spokesmen retorted by reeling off a whole list of the perks those of them employed in government service had enjoyed under the British – varied and regular food, punctual wages and overtime pay, free housing and medical care and special schools for their children.[164]

This nostalgia however was not necessarily all it appeared. In some cases the expression of pro-British feeling may have reflected not so much an appetite for the old pre-war order as a pragmatic desire to be on the winning side. Emily Hahn observed with her usual acidity how in the summer of 1943 'a lot of people were suddenly remembering their British passports'.[165] One former Stanley internee recalled innocently that 'as time went on the growing support for the camp [from the Asians in town] made it apparent that the tide of war had turned in our favour';[166] and certainly several episodes that took place in the second half of 1943 had a strong whiff of opportunism about them. In September a deputation from the Triad gangs – a segment of society not known for its sentimentality – were arrested by the Kempeitai on their way to make contact with the British in Stanley.[167] A Sikh constable whose zeal in guarding the camp on behalf of the Japanese had earned him threats of reprisals from some of the British inmates surreptitiously offered a bottle of rum to his former chiefs in the Hong Kong Police and assured them, 'Sahib, Sahib, the Union Jack forever fluttering in my heart!'[168]

The nostalgia seems in any event to have been displayed chiefly by either the minority groups or the Westernized, English-speaking Chinese. It is not quite so clear how much yearning for the British was felt among the great mass of the Hong Kong Chinese public. One police sergeant of Canadian origin who had worked for the Special Branch on the eve of the war and could speak Cantonese found an opportunity to sample local opinion when he was brought from Stanley into town for questioning in the latter part of 1942. His impression was that the public were simultaneously anti-Japanese and anti-British – but pro-American.[169] This attitude to the British seems not to have changed altogether six months further on. A Portuguese merchant observed in the summer of 1943 that the Japanese whatever their other failings had been 'extremely successful in their anti-foreign, particularly their anti-British propaganda'.[170]

Even the young people who slipped away to sign up with the British resistance were not always filled first and foremost with a passionate loyalty to the Crown. Some may simply have wanted to strike a blow against the Japanese by any means possible, and others may have felt they were serving the Chinese as much as the British cause. Paul Tsui, who had nursed a boyhood dream of becoming President of China, initially tried to find a job with the Nationalists when he left Hong Kong in March 1942: it was only after he failed in that objective that he joined the BAAG.[171] One or two curious ripples were reported from Guilin, the south-west Chinese city to which the BAAG had transferred their headquarters in August 1942. At one point, for example, a Chinese who had formerly been a student of Ride's and had served under him in the Hong Kong Field Ambulance set up an Overseas Chinese Volunteer Unit (OCVU). This unit, which was said to have attracted 'a surprisingly large number' of former students of Hong Kong University and former members of the Hong Kong Volunteer Defence Corps, appears to have had the prime object of spreading propaganda against the British in general and Ride in particular. Too much importance should probably not be attached to this breakaway faction, which may well have owed something to the activities of Japanese *provocateurs*; but it is a reminder that all was not wholly secure for the British even at their own wartime base.[172]

Many Hong Kong Chinese were undoubtedly glad and grateful to line up with the British against the detested New Order. It didn't necessarily follow that they wished to find themselves back under British control when the war had been won. Large numbers of refugees from the colony had congregated in Guilin with their wives and children (incidentally earning the city the nickname of Little Hong Kong); and in August 1943 these refugees were subjected to a kind of informal opinion poll. The poll was conducted by Father Thomas Ryan, an Irish Jesuit priest who had ministered vigorously to the colony's subject communities in the pre-war years. Ryan found that the refugees subscribed to three basic outlooks. Some young people maintained 'ardently and vocally' that Britain should return Hong Kong to China without conditions at the end of the war. Persons of a 'sober and more intelligent disposition', who were often businessmen 'with a stake in Hong Kong', plumped for one or the other of two more moderate views. The majority felt that Hong Kong should be handed back after a transition period of some years during which local Chinese should be given access to the higher posts in the civil service and should by degrees take over the whole of the administration. A smaller group had been sufficiently disillusioned by what they had seen of Nationalist China to have no apparent wish for the colony to return to the mainland; but even they hoped for an 'improved version' of the political and social arrangements which had prevailed before the coming of the Japanese.[173]

The British regroup: 'A new angle of vision'

In the course of 1943 the authorities in London began to exhibit a steadily growing determination to get Hong Kong back. One reason was that the pressures from their Allies had diminished considerably. Following the con-clusion in January of the treaty abolishing British leases and privileges on the Chinese mainland Chiang Kai-shek and the Nationalist regime were quiescent so far as Hong Kong was concerned. This quiescence did not imply any sort of decline in Chinese irredentism. Rather the Nationalists seem to have judged, in the light of Britain's agreement to talk about the future of the New Terri-tories at the end of the war, that the colony was now in the bag. In his auto-biography *China's Destiny*, which appeared in March, Chiang remarked placidly that he was sure the British government would not 'allow the endur-ing friendship between China and England to be injured on account of this tiny plot of land'.[174] But at any rate Chungking saw nothing to be gained, for the moment, from a renewal of its diplomatic offensive. On a visit to London in July T. V. Soong, the Nationalist Foreign Minister, never so much as brought up the Hong Kong question.[175] President Roosevelt still hoped that the colony would be retroceded to China, and he and his colleagues continued sporadi-cally to suggest such a course in their meetings with British officials.[176] But the heat had gone out of the issue. The administration had no wish to goad the British unduly, and a junior minister at the British Foreign Office who trav-elled to the United States at the end of the summer observed that in general 'the Empire was not so much under fire as it had been'.[177]

In the meantime Whitehall had begun to come under a strong counter-vailing pressure to dig in its heels. Precisely because they had lost their old footholds on the mainland, British businessmen were adamant that Hong Kong must be kept after the end of the war as an offshore base. In February 1943 Edward Gent, the Assistant Under-Secretary in charge of Hong Kong affairs at the Colonial Office, received a visit from two prominent representa-tives of the business world. Even if the New Territories had to go, these visitors urged him, some effort must at least be made to preserve British sov-ereignty over Hong Kong Island and Kowloon. Gent assumed that this overture had been inspired by the China Association, the principal forum for British business interests in China; and sure enough on 27 May the Asso-ciation submitted a formal letter expounding the detailed argument for retaining Hong Kong. In the post-war period, they predicted, the colony would become the leading entrepot for Britain's trade with the mainland, and would probably also take the place of Shanghai as the major centre for British insur-ance business throughout the Far East. Above all it would be needed as a place of efficiency, honesty and enforceable contracts, an 'oasis of law and order' amid the turmoil which seemed likely to rage on the mainland and over the rest of East Asia for a long time to come.[178] This key point was drummed in further during the following months by two of the chiefs of the top British trading firms in the colony who had been safely absent in the Chinese interior when the Japanese launched their drive to the South. In August F. D. Roberts of Butterfield and Swire insisted to Gent that Britain should maintain its 'full position' in Hong Kong for at least ten or fifteen years, because no other 'sheltered place of business' would be available. John Keswick, the taipan of Jardine Matheson, advised Gent in September that 'until the East has settled down, to relinquish this last haven of security would be greatly detrimental to British trade'.[179]

Thinking in London was also shaped by less tangible factors. Not only the Chinese were moved by considerations of 'face'. As early as September 1942 the Under-Secretary in charge of the Far Eastern Department at the Foreign Office, Sir Maurice Peterson, had taken issue with the resigned attitude to the colony's fate which prevailed among most of his colleagues. 'In view of the ignominious circumstances in which we have been bundled out of Hong Kong', he declared, 'we owe it to ourselves to return there, and I personally do not believe that we will ever regain the respect of the East unless we do.'[180] By 1943 the same idea was beginning to be expressed in both military and intelligence circles.[181] And as British troops started to drive the Axis forces out of north Africa and southern Italy and the prospect of ultimate victory in Europe could clearly be glimpsed, officials began to display an increasing confidence that Hong Kong and the other colonies in the East could indeed be recovered, and that there was no reason why Britain should defer automatically to the demands of its Allies.

Under the impact of all these trends the authorities set about laying the groundwork for the resumption of British rule. The first step in this process was, naturally, to ensure that the British recovered physical possession of the colony from the Japanese forces. The recapture of Hong Kong became an important concern of a number of the British undercover organizations which were active in the Far East. One of these bodies was the Special Operations Executive (SOE), the organization responsible for sabotage, subversion and propaganda. Already in the first few months after the colony fell they had set up a China branch under the direction of John Keswick of Jardine Matheson, and had sought to stage sabotage operations in the Hong Kong area through a commando unit known as Z Force.[182] By the summer of 1943 they were busy devising the first in a series of projects for infiltrating British contingents back into Hong Kong. A second concerned entity was the BAAG. Formally an offshoot of MI9, the outfit in charge of promoting escapes from enemy-occupied territory, the BAAG had had from the moment of its inception a *raison d'être* more intricate than this formal purpose implied. John Keswick in Chungking observed that the BAAG would 'provide a useful force' in Guangdong province, which on account of its closeness to Hong Kong had 'always been British in outlook'.[183] From 1943 onwards, as the trickle of POW escapers dwindled to almost nothing, the strategic role of the BAAG became more and more prominent. MI9 delegates observed at a meeting with the Colonial Office in London that the BAAG through creating its widespread intelligence network had developed considerably from its original philanthropic and escape promotion activity 'which, nevertheless, still remained its cover *vis-à-vis* the Chinese'.[184]

In the light of Chiang Kai-shek's proclaimed designs on the colony any British preparations for retaking Hong Kong necessarily had to be made behind the backs of the Nationalist regime. Given however the British dependence on local help Chinese partners of some sort had inevitably to be enlisted for any workable plan. The obvious candidates were the Nationalists' deadly rivals, the Chinese Communist Party, with whose representatives British officers in the Hong Kong area had struck up such a pleasing rapport. Back in the early months of 1942 the head of Z Force, F. W. Kendall, is said to have hoped to use the East River guerrillas in an Allied reinvasion of Guangdong province, and to have supplied them to that end with money, arms, equipment and training. In July 1943 the SOE began to work out a more focused scheme which was known by the codeword Oblivion. The idea was that British agents should be landed to conduct sabotage operations in the Hong Kong docks and along the adjacent coast. The East River guerrillas would be well suited to help in these landings, since as the SOE noted approvingly 'they have no connection with Chungking and in fact have substantial prices on their heads'.[185] Based as they were in the colony's rural hinterland the guerrillas might also act as a buffer against any possible interference by Nationalist troops. In the following month the concept of British teamwork with the Communist partisans received a warm endorsement from Ride of the BAAG. In a memorandum to Brigadier G. E. Grimsdale, the head of the British Military Mission in Chungking, Ride suggested that '*de facto* recognition' should be given to the East River guerrillas. 'Their name should be changed from the Reds to the Hong Kong Guerrillas, they should be given definite prestige, armed and supported by us *and then I am certain no enemy would ever walk through the New Territories as the Japanese did*' [my italics].[186]

Once the colony had been physically secured for Britain the next step would be to instal a resuscitated colonial government. On 24 June 1943 the various branches of Whitehall concerned with Hong Kong exchanged views at a meeting of an inter-departmental committee which had been organized to work on Far Eastern Reconstruction. All agreed that the time had now come to assemble a 'nucleus administration' whose object would be to restore civil government to the colony as soon as possible after the Japanese had been overthrown.[187] In August a small band of nine veteran civil servants who had held posts in the colony in the pre-war years were accordingly formed into a Hong Kong Planning Unit within the Colonial Office, and by November they had started drafting the first British policies to be implemented in a recaptured Hong Kong.

As these various preparations moved forward, Britain's public stance on the colony's future started to harden considerably. By the autumn of 1943 British diplomats were fending off with increasing robustness the fitful American efforts to urge on them the necessity of 'doing the decent thing'. In November a political adviser to the State Department who was visiting London brought up, rather tentatively, the issue of Hong Kong's future in a discussion with counterparts from the Foreign Office and other British government bodies. 'The effect', he recalled, 'was electrifying.' The following morning he was hauled before Churchill, who delivered himself of a resounding harangue. Hong Kong, the Prime Minister explained, was a British creation which had benefited the entire world. It was British territory, and there was no good reason why it should cease to be such.[188] At the conference which took place some days later in Cairo between Churchill, Roosevelt and Chiang Kai-shek, the United States President quietly worked out with the Generalissimo the outlines of a compromise deal. The idea was that Britain would hand Hong Kong back to China as a magnanimous gesture, whereupon Chiang would with equal nobility declare it a free port and promise protection for British interests and residents. When the two Anglo-Saxon leaders adjourned in the midst of the talks to Tehran for their summit with Stalin, Roosevelt took the opportunity to propose this solution to his British comrade-in-arms. Churchill merely growled, 'I will not give away the British Empire.' We are told that he refused even to discuss the proposal.[189]

Yet for all the bravado the British position was still quite precarious. In the first place it seemed doubtful that the Nationalists would give Britain the chance to organize an effective striking force within reach of Hong Kong. In April 1942 Chiang Kai-shek had denied the SOE's Z Force the permission they needed to operate in southern China, and by the middle of the year he had personally ordered out of the country almost all of the Z Force personnel.[190] Three Z Force officers alone were allowed to remain, seconded to the BAAG on the strict understanding that they would be used exclusively for escape promotion activities. The BAAG were correctly perceived by Chungking as a British device for keeping a foot in the Hong Kong door, and their work was hedged about with all kinds of restrictions. Ride and his colleagues were only granted permission to function on condition that they would desist from engaging in political activities and would maintain close liaison with Chiang's spymaster, General Dai Li. All the BAAG's officers had to have passes issued by the Chungking government. Requests made by the BAAG to set up their own wireless stations in Nationalist-controlled areas close to the colony were persistently held up or vetoed, and it was only in 1943 that the outfit finally received the authority to instal a station at their new headquarters in Guilin.

Nationalist obstruction was only made more intense by the British efforts to team up with the Chinese Communist Party. Persuaded, in Chiang's famous metaphor, that the Japanese were a mere skin disease while the Communists were a disease of the heart, the Nationalists were terrified that the British might give a decisive advantage to their hated rivals. One of the reasons Z Force were expelled was that Kendall and his officers had been found to have gone independently to Guangdong to 'negotiate' with the East River guerrillas. The BAAG had barely taken shape when word leaked out that two Royal Scots privates on the run from Hong Kong had been training Tsoi Kwok-leung's followers in the use of Vickers machine-guns and other small arms: the Nationalists promptly shrieked that the BAAG had been training Communist bandits to fight them, and Ride was obliged to ensure that the two men were spirited out of China before any connection with his team could be proved.[191] In July 1942 the officers at the BAAG's advance base in Huizhou were allowed to dispatch a Forward Operational Group to make contact with the guerrillas on the understanding that such contact should be limited to pursuing the official aims of the BAAG. But the BAAG command were denied permission to send the Group any money or supplies, and relations with the Nationalist authorities worsened so alarmingly that in September the BAAG felt obliged to pull the Group out. The abatement of Nationalist diplomatic pressure over the Hong Kong issue which began to be noticeable in the following year was accompanied by no falling-off of the tensions in Guangdong, and in June 1943 matters came to a crisis. The BAAG had concocted a plan for establishing an observation post on the colony's outlying island of Lantau to keep watch on the movements of Japanese shipping. Such a post could only be set up under the protection of the Communists, who were active in Lantau as they were in most other parts of the New Territories. The BAAG consequently appealed to the Nationalist military chiefs in Huizhou for leave to supply the partisans in Lantau with a small quantity of arms and ammunition to help guard the post. The Nationalists flatly refused, and directed that all contact between the BAAG in Huizhou and the East River guerrillas must cease at once. The British felt they had little choice, and in August (apparently only days after Ride had urged Grimsdale that the guerrillas should be given full-blooded support) the BAAG severed all their ties with the East River band. All subsequent British attempts to negotiate with the Nationalists at a high level for the resumption of this strategic connection proved unsuccessful.[192]

Even if the British did manage to recover the colony any government they installed there would still have to come to some form of accommodation with the mainland regime. If Chiang Kai-shek and his followers insisted, for instance, there could be little doubt that the New Territories would have to be given back. 'Our attitude', proposed Gent of the Colonial Office in July 1943, 'should be in favour of retaining possession of the New Territories . . . *if that course is found to be politically practicable in postwar conditions vis-à-vis China*' [my italics].[193] If the New Territories were given back some attempt might conceivably be made to hang on to Hong Kong Island and Kowloon; but such an

endeavour would only be possible with a large helping hand from the mainland authorities. The reduced colony, Gent and his colleagues observed, would
have lost both Kai Tak airport and the water supply from the Shing Mun reser-
voir, and some sort of an Anglo-Chinese condominium would have to be
organized to ensure British access to these vital facilities. Even Churchill seems
tacitly to have accepted the need for a certain measure of compromise. In the
middle of the dressing-down he administered to the State Department adviser
in November the Prime Minister conceded that some new arrangement might
perhaps be devised with the Nationalists under which formal sovereignty
would be transferred to China, but the colony would remain under British
control.[194]

A restored colonial government would also need to find ways of rebuilding
its local support base. First and foremost the British faced the awkward
problem of how to handle the gentry. In the months after the colony fell there
had been signs of a massive backlash in expatriate circles against the community leaders who had acquiesced so tamely in the Japanese takeover. Angry
reports had made their way back to London from a whole range of sources –
from individual British and other Europeans who had managed to get out of
the colony, from Ride and his assistants at the BAAG headquarters in Guilin,
from Reeves at the British consulate in Macao. Particular opprobrium had
been heaped on the head of Sir Robert Kotewall. Rumour maintained that
Kotewall had been chosen by the Japanese as their Puppet Governor, and he
was said to have 'publicly made some venomous anti-British and fervently pro-
Japanese speeches'.[195] An Irish doctor debriefed by Ride added that Kotewall
was 'reported to have the tobacco monopoly in Hong Kong', that he now had
'plenty of money' and was 'buying up all kinds of silver, crystal, etc.'; and a
White Russian lady declared that Kotewall's daughters were 'among the few
women who seemed able to shop for anything save the bare necessities of
life'.[196] Sir Shouson Chow had been castigated alongside Kotewall as one of the
'two local bigwigs' who was vying with his colleague in 'pro-Japanese fervour
and anti-British advocacy'.[197]

The other gentry figures had also come in for their share of vitriol. Sir
Robert Ho Tung, for instance, had attracted some notice as he slipped to and
fro between Macao and Hong Kong in the spring and summer of 1942. An
employee of the British firm Dodwell and Company pointed out that the old
tycoon was said to have made a speech at a Japanese dinner praising the Co-
Prosperity Sphere and thanking the conquerors for all they had done for
China. The Dodwells man remarked grimly, 'He is a lad who is marked for the
gallows when we get back.' The critics were slower to catch up with Aw
Boon-haw, but catch up they did. One intelligence report drew attention to
the newspapers the Tiger Balm King was sponsoring under Japanese auspices
in both Hong Kong and Canton, describing him as 'a typical rich Overseas

Chinese, enterprising but politically an opportunist'. Reeves in Macao called him simply 'the damned old man'.[198]

But could Britain afford to write off the whole body of local leaders whom it had relied on for upwards of twenty years? From the perspective of Whitehall the answer was plainly no. The Colonial Office duly opened a file to house the accumulating sheaf of reports about 'Quislings and Collaborators', and the view was expressed that Kotewall and Chow might eventually have to be stripped of their knighthoods.[199] But no one was in any hurry to rush into action. As early as February 1942 W. B. L. Monson, the official who had charge of the quislings issue, remarked of the supposed choice of Kotewall as Puppet Governor, 'It is safer for us to reserve judgement of the person selected until the facts of his selection are clearer'.[200] From the summer of 1943, as the gentry started visibly to shift their ground, the officials in London began to display a marked tendency to give their former protégés the benefit of the doubt. In an analysis of Kotewall's Christmas broadcast that year Monson observed that the speech had been 'very carefully phrased' to compare Isogai's regime favourably with the chaos of the Gunseicho period rather than with the pre-war British era. 'I therefore read his speech as a sign that despite his eulogy of the [Isogai] administration Sir Robert Kotewall was really "hedging".'[201] A second official who came across the same broadcast a year later agreed with enthusiasm:

> I am most pleasantly surprised at the content of this speech. It seems to boil down to this – things got in a bloody mess at the time of the [initial] occupation but the Nips do seem to be trying to get things a bit better and to our surprise the arrangements often work out smoothly . . . That is what our Robert seems to be saying . . .
>
> I'm glad to see that he refrains from saying anything derogatory of our Government – if he refrains from comparisons, it may have been from the feeling that he's playing on a sticky wicket.
> Harmless stuff![202]

Sir Shouson Chow was viewed with even greater indulgence. N. L. Smith, a pre-war Colonial Secretary who had been named the first head of the Hong Kong Planning Unit, insisted that Chow had been 'a loyal servant of the British' and was 'violently anti-Japanese'. In any event he was 'too old to matter much now'.[203] Lesser figures on the two Chinese Councils such as Li Tse-fong, his brother Li Koon-chun and the comprador Kwok Chan seemed to Smith 'not a great deal worse than the postmen or sanitary employees who carried on the machinery of government'.[204] As for Sir Robert Ho Tung, Monson 'would not be prepared to say anything other than that he is keeping a foot in both camps'.[205]

Rather than harp on the possible sins of the bulk of the gentry, officials in London seized eagerly on the one gentry figure whom reports from Hong

12. Japanese soldiers advance to the Kowloon waterfront, 12 December 1941. Their approach is somewhat leisurely. The British have already left under fire from fifth columnists.

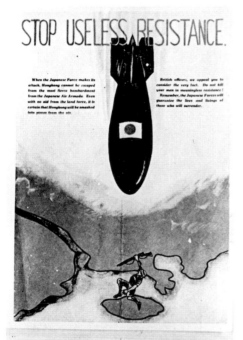

STOP USELESS RESISTANCE.

When the Japanese Force makes its attack, Hongkong cannot be escaped from the most fierce bombardment from the Japanese Air Armada. Even with no aid from the land force, it is certain that Hongkong will be smashed into pieces from the air.

British officers, we appeal you to consider the very fact. Do not kill your men in meaningless resistance! Remember, the Japanese Forces will guarantee the lives and livings of those who will surrender.

British officers and men! What do you expect in your useless resistance after having deen cornered in this small island of Hongkong? If you are waiting for the Chungking troops to stir up the Japanese rear it will only end in a fool's dream. The Malay Peninsula and the Philippines are now under the sway of Japanese forces and their fate is completely sealed.

Your comrades brought to Kowloon, have already been sent to Samchun and they are calmly enjoying a peaceful X'mas. you are et the cross-road now. It's all up to you whether you prefer death or save your life for the future.

We will give you the last chance for your reconsideration, If you surrender to us, the ultimatum ends at midnight of Dec. 26th

JAPANESE ARMY COMMANDER

13. Statue of Queen Alexandra pictured against the smoke from a burning oil tank.

14. In the days after the fall of Kowloon, Japanese propaganda leaflets were dropped to soften the Allied resistance on Hong Kong Island. Note the allusion to the Nationalist Chinese relief force on which British hopes were now pinned.

9. Only the small cluster of British radicals in Hong Kong were prepared to join forces with the Chinese against the threat from Japan in the pre-war years. Hilda Selwyn-Clarke (second from right) helps Mme Sun Yat-sen to ship relief supplies to the Chinese interior.

10. As the threat of invasion looms, the Hong Kong Volunteer Defence Corps drill outside the Southorn Stadium. Note the absence of Chinese members.

11. The new Governor, Sir Mark Young, confers with his generals in the New Territories, autumn 1941.

6. A contingent of the Hong Kong Police, about 1906. Note that the Indians are armed with guns, and the Chinese are not.

7. With admirable sang-froid, the Governor, Sir Henry May, inspects a guard of honour in Connaught Road shortly after his arrival in 1912. He has just been the object of an assassination attempt by a disgruntled Chinese. In the background a Japanese business hints at a threat for the future.

8. The Japanese threat draws closer. Friction at the Hong Kong border shortly after the Japanese capture of Canton in 1938.

4. Educating the gentry. Staff and students of Queen's College pictured in 1929.

5. Some of the products of this education went on to make fortunes. A signed photograph of Sir Robert Ho Tung.

Fanling Old Course 5th green.

2. The expatriate life. A British golfer attended by his Chinese caddy.

3. An expatriate party approached by Chinese beggars. Sometimes the contrasts could be stark.

1. Hong Kong in the late 1930s. The Hongkong and Shanghai Bank (right centre) dominates the Victoria skyline, but faces a challenge (left centre) from the Chinese-owned Bank of East Asia.

15. Japanese landing party storming ashore on Hong Kong Island. It was here that the British resistance got tough for a while.

16. Christmas night, 1941. The British leaders surrender in the Peninsula Hotel. On the right of the picture is General Maltby. In the centre, obscured by the blaze of the candlelight, is Governor Young.

17. The ones that got away. Admiral Chan Chak and his party of escaped British officers pictured on arrival at Huizhou, 29 December 1941. His arm in a sling, Chan Chak occupies a commanding position at the centre of the group.

18. Riding in triumph through Persepolis. Lieutenant-General Sakai leads his 23rd Army in its victory parade, 28 December 1941.

19. Victorious soldiers of the 23rd Army lounge beside one of the bronze lions guarding the entrance to the Hongkong and Shanghai Bank.

20. The first weeks of occupation, January 1942. Japanese propaganda van makes its way down Queen's Road Central proclaiming the new doctrine of Pan-Asiatic solidarity.

21. British POWs being marched off to internment.

22. The face of defeat. A contingent of British and Indian POWs. Soon the Indians will be separated from the British and subjected to 'intense propaganda'.

23. The uninterned. Watched by curious Chinese bystanders, a procession of British bankers are marched to work through the streets of occupied Hong Kong. They have been forced to help liquidate their own businesses for the benefit of the Japanese.

24. Shorn of their pre-war comforts, the British bankers gaze out from the dingy balcony of the Sun Wah Hotel.

25. Lieutenant-General Isogai Rensuke. The first Japanese Governor of Hong Kong showed some initial desire to court local favour, but the Imperial war effort mattered more.

26. Governor Isogai with the leaders of the two Chinese Councils. Putting a brave face on an unenviable situation are Sir Shouson Chow (to Isogai's right) and Sir Robert Kotewall (behind Isogai's left shoulder). Looking on grimly behind Chow are the pro-Japanese activists Chan Lim-pak and Lau Tit-shing.

27. The New Order. The Hongkong and Shanghai Bank building is now the Japanese Governor's Office. An Imperial Rescript has been enshrined in the monument which once housed the statue of Queen Victoria. And in the absence of motor transport the streets are dominated by rickshaws.

28. A source of resistance. Professor Lindsay Ride with his students in the Hong Kong University Physiology Department, 1941. Many of these students would go on to join his British Army Aid Group.

29. Convinced of his duty to take care of the uninterned Asian populace, SelwynSelwyn-Clarke persuaded the Japanese to let him continue in office as Director of Medical Services. Under this cover he also channelled surreptitious relief supplies to the Allied POWs and internees.

30. Racing at Happy Valley, 1944. Diversions were still available for the well-heeled.

31. Franklin Gimson's dogged assertion of British authority helped to fend off rival claims to Hong Kong in the uncertain fortnight that followed Emperor Hirohito's surrender broadcast. But he was forced to call in a bizarre range of allies.

32. 30 August 1945. Warships from Rear Admiral Harcourt's squadron creep across the deserted harbour towards Victoria. The unfinished Japanese war memorial still looms over the city. Note the relative lack of damage to buildings after four years of war.

33. Newly arrived British marines venture out from the Naval Dockyard. The name of a Japanese regiment is still scrawled on the entrance.

34. Rear Admiral Harcourt reads out the surrender terms to the Japanese Army and Navy chiefs. Looking on rather balefully at Harcourt's right is the Chinese Nationalist representative, General Pan Huaguo. The British had judged it advisable to offer the Nationalists a presence at the ceremony.

35. British troops celebrating outside the Luk Kwok Hotel in front of a captured Japanese flag. Mixed with them are a number of joyful Hong Kong Chinese. The war has brought the communities closer together.

36. Chinese labourers arrive to work in the dockyards, presenting their pre-war passes. Note their emaciation. Fearful of social unrest the restored British rulers took rapid action to create employment.

37. The reckoning. A first group of Japanese face trial for war crimes in March 1946. Most of the sentences passed, however, were surprisingly mild.

38. The inheritors. The post-war gentry leader Sir Sik-nin Chau signs a contract in 1970 with a director of Ikeda Construction Ltd, while the British look on.

Kong and south China had tended to depict in a favourable light. M. K. Lo, they observed, was reported to have 'worn the armband unwillingly', to have joined the Rehabilitation Advisory Committee 'only after being subjected to considerable pressure', to have been 'so violent in his opposition to everything Japanese that he was in considerable personal danger'.[206] As such he represented the natural starting-point for any British bid to reconstitute a gentry following, and attempts were accordingly initiated to reach out to him. As early as September–October 1942 a BAAG deputation made contact with Lo, who was said to have voiced gratifying pleasure that he 'had not been forgotten'.[207]

In the meantime steps were taken to cement the allegiance of those young Hong Kong Chinese and Eurasians who had left the colony and – for whatever reason – joined up with the BAAG. 'Wartime degrees' were conferred on a number of final-year students from Hong Kong University whom the invasion had deprived of the opportunity to sit their exams. (One of the beneficiaries was Paul Tsui.) All other students were given certificates in recognition of the parts of their courses which they had completed, and arrangements were made for them to continue their studies at universities in Free China, with the British government providing the funds.[208] Measures were also adopted to meet the needs of Asian ex-members of the Hong Kong Volunteer Defence Corps, of the Police Reserve and of the various branches of the old civil service. Relief payments were sent out from London by way of Chungking and distributed to almost 1,000 of the exiled Hong Kong Chinese in Guilin.[209] By September 1943 British officials in London were pleased to hear from one of their diplomats who had spoken to Father Ryan in 'Little Hong Kong' that this relief drive had 'created a very favourable impression'.[210] In Macao similarly one of Reeves's tasks was to care for the stream of Chinese, Indian, Eurasian and (especially) Portuguese refugees who poured in from Hong Kong. Modest subsidies were made available to all British subjects, and an English-language curriculum was organized for Hong Kong boys at the St Luiz Gonzaga School.

All these thoughtful measures, however, were still not entirely enough to produce the desired local enthusiasm for a British return. By September 1943 the officials in London were also getting news, once again through the medium of Father Ryan, of the appetite which existed among the Hong Kong Chinese refugees in Guilin for post-war social and political change.

Virtually from the earliest days of the occupation Whitehall had begun to appreciate that if British rule were to be restored in Hong Kong it would have to be on an altogether different basis from that of the past. The point was made less than a month after the fall of the colony by Ronald Hall, the saintly and impulsive Bishop of Hong Kong who had unsettled the expatriates in the pre-war years through his championship of the Chinese subject masses. Bishop Hall had by accident been away from Hong Kong when the Japanese attacked, on sabbatical giving a series of lectures at a theological college in the United States.

Unable to travel straight back to his see, he instead made for London and on 16 January 1942 called at the Colonial Office for a conversation with Gent. At the end of the meeting he left behind a memorandum, humbly handwritten on a few scraps of paper. 'The recent disaster', he observed, 'gives a chance for radical changes when the administration of Hong Kong by Britain is resumed.' In the first place he recommended that the upper reaches of the colony's civil service should be thrown open to all Hong Kong Chinese and Eurasians who were British subjects. Secondly he proposed that the tiny move which had been made towards representative government in the pre-war decades should be 'advanced a stage'. An electorate should be constituted to choose all the 'unofficial' members not merely of the feeble Urban Council but of the Legislative Council as well; and all men and women who had obtained school certificate qualifications should be entitled to vote. Finally he advised that the colony's post-war government should provide larger subsidies to the social services, and that public housing should be created with vision and energy as 'a matter of justice for the poor'.[211] His message delivered, the Bishop moved on to the still unconquered parts of his diocese in the south China hinterland, where he devoted himself to relief work, including the maintenance of the Hong Kong Chinese refugees. (Two years later he would earn himself a niche in history by ordaining a Chinese deaconess, Florence Lei Tim-oi, to minister to the Protestant refugees in Macao as the Church of England's first woman priest. Anglican thought was still fifty years away from accepting this novelty, and the *Church Times* referred to the Bishop as 'a wild man of the woods'.)[212]

Gent and his colleagues were not firebrands in the mould of the Bishop. Their vocation was not to pursue social justice for its own sake, but to do what they could to make sure that Hong Kong carried on as a British domain. But they too were compelled to admit there was force in the Bishop's demands for reform. Sydney Caine, who had served as the colony's Financial Secretary in the pre-war years and at that time had looked on the Bishop's activities with a certain amount of sardonic amusement, now agreed with him that any future British administration would have to be 'radically changed in all sorts of ways'.[213]

Some of the grounds for the new thinking in the Colonial Office have been preserved in a series of post-mortem-type documents written by David MacDougall, the sensitive information chief who returned to Whitehall in the spring of 1942 after breaking out of the overrun colony in the company of Admiral Chan Chak. On his way back to London MacDougall had thought long and hard about the reasons for the December catastrophe; and in particular he had been impressed by the critique of Britain's performance that he had found circulating among the Nationalists in Chungking. He agreed with the Nationalists that the fall of the colony had been due in large part to the British failure to make any adequate use of Hong Kong Chinese manpower.

Even if you allowed for fifth columnists and 'jellyfish who ooze quietly to the winning side' there could not, in his view, have been fewer than 75,000 out of a total of 300,000 able-bodied Chinese men who might have been mobilized to resist the invasion; and the exclusive reliance which the British instead chose to place on less than 12,000 European and Indian troops could 'hardly have been duplicated in history since small mercenary armies defended the rich cities of mediaeval Europe'.[214] He agreed, too, with the judgement expressed in Chungking that the colony might have been saved if the British had made up their minds to work wholeheartedly with the Nationalists in the year which preceded the onslaught, rather than turning to them at the very last minute – yet another manifestation of the chronic British unwillingness to trust the Chinese.[215] Looking back further MacDougall deplored the lack of a 'larger purpose' in the pre-war running of the colony. 'Something', he noted, 'was missing from both Government and governed which prevented the fusion of the community into a living whole.' Seen from this standpoint the Japanese conquest might not necessarily be a total disaster, but a chance for the British to start out again with a clean slate. 'I hope it is true', MacDougall wrote glee-fully, 'that the statues have been removed from Statue Square.'[216]

The Colonial Office were also aware that internal reform was one way to protect British rule in Hong Kong from the external challenge. Even suppos-ing the British contrived to win back full control of the colony any policies they pursued would require the tacit consent of the mainland Chinese gov-ernment. And some signs of enlightenment would be essential if Britain were to fend off the likely pressure from its United States ally to give Hong Kong up. 'I am near thinking', MacDougall observed after running the gauntlet of hostile comment at the Mont Tremblant conference of December 1942, 'that nothing would be less to the liking of American liberals than that we should reform beyond the possibility of reproach or attack.'[217]

On these grounds the Colonial Office began to apply to Hong Kong what they themselves described as 'a new angle of vision'.[218] Right from the outset Gent's team appear to have accepted the Bishop's contention that the time had now come to remove the absolute bar which existed to the advancement of non-Europeans in the civil service. The idea of elections to the Legislative Council was viewed with more caution; but by the middle of 1943 the team had concluded that they would 'probably have to consider a more representa-tive form of local government'.[219] The embryo post-war administration that had been set up in the shape of the Hong Kong Planning Unit was given the brief of advising on the attitude of the subject communities and the approaches most likely to win their support. And to comply with the wishes of the United States it was laid down that the government traffic in opium should at last be abolished and that the consumption of opium should be completely stamped out.

Everything must change, so that nothing might change.

New ideas were also beginning to make a certain amount of headway among the British held captive in Stanley camp. In May 1942 Kenneth Uttley the government doctor recorded that many of the internees were 'quite obviously doing a lot of very serious thinking'.[220] The enforced leisure of internment left ample scope for reflection; and the mood of despair and nostalgia which had engulfed the expatriates after the British surrender seems by this stage to have given way, in some quarters at least, to a more positive frame of mind. Two weeks later internees were 'going about quite cheerily making preparations to carry on and reconstruct the colony after the war'; and by the following April a group of them were meeting on a regular basis to discuss the problems which would have to be grappled with in a post-war Hong Kong. 'We are alive', Uttley noted, 'to the necessity of thinking ahead'.[221]

Underlying this mood was a definite shift in attitude towards Hong Kong's subject peoples. Some at least of the internees had learned from their suffering. One recalled that captivity 'gave us a new understanding and respect for the poor and destitute of every country'.[222] Mixed in with the camp's other inmates were a number of Eurasian women married to lower-class Europeans who had come into Stanley voluntarily to be with their spouses. The more thoughtful expatriates started to view these Eurasians with new eyes and to draw close to them for the first time. In such basic conditions, one lady remembered, the people you came to value were the ones (irrespective of race) whom you found most congenial and not, as before the war, those who dressed the most elegantly, or who gave the best parties. Some of the internees had also grasped that the Asian population beyond the camp boundaries were worse off than they were – that if they were malnourished, the townsfolk were starving. And in Stanley as in Whitehall there seems to have been a dawning perception that the debacle of December 1941 had been more than just military; that it had in some measure been due to grave flaws in the pre-war order of things. An interned clergyman informed his congregation one Sunday that they were in the camp 'as a punishment for the bad ways into which Hong Kong had got'.[223]

The change of heart was undoubtedly not universal. Many of the captive British persisted in the troglodyte attitudes they had held to before the war. Quite a number, for instance, were heard to mutter that if it wasn't for all these Eurasians there might be more food for them.[224] Little wish for reform was displayed, on the whole, by the businessmen and professionals, the rebels who at the start of internment had thrown off the authority of the pre-war administrators and had got the camp operating on democratic lines. Most of these rebels were simply the heirs of the disgruntled expatriates who had agitated against the colonial government in 1894–6 and 1916–23. The democracy they were after was strictly for Europeans. One of them put the case for the insurrection in terms that hadn't perceptibly altered in the last fifty years. His creed was that 'in a British Crown Colony the European subjects of His Majesty were not bound by the same laws as the natives of that Colony and were not subject to the authority of the Governor'.[225]

Among the discarded officials, however, the spirit of renovation was lively. Several of these officials had tinkered before the invasion with ideas for economic and social improvement – modest schemes which they now felt impelled to elaborate in their seclusion behind the barbed wire. One of the more active planners was a Dr G. A. C. Herklots, a Reader in Biology at Hong Kong University who in 1941 had been made head of a newly established Fisheries Research Station. Herklots settled down to devising a programme for the development of local fisheries which included, as one of its principal features, a system for the cooperative marketing of the fishing catch. (Presumably unknown to Herklots, his plan tallied closely with the actual measures the Japanese were introducing to modernize the colony's fishing arrangements at exactly this time.) Herklots also helped to draw up a project for the wholesale marketing of vegetables as part of an overall bid to improve the conditions of villagers in the New Territories. In October 1943 the interned Police Commissioner, John Pennefather-Evans, completed a document he entitled an 'Interim Report on the Hong Kong Police'. 'The complete break with old Hong Kong caused by the war', he declared, 'is a unique opportunity to start afresh.' Pennefather-Evans was all too aware of the massive defection of non-Europeans from the Police Force which had taken place during the two weeks of the Japanese onslaught: in his eyes, however, the solution was more trust, not less. First and foremost he urged that the Force should make a point of employing more Asiatics in responsible jobs. 'A more educated type of Chinese' should be recruited, along with 'a few Eurasian lads of good standing'. The suspicious old practice of taking HK$50 from each Asiatic recruit as a bond for good behaviour should be done away with, and the recruits should be given better training and more acceptable living and working conditions. The European contingent who monopolized the rank of inspector should be phased out: in the meantime they should be given more strenuous instruction in the Cantonese language, and in general 'every effort should be made to enlarge the outlook and contacts of European members of the Force'. A devout, sober-sided adherent of the Oxford Christian Group, Pennefather-Evans wasn't altogether a model of enlightenment. He still thought that European police alone should be allowed their own quarters since 'Asiatics do not mind communal living'. He still believed that it was desirable to have non-Cantonese policemen to deal with Cantonese crowds. And he remained vehemently opposed to mixed marriages between European policemen and Asian women because of the 'low standards of morality' typical of the lower-class women who contracted such marriages and because it was 'difficult to have mixed partners in the European quarters without causing dissatisfaction'. But he was able to see that the post-war Hong Kong would be a substantially different place from its former self. He also reckoned that China, as a 'modern, progressive and energetic' country, was likely to be 'extremely critical' of any retention in Hong Kong of what it considered to be 'outmoded ways'.[226]

The prime mover behind the conceptual ferment, however, was not a long-standing Hong Kong civil servant but Franklin Gimson, the Colonial Secretary who had arrived in Hong Kong on the day before the 23rd Army attacked. We last met Gimson struggling to assert his authority as the King's representative in the camp in the teeth of the insurgent expatriates. Within a few months he had managed to come out on top. By May 1942 he was said to be 'slowly but surely' prevailing over the democrats in the British Communal Council.[227] By July, with the help of a petition submitted by 1,300 internees who had been unimpressed by the performance of their elected delegates, he had purged the Council and its chairman, Nielsen, and had taken over as chairman himself. In August he was able to bring about the replacement of the Council with a tamer body, the British Community Council, which was limited to a largely advisory role; though he was still not allowed to appoint any members of the old pre-war government, and he continued to have to live with block elections and the carping of elected block spokesmen for at least two more years.[228]

The Colonial Secretary was not, at first glance, one of nature's liberals. A diary he kept in the camp indicates that he found any criticism to be almost intolerable. In his eyes Nielsen and all the rest of the expatriate democrats were members of 'a subversive organization', and even the defanged British Community Council was 'a revolutionary body'. On one occasion he permitted himself the Cromwellian thought that 'if [the Council's] antagonistic attitude continues or is in any way accentuated I shall have to see whether the services of this body are really of any value to the administration'.[229] Only Gimson would have 'had a dream in which I refused to discuss anything about the military operations in Hong Kong'.[230] Only Gimson, in the context of a Japanese prison camp, would have chosen to describe himself as the Camp Commandant (he was later obliged to soften this title to Representative of Internees).[231] Viewing himself – with some justice – as the only figure in camp with a sufficient sense of diplomacy to deal with the Japanese authorities, he seems at times to have felt more at home with his captors than with his own unruly compatriots.[232] He was even willing, when his own remonstrations appeared ineffective, to call in the Japanese camp supervisors to help him keep order. In August 1943, for example, he appealed to the ex-barber Yamashita to help him sort out a British delinquent. Yamashita obligingly promised to deal with the man 'by threatening to send him to gaol if he did not reform'.[233]

Yet this crusty autocrat was also keenly conscious of the need for social, economic and political innovation in a post-war Hong Kong. In common with most of his colleagues in the Colonial Service, he combined a firm faith in the benefits of British rule with a sense of duty towards the whole population. He looked with disdain on the self-absorbed expatriate merchants, 'unable to consider any other world than that in which they can make money and retire'.[234] Much of his previous career had been spent in Ceylon, a colony of progressive complexion which had brought in a large measure of representative government and where he had 'naturally identified himself with the local inhabitants'. From this standpoint he had equally little use for the pre-war officials in Hong Kong, most of whom he found 'woefully backward' in their views on the way in which colonies ought to be run.[235] And regardless of his personal inclinations, Gimson saw himself as the faithful executor of Whitehall's designs. He had entered the camp well abreast of the latest advances in British imperial thinking, and in some subterranean way he contrived to remain so. By the summer of 1942 he was smuggling messages out of Stanley to the Colonial Office. It isn't clear what replies he received, or how they may have travelled, for Gimson was careful not to entrust any hint of outside contacts to a diary which might very easily be seized by the Japanese. Other internees however have testified that he knew all about the wireless link which a group of his colleagues maintained with the BAAG between April and July 1943 – the very period when the Colonial Office made up their minds that a more liberal constitution would probably be required for Hong Kong and decided to organize the Hong Kong Planning Unit.[236]

Whatever the truth about his channels of communication, from the moment he started to gain the upper hand in the Stanley power struggle Gimson went hammer and tongs to promote the new thinking. In a memorandum of 23 July 1942 he informed the Colonial Office that steps were 'being taken as fast as possible to educate public opinion'.[237] He launched or encouraged most of the committees which were being formed to discuss post-war reconstruction, and chose suitable experts to serve on them. He himself played a vigorous, even a dominating part in these discussions, trying as he put it 'to persuade people to attune their minds to post-war conditions'.[238] Between June 1943 and June 1944 he was busy arguing in one group or another that more concern should be shown for Hong Kong Chinese labour, that the banks should play a more active role in financing commercial enterprise and that more intensive training should be given to entrants into the Hong Kong civil service. He urged the admission of popularly elected Chinese representatives to the Legislative Council, and stressed that 'in future the Chinese will have to play a bigger part in Hong Kong and the Europeans will have to rely on their cooperation more than they have done in the past'.[239] He suggested that the antipathy between Europeans and Asians which was to be found in Hong Kong was based on more than mere skin colour, and that when the war was over, the standard of living of upper-class Europeans would have to be

'considerably reduced'.[240] In December 1943 this sniffer-out of expatriate revolution was pleased to find Police Commissioner Pennefather-Evans 'quite
receptive' of 'the rather revolutionary ideas that I hope will be introduced into
Hong Kong when we reoccupy it'.[241]

These suggestions were not designed to prepare Hong Kong for its rever-
sion to China. For Gimson as much as for the Colonial Office in London, the
name of the game was to restore British rule; and he made the first practical
moves a full year before they did. At the end of June 1942 the American contingent in Stanley were shipped off home as part of a prisoner exchange which
had been agreed between the United States and Japan. The British internees
not surprisingly urged that their government should be asked to make a similar
arrangement for them. But Gimson said no. He informed his compatriots that
they had no case for demanding repatriation: Hong Kong was 'British territory as much as Britain itself', and in any event the shipping which would have
to be sent to collect them was needed elsewhere.[242] His underlying reasons were
set out in the secret memorandum which he addressed to Whitehall on 23 July.
While a certain number of internees could perhaps be evacuated to ease the
food shortage it was, he insisted, imperative that 'a nucleus of British officials
and residents' should remain in the camp. In effect they were Britain's stake in
the colony. Any wholesale repatriation would be construed as implying that
the British had abandoned Hong Kong to its fate. It would highlight the colonial aspect of the British presence, and could jeopardize Britain's chances of
prevailing in any diplomatic tussle that might break out over Hong Kong with
the Americans and the Chinese Nationalists at the end of the war.[243] Once again
the expatriates found that their personal welfare had to take second place to
strategic considerations. We are told that a group of them went over Gimson's
head and petitioned their Japanese captors to let them go. In the end they were
forced to accept the bleak fact that they would have to languish behind the
barbed wire for as long as the war went on. But they seethed with resentment,
and Gimson's obstruction still rankled in the memories of some of them over
forty years later.[244]

The Colonial Secretary pressed on imperturbably. His other concern was to
fill the power vacuum that a Japanese collapse would create in Hong Kong. He
was trying, he explained to Whitehall, to line up a skeleton government of 'men
loyal to the best interests of the Empire' who could march out of the camp and
impose their authority the moment the war was won.[245] Britain would have
to help him by rushing in a supply of the old colonial currency – HK$100 m-
worth of freshly minted banknotes, of which half should come in the lowest
denomination of HK$1. Immediate military support would be needed, if pos-
sible from the air, as there would be many armed Chinese at large in the colony:
at the same time officials aware of the new imperial thinking would have to
be sent to assure the Chinese public that Britain intended no return to the

alienating policies of the past.[246] In the course of 1943 Gimson continued to 'meditate on the possibilities of the reoccupation of Hong Kong by the British', and to siphon his ideas back to the Colonial Office through any courier who presented himself.[247] Gent and his colleagues initially smiled at the exertions of this 'stout-hearted personage'.[248] But Gimson had grasped earlier than anyone else that as soon as Japan was defeated a race would be on between the Allies for the *de facto* control of the colony; and it was a race which the British would have to win.

CHAPTER FIVE

The End Game

The Japanese shrug their shoulders

From the final quarter of 1943 conditions in Hong Kong were growing worse by the day. The American air raids were becoming incessant, and combined with the onslaught of prowling submarines were choking off all the colony's communications and trade. Japanese ships 'couldn't stick a nose out of the harbour' without getting strafed, bombed or torpedoed, and a number which tried to break out, by themselves or in convoy, were observed being miserably towed back again.[1] Food was no longer arriving, and in mid-April 1944 the Governor's Office were obliged to abandon the rice distribution scheme which had been devised two years earlier by the 'Mayor of Hong Kong'. Similar difficulties were mounting with fuel. Firewood was said to be as scarce and expensive as cassia: even where food could be found, there might no longer be any way to cook it. Buses and trams disappeared from the streets owing to the shortage of petrol, and the media proudly announced the introduction of hand-cart, rickshaw and tricycle services. By August the coal stocks were exhausted. The power stations could no longer supply electricity, industrial activity ground to a halt and the colony was plunged into darkness as soon as night fell. Prices of all goods shot up uncontrollably: the regime churned out vast amounts of their scrip in a bid to keep pace with the soaring inflation, but the only result was that the scrip lost what little value it had had. By November a military yen was reckoned to be worth about two thirds of a farthing on the international market. The colony's plight was summed up by Beth Woo, a former Chinese resident who passed through briefly during 1944 and called on some friends who had chosen to stay put. 'Hong Kong is dead', she reported informing them, 'and so they will be too.'[2]

In the meantime the news that seeped into the colony spelled more and more unmistakably the approaching demise of the Japanese Empire. In June 1944 Anglo-American troops staged their landing in Normandy – the begin-

ning of the end for Japan's German ally. In the following month the fall of
the Pacific island of Saipan gave the United States Navy its first foothold on
pre-war Japanese soil, and by the last week of October the Marines were across
the whole ocean and storming ashore in the Philippines. In November B-29s
of the United States Air Force started launching large-scale raids against
Japanese cities, and before the end of February 1945 the first fire-bombs were
falling on Tokyo.

Against this sombre background the regime made an effort to keep up
appearances. On 20 February 1944 the second anniversary of the founding of
the Governor's Office was celebrated at the first function to be held in the
newly completed Government House. The festivities had to be toned down in
keeping with the colony's reduced circumstances; but Governor Isogai told
Kotewall and his colleagues to make sure the public did not get the mis-
leading impression that the war wasn't going too well. In the course of the next
year the United States advance across the Pacific was portrayed as a series of
Pyrrhic victories that were draining the life-blood from the American forces;
and the fire-bombing of Tokyo was announced in a statement of incoherent
mendacity worthy of Bunter. 'Tokyo had not been bombed, the damage was
very slight and only a few fires had been started. Three American planes
brought down over Tokyo were on exhibition. No raid had taken place.'[3]

The authorities still sought to play on the old theme of pan-Asiatic frater-
nity. Hong Kong went on being held up as a testing-ground for developing
a model friendship between the Chinese and Japanese peoples,[4] and the
Governor continued to advertise his personal dedication to achieving that
goal. In the spring of 1944, on a brief tour of the New Territories, he paid his
respects at a shrine which had been put up by residents of the market town of
Yuen Long to commemorate a number of their ancestors who had been killed
resisting the British occupation of the area half a century earlier. In October
he once again displayed his enthusiasm for Chinese culture by buying the
work of a local painter which had been included in an art exhibition at the
Matsuzakaya department store.

The regime even took one or two new initiatives in an apparent attempt to
respond to the groundswell of discontent and recoup the support of the gentry
and middle classes. In October 1943 Isogai announced the establishment of a
new civilian law court divided into a civil and a criminal branch. The previous exclusive reliance on martial law, he observed to Kotewall and the other
Chinese Representatives, had been ineffective from the point of view of reassuring people and 'enabling them to live in peace and work contentedly'.[5]
In December a general drive was proclaimed to cut down on red tape. All
the decrees which had been issued since the takeover were to be looked at
again, in particular the rules which had been drawn up to provide for the close
supervision of every movement in and out of the colony and every change of

residence inside its limits. Fitful efforts were now at last made to address the gentry's complaints about Kempeitai lawlessness. Isogai told Colonel Noma to carry out 'some rectification' of the way in which arrests were being conducted as part of the mass deportation scheme. He foresaw that the random arrests which were taking place of respectable citizens would 'affect the feelings of the population very much'.[6] Similar mild reproaches were voiced in the following year about the widespread use of torture in Kempeitai prisons. On three occasions between September and November 1944 the Governor is said to have passed on complaints to Noma and asked him to tighten up on the conduct of his gendarmes.[7]

Much publicity was given to a new deal designed seemingly to improve the conditions of the local business community. One of the major features of the cutback in bureaucracy which the regime announced in December 1943 was a relaxation of the curbs on trade. From now on permits would no longer be needed to bring foodstuffs into the colony from most outside ports, though the shipments would still have to be reported to the authorities on arrival. Merchants wishing to launch a new company would still have to submit particulars to the Governor's Office; but they would no longer be called on, as they had been formerly, to obtain the approval of the Kempeitai. In a typically cloying simile Isogai likened the regime's policy towards local business to the 'handling of an infant who has to be given a special diet of milk etc. at first until it is able to assimilate other food, after which a change is then made'.[8]

In the course of 1944 this new liberal policy was carried forward amid still more fanfare with the lifting of a whole series of irksome constraints. In February compensation at last began to be paid to the gentry for the goods that had been sealed off in the godowns, and the repayments went on intermittently through the first half of the year. 'Nothing like this', the *Hong Kong News* observed proudly, 'has ever occurred in any occupied territory during wartime'.[9] At the start of September the Japanese-only Hong Kong Commercial Federation was abolished and replaced by a new Trade Association in which local Chinese firms were allowed to take part. Prominent local businessmen now had for the first time the chance to engage in transactions outside the colony's immediate neighbourhood.[10] In mid-November a certain amount of new scope was created in turn for the banking sector. An announcement was made that Chinese banks were now free to accept remittances from the public for Shanghai and other nearby ports. Some days later it turned out that this particular privilege had been extended to the Bank of East Asia only; but other Chinese banks along with the Bank of East Asia now had clearance to deal for the first time in mortgages and loans.[11] And in the background to all this the restrictions imposed on routine import business continued to be pared away. In the first months of 1944 the authorities lifted all the remaining curbs on the import of firewood and textiles. By November approval was no longer required from the government for the import of goods of any kind.

Some solicitude still went on being shown by the Japanese for the physical sustenance of the local elite. In November 1943 the garrison troops joined hands with the South China Expeditionary Force on the mainland to clear the Nationalists from the stretch of the Kowloon–Canton railway line between Shenzhen on the border and the town of Shilong, and the following month the line was formally declared open for the first time in six years. Hope was now held out for new shipments of rice and vegetables overland from Guangdong province which would offset to some extent the colony's near-total inability to bring goods in by sea. In the meantime the elite were to be shielded from the worst effects of the regime's decision to abandon the distribution of rice to the Chinese masses. In the spring of 1944 the authorities made it clear that rice rations would still be maintained for those people directly involved in the war effort and the reconstruction of the 'new Hong Kong'. This meant in practice the members of the two Chinese Councils, the staff of the Governor's Office and the District Bureaux and the employees of firms working closely with the Imperial forces. Rice supplies were also to be kept up for the families of people in these categories. From time to time for good measure a few little extras were handed out for the upkeep of the Indian minority. On one occasion in January 1944 a special donation of M¥1000 was made by the Governor's Office to the Indians through the intercession of their guardian angel, Lieutenant-Colonel Endo.

In addition concern was being displayed for the first time for the non-material side of the elite's existence. In line with their general push to root out Western influence the Imperial forces had treated with contempt and hostility the Christianity which (in its various guises) had been widely practised by the gentry and middle classes and in particular by the Eurasians and Portuguese. All religious societies had had to be registered, and many churches had been used for secular purposes: St John's Cathedral, for instance, had been relieved of its role as a stable only to be converted into a social club for the Yamato-kai. From the autumn of 1943, however, an improvement began to be engineered by Major-General Suganami Ichiro, who had taken over from Arisue the previous December as the regime's Chief of Staff. Suganami appears to have had a certain amount of puzzled respect for the Christian faith. When a group of young officers were proposing to turn the Baptist Church in Kowloon into an army brothel, he expostulated that they might as well burn it down and have done with it. But more to the point he considered that their attitude to religion had been one of the reasons why the Japanese rulers had been 'losing the hearts of the people'.[12] He accordingly arranged for a Protestant clergyman named Samejima Moritaka to come out from Japan and assume the task of guiding and helping the local Christian communities and mediating between the troops and the Church. He told Samejima to mention his name and inform him if trouble arose with the military and (especially) the Kempeitai, and promised that he would do his best to step in.[13] By 1944 Christian services were getting respectfully publicized in the pages of the *Hong Kong News*; and in August Samejima and his Chinese colleagues were able to hold a five-day series of revival meetings in Wanchai.

Finally an endeavour was made to keep up the spirits of the more prosperous classes through recreation. The media carried regular notices of softball or basketball matches, of miniature football fixtures with Canton or Macao. Gaunt, sweat-streaked ponies brought in from Japan limped around the Happy Valley racecourse each Sunday, while a band played the popular hit 'Miss Canton'. The public must still have their circuses, even if the bread had run short.

At the end of 1944 the attempt to rebuild local sympathy seemed to gain further impetus from an unexpected leadership change. On Christmas Eve it was announced suddenly that Governor Isogai was being transferred to a post in Japan. Festooned with tributes to his 'Rule of Love',[14] Isogai set off home early in the New Year and was replaced by Lieutenant-General Tanaka Hisakazu – the same Tanaka who had directed the Japanese landing in Guangdong province in October 1938. In the subsequent years Tanaka had continued to head campaigns in the province, and he now occupied Sakai's former post as commander of the 23rd Army in Canton. Then in February Colonel Noma was recalled and succeeded as chief of the Kempeitai by Lieutenant-Colonel Kanazawa Asao, a Kempeitai officer who had been brought down from Manchuria and had served for the previous six months in the Governor's Office as assistant to the Chief of Staff.

Up to a point this changeover was a matter of straightforward court politics. In July 1944 Premier Tojo had fallen from power in Tokyo as a result of the loss of Saipan. And with that the writing had been on the wall for the elderly Isogai, who owed his position entirely to Tojo's patronage.[15] Isogai's fall in turn meant the end for his old associate Noma. According to Noma the outgoing Governor summoned him and informed him that since he was going back to Japan he was making arrangements for Noma to go back too. But there are also signs that the change was inspired in some measure by a wish on the part of the Army to check the power and abuses of the Kempeitai in Hong Kong. Talk had been current for some time in both the Army Ministry in Tokyo and the Army garrison in the colony that the Hong Kong Kempeitai were 'deteriorating'. Colonel Noma is said to have been sent back to Japan 'partly for this reason';[16] and certainly the first few weeks of the new administration were marked by a systematic drive to clip the Kempeitai's wings. In the course of February 1945 about 100 of the 150 members of the Kempeitai in the colony were replaced by new personnel shunted in from Canton. At the end of that month Governor Tanaka stripped the Kempeitai of the extraordinary additional power they had assumed of directing routine police affairs, and confined them to their proper functions of military policing and counter-subversion. Kanazawa, who from now on wore two hats as Kempeitai chief and Police Commissioner, seems to have made some attempt to correct the abuses that had been rife in the Kempeitai during Noma's reign. Corruption and torture, he later claimed, were curtailed, and the gendarmes were instructed to be 'kind and bright' in performing their duties.[17] Local testimony suggests that there was a grain of truth in Kanazawa's assertions. Random killings are said to have diminished, and a number of citizens who had been imprisoned for years are said to have been released.[18]

In several other areas the display of improvement which had been made during the last year of Isogai's rule was pushed ahead with new vigour. The measures designed to free up local business were carried to still greater lengths. Export as well as import procedures were now being simplified, and in February 1945 clearance was given to export virtually anything from the colony except precious metals, machinery and electrical equipment. The regime by this stage appeared to observers to have 'abandoned any attempt at interference or control'.[19] In March, one more step in the overall drive to cut down on bureaucracy, the apparatus of the Governor's Office was streamlined: the various sections which had handled civil affairs, finance, communications and so forth were amalgamated into two super-sections, a No. 1 Department and a No. 2 Department, whose principal tasks were respectively to increase production and to promote communications and trade. More and more stress was placed on the bid to get food supplies in from Guangdong province, and Tanaka was indeed on record as advocating the economic 'unification' of Hong Kong and Canton.[20] Still more endeavour was made to lay on diversions. One of the new Governor's first acts was to rescind the order issued by his predecessor in the name of Oriental morality banning the opening of 'dancing and other recreational centres'.[21] No longer, furthermore, would certain choice resorts such as the red light district of Wanchai be restricted to Japanese only. At the end of March Kanazawa announced that from now on 'all other persons' would be permitted to enter the various 'places of amusement' in Hong Kong.[22]

But it was all so much window-dressing. In the first place, however much their press might bleat about imminent victory, the leading Japanese in the colony were well aware they were beaten. As early as January 1943, two months after the first American air raid, Colonel Noma the Kempeitai chief had called a meeting of all the Japanese residents. He had told them that the Allies were bound to fight to recover the colony, and that they should expect to die in a last-ditch stand.[23] The general foreboding grew steadily in the course of the next two years. In July 1944, when Saipan fell, one or two of the camp officials in Stanley started asking British internees to provide them with references, seemingly with a view to the prospect of post-war tribunals. At a meeting with one of these officials, Maejima, Gimson mentioned a rumour he had heard that the Navy would shortly take over the running of the camp. Maejima asked glumly if it was the American Navy.[24] In February 1945 orders were issued by the Army Ministry in Tokyo for the evacuation of all Japanese women and children from the colony. Japanese businessmen started whispering (when the military were safely out of earshot), 'It looks as though this war can't go on for much longer', and a number of them contrived to get themselves evicted along with their families to Shanghai and other points to the north.[25]

Caught in the throes of a desperate war effort, the regime had no interest in making a serious move toward liberalization. Even as he proclaimed the creation of a new civilian court Isogai felt obliged to remind Kotewall and his colleagues that military government was 'still the main idea'.[26] Placed at the head of the criminal branch of the new court was a Public Prosecutor named Kashiwagi, who handed out death and gaol sentences with a relish that made Judge Jeffreys look like a penal reformer. He is said to have asked a local Kempeitai commander 'how his station could provide its prisoners with so much food'.[27] And while Kashiwagi struck terror into common malefactors, the crack-down on subversion continued with little obvious slackening throughout the old Governor's final years. At Yuen Long, the same market town which Isogai toured that spring in a flurry of pan-Asiatic symbolism, a local resident named Du Riwei was decapitated because the characters in his name could be read to mean 'Stop the Might of Japan'.[28] In early June the Kempeitai lashed out with a new wave of savagery as rumour began to spread of the Normandy landings in Europe. (This would seem to have been the first time that the Japanese in Hong Kong were really unsettled by events taking place beyond the Pacific theatre.) Dr V. N. Atienza, a Portugese who had helped spread the news, was hung up by a beam in the Supreme Court torture cells till he lost consciousness. An Indian named Ghilote had his tongue scorched and his hands crushed. A Chinese called Wong Pui had the flesh of his back burned away with a piece of red-hot metal. The complaints relayed by Isogai to Noma during the autumn appear to have made little impact, and in December the repression was still in full swing. At a celebration of the third anniversary of the assault on the South two of the Kempeitai's executioners were overheard discussing the techniques of beheading. 'Ishikawa said that his sword could cut off heads at one stroke but that he did not care to cut off a woman's head as their hair got in the way and they screamed. Nagakawa said that he could cut off women's heads but when that was done, the blood usually stained the boots.'[29]

The breakthroughs which were publicized in economic conditions turned out to be almost as much of a sham. The compensation the government paid to the gentry for the goods they had removed from the godowns was grotesquely low.[30] And the relaxation of import controls was a near-mockery at a time when there was so little prospect of importing anything. The clearing of the Kowloon–Canton railway in November 1943 made little difference to the worsening food crisis. Reports from 1944 indicate that the railway still wasn't back in working order. Repairs to the tunnels on the New Territories side proved to be necessary during much of the spring: the first official through service into Guangdong province only started in June, and even then it only went a short way past the border, as far as the town of Zhangmutou. Most of the food that did come in appears to have been sequestered by the military. By mid-November the shortage was such that the families of those locals employed by the government had to be excluded from what remained of the rice ration scheme: only the employees themselves would from now on be entitled to draw food supplies. And in the meantime the Governor's Office pressed on indefatigably with its drive to relieve Hong Kong of the destitute rabble. In March 1944 recruitment posters went up inviting able-bodied young men to come out of the colony and earn good money working in the gold mines on Hainan island, near Vietnam. Over the following months a total of 7,000 Chinese applied to take part in the programme. They were packed off to Hainan without ceremony and put to work on road building sites and in iron mines (not gold ones), where 5,000 of them eventually died from starvation, overwork and disease. The turn of 1944–5 was recalled as the worst period for the mass deportations. Smart and shabby alike were picked up on the streets and corralled behind rope barriers, ready to be consigned to the transit camps and the deportation boats.[31]

The arrival of the new Governor Tanaka brought no substantial improvement. In a sort of way it marked a belated victory for the old China faction. Hong Kong was now once again under the control of the 23rd Army in Canton. But this no longer implied, as it had three years earlier, that the colony would be coddled in the hope of creating a political opening to the Nationalist regime. Hong Kong was no longer packed with Nationalist politicians who might be persuaded to make overtures to Chungking on Japan's behalf. Even if it had been there was no longer any prospect that Chungking would have the remotest interest in peace talks with Tokyo.[32] The resumption of control by the 23rd Army was instead prompted by strictly operational thinking. With United States forces now entrenched in the Philippines Hong Kong was becoming vulnerable to a seaborne offensive. Allied forces were also gathering strength in the Chinese interior, and it seemed quite conceivable that Tanaka's troops might before long be obliged to abandon Canton and fall back on the colony for a last-ditch stand. By absorbing Hong Kong the 23rd Army would be able to organize a unified defence of the whole Guangdong region.[33] It was time to remove the anomaly of Hong Kong's special status – an anomaly which had become all the more meaningless now that the colony was dependent on Guangdong for such little food as it had.

With logistics, not politics, now wholly dominant Tanaka and his colleagues had no compelling reason to lighten up on the local inhabitants. Whatever modest measures Kanazawa may have introduced to clean up the Kempeitai the battle against subversion still went on – and with new forms of terror. In the spring of 1945 Dracula walked abroad in Hong Kong. Army dogs were unleashed to prowl the streets from midnight until shortly before dawn and hunt down any Allied agents who might be operating during these hours of curfew. The dogs bit the throats of any people they found loitering in the open, and then gnawed their stomachs.[34] The food crisis was graver than ever, and by February general starvation seemed imminent. The regime stressed the need to step up local food production, even growing vegetables in the middle of the Happy Valley racecourse. But they took no step to disgorge their own food supplies. In July Tanaka decreed that 200,000 to 300,000 people should be driven out of the colony in a further great deportation campaign. Deportation was, he explained, 'absolutely necessary' in order 'to maintain the food problem on a sound basis'.[35]

Terminating Hong Kong's special status indeed made an impact; but the most obvious consequence wasn't reform, but neglect. Governor Tanaka, to begin with, was seldom even there. He spent the bulk of his time in Canton, coming down to the colony for a maximum of one week per month. And in his absence the sinews of the occupation regime grew increasingly feeble. Chief of Staff Suganami had gone back to Japan the previous July and had been replaced by a string of successors whose tenures became ever shorter as more and more officers were recalled to take part in the defence of the Japanese homeland.[36] Many of the key civilian heads of department were transferred in the same way, and by early 1945, as one Japanese witness commented, the Governor's Office was 'unable even to look after itself'.[37] Tanaka grumbled on one of his rare visits that the number of civilian officials was now too small to keep the government going. The creation of the No. 1 and No. 2 Departments was not in reality so much a mark of efficiency as an effort by Tanaka and his team to maintain control within a sharply reduced sphere of operations.

The regime now had neither the means nor the inclination to attend to the finer details of running this enclave which had become nothing more than an appendage of Canton. By the summer of 1945 grass grew on the streets. The old focus on public health was visibly wavering, as the Governor's Office failed to maintain the cleansing of filters and the chlorination of drinking water. Even some of the most cherished Japanese prestige projects were being discontinued. Progress on the grand war memorial in the Wanchai Gap slackened under the impact of failing government finances, a shortage of local construction materials and American bombing; and in July orders came through from Tokyo that all work on the scheme was to stop.[38]

Little by little Hong Kong was sliding back into the anarchy that had characterized the opening months of the occupation. As the mass hunger grew keener not even the most drastic efforts of Public Prosecutor Kashiwagi proved adequate to discourage a mushrooming of petty crime. Parcels were snatched on the streets, and any contents that seemed to be vaguely edible were devoured in full view of the owners. Empty houses were gutted of anything that could be used as firewood, including their wooden floorings, window-frames, staircases and even front doors. Bands of 'ghouls' raided graveyards to dig up the corpses and strip them of any gold rings and bangles.[39] The police force now consisted of some 2,200 to 2,300 members, of whom about fifty were Japanese; and that as one of the police chiefs lamented was 'by no means sufficient to maintain peace'.[40] Criminals were by now coolly posing as local policemen to accost citizens at gunpoint and relieve them of their money and jewellery. One gang even stole arms from the Governor's Office.[41] In July 1945 Kanazawa in his capacity as Police Commissioner negotiated with the Foreign Ministry in Tokyo to have an extra fifty police sent down from the Japanese consulate in Canton; but this reinforcement was too feeble to make any real difference. At the beginning of August Governor Tanaka voiced at a press conference his conclusion 'that there would be no peace and order in Hong Kong until the food problem was satisfactorily solved'.[42]

In the last year of Isogai's reign, as Hong Kong embarked on its descent into breakdown, the true feelings of the Japanese for their subjects began to show through in displays of indifference verging on cynicism. In February 1944, for example, noting that before long there might not be a single ship putting in at the colony, the old Governor summed up the economic predicament with unadorned frankness. 'If rice is available the people will have rice to eat. If there are only sweet potatoes they will only have sweet potatoes and if there are only beans they will have beans.'[43] To underscore further the need for belt-tightening the Governor's Office released for public consumption a quantity of laundry starch which, they maintained, could be made into a luscious pastry by the simple addition of groundnut oil or sugar. 'Since the supplies of oil and sugar had by then been totally exhausted', Selwyn-Clarke observed drily from Stanley gaol, 'one was left with the impression that Marie Antoinette was working for the Japanese department of propaganda.'[44]

In December 1944 the *Hong Kong News* started to adopt a valedictory tone. Great advances, it insisted, had been made in the course of the last three years. All the old racial and class barriers had been lifted: in the local Japanese firms, for instance, employees were treated alike whatever their ethnic background, employers mixed freely with the lowest-paid members of their staff and 'there was a complete absence of the "boy" and "coolie" cry that was so prevalent in the bad old days'.[45] Having said this, however, the paper was obliged to admit wearily that the attempt to turn Hong Kong into a laboratory for

Sino-Japanese friendship had failed. Even after three years it could not 'be truthfully asserted that the Japanese understands the Chinese and vice-versa'. To a 'very great extent' this was due to the language barrier.[46] If social relations between the Japanese and the local residents had been closer, the latter would have realized that the former were 'undergoing the same hardships and facing the same difficulties'. It was 'regrettable, but unavoidable, that the really creditable successes achieved by the Administration should have been offset by the circumstances brought about by the war'.[47]

Hand in hand with this attitude of resignation went a growing tendency to let the locals sort out their own difficulties. Isogai's sudden lifting of import controls may be seen as the first step in this general process of abdication. In December 1943, a fortnight before the new liberal rules for importers were unveiled, the old Governor remarked 'with a smile' that in due course the authorities might 'have to turn to the people for supplies of rice'; and at the end of the year Domei, the official Japanese news agency, envisaged that 'leading Chinese residents of the colony' would 'presently play the vital role of accelerating the exchange of staple commodities between Hong Kong and the other parts of Greater East Asia'.[48] In April 1944, the same month that the rice distribution scheme was abandoned, Tomari, the Secretary-General of the Governor's Office, noted that local merchants were being given 'every encouragement' to import rice into Hong Kong. The authorities felt, he explained, 'that the import and sale of rice could be handled much better by the people themselves'.[49] Relief work more than ever was left to the gentry. In September the Governor's Office appealed for the support of charitable institutions, and expressed the hope that the wealthy would contribute generously to these institutions 'for the relief of their fellow countrymen'.[50]

With the advent of Tanaka this inclination to shuffle off responsibility on to the locals grew steadily more pronounced. In February 1945, shortly after the new Governor assumed office, small increases were announced in the membership of the two Chinese Councils. The Chinese Representative Council was increased from a total of four to five and Chinese Cooperative Council from twenty-two to twenty-four. The idea, according to the official media, was 'to strengthen the civil administration of Hong Kong'.[51] The gentry were now expected to help not only in importing and distributing food but in shoring up the whole crumbling infrastructure, and above all in the preservation of order. In April a Police Affairs Committee composed of sixty 'prominent citizens' was set up under the chairmanship of the aged Sir Shouson Chow. Part of the Committee's task was to advise Kanazawa, who 'felt the necessity of getting in touch with the real voices of the general populace'.[52] Its main function, however, was to keep the local police on the beat by raising funds for their upkeep and that of their families.

Farther down on the social scale a new emphasis was placed on the role of the Chinese-run District Bureaux. On 12 January 1945, the day after Tanaka took over, the Governor's Office declared rather peevishly that Hong Kong people had always been accustomed to having their street cleaning and refuse clearance done for them: 'they should try to do this work themselves'.[53] The task was promptly handed down to the districts. By the end of February the Bureau in the Central District of Victoria had been divided into fifty-two sections, each of which was supposed to raise funds from householders to pay the wages of the local 'sanitary coolies'.[54] The District Bureaux were also called upon to maintain order by backing the police and by helping to rid the colony of its destitute masses. Two or three Chinese from each district were asked to join the gentry on the Police Affairs Committee, and Bureau staff are said to have been present regularly at Kanazawa's police stations. In late March the Bureaux were assigned the job of distributing Residents' Certificates, a new device which had been introduced to help track down subversives and vagrants, and in June they were given the power to issue exit permits, 'to simplify the procedure for people wanting to leave'.[55] By July they appear to have been on the point of inheriting almost all the routine functions of local administration. In the middle of that month a meeting of District Assemblymen was held at the Central District Bureau of Victoria to discuss the 'work of self-governing by residents' and to examine a plan which had been drawn up to that end.[56]

Finally the authorities started to fall back once again, as they had in the early weeks of the takeover, on the last-ditch support of the Triad gangs. In spite of the initial attempt which was made under Isogai to curb Triad activities the gangs had, as we saw, never really been stamped out; and from late 1943 onwards the slackening of the Japanese grip on the colony had been paralleled by a steady revival in the importance of the Triad-based Street Guards. Officially reckoned 'necessary to assist the administration of the District Bureaux',[57] the Street Guards had been used to spearhead a series of censuses which were conducted with brutal thoroughness for the purpose of flushing out vagrants and resistance elements. And in March 1945 they were earmarked by Tanaka and Kanazawa as the basis for a new corps of vigilantes which was to be formed to supplement the regular police. A Protective Guards Body was to be elected by the Street Guards in each district to keep order under the auspices of the District Bureaux. Armed with batons and given a basic police training, these Protective Guards were deployed in the following months around the neighbourhoods of Kowloon and Victoria to guard against theft. By mid-June they had been consolidated into a standing force of around 2,000 in each of the cities, and by early July an auxiliary corps of a further 2,000 was being recruited in the Central District of Victoria. The heads of the Protective Guards on Hong Kong Island were invited to dinner to discuss plans for keeping order with the chairmen of the Police Bureau and Police Committee for the Island, and to highlight their importance still further Kan Man, a District Bureau chief who had recently been promoted to a seat on the Chinese

Cooperative Council, acted as their spokesman. Together with the more exalted local organizations the Protective Guards were called upon to contribute to the maintenance of government in a broader sense. They were expected to play their part in rubbish disposal and to report any outbreaks of infectious diseases. Through the black market (itself organized by the Triads) the Protective Guards are also said to have virtually taken over the distribution of food to the populace during these months of collapse.

The basic needs of these gangsters were met by the Triad leaders themselves. One of the main Triad chieftains, a certain Wan Yuk-ming, is said to have organized a Hong Kong Law and Order Assistance Group to look after their welfare and to have funded it out of his own pocket.[58]

The quid pro quo was the same as it had always been. The new tolerance for 'amusements' with which Tanaka inaugurated his rule was in fact a green light to Wan Yuk-ming and the other Triad bosses to go ahead with the unrestrained propagation of vice.[59] During the following months gambling joints multiplied once again. The red light districts boomed, and the colony became dotted with an estimated 8,000 opium dens, many of them large-scale and operating in full public view.[60] Overall it seems likely that the Protective Guards did help to stave off a descent into absolute anarchy. But public opinion remembered them unkindly as 'a lot of brothel keepers and their runners'.[61]

The elite get ready for change

Disenchantment with the Japanese and their works was by now pretty well universal. For the top gentry leaders the strain of their association with the regime was beginning to manifest itself in a variety of physiological ways. Sir Robert Kotewall, for instance, was subject to repeated bouts of angina pectoris.[62] Li Tse-fong of the Bank of East Asia, who sat with Kotewall on the Chinese Representative Council, developed hypertension and had to be put on a special diet of steamed fish and vegetables. Li Koon-chun, Li Tse-fong's elder brother, the rice merchant who served as vice-chairman of the Chinese Cooperative Council, also came down with an unspecified illness which was aggravated by a direct encounter with the colony's crime wave. He arrived at his office to find it being rifled by a gang of knife-wielding robbers, who abandoned their hunt for cash and instead made for him yelling, 'Kill the fat fellow first'.[63] In some cases the physical symptoms were accompanied by clear signs of mental anguish. In the course of 1944–5 several members of the Li family took advantage of the regime's lifting of controls on religion to seek consolation and guidance from the Christian faith. They included Li Tse-fong, who was baptized in March 1945 under the name of Peter.[64]

While there is no reason to doubt the authenticity of these afflictions, physical or mental, it is evident that many of the top leaders used them as a pretext for keeping the maximum possible distance from the Japanese. From 1944 onwards, we are told, members of both Chinese Councils tended increasingly to 'slacken off' and duck out of meetings with the Governor's Office on grounds of ill health.[65] Kotewall seems to have been especially prone to this absenteeism. In the spring of 1944 he was 'indisposed' for the best part of three months. In February 1945, when the new Governor Tanaka invited him and his fellow Council members to a special interview, he was 'unable to be present owing to illness'. At the beginning of August he was once again 'convalescing'. In a statement put out by the two Chinese Councils he explained that he had been attending to Council business by telephone or through 'personal contact at his residence'; but he had now been advised by his doctor to have 'a complete rest'. He was, therefore, 'reluctantly compelled to give up all public duties for one month'.[66] Li Koon-chun too exploited his own ailment for all it was worth. By the start of 1944 he had stepped down from his post on the Chinese Cooperative Council and taken to his bed.[67] Most of the leaders were still too prominent and too closely watched to have any realistic chance of getting out of the colony; but Li Koon-chun after several months of bed-ridden seclusion seems to have felt unobtrusive enough to attempt an escape. In September 1944 he slipped off with his family on a rickety boat to Macao. Tung Chung-wei, the chairman of the Hong Kong Chinese General Chamber of Commerce, made a similar exit.[68]

Under these circumstances the bulk of the broadcasts and public appearances were increasingly made by the Laval figures who had committed themselves heart and soul to the Japanese cause. The Lavals too, however, were starting to disappear from the picture in one way or another. In mid-December 1944, having issued an appeal to the public to keep calm and place their full confidence in the occupation authorities, Chan Lim-pak the far-right businessman applied for and was granted a month's sick leave. He had apparently grasped that the game was up for the Japanese, and was planning to go into hiding in Macao. He never made it. On Christmas Eve United States fighters attacked his steamer as it was crossing the Pearl River estuary, and Chan Lim-pak fell in a hail of machine-gun bullets. Chinese legend has it that he drowned trying to rescue his concubine, on account of a bag of gold she had tied to her waist: she 'unexpectedly clasped him with all her strength, and they both sank together'.[69] The following April Lau Tit-shing, the pan-Asiatic enthusiast, dropped dead of a heart attack. The Japanese seem to have felt the loss of their last fervent gentry backer. A staff officer representing Governor Tanaka brought a special letter of condolence to the dead man's family – a unique honour conferred in token of 'the meritorious services given by the late Mr Lau'.[70]

The same pattern of stress and withdrawal can be made out in the conduct of the middle classes. The petty functionaries employed by the Governor's Office were well aware that Japan was heading for defeat. Chinese and Indian constables in the police force had been thrown, their employers remarked, into 'mental chaos and worry' and hence 'were not eager in discharging their duties'.[71] The heyday of the Eurasian and Portuguese brokers was long since past. Joseph Carroll, the Eurasian who had made a packet supplying the needs of the Japanese Navy, found by 1944 that there was practically no brokerage to be done, and 'hardly went to his office'.[72] In June 1945 he closed his office altogether and joined in the exodus to Macao. Small Chinese businesses were going from bad to worse. Between April and June 1944 the pawnbrokers increased their monthly rates from 10 to 20 per cent, and in January 1945 one of the larger pawnbroking fraternities was obliged to close down through lack of funds. In April 1945 the Match Distribution Syndicate was dissolved, and in June nineteen authorized cigarette depots applied to the Tobacco and Cigarette Distribution Syndicate for permission to shut up shop. Managers and assistants in numerous other firms were reported by the official media to be planning either to suspend operations or to clear right out of Hong Kong.

The last redoubts of middle-ranking support for Japan were now cracking up rapidly. By the summer of 1944, for example, major ructions were taking place in the Hong Kong branch of the Indian Independence League. The branch chairman, a Dr Naidu, was replaced at the end of June in an internal *coup* by a colleague, P. A. Krishna, who explained to the media that it had been necessary to reorganize the League 'owing to the slackness of the Indian public in responding to the fight for freedom'. Contrary to the belief of some Indians, he insisted, the Japanese were 'only interested in helping us to stand on our own two feet'.[73] A few days later 'several hundreds' of local Indians (no attempt was now made to claim the thousand-strong attendance figures of former League rallies) were assembled on the old Cricket Ground to reaffirm their loyalty to the Provisional Government of Free India and to be told by Krishna that they 'sank or swam with Japan'.[74] Even the Sikhs who had been among the keenest partisans of the New Order had now dropped away, and some of them were engaged in active conspiracy. In May 1945 the Kempeitai uncovered a spy ring which had been funded by Reeves and the British consulate in Macao. The ringleaders turned out to be Mohinder Singh, once a prominent figure in the Hong Kong branch of the League, and a couple of his co-religionists.[75]

Clinging on to the end were George Wong, Call Me Howard and the other thugs who had made a niche for themselves in the Kempeitai's service. Even the Kempeitai no longer had much use for them. But they were uneducated and doglike, and had nowhere else to go.

The elite's final defection was symbolized by the withering of what little remained of elite social life. In April 1945, when the bulk of the starving

Japanese ponies at Happy Valley had died and been eaten, the authorities sub-stituted miniature wooden horses which were trundled round the racecourse on wires in a frantic attempt to keep up the general jollity. But the punters weren't interested. The first venture into miniature racing was reported to have been only 'moderately successful'; and at the beginning of May, after two more Sundays of 'very poor' attendance, the Happy Valley races were closed down for good.[76]

And in the midst of all this an ironic chorus was kept up in the pages of the elite's own newspaper, the *Hong Kong News*. Commander Faure, the editor who had so ingeniously subverted the paper from within, had long since been removed from his post and cast into a Kempeitai prison;[77] but the technique he invented seems to have lived on. In the summer of 1944 the *Hong Kong News* began publishing a series of 'Fruits of Wisdom' – quotations distilled from clas-sical authors and savants of the Enlightenment which could be identified by any discerning reader as a coded denunciation of the Japanese and a bracing prediction of their imminent ruin. In September, for instance, the eighteenth-century Swiss educationist Pestalozzi was quoted as observing, 'There is no happiness for him who oppresses and persecutes; there can be no repose for him. For the sighs of the unfortunate cry for vengeance to heaven.' Aristotle added a few days later, 'A king ruleth as he ought; a tyrant as he lists; a king to the profit of all; a tyrant only to please a few.' In October Horace weighed in with an apparent warning to collaborators, 'Those unacquainted with the world take pleasure in intimacy with great men; those who are wiser fear the consequences', while Polybius counselled the Allied resistance, 'Some men give up their designs when they have almost reached the goal, while others, on the contrary, obtain a victory by exerting at the last moment more vigorous efforts than before.' And in April 1945, with Japan's Empire tottering, Fichte exulted, 'My mind can take no hold of the present world nor rest in it a moment, but my whole nature rushes onward with irresistible force toward a future and better state of being.'[78]

The great mass of the Chinese were, as Police Chief Kanazawa remarked deprecatingly, 'not bright and cheerful'.[79] Tucked away in the newspaper columns most weeks were reports of anonymous individuals who had opted to put an end to their wretchedness by jumping off buildings or ferries. Many residents who contrived to avoid starvation were picked off instead by the frequently misdirected American air raids. On 18 April 1945, for example, American planes machine-gunned a crowded ferry crossing from Hong Kong Island to Yaumati in Kowloon, and on 12 June fifty-nine American raiders dropped incendiary bombs on the Central District. But in spite of the deaths of almost 10,000 Chinese civilians in these attacks the bulk of the populace by all accounts steadfastly refused to blame the United States. The attacks were laid squarely at the door of the Japanese military, who had no business to be in the colony, and even seem to have been welcomed as evidence that the occupation was nearing its end.[80] The Chinese public could smell the impending fall of the Japanese as surely as they had smelled that of the British four years earlier. 'How long', they whispered, 'will the Japanese forces be able to hold on? . . . How long will people go on accepting the military yen?'[81] Going the rounds was an epigram ascribed to the poet Dai Wangshu:

> Greater East Asia,
> What a surprise –
> All that hot air
> Was a pack of lies.[82]

In spite of all this it is clear that the colony's upper and middle classes did step forward where needed to fill the void created by the Japanese abdication. The gentry were quick to respond to the Japanese promptings to help out with the question of food supply. At the end of November 1943 a Hong Kong People's Food Cooperative Association was formed on the initiative of Aw Boon-haw, the Tiger Balm King. The task of the Association was to negotiate with the authorities in neighbouring centres for the import of rice. A firm called the Chung Kiu Company was set up under the auspices of the Association to handle the importing of any rice which might be secured as a result of these efforts. The firm had a capital of M¥10 m: the Tiger Balm King was the largest shareholder, with a stake of M¥500,000, but 'most of the wealthy Chinese' in Hong Kong were said to have bought shares, and the share issue was underwritten by the Bank of East Asia.[83] Over the following year a succession of gentry leaders were sent to Canton to take advantage of any new opportunities for importing that might have arisen from the tentative reopening of the Kowloon–Canton railway. Prominent among them was the Wang Jingwei groupie, Kong Kai-tung, who was twice dispatched to persuade his counterparts in the Chinese puppet government of Guangdong province to relax various restrictions they had imposed on the shipment of rice to the colony.[84]

In the same way the gentry complied with the summons they had received from the Governor's Office to step up their charity work. A fund-raising campaign which was launched in August–September 1944 by their coordinating body, the General Association of Chinese Charities (GACC), was reported to have been 'far more successful' than the initial one of the previous year.[85] Flag days and concerts and performances of Cantonese opera were all organized to rake in the cash. In the winter of 1944–5, despite worsening financial strains and the near-bankruptcy of such major individual charities as the Tung Wah and Kwong Wah hospitals, the GACC managed to open a number of food kitchens for the distribution of congee; and Sir Robert Kotewall became chairman of a committee set up to arrange relief for the victims of the American air raids.[86] Finally the gentry shouldered with some vigour the responsibilities which had been thrust on them by the incoming Governor Tanaka in the sphere of public order. In May 1945, in his capacity as head of the Police Affairs Committee, Sir Shouson Chow announced the establishment of a Cooperative Society whose brief was to be to raise money from each social group so that rice and other essentials could be bought at cheap rates and distributed to all members of the police.[87]

Two likely reasons may be suggested for the gentry's visible willingness to help out in these spheres. In the first place they were still managing to make money. Beth Woo, the Chinese who returned to the colony in the spring of 1944, was still able to refer at that date to 'those making millions'.[88] If they weren't making millions they were at any rate sitting on millions: the Governor's Office explained that the reason the Bank of East Asia, unlike the rest of the Chinese banks, had been given the privilege of handling remittances to Shanghai and its sister ports was that no other bank had so large a capital base, or so many facilities.[89] And empowered by those millions, many top tycoons were still able to enjoy a remarkably good lifestyle in the midst of the general deprivation.[90] The Comte de Sercey, a Frenchman formerly employed in the Chinese Postal Service who got out of the colony at about the same time as Beth Woo entered it, reported that though the cost of living was higher there than it was in Chungking 'with money anything could be had'.[91] Li Tse-fong of the Bank of East Asia had been eating Chinese delicacies such as shark's fin before his doctor put him on a diet, and his brother Li Koon-chun had plainly got through enough meals to catch the eye of the looters in his office who bore down on him as 'the fat fellow'.[92] As late as July 1945 advertisements were being placed in the *Hong Kong News* by the Alex Chocolate Shop in Ice House Street. Given this background it followed that the gentry might have something to gain from the new Japanese invitations to import, and they quickly seized the chance to improve their position still further. The rice which was to be brought into the colony by the Chung Kiu Company was earmarked 'primarily' for the company's shareholders.[93] It followed equally that the gentry had much to lose from a drift to complete social chaos; and their efforts to shore up the colony's crumbling police force should be seen in this context. In July 1945 the Cooperative Council held a meeting to discuss ways of working with the police in Tanaka's new drive for the deportation of 'undesirable characters'.[94] The Council members regretted that the lower-grade police still showed a tendency to rope in 'respectable persons' by tearing up residence permits and identity cards. But they agreed – and continued to state in post-war testimonials – that the idea underlying the scheme was a good one.[95]

Secondly however (the other side of the coin that is always apparent in their behaviour), the gentry still retained their traditional sense of duty to the public at large. Even if most of the rice imported by the Chung Kiu Company was to go to the shareholders, the idea was that the rest should be put on the market at a favourable rate; and as the shortages worsened more strenuous efforts were made to ensure that such rice as came in did get through to the masses. At the beginning of May 1944, soon after the suspension of the government's rice ration scheme, 'a number of wealthy members' of the United Christian Church of Hong Kong were reported to have formed a Consumers' Cooperative for the exclusive purpose of bringing rice into the colony and selling it cheap. The office of the Cooperative was in the Bank of East Asia.[96] In November, again with some help from the Bank of East Asia, a Hong Kong Wholesale Rice Merchants' Association was organized in an effort to keep the rice price as low as possible. The experiment foundered after only two weeks, as the bulk of the rice merchants were unwilling to agree to 'losing all the time'.[97] But Kotewall pleaded with them to cooperate; and the two Chinese Councils embarked on a week-long series of conferences with the merchants in the hope that the Association might be revived.

The charity offensive of 1944–5 was sustained in large measure by the contributions of individual gentry leaders. Once again the leading role was played by the stupendously wealthy Tiger Balm King. On frequent occasions he helped both the GACC and the various individual charities with donations of rice from his huge share in the Chung Kiu Company, other food supplies in the form of salt and sugar and beans, summer suits, winter jackets and money for the schooling of orphans and the care of the old. Cash injections of the order of M¥10,000 a time were also dispensed to the charities by Li Tse-fong, Ho Kom-tong of the Jockey Club and Kwok Chan, the acting chairman of the Hong Kong Chinese General Chamber of Commerce.[98] The *Hong Kong News*, which seems to have adopted an increasingly acid tone as the war neared its end, commented scathingly on the exertions of these plutocrats who wished to earn a reputation for philanthropy by 'subscribing enormous sums out of their fabulous fortunes'.[99] Charity, it observed with a nod to I Corinthians 13, needed to be prompted by a genuine feeling of sympathy with the sufferers. But the gentry must take some credit for the remarkable fact that the GACC remained comfortably solvent right through to the summer of 1945.[100]

Throughout these months the gentry kept up their sporadic endeavours to bend the ears of the Japanese rulers. Some of their pleas seem chiefly to reflect a desire to promote their own businesses and maintain their own comforts. In September 1944, for instance, the two Councils submitted to Isogai the proposal that an Enquiries Section should be attached to the newly created Hong Kong Trade Association so that help could be given to those Chinese merchants who were now entitled to join the Association and take part in long-distance trade. The Councils also pressed for a resumption of the electricity supply so that 'the numerous factories' could carry on.[101] In November Kotewall and his colleagues appealed to the Governor to reconsider a suspension of the water supply which had been imposed on certain districts in the upper levels of Victoria – where most of them lived. Various other overtures, however, were made pretty clearly with the general interest at heart. In November 1943, after the regime had started to substitute beans for rice in the government rations, the Council members urged that the novelty should be discontinued because the Chinese population did not consider a diet of beans to be good for their health. In the summer of 1944, after the rice rationing scheme had been discontinued, Li Tse-fong proposed in a press interview that workers in factories and business firms should be given a pay increase, and that those of them who did not get board and lodging as part of their package should continue receiving a certain quantity of rice every month.[102] And in December, following a sudden drastic surge in the rice price, Kotewall and the other Chinese Representatives paid several calls on the Governor's Office to ask the authorities what they intended to do.[103] No doubt gentry interests were involved here (Chan Lim-pak commented that the price increase had caused much anxiety to Council members 'as it not only affected the poorer classes but even the rich');[104] but it seems fair to deduce that the gentry leaders were trying their best to save lives. From the autumn of 1944 efforts were also made to induce the regime to reopen the air-raid shelters so that the public could have some protection from the American bombing. Keen though they were, in the interests of social order, that the colony should be rid of its 'vagabonds' the gentry leaders did, lastly, attempt once or twice to prevail upon the Japanese to improve the conditions of the wretched repatriates. In November 1943 the two Chinese Councils asked the Harbour Department to allow repatriates to take with them a small bag containing their personal effects; and a year later Kotewall and the other Councillors requested the abolition of the compulsory stool tests and vaccinations which were inflicted on repatriates before their departure.

As the Japanese grip slackened the gentry seem to have recovered a little of the official attention they had enjoyed at the start of the take-over. True to form the authorities were more prepared to respond to appeals calculated to further the gentry's own interests than to entreaties submitted on behalf of the masses. An Enquiries Section was attached as requested to the offices of the Hong Kong Trade Association. The resumption of electricity for industrial purposes was quickly conceded, and Isogai promised to have another look at the question of maintaining a water supply to the upper-level districts. The cancellation of stool tests and vaccinations for repatriates, on the other hand, was declared to be 'impossible'.[105] No known effort was made to ensure the sustenance of industrial and commercial employees; and while Kotewall emerged radiating good cheer from a final round of talks with the Governor's Office at Christmas 1944, the price of rice continued remorselessly up. Even for the masses, however, the gentry did manage to secure one or two modest gains. The Governor's Office refused to eliminate beans from the rice rations, but they did at least agree to replace the green beans they had issued with yellow ones which were 'better appreciated by the public';[106] and the rules about luggage for repatriates were somewhat relaxed. In June 1945, after months of foot-dragging, a number of air-raid shelters were belatedly made available for public use.

Whatever their inner misgivings the low-grade officials who served the regime also showed themselves willing to take on new duties. In their case the motive was brutally clear. After the rice ration scheme for the general public was jettisoned in April 1944 it was a choice between government work and starvation. Jobs with the government remained at a premium: that same spring 1,200 citizens were reported to have applied for 200 secretarial posts advertised by the Governor's Office.[107] Like the gentry these minor local functionaries seem to have sensed the new Japanese need for back-up, and like the gentry they seized the chance to angle for certain concrete improvements in their conditions. In October 1944, for example, the heads of the District Bureaux sought permission to impose their own taxes on the districts so that they could generate extra income for their staff and themselves. The Governor's Office were reported to be 'unsympathetic'.[108] Five months later, however, after Tanaka had arrived and responsibility was being sloughed off on to the Bureaux at an increasing rate, the regime changed its tune. The Bureaux were now to be allowed to raise funds from local residents at a monthly rate of some M¥30 per family.

Quite a few of these petty officials seem to have been all too conscious of their enhanced status. Heads had been turned after three years of unexpected advancement, and the effect was to trigger a certain amount of unconcealed public wrath. In July 1944, in an early display of its new penchant for invective, the *Hong Kong News* launched a swingeing attack on the 'beggars in purple' who staffed the District Bureaux. It condemned their inertia, their 'intolerable rudeness', their 'exaggerated idea of their own importance'.[109] In March 1945 this government propaganda organ even went so far as to publish a critical editorial opposing the Tanaka administration's plan to let the Bureaux raise their own funds and denouncing them as 'sanctuaries of complacent egotists' which had 'outlived their usefulness'.[110] But the low-grade functionaries also seem to have done their share of good works. From the end of 1943 the Bureaux chiefs were said to be spearheading a renewed effort to organize free schooling for children of the poorer classes. Several Bureaux were reported to be operating free medical centres, and to be raising funds for the rescue of new-born babies and invalids who were being found abandoned at the roadside. In May 1945 Chan Kwai-pok, who had taken over from the 'Mayor of Hong Kong' as head of the key Bureau in the Central District of Victoria, appealed to the rice merchants to desist from their habit of profiteering and to play their part in providing affordable food.

   In the meantime both gentry and middle classes were starting quietly to
position themselves for change. Some clue to the evolution of gentry thinking
may be found in an assessment given by Li Shu-fan, the doctor and big game
hunter who had escaped to Free China so dashingly in the summer of 1943. In
February 1944 Li appeared in London and presented himself for debriefing by
the Colonial Office, the Foreign Office and the SOE, who questioned him
closely about the mood in Hong Kong. In response to their grilling he drew
attention to the difference between the transient mass of the Hong Kong
Chinese population whose views on the colony's future (so far as they had any)
probably corresponded to those of their counterparts on the mainland, and
those Chinese who had been born in the colony and had property interests
there. A high percentage of the latter, in his estimation, had doubts whether
post-war China would be 'a haven of law and order', and 'felt considerable
qualms as to whether they would find under a Chinese government the security for their property which they had enjoyed under British rule'. In the last
analysis, he believed, the men of property might prefer to see Hong Kong
reclaimed by the British rather than given up to the mainland.[111]
   That this preference wasn't necessarily set in stone was apparent from the
conduct of Li himself. During his spell in China Li hadn't linked up with the
BAAG, like so many of the upper-crust refugees from the colony. Instead he
had hastened to Chungking, where he had resumed his decades-long intimacy
with the Nationalist establishment, spending nearly four months in the house
of Foreign Minister T. V. Soong. He averred to the officials in Whitehall that
he had been looked on with suspicion by the Chungking leaders as 'too pro-
British'; but his subsequent performance in London did not altogether seem
to bear this out. Sir George Moss, the SOE's regional adviser for the Far East,
wrote to John Keswick that he had found Li 'very cagey', maintaining 'the bland
and rather stupid attitude which Chinese generally adopt when they do not
want to disclose their real thoughts'.[112] The doctor had evaded a point-blank
request for his personal views as a Hong Kong property owner. Some days after
the meeting he had been invited to lunch by F. W. Kendall, the former chief of
the SOE's Z Force, who had done business with him in previous years; and
on this occasion he had sung a rather different tune. He spoke 'bitterly and
stupidly' about how kind the Americans had been to China and how unkind
the British had been, and in general struck Kendall as being 'fundamentally
anti-British and pro-American'.[113] And now rather than linger in London he
was on his way once again – to the United States. In other words Li was clearly
signalling that he was well aware of the alternative to a British restoration, and
was prepared to embrace it if this proved expedient. The fact was that for Li,
like the rest of the gentry he spoke of, it all boiled down to a question of money.
The worldly physician was highly exercised about the HK$1m he had lost as a
result of the fall of Hong Kong. He wanted assurances that this loss would be

made good by the British authorities, and that his currency holdings in the Hongkong and Shanghai Bank would be fully honoured by the British at the end of the war. Provided his concerns were taken care of there was no reason why he should not throw his weight behind a British comeback. Moss surmised that the doctor might well be planning to promote a deal in the course of his American visit under which the United States would give its diplomatic support to Britain's attempt to recover the colony in return for a British agreement to pay compensation for American and Chinese losses – including Li's own.

Other reports in the following year confirm the broad picture of gentry preference for a British return. The Comte de Sercey, the French official who left the colony in April 1944, brought word to the British embassy in Chungking that the Hong Kong Chinese with whom he had dealings were 'even more pro-British than pro-Chinese'.[114] Some of them had informed him that if Hong Kong were handed over to the mainland after the victory they would emigrate to Singapore. In February 1945 K. C. Lee, the Chinese adviser to the Hongkong and Shanghai Bank – a classic comprador figure – gave the British ambassador, Sir Horace Seymour, his ideas about Britain's most promising strategy for regaining Hong Kong. The best plan, he suggested, would be for Britain to make an immediate offer to hand back the colony – subject to the proviso that British control should be maintained for a certain period after the end of the war so that Britain could clear up the mess. This would cut the ground from under the more chauvinistic elements in the Chungking government while 'putting the whole question in storage for an indefinite length of time'. Lee's backing for this scenario however clearly rested on the same assumption Li Shu-fan had been making – that the British would look after the gentry's assets. The extension which Britain would win under his plan would be used by it to 'sort out the interests of British nationals' and to make 'equitable adjustments' regarding 'property rights and compensation'.[115]

In the most literal sense both the gentry and the middle classes were putting their money on a British outcome. From June 1943, when the Hong Kong dollar was banned, local merchants were reported to be hoarding up their old colonial banknotes on the calculation that the British would return at the end of the war and redeem them at par. Many businessmen were setting out to accumulate as much as they could of the former currency, and Hong Kong dollars were even accepted in exchange for stocks of tinned food. Next to real estate and jewellery the Hong Kong dollar had now become the favoured form of investment; and it gained value with dizzying speed against the collapsing military yen. For a year or so after June 1943 a Hong Kong dollar was worth some M¥1 to M¥2 on the black market – an exchange rate already in sharp contrast with the official rate of M¥1 = HK$4 which had prevailed at the time the dollar was suppressed. By March 1945 it fetched M¥25, by April M¥30 and by August approximately M¥250. The Hong Kong Chinese are nothing if not gamblers, and in the uncertainty which lay ahead after Japanese rule a chance of making the ultimate killing presented itself.

'We must get there first': the British and their competitors

The British determination to recover Hong Kong hardened steadily as the European victory drew ever closer in 1944–5. Typical of the mood in official circles was a memorandum submitted to the Colonial Office on 1 May 1944 by Sir George Moss, whom we have just met in his capacity as a leading light in the SOE. Moss had held high office in the British consular service in China, and his views on the colony's future were considered to 'carry great weight'. Hong Kong, he declared, was 'like a hulk off the mainland of China' – an indispensable springboard for British trade. If Britain were to hand over Hong Kong 'we should have given up our last base on the China coast and might well find ourselves back in a position similar to that which we occupied in 1840'. In addition Moss saw Hong Kong as a 'last stronghold' against the overweening ambitions of a resurgent post-war China which was likely to overshadow the whole of South-east Asia and might in due course propel 'swarming millions of Asiatics' as far as Australia. In this context Moss wasn't disposed to draw any sharp distinction between the Chinese and Japanese. The Nationalists, he observed, had 'already profited much indirectly from Japanese pan-Asiatic propaganda, the results of which will persist in Asia long after the defeat of Japan'. It was possible that they might even obtain reinforcements after the war from 'certain pan-Asiatic Japanese elements'. For Moss like his colleagues the retrieval of the colony had also become entwined inexorably with questions of British confidence and 'face'. 'When we have faith and trust in ourselves and let others see that we are self-confident and true to ourselves, that faith in our power and our good intentions will communicate itself to others . . . Our prestige has suffered greatly in Asia, it must be restored.' In a word Moss was 'inclined to think that it would be most unwise even to entertain the idea of giving up Hong Kong'. He advocated 'reserving all British rights . . . until the problem can be seen and weighed in the perspective of post-war conditions'.[116]

Most of these sentiments were fully shared by the leading players at the Colonial Office. Gent, for example, the chief day-to-day strategist on Hong Kong, found the Moss memorandum 'convincing'.[117] At a meeting which took place in August 1944 between the Colonial Office and the SOE Gent pronounced himself to be 'in favour of any action which could be taken . . . to bring home to our Allies that it was intended to reinstate Hong Kong as British territory'.[118] Less and less was now heard about the idea of handing back the New Territories to Chiang Kai-shek. In December the Colonial Office wrote to the Far Eastern Reconstruction Committee of the War Cabinet that the remaining fifty years of the New Territories lease was 'manifestly much too short a period on which to base long-term reconstruction plans'.[119]

There were still a few timorous voices at the Foreign Office. At the end of 1943 Ambassador Seymour commented in the course of a visit to London that in view of mainland Chinese opinion regarding the Hong Kong issue it would be hard for the British not to accommodate China 'at least to some extent'.[120] In late March 1945 an attempt was still being made by Foreign Office staff to tone down a Colonial Office assertion that Britain was 'determined to hang on to Hong Kong at all costs'.[121] These hesitations were reinforced by a certain E. T. Nash of the British Overseas Press Service, who sent in to Whitehall a report urging the retrocession of Hong Kong in the light of a widespread opinion he had detected among 'influential Chinese' in New York. But the Colonial Office now had the bit firmly between their teeth. Nash's observations were greeted by Gent with an un-civil-service-like snarl. 'It is a pity', the Assistant Under-Secretary noted, 'that for official British purposes "Chinese opinion" is left to be appreciated and propagated by a man who seems to have the qualities, principally, of a defeatist.'[122] In May 1945 the Secretary of State for the Colonies, Oliver Stanley, complained to Foreign Secretary Eden about the 'expressions of doubt' which had been encountered 'in some unexpected quarters' about Britain's intention and capacity to resume the administration of the colony, and received an abject assurance that no doubt whatever was being thrown upon this.[123]

The business community continued to chime in influentially from their corner. On 23 November 1944 the China Association sent in a second letter to the Colonial Office. They were still prepared to contemplate an effective relinquishing of the New Territories subject to an agreement for the joint Anglo-Chinese management of the airport and the water supply. They agreed that Britain should have in mind 'the possibility of a more "liberal" form of government than in the past' and should aim to give the Hong Kong Chinese 'a great if not a preponderant voice in municipal affairs'. To retrocede the colony, however, they insisted, 'would not only weaken our position but that of all other Western nations' and 'would be interpreted as a sign of weakness and abdication'. Sovereignty over Hong Kong, they were clear, 'must rest firmly in the British Crown'.[124] The China traders were well represented in the House of Commons, and on two occasions in 1944 one of their leading spokesmen, William Astor, got up to point out that Hong Kong was 'undoubtedly British' and to demand reassurance that it was covered by Churchill's ringing declaration that 'he had not become the King's First Minister to preside over the liquidation of the British Empire'.[125] The reassurance was promptly given.

Broader geopolitical considerations had also started by now to obtrude on the picture. With Germany beaten the might of the Soviet Union would be available to help out in the Far East with the Anglo-American war effort against Japan. In return, Churchill noted at the end of October 1944, it would be essential to offer the Russians 'substantial war objectives' in the form of such places as Port Arthur in Manchuria. And, he added cheerfully, 'any claim by Russia for indemnity at the expense of China would be favourable to our resolve about Hong Kong'.[126]

From the middle of 1944 the United States started to exert fresh pressure on Britain over the Hong Kong issue. Some voices in the State Department had been urging that an attempt should be made to impose the American will on Britain over colonial matters while the British were still dependent on the United States for their survival. And there was, once again, the Soviet factor. Roosevelt even more than Churchill was anxious to bring the Soviet forces into action in East Asia; but the conclusion he drew from this was precisely the opposite to the conclusion that Churchill had drawn. He too thought that the Russians would have to be rewarded with concessions in Manchuria; but in view of this he believed it was all the more vital that Chiang Kai-shek should be mollified with the recovery of Hong Kong.[127] At the second Big Three conference held at Yalta in February 1945 the Hong Kong question was not addressed formally any more than it had been at Tehran. The United States President however expressed at a secret meeting with Stalin his hope that Britain would return the colony to China or at any rate turn it into an internationalized free port. Still convinced that 'colonialism must be abandoned by our Allies',[128] Roosevelt dispatched to London in April his newly designated ambassador to Chungking, General Patrick Hurley, with instructions to bring up Hong Kong and find out just how adamant the British views really were.

The Nationalists remained relatively quiescent by comparison with their American sponsors. In June 1944 Chiang Kai-shek indicated that he hoped an agreement might be arrived at about Hong Kong which would satisfy everyone, and in November T. V. Soong remarked at a lunch with American journalists that China should not, in his view, exert any pressure on Britain to disgorge the colony. Soong however went on to explain he was against using pressure for the simple reason that there was no need for it. The Japanese conquest three years before, he observed, had shown Britain that without a friendly hinterland Hong Kong was militarily untenable: all that the more powerful Chinese state of the future would need to do would be to show its interest in the colony and 'the processes of good sense would work upon the British government'.[129] British visitors to Chungking were left in no doubt of the strength of feeling on the subject, in intellectual circles especially.[130]

By this stage, however, all such attitudes were meeting with flinty and unequivocal British resistance. From the spring of 1944 the British Information Services in New York were engaged in a counter-offensive designed to win over American opinion. Booklets were issued explaining how Britain's rule in the colony had benefited the Chinese as much as Britain itself. (One of the chief illustrations advanced in support of this claim was Hong Kong University, with the fine educational opportunities it had offered to Chinese both inside and outside the colony.) Churchill is said to have 'exploded' when he found out after Yalta that Roosevelt and Stalin had been discussing the possible amputation of Hong Kong from the Empire behind his back;[131] and when Hurley descended on London in April 1945 he encountered not even the hint of concession over the issue of sovereignty that had underlain the Prime Minister's previous stance on Hong Kong. Churchill by his own account 'took him up with violence about Hong Kong and said that never would we yield an inch of the territory that was under the British Flag'.[132] Even the New Territories now seemed to have been placed beyond the scope of negotiation. The question of the lease would not, Churchill noted, come up until about 1998 – and 'in the meantime we would set up distilling machinery which would give us all the water we wanted and more'.[133]

The Nationalists were slapped down a little more gently, but they were slapped down all the same. Part of the task of spelling out Britain's purposes was assigned to David MacDougall, the former information chief in the colony who in September 1944 had been appointed director of the Hong Kong Planning Unit and as such was in the thick of the groundwork being laid in Whitehall for a post-war colonial order. In April 1945 MacDougall was sent on a trip to Chungking. The main purpose of his mission was to track down British China hands who could help run Hong Kong after Britain recovered possession. But he also appears to have taken the opportunity to impress on the Nationalist leaders that they should not expect to gain possession of Hong Kong 'the day after tomorrow'.[134] That same month British and Nationalist delegates made their way to San Francisco for the founding conference of the United Nations. In a note issued for guidance to its representative the Colonial Office stressed that 'nothing should be said which might be interpreted as suggesting that we are willing to bargain about or even expecting to discuss the future of Hong Kong'.[135]

All of this diplomatic assertiveness would, however, in the last resort count for very little if the British were unable to win the rapidly developing race on the ground. Ever since the avenging American forces had begun to push the Japanese back across the Pacific in 1943 the British had had to reckon with the strong probability that Hong Kong's liberation would take the form of a seaborne landing conducted not by themselves but by the United States. British planners in Whitehall assumed that the colony would most likely be captured by the United States Navy under the command of Admiral Chester W. Nimitz; and so, with less obvious thought for the implications, did the inmates of Stanley camp. 'We hope', wrote one internee in his diary in March 1945, 'that Nimitz will come quickly.'[136]

To this primary challenge was added the headache posed by the increasing predominance of the United States military in the unoccupied parts of the Chinese mainland. Ever since the Pacific War started the Americans had enjoyed pride of place among the various Allied contingents in China. Major-General V. W. ('Vinegar Joe') Stilwell, the Commander-in-Chief of United States forces in the China–Burma–India theatre, had served simultaneously as Chief of Staff to the Supreme Commander in the China theatre – Generalissimo Chiang Kai-shek. The Americans had also been setting up branches of their intelligence networks, in particular the Air Ground Air Service (AGAS) and the Office of Strategic Services (OSS), the wartime predecessor of the CIA. And this growing United States establishment on the mainland exhibited, in a more intense form, the antipathy which prevailed in Washington towards British purposes in the Far East. At an inter-departmental meeting which took place in Whitehall in June 1944, officials lamented that many of the OSS personnel had 'a complex about British Imperialism and, in some cases, a definite anti-British bias'.[137] In October this outlook received powerful reinforcement when General Albert C. Wedemeyer stepped into Stilwell's shoes. The intention was clearly that (with Chiang's authority and approval) Wedemeyer should serve as Commander-in-Chief of all Allied forces in China – the Eisenhower of the East. And Wedemeyer, if not on his own insistence an Anglophobe, was keenly suspicious of what he perceived as the British aim of subjecting a post-war China to renewed colonial control. 'Intent mainly on their commercial aspirations', he wrote, 'the British opposed America's fumbling efforts to help China become strong and independent.'[138]

All of this spelled bad news for the BAAG, the SOE and the other British military and intelligence outfits that were hatching schemes to recover Hong Kong. The appearance of AGAS in September 1943 resulted in an immediate constriction of the BAAG's operations. The War Department in Washington secured an agreement from the British War Office that the United States was to have 'primary responsibility' for clandestine activity on Chinese soil. The BAAG would be permitted to carry on with their official task of extracting Allied POWs and civilians from behind the Japanese lines, but the scope of their work was to be reduced from a large part of south China to the region around Canton and Hong Kong. With the advent of the OSS even that domain seemed to be threatened: at their meeting in Whitehall in June 1944 the British officials predicted with foreboding that the new American agency would be 'likely to move towards Hong Kong'.[139] Shortly after his arrival in October Wedemeyer took advantage of the growing scale of United States undercover activity to veto Operation Oblivion, the SOE project under which British saboteurs were to be infiltrated into the Hong Kong area with the help of the East River guerrillas. The reason formally given was that such a scheme would entail needless duplication of effort; but the SOE were in no doubt that the underlying intention was to tie Britain's hands. On a typical occasion in May 1945 Wedemeyer hauled in for a dressing-down at US Army Headquarters General Zheng Jiemin, Chiang's staff officer who was also the head of the Nationalist International Intelligence Service (IIS). Wedemeyer had been irked by Zheng's apparent acquiescence in a proposal the British had made for the joint training of a spy team to operate in Canton and Hong Kong. Why, he demanded, had Zheng not told him about this proposal before? Why couldn't the Nationalists do their intelligence gathering by themselves? Why did they have to cooperate with the British? As Chiang's Chief of Staff, he declared, it was his job to protect China's interests; and Zheng should at all times inform him of any requests made to carry out secret intelligence work by countries other than the United States.[140] In late July Major-General E. C. K. Hayes, the General Officer Commanding, British Troops China, reported to the War Office that the American attitude towards British military organizations in China was 'still tending to harden', that the Americans 'regard China as their theatre and barely tolerate our presence there at all'.[141] On 4 August the head of the SOE team at the headquarters of Mountbatten's South-east Asia Command at Kandy in Ceylon sent a cable to his chief in London inquiring pathetically whether there were 'any indications of steps being taken to *save* repeat *save* the BAAG'.[142]

In spite of their passive diplomatic posture the Nationalists too were posing an increasing menace to British ambitions. As Japan's grip on Hong Kong became more uncertain they quietly started rebuilding the underground presence which had been smashed by the Kempeitai in April 1943. At some point in the latter part of that year an irregular organization of some 2,000 men known to the British as the Chungking Gang was infiltrated into the occupied colony. The Gang was led by Shan Chit-son, a follower of the one-legged Admiral Chan Chak: he and his lieutenants were reported to be 'of a better class type', but the rank and file were described as 'just gangsters'. Their formal brief was to gather intelligence, commit sabotage and assassinate Japanese personnel. In addition however it was said that their aim was to secure control of Kowloon and Victoria 'at least temporarily' after the Japanese had been overthrown.[143] From the autumn of 1944 this revived Nationalist *maquis* were hoarding up arms and making preparations for an uprising to coincide with the expected landing by United States naval forces. By May 1945 the one-legged Admiral was himself hard at work at Xingning, in the south-east of Guangdong province, finalizing the plans for the Hong Kong revolt. Large bodies of irregular troops under local warlords were also said to be encamped in the neighbourhood of Kowloon, ready to march in if the right price were paid for their help in returning Hong Kong to the motherland.[144]

Yet another concern stemmed from the growing vigour and scope of the East River guerrillas. Unscathed by the Kempeitai crackdown of 1943, the Communists of the East River had also benefited indirectly in November that year when the Japanese cleared the Nationalists from the Shenzhen–Shilong stretch of the Kowloon–Canton railway line. This enabled them to broaden their operations without being exposed, as they had been till then, to incessant attacks from Nationalist forces far more enthusiastic about mauling the Communists than resisting the Japanese. With a total strength that by this time approached 6,000 partisans, including 1,000 or so inside Hong Kong territory,[145] the East River Column, as they now styled themselves, were starting to inflict ever more telling blows on the Japanese garrison in Hong Kong. Early in 1944 the dashing Blackie Lau led five associates in a raid on the newly expanded Kai Tak airport. They planted time bombs, blew up military oil depots and planes and, we are told, 'stayed for tea' before pulling out.[146] By the spring Blackie Lau's Pistol Squad, so called for their summary shootings of detected collaborators, were staging their first forays into the colony's urban areas. In April they blew up a railway bridge over Argyle Street in Kowloon. They distributed leaflets at night at the entrance to the Central Market in Victoria, and even had the audacity to scatter some around the sentry posts outside the Governor's Office. By the turn of the year they are said to have managed to infiltrate all the key departments of the occupation regime.[147] Their activities had become rather more than just fleabites, and the Japanese were under visible pressure. One of the main priorities of Tanaka's new administration was to launch a security programme in the New Territories aimed at stamping out the guerrilla campaign. By May 1945 the 23rd Army were deploying three whole divisions to hold down the Hong Kong–Canton area.[148] The Kempeitai were drafted in to help with the pacification in places where the Army were thin on the ground, but themselves got subjected to constant harassment and had to be reinforced by Koreans and local auxiliaries.

All of this should in theory have been fairly palatable to the British given the close partnership they had developed with the Communists in the first two years after the colony fell. But this partnership had been brought to an end, for all practical purposes, when the BAAG under Nationalist pressure broke off their ties with the East River guerrillas in August 1943. Tsoi Kwok-leung and his band soon took the opportunity to send a clear signal that they weren't to be lightly spurned. In October a team of five of the BAAG's Hong Kong Chinese agents who had ventured into the New Territories to set up a coast-watching station were captured by a bandit leader allied to the Communists and held for three months before the guerrillas stepped in to negotiate their release.[149] For some months during 1944 the East River Column also showed signs of transferring their interest to the Americans. They rescued a total of eight American airmen who had been shot down in the course of bombing raids over the colony, and carried out a substantial amount of intelligence work for both the 14th United States Air Squadron (the 'Flying Tigers') which operated on the mainland under General Claire Chennault, and more generally for the United

States Theatre Command.[150] The result was that the British began to regard their former comrades with a marked access of wariness. In July 1944 Major Ronald Holmes, who had led the BAAG's Forward Operational Group that worked with the guerrillas in the New Territories two years earlier, penned a report in which he expressed his opinion that their prime aim was, and always had been, to expand their military and political presence in the Hong Kong region. In September the SOE gave some thought to a possible scheme for smuggling in agents on Portuguese merchant ships sailing from Macao to Hong Kong precisely because this would enable them to 'avoid the Red area' on the fringe of the colony.[151] And in March 1945, when a Communist representative approached Reeves in Macao with a request for funds and weapons which would help his counterparts in Hong Kong to stage a revolt as part of the preparations for the expected Allied landing, the consul is said to have declared that he had recently been instructed by the British government to have absolutely no dealings with the Chinese Communist Party.[152] Over the following four months both the Colonial Office and the War Office in London warned of the danger of a possible seizure of Hong Kong by Chinese irregular forces and the resultant establishment there of a Chinese administration. And by irregular forces they meant the East River guerrillas as well as the Nationalists.[153]

By this time, however, a still more terrible spectre was rearing its head as the Nationalists and Americans combined their resources for a conventional land advance on Hong Kong. In early 1945 Wedemeyer began to lay plans for an offensive he entitled Operation Carbonado. The idea was that Nationalist regular troops, possibly with American officers and advisers and backed by some American air support, should drive south and east from their bases in Guangxi province and retake the entire Canton–Hong Kong area from the Japanese. In March Wedemeyer put this project to the Joint Chiefs of Staff in Washington, and by June he had secured their consent for substantial United States participation in the campaign. Midway through that summer, the Eisenhower of the East recalled in his memoirs, 'we actually were ahead of schedule in our preparations for the drive against Canton and Kowloon'.[154] Wedemeyer's and Chiang's agents were hard at work in Hong Kong handing out both the Stars and Stripes and the White Sun flags of the Nationalists so that citizens would be ready to welcome the conquering army when it arrived. In mid-July, when the Big Three powers met for the third time at the Potsdam conference, the Joint Chiefs (rather belatedly) advised their British opposite numbers that the current Japanese withdrawal on the south China coast was bringing Nationalist forces nearer the Canton area, and that a Nationalist drive on Canton and Hong Kong under United States direction could be expected in the near future. By the beginning of August the Nationalist regular army mobilized by Wedemeyer had reached the port of Guangzhouwan, just 210 miles to the south-west of the colony.

The British responded to this hydra-headed challenge in a number of different ways. In September 1944 they contrived, in the course of some quiet discussion with Washington, to get the prospect of an American naval landing in Hong Kong made a little more palatable. The Americans agreed that in Hong Kong, along with any other British territories in the Far East which might be relieved by United States forces, the policies to be followed immediately upon liberation should be laid down by the British government and accepted by the American commander on the ground. The commander would be accompanied by a British Civil Affairs staff whose function would be to prepare the colony for an early return to civilian rule. In other words the British would be given a piggy-back. They would be allowed to establish themselves in Hong Kong once again, and would have the chief say in the colony's management for at least the first few weeks or months of peace. This Civil Affairs Agreement was attainable because of a certain ambivalence in American thinking. Roosevelt's administration might be aiming to prod Britain into relinquishing its rights in Hong Kong; but wartime solidarity was still all-important, and they had no wish to provoke a major rift with their British ally by actively blocking British claims to the colony while the victory over the Axis powers still remained to be won. Such a deal was still not pleasing to the more zealous advocates of the British cause. 'When Hong Kong is retaken (by the Americans!) and handed back to the British on a platter', fumed the de Gaulle-like Ride, 'it will take British prestige a generation to live it down.'[155] But the Agreement at least held out to the British the hope of restoring their rule in Hong Kong in the short term, whatever ultimate solution might be worked out at a higher diplomatic level. The role of Civil Affairs staff was assigned, logically enough, to MacDougall's Hong Kong Planning Unit, whose total strength was increased from nine to thirty-eight. By the spring of 1945 arrangements were being made for MacDougall and his team to be given formal military rank and rushed into the colony with the putative United States force.

The threat from Chinese irregulars had to be headed off by somewhat more drastic methods. In his memorandum of 1 May 1944 Sir George Moss of the SOE urged that in view of the likelihood of fifth-column activity on the part of the Nationalists, the British should 'insist on a free hand in conducting our own para-military preparations in the Hong Kong area'.[156] By the following month the first in a series of SOE schemes for frustrating a *coup* by the Nationalist underground was being sketched out. The scheme entailed the smuggling of large quantities of Union Jacks into Hong Kong 'to stimulate an apparently spontaneous demonstration of pro-British feeling' on or, ideally, just before the reoccupation of the colony by Allied troops. It might, the proponent observed, be possible to have the flags produced in such a way that they would seem at first glance to be plain squares of silk, 'the design only appearing on contact with light or water'. These objects would be distributed with the suggestion 'that the display of such a flag on one's house or person at the moment when Allied troops re-entered was the best guarantee for the safety of one's person or one's goods'. The distribution would also 'give those Hong Kong Chinese who are loyally pro-British the opportunity to display the flag'.[157] The demonstration to be manufactured by this technique would presumably strengthen the hand of any British contingent that had managed to tag along with the American landing force. The scheme was said to have received a 'somewhat enthusiastic' reception from the SOE's China supremo, John Keswick.[158]

At the end of 1944 the SOE came up with a new idea. The idea was refined over the next three months by a series of Cabinet committees in London, and in late March 1945 it was forwarded to the British embassy in Chungking for the consideration of Ambassador Seymour. The proposal this time was that a single new organization should be set up from the combined resources of the SOE, the BAAG and the British Military Mission in Chungking. The role of the new body would be to train, equip and direct the operations of some 30,000 specially recruited Chinese guerrillas in the provinces of Guangxi and Guangdong. The 'primary aim' would be 'to contain Japanese forces and disrupt their communications'; the 'ulterior aim' would be 'to facilitate, at the appropriate moment, the reestablishment of British administration in Hong Kong'.[159] Seymour poured a dash of cold water over this suggestion, pointing out, understandably, that the control of a massive band of Chinese guerrillas would be 'very difficult', and that 'arming so large a force at first attempt was too risky'.[160] Some element of the concept, however, still seems to have survived in the following month when Ride received a proposal from London that he should recruit Hong Kong Chinese of a pro-British disposition in southern Guangdong with a view to infiltrating them into the colony.[161]

By mid-July the SOE were advising Whitehall on a still further scheme, this time aimed at frustrating irregular forces of either the Nationalist or the Communist kind. The scheme had been initiated by the Colonial Office, who had suddenly awoken to the possibility that the Japanese might execute a tactical withdrawal from the colony, leaving a power vacuum behind them. The essence of the project was that at the first sign of a Japanese pull-out the BAAG and the other British military outfits would smuggle in British personnel with instructions to form an emergency administration pending the arrival of MacDougall and his Civil Affairs staff. This administration, it was proposed, might be headed by Ride. The problem was how Ride and his group were to evict any government which might already have been organized by Chinese irregulars; and it was here that the SOE came in. All talk of recruiting pro-British loyalists among the Hong Kong Chinese population had now been abandoned. Instead a more realistic, not to say cynical, approach was proposed by REMORSE, the SOE's financial wizards who had raised huge amounts of cash on the Chinese black market:

I believe there is only one way of achieving the objective of this proposed operation, and that is by the use of money and bribery. Whatever Chinese group organises itself into a *de facto* Government in Hong Kong before [Allied] occupation, the only way of moving it out, or of getting permission to put in selected Europeans at the head of it, will be by purchase. There will be no force of arms to back up selected Europeans, and promises of future benefits will weigh considerably less than actual cash, or its equivalent in munitions or gold. Alternatively, if Europeans are infiltrated into Hong Kong before the Government is actually set up some inducement may be successful in forestalling the Chinese *coup*, and substituting one with a European facade. I cannot see how a small British unit, with no force of arms behind it, can hope to do the job . . .

I think the right way to handle this difficult-as-possible operation is for Ride to carry on with the organization of getting European personnel into Hong Kong, but for REMORSE to be put fully in the picture to know whom to bribe in the new [Hong Kong] Chinese Government, and to put one of their men into Hong Kong with the necessary inducements as soon as possible, so that the good work of bribery and corruption can start now.[162]

Within a couple of weeks doubts had started to be voiced about the feasibility of this idea too. The Foreign Office were worried that the incoming British might actually find themselves fighting their way into the colony against Chinese guerrillas claiming to owe allegiance to Chungking. This in turn might provoke a diplomatic clash between the British and Nationalist governments, which would place Britain in an 'extremely embarrassing situation'. Major-General Hayes in Chungking observed that in any event the only British available for the task contemplated were 'small elements of the BAAG'. It was hard, he went on, to see how 'even a bare minimum' of the BAAG's personnel could be freed to move into Hong Kong without the consent of the Nationalist and United States military authorities; a consent which seemed unlikely in view of the progress both these had made in constricting the BAAG to the point of paralysis.[163] But before the discussion could get any further the attention of the British was jerked away by the awful news of Wedemeyer's offensive and the approaching tramp of the Nationalist regular troops from Guangxi.

The basic risk of a lunge by a conventional Nationalist army had been foreseen at a quite early stage. Already in February 1944 Brigadier Grimsdale, the head of the British Military Mission in Chungking, had written to the Colonial Office:

I feel very strongly that it is absolutely essential for the future status of Hong Kong as a British possession that the first people to enter the Island should be British.

I have little doubt that the Chinese will do their best to be first when the time comes; *actually of course they could take it tomorrow if they really wanted to*! [my italics].

It may not be at all easy to stop this. But however difficult it may prove to be to our forces – whether naval, military or air or in combination – to get there before the Chinese, we MUST make every effort to do so.[164]

But where were these forces to come from? No significant British contingent of any kind was to be found within thousands of miles of the China coast. The only real hope seemed to lie, once again, in securing a piggy-back – not now from the Americans but from the Chinese.[165] At a combined meeting held on 23 July 1945 of the Foreign Office, the War Office, the Colonial Office and the Hong Kong Planning Unit it was decided that an attempt should be made with American help to obtain Chiang Kai-shek's blessing for the attachment of a British Civil Affairs team to Wedemeyer's advancing Nationalist troops. On 4 August Gent reported in a memorandum to his Permanent Secretary, Sir George Gater, 'We are preparing to reach an understanding with the Chinese that their military command will be instructed, in the event of a successful assault on Hong Kong, to accept and implement British Government policy on Civil Affairs in the Colony, and to accept and take in British personnel to conduct the Civil Affairs administration under the military commander.'[166] This was a somewhat tall order, however. As a Chinese enterprise under Chiang's formal authority, the Wedemeyer expedition was in no way obliged to consider itself bound by the provisions of the Anglo-American Civil Affairs Agreement, which Chiang's government hadn't signed. And Washington displayed no inclination to press Chiang to agree to a similar deal. In the spring the Joint Chiefs of Staff had referred Wedemeyer's proposed offensive to the scrutiny of an inter-departmental State–War–Navy Sub-Committee for the Far East. The Sub-Committee had ruled that so far as they were concerned Operation Carbonado was a venture being prepared with a view to attaining a strictly military end. Arrangements for the subsequent civil administration of Hong Kong were a separate matter to be worked out between Britain and China. This verdict of the Sub-Committee left Chiang full scope to demand that he should be consulted about the running of the colony as soon as Wedemeyer's forces had established control. Any such consultations, the Foreign Office observed, might 'bring to a head the whole question of the future of Hong Kong'. It was, Gent sighed, 'not an easy situation for us'.[167]

Operation Ethelred: the British slip back

There was, however, a tiny, a very tiny, window of opportunity. Wedemeyer for the moment was keeping his Nationalist army static in Guangzhouwan while he built up their supplies. He wanted, as he later explained, to ensure that once the 'final drive' was launched against Canton and Hong Kong the attacking forces 'would be appropriately supported and would not bog down due to the lack of strong air support and ammunition or replacements'.[168] Like everyone else up to this stage Wedemeyer was assuming that the Allies would need to reconquer the Canton–Hong Kong area in a bloody assault. By early August, however, Gent and his colleagues in the Colonial Office were starting to have intimations of a more rapid dénouement. 'There remains', Gent observed in his memorandum of 4 August, 'the possibility that Japan may capitulate . . . '[169] In that event there might just be scope for the British to rush a naval force through to the colony before their competitors were ready to move in. On the direction of his boss, Sir George Gater, Gent accordingly drew up a contingency plan to be put before the British Chiefs of Staff. The plan was that instructions should be issued to 'two or three fast moving fleet units' to place themselves at convenient points so that if Japanese capitulation looked probable they could 'steam at once for Hong Kong under sealed orders on a given signal'.[170] Landing parties from such a force would be able to deal with any Chinese irregulars far more effectively than a few scattered commandos from the BAAG: in addition the advent of an independent British force would be vastly preferable to the piggy-back option from the point of view of asserting Britain's authority. On 10 August a further memorandum, also drafted by Gent, was submitted by the Secretary of State for the Colonies in the new Labour government to the new Prime Minister, Clement Attlee. At a Cabinet meeting held the same day the Chief of the Imperial General Staff came out in support of the Colonial Office design, and on 13 August the Cabinet's Defence Committee decided formally on the dispatch of a naval squadron to Hong Kong as soon as the Japanese had announced their surrender.

In the meantime the prospect of such an announcement had been brought dramatically closer by the dropping of atomic bombs on Hiroshima and Nagasaki and the Soviet attack on Japan in Manchuria. On 10 August the Japanese Foreign Ministry issued a note through their consul in Stockholm seeking peace terms from the United States, Britain, the Soviet Union and China. And on 15 August, in spite of some last-minute ructions from diehards in the Imperial Army, the announcement was made. Emperor Hirohito declared in a broadcast to his people that the war had 'developed not necessarily to Japan's advantage'.[171] He accepted the terms for surrender which had been issued by the Allies at the Potsdam conference and instructed his forces in every part of East Asia to lay down their arms.

The war was over: the dash was on.

The naval force visualized by Gent could in theory be furnished from the British Pacific Fleet which had been created at the end of the previous year to assist the United States Navy in the rolling back of the Japanese. The snag was that the British Pacific Fleet did not constitute an autonomous unit. Although on paper 'the greatest British fleet ever assembled',[172] it had been integrated for operational purposes with the still vaster United States Pacific Fleet; and no squadron could be detached from it without first obtaining American permission. This meant that Britain would need to execute a certain amount of rapid diplomatic footwork in Washington before any military move could take place. Shortly after the Cabinet took their decision to rush in a squadron urgent overtures were accordingly made to the United States Joint Chiefs of Staff. But these overtures were not enough. On 14 August the Joint Chiefs agreed to the detachment of a force from the British Pacific Fleet; but they made it cagily clear that they viewed this release as being 'unrelated to any British proposals concerning Hong Kong'.[173] On the following day, within two hours of Hirohito's broadcast, a task force intended for Hong Kong was dispatched from Sydney under the command of Rear Admiral Cecil Harcourt: this force's immediate destination, however, was the United States naval base at Subic Bay in the Philippines, and it could go no further until the underlying diplomatic question had been sorted out. The fact was that the British request would have to go up to the White House – and the White House would have to be asked to make an unambiguous judgement as to whether Britain or China was to move into Hong Kong. Already at the Cabinet meeting of 10 August Prime Minister Attlee had expressed his feeling that in view of the political considerations involved the issue would have to be settled at the very highest level through a personal telegram from himself to the new United States President, Harry Truman, who had succeeded Roosevelt on the latter's death in mid-April. On 18 August he accordingly cabled to Truman that Harcourt's fleet was on its way, and asked him to instruct General Douglas MacArthur, the Supreme Commander for the Allied Powers in the Pacific, to ensure that the Japanese military chiefs in Hong Kong made their surrender to Harcourt when he arrived.

Diplomatic steps also had to be taken to neutralize any possible obstruction from Chiang Kai-shek. The initial British tactic was simply to present Chiang with a *fait accompli*. On 14 August the Foreign Office sent a telegram to the British embassy in Chungking instructing them to inform the Generalissimo that Britain was moving to reoccupy the colony and restore its administration there. Two days later, when he went across to the Nationalist Foreign Ministry to receive their reply, the British Counsellor added that in the light of the new arrangements he 'did not think His Majesty's Government would like the idea' of Chinese divisions arriving in Hong Kong to take over from the Japanese. It would 'create disquiet' in the colony, and would also make for an 'added complication' now that a British force was available.[174] This breezy gambit however ran up against the immediate obstacle of the General Order No. 1 which Truman had already issued to MacArthur in response to Hirohito's broadcast. Under the terms of this order each of the regional Allied commanders in the

Pacific was to accept Japan's surrender in his respective theatre of war. As it happened the fate of Hong Kong hadn't been spelled out in this document. Possibly it had just been overlooked, caught in its usual limbo between China and South-east Asia. But it had not been included, like the rest of Britain's Far Eastern colonies, under Mountbatten's South-east Asia Command; and it was clear even to many of the British (including the Chief of the Imperial General Staff) that it belonged logically in the China theatre – of which Chiang was the Supreme Commander. On 18 August, consequently, the new British Foreign Secretary, Ernest Bevin, dispatched a cable to his Chinese Nationalist counterpart setting out a new and subtler British line which the Foreign Office and Colonial Office had concocted between them. The line was that Britain was entitled to resume its authority in places like Hong Kong where it was the sovereign power irrespective of the operational area, provided that it had sufficient forces on hand. Bevin followed this up with an argument based on British 'face' that was clearly designed to appeal to the Chinese way of thinking. He felt confident, he wrote, that 'as a soldier himself' Chiang Kai-shek would understand that as Britain was forced to relinquish Hong Kong to the Japanese it was 'a matter of military honour' to the British government to accept the Japanese surrender there.[175] As a concession to Chiang's 'face' he added that Britain would welcome the presence of a representative of the Generalissimo in Hong Kong at the ceremony which it planned to hold to receive the surrender of the Japanese garrison.

This British eloquence had little obvious impact where Chiang was concerned. The Generalissimo's 'face' had already been put very much on the line by Britain's basic decision to send troops to 'his' theatre of war without first obtaining his authorization.[176] In addition (like everyone else) he was well aware that the issue wasn't merely one of who received the surrender, but entailed the whole question of sovereignty over Hong Kong. At the very least he needed to stake a claim to Chinese sovereignty with a view to strengthening China's position in the post-war discussions about the New Territories which were due to be held under the protocol to the 1943 extra-territoriality treaty. He accordingly fought back by making his own appeal to his long-time backer, the United States. On 16 August he sent off, through Ambassador Hurley, a personal message to Truman insisting that he, or a representative appointed by him, had the right to receive Japan's surrender in the colony under the terms of General Order No. 1. On 18 August Foreign Minister Soong in Washington reinforced this message with a plea to the United States Secretary of State, James F. Byrnes.

Times however had changed in America. Truman had none of his predecessor's emotional commitment to the Chinese cause. Unlike Roosevelt he wasn't noted for his anti-colonial views; he was disillusioned with Roosevelt's erstwhile hero, Chiang Kai-shek; and he was far more preoccupied with the relations among the Allied victors in Europe than with anything going on in East Asia. His preference was for a cautious policy based on 'recognition of the established rights'.[177] In this attitude he was backed by Byrnes and the State Department, and for good measure by General MacArthur, who was known for his support of the British Empire in the Far East and had remarked as early as October 1944 that he 'fully appreciated the need for British forces to recapture Hong Kong'.[178] On 18 August Truman consequently cabled back to Attlee that he had no objection to the surrender of Hong Kong being received by a British officer, provided that 'full military coordination was effected beforehand' with Chiang to ensure Britain gave any help needed by the Nationalist and American troops who were still busy fighting the Japanese or securing their surrender in the hinterland.[179] On the same day he responded to Chiang and Byrnes responded to Soong in similar terms. In effect the line taken was identical to that which had been adopted just two months earlier by the State–War–Navy Sub-Committee for the Far East in their endorsement of Operation Carbonado. The recapture of Hong Kong was regarded as being a strictly military exercise, and the decision implied nothing about the Administration's views as to the future status of the colony. For immediate purposes, however, the Truman decision gave the British everything they had hoped for. The Foreign Office in London reported jubilantly that the question of Hong Kong had been 'dealt with' by Truman's cable, and a Colonial Office staffer crowed that the cable was 'the key document in the whole shooting match, in my opinion'.[180]

Bitterly disappointed by Truman's response, Chiang proceeded to wage a subtle diplomatic rearguard action. On 21 August he came up with a 'compromise'. The Japanese garrison in Hong Kong, he proposed, should surrender to his representative: British and American troops could take part in the ceremony, and as soon as it was over he would authorize the British to land their forces for the reoccupation of the colony. The British however would have no truck with this suggestion. If a Chinese commander received the surrender, the next step would be for him to declare that he was in Hong Kong to stay. And Truman upheld Britain's veto. On 23 August Chiang advanced a second proposal that was, if anything, slyer than the first. He would delegate his authority as Supreme Commander in the China theatre to a British commander who would receive the surrender on his behalf – after which the British would take control. Truman thought this idea 'quite reasonable';[181] but the British jibbed once again. The Colonial Office and Foreign Office had no doubt that for Britain to receive back the colony formally from Chinese hands would constitute an irreparable blow to British prestige.[182] Informed of this further rebuff Truman deplored the friction between his British and Chinese allies, but made it clear to Chiang that there was nothing more he could do.

For all the headway they were making on the diplomatic front the British still faced the risk that their dash for the colony might be thwarted by some rival military move. In the first few days after the Japanese surrender announcement they continued to run up against the antagonism of the United States military chiefs on the Chinese mainland. Hirohito's broadcast had found Wedemeyer still taking his time as he made ready the 'twenty thoroughly equipped and trained Chinese divisions' he expected to throw into the all-out offensive against Canton and Hong Kong in the course of September.[183] But the Eisenhower of the East carried on doing all in his power to obstruct British aims. On 14 August the AGAS intelligence staff, who along with the BAAG were now based in the south-western city of Kunming, unveiled a plan to parachute an American squad into the colony to make an initial contact with the POWs and internees in the camps. Ride and some of his BAAG colleagues were to be allowed to come too; but it was made clear that they would be brought along strictly as guests. The operation was to be led by an American officer; the stores included United States flags but no British ones; and the POWs (if successfully reached) were to be issued with American uniforms. Informed of these proposals the British intelligence bosses assumed Wedemeyer must be hell-bent on getting Americans in to Hong Kong, if only to make headlines in the American papers. 'We vomit with disgust and pray for further details.'[184] Ride – an enraged de Gaulle cheated of his entry into Paris – sent frantic signals conveying his fear that Wedemeyer might try to fly in Nationalist officers to receive the Japanese surrender; and as late as 18 August the Foreign Office were 'seriously concerned'.[185] At this point, however, the Truman decision resulted in an abrupt reining in of the American military. On 19 August the Joint Chiefs of Staff issued instructions to General MacArthur to arrange for the surrender of the colony to Rear Admiral Harcourt. The instructions were copied to Wedemeyer. 'Belatedly', Wedemeyer recalled in a grim undertone in his memoirs, 'I received information that this was a question that should be settled between the Chinese and the British.'[186]

This did not however remove the possibility that Chiang Kai-shek might attempt a military lunge on his own initiative. To all appearances he had dismissed any thought of resorting to force. On 24 August, in a speech to a joint session of his Supreme National Defence Council and the Nationalist Party's Central Standing Committee, he declared:

We will not take advantage of this opportunity to dispatch troops to take over Hong Kong . . . Now that all the leased territories and settlements in China have been one after another returned to China, the leased territory at Kowloon [sc. the New Territories] should not remain an exception; but China will settle this last issue through diplomatic talks between the two countries.[187]

The British ambassador to Chungking, Sir Horace Seymour, observed however that Chiang's assurances were 'not entirely unequivocal';[188] and there is in fact evidence to suggest that the Generalissimo had troops closing in on the colony at the very time he delivered his speech. On 15 August, after Hirohito's broadcast had been picked up in Chungking, he had cabled orders that the Nationalist forces in south China should receive the surrender of the Japanese 23rd Army in a series of places throughout Guangdong province. In conformity with his diplomatic posture, the list of designated places included Hong Kong.[189] And on 21 August, *after* his rebuff by Truman and *after* the Joint Chiefs of Staff had taken the steps necessary to rein in Wedemeyer, Chiang reissued his orders and fleshed them out. The New 1st Army and the 13th Army were to advance from their bases in Guangxi province to receive the surrender of the Japanese garrisons in Canton and Hong Kong. Overall charge of the mission was given to a rugged and independent-minded Cantonese warlord, General Zhang Fakui, the commander-in-chief of the Nationalist Second Military Region, and responsibility for the Hong Kong operation was assigned to the 13th Army under Lieutenant-General Shi Jue. One portion of Shi's army was to proceed from Canton along the railway line to Kowloon to receive the surrender of the local Japanese forces: this contingent was then to take over as the colony's garrison, while the displaced Japanese troops were to be concentrated on the other side of the Shenzhen River at Bao'an. The new garrison were then to appropriate the bulk of the Japanese arms (apart from infantry guns, light machine-guns and a small amount of ammunition), and were also to effect the release of the Allied POWs and civilian internees. Details of the advance which took place in the next few days were provided the following year in a memoir composed by General Zhang Fakui himself. One after another, Zhang recalled, the units moved forward from their existing positions towards their designated goals. Although it was still summer and the summer sun burned like fire, the morale of the officers and men was soaring, and they 'pressed on day and night'.[190]

The Communists also were making their move. On 10 August (the day it became known that Japan was seeking to surrender) Zhu De, the Red Army commander-in-chief in Yan'an, made a wireless broadcast to his forces in all parts of China, instructing them to receive the surrender of the Japanese Army units stationed in their neighbourhood and to make a collection of Japanese arms. Among the partisan leaders who picked up these instructions was Zeng Sheng, the commander of the East River Column in Guangdong. On 11 August Zeng Sheng and his staff in turn issued an emergency directive. Each of their guerrilla bands was to advance on the nearest Japanese outpost and confiscate the arms held by the Japanese troops and their local collaborators. The guerrillas were then to keep order, to protect life and property and to 'suppress banditry and the subversive activity of spies'. Every moment was precious, and 'there should not be the slightest delay'.[191] The guerrillas accordingly swung into action. In the course of the next two weeks the Hong Kong and Kowloon Independent Brigade took control of Taipo and Yuen Long and all the other market towns in the New Territories, as well as the colony's outer islands. At one place, Silvermine Bay on the island of Lantau, they encountered resistance from an Imperial Army contingent who had either not heard Hirohito's surrender announcement or refused to accept it:[192] everywhere else the Japanese gave up meekly or fled as soon as the guerrillas approached. The Brigade collected a total of 400 rifles and pistols, twenty-odd machine-guns, five pieces of artillery and several hundred shells, along with military vehicles and other equipment. In each centre they organized local administrations and encouraged the villagers to set up self-defence forces and youth groups and to raise money with which to buy further arms. In the general hunt for Japanese weapons and other assets a squad of guerrillas under a certain Fang Lan went so far as to march into the colony's urban area. It is not quite clear on which day they did this, but there seems to be no doubt that they were the first Allied unit to enter Kowloon.[193]

Yet in neither the case of the Nationalists nor the Communists was this activity quite what it seemed. In the days following Hirohito's broadcast Chiang Kai-shek was engaged in a wide range of strategic manœuvres. He was rushing administrators and troops to the east to reoccupy his former capital, Nanking, and his old commercial metropolis of Shanghai. He was readying armies to move back into the major centres of north China and the industrial heartland of Manchuria. His overwhelming concern was to regain control of as much territory as possible before the inevitable showdown with his former Communist partners.[194] And the same applied in south China too. Already back in April Chiang was said to have issued orders for the annihilation of the Communist forces to the south of the Yangtze river.[195] Seen in this context a military thrust designed to prevent British forces getting back into Hong Kong made little sense. Disappointed as Chiang might have been by the Truman decision, he still had reason to suppose, under the terms of the protocol to the 1943 treaty, that talks with Britain over at least the New Territories would be under way in the near future. He had nothing to gain from antagonizing the British, still less the Americans, by a sudden grab for the colony: on the contrary he was going to need their support in the conflict ahead. In the light of these factors the Generalissimo's surreptitious advance on Hong Kong starts to look rather different. He may not necessarily have been lying when he declared to his followers that he had no thought of wresting Hong Kong from the British by force. His intention may rather have been to prevent the Communists winning both the colony and the kudos that would come with its liberation *if the British failed to get there in time.* In late August newspaper dispatches were filed in Chungking claiming that the Nationalists were after all racing troops to beat the British to the colony. The Nationalist authorities did not deny that their armies were on the move. They are merely said to have stated that even if their troops reached Hong Kong first 'they would only do so to hold it until the British returned'. Major-General Hayes was informed by his Nationalist counterparts that one Chinese division was to be moved to the border of the New Territories 'to prevent movement of Communists and other non-Central Government troops into it' but that on no account would the border be crossed.[196]

A similar explanation may be proposed for the acts of the Communists. They too were busy building up their position in all parts of south China in readiness for the approaching civil war.[197] As early as the summer of 1944 it had become evident that one of the main functions of the East River guerrillas in the New Territories was to block the path of a Nationalist advance on Kowloon. True, their total strength inside the colony numbered no more than 1,000, and they didn't have any permanent bases: one observer judged them none the less to be perfectly capable of harrying the flanks of a Nationalist invasion and obstructing the progress of the enemy vanguard with crude mines and booby traps.[198] In the days after Hirohito's broadcast they were clearly hoarding up both land and arms in the expectation of waging an imminent battle for the control of the area; and their exertions were, equally clearly, not aimed at the British. They disclaimed any wish to recover the colony for China, taking refuge behind the Allies' Potsdam Declaration under which Hong Kong was to be handed – in the first instance, at least – back to Britain following the defeat of Japan.[199] They took no steps which might have impeded the entry of Harcourt's marines from the seaward side, and indeed indicated that they were doing what they could to promote that development. In Cheung Chau island, where they arrived on 20 August, they declared frankly that they intended to move out as soon as the British were ready to take over.[200]

The upshot was that the Nationalists and Communists cancelled each other out. Each side preferred to see the colony recaptured by the British than to have it liberated by their Chinese rivals. Chiang, with high-calibre troops and a competent local commander in the form of Zhang Fakui,[201] could in theory have taken Hong Kong with some ease against any likely British opposition. But he desisted from pressing home his advantage, permitting his troops to advance on the colony at the same relatively slow pace that had characterized their progress in 1941.[202] And Chairman Mao and his cadres, by throwing up an obstacle to any possible Nationalist adventure and at the same time leaving the way wide open for Harcourt, played a small but perceptible part in enabling the British to recover their colony for another fifty years.

In spite of these shifts in the diplomatic and military kaleidoscope the British were not yet assured of regaining Hong Kong. Much still hung on the course of events inside the occupied city. In Kowloon and Victoria the reaction of the Japanese to their Emperor's broadcast was one of dazed trauma. 'Maybe', one official remarked, 'we didn't expect to lose like this – suddenly, like a bat swooping out of the night.' Lieutenant-Colonel Endo, the India expert, rushed back to his office with tears streaming down his face and told his local assistants, 'Now you can be happy . . . It's over for us.'[203] And the rank-and-file soldiers listened on their knees or with bowed heads as the words of surrender from the divine Mikado were relayed to them over loudspeakers. As the Japanese reeled, the streets and districts around them embarked on a rapid descent into ultimate chaos. The starving population looted unrestrained: one Stanley inmate reported that 'no law and order now existed in town'.[204] Hong Kong had now visibly entered into the long-awaited political vacuum. A real danger existed that a local Chinese faction might seize control, posing an embarrassing and perhaps fatal obstacle to a British return.

The hour had now struck for Franklin Gimson and the schemes he had meditated in Stanley camp.

The Colonial Office had been alive from the start to the importance of activating Gimson. On 11 August, when the main concern in Whitehall was still to uphold Britain's rights in the face of Wedemeyer's expected takeover, an initial message had been sent to the doughty Colonial Secretary 'to instruct him to forestall any consequence of a military liberation of Hong Kong by re-forming the existing administration there'. Two days later this message was reinforced by a second, 'We are endeavouring urgently to secure the consent of the American Chiefs of Staff to detach British Naval Force from British Pacific Fleet to steam for Hong Kong.'[205] The Foreign Office transmitted these messages to Seymour in Chungking, who in turn passed them on to the BAAG – thereby giving Ride's frustrated outfit the one chance which came its way in the whole of this critical fortnight to play a conspicuous role. On 14 August the BAAG announced that the messages had been sent to Forward Headquarters, which would arrange for an agent to carry them on. Communications however were slow (some reliance had to be placed on a Chinese government runner),[206] and it was only on 17 August that the message got through to an appropriate agent in the form of Phoenix in Macao. Phoenix for his part took several days to get moving, because the sea passages from Macao to Hong Kong were heavily mined; but on 21 August he set off for the colony. On the following day he arrived, and went looking for Gimson with Whitehall's official command to take power in the interval pending the arrival of Harcourt's fleet.

All these exertions however turned out to be needless, for Gimson of course had not bothered to wait for Whitehall's go-ahead. Already on 16 August the end of the war had been announced in the colony's press, and the first rumours had started to seep into Stanley. On the following morning the Colonial Secretary sought confirmation from the current Japanese camp commandant, Kadowaki. The commandant drew himself up and declared, 'His Majesty the

Emperor has taken into consideration the terms of the Potsdam conference and has ordered hostilities to cease. In other words you've won; we've lost.'[207] Gimson at once called together a group of senior officials and businessmen to discuss the practical steps that would be involved in taking control of the colony's administration. Some doubt was voiced as to whether Gimson could assume authority in the absence of a formal mandate;[208] but at this point a weird incident helped to spur matters on. On 18 August Gimson received a visit from a 'mysterious messenger' who appeared in his quarters 'with the air of a conspirator making a secret rendezvous'. This Chinese stranger proceeded to give the Colonial Secretary a breakdown of developments in the outside world. In a scene that might almost have come from a fairy-tale he asked Gimson if he wanted any money 'and from a bag poured on to a small table in the room a quantity of golden sovereigns'.[209] The identity of this unknown Chinese benefactor remains obscure, but he seems to have been an additional, Hong Kong-based agent of the BAAG whom the BAAG's Forward Head-quarters had sent to anticipate Whitehall's orders to Gimson with a kind of informal tip-off.[210] This visit at any rate gave Gimson all the justification he required. He promptly summoned his leading officials and got himself sworn in by the Chief Justice, Sir Atholl MacGregor, as the Acting Governor of Hong Kong. On the following day, with some help from Selwyn-Clarke, who had just emerged from a POW camp to which he had been consigned for the final months of the war, Gimson managed to arrange a meeting with Lieutenant-Colonel Simon White, the senior British army officer left in the colony, and secured his agreement that a British civilian authority must be established right away. (Gimson was worried that the installation of a military government might have the effect of placing the colony under the orders of an American commander-in-chief.)[211] And 'after a day or two', during which Phoenix made his appearance with the formal orders from Whitehall, the new Acting Governor led his colleagues out of Stanley and set up his long-planned skeleton government in the heart of Victoria, in the former French Mission building.[212]

It was a skeleton government in a horribly literal sense. Emaciated, their bones protruding, the newly freed internees sat in rags around tables on which blankets had been spread 'to procure some dignity', while the Chief Justice, mortally sick, dispensed legal advice from a palliasse on the floor.[213] In the course of the following week Gimson and his team made a number of largely symbolic moves to assert Britain's presence. Gimson made contact with London to order a new supply of Hong Kong dollars (repeating his early demand in 1942). On 28 August he broadcast to the world that Hong Kong was once again British, and on the next day a single-page issue was printed, for the first time in nearly four years, of the *South China Morning Post*. But no amount of symbolism could disguise the fact that Gimson and his colleagues wholly

lacked the means to enforce public order, or to make their authority felt in a
tangible way. To achieve those objectives they had to resort to the help of some
curious partners.

The Japanese, to begin with, were down but not out. Traumatized though
they might be, the 20,000-odd troops of the Imperial garrison were still far
and away the most substantial force in the city. Gimson and his team were in
no position to do anything without their say-so, as Gimson himself tacitly recognized. On the morning of 18 August, after the initial discussion with his colleagues in Stanley, Gimson addressed himself to two leading Japanese who had
just arrived on a visit – Colonel Tokunaga, the commandant of all the camps
in Hong Kong, and K. Makimura, the civilian head of the Foreign Affairs
Department. He informed them that he was proposing to take charge of the
colony in his capacity as Senior Official of the Hong Kong government, and
asked them to facilitate this by arranging office space in town for himself
and his colleagues and providing him with the use of a wireless station. In
a message sent to the Colonial Office on 23 August, after Phoenix had presented him with Whitehall's formal blessing, he further underlined this dependent relationship, reporting that he was 'negotiating with the Japanese with a
view to the resumption of civil administration'.[214] In particular Gimson's team
had no chance of holding down the city unless the beaten occupation regime
was prepared to play ball. In a second message dispatched to Whitehall on 27
August the Acting Governor drew attention to this vital point. In his judgement 'an attempt to set up formally a British civil administration before the
arrival of our forces would be unwise in view of the fact that we have not the
necessary force to maintain law and order if the Japanese troops are withdrawn
to delimited areas'. Gimson went on to spell out his most pressing anxieties:

> It is reported that Chinese irregulars have entered the New Territories
> and that armed gangs are being organized, particularly in Kowloon where
> looting has been observed. Am making representations to the Japanese, but
> am apprehensive that this threat may increase.[215]

It was far from clear at the outset that Gimson was going to get the assistance he sought. Governor Tanaka was (as usual) away in Canton, and had
been issued with no instructions as to which Allied power was to receive the
surrender of his garrison. Some of the Japanese high-ups expressed their
support for the view that Hong Kong should be yielded to Chinese forces
insofar as it lay in the Chinese theatre of war. Tokunaga and Makimura
observed to Gimson at the interview on 18 August that the colony's future was
still undecided and there was no certainty it would carry on being British.[216]
On the same day Arthur May, an enthusiastic POW who had slipped up
the Peak with a fellow detainee and hoisted a long-secreted Union Jack, was
politely but firmly requested to haul it down again after just a few hours.[217]

A number of factors were none the less quietly operating in Gimson's favour. Over the last three and a half years he had managed to build up a fair stock of credit among the Japanese administrators as the one internee they could deal with satisfactorily, both for practical and social purposes. Plump Tokunaga loved few things more than a seven-hour bridge game, and from 1944 onwards each time he descended on Stanley 'bridge with the Colonel' had become an inescapable item on Gimson's schedule.[218] Whatever the logical case for surrendering to Chinese forces (and many officers argued with equal cogency that since the 23rd Army had captured Hong Kong from the British it was to the British that they should hand it back), most Japanese in the colony were in no hurry to fall into the clutches of the Chinese – least of all into those of the East River Column.[219] Much more generous treatment would, they surmised, be forthcoming from the fellow imperial power. Dozens of Japanese civilians are said to have been sure that they would be back in business within weeks of a British return; and the military chiefs were sufficiently confident of Britain's benevolence that they drew up a document offering their surrender to Harcourt's approaching squadron on the most congenial possible terms to themselves. Japanese lives and property, they proposed, should be safeguarded, and all Japanese should be allowed to hold on to their money. Farms should be placed at the disposal of the Imperial troops, and the British should offer them construction work. The civilian settlers should be allowed to stay on in the colony, with their own hospitals, schools, temples and Association; and no 'unjust oppression' should be inflicted on them. 'Apparently', a subsequent British report concluded, 'the Japanese thought they were going to live alongside us, with a good time to be had by all.'[220]

Any instinct the Japanese had to work with Gimson may have been given an additional nudge by Whitehall. According to one account the Foreign Office contacted the British ambassador in Lisbon with an urgent message for his Japanese counterpart. The Japanese envoy was asked to cable the Governor's Office in Hong Kong with instructions to hand over power to Gimson's team.[221]

Even if the Japanese weren't inclined to recognize Gimson's right to take over the colony, their general mood suggested that they could at least be relied on to play the stabilizing role which the Acting Governor had envisaged for them. By late August they had 'recovered from the initial shock of defeat and showed signs of recovering their morale'.[222] Regardless of who was to step into their shoes they were said to be quite convinced that it was their responsibility to maintain public order until a formal surrender could be organized.

Whatever precisely the course of this thinking, the outcome was that the Japanese command in the colony fell in like a dream with Gimson's designs. Even in the first hesitant hours they complied with his basic requests for practical help. They provided a bus to transport him and his officials from camp into town, and accommodation in the form of the French Mission building.[223] On 23 August the Acting Governor was able to report to London, 'Their attitude appears favourable though progress will be slow. Preliminary liaison already established with certain departments.' Four days later any lingering unwillingness to support Gimson's enterprise had seemingly dropped away. Gimson reported that the Japanese had now 'agreed to facilitate unofficial liaison with their civil and military organizations'.[224] Consultations between the occupation regime and its would-be British replacement were by this stage taking place on a day-to-day basis. 'Smartly clad Japanese officers' walked from their headquarters in the Hongkong and Shanghai Bank up Battery Path to the French Mission building, 'their swords clanging at each step'.[225] Pending the arrival of the new supply of Hong Kong dollars from London the Governor's Office enabled the British to take back control of their banks from the Japanese liquidators, and to overprint the existing unused stocks of military yen with the legend, 'Hong Kong Government One Dollar'. And they also gave access to the wireless station from which Gimson made his broadcast to the world on 28 August. They agreed not to cut off the water, gas, electricity and telephone services, thereby enabling Hong Kong to avoid the breakdown of facilities that had taken place following the invasion of 1941. Most important of all, the Army remained on duty while the Kempeitai stayed at their posts – very much as the British police had done in the immediate aftermath of the Japanese victory almost four years before.

The British responded to all this with their own brand of imperial cosiness. The Japanese, they felt, had 'behaved admirably'.[226] Kenneth Uttley, the government doctor, observed placidly in a letter to his wife that the Japanese were 'still in control, holding and policing the place until the British Authorities arrive to take over'.[227] It is somewhat hard to imagine a band of released British POWs in Europe making similar use of the Nazi supervisors of Colditz or Mauthausen. In several parts of East Asia, however, the resurgent British were looking in much the same way to their Japanese enemies for help in restraining the passions of the newly freed subject populations.[228] For the Acting Governor, who had more than once in the last three years called in the Japanese to help him discipline the unrulier of his own fellow inmates in Stanley, such a tactic may have seemed only natural. Gimson later recalled ruefully that his administration had been styled in some quarters 'the puppet Government'. This, however, he noted, had been 'by those who did not appreciate its true purport'.[229]

Japanese military back-up was still not enough in itself to keep the town calm. For the past several months, as we have seen, the Japanese had themselves been losing the fight against lawlessness, and had been obliged to fall back on the help of the Triads in the form of the Protective Guards. Gimson had little choice but to use the same weapon. 'The small nucleus of the [British] police force available', he later recorded, 'necessitated improvisation of a scheme dependent on cooperation with certain criminal elements of the local population whose assistance might in other circumstances not have been evoked'.[230] F. W. Shaftain, the Director of Criminal Investigation, who had managed the government's dealings with the Triad underworld during the desperate crisis of mid-December 1941, reassembled his staff, 'getting his finger back', as one account notes with relish, 'on the Colony's crime pulse – which was a very vigorous and quick-beating pulse indeed'.[231] Shaftain and his colleagues received an initial approach from none other than Wan Yuk-ming, the Triad chieftain whose 3,000-strong following (the British called them the Gambling House Gang) had latterly played the main part in holding back crime for the Japanese in return for the privilege of running the casinos. Wan offered the British his services on condition that he should be allowed to continue his lucrative racket. Wan's offer was refused; but 'the position was difficult, as he had more armed forces at his disposal than the police had'. Instead the British leaders decided to plump for a rival Triad outfit – the Chungking Gang headed by Shan Chit-son. By the last days of August Gimson was deploying an auxiliary police force composed of around 700 of these Chinese thugs. The Chungking Gang auxiliaries were allowed to wear armbands of office. They were given police wages and were promised that in return for their help at this critical juncture they would be allowed to make themselves scarce when the British resumed full authority, with no questions asked.[232]

This of course was potentially a high-risk approach insofar as the Chungking Gang policemen were members of a Nationalist-affiliated group. Venal ruffians though most of them were, they might none the less be mobilized at any time in a local Nationalist attempt to seize power. To counter such a prospect the British inescapably had to seek some support from the established community leaders. On 23 August a young Chinese aged about thirty and 'immaculately dressed in a white silk robe' appeared, like an angel out of the Gospels, at the house of M. K. Lo. It was Phoenix, the BAAG agent newly arrived in Hong Kong with his message for Gimson, who had been assigned the additional task of 'prompting local initiative'.[233] No British effort appears at this stage (perhaps significantly) to have been made to contact any gentry leaders apart from the trusted Lo. Gimson's skeleton government was composed exclusively of the former European members of the Executive and Legislative Councils whom the Acting Governor had assembled in Stanley. But the old gentry leadership had set their own plans in train.

News of Japan's collapse had provoked an instant resumption of the familiar partnership of Kotewall and Chow. On 16 August Kotewall (who seems to have made a rapid recovery from the illness which had immobilized him two weeks earlier) arrived with his colleague for several hours of talks with

Rakuman Kinji, the civilian head of the No. 1 Department of the Governor's Office. Kotewall and Chow then moved on to the Police Headquarters, where they exchanged views with Kanazawa, the Police Commissioner and Kempeitai chief. On the following day the two men gave a press conference at which they declared that the situation in the colony was now 'on the verge of change', and praised the Chinese public for their 'patience and good behaviour' during the past three years and eight months.[234]

Kotewall and Chow were clearly making a bid of their own to fill the vacuum of authority in the stupefied city. In the first place they were driven by the constant gentry concern to fend off social chaos. At their meeting with Kanazawa they discussed ways of strengthening the existing police apparatus, and stressed to the Kempeitai boss that 'law and order must be fully protected'.[235] On the afternoon of the next day Chow attended, in his capacity as chairman of the Police Affairs Committee, a meeting of the directors of the Cooperative Society which had been set up in May to raise funds for the police. 'Sparing no effort to devise protection for the Hong Kong Chinese' in spite of his eighty-six years, Chow returned on 18 August for a second session with Kanazawa. A decision was taken that the Cooperative Society would distribute rice to the police free of charge, and that the Police Affairs Committee would foot the bill.[236] Kotewall and Chow also organized a gentry drive to sustain the activities of the auxiliary Protective Guards. Over the following week most of the Guards' expenses were met out of voluntary donations made by 'wealthy people' in each district. These donations gradually began to flag as the days went on, but they seem to have had some effect: on 26 August the Protective Guards were still reported to be 'continuing their efforts to help maintain order'.[237]

Second and equally urgent, the two gentry leaders were seeking to manage a smooth transition from one regime to the next. Throughout these final days of the occupation they kept up an outwardly cordial relationship with the beaten Japanese. On 20 August they attended a farewell banquet which Governor Tanaka threw for the chairman and vice-chairmen of the two Chinese Councils and the editors of the local Chinese newspapers to thank them for their assistance over the best part of four years. On 29 August they returned the compliment, treating Tanaka to a banquet at the East Asia Chinese Restaurant. They made speeches expressing thanks to the Japanese Governor for his past administration and his kindness to all the residents of Hong Kong.[238] At the same time however they were quietly starting to beat a path back to the British door. By the last week of August they had placed themselves in contact with Gimson's officials. Kotewall is said to have made a daily trek to the French Mission building to call on R. A. C. North, the former Secretary for Chinese Affairs, and Brian Hawkins, who had been designated as North's successor; and a newspaper report from some days afterwards confirms that Hawkins had been engaged ever since his emergence from Stanley in discussions with 'a number of Chinese residents' about matters relating to the reconstruction of the colony.[239]

The rest of the gentry moved with equal dexterity to adjust themselves to the likely post-war shape of things. They severed unobtrusively their more gratuitous ties to the beaten regime. Already on 16 August Ho Kom-tong, the master of ceremonies, handed in his resignation as chairman of the Hong Kong Jockey Club.[240] And as if to underline their renewed British loyalties, they took action to stifle a first, somewhat belated challenge which presented itself from the local Nationalists. On 27 and 28 August two Nationalist outfits, the Nationalist Party Headquarters for Hong Kong and Macao and the Hong Kong and Kowloon branch of the Three People's Principles Youth League, sent letters to the Hong Kong Chinese General Chamber of Commerce. They proposed, they explained, to convene a meeting of public bodies in the colony to discuss the staging of a general peace celebration. The meeting would be held at 10.30 a.m. on 30 August: they wished the Chamber to lend them the fourth floor of their premises as a venue and to designate a couple of representatives to attend. The Chamber's acting chairman, Kwok Chan, rebuffed the request, pointing out that the letters were unsigned and the writing paper gave no official addresses. It was hard, he observed, for the Chamber to make their premises available at such short notice; and in any case the petitioners ought first to seek permission to hold such a meeting from the residual Japanese public order authorities. (Kwok moved rapidly to discourage the granting of any permission, declaring at a meeting with Kanazawa that the Chamber were unable for the time being to enter into any discussion of this kind with Nationalist delegates.)[241]

Some of the thinking which underlay the gentry's manœuvres may be traced in the pages of the *Wah Kiu Yat Po* (Overseas Chinese Daily), one of the few local newspapers which went on appearing throughout this fortnight of limbo. On 17 August the paper reported Hirohito's broadcast in language still infused with considerable deference to the Japanese. The Governor's Office, it noted, were 'ensuring law and order and maintaining supplies of foodstuffs for the people'.[242] This initial deference soon disappeared as the paper permitted itself ever bolder rejoicing in the Allied victory.

On 19 August, and for several days afterwards, the editors conveyed strong signs that Chinese Nationalist forces were on the way. They relayed the order which Chiang Kai-shek had issued announcing the victory and enjoining all Chinese to stay at their posts. They announced the successive return to Chinese sovereignty of Manchuria, Taiwan, the Pescadore islands and the former French enclave of Guangzhouwan. Most portentously they carried news of the official appointment on 23 August of General Zhang Fakui to take over Hainan island, Canton and Hong Kong.[243] The editors viewed this prospect with painfully mixed feelings. 'China', they observed, 'is a great country and we are the citizens of a great country . . . We are now one of the four powers leading the world.'[244] At the same time they looked back on their own recent record – and squirmed. Hong Kong Chinese who had stayed in the colony, they lamented, should ask themselves what contribution they had made to the motherland over the last four years. 'With what self-respect will we behold the Old Father from East Zhejiang [sc. Chiang Kai-shek]?' 'The only way for us to atone for our crimes is through absolute compliance with the orders of our Supreme Leader.' Everyone should remain at their posts and wait calmly for the Central Government to sort things out.[245]

By 25 August, however, the paper had got wind of yet another dramatic turn of events. Premier Attlee, it said, had announced in the House of Commons in response to a question from Churchill that a British commander was to receive the Japanese surrender in Hong Kong. Wedemeyer had denied that a Chinese Nationalist army would take the surrender, and a British fleet was about to move in. 'This without doubt indicates that Hong Kong is to be a British colony.'[246] Two days later the notion that Zhang Fakui might march in was roundly dismissed: 'Our country hasn't sent forces to recover Hong Kong.'[247] By 29 August the paper was referring, for the first time, to the setting up of Gimson's skeleton government and the various preparations the British were making to resume control. 'As regards Hong Kong Chinese feelings concerning this question', the editors noted, 'it can't be denied that there are still historical factors at work.' But they considered that for China to resolve the issue by using 'Metternich-style diplomacy backed by armed force' would be 'totally unsuited to the newly evolving world situation'.[248] The need now was to concentrate on restoring Hong Kong to its former prosperity. In any event the old rulers had much to recommend them. The editors cheerfully drew attention to a recent speech made in Belfast by General Eisenhower in which the American supremo had declared, 'From ancient times Britain has emphasized freedom.'[249]

Keen as they had now become to assist in the safe restitution of Hong Kong to their fellow imperial rulers, the Japanese command seem to have encouraged the pro-British drift of the local elite. Efforts were made to provide Kotewall, Chow and the rest of the gentry with what a later generation would call a 'through train'. On 29 August the Governor's Office were said to be trying to hold on to the Hong Kong Chinese working in 'the various organizations': the organizations were not being disbanded, 'so that after the handover has taken place they may continue to be consulted and employed by the British military authorities'.[250] The same principle was applied at a more mundane level. In accordance with the promise made by the Governor's Office to keep the public utilities in working order, Chinese personnel were retained at their posts in the telephone and telegraph offices, at the Tramways Company and in the Electricity Works.

The conditions had thus been created for a successful British return to Hong Kong.

On 27 August Rear Admiral Harcourt was given clearance by the Americans to proceed with his task force from Subic Bay. Rushed out at no notice to take advantage of Japan's unexpected collapse, Harcourt's expedition was known to the participants as Operation Ethelred. The task force was, in fact, fairly well prepared from a naval point of view. The original squadron consisting of two aircraft carriers, four destroyers, two cruisers and an auxiliary anti-aircraft ship had been reinforced with eight submarines, a submarine depot vessel and six Australian minesweepers which had by coincidence been lying off the Philippines. On 29 August, when it reached Hong Kong waters, the force was joined by a battleship and two more destroyers; and Harcourt was now able to claim possession of 'a very strong fleet'.[251] For all that, the contingent neared Hong Kong in a spirit of marked apprehension. The need for caution was drummed in repeatedly, in the briefing given to Harcourt, and in the instructions which Harcourt passed on to his men. All Orientals, it was stressed, must to begin with be viewed with suspicion. The Japanese naturally had to be approached with 'the utmost vigilance'; and they might not be too easy to identify in a crowd. 'A favourite Japanese trick is to adopt Chinese dress and hide a bomb, grenade or machine-gun under the long gown.' Japanese officers and NCOs might try to hide their samurai swords – or they might, indeed, 'turn them over to Chinese friends'. Chinese goodwill wasn't by any means to be taken for granted. Even among those Chinese who had been born in the colony, 'only a very few' were 'loyal and patriotic to the British Crown'. Marines should move in pairs or ideally in groups of three or four.[252] Souvenirs might be booby-traps. 'TOUCH NOTHING UNLESS YOU ARE ABSOLUTELY SURE IT IS SAFE.'[253]

Even assuming these physical hazards were safely surmounted, the task force would still be confronted by the challenge of winning over the local population. '"Face"', Harcourt's briefing observed, 'is important to the Orientals. When we surrendered Hong Kong we lost face; we now have to regain Hong Kong and face. The Chinese will judge us by our behaviour ashore and first impressions will count.' A smart appearance would 'go a long way in helping to restore our prestige in the Colony'. Troops 'should be marched in an orderly fashion giving the impression that we are moving back into what is rightfully ours, rather than taking an area by assault against resistance'. The conduct of the force had to be exemplary, and like Kitchener's volunteers in 1914 they had to avoid 'misbehaving with wine or women'. Any such indiscipline would 'do us no good at all'. If these guidelines were followed, on the other hand, there was good reason for thinking that those Chinese who had worked with the pre-war British rulers would 'fully appreciate' that a benevolent, stable government was in their own interests, and would be 'even more cooperative' than they had been in the past.[254]

On the morning of 30 August the task force arrived off the Stanley penin-sula, and towards midday they began to glide slowly through the Lei Yue Mun channel and into the ruined harbour. There was almost no sign of the expected resistance from Japanese diehards. Three Japanese boats were seen moving out of a bay on the nearby island of Lamma on an apparent suicide mission; but the British dealt with this threat briskly by bombing both them and the rest of the craft in the bay.[255] Scattered shots were directed at Harcourt's flagship from the Naval Dockyard, but these were soon brought to an end after the flag-ship had made wireless contact with the garrison commander, Major-General Okada Umekichi. Otherwise the Japanese were quiescent. British doubts about the response of the Hong Kong Chinese to their coming were, however, to some extent justified. The fleet crept through Lei Yue Mun in an eerie silence. Scarcely any of the local fishermen bothered even to look up. An Australian journalist on Harcourt's flagship described the scene:

> On the rocks a coolie whistled shrilly. It was like an obscenity in that still-ness. Then we were in Victoria Harbour. And still there was no movement . . . There was not a launch or a sampan moving on the water. A few Chinese – not more than about fifty – stood on the waterfront opposite the Penin-sula Hotel, watching. We walked into our berth in Kowloon and tied up. The Chinese clapped and cheered. It was a watery reception and made prac-tically no impression on the oppressive silence. It was like entering a near dead city.[256]

Gradually, to be sure, the crowds thickened; the smiles broadened; the fire-crackers began to go off. But it was still not clear that the welcome was for the British as such. Arguably the populace would have been pleased to see anybody. An old Chinese clerk well disposed to the British authorities mixed with his fellow citizens on the waterfront and reported that no one cared whether the incoming ships were British, American, Russian or Chinese. 'All they said was, "Now we will eat".'[257] If the Chinese masses were expecting any particular saviour, it didn't seem to be Britain. Many buildings and virtually every junk flew the White Sun flag of the Nationalists. And the White Suns outnumbered the Union Jacks by four to one.[258]

Still, the British had made it. Harcourt's squadron had got through to Hong Kong ahead of any possible Chinese or American force. And Gimson had hovered for two vital weeks in the vacuum which might so easily have been filled by local Chinese activists. At 7 p.m. Duncan Sloss, the Vice Chancellor of Hong Kong University, who had been appointed Publicity Officer in Gimson's government, gave the first press conference to be held by the British in the reoccupied colony. There was still, he observed, danger from 'lawless elements' which might try to cross into the colony 'with a view to creating disturbances'. But he was able to brush off the 'rumours' which had been circulating about the 'political future' of Hong Kong.[259] And he was in particular able to confirm that no Chinese army had made its appearance.

Chiang Kai-shek had not yet in fact taken the steps necessary to reverse the advance of his troops on Hong Kong. Possibly he was waiting for confirmation that the British had indeed taken over, and that the colony had not fallen into the still more unwelcome hands of his Communist rivals. Four days later, however, a new set of instructions were finally sent to Lieutenant-General Shi Jue and his buoyant 13th Army at the latest point they had reached, about two days' march from the border. The Generalissimo, they were told, had decided to authorize the British to send in marines to receive the surrender of the Japanese in the Hong Kong area. There was, therefore, no longer any need for Shi's forces to perform this particular duty, and they should instead make their way to Canton.[260] Shi's troops consequently turned back at the last minute, just as Yu Hanmou's relief army had done nearly four years earlier; and Shi's commander-in-chief, Zhang Fakui, rounded off his account of the episode with the sour observation that 'Hong Kong and Kowloon reverted to their original guise'.[261]

CHAPTER SIX

A Frail Restoration

Harcourt, MacDougall and a season of spring-cleaning

For the first eight months after the Royal Navy's warships crept into Victoria Harbour charge of Hong Kong was entrusted to the benign and very British hands of Rear Admiral Harcourt. The Rear Admiral ambled around in his shorts, on his small, chubby legs, radiating good humour and welcoming all visitors to his office with the invariable greeting, 'Glad to have you aboard.'[1] At his side was David MacDougall, the sensitive, articulate chief of the pre-war Information Bureau who had served in the final year of the conflict as head of the Hong Kong Planning Unit in Whitehall. MacDougall flew into the colony on 7 September 1945 to take up the post of Chief Civil Affairs Officer in the new British Military Administration (BMA), which had been formed by Harcourt, and soon found that almost all of the day-to-day decisions were down to him. 'I know all about cruisers', Harcourt said cheerfully: 'I will run the cruisers. You are supposed to know about Hong Kong, so you run Hong Kong.'[2]

These new British rulers now set about expunging the traces of their Japanese predecessors as quickly and thoroughly as the Japanese had wiped out the vestiges of the pre-war British regime. One by one all the trappings of Japanese overlordship were removed. On 2 September the Rising Sun flag was hauled down from Admiralty House. In the following days Japanese street signs started to be dismantled, and on 14 September the military yen, the bogus occupation currency, was banned from circulation by official decree.

Rapid action was taken to corral the colony's population of Japanese settlers. Two days after Harcourt's landfall the grand round-up of enemy aliens on Hong Kong Island which the Gunseicho had organized in January 1942 was re-enacted – with the boot on the other foot. 'From Garden Road, from Wanchai, from the Central District', proclaimed the newly resurrected *South China Morning Post*, 'streams of Japanese civilians, including women and children, were converging on Queen's Pier.'[3] After some weeks of detention in

houses and barracks in Kowloon the bulk of the settlers were moved on, like
the vanquished British civilians nearly four years before them, to await repatriation in the more spacious surroundings of Stanley internment camp.
During their confinement the assets which they had snatched from local
British interests in their days of supremacy were systematically snatched back
again. In November the Lane Crawford company were appointed liquidators
of Matsuzakaya, the Japanese firm which had seized their department store;
and a general take-over was ordered of property belonging to Mitsui Bussan
and Mitsubishi, the Yokohama Specie Bank and the Bank of Taiwan, the proprietor of the *Hong Kong News* and the former manager of the Matsubara
Hotel. By April 1946, when the BMA period came to an end, the process of
restitution had been for the most part accomplished, and almost all of the
wartime community of Japanese carpet-baggers had been packed off home.

The 10,000-odd POWs of the Imperial forces were handled with the same
pleasing symmetry. Most of them were consigned to the same place where they
had imprisoned the colony's British garrison – the Shamshuipo barracks. Like
the British before them they were put to work sweeping the streets and
removing the rubble left over from the war: in the view of a BMA intelligence
officer it constituted 'a very suitable job for the Japanese, who were responsible in the main for the damage done'.[4] Parties of them were also deployed, as
the British POWs had been, to improve Kai Tak airfield.[5] After some months
of this labour all but a few hundred of them too had been shipped home, along
with their Taiwanese and Korean auxiliaries.

Finally special measures were taken to round up a hard core of suspected
perpetrators of war crimes. A blanket order was issued to detain all of the
former members of the Hong Kong Kempeitai. By early November 1945 a total
of 271 suspects had been winkled out from Shamshuipo and various lesser
camps with the help of some special 'intelligence assault units' supplied by the
SOE. Colonel Noma, the Kempeitai's long-time chief, was tracked down in
Japan and flown back to join them. Hauled in too were a number of officers
of the 23rd Army who had presided over the bloody conquest of Hong Kong
Island in December 1941. All of these suspects would have to remain in the
colony for a little while longer. Once again with a touch of poetic appropri-
ateness they were shut away in a cell block in Stanley gaol, scene of some of
the beastlier of the wartime atrocities. There they were held pending investigation by one of the two war crimes courts which the British high command
in South-east Asia were preparing to set up as part of Britain's contribution to
the joint Allied effort to bring offenders to justice.[6]

By the end of the BMA period little visible trace of the Japanese presence
remained at all. The unfinished hulk of the Shinto war memorial on Mount
Cameron continued to loom over Victoria for a few months longer: it was
finally dynamited (after a number of unsuccessful attempts) in February 1947.

A further couple of construction projects which had been completed under the New Order were left intact. Harcourt reckoned, in common with most British observers, that the Japanese had made 'an extremely good job' of the reconstruction of Government House.[7] There seemed little point in running up the expense of a whole new mansion, and the Osaka architect's confection with its pagoda-type tower was left intact to provide a home for successive British governors for the next fifty years. A road that the Japanese had started building into the Saikung peninsula in the New Territories in a bid to control local smuggling was found to be handy and was finished off.[8]

There were a few other random mementoes. MacDougall complained of the way local people persisted in 'bawling like the Japanese', and a fairly large number of them appear to have retained a smattering of the Japanese language.[9] Japanese slogans lingered on in some of the schools. One Chinese schoolteacher who had travelled back from the mainland reported that on the first day she went into her old classroom in the autumn of 1945 she had the shock of her life: the children 'opened their mouths and said "East Asian Co-Prosperity", then closed them saying "Japanese Guidance, Chinese Support"'.[10] The prostitution and open consumption of opium which the Triads had been allowed to promote in the final months of the occupation continued to disfigure the streets for a good many weeks. In the final days of their power the Kempeitai had let loose in the hills the vicious Army dogs which they had used to terrorize the public, and two children in Stanley village were reported to have been bitten by semi-wild Alsatians. For about a year, too, bathers swimming off the beach below Stanley gaol were attacked periodically by marauding sharks. The sharks were believed to have been drawn to the beach by the scent of blood it had given off during the years it was used as an execution ground. But all this formed part of a short-term hangover.

On the face of it there seemed to be little sign that the Japanese had bequeathed any more profound legacy. Looking back from the standpoint of the late 1960s one local historian judged that 'for the most part' Japanese influence on the creation and character of the new Hong Kong had been 'virtually nil'.[11]

In the meantime the BMA had begun supervising an all-out drive to bring the colony back into working order. Hong Kong in the aftermath of nearly four years of war was a pitiful sight. The harbour was clogged with rusting hulks and unexploded mines. Thousands of buildings lay derelict, engulfed by vegetation and crawling with rats. The roads were unlit by night, and the road surfaces gaped with potholes, and heaps of barbed wire by the roadside tore at the clothes of passers-by. But the problem was mess and neglect, not destruction. Bomb damage inflicted at various times by the Japanese and Americans had been very minor, and there was little amiss with the infrastructure that couldn't be quickly put right. Within two weeks of Harcourt's arrival large numbers of the docks had been brought back into operation, and a month after that the electricity supply had resumed. By early October 1945 Harcourt was reporting to London that 'the situation was generally satisfactory, with signs of a return to normality daily apparent',[12] and by November he felt in a position to send in an upbeat account of the public response. The shops had reopened, packed with goods which had been hidden away during the occupation years. Young Chinese women were coming out on the streets in pretty dresses instead of the drab-looking garments they had worn in the war to escape the attentions of the Japanese soldiery, and the streets were 'full of people who are very cheerful and appear contented'.[13] By January 1946, when the gas supply was restored, all the basic utilities were back in place. Government and society were once again functioning, and Hong Kong had begun to earn plaudits for the 'remarkable progress' it had made towards rehabilitation – progress faster, it has since been suggested, than that achieved in any other territory occupied in the course of the Second World War.[14]

The BMA's endeavours were rounded off with a dapper resumption of Britishness. By as early as the first few days of September 1945 English lettering was starting to reappear on the street signs and hoardings. English place names came back into use: the Toa Hotel was once more the Peninsula, and the Matsubara became the Gloucester again. On 11 September the old colonial currency began to make its comeback as the BMA took delivery of the consignment of Hong Kong dollars ordered from London by Gimson during the interregnum of the previous month. In October the first moves were made to recover the totems of British majesty which the 23rd Army had looted from Statue Square. The two bronze lions which had guarded the entrance of the Hongkong and Shanghai Bank were spotted in a dockyard in Tokyo Bay, and a priority signal was issued from Harcourt's Naval Headquarters to have them retrieved. Similar orders were issued for the rescue of the battered bronze statue of Queen Victoria which had been found on the scrap heap of an Imperial Army arsenal at Osaka. The restoration of normality was celebrated with a return to the colony's pre-war social round. Golf, race meetings, bathing picnics were all quickly got going again – 'so far as possible', we are told, 'in the old British way'.[15] And to crown the effacement of the Japanese interlude the termination of military rule at the end of April 1946 was followed by the ghostly return to his post, gaunt from a series of prison camps in Taiwan and Manchuria, of the colony's last pre-war Governor, Sir Mark Young.

'A critical shortage of supervisory staff'

But the continuity was more apparent than real. Behind all the panoply of their re-entry, behind the grim grey warships and shining white uniforms, the

British rulers of Hong Kong were feeble as never before. Harcourt had made his appearance on 30 August 1945 with a total strength of some 2,000 men. Of those about 350 were land troops immediately available for deployment – a force just about adequate, in the first few hours, to secure a narrow strip of the Victoria waterfront and to guard the ships tied up at the jetties.[16] On 4 September 3,000 Royal Air Force men arrived from the Admiralty Islands, and on 11 September 2,000 commandos were shipped in from Trincomalee in Ceylon. The British had by this time built up a force strong enough to patrol the streets and to shepherd the Japanese troops in town into the POW camps – but that was close to being the limit of their capacities. Like the 23rd Army four years earlier they had arrived on a scene of swirling confusion.

Victoria and Kowloon lay prostrate at the mercy of Triad gangs who were busy turning the colony, in the words of one BBC commentator, into 'the most thoroughly looted place on earth'.[17] The Chungking Gang recruited by Gimson to act as an auxiliary police force in the final days of the interregnum had joined in the scramble, making use of their official armbands to get an edge in the pillaging. The Gambling House Gang who had worked for the Japanese were still marauding, 3,000 strong; and the twin cities were 'honeycombed' with almost fifty other Triad outfits, highly organized and 'operating openly'. Between them the gangs wielded about 7,000 small arms, many of which had been handed out to allcomers by the Japanese soldiers before they were put in the camps.[18] For much of the first fortnight the British forces could make only a modest impact on this urban maelstrom; and some of the RAF reinforcements were actually said to have taken part in the looting spree.[19]

In the countryside the British had no kind of a grip at all. Three thousand armed Japanese still remained at large in various outposts, and in other areas banditry had begun to set in. By mid-September the BMA were agreed that it was 'priority no. 1' to 'clear up' the New Territories.[20] A month later, however, there was still no British presence in the colony's rural hinterland apart from a few commandos dotted around in the villages and a handful of police inspectors and interpreters.

Faced with this turmoil the BMA did their best to assert themselves through the adoption of a no-nonsense, muscular front. On 1 September an initial decree underlined that the new government had been set up 'for the prevention and suppression of public disorder'.[21] Any looting or rioting would be dealt with by a military court. 'Timid souls' were assured that the 'strong hand' was ready and waiting to hammer down any wrongdoers if the need should arise.[22] But there was more than a little bluff in this posture. Like the Gunseicho before them the BMA were in practice compelled by their limited numbers to strike whatever deals they could manage with whatever local partners they were able to find.

In the first days of September large sums of money were apparently sprayed around in the urban areas in a concerted effort to buy off the Triad gangs. (The source of these funds is unclear, but it seems possible that the SOE in the end won endorsement for their suggestion that money would be needed to purchase the cooperation of the local Chinese.) The Chungking Gang were awarded a 'special gratuity' of HK $5 m, on the understanding that they would disband and surrender their weapons. A similar sum is said to have been extended to Wan Yuk-ming, the leader of the Gambling House Gang: in return he was asked to break up his organization and go back to the mainland with forty to fifty of his principal henchmen. In both cases, however, the bribery operation was felt to have been no more than a 'partial success'. 'Considerable doubts' remained as to whether the Chungking Gang had kept their side of the bargain, and only 200 of Wan Yuk-ming's 3,000 followers could be prevailed upon to hand over their arms.[23] Even as they made their attempt to close down the two outfits the British also found it advisable to fall back once again on the time-honoured tactic of using part of the gangland to hold down the rest. By 4 September they had turned to the Triad-based Protective Guards who had been used to keep watch against crime in the neighbourhoods during the final months of Japanese rule. The Protective Guards had been organized into a 'special constabulary' to 'supplement' the efforts of a reconstituted colonial police force. On 10 October a report on these 1,100-odd 'special constables' admitted that it had 'not been possible to select them carefully', and that a 'bad element' had been introduced. It was only at this stage, with the gradual strengthening of the mainstream police, that the BMA's dependence on gangster cooperation began to diminish and the 'special constables' began to be 'regularized' and phased out.[24]

Similar stopgap arrangements were made in the countryside. In those places still garrisoned by the Imperial Army the BMA seem to have taken the view that Japanese order was better than no order at all. It was only in the third week of November, an expatriate historian tells us, that the last Japanese outposts in the New Territories were 'relieved'.[25] For the bulk of the policing, however, the choice of the British fell on their old wartime partners – the Chinese Communist Party. By mid-September the East River guerrillas who had kept order in many parts of the hinterland since the Japanese collapse a month earlier were quietly getting ready to pull out of the colony on the instructions of Chairman Mao. Now that the British had been reinstalled in Hong Kong in accordance with the Potsdam Declaration their work (so the Party line had it) was over: their assignment was now to redeploy to the mainland for the imminent confrontation with Chiang Kai-shek's Nationalists. But the BMA had other uses for them. On 18 September a British officer was dispatched to the command post of the Hong Kong and Kowloon Independent Brigade in the border village of Shataukok to ask for talks. The Brigade sought permission from East River Column headquarters in Guangdong, who in turn sought permission from Mao and the other Party chiefs in Yan'an; and discussions were duly initiated in that perennial centre for momentous events, the Peninsula Hotel. The British requested that the guerrillas should for the time being stay in the New Territories to carry on with their policing work. In addition they asked that the Brigade should formalize the new partnership by setting up a liaison office in town. The guerrillas agreed, and arrangements were made to slow down their withdrawal. On 28 September the bulk of the guerrilla contingent departed on schedule, leaving behind them a circular in which they bade farewell to the local Chinese villagers and hoped amiably that the British administration would help them to rebuild their homes and businesses and to better their lives. In the meantime, however, demobilized members of the Brigade were regrouped into a network of Self-Defence Forces of twenty to thirty men each. The Brigade's new liaison office assembled these units and trained them, and the British provided each man with a gun, twenty rounds of ammunition and expenses of HK\$60 a month. (Attitudes had indeed changed since the time of the Japanese invasion four years earlier, when the British had twice shied away from the prospect of issuing the guerrillas with arms.) By October the first four units were already formed and policing the districts of Saikung, Shataukok, Sheung Shui and Yuen Long. The Self-Defence Forces continued to help the British to pacify the New Territories for the best part of a year, and the last unit was only disbanded in September 1946.[26]

Even when they had overcome the initial security problems the British were still too few to establish an adequate day-to-day administration without local help. In the very earliest days of the BMA, in the first fortnight of September 1945, the civil side of the government went on being handled by Gimson and about 700 of the ex-internees. But these wasted former inmates of Stanley were in no state to manage the colony for any length of time. 'Often', one journalist wrote, 'as you talked to them you would see them shake their heads like a punch-drunk fighter'. They needed to be sent home as quickly as possible to recuperate; and within less than a month almost all of them had indeed left the colony, on a hospital ship which had been made available by the British Pacific Fleet and a pre-war luxury liner, the *Empress of Australia*.[27] The intention was that they would be replaced by an influx of fresh administrators who were to be sent out from Britain to work under MacDougall, the newly appointed supremo of Civil Affairs. But in the extreme dislocation of the post-war months transport did not exist to bring these substitute personnel round the world to the colony in anything like the numbers required. The result was that throughout the civil arm of the BMA the British contingent was minimal. MacDougall arrived on 7 September with just twenty-eight Civil Affairs officers who were supposed to make up the core of the new bureaucracy: one month later his team had increased to fifty-six, but this was still only about 10 per cent of the designated European staff. The same pattern prevailed in every department. As the year drew to its close not a single European officer was to be found in the Secretariat and Accounting Branch of the police: there had been four of them before the war. Only two of the thirty-eight posts earmarked for British officers in the prison service had been filled, and no British inspector had returned to the fire brigade. The Works Branch, charged with much of the colony's physical reconstruction, reported 'a critical shortage of supervisory staff', and the Imports and Exports Department declared itself understaffed in respect of European revenue officers. Sixteen of the seventeen Europeans who had run the colony's telecommunications had been repatriated, as had all of the European electrical staff except two; and no substitutes had appeared on the scene.[28]

In the absence of British officials much of the work necessarily devolved on the Asian subordinate grades. Throughout the administration Chinese and Indians, Eurasians and Portuguese employed before the war were reported to have returned to their posts. In the fire brigade, for example, almost the whole of the pre-war Asiatic staff were said to have reappeared. A large number of clerical workers including 'the key men' had 'reported for duty' in the Imports and Exports Department, and a fair proportion of the Chinese revenue officers were also 'back'.[29] Some of these pre-war employees may have genuinely 'returned' in the sense that they had gone underground during the occupation and reemerged after Harcourt arrived to sign up once again with their old British masters: many more, probably, had just plugged on with their jobs through the years regardless of changing regimes. The British had also seen fit in some cases to draw on the large new pool of local employees whom the Japanese had brought into the government service in the course of the war. The new regular police force that was being mustered from early September consisted for the most part of young Chinese men in the eighteen to twenty-five age band: many of them, it was noted, had been recruited originally by the Japanese.[30] Whatever their background these Asian underlings clearly kept a good deal of the government machinery going in the early months of the BMA. In the Telecommunications Department 'skeleton technical services' were said to be getting maintained 'with non-Europeans'. The Asians in the fire brigade performed with sufficient effectiveness that the Chief Officer was 'prepared to carry on without replacing Inspectors'.[31] It was all a long way from the pre-war period when almost all responsible tasks in the civil service had been concentrated in European hands.

The British had no doubt about the gravity of this state of affairs. As the autumn advanced, the breezy reports sent to London by the BMA chiefs began to be interspersed with other messages of a more sombre character. On 22 September Harcourt gave the War Office a first intimation of the looming crisis of European manpower. 'Since all [pre-war] Colonial personnel are being repatriated earliest', he cabled, 'administrative machinery will break down unless early replacements are urgently forthcoming'.[32] Welcome though it might be in itself, the dominant contribution being made by local civil service employees wasn't entirely an advertisement for restored British rule. It was 'of the utmost importance', Harcourt pursued on 6 October, that all Civil Affairs staff should be transported to the colony as fast as possible from the point of view of the BMA, of the Colonial Office, 'and of His Majesty's Government's general prestige in China and the Far East'.[33]

Pacifying the Nationalists

Perched on this rickety edifice the British now had to fend off a challenge from the mainland undreamed of in their pre-war days of supremacy.

In Chungking sat the Nationalist regime, basking in its new status as one of the victorious Allies, flushed with the glory of China's first triumph over a foreign enemy in more than a hundred years. As Chiang Kai-shek's forces prepared to take over from the beaten Japanese all those places such as Taiwan and Manchuria which Japan had annexed in the course of the last few decades, the long-standing drive of the Nationalists to claw back the country's lost territories was almost complete. Only Hong Kong, back in British hands, survived as the galling exception – the one bit of land prised away by the foreigners in the age of defeats and 'unequal treaties' that had not been regained.[34] Back in the 1930s, cash-strapped and beleaguered, the Nationalists had been obliged to stay passive as Britain had airily disregarded their claim to the colony. They would do so no longer.

The first indications of a new posture came soon after Harcourt's arrival, as British and Nationalist diplomats set themselves to sort out the still unresolved issue of the arrangements that were to be made for the surrender of the colony's Japanese troops. On 31 August Chiang was offered a 'unilateral compromise' put forward by Whitehall in the interest of saving a scrap of his face. The suggestion was that Harcourt should accept the surrender of the Japanese garrison on behalf of both the British government and the Generalissimo in his wartime capacity as Supreme Commander of the China theatre. Chiang indicated his grudging acceptance of this proposal – but raised in the meantime a formidable series of incidental demands. He wanted the surrender ceremony, which the British had fixed for 12 September, postponed to ensure that it did not take place any earlier than the date when the Nationalists planned to receive the Japanese surrender in Nanking, shortly to be restored as their capital, and the other great cities which Japan had occupied on the Chinese mainland. On no account was he going to allow China's thunder to be stolen by a European colonial power. In addition he asked for the right to collect and take over all Japanese ships and vehicles, arms and ammunition which were found in the colony. And he wanted the British to make the port of Hong Kong and any ships they were able to muster available for the passage of four of his southern Chinese armies which he proposed to send north to recover Manchuria. The main purpose of both these last two requests was to strengthen his hand for the coming confrontation with the Chinese Communist forces; but he would at the same time obtain (if the British consented) a mainland presence and level of activity in Hong Kong unimaginable in the pre-war years. As fresh wrangling broke out over Chiang's stipulations the British ceremony started to be put off and put off again, from one day to the next.

In the background of this agitation about the surrender arrangements the Nationalists began to prepare themselves for the pursuit of their more basic objective – to get Hong Kong back. Now that the war had been won they were entitled, under the protocol to the 1943 extra-territoriality treaty, to bring up for discussion at any time of their choosing the question of winding up the British lease on the New Territories. And that, as everyone knew, would in all probability lead to the termination of British rule in the rest of the colony too. By October 1945 the Foreign Ministry in Chungking were 'looking for the right moment' to open negotiations with Britain.[35] The right moment wasn't immediately identified; but from this point on any step which suggested that the British were seeking once again to entrench themselves in the colony met with a swift and aggressive diplomatic response. The first outburst of trouble erupted at the end of the month when word got about that the British were planning to build a new airport. The site they had chosen was at Pingshan, a village in the New Territories virtually on the border with Guangdong province; and the obvious implication was that the New Territories were to be cemented to the main part of the colony for the foreseeable future.[36] To make matters worse it turned out that the new airport was intended to serve as a base for the RAF. In November the Foreign Ministry summoned the British chargé d'affaires in Chungking and informed him that the project was unnecessary and ought to be cancelled. The Foreign Minister, Dr Wang Shijie, observed in a memorandum to his master Chiang that for the British to be building an air base on the edge of Guangdong was 'similar to putting up gun emplacements'. He assured Chiang that the Ministry would persist in their efforts to get the New Territories put on the agenda for talks.[37] In January 1946 a report came in that the BMA had designated a sizeable fishing zone in the waters surrounding Hong Kong. Foreign Minister Wang advised Chiang that the zone would infringe China's sovereign rights and would also have a major adverse impact upon the Chinese economy. A protest, he urged, should be lodged with the Hong Kong authorities asking them to revoke their decree. If this protest went unheeded Chungking should retaliate by announcing that it would from now on forbid British warships to navigate in Chinese waters.[38]

Shortly afterwards the BMA was indeed refused permission to send a warship to Hainan island to look into the fate of the Hong Kong Chinese labourers who had been shipped there by the colony's Japanese rulers during the last two years of the war.[39] This new diplomatic assertiveness was buttressed by editorials in the Nationalist press warning that 'unless the British hurry up and give Hong Kong and Kowloon to China there may be trouble', and by protest rallies of patriotic students who massed in the capital's streets to demand retrocession.[40] Most of what came out of Chungking, however, was sound and fury and scarcely posed an immediate danger to British control.

The cutting edge of Nationalist indignation was to be found in Canton. In charge in Canton from the middle of September 1945 was Zhang Fakui, the warlord who had briefly seemed poised to direct Chiang's southern armies in a triumphant march into Hong Kong until they had received the abrupt command to turn back. Now the effective commander of the Nationalist forces throughout southern China, Zhang continued to brood over his thwarted recapture of the colony. On 29 October, after learning about the Pingshan airport project, he cabled glumly to Chiang, 'We should have recovered the Leased Territory of Kowloon [sc. the New Territories] before ... in future negotiations are bound to be even more difficult.'[41] And Zhang had a weapon to hand. In the chaotic transport conditions of the early post-war months, when few vessels were getting through to Hong Kong, the colony had continued to look to Guangdong and the Pearl River delta for most of its major necessities – rice and vegetables, coal and firewood and cooking oil. It was a lifeline that could be severed at any time. In early November the British gave Zhang further cause for annoyance. As Chinese flooded back from the mainland to the colony in their tens of thousands to take advantage of the rapid pace of rehabilitation, the BMA felt obliged to impose some restrictions on entry. Travellers from Canton were required to obtain entry permits, and a barbed-wire fence was put up at the border to stem the tide of unauthorized immigrants. Zhang interpreted this as an insult to 'honest Chinese merchants', and a violation of the understanding which had prevailed right up to the eve of the war that all Chinese should enjoy freedom of movement both into and out of Hong Kong. He struck back immediately, by banning the export to the colony of foodstuffs and all other essential supplies.[42]

The challenge of the Nationalists also loomed up, in a form more obscure but no less intimidating, in Hong Kong itself. Still at large in the colony was Shan Chit-son, the Nationalist Party's self-styled Director-General for Hong Kong and Macao. From his base at 257 Prince Edward Road in Kowloon, where he kept in touch with the mainland with the help of a wireless transmitter, Shan set to work in the course of September 1945 to foment a campaign of anti-British agitation. As the head of the Chungking Gang Shan still had at his disposal a number of Triad thugs who had not been successfully scattered by

British bribe money; and he was joined in his efforts by the local representative of the other main Nationalist group in the colony, the Three People's
Principles Youth League. In the following weeks a succession of Nationalist
intelligence officers also started to creep into Hong Kong: several of them
either visited or even took up residence at 257 Prince Edward Road. They
included an Inspector-General to the Chinese Army whose function was 'to
coordinate Army policy at every level', a 'political Admiral from the Chinese
Navy', an official of the Hong Kong and Macao International Investigation
Bureau and a Commander of the Seventh War Zone and Inspection Commissioner of the Fifth Political District of Guangdong Province.[43] In early
October the British police were requested to help arrange a passage to Canton
for General Li Ping, an adjutant of Chiang Kai-shek's grand spymaster Dai Li
who had slipped into the colony with two of his aides. The go-between who
approached the police smiled disarmingly that General Li and his men had
not disclosed their arrival in Hong Kong to the BMA 'because they were secret
service agents'.[44] There is no evidence to suggest any kind of coordinated
Nationalist design for seizing the colony; and indeed the many factions and
entities that operated under the aegis of the Chungking regime were renowned
for their lack of coordination. But the Nationalists were well aware that the
British in Hong Kong were vulnerable as they had never been in the past. In
the words of one visiting Chinese colonel, the war had shown that the colony
could not be held against determined opposition from the mainland.[45]

The Nationalist demand for Hong Kong still enjoyed a considerable measure
of backing from the United States. President Truman's decision to let
Harcourt's squadron move into Hong Kong and receive the surrender had not,
as we saw, necessarily committed the White House to long-term support for
the restoration of colonial rule. Harcourt's arrival is said to have been followed
by a 'wave of censure' in American political circles against Britain's reoccupation of the colony which 'continued for some months'.[46] There are also signs
that the United States service chiefs in China were as keen as ever to prise the
British out of Hong Kong. General Li Ping and his aides, it turned out,
had made their clandestine trip to the colony 'to welcome Rear Admiral
Buckmaster of the United States Navy'.[47] G. A. Wallinger, the British Minister
in Chungking, who passed through Hong Kong at this juncture, reported that
a number of American officers had been turning up in the colony without
prior warning. Some of them were apparently 'talking to their Chinese contacts in a way directly prejudicial to British interests'.[48]

The British were keenly aware of the risks. No one felt any certainty that
Britain would manage to keep possession of the colony for any length of time.
In Whitehall the authorities waited for the Nationalist regime to exercise its
post-war right to bring up the question of the New Territories. Days after
Harcourt's landfall the Nationalist bigwig T. V. Soong arrived in London on a

visit which seemed all too likely to have just that aim. Much to the surprise of the British officials Soong never in fact raised the dreaded issue; but the mere prospect that he might do so had been enough to concentrate minds. On 9 September John Paskin of the Colonial Office minuted that the time had now come to examine the problems which might arise if the New Territories had to be handed back to China.[49] At Paskin's suggestion other departments were invited to contribute their thoughts through the medium of the Far Eastern Planning Unit of the Cabinet Office; and the result, in the following months, was a sort of re-run of the agonized debate over Hong Kong's future which had gripped Whitehall at the nadir of Britain's fortunes in 1942. Once again some of the senior Foreign Office administrators inclined to the view that Hong Kong was untenable. G. V. Kitson, then serving as head of the China Department, went so far as to question implicitly the actual morality of Britain's presence there: how, he inquired, would the British have liked it if the Chinese had spent the previous century in occupation of the Isle of Wight? In language reminiscent of Roosevelt's at Tehran Kitson advocated that Britain should 'as a gesture of good will and in a spirit of friendship with the Chinese nation' declare unilaterally that it was ready to enter into negotiations for the return of the New Territories 'on suitable conditions'.[50] The best option, in his judgement, was for Britain to retrocede the entire colony, while at the same time concluding a new treaty to lease it back (with or without the New Territories) for another thirty years. Failing that, Britain might set up some form of Anglo-Chinese condominium over either the New Territories or Hong Kong as a whole. In any event Kitson saw no possibility that the expected Chinese demand for the rendition of the New Territories could be turned down. Once again the Colonial Office took a harder line calculated to ensure that Hong Kong remained British if possible. They advised against any plan for retrocession or leaseback, and favoured rejecting any Chinese demand for the surrender of any part of the colony. But they too were willing to consider an option by which Britain would hand back the New Territories 'with certain conditions'.[51]

In Hong Kong itself the same sense of fragility permeated the early statements put out by the BMA. On 13 September a scale of punishments up to and including the death penalty was prescribed for anyone inciting the populace to insurrection against the authorities or publishing, possessing or circulating any printed matter hostile or detrimental to the BMA or 'in the interests of the enemy'.[52] (We detect once again that British tendency to elide Japan and China into a single antagonist.) MacDougall pronounced it 'unfortunate' in view of Hong Kong's reliance on supplies from south China that a controversial project like the new airport had to be pushed ahead 'at this particular moment'.[53] The BMA were also said to be 'worried' about the unexpected appearance of American officers and their undercover discussions with local Nationalists.[54]

Faced with this challenge the British began to give ground to the mainland regime on a scale they would never have contemplated half a decade before. Even the 'unilateral compromise' offered about the surrender arrangements the day after Harcourt's arrival carried with it a definite whiff of retreat. By proposing that Harcourt should take the surrender in part on Chiang's behalf the British were in effect recognizing that the Chinese government had a legitimate interest in the colony's fate. (They were also tacitly acknowledging the validity of Chiang's rather cogent argument that the China theatre included Hong Kong.) In the interests of giving Chiang face it was quickly agreed that the surrender ceremony should take place no earlier than the date when the Nationalists were proposing to receive the surrender of Japan's Expeditionary Force on the Chinese mainland. For almost ten days an effort was made to resist the other demands Chiang had raised as his price for going along with the British arrangements. In the end, however, Harcourt signalled that the continued postponements of the ceremony which had been caused by the stand-off were 'becoming an embarrassment in the Colony' and 'adding to our many problems';[55] and the decision was made to give way on these issues too. On 16 September, consequently, Harcourt took the swords and signatures of the local Japanese Army and Navy commanders in a terse fifteen minutes at Government House. The surrender took place on the same day that the Japanese forces made their formal submission on the Chinese mainland. The ceremony was conducted against a backdrop of British and Nationalist flags, and to emphasize China's role further Harcourt was flanked by a Nationalist general, Pan Huaguo, who had arrived in the colony six days before to help the British receive the surrender as head of a twenty-four-man Chinese Military Delegation. Three weeks later the same symbolism was employed in a grand three-day celebration of the Allied victory. The festivities were, once again, a joint British–Chinese event; and the dates chosen for them centred on 10 October, the anniversary of the 1911 Nationalist revolution which was observed on the mainland as China's National Day.

In the meantime the BMA were also letting Chiang have his way on the meatier questions. For a period of some eight weeks after the surrender ceremony General Pan and his colleagues were hard at work rounding up all the arms, ships, planes and motor vehicles that the Japanese garrison had left in Hong Kong. The British noted grumpily that Pan's team seemed to have 'somewhat exorbitant views on what constitutes military equipment', even going so far as to commandeer private cars;[56] but they made no attempt to interfere with the process. And from early October, for the next six months, a continual stream of some 100,000 of Chiang's finest troops poured into the colony, bivouacked in the suburb of Kowloon Tong and marched in serried ranks down the Kowloon streets to the dockside to rendezvous with warships which the United States had sent to ferry them to Manchuria. The first units belonged to the 13th Army of Lieutenant-General Shi Jue, which had been turned aside only six weeks earlier from its triumphant advance on Hong Kong. The passage of the mainland troops 'scared the daylights' out of MacDougall; but he saw no alternative but to make such concessions. 'The lighter forms of the gesture and protestation of friendship', he wrote to Gent in London, 'are a pre-war luxury. The 1941 technique no longer serves'.[57]

Concessions were soon being offered almost automatically in response to the pressures and pinpricks from Canton and Chungking. In mid-November MacDougall went up to the border to talk to Zhang Fakui's representatives about the export ban which had been provoked by the colony's new immigration controls. An agreement was reached that Canton would resume food supplies to the colony in exchange for the withdrawal of the offending restrictions. Enough British dignity had been preserved that MacDougall felt able to send the Colonial Office a light-hearted gloss on the whole affair: 'Incident settled. In return for food they haven't got we have given up restrictions we couldn't enforce. Satisfactory all round.'[58] Other retreats were more abject. In January 1946 Harcourt travelled to Chungking and gave a press conference to Nationalist correspondents of the Central News Agency. He explained meekly that the reported designation of a fishing zone in the waters around the colony amounted to nothing more than a provision that fish caught in those waters and brought to Hong Kong should be given the same preferential treatment as local produce. There would not, in other words, be any question of Hong Kong patrols interfering with mainland fishing boats. In addition he did his best to justify the Pingshan airport project, emphasizing among other points that the villagers displaced by the project would be given full compensation and helped to new housing.[59] In effect he was acknowledging that the fate of peasants in the New Territories was a legitimate concern of the mainland regime. This soft answer, however, was still not sufficient to turn away the wrath of Chiang Kai-shek's Foreign Ministry. Three months later, 'to avoid political entanglement' as a subsequent British account expressed it, the BMA put out an announcement that the Pingshan project was being shelved.[60]

The Nationalist underground in the colony were too numerous and too well armed to be swatted lightly aside, and the BMA knew it. They embarked on their dealings with the local Nationalists by punctiliously tying up a loose end from the war. In the course of September discussions were launched with a view to repaying the huge debt Britain owed to Zhang Zilian, the Shanghai Triad boss who had used his personal wealth to dissuade his fellow godfathers from wiping out the colony's European population at the height of the Japanese onslaught in 1941. The British were coy about the means they employed to arrive at a settlement ('That *must* remain my secret', wrote Shaftain of the Special Branch in his memoir); but they had clearly gone ahead in full recognition of the ties between the Nationalist-affiliated gangster and his parent regime. For the talks were conducted not with Zhang personally, but with Zhang's superiors in Chungking.[61]

Steps were indeed taken to put a stop to Shan Chit-son's campaign of sub-version. On 6 October the police swooped on Shan's headquarters in 257 Prince Edward Road, arrested Shan and a number of his lieutenants and confiscated a quantity of illicit arms. In the aftermath of the raid a ban was imposed tem-porarily on Nationalist activities in the colony, and the Chungking leaders were quietly prevailed upon to pull Shan from the scene. But all that turned out to have happened for practical purposes was the substitution of an overt Nationalist presence in Hong Kong for an underground one. Given both the armed strength of the Nationalist partisans and the now pressing need to establish smooth relations with the regime on the mainland, the BMA had concluded that they had no choice but to abrogate the outlaw status in which the Hong Kong branch of the Nationalist Party had languished in the pre-war years.[62] Less than a month after Shan's arrest his successor, Chan Su, reported to MacDougall as the Party's first officially accredited representative in Hong Kong. The British observed that Chan's official position would help to 'clarify' Nationalist affairs in the colony and to 'put them on a satisfactory basis'. But they also admitted that under this new open system the local branch of the Party had 'strengthened its position' and 'might be expected to become increas-ingly active'.[63] And along with the Party there arrived in the course of the autumn the entire sprawling matrix of Nationalist organizations – all of those government and semi-government entities which had operated in Hong Kong unofficially after the outbreak of the Sino-Japanese war and which now hoped to re-establish themselves on a permanent footing. Staff of the Ministry of Information moved in to produce a Hong Kong edition of the Party organ, the *Guomin Ribao* (National Times). Staff of the Ministry of Communications embarked on the task of reconstituting their pre-war wireless network. The Ministry of Education sent an official down to assess local schoolchildren with the object of reviving the colony's Chinese language schools. And back too came the branches of the Bank of China and a series of other state commer-cial concerns. By the end of October there are said to have been no less than fifteen quasi-official delegations trying to establish themselves in the colony on various pretexts; and the Peninsula Hotel was reported to be 'mostly occu-pied' by Chinese government bodies.[64]

To crown the whole process the British agreed to accept the appointment of a mainland diplomat, T. W. Kwok, to serve as the Nationalist government's Special Commissioner for Hong Kong. The BMA seem to have been rather pleased by the advent of this functionary, who they hoped would be able to take responsibility for the whole hydra-headed Nationalist set-up. But by accepting him they had acquiesced in an innovation which successive Governors of the colony had resisted right up to the Pacific War. For the first time Britain was making room in Hong Kong for a formal representative of the mainland administration who would be able, if he chose, to set himself up as a rival focus of allegiance for the local Chinese. To underscore his potential claims Kwok had been deliberately styled Special Commissioner rather than Consul-General (which would have implied recognition of British sovereignty), and Special Commissioner *for* rather than *in* Hong Kong (which conveyed that he was responsible for looking after Hong Kong and its people).[65]

These retreats were combined with a number of rather more proactive measures. Among the motley ranks of the Nationalists the British were able to identify a certain number of prominent figures who viewed them with a fair amount of goodwill. One of the most senior members of General Pan Huaguo's Military Delegation was Colonel S. K. Yee, who had served as the right-hand man to Admiral Chan Chak in underpinning the British defence of the colony in December 1941. The British had had the foresight to reward Yee for his services by presenting him with a CBE, the first such honour to be conferred on a Chinese army officer; and this display of esteem had made the intended impression. In a conversation with BMA contacts Yee intimated that he was not a committed Nationalist and was indeed thinking of withdrawing into private life.[66] And in Canton, newly raised to the dignity of the city's first post-war mayor, was the one-legged Admiral himself. He too had been honoured before the war ended, in this case with a knighthood; and the BMA judged him to be 'a convinced advocate of Sino-British cooperation' and 'very much our friend'.[67] Every effort was now made to build on these and other Chinese contacts. Harcourt wrote to the Admiralty that he and his colleagues were 'gradually making contact' with leading Chinese in Canton, Chungking and other points outside the colony in an attempt to 'build up confidence' in the intentions of the Hong Kong government.[68] An RAF plane was dispatched to bring Special Commissioner Kwok to the colony, and he was quickly befriended by MacDougall and the other British leaders who found him to be, reassuringly, a plump, Western-educated *bon vivant* and man of the world. Harcourt even reported that the BMA were 'not without hopes' of getting better relations with General Zhang Fakui.[69]

Conceding when necessary and coopting where possible, the BMA were largely successful in heading off the immediate Nationalist threat. Confident that Hong Kong would be theirs before too much longer the Nationalists bore themselves with restraint throughout the tense first autumn of the British return. General Pan Huaguo's Military Delegation, for instance, was judged by the Hong Kong authorities to have behaved 'very well'.[70] In a speech which he made a couple of days before the surrender ceremony Pan even urged the Hong Kong Chinese to support the BMA in its work of rehabilitation. They should not, he insisted, spend time second-guessing the future relationship between Hong Kong and the mainland, which would be resolved satisfactorily in the

course of negotiations between the diplomats in London and Chungking. Pan
was at pains to make clear that his own task was not to assert Chinese rights
in the colony but merely to take over the Japanese war *materiel*. The transit
through the colony of Chiang Kai-shek's armies passed off with remarkable
uneventfulness, given the size of the forces involved. The Nationalists deployed
a small squad of military policemen to help keep their legions in order. On
one occasion a riot came close to erupting when a British naval patrol arrested
a Chinese officer on suspicion of theft. Trouble was however headed off by a
Nationalist general who happened to be strolling through the district in mufti.
The general offered to mediate, and after a brief altercation with the patrol
leader ('. . . and I'm the Archbishop of Canterbury') was permitted to do so.[71]

Several of the key Nationalists courted by the BMA also played their part in
ensuring a tranquil outcome. A British intelligence report at the end of September observed that Yee 'continued to be friendly and helpful'; and he appears
to have given the BMA some information which led to the crackdown on Shan
Chit-son and his group.[72] In the thick of the crisis provoked by Zhang Fakui's
trade embargo Chan Chak sent private messages assuring the BMA of his
'continued efforts to maintain and expand the cooperation essential to mutual
prosperity'; and when MacDougall went up to Canton shortly afterwards the
Admiral received him with a 'royal welcome'.[73] As for the Special Commissioner, he made himself 'most helpful in all kinds of ways, official and unofficial'.[74] On one occasion he arranged the return of some locomotives and rolling
stock belonging to the Hong Kong government which had been taken to the
interior during the war. He gave MacDougall a lot of 'very good tips', and told
him incidentally 'one or two things which, if he had kept them to himself,
would have made it very awkward for me'.[75]

Absolving the gentry

But the new pressures from the Nationalists represented only part of the
overall problem the British now faced. An equally pressing task for them was
to reassemble a supportive local elite with whose backing they could once more
govern Hong Kong. To secure local partners, however, they first had to sur-
mount a whole series of obstacles.

Obvious candidates, to be sure, were at hand in the form of the old pre-war
gentry. Within days of Harcourt's arrival Kotewall and his colleagues had
quietly taken up their familiar role as the chief representatives of the Hong
Kong Chinese. On the strength of the contacts they had made with Gimson's
officials in the final days of the interregnum they were enrolled by the BMA
as members of a new Chinese Advisory Council.[76] Kotewall, Chow and Li
Tse-fong were all received with 'high favour' at Government House, and 'formed

the backbone of the group of VIPs at all functions'.[77] Other prominent figures
of the occupation lost equally little time in showing their faces again. On 4
September Peter H. Sin, the wartime 'Mayor of Hong Kong', joined his fellow
solicitors at a meeting convened by Chief Justice MacGregor to announce the
reestablishment of the colony's lawcourts. On 20 September Tung Chung-wei,
formerly of the Rehabilitation Advisory Committee, and Kwok Chan, lately of
the Chinese Representative Council, presided at an early post-war session
of the Hong Kong Chinese General Chamber of Commerce. And the Allied
victory celebrations which were held throughout the colony in mid-October
were organized by the selfsame impresario whom we last saw directing the
Jockey Club races on behalf of the Japanese, the perennial master of ceremonies, Ho Kom-tong.[78]

Other citizens, however, were not disposed to allow this deft footwork to
take place unchallenged. Many of the expatriates who poured out of Stanley
were outraged to discover, as they put it, that the same people who had shouted
'*Banzai!*' yesterday were singing 'God Save the King' today;[79] and the result
was a torrent of protest in the resuscitated English-language press. On 12
September an editorial in the *South China Morning Post* commented on 'the
ease wherewith the scallywags who worked for the Japanese have been able to
ingratiate themselves anew not only with the restored Hong Kong government
but also with the public utility managements and private firms'.[80] Two days
later an ex-internee urged the paper to print a list of such culprits, and on 17
September 'a Jail Sufferer' cheered on the campaign. 'The traitors themselves',
he declared,

> were quite frightened three weeks ago, and only the tenderness of Govern-
> ment officials made them more brazen as the weeks passed by . . . The
> Government should let the public realize in no uncertain terms that men
> who can turn their coats with chameleon-like rapidity are not the type of
> men to assume the responsibilities of public service.[81]

The expatriates were not alone in their outcry. One Chinese correspondent
wrote in with a scathing allusion to 'the fawning gentries'; and calls started
mounting for the immediate detention and trial of the gentry leaders, and
Kotewall in particular.[82]

The gentry's reemergence thus threatened to create more difficulties than it
solved. A real danger existed that the reclaimed Hong Kong might be torn
down the middle by recriminations. 'Few substantial citizens of the colony',
MacDougall lamented, 'escaped contact with the occupying forces in one form
or another . . . It seems certain that a proportion of them behaved very badly.'
It was all 'hideously embarrassing'.[83]

But the British officials continued to feel the same deep reluctance they had
shown throughout the war to rush into a blanket condemnation of the local

leaders. MacDougall, for instance, had no time for the accusations of treason which were being levied at Kotewall:

> The Kotewall business is a mess. So far as I can see no one has a scrap of real evidence, and all I have seen so far would not stand up in court for two seconds. This does not stop people pressing for his immediate arrest and trial (K. was always a man who inspired violent personal dislike.)[84]

In support of his judgement MacDougall was able to draw a distinction which marked Kotewall and his associates off from many of their counterparts in occupied Europe. The gentry of Hong Kong, he observed, might have shouted '*Banzai!*'; but there was no suggestion that they had betrayed a single soul to the Japanese.[85]

Plentiful evidence, on the other hand, could be found of the effort the gentry had made to attend to the needs of the Hong Kong population. It was they, after all, who had directed and funded and generally kept alive the whole network of local charities. Most of the charities were still hard at work when the British took over, and in the following weeks they played a key role in distributing such food as the BMA managed to bring in to Hong Kong. MacDougall remarked that in their 'long and honourable history' those bodies had 'never given better service than now'.[86]

There were other, more pragmatic considerations. If the gentry were toppled the British authorities were still going to need interlocutors able to deal with them on behalf of the Hong Kong Chinese masses. The press called vociferously for 'new blood' in the leadership of the Chinese community and 'a brand new set of advisers to Government'.[87] But where would the new blood be found? The fact was that in spite of the brickbats none of the local people were willing to come forward and challenge the Anglicized Chinese and Eurasian oligarchy who had represented them for the last fifty years. And the British knew no one else. In a letter to Gent at the Colonial Office MacDougall summed up the dilemma. 'We have dusted out the marriage chamber, cleaned the windows, put in some (almost) fresh linen and turned back the covers. But there is no sign of the bride, and the groom grows restive.'[88]

The local public were not, furthermore, the sole group to be clamouring for the gentry's heads. Many of the Nationalists wished to see Kotewall and his associates called to account for their other hypothetical treason – to China. A correspondent for one of the Chungking papers described the disgust that he felt as he looked around Government House on the day of the Japanese surrender ceremony:

> In one room there was still a scroll presented to the Japanese by 'Chinese representatives'. How shameless that our lovely [Chinese] characters should be used for such a purpose! And these 'representatives' cannot examine their hearts, but today are busy felicitating another master.[89]

Shan Chit-son compiled dossiers on the 'Chinese traitors' with a view to arranging their execution.[90] Following Shan's removal the methods envisaged were less extreme; but both the legalized branch of the Nationalist Party which took his place and the teams which were sent to Hong Kong by the various Chungking ministries made it clear that they expected Hong Kong to hand any quislings over to them in conformity with a decision of the United Nations.[91] From the BMA's angle this agitation looked all too much like another prong in the multi-pronged drive by the Nationalists to embed themselves in the colony.[92] And it lent the beleaguered gentry a certain extra appeal. By choosing, when the British surrendered, to work with the Japanese rather than rallying to Chungking like model Chinese citizens they had proved that their loyalty was, in the last resort, to Hong Kong exclusively. For the sake of Hong Kong they would strike an accommodation with whoever happened to rule it. They were thus, paradoxically, the segment of society on whom the returning British could now best rely in the face of the intensified threat from the mainland.[93]

So the gentry had to be saved. Little more than a month after Harcourt's arrival the first action was taken to put an end to the hue and cry.[94] On 2 October a statement was issued to the newspapers by R. A. C. North, the pre-war Secretary for Chinese Affairs who was on the point of embarking for Britain along with the rest of the ex-internees. North described what had happened at the fateful meeting in January 1942 when he called on Kotewall and Chow in the China Building and asked them 'to take upon themselves what should have been my duty in working with the Japanese'. As a result, he went on, the two gentry leaders and their colleagues had been not merely humiliated by the conquerors but also 'misrepresented and abused' by some of their friends. 'I regret more than I can say that misunderstandings should have arisen over this matter, and I sincerely hope that the true facts will now be realised'.[95] More direct methods were also used to stem the outburst in the newspapers: the details are unclear, but MacDougall in later years recalled tersely, 'We jumped on it; I jumped hard on it.'[96] By the second week of October, at any rate, the topic of collaboration had disappeared suddenly and completely from the colony's press. In keeping with a policy worked out during the latter part of the war the BMA set up a War Activities Committee to look into the conduct of 'quislings and renegades'; but the wheels of the Committee had barely started to turn before a foot was applied to the brakes. Harcourt rejected at once the Committee's recommendation that Sir Robert Kotewall should be put on trial.[97] The focus then shifted to Li Tse-fong of the Bank of East Asia, Kotewall's former colleague on the Chinese Representative Council; but by this point the gentry themselves were starting to protest.[98] In December MacDougall dispatched an envoy to London to confer with the Colonial Office about the Li Tse-fong case and more generally about the whole quisling dilemma. The envoy selected was

T. M. Hazlerigg, an official who had served before the war in the legal department of the Hong Kong government and who was now attached as a special
adviser to MacDougall's Civil Affairs staff. In his talks in Whitehall Hazlerigg
was emphatic that the drive to prosecute the gentry should be brought to a halt.
He considered it 'reasonable' to assume that their wartime pronouncements
had been delivered in a state of fear and duress, and that they would have tried
to get out of the colony if the surveillance imposed on them hadn't been too
intense to permit an escape. In any event the BMA had been unable to find any
other 'informed and representative' Chinese advisers, and now that the public
mood had begun to grow calmer 'it would seem highly impolitic to stir up ani-
mosities'. The outcome was that, as MacDougall expressed it, 'we cleared the
whole thing'.[99] The Colonial Office agreed that Li Tse-fong should not be tried,
and within a few weeks had endorsed the whole tenor of the BMA's thinking.
On 30 March 1946 formal instructions were issued from London that only those
persons who had helped the Japanese to inflict acts of cruelty on the Hong Kong
population should be brought to trial.

This did not mean that the gentry escaped altogether. A 'very general feeling'
existed that those personalities who had been associated with the Japanese
regime should at least not 'continue to bask in the sunshine of official favour'.[100]
The most prominent gentry leaders were, consequently, edged into retirement.
In October 1945 Harcourt instructed MacDougall to let Kotewall know that he
should withdraw from public life until investigations into his wartime record
could be completed; and action was taken to bar him from attending the sessions of the newly formed Chinese Advisory Council. A British officer recalled
sorrowfully, 'I was under strict orders not to admit [Kotewall] to a Council
meeting, and it was a terrible moment in my life to have to tell Sir Robert that
he could not come in, for I had dined many times in his house before the
war'.[101] When civil government was restored the following May Kotewall was
obliged to resign without ceremony from his pre-war seat on the Executive
Council. MacDougall had argued that the fallen leader should be allowed to
attend the first session of the Council, after which he could bow out in a face-
saving manner on grounds of ill-health, but the returning Governor Young
was dead against such a gesture ('It was this *Banzai* thing').[102] There is no doubt
that Kotewall was cut to the quick. He had apparently counted on being praised
for his wartime attempts to improve the lot of the Chinese population. He
appealed to his old British patrons in a piteous circular:

> A Scottish verdict of 'not proven' is insufficient to drive away the unjusti-
> fied odium which, in ignorance, is permitted to besmirch the good name of
> one who has given the Crown half a century of loyal, wholehearted and
> faithful service.[103]

But for all his protests he was never allowed back on stage. To a lesser extent shadows fell over the other leading figures. Sir Shouson Chow, Kotewall's long-time partner, is said never to have returned completely to public life. Li Tse-fong failed to win reappointment to the Legislative Council when it came back into being in 1946. And Peter H. Sin, the 'Mayor of Hong Kong', had some difficulty in getting his lawyer's licence renewed.[104]

All in all, though, the purging of the community leaders was remarkably mild. In each case ways were found to cushion the fall. In the month Kotewall resigned from the Executive Council the House of Lords in London passed a motion endorsing his conduct, and both Harcourt and Young were induced to write letters assuring him of their continued regard. Neither Kotewall nor Chow were deprived of their knighthoods, in spite of the wartime murmurs at the Colonial Office. Following his exclusion from the Legislative Council Li Tse-fong seems to have found it judicious to absent himself for a ten-month period in the United States. When he came back, however, in February 1947, to take up his old post as manager of the Bank of East Asia, he was once more invited to public functions and he continued to sit on a number of advisory bodies and on the boards of a number of charitable concerns.[105] By the end of 1945 the 'Mayor of Hong Kong' had secured the right to appear as an Authorized Advocate in the defence of persons brought up before the military courts on charges of war crimes.[106]

More peripheral figures received a complete absolution. Towards the end of 1945 Sir Robert Ho Tung was 'invited' by the BMA to come back from his retreat in Macao, to take charge of his business and participate in rebuilding the colony.[107] Aw Boon-haw, the Tiger Balm King, went on running his newspaper, which had now dropped its occupation-period name and reverted to its pre-war title, the *Xing Dao Ribao*.[108] And Tung Chung-wei and Kwok Chan were left undisturbed at the head of the Hong Kong Chinese General Chamber of Commerce.

In the meantime the British set to work constructing a new gentry leadership out of the handful of personalities who were felt to have been relatively untainted by the events of the war. Foremost among them was M. K. Lo. Lo was not altogether free from controversy. He had, after all, served successively on the Rehabilitation Advisory Committee and the Chinese Cooperative Council, and he had put his signature to one of the early gentry statements saluting the puppet Chinese regime of Wang Jingwei. Almost all the wartime reports that came through to Whitehall had, however, testified to the extreme reluctance with which he had performed these duties; and by October 1945 there was said to be a 'general feeling' that he might be the 'best representative' of the local Chinese.[109] MacDougall recommended him to Harcourt as a natural for the newly formed Chinese Advisory Council, and he was made Rice Controller, with the key assignment of organizing the food supply. In the spring of 1946, as the BMA got ready to make way for the new civil government, MacDougall further earmarked him for a seat on both the Executive and the Legislative Councils. When a query about Lo's wartime activities was tabled in the House of Commons, the Colonial Office arranged an indignant rebuttal. The reply stressed that Lo had acted 'in accordance with the instructions he was given, and was inspired by no motive other than those of concern for the suffering and distress of the people of Hong Kong'.[110] Singled out for advancement along with Lo was T. N. Chau, the senior member of the pre-war Legislative Council who had slipped off to Macao a few weeks after the Japanese takeover. MacDougall described him as 'the only public figure who appears to have entirely clean hands'.[111] He too was put forward for both the Executive and Legislative Councils. Finally the authorities lighted on Sik-nin Chau, the eye specialist nephew of Sir Shouson Chow who had won the gratitude of the captive British bankers in the Sun Wah Hotel by attending to their medical needs. Harcourt recommended him for the Legislative Council, pointing out that his wartime record had earned the high praise of both the British and Chinese governments.[112] These three 'good' gentry leaders soon began to be sanctified in the classic British way. By the end of the BMA period T. N. Chau had been awarded the CBE; and two years later Lo was given a knighthood for his 'outstanding service in Hong Kong's rehabilitation programme'.[113]

'The Lees are building!'

Mere absolution, however, was not quite enough. The gentry also had rather more concrete expectations of the British return. With the war at an end many local magnates were looking to see what was going to become of their money. Would their pre-war holdings of Hong Kong dollars turn out to have kept their original value? Would their secret hoarding of the old colonial currency over the last two years prove to have paid off? Would any trouble be taken to honour the cheques drawn on the various British banks which they had accepted during the occupation in payment for the food and medicines they had channelled to the expatriate internees? Above all, what would happen to their piles of dud notes? During the final days of the interregnum the currency speculation which had been on the rise ever since the middle of 1943 had taken a fevered new turn. Millions of the celebrated duress notes, the fake Hong Kong dollars issued by the Japanese under the signature of the captive British bankers, had been bought up by a small band of speculators gambling, in true Hong Kong style, that they would eventually manage to get them redeemed. It was the same story with the military yen. In the days after Harcourt's arrival the bogus Japanese scrip actually rose against the Hong Kong dollar to a level about five times that of the week before as the speculators gambled that the

BMA would convert their wartime cash. Some optimists even bet that the BMA would give them a rate of HS$1:M¥4.[114] In the thick of all this speculation, by many accounts, was one of the 'clean' gentry personages soon to be marked out for promotion to the new gentry leadership, the eye specialist Sik-nin Chau.[115]

Financial questions apart, the gentry were still waiting to see whether the restored British Hong Kong would turn out to be durable, and if durable, whether it would be a place where prosperous non-Europeans could expect to maintain and increase their wealth. The initial British plan was that the BMA would monopolize all import and export transactions in the colony for the first six months of the restoration. By November, however, Harcourt was reporting widespread discontent in the local business community at 'a situation represented by a harbour full of men-of-war instead of merchantmen'. There was, he informed the Colonial Office, 'a latent suspicion that the reoccupation of Hong Kong is being turned exclusively to the British advantage'.[116]

As a second step, therefore, the BMA had to convince the gentry and the moneyed classes in general that the return to British rule would be likely to work in their interests. A key role in this effort was played by the Hongkong and Shanghai Bank. Even before the war ended the Bank had contrived to safeguard the assets of numerous magnates through the foresight of its exiled head office in London, which had prudently husbanded several millions of silver dollars as backing for the old colonial currency. Back in the colony under the leadership of a vigorous Ulsterman named Arthur Morse, it now got to work settling the vast majority of its wartime IOUs. Dutiful action was taken, for instance, to repay the HK$2m which had been diverted from the accounts of local clients for the benefit of Selwyn-Clarke and his medical team. More spectacularly, the decision was taken to accept the duress notes. Clearly it was of some importance for the Bank's reputation that its staff shouldn't be seen to have been embroiled, however inadvertently, in a large-scale racket; and Morse was also convinced it was vital for British prestige in Hong Kong and the Far East in general that Britain's word should be demonstrated to be its bond. On 1 April 1946 the Bank announced that the HK$119m worth of duress notes were to be recognized as legal tender. Morse and his colleagues bought up every one of the notes they could track down, and paid full value for each of them.[117] Indications were even apparently given that the Bank would redeem the military yen – albeit at a highly unfavourable rate.[118]

While the bankers endeavoured to please their big customers MacDougall and his team of officials set about demonstrating that the restored colony was a promising place in which to do business. One approach was to get a suitable gentry figure embarked on a large building project in order to convey the impression that the British were there to stay. Dick Lee, a tycoon who had aided the BAAG and was viewed as another of the 'cleaner' leaders, was persuaded (with some difficulty) to start putting up a new edifice in the Happy Valley district of Hong Kong Island on the understanding that the authorities would guarantee half the funds.[119] Another approach was to open up private trade. On 23 November 1945 all official controls were abolished, three months ahead of schedule. The first steps had been taken towards a new dispensation in which the colonial government would see its main function as giving backing to business – whether by lending money, by pushing local products and services in overseas markets, or simply by keeping out of the way.

The gentry appear to have been duly gratified by the thoughtful British display of concern for their wealth. The financial arrangements went down especially well. In November 1945 Li Shu-fan, the exuberant physician and sportsman, 'hastened back' to the colony from his eighteen-month sojourn in the United States. Finding his fortune still largely intact he observed happily that by keeping hefty reserves of silver in London as backing for the Hong Kong dollar the British authorities had 'justified the faith placed in them'.[120] In April 1946 the decision of the Hongkong and Shanghai Bank to accept the duress notes brought joy to a number of top local speculators. Three tycoons who had hoarded large quantities of notes before the decision was announced are said to have made instant profits of more than HK$10m.[121] Coming at a time when little currency was available, the Bank's decision was also welcomed as a vital stimulus to the Hong Kong economy. One gentry member recalls that no other British measure did more to get the colony moving again.[122]

A warm welcome was also accorded to the British efforts to recreate a good business environment. As Dick Lee and his clan buckled down to their construction project in Happy Valley the joyous cry of renewed optimism rang out, 'The Lees are building!'[123] Faith in the durability of the restored British order grew swiftly, and by March 1946 local merchants in Hong Kong were said to be 'planning ahead for the resumption of peacetime trade, with the conviction that there will be no change in the status of the colony for many years to come'.[124] Prominent among the planners was Sir Robert Ho Tung. In December 1945 the venerable plutocrat had accepted the BMA's 'invitation' to return to the colony, and over the next two years he displayed (indeed underlined) his commitment to its future with a series of bequests and investments. In 1946 he endowed the Central British School and disbursed HK$1m for a women's hall of residence at the University of Hong Kong, and in 1947 he embarked on the construction of a modern office building called Victory House.[125]

Finally, and predictably, the gentry warmed to the various obscure measures the BMA had adopted to curb crime and looting and to break up the Triad gangs. In a speech he delivered in May 1946 to greet Governor Young at the first session of the reconstituted Legislative Council M. K. Lo, the newly anointed gentry leader, declared that the colony had learned during the last few months to appreciate 'the inestimable boon of law and order'.[126]

'The 1946 outlook': a drive for reform

But this still wasn't enough to secure for the British the solid core of support that they needed to have. Widespread murmuring had developed among both the gentry and the middle-class dogsbodies on whose efforts every branch of the administration relied. These local Asians didn't rise up to resist the return of the British in the same way that the peoples of Vietnam and Indonesia rose up to resist the second coming of the French and the Dutch. But they did make it very clear that they weren't prepared to accept a re-erection of the barriers which had hemmed them in so efficiently in the decades before 1941.

The first protests were being voiced within less than a fortnight of Harcourt's landfall. As the BMA fussed over the care and repatriation of the newly freed inmates of Stanley and Shamshuipo, little if any attention appeared to be getting paid to the needs of the non-European public. One indignant Chinese wrote to the *South China Morning Post*,

> We in our greater Concentration Camp have had our share of suffering during the past four years. For one who has felt hunger in the little Con-centration Camp, thousands have starved and died outside . . .[127]

On 28 September the BMA compounded their initial *faux pas* by issuing a decree which provided for repatriation or cash benefits to be made available to former members of the Hong Kong Volunteer Defence Corps. The pro-vision seemed generous, but it applied in effect only to the Europeans. All those Chinese, Eurasians and Portuguese who had fought for the Crown in December 1941 were reckoned to have been demobilized from the date of the British surrender and not, consequently, to be eligible for any further pay or allowances. The decree provoked 'considerable public resentment and discus-sion'.[128] And on top of all this the British were ruffling local sentiment through their handling of that ever-important issue, the goods in the godowns. Approaches had been made to the BMA by businessmen of both British and non-European origins seeking compensation for goods belonging to them that had been looted by the Japanese. Compensation was duly paid to the British merchants but denied, in many cases, to the locals on the grounds that they had been given the chance by the Japanese rulers to withdraw at least some of their goods from the godowns while the British had been cooped up in Stanley.[129] An impression began to form that perhaps not a lot had been changed by the British restoration. Three weeks after the British return a 'little chap' came up to MacDougall and whispered, 'You know, being reoccupied is very much like being occupied. Somebody takes all the big houses and all the big cars'.[130]

By October the specific grumbles of the first few weeks had expanded into a barrage of general comments about the shortcomings of pre-war British rule. In letters to newspapers, in conversations with Western acquaintances, bankers and compradors, teachers and journalists, junior civil servants and company clerks all began to give vent to their distaste for the old colonial system and to come up with their suggestions of ways in which it should be changed. In the first place, they urged, there should be an end to the 'old order based on race and privilege' under which Asians had been denied the right to live on the Peak and debarred from admission to the Hong Kong Club. The old stigma attached to miscegenation should be done away with, and it should be accepted that for a European to marry 'a well-bred Chinese or Eurasian' was 'no sin against society'.[131] No more discrimination should be allowed in the workplace. More positions, including high-ranking government posts, should be thrown open to non-Europeans, and a plan should be drawn up for training young Chinese for government service. And equal pay should be given for equal work. Now that the cost of living was ten times what it had been before the war a Hong Kong Chinese who had spent fifteen years on the government payroll could no longer be expected to get by with a fraction of the salary drawn by his European colleagues, regardless of how unfavourably the latter might compare with him in terms of experience or ability. 'Such a state of affairs can have only one result – namely, the transfer of the victims' friendship and likings to the Americans, a trend already apparent in China'.[132] On the political side steps should be taken to ensure greater representation of the Chinese in the running of the colony. A number of them, for example, should 'sit on the Legislative or the Executive Council to coordinate public opinion and the Government'. Urban and District Councils should be organized so that 'lesser fry' too could have opportunities for public service. And the censorship which had been slapped on the Chinese press in the twenties and thirties should be repealed.[133]

Quicker on the uptake than their pre-war forerunners, the BMA soon became aware of the existence among their more articulate Asian subjects of an 'undercurrent of discontent'.[134] It was clear in particular that any British behaviour which smacked of the pre-war mentality was 'absolutely taboo'. Local people were counting on a new dispensation, to be brought in as soon as civil government was restored to the colony in the coming year. Harcourt called it 'the 1946 outlook'.[135]

The British themselves, as it happened, were now strongly predisposed to a drive for reform. In London the new Labour government headed by Clement Attlee were pledged to the goal of decolonization in every part of the Empire. And the top officials whom London sent to pursue that objective in Hong Kong

were personally sympathetic to the '1946 outlook' of the local public and convinced of the need to accommodate it. First and most obvious of these agents
of reform was MacDougall. A liberal by the standards of the Colonial Office
even before the war, he had pressed, as we have seen, for a rethink of policy
in the light of the 1941 cataclysm and had presided at the wartime meetings
of the Hong Kong Planning Unit at which the blueprint for future change
was drawn up. Second, and more surprising, was the restored Governor, Sir
Mark Young. No one had fancied that Young, the stern, the forbidding, the
Churchillian, would turn out to be a reformer. He was allowed to come back
for a stint in his old post as a matter of personal honour – a chance to wipe
out the trauma of his deeply reluctant surrender to the Japanese forces half a
decade before. The Foreign Office were sharply opposed to his reappointment,
regarding him as yesterday's man. Some of the British expatriates, impatient
with the slow rate of progress in areas such as price control and the provision
of housing, referred to him unkindly as Sir Mark Time.[136] Yet Young in his
second coming proved more inclined to innovation than any Governor Britain
had placed in the colony for the past twenty years. Like Gimson, that other
improbable advocate of reform, he had spent much of his career in the
Colonial Service in Ceylon, with its progressive institutions and relaxed racial
climate. He was no China hand, but was said to have been 'very considerably
influenced' by the Chinese and their culture.[137] Initially wary of the Hong Kong
Planning Unit's proposals, which had been drafted while he was still lan-
guishing in the Japanese camps, he decided upon his arrival that the proposals were right and should be pushed even further. And he kept MacDougall
beside him in the key supporting role of Colonial Secretary.

The same will for change permeated the greater part of the British community. The pre-war radicals, who had never doubted the need for a more
humane social order, were back in full cry. Bishop Hall warned his flock in a
ringing sermon preached in St John's Cathedral on Armistice Day 1945, 'Under
God we dare not stay in Hong Kong unless it is our purpose to build there, as
part of the great Pacific civilization of the future, a city in which truth and
freedom and justice are not tainted by national pride and racial fear'.[138] And
for the first time the radicals were in tune with the feeling of most of the expatriate rank and file. Out on the evacuation ships went the bulk of the old guard
– the pre-war blimps who had learned nothing and forgotten nothing. In
with the BMA came a new breed of soldiers and officials, no longer convinced
altogether of the white man's mission to rule, disposed by and large to look
sympathetically on the non-European peoples. Widespread throughout the
community was a keen sense of the shame which the Japanese conquest had
inflicted on Britain in the eyes of its Asian subjects, and a consciousness that
the restored British masters were back in the colony strictly on trial. The *South
China Morning Post* pointed out to its readers that the old pre-war order could

never return: rather than hanker after it they should seize the chance which now offered 'to rid ourselves of some past blemishes and so justify our salvation'.[139] There was at the same time a sentiment that those Asians who had rallied to the Crown in its hour of need now deserved 'the best that we can give them'.[140] 'Everyone', MacDougall wrote drily to Gent at the Colonial Office, 'seems now to say and to think what would have been usefully said and thought any time from 1937 to 1941'.[141]

Once again generous instincts were reinforced by a certain amount of hard calculation. Most of the movers and shakers were more persuaded than ever that reform was essential if Britain was to hold on to Hong Kong. Gent in London considered that a new deal delegating a real share of power to local people would help to reduce Nationalist Chinese pressure on Britain to return the New Territories. John Keswick, the taipan of the Jardine Matheson company, thought an end should be put to all forms of racial discrimination; but he saw this in part as a necessary manœuvre through which Britain might cut the ground from beneath its Nationalist Chinese and American critics.[142]

Hong Kong was accordingly treated to a reworking of a familiar recent motif. Just as the colony's British rulers in the 1920s had been galvanized (for a time) into bringing in social changes by the shock of the great strike and boycott campaign, so their post-war successors were prompted by the upheaval of the Japanese occupation to address the whole new gamut of social and political discontents. The BMA, as an interim government, did not have the authority to push through any sort of long-term institutional change; but they did use their eight months in power to signal the dawn of a new age in which Asian murmurings would be listened to. From the start they adopted a posture of openness. Duncan Sloss, the Publicity Officer appointed by Gimson, carried on at his post for the first few weeks, doing his best to explain British policies to the population; and a daily press conference was organized at which the heads of the various departments of Civil Affairs were encouraged to talk about matters of public interest within their spheres. With the help of this new public relations machinery the BMA took rapid action to limit the damage inflicted by their early *faux pas*. On 9 September 1945, for example, Sloss made a press announcement designed to allay the furore which had broken out over the alleged favouritism being shown by the authorities to the ex-internees. He informed readers that the administration was 'working ceaselessly to ensure the well-being of people of all races'.[143] Two weeks later MacDougall issued a similar reassurance denying any intent to discriminate in the unpopular decree which had, in effect, provided for back payments to be made to the European members of the Hong Kong Volunteer Defence Corps but not to the others; and the decree was in due course modified with the purpose of guaranteeing 'a greater degree of equality of treatment'.[144]

The BMA also took the opportunity to make a number of concrete advances – *ad hoc*, not definitive, but pointing the way to the future. In the first place they interpreted the lack of British and abundance of Asian candidates for every sector of public employment as an obvious signal to 'open the whole thing up'.[145] MacDougall perceived, for example, that the colony was packed with first-rate local barristers and solicitors who had been trained in English law. Brushing aside the protests of a few diehards that 'we must keep the system British' he promptly appointed three or four Chinese magistrates; and by the end of October twenty-one out of thirty of the Authorized Advocates designated by the BMA's Military Courts were Chinese, Eurasians or Portuguese.[146] As with the judiciary, so with the executive. By the end of October a Eurasian, a veteran of the Hong Kong Volunteer Defence Corps, had been appointed Deputy Director of Education; and local Chinese were said to be occupying a whole range of executive posts 'with responsibilities unknown before the war'.[147] With a similar briskness the BMA swept aside some of the restrictions on freedom of expression that had been imposed in the twenties and thirties on the Chinese, but not on the Europeans. A decision was taken that there should be for the moment no further censorship of the press or of letters.

With the advent of Young the door was thrown open to long-term, systematic, legislated change. One spectacular break with the past followed almost immediately. On 27 July 1946 the restored civil government announced the repeal of the carefully crafted 1918 ordinance which had debarred Asian citizens from living on the Peak. From now on anyone who could afford to could make their home on the prestigious heights overlooking Victoria. Abolished at the same time was a ruling designed to prevent local settlement in the hills on the island of Cheung Chau, another choice part of the colony which had been earmarked for Europeans. Residential apartheid was at an end.

Young confirmed and expanded the tentative moves which the BMA had made to provide local Asians with new opportunities. Soon after his return he gave it out officially that more local people were to be recruited for government jobs; and by the autumn of 1946 a broad push for 'localization' was well under way. In October a Hong Kong Chinese was enrolled for the first time in the Cadets, the elite stream of the colony's civil service. The choice for this privileged posting fell on Paul Tsui, the wartime loyalist who had played the major role in selecting local Chinese for the BAAG. Lower down in the hierarchy Young and his team aimed at nothing less than a complete substitution of local for expatriate personnel. Radical ethnic changes were launched in the police force. In keeping with the ideas which had been mooted in Stanley by Police Commissioner Pennefather-Evans, plans were readied for the phasing out of European inspectors – a project favoured by the fact that the bulk of the pre-war European officers had been sent home to recuperate. In 1946–7 1,002 local Chinese were recruited into the police force, but no Europeans; and the Chinese contingent rose to exceed 50 per cent of the total police numbers for the first time.[148]

Lastly Young set to work on an overhaul of the colony's political system. As in the late 1920s steps were taken to provide for a slight enlargement in the number of gentry leaders attached to the Governor's side. Young advised the Colonial Office that it would be 'useful as well as politically expedient' to increase Chinese membership on the ten-seat Executive Council from one to two (hence the combined elevation of M. K. Lo and T. N. Chau).[149] But the objective this time went a great deal further. In an inaugural statement made following his arrival in May 1946 the restored Governor proclaimed Britain's purpose of giving the whole Hong Kong population 'a fuller and more responsible share in the management of their own affairs'.[150] Young had brought with him a scheme for reform which had been sketched out in the final months of the war by the Hong Kong Planning Unit in London. In its essence the Young Plan, as it came to be known, entailed nothing less than the transformation of Hong Kong from an autocratically managed Crown Colony into a self-governing city state. The old Urban Council with its modest element of election was to be expanded into a thirty-seat Municipal Council set up 'on a fully representative basis'. Half of the seats would be occupied by Hong Kong Chinese and half by Europeans: two-thirds of the seats would be directly elected, and the remainder appointed by representative bodies such as the Chinese professional guilds. Vastly more muscular than its predecessor, the Municipal Council would operate in tandem with the established government, gradually taking over such major spheres of activity as education, social welfare, town planning and public works. During the course of the summer the Young Plan was submitted for the consideration of the Hong Kong Chinese General Chamber of Commerce and other local bodies, and in October it was formally recommended by the Governor to the Colonial Office.

A more tentative puff of democratization was to be breathed into the established government as well. The 'Unofficial' members of the Legislative Council, the members appointed from the major firms and other non-government bodies, were to have for the first time a majority (of one) over the *ex officio* members who were obliged to vote as the Governor ordered; and two of these Unofficials were to be nominated by the new – and partly elected – Municipal Council. The push for democracy even extended into the colony's hinterland. In the course of 1946 elections were held for the first time in some of the districts of the New Territories, where representatives of twenty-eight sub-districts were chosen to sit on a network of rural committees.[151]

The long-term thrust of these policies was underlined by a general lowering of the British profile. In his inaugural statement of May 1946 Young referred to Hong Kong as a 'territory': for the first time the term 'colony' wasn't felt to roll comfortably off the tongue. At a meeting in October the Executive Council decided to go slow on the reinstallation of the old royal effigies in Statue Square. Young and his advisers agreed to defer taking action to replace any statues of British royalty which could not be tracked down in Japan, and to drop a proposal which had been made for adorning the empty pedestals with commemorative plaques.

Many of these official advances were matched by the general run of expatriate society, in letter, or spirit, or both. The Jockey Club was revived, but a consensus had now formed that there could be no going back to the all-European club committee of pre-war days; and a Chinese steward was consequently appointed in the person of Sik-nin Chau. 'Quite a feeling' had grown up, in the same way, that the sacrosanct European bathing beaches which had in the past lined the Castle Peak Road on the south coast of the New Territories should from now on become free for all, and both these and a number of other bathing and picnic resorts were duly opened up to the local inhabitants.[152] Certain features of pre-war expatriate conduct towards the subject peoples were no longer reckoned to be quite acceptable: little by little, we are told, the cries of 'Boy!' which had rung out to summon elderly Chinese waiters in the colony's bars died away.[153] In the private sector as in the administration new jobs began to be offered to Asian employees. Late in 1945 the Eurasian M. H. Lo, a brother of M. K. Lo, became the first local to be allowed to join the Private Office of Jardine Matheson and to be given the responsibility of signing 'p.p.' letters on behalf of the firm.[154]

These various innovations had the intended effect. The gentry hailed with much pleasure the lifting of the pre-war racial barriers that had constrained them along with the rest of the non-Europeans. M. K. Lo, who had inveighed against British discrimination so fiercely throughout the late 1930s, declared in the speech of welcome he delivered on Young's arrival in May 1946 that the Governor's return signified 'the birth of a new Hong Kong' which was 'resolved to advance the interests of the Colony as a whole and not those of any particular section of the community'.[155] He expressed his approval of the newly proclaimed 'long-term policy of replacing European officers by local officers', and of Young's promise to endow Hong Kong's citizens with a new 'sense of responsibility' by introducing 'a greater measure of self-government'.[156] When the Peak District (Residence) Ordinance was repealed in July Lo observed that the ruling had been 'a source of resentment to the Chinese ever since its enactment', and voiced his belief that its removal would give them 'universal satisfaction'.[157] In a very short time the first local tycoons were moving to take advantage of the new dispensation on the Peak. Before the year was out Li Shu-fan had completed the building there of a mansion called White Jade – a 'modest landmark' which the pleasure-loving doctor went on, in the next two decades, to embellish with twelve gardens of different sizes standing in tiers and 'more than 2,000 rose bushes of many varieties'.[158]

The same appreciation appears to have been widely felt among the upper and middle classes. Less than a month after Harcourt arrived a young, university-educated Hong Kong Chinese with a Eurasian wife had already begun to detect promising signs of a new atmosphere which he pointed out in the course of a conversation with an Australian journalist. After noting how the Chinese in the colony had been drawn, in their turn, closer to the expatriates by the common experience of Japanese maltreatment, he went on,

> Then these English occupation troops came. And we found that they put a friendly hand on our shoulder and accepted us and talked to us as they talk to each other – not down to us, or through us.
>
> They come into our homes, these men, to sit and talk and drink and eat with us . . . There is no racial snobbery in their make-up . . . They are not the people who say that if you marry a Chinese or Eurasian girl your Public Service career is finished and your social status wrecked.[159]

As the reforms started to take effect a greater mixing of the races was clearly perceptible. Friendships that had grown up during the war between British and Chinese in the BAAG or the occupied city lingered on in the form of an 'unexpected if discreet camaraderie'.[160] For the first time British women felt able to venture into Chinese households, and for the first time Chinese households felt happy to receive them. As the old restraints on social intercourse were pared away Chinese residents of the more prosperous classes tended more and more to become Westernized. They shed their traditional long gowns for Western suits, gave their children Western names and were observed increasingly to favour 'the European type of house'.[161] As the old racial barriers to employment began to be raised growing numbers of young Chinese were emboldened to enter the legal, medical, accounting and other professions and to compete with Westerners in the various professional exams. The deep-rooted prejudice against intermarriage, already weakened by the scattered unions formed at the resistance headquarters in southern China, showed further signs of abating. In the autumn of 1945 a senior civil servant who had become engaged to a 'charming, educated' Hong Kong Chinese girl declared cheerfully, 'I'm going to try it, anyway. I'd say it's never really been tried out properly'.[162] His example was apparently followed over the next couple of years, and in 1947 a total of forty-seven mixed marriages were recorded by the Registrar-General's office.[163] One side-effect of this process was that the old pre-war stigma attached to Eurasians began slowly to disappear. Less and less the Eurasians were viewed, by themselves and by others, as a distinct community, more and more they were absorbed as individual members of the larger Chinese and European groups.

A new fluidity was becoming apparent not only between the races, but also within them. By the end of the war the old stuffy antagonism which had kept the British officials and businessmen at arm's length of each other had melted away. In spite of the feud which had ground on in Stanley between Gimson and the leaders of the businessmen's mini-revolution, the bulk of the civil servants and expatriate merchants emerged from the camp with a new fellow-feeling born of the years they had spent 'in the bag together'.[164] The *rapprochement* was hastened by the clear intention of the restored British rulers to throw their weight behind trade. In an interview given in 1947 MacDougall recalled 'how correctly it was realized on all sides' that it was only through 'the closest cooperation between Government and the business community' that Hong Kong could regain its former prosperity.[165]

Inside each British sub-group a marked decline could be sensed in the pre-war obsession with social status. One old-timer who came back to the colony in 1947 noted that

> The *taipan* and the senior government official were no longer regarded, nor did they regard themselves, as demi-gods. They were now simply ordinary human beings who, on account of their age and seniority, attracted a degree of respect.[166]

The bigwigs for their part seem to have shown an increased courtesy to lower-grade Europeans on their staffs, in the shops and in the armed forces. Gone, to a great extent, was the pomp of yesterday. Mountain Lodge, the mansion on the Peak which had served as the Governor's summer residence since 1867, was demolished on the advice of the Public Works Department, and never rebuilt; and the grounds were turned into a public garden. The Fanling Hunt was abandoned, squeezed out by the expansion of chicken farms and fruit orchards in the New Territories. And the lush festivities which the expatriates had once enjoyed in the Hong Kong Club and the Repulse Bay Hotel were never quite the same again. In place of these glories, however, came a vastly wider range of social circles and shared interest associations.

Evidence for the Chinese and the other Asian communities is more fragmentary; but there are one or two signs that a similar process of relaxation was at work there as well. In the Li family, for example, the great Chinese clan which produced Li Koon-chun and Li Tse-fong, the strict hierarchical rules which had governed relationships are said to have loosened up, in part owing to the wartime conversion of many family members to Christianity. In 1947 the family matriarch who held sway over all domestic affairs was induced to extend formal recognition to the common-law wife of one of her sons, a woman whom she had cold-shouldered for years.[167] The grand family gatherings which had taken place in the pre-war decades at the Ho Tung mansions were now smaller and less frequent. The Ho Tungs, like a good many of the

Eurasian families, had been dispersed by the war. Jean Gittins, the daughter of Sir Robert, who had spent the war years interned with the British in Stanley, had been offered the chance to recuperate in Australia, and had chosen to stay in her interim home. But the family ties were in some ways more real than they had been in the old days of grandeur: Jean Gittins found that in their new state of separation she and her father for the first time 'grew to understand and love one another'.[168] In other areas also a trend seems to have set in for change and modernity. The entrenched Chinese custom by which girls from poor families were sold off to work as unpaid servants in wealthier households – the custom against which well-meaning Europeans had campaigned unavailingly twenty years earlier – is said at this juncture to have 'come naturally to an end'.[169]

Other new social breakthroughs had meanwhile begun to be made that transcended the ethnic distinctions. The immediate post-war years saw the appearance of the first woman political representative, the first woman lawyer and (amid some sensation) the first woman Justice of the Peace.[170] Chastened by hardship post-war Hong Kong was, in short, a kinder, a more tolerant and a more open society. It was also, as one expatriate remembers, a much more *interesting* one.[171]

Retribution and rice bowls

But even this was not the end of the task that confronted the British in the autumn of 1945. In addition to reconstituting a pliant elite they had also to satisfy the expectations of the Hong Kong Chinese masses. In the first place the masses were hungry for revenge on their wartime tormentors. In the days after Harcourt's arrival Japanese soldiers had been hauled off a tram outside the Naval Dockyard and beaten to death. The Kempeitai executioner from Stanley gaol had been trussed up and flung into the harbour by a band of labourers who spotted him trying to make his escape on a Kowloon-bound ferry; and for want of an animate target the tablet bearing Isogai's inaugural Rescript in Statue Square had been pulverized by a furious mob. The cry was that the BMA should hunt down all of the principal Japanese killers and bring them to justice. But the British were not felt to have been carrying out this task with anything like the enthusiasm required. There was a sense that the BMA's efforts were for the most part directed at catching the Japanese who had victimized the European internees and POWs rather than those who had preyed on the Chinese public in town. Widespread indignation was voiced that a number of arch-villains such as the savage Public Prosecutor, Kashiwagi and three or four of the Kempeitai district bosses had been allowed by the British to slip through the net.[172]

By the same token the masses were quivering to get even with the Kempeitai's local hirelings. In the absence of any conspicuous steps by the British to hunt down these rascals local vigilantes were starting to mete out their own form of justice. Kangaroo courts were being held, and a number of alleged informers or torturers were found shot, Chinese-style, through the back of the neck.[173]

In the light of the victory over Japan the Hong Kong masses were also filled with a new pride in being Chinese, and a greatly increased disposition to identify with the mainland regime. In the first days of September the Nationalist flag continued to fly from 'all buildings' in the colony. During the Allied victory celebrations of 9 to 11 October rallies staged by the local agents of the Nationalist Party attracted crowds of over 10,000 Hong Kong Chinese: 40,000 to 50,000 joined in one 'massive' parade led by the Three People's Principles Youth League, and shouts rang out, 'Long Live the Republic!'[174] The return of the colony to the motherland was confidently expected to follow at no distant date: 'Wherever you looked and listened', one journalist wrote, 'on every hand there was being said, in a hundred ways, "When China takes back Hong Kong . . ."'[175] In this context the masses were in no mood, any more than the better-off Asian residents, to put up any longer with the kind of slights which had come their way in the pre-war years. On the night of 5 October a seven-year-old Chinese girl was thrown to her death from a balcony in the Wanchai district by a drunk British naval rating. Official reports coyly stated that 'the reaction was very noticeable': riots broke out, and the public made it plain that they looked to the BMA to take swift and well-publicized action against the offender, with the death penalty at the end of it.[176] And in cases where the British seemed to ignore local interests, the masses were no longer willing to accept Britain as the sole source of authority. Signs of this became apparent at the end of October, when the 10,000 villagers due to be displaced by the Pingshan airport project were issued with their eviction notices. Some of them sent the notices back through the post, torn in half: others went to Canton and implored General Zhang Fakui to secure for them the support of 'our government'.[177] Special Commissioner Kwok, the Nationalist representative who arrived in the colony at the same period, soon began to be viewed by large numbers of local Chinese as their leader, and his office was regularly called upon to take up the cudgels in disputes between Chinese and Europeans.

Last and most basic, the masses were preoccupied with the struggle to survive. Hunger was universal, and '1940 clothes hung on wasted 1945 frames like wet rags on broomsticks'.[178] Wages were still fixed at the levels prevailing before the war in spite of the tenfold rise that had since taken place in the cost of food, fuel and other essentials. And the British had in certain ways even made matters worse. The overnight suppression of the military yen, carried out at a time when the new stocks of Hong Kong dollars were still, in MacDougall's words, 'dangerously inadequate', had for a short while reduced about 90 per cent of the populace to virtual destitution.[179] Landlords had been allowed to raise rents, frozen during the occupation, and in some cases were even trebling them. Within a few weeks of the British re-entry the cost of living was higher than under the Japanese, and people were said to be 'forgetting their liberation from Japanese rule because of the concerns of the moment'.[180]

In the course of the autumn the articulate Chinese citizens who chatted with European officials or journalists or wrote to the English-language press came up, along with their other ideas, with a set of suggestions for improving the lot of the poor. Free education, they argued, should be laid on by the government for all children who couldn't afford to pay for their schooling. Health and employment insurance should be brought in and made compulsory, and a Poor Law-type system should be organized by compiling a register of *bona fide* residents. Slums should be cleared and factory workers rehoused in sanitary conditions, and the feeble pre-war efforts to promote farming and fisheries in the rural parts of the colony should be taken up with a new vigour.[181]

The masses themselves did not come up with any formal manifesto, but they made it clear that there would be trouble if their distress was ignored. For the first time since the 1920s there began to be hints of industrial turmoil. In early November unrest was reported among drivers, and fitters, and labourers in the Taikoo dockyard, and by December the colony's machinists were demanding a wage increase.

The British saw well enough that this disaffection among the mass of the Chinese populace posed potentially the gravest crisis of all. On 2 November MacDougall drew London's attention with his usual eloquence to the desperate shortage of foodstuffs and other necessities, now exacerbated by the embargo imposed from Canton. Up until now, he observed, the BMA had succeeded in keeping the colony 'one jump ahead of a breakdown', but

> with increasing difficulty the position is held . . . From now on each day until supplies reach us we lose ground. There is a limit to the amount of ground that can be lost. There is unrest south of us and north of us.[182]

One is reminded of Gordon's dispatches from beleaguered Khartoum. MacDougall intimated unmistakably that British control might not survive a continued failure to deliver. 'By shifts and evasions,' he wrote on 7 November, 'we have carried on for nine weeks to conceal the essential weakness of our position, which is that the larder is bare, that the godowns are empty and that the liberators brought nothing that fills stomachs or furnishes houses'.[183] Already, he noted, the local trade unions were beginning to take shape once more. Sooner or later they would be given a lead by political forces outside Hong Kong, and if by that time the colony had not 'been able to make manifest the promise of prosperity by reviving trade and industry', the consequences were 'likely to be serious'.[184]

As their final piece of spring-cleaning, then, the British set themselves to addressing the grievances of the common people. They were unable by this stage to do very much about the clamour for the detention of more Japanese villains. Many of the leading suspects had managed to get out of the colony to Macao or Canton before Harcourt even arrived. In response to Chinese pressure an order was eventually issued for the arrest of Public Prosecutor Kashiwagi; but Kashiwagi was never tracked down. Scope did however exist for meting out justice to the principal local thugs who had joined in with the Japanese. In April 1946 George Wong, the Kempeitai's leading henchman, who had been discovered in suitably Stygian circumstances squatting underneath a woodpile on Nathan Road, was brought before a military court on the colony's first ever charge of high treason. Duly convicted, he went to the gallows that summer along with a couple of other Chinese hirelings who had worked with him in the Kempeitai's torture chambers. Prosecutions were also brought against a succession of lesser Kempeitai hangers-on, and the bulk of them were handed down prison sentences of up to fifteen years with hard labour. Thrown in with this crew were the various seedy figures whose sympathy for Japan had been manifested in less violent ways. These included the two Eurasians, Joseph Richards and Joseph Carroll, who were brought to court on a series of charges which ranged from gathering intelligence for Japan in the pre-war years to procuring strategic materials for the Japanese forces. They were convicted on the lesser count of breach of the Defence Regulations, and received prison sentences of one year and six months respectively. Finally steps were taken to deal with some of the Indians who had espoused the Japanese cause with such zeal in the early months of the conquest. A large number of Indian policemen and prison warders were sent back to their homeland, and no Sikhs were ever again recruited for the police force.[185] All these moves still amounted to little more than a token display. Only twenty-eight people in all were found guilty,[186] and many other culprits were never brought to trial.[187] Howard Tore (Call Me Howard), for instance, the greasy extortioner, slipped across the border to the mainland before anyone could catch him, returning to the colony some time later under a different name. But enough had been done to give at least an impression of retribution. The phasing out of the Sikh police also had the side benefit of removing an old Chinese gripe. Chinese crowds, it was reckoned, might still, at a pinch, obey the orders of a British police officer; but they would not now take kindly to being hectored by an auxiliary foisted on them from another colony thousands of miles away.[188]

The BMA quickly seized the chance to display sensitivity to the public's new access of national pride. After the killing of the Chinese girl in Wanchai a statement was at once put out that the seaman in question had been detained and that the affair was being investigated by the Navy authorities.

Most important of all the restored British rulers addressed themselves, with an energy never witnessed in the pre-war period, to tackling the squalid hardship endured by the mass of ordinary Hong Kong Chinese. A sharp break with the old days was made soon after Harcourt's arrival, on 20 September 1945, when Proclamation no. 13 of the BMA, issued in accordance with the joint announcement of the Allied colonial powers almost two years earlier, decreed, at long last, the end of the government opium traffic and the complete prohibition of opium smoking within Hong Kong. And in the meantime the Civil Affairs staff were doing their utmost to demonstrate their concern for Chinese well-being. MacDougall had flown in from London with instructions to promote social welfare, and in the course of the autumn he struck out on a dozen fronts to alleviate the immediate post-war distress. A sum of HK$150,000 was allotted for feeding the destitute, and up to 40,000 free meals were provided each day at thirteen food kitchens. For good measure the government opened a network of 'economical' restaurants where rice or noodle dishes could be had for as little as HK$2, and the price of rice in the shops was held down at a subsidized level of HK20¢ a catty. Thirty to forty thousand unskilled labourers were given jobs every day cleaning up the war-ravaged streets, and a major programme of public works was launched in a broader effort to relieve unemployment. The minimum daily wage was increased 'within half an hour' from HK60¢ to HK$2, and MacDougall recommended to Harcourt a rehabilitation allowance of HK$1 a day to be paid to every non-European essential worker. To soothe the unhappiness that had been caused by the initial rent increases, rents were frozen by proclamation at the levels of 1941, and tribunals were set up to adjudicate individual disputes between landlord and tenant.[189] 'I will not pretend', wrote the irrepressible Chief Civil Affairs Officer, 'that I am not enjoying myself'.[190]

In the countryside too a new effort was made by the BMA to raise living standards. Dr Herklots, the government biologist, emerged from Stanley with the new title of Secretary for Development and the chance to put into practice the ideas he had worked out behind the barbed wire for upgrading the colony's fisheries. By 6 September he had set up a new Fisheries Organization designed to rescue the fisherfolk from the clutches of the pre-war middlemen and enable them to sell their produce in a wholesale market through a cooperative marketing scheme. Partly at the prompting of Herklots Hong Kong was also endowed for the first time with a Department of Agriculture. The farmers, like the fisherfolk, were encouraged to group together on a cooperative basis and sell their crops through a newly formed wholesale vegetable market; and an experimental farm was set up in the New Territories to develop new techniques of arable cultivation in difficult soil.

Here again Young put flesh on the bones of the BMA's improvisations. In August 1946, in a sign of a new sensitivity to working-class feeling, the Executive Council lifted the ban which had been imposed in the twenties and thirties on a dozen Chinese trade unions. A Labour Office was organized, and a Labour Arbitration Committee established to help bring an end to industrial feuds. A Social Welfare Office was also created in embryo, in the guise of a sub-department of the Secretariat for Chinese Affairs. Underlying these moves was a growing sense that the management of the colony's poor was too weighty a matter to be left to the mercies of firms and the efforts of a handful of charities. From his seat on the Executive Council, where he had resumed his duties as Director of Medical Services after a spell of home leave, the pre-war maverick Selwyn-Clarke argued tirelessly for government intervention to aid the less privileged. He pressed for a stop to be put to a planned hike in the fares on the cross-harbour ferries; for new housing to be constructed for vagrants; for more generous pay and conditions to be arranged for local officers in the public service.[191] In the course of 1946 serious thought was even given to funding the government's increased social expenditure through the introduction of an income tax.[192] Free-market Hong Kong found itself peering into the bewildering landscape of the Welfare State.

Various negative signs suggest that the Chinese masses were gratified in their turn by the British exertions on their behalf. The initial surge of support for the Nationalists died down rather quickly. As early as October 1945 the British police raid on Shan Chit-son's illegal headquarters was said to have met with 'no discernible local repercussion';[193] and in the following year more and more of the public apparently disregarded the efforts which were made to recruit them by Chan Su's newly legitimized Party branch. Shopkeepers ignored pressures to pay taxes to the mainland government, and young men brushed aside exhortations to join up with the Nationalist army. In spite of the British apprehensions, no serious labour trouble broke out in the colony up to the end of the BMA. Harcourt and MacDougall were sure that the lack of disorder was a direct result of their great push to provide economic relief.[194] Following Young's return the industrial scene grew more turbulent. Gas and electricity workers came out in May 1946, and in July the Star Ferry crews went on strike for a wage increase. Jean Gittins, dropping in from Australia to call on her father, was startled by the Star Ferry disruption, which contrasted rather sharply with the dead social calm of the 1930s. But the walk-outs were accompanied by almost no violence, and the Star Ferry disruption was followed by a further year of relative tranquillity before the outbreak of the next major strike. Jean Gittins was left with the feeling that while there were 'moaners in the hotel lobbies and beggars on the streets', people on the whole were 'happy and contented'.[195]

The Japanese and the post-war transformation

Contemplating the changes which took place in the first two years of the British return it becomes rather hard to accept the contention that the Japanese interlude had no significant impact on post-war Hong Kong. In a general sense, at least, the role played by the Japanese was clearly of the utmost importance. By overthrowing the British in December 1941 they had shattered for ever the myth of supreme British power. And every day from then on for just under four years they had drummed in the message of that overthrow, ceaselessly inculcating in the local public their doctrine of Asian self-government and hostility to the whites. Westerners who spent part of the war in the occupied city had no doubt that this doctrine would leave its mark: their side would win, but as one of them put it grimly, 'ours will be no victory'.[196] The effects of all this showed themselves straight away in the calls for reform which broke out among articulate Asian citizens in the weeks after Harcourt's arrival. The clamour for an end to social and political discrimination recalled, almost point for point, the critiques of pre-war British rule which had filled the pages of the Japanese-sponsored *Hong Kong News* in January–February 1942. On top of this local people were filled with the new confidence stemming from the joint Chinese–British resistance to Japanese tyranny and from China's new status as one of the victorious Allies. One local schoolmaster summed up his ideas for reform by observing that the Chinese had now 'risen in the social scale' and 'wished to live on equal terms with the Europeans'.[197]

More specific connections between Japan's policies and the upsurge of the '1946 outlook' are inevitably harder to trace. In view of all the suffering inflicted by the New Order few citizens were likely to allow that the Japanese had done anything positive which might have given rise to their demands for reform. One or two of the post-war suggestions were none the less ascribed explicitly to a Japanese precedent. The correspondent who wrote to the *South China Morning Post* advocating a system of District Councils to increase opportunities for 'lesser fry' to take part in government declared frankly that 'the Japanese introduced it here and it might be revived for the new Hong Kong'. The same writer went on to allude to the grass-roots control measures employed by the wartime regime as a possible basis for his proposed Poor Law arrangements: 'the Japanese', he pointed out, 'made use of the District Bureaux to compile a register of residents, and a new Hong Kong should have little difficulty in compiling a better one'.[198] In the last days of August 1945 a report was drawn up by a certain S. Y. Lin, a one-time Superintendent of Fisheries Research, for the benefit of his pre-war chief, Dr Herklots, who was on the point of launching his new Fisheries Organization. Lin gave a surprisingly positive account of the 'considerable success' achieved by the fish-handling system introduced under Japanese rule, and advised that the wholesale fish market to be founded by Herklots should be 'similar in the main to that which the Japanese had adopted, with some modification'. For example the district syndicates of the Japanese period could be 'changed easily into a Fishermen's Cooperative Society'.[199]

The same picture emerges from the British response to the calls for reform. In abolishing petty apartheid in housing and clubs, in holding better government and private jobs out to Asians, in suppressing the remains of the opium business, the restored British rulers of Hong Kong were belatedly quelling evils to which the Japanese had drawn awkward attention in their anti-colonial propaganda. In the first two of these areas it may even be argued that the British were merely ratifying advances which the Japanese had already made during the show of reform which marked the early weeks of their rule. Never mind that the Japanese then went on to make a mockery of their own professed enlightenment: once they had introduced the first, outward changes it was impossible for the British not to follow up. The Japanese had also helped to prompt the post-war British spring-cleaning in other broad ways. The conquest of December 1941 had given the old colonial rulers a sort of enforced sabbatical in which to sit back and take stock of their pre-war deficiencies. And the sharp decline in their power and prestige following their defeat had compelled them to recognize a new need to accommodate the expectations of the Americans and of both the mainland and local Chinese.

Few of the British at the same time were likely to acknowledge that any specific reform they brought in had been inspired in any way by Japan. Possible legacies of Japanese wartime practice may be suspected, for instance, in the holding by the restored British rulers of regular press conferences to keep the public abreast of their latest decisions, and in the post-war promotion of intensive crop-raising in the New Territories; but such links can at best be conjectural. Here too however it is possible to identify a limited number of more certain debts. Dr Herklots recorded that his eventual scheme for cooperative fish marketing had 'incorporated a number of Mr Lin's suggestions';[200] and the similar system which was introduced for marketing vegetables has also been traced, in part at least, to a Japanese source.[201] The rural representative committees to which Young and his officials began to organize elections in 1946 were essentially those which the Japanese had set up during the occupation as a more efficient substitute for the loose pre-war British system of rule through the village headmen. Japanese-sponsored committees had been found intact and still functioning in Saikung and other districts at the time of the British return; and the post-war period is said to have seen in the countryside a general spread of representative bodies 'owing something to Japanese-inspired wartime creations'.[202]

The Japanese may, then, fairly be said to have acted as catalysts for the post-war burst of reform – whether through the spotlight they threw on past British inadequacies, through the handful of constructive measures they brought in themselves or through the reaction provoked by their monstrous excesses. By storming in with their bogus New Order they had in the end cleared the way for the more genuine new order of Harcourt, MacDougall and Young. Hong Kong had escaped from their grip to embark, in 1945–7, on the most striking social and political advance in its history. Whether that advance would be durable, and whether the Japanese interlude would turn out to have any more profound repercussions, were questions to be answered by later decades.

Epilogue

The past exorcised

Between March 1946 and March 1948 the last episode took place in the lurid drama of the occupation. In the course of those two years the two military courts which had been set up in Hong Kong to try war crimes suspects sat in judgement on a total of forty-eight cases involving 129 Japanese. The trials were character-ized by the observance of a rather conspicuous British fairness. All of the cases were meticulously investigated. All the accused were represented, often with some spirit, by British army officers assigned for the purpose; and after the first three months, from July 1946, they were also permitted the services of a team of Japanese lawyers. Twenty-one of the accused were sent to the gallows, and twenty-eight received prison sentences of ten years and upwards: for the most part, however, the sentences were restrained to the point of leniency. Fifty-seven defendants were given prison sentences of less than ten years, fourteen were acquitted, and the charges against the remainder were dropped.

At the same time the trials reflected the marked changes that had taken place in the relations between the British and their Asian neighbours, both outside and inside Hong Kong. Missing rather conspicuously from the proceedings were the three most senior figures of the occupation regime – Sakai, who had led the invasion of December 1941 and subsequently served as head of the Gunseicho, and the two wartime Governors, Isogai and Tanaka. Sakai and Tanaka had both been captured by Nationalist forces on the mainland, and Isogai had been arrested in Tokyo by the Americans and sent on to China by them; and all three were accordingly put on trial by the Nationalists as part of their contribution to the Allied war crimes inquiry. Sakai was found guilty and shot in Nanking in September 1946. Tanaka faced a firing squad in Canton in March 1947 – the first and only Governor of Hong Kong to be executed. (We are told that he grunted defiantly on the eve of his execution, 'Let's see who's calling the shots in East Asia in ten years' time!')[1] Old Isogai by contrast got off unexpectedly lightly. Following a brief hearing in Nanking in July 1947 he was given a life sentence, largely for his part in the compulsory evacuation scheme. The sentence was subsequently twice commuted, and he ended up serving no more than five years in gaol.

The British had initially hoped to have a say in at least one or two of these mainland trials. But the Nationalists had no wish to let Britain take part. From their point of view any crimes these men had committed in the colony fell properly within China's jurisdiction. In addition they wanted to call the three men to account for their record outside Hong Kong, during the years they had spent as commanders of troops on the occupied mainland. In keeping with their new post-war attitude of assertiveness the Nationalists consequently rebuffed each effort Whitehall made to secure permission for a British prose- cutor to sit on the mainland courts. And the British, after a certain amount of inter-departmental discussion, took it all lying down. The sentence passed on Sakai was picked up from the Nanking authorities and meekly put on display in the British Library in London. When Isogai's turn came the sole British rep- resentative to make an appearance was an obscure Captain F. V. Collison, who was dispatched to Nanking in the capacity of an observer. He arrived too late to attend the half-day hearing, but was in time to witness the passing of the sentence a week later.[2]

There were in fact a number of cogent reasons for the British to desist from taking a hand in the trials of these senior Japanese. Generally speaking they had no wish, in the new post-war climate, to exacerbate relations with the Nationalist government by pressing their claims. And in the case of Isogai they had one very specific reason for keeping quiet. The British were, as it happened, in possession of a certain amount of information implicating the old Governor in the opium racket which the Japanese had operated in wartime Hong Kong. But the same information also implicated the old mainland warlord Xu Chongzhi, who had acted as Isogai's partner in the racket through his role as head of the Opium Sale Syndicate. And Xu, as we have seen, had at one time over twenty years previously been Chiang Kai-shek's commanding officer. The War Crimes Investigation Unit in Hong Kong consequently 'hesi- tated to name' either Xu or the Syndicate for fear of the massive offence which an exposure of Xu would cause to the Generalissimo; and in March 1947 the Unit received firm orders from the War Office that 'on no account' should any details about Xu be divulged or any further inquiries be made.[3] It followed that a discreet silence was advisable in the case of Isogai too. (This British silence undoubtedly helped to lighten the sentence passed on the old Governor. He was actually given some credit by the Chinese court for his much-vaunted pro- gramme to rid the colony of its opium traffic.)

More compelling than either of these arguments was the British desire to guard the backs of the Hong Kong gentry. If Britain clamoured loudly enough for a voice in the mainland trials, Whitehall reasoned, it might well turn out that the Nationalists would give way in the end. But their price would undoubtedly be a mainland presence on the war crimes courts in Hong Kong – which they would almost certainly use to bring up the record of the local Chinese leaders. To avoid any possible unpleasantness it seemed best to back down.[4]

In the absence of the top Japanese commanders pride of place in the dock was given to Colonel Noma and Lieutenant-Colonel Kanazawa, the two successive chiefs of the Hong Kong Kempeitai. In the case of these two men the British courts showed themselves indisposed to adhere to their overall attitude of restraint. Colonel Noma endeavoured to present himself as a well-meaning, misunderstood individual deeply impressed by a 'very specific experience with mercy' he had undergone during a visit to London in 1923, when he had watched a small girl feeding the sparrows in Hyde Park.[5] His defence cut no ice, and he was sentenced to hang. Kanazawa attempted to lay all the blame for the Kempeitai's savageries at Noma's door, drawing attention to the steps he took to clean up the organization and to institute a policy of 'kindness' and 'brightness'.[6] He too was marched off to the gallows. Hanged along with their chiefs were nineteen other high-ranking Kempeitai officers. Two of the other most prominent Japanese defendants, by contrast, benefited from the generally mild approach of the British military judges. Major-General Tanaka Ryozaburo, whose assault column had been responsible for almost all of the massacres of Allied troops carried out during the 23rd Army's conquest of Hong Kong Island, wound up with nothing more than a twenty-year prison term. Colonel Tokunaga, the portly commandant of the internment camps, was initially given a death sentence; but his sentence was soon commuted, at first to life imprisonment, and subsequently to twenty years.

The difference in these sentences can be explained primarily by the new British concern to satisfy the expectations of the Hong Kong public. Tanaka Ryozaburo and Tokunaga could be shown a degree of magnanimity because their crimes had been committed for the most part against Allied soldiers and POWs. Noma, Kanazawa and their subordinates, on the other hand, had preyed widely on the local Asian townsfolk. Much of the testimony against them was provided by a series of Chinese, Eurasians and Indians who had suffered in their cells – and it was this testimony which weighed with the judges. Kanazawa, for instance, who is said to have been flabbergasted to be brought to trial,[7] and who had been responsible for no reported atrocities against British victims, might have had some grounds for expecting a commutation; and such a course was initially recommended by the Deputy Judge Advocate General. But the evidence of torture brought by his Asian captives, and in particular by the Indian spy ring arrested in May 1945, seems in the end to have tipped the balance against him. Following their convictions the Kempeitai chiefs and underlings were briefly paraded around the streets for the gratification of the Chinese masses.[8] The British had not caught as many of the Kempeitai killers as the public had hoped for. But with regard to the killers they had caught they meant to make sure that justice would, very literally, be seen to be done.

Thanks to these efforts the whole saga was finally and successfully buried. By the end of March 1948, when the last trials closed, all of the war crimes suspects had either been executed, or dispatched to serve out their terms in the Sagamo war crimes prison in Tokyo, or released to return to their country; and the British had seen off the last representatives of Japanese rule in Hong Kong.

Or almost the last. Afraid of retribution, and ashamed to go home, a small number of Japanese had slipped through the original British dragnet. Some of them obtained shelter through bribery or gangland connections, while others were able to secure the protection of Chinese mistresses they had picked up during their days in power. To conceal themselves further they assumed Chinese names, started speaking Chinese, even married their Chinese women.[9] But by those very steps they effaced every hint of their origins – in some cases for decades. An elderly street sleeper known as Ho Chun-wing whose skeleton was found lying under a Kowloon flyover in 1995 was said before his death to have confided to his fellow derelicts that he was a Japanese who had decided to stay on in the colony at the end of the war.[10] The war also left behind it a glut of half-Japanese children. Many of them had been born in September–October 1942, products of the orgy of rape which had been perpetrated by the Imperial forces during the sack of Hong Kong nine months earlier. But they too are said to have been quietly absorbed into the general population.[11]

In the meantime the British continued to douse the last smouldering embers of the collaboration issue. In May 1949 Sir Robert Kotewall died, from his heart trouble and (according to one Chinese version) from grief.[12] His sidelining had undoubtedly inflicted a deep wound on him and his family. At least two of his children were deterred by his fate from pursuing a public career, and one of his daughters maintains to this day that her father's treatment was 'the most unfair thing the British have ever done'.[13] Yet the British did their best to keep up appearances. Kotewall's funeral was attended by the Governor's Aide-de-Camp and the Acting Secretary for Chinese Affairs (a lower-key send-off than he might once have expected, but better than nothing), and an 'appreciation' of him was published in the *South China Morning Post*.[14] In later years British officials went to some lengths to head off any prurient depiction of his wartime activity, and MacDougall recalled kindly that he 'was a poor man . . . the only one of the bunch who was a poor man'.[15] In Hong Kong today his memory is preserved by Kotewall Road in the Mid-Levels, named after him in his pre-war days of glory; and a bronze bust of him adorns the Sir Robert Kotewall Room in the Hong Kong Public Library, to which he donated his large collection of books.

Sir Shouson Chow did a great deal better. By the 1950s he was fully restored, to all outward appearances, to his pre-war status as one of the 'grand old men' of the Chinese community.[16] At the annual banquets which were held in Government House for the local Justices of the Peace he was seated at the Governor's side; and when he died in 1959, at the prodigious age of ninety-eight, his family received a message of sympathy from the Duke of Edinburgh. One post-war Governor's memoir recalled him as having been 'jovial, human and everybody's friend'.[17] His name too lives on, in Shouson Hill on Hong Kong Island and in the Shouson Theatre of the Hong Kong Arts Centre.

The charges of fence-sitting which had been levelled at Sir Robert Ho Tung in the early months of the occupation had long since been swept into the obscurity of the government files. By the 1950s the veteran plutocrat had once again been ensconced, like Sir Shouson, in the status of a 'grand old man'. The last years of his life were passed in a glow of directorships. In 1955 his knighthood was upgraded to a KBE, and when he died in the following year the Hongkong and Shanghai Bank (at his special request) flew its flag at half-mast.[18]

Kwok Chan, the one leader to have had the distinction of serving on both the wartime Chinese Councils, was elected in 1951 to the chairmanship of the Rotary Club. By 1957 he was also an OBE and the Honorary Vice President of the Hong Kong University Economics Society.

Various lesser figures who had done a spot of business with the Japanese wartime rulers carried blithely on with their lives. One example was Xu Chongzhi. After a brief disappearance in Macao the old warlord seems to have slipped back to the colony, where he was sighted in the spring of 1950 carousing at a night-club in West Point:

> Amongst the newcomers was a general to whom Chiang Kai-shek had once been Chief of Staff. He had two sing-song girls with him and introduced a note of boisterous hilarity into the proceedings . . . The general was restless and leaped about between his two girls on the sofa and the card players, giving the former slaps and tickles and the latter a great deal of noisy advice.[19]

As for the 'good' gentry leaders who had been picked out and approved by the post-war authorities, they made their way ever further into the sunlit uplands. Nothing perhaps illustrates the success of post-war British policy in Hong Kong more dramatically than the transmogrification of M. K. Lo. As can be seen from the speeches he made welcoming Governor Young, Lo had undergone a complete change, from pre-war gadfly to pillar of the post-war colonial establishment. In 1947 we find him presenting 'a very fine challenge cup' to the Police Sports Association 'to stimulate inter-divisional football'.[20] In the 1950s he became a permanent fixture on the Executive Council, where he was admired by the Governor for his 'first class brain' and 'great moral courage', and a member of dozens of public commissions.[21] In 1959 he died suddenly while getting ready to attend an official reception at Government House in honour of the Duke of Edinburgh.

The British had once again made an effective job of papering over the past. By the summer of 1947, it appears, the furore surrounding the wartime role of the gentry was largely forgotten.[22] Any lingering odium was attached to the two Laval figures, Chan Lim-pak and Lau Tit-shing – both of whom, of course, were conveniently dead. And the record of the others was screened by a pious mythology. By 1952 Harold Ingrams, a British writer who published an account of Hong Kong under the auspices of the Colonial Office, felt able to state that the loyalty to the Allied cause of those Chinese who remained in the colony during the Japanese occupation was 'never in doubt'.[23]

'Hong Kong's second century': the resurgence of British morale

By the late 1940s the British position in Hong Kong was appreciably stronger. This was due primarily to a steady decline in the external threat. From 1946 onwards the Nationalists on the mainland were locked in the final, all-out struggle for control with their Communist rivals. By 1947 they were losing ground, and by the end of 1948, as the crack troops they had shipped through the British colony three years earlier lost battle after battle in the crucial theatre of Manchuria, they were spectacularly on the way out.

Under these circumstances Chiang Kai-shek and his followers had less and less inclination to press ahead with their goal of regaining Hong Kong. As early as March 1946, when the conflict in Manchuria began to warm up, the Foreign Ministry in Nanking pointed out in a memorandum that now was not the time to enter into negotiations about the New Territories. At present, they noted, the 'problems in the North-East' were 'extremely serious'. Better to put off the opening of any talks until the 'international situation was more favourable' to the Nationalist cause[24] – or in other words, till the Communists had been vanquished and the Nanking government could be expected to carry more international weight. In June Chiang probed Britain's intentions regarding the colony, both at a meeting he held himself with the departing British ambassador, Sir Horace Seymour, and through a meeting conducted at the Foreign Office in London by his own departing ambassador, Wellington Koo. He emerged with a firm sense that Britain was not disposed to give ground at this juncture, and from then on was ever more clearly on the retreat. In the course of 1947 two of the Generalissimo's topmost associates publicly announced the regime's decision to defer the addressing of the Hong Kong question.[25]

Pressure was still intermittently brought to bear on the British by hardline elements in the Nationalist Party, and in particular by the Nationalists in Canton. In November 1946, for instance, a whole array of organizations in Canton, including the Canton Labour Union, the Engineers' Guild and the Chamber of Commerce, called for a massive campaign to strangle the colony through (among other methods) a general strike of Hong Kong Chinese workers and a boycott of Hong Kong trade. It was to be the great confrontation of the mid-1920s all over again. In April 1947 a British training aircraft which had strayed across the border into Guangdong province got riddled with machine-gun bullets for 'not heeding Chinese territorial sovereignty'.[26] And in January 1948, trouble flared up once more over the ever-sensitive issue of the enclave claimed by China within the New Territories – the Walled City of Kowloon. The Hong Kong government had embarked on a drive to clear the enclave of several thousands of squatters who had moved back there since the end of the war. In the course of the clearances the police had opened fire on an angry crowd, killing one of the squatters and wounding a number of others. The response in Canton was dramatic. On 16 January over 40,000 outraged Nationalist supporters assembled in a protest rally in front of the Sun Yat-sen Memorial Hall: a portion of them then advanced to the British consulate on Shamian Island and burned it to the ground. The irredentism of the hardline Nationalists continued to receive a certain amount of support from United States circles in China. In March 1948, two months after the Walled City episode, the United States minister in Nanking, Lewis Clark, remarked in the course of a chat with the Canadian ambassador that he viewed the continuing British presence in Hong Kong as a 'perpetual provocation' to the Chinese. He thought that the Nationalists should adopt a policy of economic pressure to drive Britain out – for example by dredging the Pearl River, which would allow them to ship goods directly to Canton from overseas and deprive Hong Kong of the bulk of its freight business.[27]

Mainstream feeling within the regime was, however, against any kind of aggression. In October 1947 Chiang Kai-shek's brother-in-law and factotum, T. V. Soong, was appointed Governor of Guangdong province, a move that sidelined the Generalissimo's over-mighty subject, Zhang Fakui. Soong brought with him a markedly softer approach to the issue of Hong Kong's future. 'In 25 years' time', he observed on a trip to the colony, 'I, or rather my successor, will ask for Hong Kong back, and we shall expect to get it.'[28] The objective was unchanged, but the timescale was suddenly a great deal longer. When the colony's police opened fire on the squatters in the Walled City the following January, Soong advised Chiang that he saw no advantage in breaking off relations with Hong Kong. He gave his blessing to the staging of a 'planned and regular' protest demonstration in the Canton streets, but next day, when the hardliners in the crowd ran amok, blamed the excesses on 'bandits' and ordered his military police to move in and suppress them.[29] A mild note was dispatched from Nanking to the British government voicing regret at the burning of the consulate and hoping that a fair solution might be worked out to the Walled City problem once the arsonists had been brought to book; and strict orders were issued to all ministries and to every branch of the media that the Hong Kong police attack on the squatters should be played down. In Hong Kong Special Commissioner Kwok sent a note to Colonial Secretary MacDougall declaring affectionately, 'Without you here, Mac – you with your friendly understanding, your mature judgement, your spirit of cooperation and your foresight into the future of Sino-British amity – I shudder to think how we could have passed those months since 1945.'[30] The Nationalist chiefs also took the opportunity to spell out their new line unequivocally to their American backers. In a private conversation with the United States ambassador, Foreign Minister Wang Shijie discussed the Hong Kong question in terms very different to those he had used when he urged Chiang to assert China's rights only two years before. He felt deeply, he said, that friendship between China and Britain was 'essential to the broader world picture'.[31] He was not, of course, able to prevent a popular clamour from breaking out for Hong Kong's retrocession; but he was determined to ensure, so far as he could, that it didn't unsettle the overall tenor of Sino-British ties.

The ascendant Chinese Communist Party was, for its part, in no hurry to get Hong Kong back. At the end of 1946 Chairman Mao Zedong was airily dismissive when the issue was raised with him by a British journalist during an interview at his north-western base in Yan'an. Mao's timetable for retrieving the colony seems if anything to have been more leisurely than the one suggested by T. V. Soong a year later:

> Perhaps 10, 20 or 30 years hence we may ask for a discussion regarding its return; but my attitude is that so long as your officials do not maltreat Chinese subjects in Hong Kong, and so long as Chinese are not treated as inferior to others in the matter of taxation and a voice in the Government, I am not interested in Hong Kong, and will certainly not allow it to be a bone of contention between your country and mine.[32]

The same placid attitude was adopted by the Communist organizations in Hong Kong itself. From 1946 onwards the Communists, like the Nationalists, were rebuilding the presence they had maintained in the colony on the eve of the Japanese invasion. A South China Bureau of the Party was set up once again under the leadership of Liao Chengzhi. The Shanghai intellectual Qiao Guanhua reappeared as director of the Hong Kong branch of the Party's newly created propaganda organ, the New China News Agency, and the journalist

Xia Yan joined in with a group of other left-wing writers from the mainland to revive the *Hua Shang Bao* (Chinese Commercial Daily), the innocently entitled paper which they had launched five years earlier as a mouthpiece for the Party's determination to stand up to the Japanese. But the Communists showed no desire to make trouble. Most of the rank and file of both the South China Bureau and the Hong Kong branch of the New China News Agency were veterans of the East River Column; and the first pronouncements they issued through their newspapers were filled with nostalgic allusions to the Column's wartime partnership with the British forces. In an editorial welcoming the return of Governor Young the *Hua Shang Bao* recalled the weeks of the Japanese invasion when the Governor had 'led the Hong Kong resistance'. Subsequently Young had suffered 'hardship and humiliation' along with the rest of Hong Kong's citizens; and the paper was sure that this shared experience would have 'redoubled his feeling of closeness to them'. All in all, the editors concluded, the British and Chinese in Hong Kong had a wide range of common interests, and they should pull together today with the same resolution they had shown when the 23rd Army marched in.[33] Proceeding from this basis the Communist journals went on to give the restored British rulers a strikingly easy ride over policy issues. The *Hua Shang Bao* embraced the Young Plan with much more enthusiasm than the Nationalist press. Over the Pingshan airport dispute it advised that Britain and China should seek a 'realistic solution' based on 'mutual understanding'; and when the police shot the Walled City squatters in January 1948 it confined itself to observing that the Hong Kong authorities had made a mistake in using force.[34]

The main reasons for this Communist affability were not, of course, sentimental. Mao and his colleagues had their hands full, every bit as much as their Nationalist opponents, with the civil war on the mainland. They had no wish to add the British gratuitously to the ranks of their enemies; and they had much to gain from preserving a friendly relationship with British Hong Kong. In keeping with its long tradition of sheltering dissidents at odds with the mainland regime of the day, Hong Kong offered the Communists and their left-wing allies refuge from the attentions of Chiang Kai-shek's armies and police. It could serve as a base for supporting the Party's political effort throughout southern China, and at the same time for winning adherents among the Chinese communities in South-east Asia and sympathizers in the Western world. But whatever the motives of the Communists the effect was that the British in Hong Kong were spared the immediate substitution of one outside threat for another.

The internal challenge was also on the decline. From late 1946, as the civil war on the mainland intensified, a great wave of refugees started to pour in seeking shelter from both the chaos of the fighting and the corruption and petty restrictions that had become the chief features of the declining

Nationalist regime. These refugees had no interest in challenging the political order which greeted them in their chosen home. Their very reason for coming to this British outpost was that it appeared to offer stability and the rule of law. Partly because of their advent, and partly because of the steady economic revival, the mood in Hong Kong at every social level became more and more one of acquiescence in the colonial come-back. Support for the Nationalists was diminishing fast. The appeal to the colony's workers to stage a general strike which was issued from Canton in November 1946 evoked nothing more than a scattering of small-scale demonstrations, and the burning of the British consulate a year later had no discernible echo in Hong Kong at all. Nor was there any great rallying to the Communist Party. Communist publications lamented the way local students were succumbing to 'Hong Kong Head' – a syndrome made up of arrogance, materialism and a tendency to forget their Chinese identity.[35] Contemplating the colony in the aftermath of the Walled City drama the Canadian ambassador in Nanking had no doubt that the rich Chinese there were pinning their hopes on a continuation of the British status quo. In his judgement they looked on Hong Kong as a 'nest' for themselves and their wealth.[36] The ambassador was not so sure about the mass of the public; but once again there are clues to be found in the industrial data. In 1947 the colony's workers came out twenty-three times, but none of the strikes appeared to have any political motive. In 1948 the number of strikes fell to five.

In the light of these changes the British began to display a new confidence and determination to stand their ground. In 1947 a joint paper on Hong Kong which had been concocted by the Foreign Office and Colonial Office for the Cabinet in London was withdrawn unsubmitted. The intention had been to set out the range of possible stances which might be adopted in discussing the colony's future with the Nationalist regime. Given the deepening civil war on the mainland, however, Foreign Secretary Bevin concluded that Britain could get away with not raising the issue at all. In Hong Kong the revival of British morale was equally striking. 'I knew', recollected MacDougall, 'that the Nationalists were never going to make an assault which would make them confront a major nation with their mortal enemy, the Communists, knocking at the gates of Peking. I did not think it was at all likely.'[37] The expatriate mood was reflected in an article which was published in July 1947 in a new journal, the *Far Eastern Economic Review*. The writer looked forward to the prospect of 'Hong Kong's second century as a British colony'.[38]

No need was now felt to placate Nanking with the frantic concessions which had been made in the first few months of the British return. Already by the autumn of 1946 the RAF were quietly getting back to work on the building of Pingshan airport, in blithe disregard of a flurry of Nationalist protests.[39] When the Walled City squatters resisted eviction on the grounds that they owed allegiance solely to the mainland, the response of the British was to assert their authority. 'No government can lose the confidence of its people and remain in power.'[40] Following the destruction of the British consulate in Canton secret orders were issued for the surveillance of Nationalist organizations and personnel in the colony and for the deportation of any troublemakers; and a Nationalist proposal of a compromise settlement under which Britain might be permitted to retain a *de facto* jurisdiction within the Walled City if Chinese sovereignty were recognized in form was politely refused.

The British still found it judicious to keep up a show of goodwill to Nanking. Some attention was still being paid to Chiang Kai-shek's sensitivities, as we have seen in connection with the war crimes trials. And the occasional gesture went on being made. In January 1948, the same month as the Walled City crisis, the Hong Kong government finally put its signature to a customs agreement which had been requested by the Nationalists fourteen months earlier to cut down smuggling from Hong Kong to the mainland. Under the terms of the deal vessels of the Chinese Maritime Customs would be allowed to patrol within Hong Kong's territorial waters, and Nationalist officials would be given permission to set up customs houses at two points inside Victoria harbour and at the Kowloon end of the Kowloon–Canton railway. The agreement represented in principle, as the colonial rulers acknowledged in their Annual Report for 1948, 'a considerable derogation of sovereignty on the part of Hong Kong'.[41] In practice, however, it amounted to very much less than appeared at first glance. No inspection or customs collection by Chinese officials could take place inside the harbour without the consent of the shipowner; and any suspected smugglers had to be handed over to the Hong Kong police to be dealt with by British law. The fact was that by this stage the strength of the Nationalists had been so eroded that a token surrender of this kind could be made without jeopardizing Britain's grip on the colony in any concrete way.

Little threat in the meantime was perceived from the Communists. British officials in Whitehall foresaw an eventual Communist victory in the civil war, but were by no means all agreed that this would necessarily have dire implications for Hong Kong. The colonial government were even less disposed to anxiety. They were content to tolerate a profusion of Communist representative bodies ('representing was one thing and performing was another, we thought'),[42] and are even said to have offered the New China News Agency a choice of premises for its Hong Kong branch. The low profile adopted by the local Communist entities was registered with approval, and MacDougall observed that the New China News Agency differed from all the other Chinese media in Hong Kong in adopting 'a dispassionate, and in fact often friendly attitude to the Colonial Administration'.[43] To a certain extent British attitudes were still bathed in the afterglow of the joint resistance to Japan. In May 1946 arrangements had been made for Huang Zuomei, the interpreter and director of international relations for the East River Column, to take part in the parade held in London in honour of the Allied victory and to receive an MBE from King George VI. As the civil war unfolded on the mainland, memories of the help given to escaping British POWs by the East River guerrillas are said to have stimulated a fair amount of sympathy among the Hong Kong expatriates for the Communist side. The British radical set had been quick to renew their pre-war friendships with the contingent of left-wing mainland intellectuals. Selwyn-Clarke's wife, 'Red Hilda', who had now returned to London, sent cuttings from the British press to Margaret Watson the almoner for forwarding to Qiao Guanhua and his wife, Gong Peng.[44] Bishop Hall viewed the triumph of Communism on the mainland as inevitable and for the most part desirable. Like the Roman Empire, he pointed out to his congregation, the Communist Empire was a mixture of good and evil, of harshness and security. And just as the Roman Empire had provided the ordered environment in which the Gospel had been able to spread through the ancient Western world, so the Communist Empire would in the fullness of time be the seed-bed for the conversion of China's people to Christ.[45]

Anxieties finally started stirring in late 1948, as Mao's victorious armies prepared to cross the Yangtze river into southern China. The British were now confronted by a potential adversary of awesome strength, far more able than Chiang Kai-shek's enfeebled and disunited forces to press China's claim to the colony. The horrid possibility started to suggest itself that the Communists might march on Hong Kong; and for a while painful memories seemed to revive of the collapse of local support for the British that had taken place when the 23rd Army attacked eight years earlier. Absolute trust, it was felt, could not be placed in the rank and file of the now mainly Chinese police force, and only a third of them, for that reason, were armed. In August 1949 the government briefly mooted the idea of bulldozing the Walled City in order to flush out subversives who might sabotage the defence of the colony in the event of a Communist onslaught.[46] After the new People's Republic was proclaimed in Peking in October the staff of the Hong Kong and Shanghai Bank were gripped by a 'general nervousness', and two years later, when Mao's troops confronted the West in Korea, plans were laid for the transfer, for the second time in a decade, of the Bank's head office to London. To be caught napping once by an invasion might be regarded as a misfortune; to be caught twice looked like carelessness.

But if the Nationalists would but couldn't, the Communists could but wouldn't. As their forces advanced through south China in 1949 they felt, it seems, some anxiety that a lunge for Hong Kong might provoke, in the new Cold War context, a massive intervention by the United States. Later on, as the Cold War progressed, and the fighting broke out in Korea, and their new regime in Peking was consigned to political quarantine by the United States and subjected to trade embargoes by both the United States and the United

Nations, it became clear that this colonial fossil could serve Communist interests in a number of ways. It could provide the regime with a listening post
at which to pick up Western thinking, and a commercial 'ventilation shaft'
through which to smuggle in badly needed strategic materials and to draw in
remittances from sympathetic Overseas Chinese.[47] And it might incidentally
enable Peking to drive a wedge between the British and the Americans. So the
Communists continued to stay their hand. In October 1949 the People's
Liberation Army, driving south through Guangdong province, were ordered
to stop short at the Shenzhen River on the colony's border. When a contingent
of Hong Kong Chinese tramway workers who had staged a strike appeared in
newly liberated Canton two months later they were given a heroes' welcome,
regaled with speeches denouncing the colonial government – and then, in
effect, told to make themselves scarce. The policy of restraint was spelled out
some years afterwards by the Communist premier, Zhou Enlai, who indicated
informally that the new China could live with a British presence in Hong Kong,
provided only that the colony stayed a colony and no democratic experiment
was permitted that might give the local Nationalists a chance to gain power.[48]
Inside Hong Kong itself the Communist supporters remained unobtrusive.
One spring evening in 1950 Harold Ingrams, the writer engaged by the Colonial Office to pen an upbeat account of Hong Kong's post-war resurrection,
found himself on the Star Ferry next to a pleasant young man who turned out
to be the foreign editor of one of the Communist papers. On inquiring which
part of England Ingrams came from and being told Shropshire, the journalist
disclosed that he had written his doctoral thesis on A. E. Housman – and
'we quoted *The Shropshire Lad* at each other as we crossed the harbour in the
moonlight'.[49]

Far from being undermined by the massive change to the north the internal British position in the colony had in fact been bolstered still further. As the
new Communist order swept over the mainland Hong Kong was submerged
in a second great influx of refugees. By 1950 they had brought the population
to 2.5 m, as against 600,000 at the end of the war. This second wave of immigrants were, if anything, even less disposed than the first wave to fret about
the anti-colonial grievances of earlier times. They had come to Hong Kong to
get away from the Communists, and their object was to hang on for dear life.
In November 1949 Peking sealed the border, a step which debarred them from
returning even if they had wished. Some of them moved onwards to other
parts of the world, but a great many chose to remain and put down roots
in their colonial haven; and the colony was consequently endowed, for the
first time in its history, with a permanent rather than a floating Chinese
population.

The result of all this was that the flurry of panic which seized the expatriates briefly at the end of the 1940s proved to be little more than a blip in the

steady upward movement of British morale. To all outward appearances British confidence continued to revive further with each passing year. In the absence of any clear sign of Communist determination to take the colony back the authorities felt able to strike a posture of doggedness. In December 1948, and again in August 1949, the Labour government formally asserted their intention of hanging on to Hong Kong. The garrison was built up from 6,000 to some 30,000 – a larger force than the colony had possessed when the Japanese struck, and much more strongly equipped, with tanks, land-based fighter aircraft and a powerful naval unit including an aircraft carrier. 'Will the British remain?', Harold Ingrams was asked on his arrival in the colony early in 1950. 'The answer', he snorted, 'seemed obvious and was reinforced by the very evident presence of large numbers of British troops in the New Territories'.[50] Various measures were adopted to avoid aggravating the mainland unnecessarily. In January 1950, in marked contrast to their American allies, the Labour government recognized the new regime in Peking; and in August 1951 the controversial Pingshan airport project was finally scrapped. But the Hong Kong authorities were clear at the same time that they 'did not want to appease or appear to do so, or give in to unreasonable demands'.[51]

In October 1951 the recapture of power by Churchill and the Conservative Party killed off any lingering appetite for decolonization; and from this point onwards the overall British posture grew still more robust. Several times in the following years the Hong Kong authorities felt able to rebuff the Communists as firmly as they had done the Nationalists, if not slightly more so. In 1955, for example, they turned down a proposal which Zhou Enlai had floated for a new Chinese Special Commissioner to be stationed in the colony on the model of T. W. Kwok. Their refusal was justified by the contention that there was 'no room in Hong Kong for two Governors'.[52] In 1963 they would brush off a renewed mainland effort to claim jurisdiction within the Walled City.

And, exactly as had happened in the 1930s after the shock of the 1920s crises began to wear off, the revival of British confidence was accompanied by a slackening in the pace of reform. An early portent of backsliding came in May 1947 with the retirement of Governor Young. Young had not been intended to remain in his old post for more than a year. It was felt that after his ordeal in the Japanese camps he was too ill and too tired to continue much longer. But the main reason for bringing him back was that Whitehall wanted new blood – a real post-war Governor untouched, as Young inescapably if unjustly was in the minds of the Hong Kong public, by the stigma of the surrender in 1941. The choice fell on Sir Alexander Grantham, a younger man who had spent his early career in the Hong Kong Cadet Service and was reckoned to have 'an appreciation of the fundamental principles on which the future of the Colony depends'.[53] And the newcomer, ironically, turned the clock back. Honest, hardworking, efficient, fond of the old-time colonial regalia and panoply,

Grantham soon made apparent his preference for a slower and more cautious approach. And he went on to pursue it, up to and through and beyond the Communist take-over on the mainland, for the whole of the next ten years.

Even before Grantham came a new tide had begun to wash out of the colony the strange cluster of British liberal and radical figures who had been thrown up by the war. In March 1947 Selwyn-Clarke was recalled to take up a new posting as Governor of the Seychelles. On the surface this was a dramatic promotion – an unparalleled honour for a mere physician, and a tribute to the dashing campaign of surreptitious relief work which the Director of Medical Services had masterminded in wartime Hong Kong. The reality, though, was that some of his colleagues wished to see the back of a social crusader who had ruffled too many feathers.[54] With the coming of Grantham the liberals who remained were effectively doomed. In March 1949 MacDougall, the pivotal figure of the reform drive, resigned suddenly from his post as Colonial Secretary and departed for home. The immediate cause of his resignation is said to have been an indiscretion of a personal nature; but there are also signs that Grantham and others who thought like him had jumped at the opportunity which the episode offered to edge the reformer out. 'By God, it's a warning', a sympathizer of MacDougall's wrote wrathfully to him, 'do anything to upset certain types around this place, then look out for yourself – for it seems they will never rest until they get your blood.'[55] Bishop Hall proved a little more difficult to dislodge. For some years the Pink Bishop, as the mainstream now called him, sent Grantham into paroxysms of impotent fury as he denounced the government's selfishness from the pulpit of St John's Cathedral. He threw his energies into filling the all too obvious gaps in the official welfare efforts, setting up Workers' Schools for the education of the poorest classes and co-founding a Hong Kong Housing Society which built low-cost flats for some 100,000 mainland refugees. In 1956 he went up to Peking, had dinner with Zhou Enlai, and came back likening the Long March to the story of Moses and Joshua and informing his flock that China now had, for the first time in centuries, a government of which its people were proud. As the 1950s wore on, however, even the Pink Bishop lost something of his old fire, slipping gradually into a 'less aggressive, less prophetic social commentary'.[56]

Right through the upper layers of the society the lead had passed to conservative forces. The expatriate taipans were once again potent. Ransomed, healed, restored, forgiven under their new leadership, the gentry carried more weight than they had in the pre-war period; but the gentry had never been ardent for far-reaching change, and they had no intention of backing it now. Time and again they came down against new-fangled notions that threatened to constrain their ability to build up their fortunes or to rupture the basic social calm. In 1947, for instance, Dr Sik-nin Chau inveighed against the appalling suggestion of introducing an income tax; and the gentry joined with the taipans to block a proposal that the public utilities should be placed under some form of government ownership. In 1948 M. K. Lo, that much mellowed *enfant terrible*, dissented from the report of a Committee on Chinese Law and Customs which had attempted to outlaw the taking of concubines.[57] Another Governor might have used his position to face down the conservative caucus. But as MacDougall observed, 'Grantham always listened to power . . . He didn't take a single step without consulting everybody . . . The stronger side always won.'[58]

In the new age of Grantham the administrative changes which had been set in motion by the wartime upheaval were slowed down or even reversed. Little came, in the end, of the post-war leadership's effort to place local people in senior posts. The appointment of Paul Tsui to the Cadet Service turned out to be a flash in the pan. No other Chinese Cadet was recruited for years afterwards, and only three altogether had won admission to this elite corps by the end of the 1950s. In 1948 the police force went back to enrolling expatriate inspectors after a break of two years. The about-turn reflected in part the belated unease which was felt by the Hong Kong authorities at the Communist surge to power on the mainland, and perhaps even more a desire felt in London to find billets for the large number of colonial policemen who had been made redundant by the end of the British mandate in Palestine. More expatriate officers were to be drafted in for the same reason during the next two decades, as British rule was wound up in Cyprus and East Africa.[59] In one branch of the government, to be sure, modest progress in 'localization' was still taking place. At the beginning of the 1950s two local lawyers became the first Chinese Crown Counsels to serve in the legal department. But the great mass of their colleagues continued to be expatriates. And the expatriates went on enjoying superior treatment in the form of higher salaries, longer holidays and lavish and subsidized housing.

Swept away in the same tide was the trend of the immediate post-war period towards government openness and freer political expression. Grantham didn't approve of press conferences.[60] By the end of 1949, in response to the advent of Communist rule on the mainland, legislation had once again been brought in to curb the trade unions and to ban all bodies linked to the Communists, Nationalists or any other outside political group. Right through the 1950s and into the 1960s, any sign of political protest was 'fiercely suppressed', and films were routinely censored for political reasons.[61]

Most revealing of all was the sabotage of the Young Plan. Grantham was personally dead against the whole notion of democratic reform from the start. There was, to his mind, no scope for an advance to self-government in an enclave carved out of Chinese territory where the mass of the population looked to China for their political cues. The choice for Hong Kong was either to carry on as a British colony, ruled on the lines of 'a benevolent autocracy', or to be reabsorbed into Guangdong province. The British business chiefs were alarmed by the 'unknown hazards' of universal suffrage;[62] and so, even more, were the gentry. Even in 1946 they had received Young's proposals with a coolness suggesting that, from their point of view, representative government was a reform too far; and in the following years, emboldened by Grantham's arrival, they began gradually to voice outright opposition to a measure which threatened their power. In November 1948 Sik-nin Chau went so far as to call on the Colonial Office and inform British officials that there was 'no demand' for the Young Plan in Hong Kong. Grantham was only too happy to swim with the tide. For the first eighteen months of his reign no significant action was taken to move the Plan forward, and in March 1949 he made a statement conveying that Young's proposals were, in effect, to be scrapped. In August he sent the Colonial Office a substitute scheme which had been drawn up in the previous months by the taipans and gentry with his own unobtrusive guidance and support. The new scheme discarded Young's Municipal Council, with its ominous promise of evolution into a full-blooded democratic government. The post-war expectation of change was still sufficiently widespread that some sign of progress towards a representative system was considered desirable; and the drafters accordingly suggested an enlarged Legislative Council, with a majority of 'Unofficial' members, just over half of whom would be chosen by election. The implications of this were, however, reduced drastically by restricting the franchise to the tiny minority of British nationals.

This new blueprint was further diluted over the next two years by the combined efforts of Grantham, the taipans and gentry and a Colonial Office which was itself swiftly losing its zest for reform. In May 1952 the amended reform scheme was finally put to the Cabinet in London; but at this point the taipans and gentry joined forces to kill off the whole exercise. They informed Grantham that there was 'no real demand whatever' for representative government, and pleaded with him to 'stop this madness which will be the ruination of Hong Kong'. Grantham promptly requested the new Conservative government to call a halt to the project, and the Conservative government promptly obliged.[63] The feeble Urban Council was left, as it had been in prewar times, the only body in Hong Kong chosen to some extent by elections. Bishop Hall sighed prophetically to the Victoria Diocesan Association, 'I am not alone when I say I believe that Hong Kong will remain very much as it is at present for the next 40 years.'[64]

In 1957 a symbolic seal was set on the Grantham counter-reformation when the missing statue of Queen Victoria was at last erected again. Even Grantham apparently thought it best to avoid dealing out too direct an affront to the new post-war sensitivities. The statue was put up in a spot well away from the city centre, in Victoria Park in Causeway Bay. But Hong Kong was once more clearly labelled a colony.

The expatriate public back-pedalled in much the same way. By the late 1940s the tentative moves to open the colony's clubs and recreation spots to Asian residents had slowed to a halt. On one occasion when T. V. Soong and his wife came down from Canton on a visit Grantham joined them for dinner with the manager of the Hong Kong branch of the Bank of China at the latter's house in Deep Water Bay. The Royal Hong Kong Yacht Club was visible across the water, and Soong asked the manager casually if he often went there. The manager replied that he didn't 'because he was not allowed to be a member'.[65] Right up to the mid-1960s Sik-nin Chau remained the Jockey Club's only Chinese steward. The Hong Kong Club continued to be barred to non-Europeans, and so did the choice bathing beach at Shek O.[66] 'Localization' crept forward at the same snail's pace in the business as in the government sector. In the mid-1950s senior Portuguese clerks on the staff of the Hongkong and Shanghai Bank were finally given the responsibility of signing documents. At around the same time the Bank started employing a few Chinese in clerical posts; but as late as 1956 a woman who applied for a job as a secretary was informed that Chinese were only taken on there as janitors.[67]

The fact was social attitudes had slipped back, to a certain extent, into the pre-war pattern. Once again the British were starting to show signs of arrogance. A visitor who arrived in Hong Kong for the first time at this period was struck by the way the expatriates 'habitually spoke to Chinese in a hectoring or domineering tone of voice'.[68] Even in cases where the frame of mind was more amiable there was still apt to be a paternalistic whiff from the past. Grantham wrote in his memoirs of 'Ah Yau, the no.1 boy at Government House – a most admirable and kindly man'.[69] In the legal department one day in the early 1950s a junior British staff member passed one of the newly appointed Chinese Crown Counsels a stack of files and said, 'Simon, would you be kind enough to look after this now? I have to go on leave.'[70]

Once again it was normal to hold the Asians at arm's length. The segregation maintained by the clubs merely reflected the habits of most ordinary expatriate people. One old Hong Kong hand boasted, 'I've never had a Chinese cross my threshold as a guest. Never know what they might do!'[71] And to crown all of this the aversion to interracial liaisons which had shown signs of weakening during the first post-war years had begun to creep back. In the late 1940s a Eurasian girl sailing from England to Hong Kong made friends with a young British man who was travelling out to join an expatriate firm. The two agreed to meet up after the end of the voyage: a few days later, however, the young man wrote saying that he had been 'ordered not to continue the acquaintance because it was against the policy of the firm that their employees should have local friends'.[72] Asked by a newcomer to Hong Kong at a dinner in 1959 if her daughter and those of her friends would eventually marry Chinese husbands, an expatriate hostess replied laughingly, 'Oh, no, no – our daughters go to

London for the Season!'[73] The aversion may have persisted well into the 1960s. It has been widely rumoured, if never conclusively proved, that in that decade both Ronald Holmes, the BAAG officer who took a Eurasian wife, and Ken Barnett, an outstanding administrator who had married a Chinese, were denied elevation to the highest ranks of the government on account of their *mésalliances*.[74]

The retrogression, to be sure, wasn't total. Many of the post-war British business chiefs were new arrivals from Shanghai, markedly more sophisticated than the previous generation of taipans in their attitudes to the Chinese; and the alliance they formed with the gentry was reflected in a fair amount of socializing at this somewhat rarefied level. Segregation clung on in redoubts, but was no longer the organizing principle of the society. And the British had also developed by now a self-consciousness over racial issues they had never shown in pre-war days. Grantham was 'much embarrassed' by the episode of the Yacht Club.[75] One expatriate boss, though himself according to a colleague 'as racist as they come', was at pains to make out that nobody on his staff was a bigot. And some European managers now made a point of inviting their Asian employees to a 'duty party' at home – once a year.[76] The fact remained that the new friendliness and respect with which the British had approached their Asian fellow-citizens in the aftermath of the war had worn thin.

The Asians in the same way had reverted to many of their pre-war postures. Gone was the breezy outspokenness with which even humble Chinese had been used, in the war years, to proffer their views to the European bosses. Amahs and cookboys once more addressed their employers deferentially, as 'Master' and 'Missy'.[77] Gone also was the fragile solidarity which had grown from the shared ordeal of Japanese rule. When the British gunboat *Amethyst* was cornered humiliatingly by Mao's advancing forces on the Yangtze in the summer of 1949, Grantham observed that the incident was 'not unpleasing to many Hong Kong Chinese, even those unsympathetic to the Communists'.[78] And there were once again signs that British high-handedness was breeding resentment among the Asian upper and middle classes. In 1952 the first of the two Chinese Crown Counsels resigned in protest against the discrimination he encountered in the legal establishment. The second Chinese Crown Counsel was strongly inclined to do likewise, but was headed off by a friend who advised him to stay at his post and work to achieve a better deal for the colony's non-European civil servants.[79]

Inside the British community, finally, the pre-war rigidities were coming back fast. By 1950 contact between the officials and businessmen was once again said to be 'incomplete', and observers were once again noting an expatriate tendency to hive off into cliques.[80] Status had once more become a decisive factor in day-to-day social planning. One expatriate wife was heard to advise her husband, an engineer in the Waterworks Department, 'We shouldn't invite them to lunch, dear. He's only an inspector.'[81] A scathing description of the Hong Kong colonial mindset which was produced at this time by the Eurasian novelist Han Suyin might have come word for word from the pen of Stella Benson a generation earlier:

> They are afraid to lose caste within the narrow circle to which they are confined by the scope of their interests; to be rejected from the social herd for any peculiarity of thought; to lose in the struggle for conformity up the nicely graduated steps of the island hierarchy. Their aim is to attain that chimerical upper stratum of birth and financial security which only exists in the English middle-class mind but which in the Colony is still so doubtfully symbolized by that eminence called THE PEAK.[82]

The relapse into social torpor was only arrested by a fresh bout of upheavals that took place in the second half of the 1960s. In April 1966 an increase in the fares on the Star Ferry triggered off the first major outbreak of public unrest since the war, with four nights of rioting in the streets of Kowloon. Then the following year between May and December Hong Kong was caught up in the backwash of the Cultural Revolution on the mainland, as the local Communists who had for so long been quiescent came forward to challenge the colonial power. Transport networks and factories were paralysed by political strikes. Demonstrators rampaged, and crowds chanted at the gates of Government House, and thousands of bombs were planted in every part of the colony. (One of the principal bomb-making factories was discovered to be in Saikung, where the Hakka villagers had maintained their Communist loyalties and infrastructure since the days of the East River Column.) For a few weeks the government went into last-ditch mode. A curfew was briefly imposed on Hong Kong Island for the first time since the war. Emergency legislation was pushed through suspending many civil and political rights: police raids were launched on suspect schools and trade-union offices, and a total of 200 leftist ringleaders were interned. In a climate of panic large numbers of European residents were observed to be packing their bags. The gentry remained broadly solid behind the authorities, but there were one or two suggestive pieces of footwork. Dick Lee, the tycoon who had directed the crucial morale-boosting building programme in the BMA period, resigned from all his civil service appointments. He ascribed his departure to 'personal preoccupations'; but it was 'widely believed that his resignation had a political tinge'.[83]

These new crises gave rise, in the familiar pattern, to a new wave of change. The authorities suddenly woke up to a need for increased consultation with their Asian subjects. In 1968 they established a network of City District Offices whose task would be to extend the government's reach at the local level, to promote understanding of government policies and to inform the government of any discontents.[84] In May 1969 the Colonial Secretary issued a paper stating bluntly that the way to forestall any further subversive activity on the part of the Communists was to 'improve the administration' of Hong Kong. Among other things this meant 'maintaining equality under the law' and creating more opportunities for local school leavers.[85] In response to these strictures the wheels of localization were set in motion once more. The early 1970s saw the appointment of the first Chinese Secretary for Social Services, the first Chinese high court judge and the first Chinese Vice-Chancellor of Hong Kong University. A sustained effort was at last made to help Chinese civil servants to climb the career ladder, and by the end of the following decade the lower ranks of the government were filled almost exclusively by Chinese. The Colonial Secretary's paper also stressed that the government had to ensure the provision of 'basic necessities'.[86] For the first time since the reform drive of 1945–6 sweeping action was taken to better the living conditions of the colony's poor. At the end of the 1960s the construction of public housing (the one area where there had been significant progress in the intervening years) was sharply accelerated. In the first half of the 1970s the demand for comprehensive primary education which had been voiced at the end of the war was finally met when arrangements were made to provide for nine years of free and compulsory schooling. New attention was paid in the same way to raising the level of public health and amenities, and overall spending on social welfare increased nearly twentyfold. In the background to all this the authorities shifted once again to a more modest posture. In 1972 the colony became, once again and conclusively, a Dependent Territory, and the Colonial Secretary turned correspondingly into the Chief Secretary. In 1973 the Secretariat for Chinese Affairs was renamed the Department of Home Affairs, removing the anomaly under which, as a local historian puts it, 98 per cent of the population were apparently classified as a separate species.[87] In 1974 the announcement was made that the Chinese language would from now on be recognized as an official language in conjunction with English. And in the meantime, as if to sum up the whole process, the cricket ground which had occupied a swathe of the Central District was quietly converted into a sitting-out area for the use of the public.[88]

Private institutions once more followed suit. By the end of the 1960s the Hong Kong Club and the other whites-only facilities had at last opened up to non-Europeans. In 1972, after a century of existence, the Hongkong and Shanghai Bank for the first time appointed a Hong Kong Chinese to its Board of Directors. Five years later the Bank revised its recruitment system to provide for a higher percentage of non-British employees; and ten years after that Chinese filled the vast bulk of the junior executive slots in both the Bank and the rest of the old British firms. Many of the deep-seated taboos of expatriate life were again breaking down, and this time decisively. By 1968 it was regarded as chic in some expatriate circles to have a Chinese wife.[89] By the 1980s a European married to a Chinese held the leading government post of Financial

Secretary, and expatriates with Asian spouses were rising without trouble to top jobs in such British-owned companies as Jardine Matheson and the Chartered Bank. Arrogance much diminished, the British residents even appeared, in a good many cases, to have picked up something of a Chinese veneer. They ate Chinese dishes prepared for them in their homes, and displayed their sophistication (not to say their prosperity) by acquiring collections of Tang horses or Ming dynasty scrolls. Early each summer the more athletic among them took part happily in the Dragon Boat Festival, the yearly regatta held to mark the death of the ancient Chinese poet Qu Yuan, which seemed to have been assimilated in some mystic fashion to the Oxford and Cambridge Boat Race.

Even then the change could not be called comprehensive. Right up to the mid-1990s all the top posts in the government – those of the Governor, Chief Secretary, Financial Secretary and Attorney-General – remained in British hands. In 1985 expatriates still accounted for 37 per cent of the officers and inspectors in the Royal Hong Kong Police Force. The recruitment of overseas inspectors for the Force wasn't abandoned until 1994, and as late as 1996 four out of five officers promoted to the rank of chief superintendent were of expatriate background. In the early 1990s one fifth of the 450 administrative officers (the Cadets of the past) were imported, and overall more than 3,500 expatriates remained on the government payroll.[90] Much the same pattern could still be traced in the clubs and the old British companies. In 1995 the Hong Kong Club finally chose its first Chinese chairman, and in 1996 the Jockey Club appointed its first non-European chief executive since Ho Kom-tong was propelled by the Japanese into that capacity fifty-four years before. In 1982 Jardine Matheson came under fire in the press for being 'far too slow in bringing Chinese on to its Board of Directors', and a dozen years after that the Asian presence in the higher echelons of Jardine Matheson, Swire's and the Hongkong and Shanghai Bank was still reckoned to be remarkably small.[91] The decision that had been taken in 1974 to include Chinese as an official language was implemented in a somewhat leisurely fashion. Twenty years later the government's policy papers and internal memoranda were still being written entirely in English. The first new laws to be issued in Chinese as well as English only made their appearance in 1989, and in the early 1990s the translators were still hard at work rendering the existing corpus of law into a Chinese version. In 1995 summonses made out in English were still being served on uncomprehending Chinese defendants, and English continued to be the sole language which might be used to conduct the proceedings of the higher courts. Arguably there were limits beyond which institutional change could not reasonably be expected to go. After all, Hong Kong was a colony. But even at a casual level the gulf between the traditional British ruling caste and their Asian subjects still seemed in the mid-1990s to be quite considerable. Implicit in many encounters and relationships there continued to lurk a kind of ethnic subtext that startled Western visitors used to the unselfconscious equality of dealings on the mainland or Taiwan.[92] In particular the promise of relaxed social mingling which had flickered briefly after the end of the war still appeared to be a fair way from fulfilment. On one festive evening I witnessed in these years the staff of an expatriate-run firm met in their office overlooking the harbour to catch a bird's-eye view of a firework display. And the expatriates watched from one room, and the Chinese from another.

Also ran: British business

In a larger sense, however, the British never really recovered their pre-war control of Hong Kong. In the sphere which most counted, the economic sphere, they never found the strength to reimpose their accustomed hegemony. Most of the old British business community left for home on the evacuation ships in the autumn of 1945. A BMA spokesman advised the Hong Kong General Chamber of Commerce that its members should leave, since with no ships available to bring in merchandise and no banks likely for the time being to transact ordinary business there was no prospect of an early resumption of trade.[93] For the next year or so, therefore, the British commercial presence in Hong Kong was negligible. By the end of 1946 British firms were returning, and one or two major new ventures had been set up. George Marden, a former official of the Chinese Maritime Customs, had founded Marden's, a new expatriate trading house; and a fledgling airline, Cathay Pacific, had made its appearance with the backing of Swire's. But the poverty into which Britain had been plunged by the war and the uncertainty which continued to shroud the colony's future discouraged any larger-scale flow of British capital into Hong Kong. The *Far Eastern Economic Review* observed gloomily in January 1947, 'It is probably correct to say that Hong Kong has ceased to be an outpost of British trade in the Far East.'[94]

Under these circumstances, as Harcourt later recalled, 'the real work of rehabilitation had of course to be and was done by the Chinese'.[95] It was the Hong Kong Chinese, streaming back in their tens of thousands, whose efforts to kick-start the colony's business life won the admiration of outside observers. Already by the end of September 1945 evidence of their enterprise was detected in the resumption of shipping services along the Pearl River.[96] It was they, not the British, who were responsible for the colony's physical reconstruction. In January 1946 every one of the forty-seven contractors engaged by the Public Works Department for the rebuilding programme was a Chinese firm.[97] It was they, not the British, whose pressure on the BMA brought about the early lifting of restrictions on private overseas trade: the merchants who in March 1946 were reported to be rosily planning for their future peacetime trading activities were 'mostly Chinese'.[98] Lastly and naturally it was the Chinese, not the British, who reconstituted the light industrial base which they and their fathers had laid in the pre-war decades. The promising light industrial sector of the pre-war economy had certainly been ravaged by the Japanese grab for strategic plant and materials: the number of factories in Hong Kong is said to have dwindled from 800 in 1940 to 366 in 1946.[99] But the sector hadn't been wiped out; and indeed, as we saw, the enforced autarky of the occupation even caused one or two local industries such as rubber footwear and soap to come into their own. Galvanized by the coming of peace these industries promptly stepped up their output, and even enjoyed a modest boom at a time when most overseas shipping had not yet revived and large gaps were apparent in both the mainland and the South-east Asian markets. In January 1946 the owners of nearly thirty rubber footwear factories held a meeting and claimed that if the raw materials were made available to them they could produce sixty million pairs of rubber shoes by the end of the year. In the following months rubber shoe production surged forward at top speed, and the whole industry impressed British observers as 'efficient and rather modern'.[100] Thanks to the 'good foundation' which had been laid during the war local soap manufacturers were equally considered to have 'had a good start'; and other plants turning out buttons, matches and suchlike small goods were reported to have been able to 'resume business immediately' as soon as Harcourt sailed in.[101]

Most of the newly revived Chinese firms were small family ventures of only modest ambitions. But they did of course benefit in some measure from the temporary absence of almost the whole British business class. In the autumn of 1945, for example, Hong Kong government vessels which would normally have been handled in the British-owned docks were instead sent for repair to local Chinese shipyards.[102] Heartened by the new openings the Hong Kong Chinese started to expand their concerns and hoard up their profits into capital for further expansion.[103]

Into the midst of all this – and before the returning British business chiefs had a chance to get their breath back – came the refugees from the civil war on the mainland. These were not humble family traders, and their ambitions were anything but small-scale. Many of them were magnates from Shanghai where they had made fortunes running textile enterprises and other major light industrial plants. A fair number had already been in Hong Kong ten years earlier, sheltering from the onrush of the Japanese forces: they had played a leading part in the colony's pre-war manufacturing upsurge, and had marked it down as a possible centre of operations at some future date. Now they were back again – to take up where they had left off when the 23rd Army swept into the colony, and to build on the modest industrial base which had been preserved by the efforts of the local Cantonese. By the end of 1946 they could be seen every teatime packing the lounges of the Gloucester and Hong Kong

Hotels.[104] By the end of the following year they had gone into action: the urban parts of the colony had begun to be dotted with modern textile mills, the first plastic and leather goods plants had made their appearance and the total number of registered factories was observed to 'compare favourably with pre-war figures'.[105]

Reinforced by the second wave of refugees driven south by the Communist takeover, the magnates from Shanghai made an impact the British couldn't ignore. In the first place they brought with them a massive dollop of capital. Between 1946 and 1950 no less than US$500 m poured from the Shanghai area into Hong Kong in the form of merchandise, securities, gold and foreign exchange – neatly reversing the flow of investment which had taken place from Hong Kong to Shanghai in the early years of the century. As often as not the fortunes of the new arrivals were also manifested at an individual level. 'Many Europeans', noted Ingrams in 1950, 'are entertained by wealthy Chinese, but tend to avoid much of this *because they cannot compete with it* [my italics].'[106] And if any of the magnates were by chance lacking in ready cash, they made up for it with almost limitless chutzpah. Taking account of the new policy of official support for business which had been brought in by the reformist administrations of Harcourt and Young, they headed for the Hongkong and Shanghai Bank in pursuit of the start-up loans they would need to embark on their new industrial ventures. By the end of the 1940s the retreat into social conservatism of the Grantham period was well under way. Both the government and the big British firms were again, as one immigrant observed, 'high on top', and the Bank had resumed its traditional practice of dealing with the Chinese population through a comprador – that institutional equivalent of pidgin English. But the Shanghai magnates were not disposed to be cowed, like their Cantonese predecessors, by colonial haughtiness, and they were not going to be fobbed off with the comprador. Instead they demanded the manager's personal attention; and after some initial fluster, they got it.[107]

Following the great refugee influx the economic balance in the colony began to tilt inexorably in favour of the Chinese. The trade embargoes imposed on the new People's China by the United States and the United Nations obliged Hong Kong to discard much of its traditional role as an entrepot, and light industry now emerged as the leading sector. As the drowsy pre-war city began to be transformed into a seething modern metropolis, as 'Grayburn's Folly', the high-rise marvel of 1930s Victoria, was swallowed up in a thicket of gleaming skyscrapers of twenty storeys and more, as international bodies ceased to classify Hong Kong as a developing territory and instead sized it up as a possible aid donor, the motor of progress was industrialization; and the motor of industrialization was Chinese (and especially Shanghainese) money. In 1963 P. P. Tang, one of the Shanghai textile bosses, became the first Chinese chairman of the Hong Kong General Chamber of Commerce – a body which had still been known to the Chinese community as 'the Westerners' Chamber of Commerce' as little as fifteen years before.[108] Confronted by the huge forward march of Hong Kong Chinese industry the British trading houses kept more and more to their old domains of finance, insurance and up-market transportation and retail business. And even in those domains they were scarcely secure. In the mid-1960s a go-getting Chinese, Ronald Li, applied for membership of the Hong Kong Stock Exchange. The Hong Kong Stock Exchange was run by a cosy network of British businessmen trading in a handful of blue-chip shares in Swire's, the Hongkong and Shanghai Bank, China Light and Power and the other major expatriate firms. It rejected Li's application. Taking the view if you can't join them beat them, and ignoring incredulous murmurs that Chinese people could never establish a money market, Li went off and set up a much larger Chinese stock exchange, which was rapidly followed by a couple of others. Not content with encroaching on the preserves of the old British trading firms some of the Chinese magnates now started to lay an acquisitive hand on the firms themselves. In 1979 the Shanghainese shipowner Y. K. Pao bought up the old trading company Hong Kong Wharf and Godown: with it came control of the tramways and the Star Ferry. Six years later Pao went on to annex Wheelock Marden, successor to Marden's, the latecoming post-war British venture; and this takeover gave him, in passing, possession of Lane Crawford's department store. In the meantime Li Ka-shing, a refugee from Guangdong who had made his fortune by turns as a plastic goods manufacturer and a property mogul, took over the august firm of Hutchison Whampoa and even started to make ominous inroads into Jardine Matheson. The British trading houses were now ringed by countless local rivals, and in constant danger of being devoured by them.

The war also left the British faced by a massive external competitor in the form of the United States. One of the few countries in the world to have a surplus of goods available for export, the United States was overwhelmingly well placed to muscle its way into the Hong Kong market – and it lost almost no time in doing just that. Some of the American officers who arrived unannounced in the colony in September 1945 were reported to be 'blatantly approaching Chinese firms with offers of business';[109] and one comprador warned the British that unless they could send well-stocked cargo ships down to the colony as quickly as possible, they would 'be beaten to it by the Americans'.[110] Heavy pressure was brought to bear on the BMA by the agents of United States companies to permit the export to Hong Kong of goods which the agents declared to be ready and waiting on the American Pacific coast. The American consul demanded assurances that Hong Kong was contemplating no policy of exclusion or discrimination against United States products, and the first soundings were taken about the provision of air facilities for American firms.[111] In 1946, following this initial barrage, the United States duly supplied a higher proportion of the colony's imports than any other country. Later on in the decade the exporting push seems to have slackened a little, as the Marshall Plan diverted American energies from East Asia to Europe. But America's long-range designs on the Hong Kong market could still be discerned. The Canadian ambassador to Nanking was left in no doubt by his conversation with his American colleague in March 1948 that a major reason for the latter's clearly expressed wish to see Britain driven out of the colony was the aim of the United States 'to eliminate British commercial competition in this area'.[112]

The influx of American goods soon produced a sea change in the appetites of the Hong Kong consumer. Harold Ingrams reported with mild distaste on the spectacle that greeted him as he strolled around Victoria one evening in early 1950:

> From up on high one was exhorted to drink beer in violet and green, but Coca-Cola always in the lucky vermilion of China. So prevalent was this latter invitation that one began to believe that Coca-Cola had become the staple food of China.
>
> Indeed, one of my first impressions was that there was an American air about parts of Hong Kong. Further east up Queen's Road, 'Battleground Annie' shrieked all too loudly for attention, and other cinemas at that end of town seemed overpoweringly American. The films had endowed many a citizen of Hong Kong who had never been out of China with a strong American accent, and large, glossy and opulent American cars added a good deal to traffic problems.[113]

Ingrams deduced that there was 'something flamboyant in the outlook of Westernised money-making Chinese to which the American way of life makes a strong appeal'.[114]

The growing local penchant for things American also obtruded itself in a more refined sphere. In the late 1940s the United States started to take Britain's place as the country to which the gentry sent their offspring for a higher education. Grandchildren of Sir Robert Ho Tung went variously to Stanford, the Harvard Law School and the Columbia School of Journalism in New York. Li Koon-chun sent his sons to MIT and the Wharton School of Business, and a nephew of Dick Lee took successive degrees from MIT and Stanford.[115] The switch was in part caused by (once again) the new poverty of post-war Britain and the meagre number of scholarships that were offered to enable students from Hong Kong to attend universities there. But it also seemed evident that Britain's grip on the loyalties of educated young people in the colony was getting undermined by a challenge very nearly as insidious (to some minds at least) as that posed by Communism. A Conservative MP proclaimed that the British did not want their way of life, 'the knowledge of our past and above all of our literature', to vanish from Hong Kong and be 'replaced by the American or any other ideology'.[116]

Momentum faltered briefly in the early 1950s, when United States residents were advised by their government to pull out of Hong Kong following the outbreak of the Korean War and the imposition of the trade embargoes. But Korea proved to be no more than a hiccup in the American business advance. By 1954, the year after the Korean War ended, fifty American firms were back at work in the colony; and not long after that the United States was busy scrambling aboard the new Hong Kong bandwagon of industrialization. In 1956 the surging textile industry received its first injection of American capital. Over the next decade, as the Shanghainese textile magnates diversified nimbly first into plastics and later into electronics, United States investment was seldom far behind. In 1963 the Fairchild Corporation installed the colony's first plant for the assembly of silicon planar transistors. By 1971 the United States was easily the largest outside investor in the colony's industries: American investments accounted for 44 per cent of the total, with the British lagging at a mere 20 per cent.[117] During the 1980s a host of American finance houses sprang up in Hong Kong, posing a further threat to the dominance of the old British trading establishments. By the end of the decade no less than 900 United States companies were operating in the colony; and individual American executives were starting to gain footholds in the old British firms. In 1987, for a few months of sacrilege, an American even occupied the position of Managing Director of Jardine Matheson. Keeping pace with these inroads came the inexhaustible march of American popular culture, hastened from the mid-1950s by a steady rise in the numbers of United States tourists and then from the 1960s by the regular visits of GIs on 'rest and recreation' from Vietnam. One commentator remarked that the onslaught of McDonalds and Disney and Dallas had done more to transform the daily lives of the Hong Kong Chinese population than any edict the British had ever put out. The business conquest was underpinned by the periodic descent of American battleships and aircraft carriers, with their implicit suggestion (though no commitment was ever actually made) that the United States might step in to protect Hong Kong from a mainland attack. Small wonder, perhaps, that a senior official at the huge United States Consulate General was heard in 1986 to boast to a visiting grandee from New York that it was right there, in the consulate, that Hong Kong was really run.[118] Diverted by the Cold War from its old objective of turfing the British out of the colony, the United States had settled to eclipse them instead.

From the late 1940s the British were also confronted by the beginnings of a second and deeply ironic external challenge – the return of the Japanese. Prostrate at the end of the war, Japan quickly began to revive under the supervision of the United States occupation forces; and the dust from the conflict had scarcely settled before Japanese exports were making a significant impact on post-war Hong Kong. In the first post-war years it was Japan, more than anywhere else, that churned out the machinery and raw materials needed to power Hong Kong's incipient industrial take-off. In October 1946, for instance, the colony entered into negotiations with Japan for the shipment of a large number of cotton spindles which, it was hoped, would 'form the backbone of a Hong Kong cotton industry'.[119] Arrangements were also made for the import of Japanese cotton yarn. The *Far Eastern Economic Review* explained to its readers in February 1947 that cotton yarn was in short supply the world over. Hong Kong 'would use British yarn if it could get it' – in the meantime, however, Japanese yarn would have to be imported in order to restart the local textile mills.[120] Japanese coal was shipped into the colony at a rate of about 9,000 tons a month, and so was a quantity of miscellaneous Japanese industrial plant and equipment. In the same years, too, Hong Kong was beginning to buy from Japan large amounts of consumer goods, foodstuffs and bicycles, glassware and porcelain and cigarette paper.

All of this traffic was strictly governmental, conducted between the Hong Kong authorities and General MacArthur's headquarters in Tokyo. The industrial plant and materials were delivered to Hong Kong by the United States occupation regime as part of the Japanese war reparations, and the consumer goods were thrown in as a method of earning the foreign exchange that was needed to pay for the import of essential commodities into Japan. For the first two years after the end of the war no private trade between Hong Kong and Japan was even allowed. Japanese businessmen were, however, stirring back into life; and as they did so their attention was naturally caught by the broadening flow of their country's goods to the colony. By September 1948 three Japanese trading companies were said to be looking for ways to export to Hong Kong.[121] Grander plans altogether were cherished by Mitsui Bussan, which had been the chief Japanese trading house in the colony during the pre-war and wartime years. Mitsui Bussan were determined to get back into Hong Kong and rebuild their old presence. To spearhead their re-entry they chose Fujita Ichiro, an executive who had worked in their Hong Kong office in the 1930s and had then gone on to preside over its General Trading Department for the greater part of the war. During the final stages of the American occupation all of the company papers relating to the colony were dug out, copied and circulated to the Mitsui Bussan staff under Fujita's supervision. In 1952, with the occupation at last at an end and a peace treaty signed between Japan and the wartime Allies, Fujita set about briefing his employees on the conditions they could expect in Hong Kong and the local contacts they might hope to take up again. By the autumn he was ready to venture back to the colony for the first time to prepare for the reopening of the firm's Hong Kong branch.[122]

Any large-scale resumption of private trade would of course need to have proper financial back-up. In 1950 an emissary of the Japanese banking world approached several banks in the colony looking for one in which he might be able to invest US$500,000 in cash; and a year later 'chief executives handling the preparatory work' were reported to be trying to negotiate premises for the first post-war Japanese bank in Hong Kong. The idea was that the bank's representatives would approach the Hong Kong government for registration as soon as the peace treaty was signed.[123]

The return was, of course, fraught with obstacles. After nearly four years of subjugation the colony's official attitude to the Japanese was one of stiff antipathy. Since the last contingents of occupation troops, settlers and war criminals were packed off home in 1946–8 the British authorities had, for all practical purposes, allowed no Japanese to come back to Hong Kong. Any Japanese wishing to make the journey had first to apply for a visa to the Hong Kong government's representative in Tokyo. In the early 1950s this representative was W. J. Anderson, a former inmate of Stanley who had been thrown into prison by the Kempeitai during their crackdown on resistance activities in 1943. Anderson kept a notebook in which he had recorded the names of all the Japanese he encountered in the course of the occupation; and any would-be business visitor whose name appeared in his notebook could forget about going to Hong Kong.[124] The tiny handful of Japanese who were granted visas were generally permitted to remain in the colony for no more than two weeks. In October 1952 a diplomat, Itagaki Osamu, was given leave to open the first post-war Japanese consulate in the colony to 'develop trade'[125] – but the visa restrictions remained in force.

In the early stages a similar aversion was widely in evidence in business circles, both expatriate and Chinese. In August 1947, when the ban on private commerce was lifted, the *Far Eastern Economic Review* noted that there was 'still some opposition to trading and the resumption of ordinary relations with Japan and the Japanese people which is obviously a consequence of the prolonged impact of war experiences'.[126] The aversion was markedly reinforced by the influx of industrialists from Shanghai. These mainlanders brought with them their own bitter memories of Japanese conquest; and on top of that they were alarmed at the threat which seemed likely to be posed to Hong Kong's infant industries as Japan's export effort came back to full throttle. Early in 1948 a number of textile manufacturers in the colony led by a certain C. L. Hsu organized a 'Hong Kong Chinese Association to Oppose the Promotion of the Revival of Japanese Industries', and that summer a boycott of Japanese products was briefly considered.[127] In the autumn of 1951 the proposed setting up of a Japanese bank in the colony was reported to have aroused keen anxiety in the local business community, which interpreted it as 'the vanguard of an all-out Japanese campaign to overrun Hong Kong and its neighbouring market'.[128]

But the barriers were not impermeable. In June 1948, less than a year after its earlier downbeat assessment, the *Far Eastern Economic Review* was reporting on the 'rather fast dying-out anti-Japanese bias' in the business world. 'Businessmen on the whole', the *Review* observed, 'are never sentimentalists, and therefore any propaganda based on the Japanese bogey cannot be successful.'[129] The *Review* was above all the mouthpiece of expatriate business, and it seems clear that the resistance in that quarter was especially soft. Relatively few of the British taipans by now were old-timers like Anderson with direct experience of maltreatment by the Japanese; and as the China market collapsed under the impact of the civil war many of them were only too eager to trade with Japan. Within weeks of the unbanning of private commerce the Hongkong and Shanghai Bank had opened branches in Tokyo and three other Japanese cities, and in the following years it is said to have played a key part in the opening up of a limited trade between Japan and the sterling area. By the early 1950s the Bank was ready to take the first steps to facilitate the re-entry of Japanese businessmen into Hong Kong. In 1952, just after the conclusion of the peace treaty, Arthur Morse and his colleagues played host to two visitors from the Foreign Exchange Control Board and the Banking Section of the Ministry of Finance in Tokyo. Accommodation was laid on for the Japanese guests in the Bank's head office, and Morse even took them to the races in Happy Valley. Other British firms also made their contribution. That October Fujita of Mitsui Bussan was enabled to set out on his pioneering trip to the colony by the sponsorship of Lane Crawford's department store. The support of Lane Crawford's induced Anderson to grant an entry visa to this potentate from Mitsui in spite of his lengthy presence in wartime Hong Kong, and he was for good measure allowed to come in for an exceptional spell of three months.[130] Encouraged by these beginnings the British merchants began to agitate for the Hong Kong government to abolish its entry restrictions on the Japanese. The *Far Eastern Economic Review* complained that the difficulty experienced by Japanese businessmen in obtaining entry visas was 'most unsatisfactory and ought to be speedily corrected'.[131] In November 1954 the government finally gave way to the pressure, and permission was granted to Japanese firms and their staff to come freely back to the colony and open up offices there.

Other cracks in the wall of antagonism were to be found in the gentry. When Fujita came back in October 1952 to relaunch the Hong Kong branch of Mitsui Bussan no one initially was willing to lend him so much as a square foot of office space. Rescue, however, was soon forthcoming – from the Bank of East Asia. Following the intervention of the Bank's chief manager Kan Tong-po and his son Kan Yuet-keung (Y. K. Kan), Fujita was 'provisionally' installed in a room in the Bank of East Asia building, which continued to serve as the Mitsui Bussan office after the formal reopening of the firm's Hong Kong branch in late 1954. At the same time that Fujita arrived the new Japanese consul-general, Itagaki, ran into identical difficulties when he tried to obtain premises for his mission. Once again the Kans stepped in, and once again a solution was found in the form of a room in the Bank of East Asia building.[132] Asked in later years why he and his father had been prepared to do such kindnesses to the Japanese in view of the war record, Y. K. Kan by his own account answered, 'I don't know myself'.[133] But the Kans were an old clan whose business ties with Japan went right back to the late nineteenth century. One former Japanese colleague of Fujita's believes that in the case of Mitsui Bussan the help was a thank-you for extensive business which the firm had done with the Bank of East Asia both before and during the war.[134] Help was also given to the returning Japanese by Kenneth Fung Ping-fan, another member of the Bank of East Asia nexus whose father Fung Ping-shan had made his fortune importing foodstuffs from Japan in the Meiji period.[135]

Heartened by this assistance the vanguard of Japan Inc. started slowly but systematically to work their way in. For a few years their activities were fairly small-scale. Mitsui Bussan and half a dozen similar trading houses conducted a modest import business and were serviced by local branches of the Bank of Tokyo and the Tokyo Fire and Marine Insurance Company. By the late 1950s, however, the Japanese were beginning, like the Americans before them, to seize the opportunity that presented itself to invest in the colony's industrial take-off. In 1959 large amounts of Japanese capital started to flow into Hong Kong and 1960 saw the completion of the first wholly-owned Japanese textile mill to be established there since the end of the war. Within a year or two after that Japanese money was moving into new sectors like electronics and steel, and by 1964 steel rolling was said to be emerging as a major local industry 'largely due to Japanese investment'.[136] From the early 1960s, too, as mounting efforts were made to create an infrastructure adequate to cater for the surging population and the colony echoed to the sound of the jackhammer, Japanese companies were beginning to put themselves forward as suppliers and contractors for the proliferating construction schemes. In 1962 the Nishimatsu construction firm won a contract to build the Lower Shingmun Dam in the New Territories – a project located, ironically, close to the site of that Shingmun Redoubt where the British forces had been overwhelmed by the 23rd Army in December 1941. Other Japanese interests were in the meantime working busily to secure a foothold in the fast expanding consumer market. In 1960 the Daimaru company opened the first Japanese department store in Hong Kong. 'Its spacious, skilfully dressed halls', reported an expatriate visitor, 'its Japanese dining room, its Italian tea room and large car park pamper the Hong Kong shopper to a degree unknown in post-war years and set a new standard for Hong Kong's retail trade.'[137] Enthusiasm for the prospects of the Hong Kong market even swept up the colony's wartime governor, Isogai Rensuke. Sighted in the course of the 1964 Tokyo Olympics by a contingent of Hong Kong journalists, the old man, now approaching his eighties, declared affably that he was making plans to return to the colony – as a businessman.[138]

The going was still far from easy. Outside the business elites, among the mass of the Chinese public, memories of the occupation still ran very deep. The Cantonese of Hong Kong are a famously superstitious people, and all over the colony, everywhere that atrocities had been committed, they were conscious of the presence of ghosts. Ghosts of Kempeitai victims were said to haunt the Supreme Court building where the torture chambers had stood, and the Ratings and Valuation Department which had once been a barracks, and the Rediffusion broadcasting station which had been used as a burial ground. Shrieks and groans were reported to echo nightly in the Reuters office and in the neighbourhood of the Bank of China. Stretches of coastline were shunned for their evil reputation, and the British naval headquarters was known as Ghost Base. Pressing in to exploit this enticing new market the fresh cohorts of Japanese investors and contractors had as often as not to inch their way uneasily forward in an atmosphere of continuing hate. In 1962 the Nishimatsu construction company encountered 'a lot of hostility' when they embarked on the building of the Lower Shingmun Dam. Local labourers disrupted the work and even sabotaged the machinery.[139] Effects of the fiasco were felt two years later when Nishimatsu failed to win a similar contract for the Plover Cove Water Scheme: ascribed by the local building industry to budgetary factors, their rejection was unofficially put down to 'certain problems of language and temperament which can arise between Chinese and Japanese co-workers'.[140] The Daimaru department store opened amid controversy, and it too was plagued for some time by friction between Japanese management and Chinese labour. And those gentry leaders who were attempting to ease Japan's way back into the colony were reviled in the Hong Kong Chinese press as 'the new collaborators'.[141]

By the mid-1960s, however, the Japanese bid to reach out to the Hong Kong consumer was beginning to have its effect. In 1966 a British journalist reported that

> there would be nothing particularly surprising about a Hong Kong resident dressed in Kurashiki fabrics parking his Isuzu saloon outside the Daimaru in Causeway Bay, eating a Kobe beef sukiyaki in the store's restaurant, then going on to see Toshiro Mifune at a local cinema and rounding off the evening with an Asahi beer somewhere.[142]

From the 1970s onwards a new generation of Hong Kong Chinese were emerging without memories of the war. Japan's attraction for these younger people grew steadily, and by the last decade of the century it had come to exert a pull at least comparable to that of the United States. Buoyant 'chuppies'

(Chinese yuppies) spent their leisure hours in the growing numbers of sushi bars and karaoke clubs and enthused over the streamlined management skills of Japanese firms. Teenagers thrilled to Japanese pop music and hairstyles, television programmes and *manga* comics. And small children went around in Hello Kitty T-shirts and looked after mechanical Tamagotchi pets. To the 'chuppie' types, who had mostly turned their backs on the Communist mainland, Japan shone forth as a beacon of modernity. Poorer Chinese at the same time were said to identify more with Japan than the United States because it was culturally closer to them. The mounting passion for things Japanese was reflected in the tourism figures. In 1970 an early trickle of 30,000 Hong Kong tourists made their way to Japan for their holidays: by the late 1980s the annual total had risen to 200,000, and it was approaching 300,000 by 1991.[143]

Even now the old grievances had not entirely vanished. Right through these last decades of the century deputations of elderly Hong Kong citizens marched periodically on the Japanese consulate in a fruitless bid to secure the redemption of their holdings of wartime military yen. And young people as well as their elders gave vent every few years to spectacular outbursts of anti-Japanese anger. In 1971 riots broke out after police tried to curb an unauthorized protest meeting which Hong Kong Chinese students had staged in Victoria Park. The protest had been caused by Japan's continued refusal to relinquish to China the disputed Diaoyu islands in the East China Sea – a refusal seen by the students as presaging a new wave of Japanese expansion. More disturbances followed in 1982 when the Ministry of Education in Tokyo set about rewriting Japan's history textbooks in such a way as to gloss over the enormity of the country's wartime misdeeds. Ten thousand demonstrators mustered in Victoria Park, Japanese goods were boycotted, a bomb went off in a local Japanese business and taxis in East Kowloon displayed signs saying 'JAPANESE ARE NOT WELCOME'. In 1989 a self-styled Blood and Light Dare-to-Die Squad issued threats against Japanese in the colony, and in 1996 a local activist, David Chan, was drowned in the course of a quixotic attempt to land on the Diaoyus.[144] Even in quiet years posters seldom failed to appear in the streets on the appropriate anniversary dates reminding passers-by of Japanese crimes as far back as the Manchurian Incident and the Nanking Massacre. Yet these manifestations may not have been quite what they seemed. According to one theory the campaigns to secure the redemption of the military yen were a good deal more about money than moral outrage. The holders of the military yen, it was pointed out, had in fact been offered compensation for their bogus notes in the wake of the British return by the Hongkong and Shanghai Bank. Finding the rate offered too low (and perhaps not wishing to answer too many questions about how those notes were amassed), they had preferred to sit tight in the hope of eventually getting a better deal from the Japanese government and had now, decades later, been prodded into action by their acquisitive offspring.[145] And the young protesters were reckoned to be for the most part mainland sympathizers who wished by assailing the Japanese to proclaim their allegiance to China without drawing down on themselves the stigma of Communism.[146] In neither case did the agitation appear to reflect the concerns of the mass of the Hong Kong Chinese. In February and June 1995, when gatherings of local residents met to commemorate the fiftieth anniversary of the defeat of Japan, it was noticeable that the bulk of those present were immigrants from north China, and that the dominant language of the proceedings was Mandarin rather than the Cantonese of Hong Kong.

As the Chinese majority lost touch with the past and the old rancour was kept alive largely by a small number of special interest groups, the Japanese business juggernaut crashed triumphantly on. By the 1980s Japanese construction firms were securing a leading role in some of the colony's most spectacular projects. The second tunnel built under the harbour from Hong Kong Island to Kowloon in those years received significant Japanese investment, and so did the extension to the sparkling underground system, the Mass Transit Railway. The Daimaru company was followed into Hong Kong by a host of other retail operations, including Matsuzakaya, the firm that took over Lane Crawford's during the war; and by the end of the 1980s the Japanese were said to own 40 per cent of the colony's department stores. More awesome still were the inroads of Japanese finance. From the late 1970s a long procession of Japanese banks started setting up branches in Hong Kong to evade the tight financial regulations imposed at home, and by 1987 Japan had more banks in the colony than any other foreign country. The combined assets of these fifty-eight banks were reckoned to be HK$980.5bn – rather more than 45 per cent of the total assets of all the financial institutions in Hong Kong.[147] One effect of this surge was to drive the British to the wall. By 1971 Japan had already outstripped Britain's share of investment in the colony's manufacturing industry, with 23 per cent to Britain's 20 per cent. By 1989 the Japanese had increased their share to 27 per cent, way ahead of Britain at 8 per cent and a mere seven percentage points behind the United States.[148] Some Japanese investors were even said to have talked openly of becoming 'the natural successors to British capital in Hong Kong'.[149]

Throughout the first few years of their return Japanese in the colony had quailed in the long shadow thrown by the occupation. In 1952 the pioneering visitors from the Foreign Exchange Control Board and the Ministry of Finance asked anxiously if it was safe for them to go out on the streets; and when they were taken to the races in Happy Valley by their hosts in the Hongkong and Shanghai Bank they 'stayed close in the Chairman's box'.[150] Japanese personnel working in Hong Kong in the 1950s and early 1960s were reported to be passive, taciturn and unwilling to mix. Only a handful of Japanese even joined a Japan Society which was organized in 1962 at the University of Hong Kong by the poet Edmund Blunden and a like-minded British academic.[151] From the late 1960s, however, under the impetus of its own immense business advances, the Japanese community in Hong Kong started rapidly to recover its pre-war vigour and confidence. In 1968 a new Japanese School, the first since the war, was established by Fujita of Mitsui Bussan with help from his gentry friend Kenneth Fung, and the next year it was followed by a first post-war Japanese Chamber of Commerce. Other institutions soon sprang up to cater for the growing numbers of businessmen from Japan, culminating in the early 1980s in the Volvo Club, 'the largest Japanese-style nightclub in the world'.[152] By the late 1980s more than 1,000 Japanese firms were active in the colony, and the community was back to its wartime level of 10,000 residents.[153] Japanese nationals now outnumbered the British, and were indeed thought to constitute the colony's largest expatriate business group. Accommodation was naturally required for all these companies, and for their employees and their employees' dependants. In the course of the decade Japan became the leading investor in the colony's property market: no less than HK$5bn was invested by Japanese interests in 1987 alone. And early in 1990, in a move of inescapable symbolism, Wada Kazuo, head of Yaohan, one of the proliferating Japanese retail chains, bought Sky High, a palatial mansion on top of the Peak where the chairman of the Hongkong and Shanghai Bank had been in the custom of entertaining his guests.

Another takeover: China recovers possession

It was left to the mainland to deliver the *coup de grâce.*

For many years Mao and his colleagues in the Communist Party leadership had persisted in their strange policy of forbearance towards Hong Kong. Even during the turmoil of 1967 when the Cultural Revolution spilled into the colony the Hong Kong authorities received private assurances emanating from Premier Zhou Enlai to the effect that his government was not encouraging the local left-wing activists and had no intention of driving the British out. In 1972 the Chinese Foreign Minister Huang Hua indicated in a letter to the United Nations that Peking meant eventually to settle the Hong Kong issue – but the timing of this settlement was assigned to an indefinite future date 'when conditions are ripe'.[154] After Mao died in 1976 all this started to change. With Communist ideology discredited in large measure by two decades of calamitous domestic experiments nationalism – with a small 'n' – began to emerge more and more as a vital plank in the regime's manifesto. The new leadership of Deng Xiaoping set the Party's sights for the first time on the recovery of China's lost territories. In 1978 a Hong Kong and Macao Affairs Office of the State Council was organized for this purpose under the direction of Liao Chengzhi

– that same Liao Chengzhi who had overseen Communist operations in Hong Kong four decades earlier at the time of the Japanese conquest. In the following year, in response to a tentative British inquiry as to China's future intentions, Deng made it quietly clear that he expected the British to leave the whole colony, bag and baggage, when the lease on the New Territories expired in 1997; and from this point on the attitude of the Communists to the British presence in Hong Kong increasingly resembled the truculent stance of their Nationalist predecessors. A consistently hard line was maintained by Peking during the two years of talks which led to the Sino-British Joint Declaration of 1984, and Deng brushed aside with some venom an attempt by Prime Minister Thatcher to defend the validity of the nineteenth-century treaties under which Hong Kong was acquired. During the thirteen years which elapsed between the signing of the Joint Declaration and the agreed restitution of the colony in 1997 China's rights as the incoming power were dinned in repeatedly. In the years 1990 to 1994, for example, mainland anger was once again concentrated, as it had been in the late 1940s, on a Hong Kong government project to build a new airport: the Communists were suspicious that the departing rulers aimed to spend their last years of empire siphoning off the colony's wealth into the pockets of British construction firms. In March 1995, in a gesture of cool disregard for colonial sovereignty, a mainland security vessel armed with machine-guns crossed into Hong Kong waters to capture a couple of Hong Kong Chinese smugglers. Inside the colony agents were deployed by a variety of mainland bodies, including the Ministry of State Security and the Central Party School. Officers of the New China News Agency worked (by their own admission) to drum up support for candidates sympathetic to Peking in the elections to the Legislative Council and the district councils which had been belatedly pioneered by the British in these final years of their rule;[155] and the mainland warned that as soon as it had taken over the colony all last-minute innovations of this kind would be swept aside. By 1996 a shadow government had, in effect, been established across the border in Shenzhen in the form of a Preparatory Committee: at the end of the year the Committee chose members of a Provisional Legislature, which sat waiting to move in and replace the colonial Legislative Council the moment the British flag had been lowered. In the meantime a special clock which had been set up in Tiananmen Square ticked away the last days of British dominion, and word leaked out that 15,000 troops of the People's Liberation Army would be sent into the colony on 1 July 1997 to symbolize its long-awaited return to the Motherland.

The growing mainland challenge to British authority was underpinned by a quiet but devastating economic advance. Already in the late 1970s mainland enterprises were being encouraged to invest in Hong Kong industry. Following the decades of Maoist upheaval China's overriding objective was modernization: market economics were starting to be substituted for Marxism as the way to achieve this, and Deng and his followers sought to tap into the colony's wealth of capital and its abundance of technical and managerial skills. From the mid-1980s the pace quickened dramatically, as the mainland reached out for a slice of the local business action commensurate with its status as the future sovereign power. Several thousand firms, in the words of the New China News Agency, began 'pouring money in and establishing footholds in every corner of the territory'.[156] By 1986, only two years after the signing of the Joint Declaration, the mainland had turned into the largest external investor in the colony after the United States and Japan. By the end of the decade the accumulated mainland investment in Hong Kong had reached US$10bn, outstripping both the American and the Japanese figures: by 1994 it had doubled to US$20bn, a sum equivalent to the total investments of the United States and Japan combined.[157] This massive onrush eroded still further what remained of the old British business redoubts. In the course of the 1980s the Bank of China, the mainland's prime vehicle for international finance, increased its turnover in the colony by approximately 82 per cent. By the mid-1990s, with its new, razor-sharp tower dominating the Central District of Hong Kong Island and over 300 branches scattered up and down town, it had built up a position sufficiently strong to command acceptance alongside its British rivals, the Hongkong and Shanghai Bank and the Standard Chartered, as the colony's third note-issuing bank. According to some sources it was actually doing more business than the venerable 'Honkers and Shangers'. Mainland firms were reported to be determined to take on the role that had once been played by the British trading houses; and like their Hong Kong Chinese counterparts they had started to show a propensity for eating the British up. One of the chief 'red capitalist' businesses to be launched in the Deng years, the China International Trust and Investment Corporation (CITIC), had established a Hong Kong offshoot called CITIC Pacific, and it was CITIC Pacific that led the assault. First of all it bought a 'strategic holding' in a key expatriate operation, Hongkong Telecom. Then in April 1996 it acquired enough shares in the colony's airline, Cathay Pacific, to deprive Swire's of the control it had exercised since the airline was founded half a century earlier.

As the return to the mainland drew closer certain echoes were detectable of that far grimmer and bloodier take-over of fifty-five years before. The gentry, for example, remained true to form. For as long as continued control from Britain had seemed possible they had adhered to a steadfastly pro-British line. In the negotiations over the colony's future which took place with Peking in 1982–4 several of them pressed for the Thatcher government to 'tough it out' with a view to obtaining a treaty by which British sovereignty, or at least British administration, could be maintained past the deadline of 1997.[158] From 1984, however, with the colony's fate settled by the Joint Declaration, they lost little time in transferring their attentions to the incoming suzerain. They accepted appointments on the Basic Law Drafting Committee, the body set up by the mainland to devise a constitution for the future Hong Kong Special Administrative Region (SAR) and on the series of other mainland-created assemblies that followed it, up to and including the Preparatory Committee in Shenzhen. In December 1996, when the Preparatory Committee got ready to choose the Provisional Legislature which would displace the colonial Legislative Council, all of the 134 candidates for this rival parliament were said to hail from 'among the elite in Hong Kong society': they even included thirty-four members of the Legislative Council, over half its total strength.[159] Of the five principal candidates for the office of Chief Executive of the SAR – or in other words, for the rank of Hong Kong's first post-colonial Governor – two derived from the old pre-war gentry, while three were representatives of the latter-day gentry born out of the post-war immigration of tycoons from Shanghai; but all had in their different ways taken trouble to advertise their allegiance to the mainland and its Communist leadership. T. S. Lo, lawyer son of the old gentry leader M. K. Lo, procured mainland Chinese identity papers and started writing his name in a suitably Oriental fashion, as Lo Tak-shing. Simon Li, an ex-judge and director of the Bank of East Asia who was son and nephew respectively of the wartime gentry leaders Li Koon-chun and Li Tse-fong, spoke out in support of the Provisional Legislature and called for a tightening of the local public order provisions to prevent Hong Kong's prosperity and stability from being 'eroded by frequent protest actions on the streets'. Ti-liang Yang (or Yang Ti-liang, as he had now restyled himself), the Chief Justice, urged that the future government 'should do nothing which might be seen to deny Peking's sovereignty', and Peter Woo, a shipowner, 'confirmed that he had consulted Peking to make sure he was an acceptable candidate before announcing his bid'. The eventual winner, the shipping magnate Tung Chee-hwa, condemned 'international forces' for trying to use the colony as a weapon to isolate China, and warned that it would not be easy to reconcile freedom of expression with the need to be alert to such threats.[160] And in the meantime the gentry began, year by year more perceptibly, to distance themselves from their British connections. Of the would-be Chief Executives, T. S. Lo showed the way as early as the mid-1980s by resigning his positions on both the Executive and Legislative Councils: ten years later he also divested himself of his CBE. Yang Ti-liang dropped his knighthood, and Tung Chee-hwa stepped down from the Executive Council to avoid any 'conflict of interests' between his job there and his role on the mainland's Preparatory Committee.[161] Everywhere gentry members were said to be fighting shy of the Governor and turning down offers of British awards. Ungrateful by some standards, their conduct could also be seen as part of a familiar and even logical pattern. One senior Hong Kong Chinese official in the moribund colonial government summed up the trend simply. 'Let's face it,' he commented, 'our loyalty has never been to the Queen. But it has been to Hong Kong.'[162]

Once again, too, the passing of British supremacy was greeted with a certain measure of anti-colonial bile. By the early 1990s, for instance, a growing hostility could be observed towards the use of the English language. Local representatives who a few years before had addressed the Legislative Council in fluent English now preferred to unburden themselves in Chinese. Many students were rejecting the language foisted on them by the outgoing rulers, and even those who perceived the importance of English as a global medium did not want their classmates to catch them practising it. Job advertisements now tended to specify Mandarin rather than English as the preferred second language for Cantonese applicants, and the nominally English television stations were more and more used to screen an assortment of international films with Chinese subtitles. Once again scattered voices were raised to denounce the iniquities of the old British order. Letters from local Chinese to the press complained of the continuing tendency of the government and the public corporations to award consultancies and engineering contracts to British and other overseas firms, of the arrogance of those expatriates who went on expecting special treatment and unfailing service in their native tongue.[163] Some of the strictures ranged widely over the whole British record. In October 1996 Lee Cheuk-yan, a member of the Legislative Council, greeted the last annual policy address to be delivered by a British Governor by voicing 'seven deep resentments' about the 150 years of British rule. He condemned in particular the way Britain had 'all along adopted colonial government' and had refused to the last to endow the Chinese population with full democratic rights. His outburst was the more striking insofar as he spoke from an anti-Peking point of view.[164] In February 1997 Dr Ming Chan, a professor of history at the University of Hong Kong, reminded the public of Britain's 'obnoxious' record of discrimination in the pre-war colony. Likening the old Hong Kong with its 'white areas' on the Peak and Cheung Chau to a 'mini South Africa', he maintained that 'insidious racism' still continued to flourish in the civil service, in the private sector and in the courts.[165]

In the last analysis, however, all these defections and brickbats were rather unnecessary. The British had not shown for years any real inclination to stand upon the order of their going. The military lessons of December 1941 had been well learned. Already at the outset of Communist rule on the mainland, when governments in London were adopting an attitude of robust resolution to fight for the colony, the underlying realities were being quietly acknowledged behind the scenes. The defence experts delivered themselves of a succession of gloomy prognoses. In December 1949 the Chiefs of Staff expressed the view that Hong Kong might be held with two army divisions and four fighter squadrons, but admitted that in the event of a global war they were unlikely to get that much; and by January 1951, with the People's Liberation Army flooding into Korea, they were stating bluntly that the military position in

Hong Kong was 'unsound'.[166] Some weeks later, when the fighting in Korea had settled into a healthier stalemate, General Sir John Harding, the Commander-in-Chief, Far Eastern Land Forces, suggested that the colony could 'probably' be defended with three brigades, or around 12,000 men, so long as Britain maintained air supremacy. But the commander in Hong Kong, Lieutenant-General Sir Robert Mansergh, wanted to know what sort of naval and air support he could count on, how quickly 2,000 reinforcements could be sent from Malaya, and how he was supposed to evacuate 20,000 European civilians in the face of a projected assault by 120,000 Chinese infantry and artillery forces.[167] The gloom of the generals had if anything deepened by the last years of the decade. In 1957 the Foreign Office are said to have conceded privately that in the event of a full-blown attack from the mainland 'all would be over before we could reinforce'.[168] The colony, experts reckoned, could hold out for perhaps a week and a half against the Chinese Communists compared with just short of three weeks against the Japanese.[169]

Under these circumstances, and in the absence of any firm guarantee from the United States to come to the rescue, the only logical policy was one of retreat. In 1958 Britain shut down the Naval Dockyard, abandoning what was left of the colony's claim to strategic importance as 'the Gibraltar of the Far East'.[170] By the end of the decade the garrison in Hong Kong had been whittled down to a level compatible only with the maintenance of internal security; and in the troubles of 1967, when a single British sentry stood guard at the entrance of Government House facing thousands of milling Communist demonstrators, it seemed barely capable even of that. In 1976 the remaining vestiges of imperial responsibility for the defence of the colony were effectively shrugged off, when Whitehall requested the Hong Kong authorities to pay for the bulk of the garrison's costs. One last admission of impotence came in March 1995 when the mainland gunboat made its incursion into Hong Kong waters. Although a British warship was anchored close by, in Repulse Bay, the Hong Kong government's security branch did not even bother to keep the Royal Navy informed of the incident; and the Marine Police were ordered to back off.[171]

Britain's ultimate powerlessness to defend Hong Kong militarily carried obvious implications on the political side. In a memorandum of March 1950 Sir John Paskin of the Colonial Office, one of the civil servants who had been involved in finessing the British return five years earlier, judged that Britain's task now was simply 'to postpone the evil day' when Peking would demand retrocession 'as long as it could'.[172] Over the next eighteen months, as war raged in Korea, the Colonial Office and Foreign Office did their best to resist any talk of negotiating the return of Hong Kong to the mainland. But they allowed grudgingly that in view of the dismal forecasts of the defence chiefs such a course might conceivably 'have something to commend it';[173] and a number of contingency plans were discussed. One or two of these projects still hankered after a compromise that might be acceptable to all the parties concerned. Some thought was belatedly given to Roosevelt's solution of making Hong Kong a free port under the management of the United Nations. But there was also a Plan Cinderella under which Britain would, in a crisis, pull out of the colony and hand it over to Peking without even trying to come to an agreement regarding its future.[174]

In the event the policy of benign neglect pursued by the Peking leadership spared the British for some time the need to accompany their military pull-out with a political one. By the late 1960s, however, as the colony swayed in the aftershocks of the Cultural Revolution, the first move in that direction was being made. In 1968 the long duel between the Colonial Office and the Foreign Office in London over how to handle Hong Kong was finally and conclusively won by the latter. The Colonial Office was merged into the Foreign Office, which thereby took over responsibility for Hong Kong affairs. In 1971 Murray MacLehose became the first Governor to be sent out to the colony with a background in the Foreign rather than the Colonial Service. The implication was clearly that Britain's management of Hong Kong would now reflect the Foreign Office priority of relations with the mainland; and from this point on British policymakers began little by little to edge towards a resolution of the Hong Kong issue. In 1972 Britain acquiesced through its silence in the assertion made to the United Nations by Foreign Minister Huang Hua that Hong Kong was not a colony waiting for independence but an occupied territory of China which would be retrieved by China 'when conditions were ripe'. (It was partly to fit in with this new Chinese formulation that Hong Kong was from now on officially referred to by the British as a territory rather than a colony.) And in March 1979 it was Britain, in the person of Governor MacLehose, which set in motion the definitive winding down of its own rule in Hong Kong by asking Deng Xiaoping to indicate what China's intentions were. In spite of the brief flurry of anachronistic protest put up by Prime Minister Thatcher the talks of 1982–4 took the form of a checkmate in two moves against any defence, as the British successively gave up all hope of retaining either their sovereign rights in the colony or their administrative machinery there. In April 1984 the Foreign Secretary, Sir Geoffrey Howe, spelled out bleakly to the Legislative Council that there was no alternative to the British withdrawal, and by December the Joint Declaration was initialled and signed. During the thirteen years which remained of their presence in the colony the British engaged in an unexpectedly spirited rearguard action, conducted both behind the scenes by their representatives on the Joint Liaison Group which the two powers had created to work out the practicalities of the change of regime, and in more colourful style by the maverick final Governor, Chris Patten. But all that they could realistically hope to achieve by this stage was some slight softening of the harsher potential aspects of mainland control.

Even on economic grounds a British disengagement was felt to be justified. In 1962 British investment in the colony was found to amount to just £16m – a figure which (even without allowing for inflation) came to less than half of the £35m recorded for 1931. Five years later two-way trade between Britain and Hong Kong was running at a mere £147m.[175] Judging by these criteria a review by the Treasury in 1967 concluded that Hong Kong was no longer on balance a positive asset for Britain. There were, to be sure, other ways by which the colony's worth to the imperial power might have been computed. If you distinguished from active British investment in manufacturing and other forms of business the accumulated value represented by land and property belonging to the British Crown and the old expatriate companies, a very different picture emerged. As late as 1996, by this yardstick, total British wealth in the colony still amounted to some US$100bn. And Britain continued to benefit indirectly from the role which the colony played as a base for British business activity in the East Asian region and a showcase for British standards and skills. None the less it is clear that by the late 1960s an incipient withdrawal was under way in the economic as well as in the political sphere. In the wake of the crisis which engulfed the pound in the autumn of 1967 the Labour government then in power in London released Hong Kong from its traditional obligation to hold its colonial funds in sterling. The Hong Kong authorities were now free for practical purposes to manage their financial affairs as they saw fit, and by 1972 they had left the sterling area and diversified their holdings into a wide range of currencies. In September 1983, at a time when the Sino-British negotiations had reached an impasse and the Hong Kong dollar was plummeting in a climate of panic, the authorities further chose, 'for simplicity's sake and to inspire public confidence', to peg the colony's currency to the United States dollar.[176] Six months later, with the end of colonial rule now a tangible prospect, the most celebrated of the old British trading houses was starting to tiptoe offstage. In March 1984 Jardine Matheson announced their intention of moving their legal domicile from Hong Kong to Bermuda in order to safeguard their ability to operate under English law. Lesser British firms followed, uneasy about the future, hard-pressed by both local and mainland Chinese interests and gripped by what one recent chronicler could only explain as an apparent collective failure of nerve.[177]

One evening in February 1997 the Royal Shakespeare Company were putting on a performance of *A Midsummer Night's Dream* at the Hong Kong Academy for the Performing Arts. The performance was attended by Governor Patten, and also by HRH Princess Alexandra, titular head of the Royal Hong Kong Police Force, who was paying a visit to the colony to say goodbye to the Force after twenty-five years. Rather belatedly, as the audience were settling into their seats, someone in the theatre management remembered that this was an occasion when the British National Anthem might perhaps be called for.

The appropriate tape was switched on, but died out after just a few bars. The audience rose, stood about raggedly for a moment or two, then dissolved into titters – in which, so far as could be judged from the stalls, some at least in the Royal Box seemed to join. The episode illustrated just how insubstantial the British presence had now become.

Four months later the moment arrived which ardent Chinese patriots had awaited for the greater part of the century. At a grand midnight ceremony in the new Convention Centre on the Wanchai waterfront the Chinese flag was raised and the British flag lowered. A beaming President Jiang Zemin proclaimed the return to the Motherland of the long-lost enclave, and troops of the new People's Liberation Army garrison crossed the border, arriving, as one or two of the more excitable Western networks put it, 'by land, sea and air'.[178] The last ghostly vestiges of British domination had been laid to rest. But the fact was that the real extinction of British supremacy in Hong Kong took place not on that evening, but on another one half a century earlier, when Lieutenant-General Sakai received the surrender of Sir Mark Young in the blazing candlelight of the Peninsula Hotel. During the second innings which they had enjoyed after the end of the Japanese occupation the British had, by fits and starts, permitted the emergence of a more fluid society. They had gradually improved the living standards of the mass of the population. And they had, by their presence and institutions, made possible an astonishing explosion of wealth. But in the process their own role had become so exiguous that it no longer really mattered, was indeed barely noticeable, when the last representatives of British authority boarded the Royal Yacht *Britannia* and HMS *Chatham* and slipped off quietly into the night.

Abbreviations

AGAS	Air Ground Air Service
ALFSEA	Allied Land Forces South-east Asia
BAAG	British Army Aid Group
BMA	British Military Administration
CD	Director of the Special Operations Executive, London
CITIC	China International Trust and Investment Corporation
CO	Records of the Colonial Office
DEFE	Records of the Ministry of Defence
DGB	*Da Gong Bao*
FEER	*Far Eastern Economic Review*
FO	Records of the Foreign Office
GACC	General Association of Chinese Charities
GMRB	*Guomin Ribao*
HK MS	Hong Kong Manuscript Series
HKN	*Hong Kong News*
HKRNVR	Hong Kong Royal Naval Volunteer Reserve
HK RS	Hong Kong Record Series
HKT	*Hong Kong Telegraph*
HS	Records of the Special Operations Executive
HSB	*Hua Shang Bao*
IIS	International Intelligence Service
JHKBRAS	*Journal of the Hong Kong Branch of the Royal Asiatic Society*
MI9	Escape and Evasion Service
OCVU	Overseas Chinese Volunteer Unit
OSS	Office of Strategic Services
RA	Royal Artillery
RAF	Royal Air Force
SACSEA	Supreme Allied Command in South-east Asia
SAR	Special Administrative Region
SCMP	*South China Morning Post*
SCMP/HKT	*South China Morning Post and Hong Kong Telegraph* (post-war joint publication)
SEAC	South-east Asia Command
SMP	*Sunday Morning Post*
SNDC	Supreme National Defence Council

SOE	Special Operations Executive
USDP	United States Diplomatic Papers
WIR	Weekly Intelligence Report
WIS	Weekly Intelligence Summary
WKYP	*Wah Kiu Yat Po (Huaqiao Ribao)*
WO	Records of the War Office
ZB	*Zheng Bao*

Notes

Introduction

1. Phrase used by Han Suyin in an article, 'Hong Kong's Ten-Year Miracle' in *Life* magazine, 1959, and taken up by Richard Hughes in his book *Hong Kong: Borrowed Place – Borrowed Time*, London, 1968.
2. Henry J. Lethbridge, 'Hong Kong under Japanese Occupation: Changes in Social Structure', in I. C. Jarvie and Joseph Agassi (eds), *Hong Kong: A Society in Transition*, London, 1969, p. 78.
3. Dick Wilson, *Hong Kong! Hong Kong!*, London, 1990, p. 84.
4. For this picture see Robert Gildea, *Marianne in Chains*, London, 2002.
5. See Parks M. Coble, 'Chinese capitalists and the Japanese: Collaboration and resistance in the Shanghai area, 1937–45,' in Wen-hsin Yeh (ed.), *Wartime Shanghai*, London and New York, 1998, pp. 62–85.
6. Lee Kuan Yew, *The Singapore Story*, Singapore, 1998, pp. 61, 66–7, 74, 77.
7. See Lieutenant-General Fujiwara Iwaichi, *F. Kikan: Japanese Army Intelligence Operations in South-east Asia during World War II*, Heinemann Asia, Hong Kong, Kuala Lumpur and Singapore, 1983; Peter Elphick, *Singapore: The Pregnable Fortress, A Study in Deception, Discord and Desertion*, London, 1995, pp. 71–2, 95–106, 113.
8. Marie-Claire Bergère, 'The purge in Shanghai, 1945–6: The Sarly affair and the end of the French Concession,' in Yeh (ed.), *Wartime Shanghai*, p. 163.
9. For example in the Dutch East Indies. See Brian G. Martin, *The Shanghai Green Gang: Politics and Organized Crime, 1919–1937*, London, 1996, p. 225.
10. See Bergère, 'The purge in Shanghai', pp. 157–78.
11. See Gildea, *Marianne in Chains*, pp. 353, 358–9.
12. The two memoirs are Li Shu-fan, *Hong Kong Surgeon*, London, 1964 and Jean Gittins, *Stanley: Behind Barbed Wire*, Hong Kong, 1982. Jean Gittins also provides a brief account of her internment in an earlier memoir, *Eastern Windows, Western Skies*, Hong Kong, 1969.

1. A Late Victorian Hill

1. Stella Benson, unpublished diaries, 11 September 1930, quoted in Susanna Hoe, *The Private Life of Old Hong Kong*, Hong Kong, 1991, p. 193.
2. The move took place in 1912. The other leading British trading house, Butterfield and Swire, had never made their headquarters in Hong Kong. They were founded in Shanghai in 1867, and their head office was established in London in 1870. See Robert Blake, *Jardine Matheson: Traders of the Far East*, London 1999, p. 217; Zhang Zhongli, Chen Zengnian and

Yao Xinrong, *The Swire Group in Old China*, Shanghai, 1991, pp. 9–10, 13. For British investment see Gary Wayne Catron, 'China and Hong Kong 1945–1967', Ph.D. thesis, Harvard, 1971, p. 19. For buildings, see Paul Gillingham, *At the Peak: Hong Kong Between the Wars*, London 1983, p. 162; Kwan Lai-hung, *Ri zhan shiqi de Xianggang*, Hong Kong 1993, p. 3; Tse Wing-kwong, *San nian ling bage yue de kunnan*, Hong Kong 1994, p. 41. With fourteen storeys the new Hongkong and Shanghai Bank headquarters was the tallest building in the Far East at this date. The only other strikingly tall buildings in Victoria were the Bank of East Asia with eleven storeys (see p. 5 below) and the Gloucester Hotel with nine plus a clock tower.

3. Major Charles Boxer quoted in Emily Hahn, *China to Me*, Philadelphia, 1944, p. 209.

4. Norman Miners, *Hong Kong under Imperial Rule, 1912–1941*, Hong Kong 1987, p. 46; Gillingham, *At the Peak*, p. 153; Jan Morris, *Hong Kong*, London 1993, p. 59. The Fanling Hunt was founded in 1924. Another favoured quarry was the South China red fox.

5. Stella Benson, unpublished diaries, 22 October 1930, quoted in Hoe, *Private Life*, p. 181; Benson, letter to Lady Eileen Orde, 29 March 1931, in *Some Letters of Stella Benson 1928–1933*, ed. Cecil Clarabut, Hong Kong, 1978, p.27; Joy Grant, *Stella Benson – A Biography*, London, 1987, p. 268.

6. Quoted in Miners, *Hong Kong under Imperial Rule*, p. 89.

7. Many of the leading expatriate merchants in Hong Kong were of Scottish ancestry. See Henry J. Lethbridge, 'Hong Kong under Japanese Occupation: Changes in Social Structure' in I. C. Jarvie and Joseph Agassi (eds), *Hong Kong: A Society in Transition*, London, 1969, p. 80, and 'Caste, Class and Race in Hong Kong before the Japanese Occupation' in Henry J. Lethbridge (ed.), *Hong Kong: Stability and Change*, Hong Kong, 1978, p. 165. Comment on Polluck quoted in Miners, *Hong Kong under Imperial Rule*, p. 131.

8. In January 1921 the Kowloon Residents' Association, a newly formed expatriate grouping, issued a statement attacking the officials of the Hong Kong government on the grounds that their 'knowledge of local conditions was gleaned from a panoramic view of the peninsula from an elevation of 1,200 feet'. Lethbridge, 'Hong Kong under Japanese Occupation', p. 80.

9. Lethbridge, 'Caste, Class and Race', pp. 165–6. The police for their part felt themselves to be unjustly scorned by the rest of the British community, pointing out that they had more responsibility than other subordinate government officers. See John Pennefather-Evans, 'Interim Report on the Hong Kong Police', 1 October 1943, p. 1.

10. Quoted Frank H. H. King, *The History of the Hongkong and Shanghai Banking Corporation*, vol. III, Cambridge, 1988, p. 266.

11. Various other white areas were designated in the same way in the course of the pre-war decades: they included choice parts of Taipo in the New Territories (1913) and the outer island of Cheung Chau (1919), Repulse Bay on Hong Kong Island and Kowloon Tong, a 'garden city' developed in the 1930s on the Kowloon peninsula. One travel guide of the period remarks on the contrast between the 'fine residences' of the Europeans on the Peak and the 'rather squalid' Chinese tenements in the city below. See Carl Crow, *Handbook for China*, Shanghai, 1925, p. 355.

12. W. J. Southorn, Colonial Secretary, letter to H. R. Cowell of Colonial Office, 3 January 1936, CO 129 555/10 pp. 5–6; Lethbridge, 'Hong Kong under Japanese Occupation', p. 94.

13. Quoted G. B. Endacott and A. Hinton, *Fragrant Harbour: A Short History of Hong Kong*, Hong Kong, 1962, p. 194. This episode occurred during a ferry strike which took place in May 1922.

14. Other major considerations were Hong Kong's strategic importance as the only British coaling station in the Far East and its exposed position on the edge of a large and potentially hostile power.

15. Comment of Governor Stubbs quoted in Miners, *Hong Kong under Imperial Rule*, p. 137.

16. Miners, *Hong Kong under Imperial Rule*, pp. 79, 85; Stanley Dzu-fang Ho, 'A Hundred Years of Hong Kong', unpublished thesis, Princeton 1946, chapter III, part 3, p. 16; 'Pure European descent' was stipulated not merely for Cadets for Hong Kong but for all candidates for the Eastern Colonial Service.

17. The three banks were the Hongkong and Shanghai Bank, the Chartered Bank of India, Australia and China and the Mercantile Bank of India.
18. See, for example, *FEER* no. 12, 19 March 1947; Harold Ingrams, *Hong Kong*, London 1952, pp. 141–2. The three shipbuilding companies were the Hongkong and Whampoa Dock Co. Ltd, the Taikoo Dockyard and Engineering Co. Ltd and W. S. Bailey and Co. Ltd.
19. Quoted Gillingham, *At the Peak*, p. 15.
20. For the evolution of these Chinese communal bodies see Elizabeth Sinn, *Power and Charity: The Early History of the Tung Wah Hospital, Hong Kong*, Hong Kong, 1989.
21. Henry J. Lethbridge, 'The District Watch Committee: "The Chinese Executive Council of Hong Kong"', *JHKBRAS*, vol. 11, 1971, pp. 116–34 and specifically pp. 116, 124–5; Norman Miners, 'The Localization of the Hong Kong Police Force, 1842–1947', *Journal of Imperial and Commonwealth History*, vol. xviii, no. 3, October 1990, p. 306.
22. Quoted in James Hayes, 'The Nature of Village Life', in David Faure, James Hayes and Alan Birch (eds), *From Village to City: Studies in the Traditional Roots of Hong Kong Society*, Hong Kong, 1984, p. 59.
23. Alexander Grantham, *Via Ports: From Hong Kong to Hong Kong*, Hong Kong, 1965, p. 113.
24. Sinn, *Power and Charity*, pp. 84–5. These startling data were brought to light by the strange, maverick Governor Sir John Pope Hennessy (1877–81), who spent his term of office in violent conflict with his British colleagues but was decades ahead of his time in his sympathy for the Chinese population.
25. Kwan, *Ri zhan shiqi de Xianggang*, p. 3; Elizabeth Sinn, *Growing with Hong Kong : The Bank of East Asia 1919–1994*, Hong Kong, 1994, pp. 1, 10, 46–7; Frank Ching, *The Li Dynasty*, Hong Kong, 1999, pp. 42–5, 80. The new eleven-storey Bank of East Asia headquarters was completed, like 'Grayburn's Folly', in 1935. Other emerging Chinese banks were the Dao Heng Bank (founded in 1921) and the Hang Seng Bank (founded in 1933).
26. For estimate of 3,000 Chinese-owned factories see Frank Leeming, 'The Earlier Industrialization of Hong Kong', *Modern Asian Studies*, vol. 9, 3, 1975, p. 340. The government Blue Book for 1927 reported a total of 1,523 factories and workshops in the colony. Government surveys of this kind, however, included only those enterprises which were registered with the British authorities: appreciably larger totals may be obtained from a study of the contemporary business directories which were published in Chinese. For size of Chinese factories see Wong Siu-lun, 'The Migration of Shanghainese Entrepreneurs to Hong Kong', in Faure, Hayes, and Birch (eds), *From Village to City*, p. 218. Only five out of 112 Chinese-owned factories analysed in a survey of 1934 turned out to employ more than 500 workers. The 1931 census figure is quoted in Miners, *Hong Kong under Imperial Rule*, p. 21.
27. Morris, *Hong Kong*, p. 52. A less spectacular but more sustained display of mainland hostility was provided some years later in the form of the customs blockade imposed on Hong Kong by the Canton authorities from 1867 to 1886.
28. For this episode, see Norman Miners, 'The Attempt to Assassinate the Governor in 1912', *JHKBRAS*, vol. 22, 1982, pp. 279–84. The assailant's father had been imprisoned for bribery in 1897, when May had been serving as Superintendent of Police. The ordinance had however provoked anger among the Hong Kong Chinese, who regarded it as an insult to the new Nationalist government in Canton. Indignation was vented in a boycott of the tram services which took place from November 1912 to January 1913. See Catron, 'China and Hong Kong', p. 13; Miners, *Hong Kong under Imperial Rule*, pp. 5–6.
29. A stoppage known as the Mechanics' Strike was staged in April 1920 by 9,000 skilled workers of the Chinese Engineers' Guild. The strike was notable insofar as it was the first large-scale, coordinated industrial protest in Hong Kong's history, and successful insofar as the participants managed to secure a wage increase from their various employers. But it was scarcely a major event by comparison with the two campaigns that followed. It did not develop into a general strike or bring the colony to a standstill. For details see Gillingham, *At the Peak*, p. 29; Miners, *Hong Kong under Imperial Rule*, pp. 9–10.

30. See Gillingham, *At the Peak*, pp. 34–8. 'Shit-tubs' or more literally 'Tower of Shit' was arrived at through a word-play on the official Chinese rendering of Stubbs's name. See Zhang Sheng, *Xianggang hei shehui huodong zhen xiang*, Hong Kong, 1979, p. 50.

31. Gillingham, *At the Peak*, pp. 33, 43–4.

32. Ibid., p. 15.

33. Miners, *Hong Kong under Imperial Rule*, p. 166.

34. See James Pope-Hennessy, *Half-Crown Colony: A Hong Kong Notebook*, London, 1969 pp. 128–36; Hoe, *Private Life*, pp. 219–20.

35. Quoted in Lethbridge, 'Caste, Class and Race', pp. 169–70.

36. Miners, *Hong Kong under Imperial Rule*, p. 129.

37. Gillingham, *At the Peak*, pp. 85, 122. Ironically the campaigns against these evils were led by the British. Most of the British officials and merchants in Hong Kong were indifferent; but shortly after the First World War concerns began to be voiced by some missionaries as well as by one or two independent-minded expatriate ladies. The agitation was then taken up by well-meaning crusaders in Britain.

38. Quoted in Lethbridge, 'Hong Kong under Japanese Occupation', pp. 86–7.

39. Quoted in Stephen Fisher, 'Eurasians in Hong Kong; A Sociological Study of a Marginal Group', M.Phil. thesis, University of Hong Kong, 1975, p. 78; Peter Hall, *In the Web*, privately published by author, Heswall, 1992, p. 118.

40. Lethbridge, 'Caste, Class and Race', p. 176; Henry J. Lethbridge, 'The Best of Both Worlds?'; *FEER*, 10 October 1968, p. 128; Fisher, 'Eurasians in Hong Kong', pp. 93, 105. In Somerset Maugham's *The Painted Veil* (1925), a novel set in Hong Kong, a character who tries to give an impression of effortless brilliance is described as being actually 'as industrious as a Eurasian clerk'. See Fisher, 'Eurasians in Hong Kong', p. 190.

41. Gillingham, *At the Peak*, p. 20. One contemporary observer however recorded that he 'looked and seemed to be less' than half Chinese. See Robert S. Ward, *Asia for the Asiatics?*, Chicago, 1945, p. 15.

42. Miners, *Hong Kong under Imperial Rule*, p. 82.

43. Frank H. H. King, *History of the Hongkong and Shanghai Banking Corporation*, vol. IV, Cambridge, 1991, p. 308.

44. Jean Gittins, *Eastern Windows, Western Skies*, Hong Kong 1969, pp. 9, 12; Gillingham, *At the Peak*, pp. 20–21; 'The Ho Tung Saga (Part 1)', *Hong Kong Inc.*, March 1990, pp. 104, 105–6. The names of the bungalows were The Chalet, Dunford and the Neuk. In 1916, while convalescing from a long illness, Ho Tung also succeeded in getting permission to be carried in his sedan chair through the whites-only Botanical Gardens. See 'The Ho Tung Saga (Part 1)', p. 102.

45. Grantham, *Via Ports*, p. 112; Robin Hutcheon preface to Hall, *In the Web*, p. xii.

46. Dan Waters, *Faces of Hong Kong*, London and New York, 1995, p. 141.

47. Professor Woo Sing-lim, *The Prominent Chinese in Hong Kong*, Hong Kong, 1937, p. 7.

48. Governor Caldecott to J. H. Thomas, Secretary of State for the Colonies, 19 February 1936, CO 129 556/17, p. 71; Hahn, *China to Me*, p. 328.

49. For the term 'gentry-merchants' (*shenshang*) see Sinn, *Power and Charity*, p. 87.

50. *SCMP*, 9 June 1938; T. C. Cheng, 'Chinese Unofficial Members of the Legislative and Executive Councils in Hong Kong up to 1941' *JHKBRAS* vol. 9, 1969, p. 24; interview with Mr Cyril Kotewall, Hong Kong, 26 June 1995.

51. *SCMP*, 9 June 1938; Gillingham, *At the Peak*, p. 39.

52. Severn to Kotewall, 17 November 1925, letter in the private papers of Mrs Helen Zimmern; *SCMP*, 9 June 1938; Woo, 'Prominent Chinese', pp. 5, 7; Cheng 'Unofficial Members', p. 22. The *SCMP* article links Kotewall's award explicitly to the 'services' which he rendered during the crisis of 1925–6.

53. Lindsay Ride, 'The Test of War' (Part 1), in Clifford Matthews and Oswald Cheung (eds), *Dispersal and Renewal: Hong Kong University during the War Years*, Hong Kong, 1998, p. 10.

54. For the Portuguese community see Leo d'Almada e Castro, 'Some Notes on the Portuguese in Hong Kong', *Instituto Portugues de Hong Kong*, Boletim no. 2, September 1949, pp. 265–76; Lethbridge, 'Caste, Class and Race', pp. 178–9.

55. d'Almada e Castro, 'Some Notes', p. 274; Gillingham, *At the Peak*, p. 38.

56. Phillip Bruce, *Second to None: The Story of the Hong Kong Volunteers*, Hong Kong, 1991, pp. 136–7, 169. See also d'Almada e Castro, 'Some Notes', p. 274. A certain number of Portuguese appear to have enlisted individually in the Corps as early as the time of the First World War. From July 1925 onwards Portuguese were enlisting in increasing numbers, and sanction for the formation of a Portuguese company was finally given in April 1927. The Police Reserve was established in 1927 at the suggestion of the Inspector-General of Police.

57. Miners, 'Localisation of the Hong Kong Police Force', p. 297. For an explicit pre-war statement of British policy see Winifred Wood, *A Brief History of Hong Kong*, Hong Kong, 1940, p. 273.

58. Lethbridge, 'Caste, Class and Race', p. 178. See also Hahn, *China to Me*, p. 218.

59. Reports of the Inspector-General of Police for 1930, 1931 and 1935.

60. For Kotewall role see *SCMP*, 9 June 1938. For Li's background and contribution, see Woo, 'Prominent Chinese', p. 15; Li Shu-fan, *Hong Kong Surgeon*, London, 1964, pp. 45–81.

61. Lecture given by Mr S. J. Chan at the Hong Kong Museum of History, 18 October 1995.

62. Kevin P. Lane, 'The Nationalist Government and the Struggle for Hong Kong's Return' in David Faure (ed.), *History of Hong Kong 1842–1984*, Hong Kong and London, 1995, pp. 103–4. See also Catron, 'China and Hong Kong', p. 25. The Manchu authorities had made a point of retaining a mini-enclave of their own within each of the various enclaves they leased to the European powers.

63. Lane, 'Nationalist Government', pp. 93, 97, 104. Raising the Walled City question with Governor Caldecott in 1936, Dr Philip K. Tyau, Chiang Kai-shek's special delegate for foreign affairs for Guangdong province, explained that 'even the Generalissimo' felt it 'necessary on occasion to bow to public opinion in Canton'.

64. A smaller British enclave, Weihaiwei on the coast of Shandong province in eastern China, had been handed back to the Nationalists in 1930 under the terms of an agreement reached at the Washington Conference of 1921–2.

65. Wang Tieya, '*Jiulong zujiedi wenti*' in Li Jinwei, *Xianggang bai nian shi*, Hong Kong, 1948, p. 102. The New Territories were regarded as being purely a matter for the British. See Steve Tsang, '*Taipingyang zhanzheng qijian Yingguo dui Xianggang zhengce miwen*' in *Xianggang Zhanggu*, vol. ix, Hong Kong, 1985, p. 101.

66. In March 1927 Clementi declared that His Majesty's Government had 'no intention of surrendering Hong Kong or of abandoning or diminishing in any way its rights or authority in any part of the adjacent mainland territories under British Administration', to the maintenance of which His Majesty's Government attached 'the highest importance'. Lane, 'Nationalist Government', p. 96. In 1927–8 Clementi proposed selling the leasehold of Crown land in the New Territories for a period extending beyond 1997, but was overruled by the Foreign Office and the Colonial Office legal adviser. Miners, *Hong Kong under Imperial Rule*, pp. 46–7. See also Robert Cottrell, *The End of Hong Kong: The Secret Diplomacy of Imperial Retreat*, London, 1993, pp. 20–4. Clementi speech quoted Gillingham, *At the Peak*, p. 145; Waters, *Faces of Hong Kong*, p. 200. For 1939 Treasury plan see Miners, *Hong Kong under Imperial Rule*, p. 288 note 53.

67. Quoted Gillingham, *At the Peak*, p. 7, Morris, *Hong Kong*, p. 67.

68. Percy Chen, *China Called Me: My Life inside the Chinese Revolution*, Boston and Toronto, 1979, p. 277; T. J. J. Fenwick, Chief Accountant, quoted in Frank H. H. King, *The History of the Hongkong and Shanghai Banking Corporation*, vol. iv, p. 36.

69. Cheng, 'Unofficial Members', p. 23; Gillingham, *At the Peak*, p. 46; Miners, *Hong Kong under Imperial Rule*, pp. 138–9. When the appointment was first proposed to Whitehall the reaction was one of considerable disquiet. The Colonial Office were doubtful that a Chinese could be trusted to observe the confidentiality of Executive Council business. In the end

the appointment was accepted; but later in the year Clementi was instructed on the insistence of the Foreign Office that secret telegrams sent to him should no longer be communicated to Executive Council members.

70. Caldecott to W. G. A. Ormsby-Gore, Secretary of State for the Colonies, 22 July 1936, CO 129 559/10, pp. 4–6; Pennefather-Evans, Interim Report; Russell Spurr, *Excellency*, Hong Kong, 1995, p. 166.

71. Quoted Hoe, *Private Life*, p. 196. The same kind of artificiality may be detected in the arrangements of the new Hong Kong branch of the Rotary Club, where throughout the 1930s the presidency alternated mechanically, a European holding the post one year and a Chinese or Eurasian the next. In functions at Government House, the role of the Aide-de-Camp was 'to mix the communities'. See Gillingham, *At the Peak*, p. 56.

72. Percy Chen, *China Called Me*, p. 277; George Wright-Nooth, *Prisoner of the Turnip-Heads*, London, 1994, p. 20. An expatriate who attended functions at Government House recalled that while on such special occasions you might have the rare opportunity of dancing with an upper-class Hong Kong Chinese girl 'you never asked them for a date because you would never have got one'. Gillingham, *At the Peak*, p. 56.

73. Interview with Mrs Margaret Watson Sloss, Oxford, 3 March 1994. See internment diary of Assistant Superintendent Lance Searle, 21 August 1942; Grantham, *Via Ports*, p. 104; G. B. Endacott, *Hong Kong Eclipse*, edited with additional material by Alan Birch, Hong Kong, 1978, p. 320.

74. For cost-cutting aspect, see Ho, 'A Hundred Years of Hong Kong', chapter III, part 3, pp. 16–17; Miners, *Hong Kong under Imperial Rule*, pp. 83–4. Caldecott himself does not seem to have felt any great sense of urgency. In the same letter in which he submitted to the Colonial Office his proposal for introducing Chinese sub-inspectors to the police force, he also wrote that while 'exceptionally able' Chinese sub-inspectors might eventually rise through the post of inspector to the commissioned rank of Assistant Superintendent, it was 'not considered desirable at present to hold out such prospects, or necessary at this stage to make recommendations as to the salary of an officer who will not in any case be appointed for at least 21 years to come'. Caldecott to Ormsby-Gore, 22 July 1936, CO 129 559/10, p. 5.

75. Pennefather-Evans, Interim Report. For the continued reluctance to 'localize' see also Miners, *Hong Kong under Imperial Rule*, p. 84; Gillingham, *At the Peak*, p. 11.

76. Gillingham, *At the Peak*, p. 85. Wood, *Brief History of Hong Kong*, p. 275.

77. See Miners, *Hong Kong under Imperial Rule*, pp. 207–77 and specifically pp. 227–8, 232, 264, 270–1, 276.

78. Wright-Nooth, *Prisoner of the Turnip-Heads*, p. 98; conversation with Dr David Faure, Hong Kong, 9 December 1995 and letter from Dr Faure, 18 November 2002.

79. See Peel cables to Secretary of State for the Colonies, 24 July and 14 August 1931, CO 129 535/3, pp. 85, 95; Shaftain, Rough Draft for Proposed Articles, pp. 15–16; Dick Wilson, *Hong Kong! Hong Kong!*, London, 1990, pp. 98–9.

80. David Paton, *RO, The Life and Times of Bishop Ronald Hall of Hong Kong*, Hong Kong, 1985, pp. 54, 80, 84, 211, 212.

81. Sydney Caine, the Financial Secretary in the Hong Kong government in the late 1930s, commented on the Bishop's concern with agricultural indebtedness in the New Territories and south China that he 'interested himself in many things besides religion'. When the Bishop visited Guangxi province in the same connection a year later Caine observed that Guangxi was now 'almost the principal field of his activities' and that there were 'reports, fortunately apocryphal' that he was 'contemplating moving his Cathedral there'. See Caine letters to G. L. M. Clauson, 3 March 1938 and 24 April 1939, CO 129 572/11, pp. 13, 18.

82. Interview conducted by Dr Steve Tsang with David MacDougall, 26 February 1987, pp. 63–4.

83. Interview with Mr Charles Sin, Hong Kong, 29 June 1995.

84. Governor Stubbs reported in 1920 that the pure-bred Hong Kong Chinese habitually referred to the Eurasians as 'the Bastards'. See Miners, *Hong Kong under Imperial Rule*, p. 128. For Chinese disdain for Eurasians see also Fisher, 'Eurasians in Hong Kong', p. 81; 'The Ho Tung Saga (Part 1)', p. 99.

85. Interview with Mr Charles Sin, 29 June 1995.

86. Woo, 'Prominent Chinese', p. 13; Cheng, 'Unofficial Members', p. 25.

87. Gittins, *Eastern Windows*, p. 15, and Jean Gittins, *Stanley: Behind Barbed Wire*, Hong Kong, 1982, p. 12.

88. Man Wah Leung Bentley, 'Remembrances of Times Past: The University and Chungking' in Matthews and Cheung (eds), *Dispersal and Renewal*, pp. 105–6. Rayson Huang, who would serve decades later as Vice-Chancellor of the University, noted similarly that the professor of Mathematics, Walter Brown, was 'one of the few teachers who took a personal interest in his students' – ibid., p. 117.

89. Gillingham, *At the Peak*, p. 130.

90. Quoted in Nakajima Mineo, *Honkon: utsuriyuku toshi kokka*, Tokyo, 1985, p. 127. Lau Ti's article, '*Xianggang de wu yue ershiyi ri*', was published in Mao Dun (ed.), *Zhongguo de yi ri: yi jiu san liu nian wu yue ershiyi ri*, Pingfanshe, Beijing, 1984.

91. Miners, *Hong Kong under Imperial Rule*, p. 166.

92. See Fujii Hiroaki, 'Japan and Hong Kong in Historical Perspective' and Ren Wenzheng, '*Shijiu shiji Gang Ri jiaotong wanglai shilüe*', in Tam Yue-him (ed.), *Hong Kong and Japan: Growing Cultural and Economic Interactions, 1845–1987*, 25th Anniversary Commemorative Volume of the Japan Society of Hong Kong, Hong Kong, 1988, pp. 103, 107, 109–10.

93. Fujii Hiroaki, 'Japan and Hong Kong', p. 103; *HKN*, 2 March 1942. For Japanese strategists in the decades before the Second World War 'the South' was a specific term referring to South-east Asia. I have accordingly capitalized the word South where appropriate throughout the book.

94. On 14 October 1854, just a year after Perry's arrival in Edo, Admiral Sir James Stirling concluded a convention with Japan which 'laid the basis' for Hong Kong–Japanese trade. See E. J. Eitel, *Europe in China*, Hong Kong, 1983, pp. 343–4.

95. Fujii Hiroaki, 'Japan and Hong Kong', p. 103; Morris, *Hong Kong*, pp. 173–4. Jardine Matheson and Butterfield and Swire were also quick to set up operations in Japan. See Morris, *Hong Kong*, pp. 107, 170.

96. Ren, '*Shijiu shiji Gang Ri*', pp. 112–13.

97. For the Kitazato mission see *HKN*, 30 May 1942 and 8 August 1945; Li, *Hong Kong Surgeon*, p. 68; Morris, *Hong Kong*, p. 107; Tam Yue-him, '*Xianggang Riben guanxi da shi nianbiao chu gao (1845–1945)*' in Tam Yue-him (ed.), *Hong Kong and Japan: Growing Cultural and Economic Interactions*, p. 166. Tam dates Kitazato's visit to a subsequent outbreak of bubonic plague which took place in the colony in 1901; but this dating is in conflict with all other sources. The honour of identifying the plague bacillus was also claimed by a Swiss pathologist, Dr Alexandre Yersin, who worked in the colony at the same time as Kitazato. Kitazato however is said to have discovered the bacillus a few days earlier than his Swiss competitor.

98. Interview given by Fujita Ichiro, retired manager of the Hong Kong branch of Mitsui Bussan, *Aji-ken Nyusu*, vol. 5 no. 10, Tokyo October 1984, p. 25; Woo, 'Prominent Chinese', p. 21; Sinn, *Bank of East Asia*, pp. 7, 14; Ching, *The Li Dynasty*, p. 42; interviews with Sir Yuet-keung Kan (Sir Y. K. Kan), Hong Kong, 24 May 1995, and Mr Okada Akira, chairman of the Japan–Hong Kong Society, Tokyo, 6 September 1995.

99. See Tse Wing-kwong, *Zhanshi Ri jun zai Xianggang baoxing*, Hong Kong, 1991, pp. 222–3 and *Xianggang kang Ri fengyun lu*, Hong Kong, 1995, p. 85. For Count Otani see also Mark R. Peattie, '*Nanshin*: The "Southward Advance" 1931–1941, as a Prelude to the Japanese Occupation of South-east Asia', in Peter Duus, Ramon H. Myers and Mark R. Peattie (eds), *The Japanese Wartime Empire*, Princeton, 1996, pp. 234–5.

100. For accounts of the Jinan massacre see Edwin P. Hoyt, *Japan's War: The Great Pacific Conflict*, New York, 1986, pp. 63–5; Tse, *San nian*, pp. 54–5.

101. Empire-building in China was not the sole motive for the Manchurian operation. The Army were also keen to secure Manchuria as a bulwark against a perceived threat from the Soviet Union. See Hayashi Saburo in collaboration with Alvin D. Coox, *Kogun: The Japanese Army in the Pacific War* (reprinted), US Marine Corps Association, Quantico, Va., 1989, p. 13.

102. Tam, '*Xianggang Riben guanxi da shi nianbiao*', p. 166. These celebrated Peking demonstrations of 1919 gave rise to the May the Fourth Movement for a political and cultural renaissance in China.

103. Nakajima, *Honkon*, p. 125. The writer was Ishikawa Tatsuzo, and the incident is described in his essay, '*Honkon yosei*' ('Night Thoughts in Hong Kong') of 12 April 1930. It is possible that the graffiti may have been inspired in part by public outrage over a local issue – the harassment of Hong Kong Chinese fishing vessels by Japanese ones, which is said to have started in the course of this year. See Tam, '*Xianggang Riben guanxi da shi nianbiao*', p. 166; Tse, *Zhanshi Ri jun*, p. 223.

104. See report by E. O. Wolfe, Inspector-General of Police, dated 15 October 1931 on Anti-Japanese Disturbances, 23 to 28 September 1931, CO 129 536/6, pp. 26–39.

105. Quoted G. R. Sayer, *Hong Kong 1862–1919: Years of Discretion*, Hong Kong, 1975, p. 120.

106. Peel statement to the Legislative Council on Anti-Japanese Agitation, 1 October 1931, CO 129 536/6, pp. 58, 59, 62.

107. Wolfe report 15 October 1931, Peel telegram to J. H. Thomas, Secretary of State for the Colonies, 28 September 1931, and dispatch to Thomas, 16 October 1931, CO 129 536/6, pp. 24, 37, 78–9. In his 16 October dispatch Peel noted that the Hong Kong government had proscribed a trades union which was 'known to be actively fomenting disaffection (*sc.* against the British) in connection with the anti-Japanese movement'.

108. Peel telegram to Thomas, 28 September 1931, CO 129 536/6, p. 79. In his statement to the Legislative Council of 1 October 1931 Peel noted similarly that the 'more responsible Chinese citizens' most strongly 'reprobated' what had happened. He added that the Chinese Council members had loyally kept a promise they had made to consult regularly during the crisis with the Secretary for Chinese Affairs, 'giving great assistance to the authorities'. Ibid., pp. 58–9, 60.

109. Dispatch from Sir Archibald Clark Kerr, British ambassador, Shanghai, to Lord Halifax, Foreign Secretary, 16 March 1939, FO 371 23516, pp. 246–9, 257–9. The original list was prepared on 27 February by J. C. Hutchison, Commercial Secretary to the Hong Kong government, with a supplement added on 7 March.

110. Article by Lady Drummond Hay in *The Egyptian Gazette*, 11 March 1938.

111. This agreement had followed the December 1936 kidnapping of Chiang Kai-shek by the 'Young Marshal' Zhang Xueliang at Xi'an (the 'Xi'an Incident').

112. Catron, 'China and Hong Kong', p. 26; Yuan Bangjian, *Xianggang shilüe*, Hong Kong, 1988, p. 163; Kwan, *Ri zhan shiqi de Xianggang*, pp. 110–11; Tse, *Xianggang kang Ri*, p. 127. Liao Chengzhi is said to have been the Party's 'eyes and ears' in the colony at this period. Wilson, *Hong Kong! Hong Kong!*, p. 28.

113. Tse, *Xianggang kang Ri*, pp. 127–30. Of the three intelligence outfits two were attached respectively to the offices of the Eighth Route Army and the North-eastern Anti-Japanese United Army, while the third was a Soviet intelligence station. The names of the two agents were Pan Hannian and Dong Hui.

114. Jung Chang with Jon Halliday, *Mme Sun Yat-sen*, London, 1986, p. 92. See also Yuan, *Xianggang shilüe*, p. 164; Chan Lau Kit-ching, *China, Britain and Hong Kong*, Hong Kong, 1990, p. 266.

115. Examples were the *Da Gong Bao* (The Impartial), the official government paper, and the *Guomin Ribao* (National Times), which was published by the Nationalist Department of Propaganda. Sa Kongliao, *Xianggang lunxian riji*, Beijing, 1985, pp. 8, 22. Hong Kong had been a centre of Chinese journalism ever since the late nineteenth century. See Paul A. Cohen, *Between Tradition and Modernity: Wang Tao and Reform in Late Ch'ing China*, Harvard, 1974, pp. 73–81.

116. Xia Yan, '*Liao Chengzhi zai Xianggang*' in Lu Yan et al. (eds), *Xianggang Zhanggu*, vol. VII, Hong Kong, 1984, pp. 154, 156.

117. Northcote secret dispatch to Malcolm Macdonald, Secretary of State for the Colonies, 13 February 1939, FO 371 23516, pp. 56–7.

118. Memorandum of R. A. C. North, Secretary for Chinese Affairs, enclosed in Northcote dispatch to Secretary of State for the Colonies, 22 January 1938, CO 129 572/6, p. 34.

119. Miners, *Hong Kong under Imperial Rule*, pp. 54–5, 293 n. 38. One or two non-Europeans had in fact managed to establish themselves on the Peak *without* official permission. See Hahn, *China to Me*, p. 231.

120. Chan Lau, *China, Britain and Hong Kong*, p. 266. In May 1941, similarly, serious thought was given to expelling Du Yuesheng after the discovery of another illicit radio station through which 'Big-Eared Du' had been transmitting messages to Chungking. On this occasion, however, the authorities were dissuaded from taking action by Colonel S. K. Yee, who intervened at the direct behest of Chiang Kai-shek. See cypher telegram from Northcote to Secretary of State for the Colonies, 19 May 1941, minutes of A. W. Scott and Sir John Brenan of the Foreign Office 28 and 29 May 1941, cypher telegrams from Northcote to Sir Archibald Clark Kerr, British ambassador in Chungking, 29 May 1941 and Clark Kerr response to Northcote, 12 June 1941, FO 371 27719, pp. 2–2 (verso), 3–4, 8, 11.

121. Catron, 'China and Hong Kong', pp. 69, 325 n. 4.

122. Sa, *Xianggang lunxian riji*, p. 84; Tse, *Xianggang kang Ri*, pp. 72–5; Kwan, *Ri zhan shiqi de Xianggang*, pp. 23–4.

123. Sir Selwyn Selwyn-Clarke, *Footprints*, Hong Kong, 1975, pp. 5–6, 52, 55–6, 59; Hahn, *China to Me*, p. 222; Hoe, *Private Life*, pp. 266–71.

124. Hoe, *Private Life*, p. 271; interview with Mrs Margaret Watson Sloss, 3 March 1994. See also Hahn, *China to Me*, p. 274.

125. For Emily Hahn background see Hahn, *China to Me*, pp. 233–4, 257–8, 283, 321; Morris, *Hong Kong*, p. 111; Hoe, *Private Life*, pp. 271–2, 276. The two other Soong sisters were Mme Chiang Kai-shek and Mme H. H. Kung.

126. Hahn, *China to Me*, pp. 222–3; Selwyn-Clarke, *Footprints*, p. 58; Hoe, *Private Life*, pp. 266, 271.

127. Gillingham, *At the Peak*, p. 172. Such views were also current at this time in official British circles. See Richard J. Aldrich, *Intelligence and the War against Japan: Britain, America and the Politics of Secret Service*, Cambridge, 2000, pp. 106–7.

128. W. H. Auden sonnet, 'Hong Kong', from W. H. Auden, *Collected Poems*, London, 1976, p. 144.

129. Leeming, 'Earlier Industrialization of Hong Kong', p. 339. The official Blue Book for 1940 gives a total of only 1,142 factories; but Leeming has drawn on the Chinese language *Gang Ao shangye fenlei hangminglu* (*Hong Kong and Macao Business Classified Directory*) for the same year. See also Wong, *Emigrant Entrepreneurs – Shanghai Industrialists in Hong Kong*, Hong Kong, 1988, p. 18; Yuan, *Xianggang shilüe*, pp. 160–1. Among the larger factories was the Ngau Tsai Wan Rubber Factory in Kowloon, which had about 500 Shanghainese and 2,000 Cantonese workers. A number of major factories had sprung up in Tsuen Wan, a town in the New Territories which was by this time industrializing at a considerable rate. They included the South China Iron Works, a concern owned by the Chinese Nationalist government, and the Beautiful Asia Silk Weaving Factory, one of the biggest plants of its kind in China. See Searle diary, 9 April 1943; WKYP, 26 August 1945; ZB, 19 April 1946. For textile weaving in Prince Edward Road see Sa, *Xianggang lunxian riji*, pp. 160–1.

130. See *SCMP/HKT*, 10 October 1945.

131. Xia, '*Liao Chengzhi zai Xianggang*', p. 156. See also Sa, *Xianggang lunxian riji*, p. 84; Tse, *Xianggang kang Ri*, p. 70.

132. Tse, *Xianggang kang Ri*, p. 118.

133. Comment of W. W. Yen (Yan Huiqing), quoted Tse, *Xianggang kang Ri*, pp. 76–7. Tse observes that the Japanese *Honkon Nippo* as well as the English-language press was spared the attentions of the censors.

134. Much difficulty was experienced, for instance, by the left-wing journalist Zou Taofen in finding a sponsor for his projected periodical *Da Zhong Shenghuo* (Life of the Masses). The sponsor finally found for the *Hua Shang Bao* was Deng Wentian, the comprador of the Sino-Belgian Bank, who happened conveniently to be a cousin of Liao Chengzhi, the local

Communist Party chief. See Xia, '*Liao Chengzhi zai Xianggang*', pp. 157, 158–60; Kwan, '*Ri zhan shiqi de Xianggang*' p. 111. The title *Hua Shang Bao* was suggested by Liao Chengzhi himself.

135. Hahn, *China to Me*, p. 37. The name of the mainland politician was Tang Liangli. Tang was an aide to the Chinese puppet leader Wang Jingwei (see p. 35, below).

136. Boeicho Boei Kenshusho (ed.), *Senshi sosho, Honkon-Chosha sakusen*, Tokyo, 1971, pp. 10–11. In 1932, following Japan's occupation of Manchuria, a British government defence committee had decided to abandon the policy of non-fortification in the Far East which had been agreed on with the Japanese and United States governments at the Washington conference of 1921–2.

137. See, for example, Chan Lau, *China, Britain and Hong Kong*, pp. 290–1. In relative terms, however, as Professor Chan notes, Hong Kong was a more important conduit of military supplies to China than any other (including the Burma Road) up until early 1939.

138. *Honkon-Chosha sakusen*, p. 4. According to one observer in the colony the proportion of China's total imports passing through Hong Kong doubled in 1940. See Endacott and Birch, *Hong Kong Eclipse*, pp. 23–4.

139. Accounts of the peace movement in the Japanese Army in China and the influence of Ishiwara Kanji may be found in Mark R. Peattie, *Ishiwara Kanji and Japan's Confrontation with the West*, Princeton, 1975, pp. 322–6; Kobayashi Hideo and Shibata Yoshimasa, *Nippon gunseika no Honkon*, Tokyo, 1996, pp. 58–9. For Operation Kiri (also known as Operation Paulownia), see Hong Kong Special Branch (Japanese Section) Quarterly Summary of Japanese Activities Fourth Quarter of 1940, 7 January 1941 and First Quarter of 1941, 15 April 1941, FO 371 27621, pp. 8 and 11 (verso); Louis Allen, *The End of the War in Asia*, London, 1976, pp. 225–7; Usui Katsumi, 'The Politics of War', in James William Morley (ed.), *The China Quagmire: Japan's Expansion on the Asian Continent 1933–1941*, New York, 1983, pp. 407–16; Tse, *Xianggang kang Ri*, pp. 154–68.

140. *Honkon-Chosha sakusen*, p. 13.

141. Reminiscence of M. Takeda, manager of the Hong Kong branch of Osaka Shosen Kabushiki Kaisha, quoted in *HKN*, 29 October 1942.

142. *Honkon-Chosha sakusen*, p. 13. For prevalence of this catchphrase see also Hayashi and Coox, *Kogun: The Japanese Army in the Pacific War*, p. 265; Hoyt, *Japan's War*, p. 205; Aldrich, *Intelligence and the War against Japan*, p. 106.

143. *Honkon-Chosha sakusen*, p. 11.

144. Reports from R. McP. Austin, British consul, Dairen, to R. H. Clive, British chargé d'affaires, Tokyo, 24 December 1935, and from Clive to Anthony Eden, Foreign Secretary, 7 January 1936, confidential letter from Governor Caldecott to W. G. A. Ormsby-Gore, Secretary of State for the Colonies, 2 April 1937, and attached report of Inspector-General of Police, and letter from G. C. Pelham, Trade Commissioner, Hong Kong, 8 June 1937, enclosing intelligence report by Hong Kong Special Branch, CO 129 562/23, pp. 7–11, 12–14, 15–16, 17–18. See also Northcote to Ormsby-Gore, 10 February 1938, FO 371 22153, pp. 166–8, and Special Branch Quarterly Summary of Japanese Activities Fourth Quarter of 1938, 6 January 1939, FO 371 23516, pp. 241–2; Gillingham, *At the Peak*, p. 169.

145. Special Branch Quarterly Summary of Japanese Activities Third Quarter of 1940, 9 October 1940, FO 371 27621, pp. 3, 4; John Luff, *The Hidden Years*, Hong Kong, 1967, p. 4; Gillingham, *At the Peak*, pp. 169, 171.

146. Special Branch Quarterly Summary of Japanese Activities Fourth Quarter of 1938, 6 January 1939, and Second Quarter of 1939, 12 July 1939, FO 371 23516, pp. 242, 268; Li, *Hong Kong Surgeon*, p. 94; Tse, *Xianggang kang Ri*, p. 87.

147. Special Branch Quarterly Summary of Japanese Activities Fourth Quarter of 1938, 6 January 1939, and First Quarter of 1939, 12 April 1939, FO 371 23516, pp. 242, 243–4, 253–4; Third Quarter of 1940, 9 October 1940, Fourth Quarter of 1940, 7 January 1941, and First Quarter of 1941, 15 April 1941, and Monthly Report on Japanese Activities August 1941, 11 September 1941, FO 371 27621, pp. 5, 6, 7, 9, 11 (verso), 12.

148. Emily Hahn, *Hong Kong Holiday*, New York 1946, p. 242; Gillingham, *At the Peak*, p. 169; Tse, *Xianggang kang Ri*, p. 86. Other Japanese agents embedded in the community included an 'electric and hand massage expert' named Miss Takamura, a jeweller in the Queen's Arcade and a Mr Mizuno who ran a sports shop in Wanchai. Mizuno subsequently turned out to be an army lieutenant. See Kevin Rafferty, *City on the Rocks: Hong Kong's Uncertain Future*, London, 1989, p. 137; Oliver Lindsay, *The Lasting Honour*, London, 1978, p. 28; Wright-Nooth, *Prisoner of the Turnip-Heads*, p. 52.

149. Special Branch Quarterly Summary of Japanese Activities First Quarter of 1941, 15 April 1941, FO 371 27621, pp. 11 and 11 (verso).

150. See Shaftain, 'Rough Draft', p. 10; Special Branch Quarterly Summary of Japanese Activities Second Quarter of 1941, 15 July 1941, and Monthly Report on Japanese Activities July 1941, 12 August 1941, and August 1941, 11 September 1941, FO 371 27621, pp. 19, 22, 30–1. These Taiwanese would mostly have spoken the Minnan dialect.

151. *Honkon-Chosha sakusen*, p. 11. See also Phyllis Harrop, *Hong Kong Incident*, London, 1943, p. 92; Luff, *Hidden Years*, p. 5. The Japanese are for good measure said to have had a British military communications chart showing telephone junctions, details of the exact number and quality of the British and other Allied troops, and information relating to the British ammunition, transport and artillery positions.

152. Tim Carew, *The Fall of Hong Kong*, London 1960, p. 28.

153. *Honkon-Chosha sakusen*, p. 13. The Army Ministry were also involved in the person of Colonel Iwaguro Goyu, head of the Military Affairs Section.

154. The Koa Kikan was a branch of the Tokumu Kikan, the Army's Special Service Organization. Earlier names for it included the Asia Development Board and the China Affairs Board. See Special Branch Quarterly Summary of Japanese Activities Third Quarter of 1940, 9 October 1940, and First Quarter of 1941, 15 April 1941, and Second Quarter of 1941, 15 July 1941, FO 371 27621, pp. 3 (verso)–4, 11 (verso), 20 (verso).

155. The Chinese edition, *Heung Gong Yat Po*, had first appeared as early as 1932. The English edition, *Hong Kong News*, followed in 1939. See Special Branch Quarterly Summary of Japanese Activities Second Quarter of 1939, 12 July 1939, and Third Quarter of 1939, 5 October 1939, FO 371 23516, pp. 268, 296–7; ibid. Third Quarter of 1940, 9 October 1940, and First Quarter of 1941, 15 April 1941, and Monthly Report on Japanese Activities July 1941, 12 August 1941, and August 1941, 11 September 1941, FO 371 27621, pp. 5, 12, 16 (verso)–17, 27; Lethbridge, 'Hong Kong under Japanese Occupation', p. 98 n. 1.

156. For Triad numbers in Hong Kong see Searle diary, 28 January 1943; Shaftain, 'Rough Draft', p. 10; *Honkon-Chosha sakusen*, p. 14; Wright-Nooth, *Prisoner of the Turnip-Heads*, p. 48. The British police estimated the Triad membership in Kowloon as 300,000 and in the colony as a whole as 450,000; but these figures seem fantastically high given that the entire population of Hong Kong at this time came to no more than 1.8 million.

157. For the foregoing see Special Branch Quarterly Summary of Japanese Activities Third Quarter of 1940, 9 October 1940, FO 371 27621, pp. 4, 5 (verso); *Honkon-Chosha sakusen*, p. 14; Tse, *Xianggang kang Ri*, pp. 97–8.

158. Special Branch Quarterly Summary of Japanese Activities First Quarter of 1939, 12 April 1939, FO 371 23516, pp. 254–5. See also Ozawa Seiichi, '*Diedu Xianggang zhi xing*' (Chinese translation by Lü Fang) in *Shijie Zhanwang* no. 1, Hankou, March 1938.

159. Special Branch Monthly Report on Japanese Activities July 1941, 12 August 1941, FO 371 27621, p. 17 (verso); *Honkon-Chosha sakusen*, p. 14; Tse, *Xianggang kang Ri*, p. 97.

160. *Honkon-Chosha sakusen*, pp. 14–15; Tse, *Xianggang kang Ri*, p. 98.

161. *Honkon-Chosha sakusen*, p. 12; Nakajima, *Honkon*, p. 130; Kobayashi Hideo, '*Taiheiyo sensoka no Honkon: Honkon gunsei no tenkai*', published in Komazawa University, Tokyo Economic Association, *Keizaigaku Ronshu*, vol. 26, no. 3, December 1994, pp. 210–11.

162. Sa, *Xianggang lunxian riji*, p. 69.

163. In June 1940 the 21st Army occupied the border town of Shenzhen, completely sealing off the colony on the land side, and in July an invasion seemed imminent. See *Honkon-Chosha sakusen*, pp. 15–16; Yuan, *Xianggang shilüe*, pp. 166–7.

164. *Honkon-Chosha sakusen*, p. 16. This Japanese source maintains that the invasion was halted 'at the beginning of September' as a result of 'the situation in Europe, the occupation of northern French Indochina and so forth'. However Japanese troops only crossed the border into French Indochina on 22 September; and it was only on 28 September that (following the Battle of Britain) the Navy general staff submitted a memorandum to the Imperial Cabinet in Tokyo stating that Britain had weathered the Nazi onslaught. It would therefore seem either that the order to halt the invasion was issued at the end rather than the beginning of September, or that it was issued at the beginning of September in intelligent anticipation rather than in response to events. The invasion of French Indochina like the planned attack on Hong Kong was intended in part as a method of cutting the supply routes to Chiang Kai-shek. See Hayashi and Coox, *Kognn: The Japanese Army in the Pacific War*, p. 26.

165. Report of Phyllis Harrop to Foreign Secretary Eden 7 April 1942, CO 129 590/23, p. 190; Lindsay, *Lasting Honour*, p. 60; Endacott and Birch, *Hong Kong Eclipse*, p. 81.

166. Tse, *Xianggang kang Ri*, p. 87. A continual stream of reports on Japanese espionage were compiled by the Special Branch of the Hong Kong police and forwarded by the Hong Kong authorities to the Colonial Office, which in turn passed them on to other departments in Whitehall. A Foreign Office staffer minuted on the report for the first quarter of 1939, 'The summary is quite dispassionate, and from it one might suppose that the Hong Kong Government remain unperturbed by this ceaseless Japanese activity.' Minute of 16 May 1939 on Special Branch Quarterly Summary of Japanese Activities First Quarter of 1939, FO 371 23516, p. 250.

167. Special Branch Quarterly Summary of Japanese Activities Fourth Quarter of 1940, 7 January 1941, and Monthly Report on Japanese Activities August 1941, 11 September 1941, FO 371 27621, pp. 9 (verso), 33. See also Gillingham, *At the Peak*, p. 171. Gillingham claims that Suzuki was left at large in the colony right up till the end of November 1941, leaving of his own accord a mere two weeks before the Japanese invasion. This assertion however is contradicted by the series of Special Branch reports. The latter state clearly that Suzuki was declared *persona non grata* and recalled to Tokyo on 30 December 1940, and that by August 1941 he was back in Tokyo working at General Staff Headquarters. See also Tse, *Xianggang kang Ri*, p. 165.

168. Selwyn-Clarke, *Footprints*, pp. 58, 62. In April 1938 the then garrison commander in Hong Kong, Major-General A. W. Bartholomew, had expressed similar views in a message sent to the War Office. 'I have . . . made it clear', he wrote, 'that troops must resist with arms any sudden attack on themselves or their charge, *but this is not to apply to any properly organised and authoritative request by a military command to enter the concessions.*' Quoted in Lindsay, *Lasting Honour*, p. 2. A precedent for the 'open city' scenario was set the following year in another part of China when Japanese forces were allowed to enter the British and French concessions in Tianjin (Tientsin). See Dick Wilson, *When Tigers Fight: The Story of the Sino-Japanese War 1937–45*, London, 1982, p. 159.

169. Quoted in Selwyn-Clarke, *Footprints*, p. 184; Endacott and Birch, *Hong Kong Eclipse*, p. 56; Edwin Ride, *British Army Aid Group: Hong Kong Resistance 1942–1945*, Hong Kong, 1981, p. 5; Oliver Lindsay, *At the Going Down of the Sun*, London, 1981, p. 51; Morris, *Hong Kong*, p. 242.

170. Minute by Colonel L. C. Hollis of Offices of the War Cabinet to Churchill embodying memorandum of the Chiefs of Staff, 10 September 1941, and letter from Hollis to J. C. Sterndale-Bennett of the Foreign Office, 4 October 1941, FO 371 27622, pp. 222–222 (verso), 223–4; Lindsay, *Lasting Honour*, p. 7; Kwan, *Ri zhan shiqi de Xianggang*, p. 15. Hollis's minute notes that Churchill concurred with the memorandum provided Eden had no objection.

171. Minute by Sterndale-Bennett of the Foreign Office, 6 October 1941, FO 371 27622, p. 221. According to an agreement reached at Singapore in April 1941 Hong Kong was to be given a more active role as an advanced *United States* naval base. Endacott and Birch, *Hong Kong Eclipse*, p. 59.

172. Hollis minute to Churchill, 10 September 1941 and memorandum from Patrick Browne of the War Office to Sterndale-Bennett of the Foreign Office, 22 October 1941, FO 371 27622, pp. 224, 254–254 (verso). See also Ko Tim Keung and Jason Wordie, *Ruins of War: A Guide to Hong Kong's Battlefields and Wartime Sites*, Hong Kong, 1996, p. 19.
173. Selwyn-Clarke, *Footprints*, p. 58.
174. For a description of Young see reminiscence of Joyce Bassett, secretary to the Governor, quoted in Alan Birch and Martin Cole (eds), *Captive Christmas*, Hong Kong, 1979, p. 6. Description confirmed in private letter to the author from the Governor's grandson, Mr Tim Young, 2 February 1994.
175. Lindsay, *Lasting Honour*, pp. 16, 23; Morris, *Hong Kong*, p. 243.
176. Recollection of Tim Fortescue, Private Secretary to the Governor, quoted Birch and Cole, *Captive Christmas*, p. 88; Hahn, *China to Me*, p. 256. Emily Hahn noted that 'it was all planned down to the last ridiculous detail'.
177. For the Bachelor Husbands agitation see letter from Major-General E. F. Norton, Officer Administering the Government, to Lord Lloyd, Secretary of State for the Colonies, 18 December 1940 enclosing petition from the Evacuation Representation Committee, confidential memorandum from Governor Northcote to Edward Gent, Assistant Under-Secretary at the Colonial Office, 8 July 1941, letters from Northcote to Lord Moyne, Secretary of State for the Colonies, 12 August 1941, and from Governor Young to Moyne, 24 October 1941 with attached correspondence and letter from Mrs. A. H. Elston to Churchill, 1 July 1941, CO 129 589/18, pp. 10–23, 30–4, 40–2, 48, 50–4; Harrop, *Hong Kong Incident*, pp. 63–4.
178. Extract from Northcote letter to Gent, 8 September 1941, CO 129 590/18, p. 7.
179. Woo, 'Prominent Chinese', p. 5.
180. Lethbridge, 'Hong Kong under Japanese Occupation', pp. 87–8.
181. Report of Legislative Council debate, 27 July 1939, CO 129 582/12, p. 21; Lethbridge, 'Hong Kong under Japanese Occupation', p. 93; Fisher, 'Eurasians in Hong Kong', p. 114. At the end of 1939, similarly, it emerged that European air-raid wardens were getting paid HK$8 a day, while their Chinese counterparts were only receiving HK$1.50. Endacott and Birch, *Hong Kong Eclipse*, p. 50.
182. Quoted Lethbridge, 'Hong Kong under Japanese Occupation', p. 93; Fisher, 'Eurasians in Hong Kong', p. 114.
183. Quoted Lethbridge, 'Hong Kong under Japanese Occupation', p. 92. Possibly with a view to keeping the gentry 'on side', the Colonial Office made a number of efforts over the following year to identify havens where the colony's Eurasians, Portuguese and Anglicized Chinese might be taken in. Destinations investigated ranged from Macao and Singapore to Fiji and Mauritius. See telegrams from Secretary of State for the Colonies to Governor of Mauritius, 15 February 1941, from Young to Moyne, 2 December 1941, and from Moyne to Sir Shenton Thomas, Governor of the Straits Settlements, 4 December 1941, FO 371 27622, pp. 104, 306, 308. See also Endacott and Birch, *Hong Kong Eclipse*, p. 17.
184. Hahn, *China to Me*, p. 217.
185. Hahn, *Hong Kong Holiday*, pp. 18–19, 43.
186. Letter from H. L. Mars addressed to Prime Minister Churchill, 28 September 1942, CO 129 590/25, p. 15. Mars appears to have been a Nationalist intelligence agent who following the outbreak of the Pacific War also offered his services to the British. One Western witness noted that the gentry were 'rarely highly regarded' by the mass of the Hong Kong Chinese. Ward, *Asia for the Asiatics?*, p. 14.
187. Harrop, *Hong Kong Incident*, p. 142. See also Mars letter to Churchill, 28 September 1942, CO 129 590/25; Sa, *Xianggang lunxian riji*, p. 7.
188. Ward, *Asia for the Asiatics?*, p. 65; Lethbridge, 'Hong Kong under Japanese Occupation', pp. 110–11; Tse, *San nian*, p. 64. According to Tse, Lau had served at one point as Vice Minister of Railways in the Chinese Nationalist government. Although one or two of the wealthier Hong Kong Chinese such as Sir Shouson Chow and Dr Li Shu-fan had a background in mainland government service (see pp. 10 and 15 above), it seems unlikely that the same would be true of the relatively obscure banker Lau Tit-shing. I suspect that Tse may be

confusing Lau Tit-shing with an unconnected mainland politician of the same name (Liu Tiecheng in Mandarin).

189. For Chan Lim-pak background see Ward, *Asia for the Asiatics?*, pp. 64–5; Lethbridge, 'Hong Kong under Japanese Occupation', p. 110; Sterling Seagrave, *The Soong Dynasty*, London 1996, pp. 193–4; Kwan, *Ri zhan shiqi de Xianggang*, p. 12; Tse, San nian, pp. 64–5.

190. Testimony of Joseph Richards, trial of Joseph Richards, HK RS 245-2-150. For Richards pre-war connection with the Japanese, see also Special Branch Quarterly Summary of Japanese Activities Fourth Quarter of 1938, 6 January 1939, FO 371 23516, p. 241; Special Branch Quarterly Summary of Japanese Activities First Quarter of 1941, 15 April 1941, and Second Quarter of 1941, 15 July 1941, and Monthly Report on Japanese Activities August 1941, 11 September 1941, FO 371 27621, pp. 11, 20, 32.

191. Special Branch Quarterly Summary of Japanese Activities first Quarter of 1941, 15 April 1941, and Second Quarter of 1941, 15 July 1941, and Monthly Report on Japanese Activities July 1941, 12 August 1941, and August 1941, 11 September 1941, FO 371 27621, pp. 12 (verso), 18 (verso), 28, 31; testimony of Ushikawa Shigeto and Shibata Kiyoshi, trial of Joseph Carroll, HKRS 245-2-208. Carroll, who had a 'Eurasian appearance', appears to have been of Irish stock on his father's side and of Chinese stock on his mother's. His mother eventually settled in Cuba. At his post-war trial he indignantly denied suggestions that he had Japanese blood.

192. Special Branch Quarterly Summary of Japanese Activities Third Quarter of 1940, 9 October 1940, and First Quarter of 1941, 15 April 1941, and Monthly Report on Japanese Activities August 1941, 11 September 1941, FO 371 27621, pp. 5, 12 (verso), 27, 31; Kwan, *Ri zhan shiqi de Xianggang*, p. 11. Other Eurasian malcontents included Charles Percival Archer alias Sidney Gidney, alias Jimmy Murphy, whom the police described as 'a known bad character and associate of the Japanese'. A British ex-schoolmaster named Darrell Drake was reported in August 1941 to be working as 'a sort of foreign "relations" officer' for Japan's Domei News Agency.

193. The British census conducted in March 1941 gave the total number of Indians in the colony as 7,379. See *FEER*, 29 January 1947; Barbara-Sue White, *Turbans and Traders: Hong Kong's Indian Communities*, Hong Kong, 1994, p. 36. This figure apparently included the Indian troops who formed part of the garrison. Figures given by the local Indians for the size of their community shortly after the Japanese take-over were in the 4,000 to 5,000 range. These totals presumably excluded the garrison troops, who had by then been interned. See *HKN*, 24 and 26 February 1942.

194. One leading dissident who took refuge in Tokyo at this early date was Rash Behari Bose (see p. 94 below). Bose went on to found the Japan branch of the Indian Independence League. See Lieutenant-General Fujiwara Iwaichi, *F. Kikan: Japanese Army Intelligence Operations in South-east Asia during World War II*, trans. Akashi Yoji, Heinemann Asia, Hong Kong, Kuala Lumpur and Singapore, 1983, p. 324 n. 55; Allen, *End of the War in Asia*, p. 133; Lethbridge, 'Hong Kong under Japanese Occupation', pp. 121–2.

195. Fujiwara, *F. Kikan*, pp. 3–6; Allen, *End of the War in Asia*, pp. 133–4; Miners, 'Localisation of the Hong Kong Police Force', p. 310; Wright-Nooth, *Prisoner of the Turnip-Heads*, p. 37. According to Lieutenant-General Fujiwara this episode represented the first establishment of contact by the Japanese Army with the Indian Independence League. Other Sikh defectors appear to have remained in Canton, where in the summer of 1941 a 'Japanese Muslim' named Sakuma was reported to be lecturing to 'disaffected British Indians'. Special Branch Quarterly Summary of Japanese Activities Second Quarter of 1941, 15 July 1941, FO 371 27621, p. 21 (verso).

196. Hahn, *China to Me*, p. 233.

197. See Tse, *Xianggang kang Ri*, pp. 48–50. In addition to the *Nan Hua Ribao*, the Wang faction published three other subsidiary newspapers, viz. the *Ziyou Ribao* (Freedom Daily), the *Tianyan Ribao* (Evolution Daily) and the *Xin Wan Ribao* (New Evening Daily). The *Nan Hua Ribao* had been founded by Wang's followers as early as 1930.

198. Lindsay, *Lasting Honour*, p. 28; Wright-Nooth, *Prisoner of the Turnip-Heads*, p. 33, 41. Fear of such infiltration was apparently a significant factor in the British introduction of immigration controls. See Gent to Sterndale-Bennett, 21 August 1941, Sterndale-Bennett to Gent

10 September 1941 and Secretary of State for the Colonies to Young, 13 September 1941, FO 371 27622, pp. 178, 180 (verso), 216.

199. For these various figures see Searle diary, 27 December 1942; Hahn, *China to Me*, pp. 349, 392; Luff, *Hidden Years*, p. 204; Wright-Nooth, *Prisoner of the Turnip-Heads*, p. 156. Howard Tore also went by the Chinese name of Tse Liang.

200. Report of Manager of the Taikoo Dockyard and Engineering Company Hong Kong to John Swire and Sons Ltd., 16 May 1941, letter from J.R. Masson of Butterfield and Swire to Gent of the Colonial Office 26 June 1941, telegram no.636 of Governor Northcote to Secretary of State for the Colonies 5 July 1941 and minute of W. B. L. Monson of the Colonial Office 15 July 1941, CO 129 590/13, pp. 2, 5, 6–8, 9–12.

201. Wright-Nooth, *Prisoner of the Turnip-Heads*, p. 48; Tse, *Xianggang kang Ri*, p. 99.

202. Alan Birch article in *SCMP*, 22 January 1978; Endacott and Birch, *Hong Kong Eclipse*, p. 49; Tse, *Xianggang kang Ri*, p. 99. The leaflets were found in Shaukeiwan, Saiyingpun, Yaumati and Kowloon.

203. Endacott and Birch, *Hong Kong Eclipse*, pp. 64–5; Birch and Cole, *Captive Christmas*, p. 1. For Kipling comments see Rudyard Kipling, *From Sea to Sea*, New York, 1906, p. 326. Porcupine quotation from British newsreel 'Gibraltar of the East', shown as part of documentary *Under the Rising Sun* on TVB Pearl, Hong Kong, 13 December 1991.

204. Frank H. H. King, *History of the Hongkong and Shanghai Banking Corporation*, vol. III, p. 571. The cheerful prognosis offered by Young and Maltby was presumably based on reports of Churchill's dispatch of the two battleships *Prince of Wales* and *Repulse* to the Far East in November 1941.

205. Li, *Hong Kong Surgeon*, pp. 91–2.

206. Letter from Lieutenant-Colonel F. C. Scott of the War Office to Gent of the Colonial Office, 22 August 1941, FO 371 27622, p. 185.

207. Wright-Nooth, *Prisoner of the Turnip-Heads*, p. 38. See also Endacott and Birch, *Hong Kong Eclipse*, pp. 55, 62. We are told that because there were not enough administrative officers to go round in the civil establishment, qualified local recruits 'had temporarily to be brought in'.

208. The earliest sign of Chinese Nationalist interest in forging an anti-Japanese partnership with the British in Hong Kong actually pre-dated the outbreak of full-scale war between Japan and China in 1937. On a visit to Canton in September 1936 Chiang Kai-shek invited Governor Caldecott to meet him there and proceeded to sound out the Governor on the possibility of British cooperation in defensive measures against a hypothetical Japanese attack on southern China. Caldecott fended off the overture by pointing out that he was responsible solely for the internal affairs of Hong Kong: he could not therefore enter into any commitment on wider issues. See Miners, *Hong Kong under Imperial Rule*, pp. 24–5.

209. Tse, *Xianggang kang Ri*, p. 173; Chan Lau, *China, Britain and Hong Kong*, pp. 294, 398 n. 9. The Nationalist approaches were made on 22 March and 5 May 1939.

210. Lindsay, *Lasting Honour*, p. 5; Endacott and Birch, *Hong Kong Eclipse*, p. 65.

211. See Harrop, *Hong Kong Incident*, p. 69; *Gang Ao xunguo lieshi jiniance*, pamphlet published by the Nationalist Party Headquarters in Hong Kong and Macao, 1946, p. 5; Hahn, *China to Me*, pp. 228–9; Endacott and Birch, *Hong Kong Eclipse*, p. 65; *Honkon-Chosha sakusen*, p. 7; Alan Birch article in *SCMP*, 29 January 1978; Lindsay, *Going Down of the Sun*, p. 6; Brian G. Martin, *The Shanghai Green Gang*, London, 1996, p. 187–8; Aldrich, *Intelligence and the War against Japan*, pp. 280–1. Chan Chak had commanded the First Fleet of Guangdong province in 1931, at a time when Guangdong was for all practical purposes an independent state. He was sent to Hong Kong in October 1938 by the Nationalist government together with Colonel S. K. Yee, who served subsequently as his right-hand man. The name of the trade union official was Jiang Qingbai. Zhang Zilian was not a member of Big-Eared Du's Shanghai mob, the Green Gang, but had been enlisted in an 'Endurance Club' set up by Du and functioned as the principal link between Du and the Triads.

212. Record of conversations of Maj-Gen L.E. Dennys with Gen Shang Zhen, Director of Office of the Military Affairs Committee, and colleagues 30 July and 6 August 1941, *Zhonghua Minguo zhongyao shiliao chu bian, dui Ri kangzhan shiqi di san bian, zhanshi waijiao (2)*,

Taipei, 1981, pp. 165–75; Lindsay, *Lasting Honour*, p. 5; *Honkon-Chosha sakusen*, p. 8; Tse, *Xianggang kang Ri*, p. 174.

213. Relations between the Hong Kong authorities and the Nationalist government, we are told, were 'never happy: they were shot through with suspicion, misunderstanding and imagined slights'. David MacDougall, 'Notes on the Siege of Hong Kong', 23 April 1942, CO 129 590/25, p. 228.

214. Chan Chak, '*Xiezhu Xianggang kangzhan ji shuai Ying jun tuwei zong baogao*', *Zhanggu Yuekan* no. 4, December 1971, p. 15.

215. Article by Alan Birch, *SCMP*, 12 October 1975.

216. Tse Wing-kwong, *Xianggang lunxian*, Hong Kong, 1995, p. 171. Tse indicates that the initial approaches which led to these two rounds of talks were made by the British. Liao Chengzhi subsequently sent reports on the talks to Mao Zedong and Zhou Enlai in Yan'an. The talks also touched on the possibility of British teamwork with the East River guerrillas – a topic which was brought up again, more urgently, in early December (see p. 50 below).

217. See report of Major Ronald Holmes, to Major Egerton Mott 12 July 1944 'The New Territories of Hong Kong and The Coastal Waters and the Seaboard of Mirs Bay and Bias Bay', pp. 15–16, HS 1/171; Selwyn-Clarke, *Footprints*, p. 76; Yuan, *Xianggang shilüe*, p. 177; *Gang Jiu Duli Dadui shi*, Guangzhou, 1989, p. 8; Tse, *Xianggang lunxian*, p. 172. According to Yuan, this third round of talks was initiated by the guerrillas, who had observed that the 23rd Army was moving south to strike at the colony and had decided to offer the British their services. All other sources, however, both Chinese and British, appear to agree that these talks (like the previous ones in October and November) were sought by the British side. With invasion looming over them, the Hong Kong authorities had brought themselves to the verge of supping with the devil: the problem was that they were only prepared to dip their spoons in about half an inch.

218. Lindsay, *Lasting Honour*, p. 24; Wright-Nooth, *Prisoner of the Turnip-Heads*, p. 40. The Communists also noted the apparent persistence of British 'illusions': see *Dadui shi*, p. 8.

219. Quoted in Carlos Baker, *Ernest Hemingway: A Life Story*, New York, 1969, p. 364.

220. Quoted in Endacott and Birch, *Hong Kong Eclipse*, p. 329. See also Hahn, *China to Me*, p. 245.

221. Original quoted in Kwan, *Ri zhan shiqi de Xianggang*, p. 21. A more literal translation would be 'The carp will return to the ocean/And the hundred years of glory will fade like a dream'.

222. Lindsay, *Lasting Honour*, p. 32. For general Chinese apprehension see Kwan, *Ri zhan shiqi de Xianggang*, p. 23.

223. Di Chen, '*Huiyizhong de yi nian*', *Xin Dong Ya* vol. I no. 5, December 1942, p. 69.

224. *HKN*, 29 March 1942; letter from William Wright of Dodwell and Co. to G. Dodwell in Watford, 3 September 1942, and memorandum of W. B. L. Monson of the Colonial Office, 1 October 1942, CO 129 590/24, pp. 8, 132; Gittins, *Eastern Windows*, p. 133; Tse, *San nian*, p. 62.

225. 'The Ho Tung Saga (Part 1)', p. 105; interview with Dr Stanley Ho, Hong Kong, 27 September 1995.

226. Interview, Mrs Margaret Watson Sloss, 3 March 1994; diary of Dr Isaac Newton, 7 December 1941, quoted in Birch and Cole, *Captive Christmas*, p. 5; report of Lieutenant-Colonel L. Ride, 'On the Conditions in Hong Kong Subsequent to the Surrender and on the Events which Led Up to My Escape from the POW Camp in Shamshuipo', CO 129 590/25, p. 203; Luff, *Hidden Years*, p. 15; Yuan, *Xianggang shilüe*, p. 168; Kwan, *Ri zhan shiqi de Xianggang*, p. 23.

227. Lindsay, *Lasting Honour*, pp. 25, 199.

2. The Debacle

1. Diary of Constance Murray, 8 December 1941. Constance Murray was a member of the Hong Kong government's Senior Clerical and Accounting Staff.

2. Fujii Kingo, '*Xianggang bianjing chongpo ji*' (Chinese translation by Lu Yu) in *Xin Dong Ya*, vol. 1, no. 1, August 1942, p. 85.

3. I am following here the figure given for the British garrison by David MacDougall, who was head of the Hong Kong government's Information Bureau when the Japanese struck, and subsequently cited in the official British war history. See MacDougall, 'Notes on the Siege', CO 129 590/25, pp. 228–9; S. Woodburn Kirby, *The War Against Japan*, vol. 1, London, 1957, p. 114. If the Hong Kong Volunteers and other auxiliaries are included, however, the figure for the defending force can be brought up to 13,000–14,000. See Ko and Wordie, *Ruins of War*, Appendix 2, p. 210; Tony Banham, www.hongkongwardiary.com. For the initial Japanese attacking strength see testimony of Colonel Noma, trial of Colonel Noma Kennosuke, WO 235/999, p. 331; Kwan, *Ri zhan shiqi de Xianggang*, p. 29. These 15,000 troops represented approximately two thirds of the Japanese unit deployed in the invasion, the 38th Division of the 23rd Army. With a force totalling 23,228, the 38th Division in turn represented about one third of the 23rd Army's total strength (see p. 65 below).

4. Selwyn-Clarke, *Footprints*, p. 184. The British naval force consisted of one destroyer, four gunboats, eight motor torpedo boats, seven auxiliary patrol vessels and an auxiliary craft used for minesweeping.

5. Lindsay, *Lasting Honour* p. 45. The force on the Gin Drinkers' Line consisted of three battalions, the 2 Royal Scots, 2/14 Punjabis and 5/7 Rajputs.

6. Kipling, 'The Song of the Cities', ll.23–4 in Rudyard Kipling, *The Complete Verse*, London, 1990, p. 143. My italics. Hong Kong with her sister colonial cities is addressing Britannia: Hong Kong's message is

> Hail, Mother! Hold me fast: my Praya sleeps
>> Under innumerable keels today.
> Yet guard (and landward), or tomorrow sweeps
>> Thy warships down the bay!

For the original apprehension which prompted this verse, see Kipling, *From Sea to Sea*, pp. 326, 331–2.

7. Quoted in MacDougall, 'Notes on the Siege', CO 129 590/25, p. 226.

8. Quoted in Lindsay, *Lasting Honour*, p. 42.

9. *SCMP*, 10 December 1941, quoted in Rafferty, *City on the Rocks*, p. 138.

10. War diary of Colonel Doi Teihichi, 9 December 1941, quoted in Lindsay, *Lasting Honour*, p. 48.

11. Tang Hai '*Xianggang lunxian ji*' in Ye Dewei et al. (eds), *Xianggang lunxian shi*, Hong Kong, 1984, p. 182; Ward, *Asia for the Asiatics?*, p. 22. The formal proclamation was made by Governor Young at a joint session of the Executive and Legislative Councils.

12. MacDougall, 'Notes on the Siege', CO 129 590/25, p. 224; Tang Hai, '*Xianggang lunxian ji*', and Chen Jitang, '*Xianggang tuoxian ji*' in Ye Dewei et al. (eds), *Xianggang lunxian shi*, pp. 190, 302; Sa, *Xianggang lunxian riji*, p. 3. See also War Diary of the Hong Kong Police compiled by L. H. C. Calthrop, Senior Superintendent of Police, Kowloon, 10 December 1941, p. 21; report by Assistant Superintendent Lance Searle, Sub-Area no.4 Commander of Police Action covering from 0200 hours on 8 December 1941 to 0200 hours on 12 December 1941, 29 August 1942; report by Sergeant Charles Hedley of the Hong Kong Police Force, 9 February 1944, CO 129 591/4, p. 21.

13. Tang Hai, '*Xianggang lunxian ji*', p. 189; Sa, *Xianggang lunxian riji*, pp. 13–14.

14. Searle report, 29 August 1942.

15. Tang Hai, '*Xianggang lunxian ji*', p. 190; Sa, *Xianggang lunxian riji*, pp. 32, 34. The rumours were substantiated by the appearance of a stream of wounded British soldiers who were getting ferried back to Kowloon from the front. See Di Chen, '*Huiyizhong de yi nian*', p. 72.

16. Diary of Dr Kenneth Uttley, 8 December 1941.

17. War Diary of the Hong Kong Police, 8 and 9 December 1941, pp. 4, 14, 17 and Preface to War Diary by John Pennefather-Evans, Commissioner of Police, 29 October 1942, p. 1; Di Chen, '*Huiyizhong de yi nian*', p. 71; Tse, *Xianggang lunxian*, p. vii.

18. War Diary of the Hong Kong Police, 9 December 1941, pp. 13–14.
19. Sa, *Xianggang lunxian riji*, pp. 39-40; Selwyn-Clarke, *Footprints*, p. 65.
20. War Diary of the Hong Kong Police, 11 December 1941, pp. 26–7, 29.
21. Ibid., p. 33; Uttley diary, 11 December 1941. The police reports speak of crowds of 200 to 300 Chinese: Uttley however refers to a mob of over 2,000 looters.
22. Tang Hai, '*Xianggang lunxian ji*', p. 197; diary of Dr Isaac Newton, 11 December 1941, quoted in Birch and Cole, *Captive Christmas*, p. 29.
23. See Fr Thomas Ryan, *Jesuits Under Fire in the Siege of Hong Kong, 1941*, London and Dublin 1944, p. 47; interview by Kevin Sinclair with Chan Pak, former waiter at the Peninsula Hotel, *SCMP*, 7 December 1991. The Chinese term was *shengli you* (Cantonese *shinglei yau*), literally 'Friends of Victory'.
24. For this incident, see Tang Hai, '*Xianggang lunxian ji*', p. 197; Ko and Wordie, *Ruins of War*, p. 167. British sources note that a contingent of the Winnipeg Grenadiers had been assigned to guard the northern approach to Kowloon. See Lindsay, *Lasting Honour*, p. 50.
25. Commodore, Hong Kong telegram no. 697 to Admiralty 13 December 1941 Fo 371 27752, p. 42; Maltby dispatch to Secretary of State for War quoted Birch and Cole, *Captive Christmas*, p. 34.
26. War Diary of the Hong Kong Police 11 December 1941, p. 33.
27. Tang Hai, '*Xianggang lunxian ji*', p. 197; Sa, *Xianggang lunxian riji*, p. 38; War Diary of the Hong Kong Police, 12 December 1941, p. 38. See also Ward, *Asia for the Asiatics?*, p. 26.
28. Sa, *Xianggang lunxian riji*, pp. 31–2, 37. See also MacDougall, 'Notes on the Siege', CO 129 590/25, p. 213. MacDougall reported having heard a rumour of the tram and bus strikes: he did not know if the rumour was well-founded, but suspected that it was.
29. MacDougall, 'Notes on the Siege', CO 129 590/25, p. 221; Hahn, *Hong Kong Holiday*, p. 77.
30. MacDougall, 'Notes on the Siege', CO 129 590/25, p. 221; Sa, *Xianggang lunxian riji*, pp. 28–9, 37; Ward, *Asia for the Asiatics?*, p. 32. MacDougall was inclined to suspect a direct fifth column intervention behind this cash shortage. Sa and Ward by contrast maintained that the small notes and coins were being hoarded by the Hong Kong Chinese public, possibly in response to Japanese leaflets which had been dropped announcing that after the fall of the colony notes in denominations higher than HK$10 would no longer be accepted. In any event the effect was to disrupt the economy.
31. Pennefather-Evans, Preface to War Diary of the Hong Kong Police, 29 October 1942; MacDougall, 'Notes on the Siege', CO 129 590/25, p. 224; Sa, *Xianggang lunxian riji*, pp. 14, 46; Endacott and Birch, *Hong Kong Eclipse*, p. 77.
32. Tang Hai, '*Xianggang lunxian ji*', p. 198. Phyllis Harrop remarked in her diary, 'We are afraid to shell Kowloon for fear of frightening the Hong Kong [Island] Chinese into riots. . . . The situation is impossible.' Harrop diary, 11 December 1941, CO 129 590/23, p. 192.
33. At the combined meeting of the Executive and Legislative Councils which was held on the afternoon of 8 December Governor Young called on the gentry to pledge the loyalty of the Hong Kong Chinese population. A pledge of support was duly given by M. K. Lo on behalf of the Hong Kong Chinese. See *HKN*, 8 December 1942; Ward, *Asia for the Asiatics?*, p. 22.
34. Mishima Bunpei, '*Chizhu youju ji*' (Chinese translation by Shen Yixu) in *Xin Dong Ya*, vol. 1, no. 1, August 1942, pp. 93–4; Di Chen, '*Huiyizhong de yi nian*', pp. 70–1; Sa, *Xianggang lunxian riji*, pp. 1–3; Searle report, 29 August 1942; Ward, *Asia for the Asiatics?* p. 33; Chan Chak, '*Xiezhu Xianggang kangzhan*', p. 16.
35. War Diary of the Hong Kong Police, 10 and 11 December 1941, pp. 20, 32, 35; Chan Chak, '*Xiezhu Xianggang kangzhan*', p. 16.
36. Shaftain, 'Rough Draft', p. 10. 'Having them shot' is the original phrase in Shaftain's typescript: he subsequently deleted this and replaced it with the more anodyne 'dealing with them'.
37. Provision for this deployment had been made in an Internal Security Scheme drawn up by the police before the outbreak of war. See Pennefather-Evans, Preface to War Diary of the Hong Kong Police, 29 October 1942, p. 1.

38. Sa, *Xianggang lunxian riji*, p. 31. Sir Shouson Chow and the members of the Li and Kan families who with him controlled the Bank of East Asia are said to have taken refuge in the Bank's vaults. See Sinn, *Bank of East Asia*, pp. 64–5; Ching, *The Li Dynasty*, p. 105.

39. Tang Hai, '*Xianggang lunxian ji*', p. 196; Shaftain, 'Rough Draft', p. 10.

40. Pennefather-Evans, Preface to the War Diary of the Hong Kong Police, 29 October 1942, p. 1.

41. Harrop, *Hong Kong Incident*, p. 69.

42. See Chan Chak, '*Xiezhu Xianggang kangzhan*', pp. 15–16. An abbreviated account of these Nationalist activities was given by the Admiral immediately after his escape from Hong Kong at the end of the month. See '*Chen Ce zongtan tuwei ji Gang zhan*', *Da Guang Bao*, 31 December 1941, cutting filed in Nationalist Party archives, Yangmingshan, Taipei, 523/137.

43. War Diary of the Hong Kong Police, 11 December 1941 and Pennefather-Evans, Preface to War Diary, 29 October 1942, p. 2; Shaftain, interview in *China Mail*, 6 October 1945 and 'Rough Draft', p. 10; Russell Clark, *An End to Tears*, Sydney, 1946, p. 91.

44. Shaftain, 'Rough Draft', p. 11. See also Chan Chak, '*Xiezhu Xianggang kangzhan*', p. 16. Chan Chak in his account makes no reference to Shaftain, but reports being approached by Police Commissioner Pennefather-Evans.

45. This account of the negotiations between the British and the Triads is based on Shaftain, 'Rough Draft', p. 11–14, and Chan Chak, '*Xiezhu Xianggang kangzhan*', p. 16. Shaftain appears to have been under the impression that all of his interlocutors (except presumably Yee and Zhang) were gangsters directly involved in plotting the massacre. To judge from Chan Chak's account, however, the persons who attended the two meetings on the Chinese side were either members of the Nationalist 'shadow government' or gangland go-betweens who had been chosen to deal with the real conspirators. It has sometimes been suggested that the Triad chiefs were simply trying to alarm the British into paying them protection money, and that no massacre was in fact being planned. See, for example, Alan Birch article in *SCMP*, 5 February 1978. Such an impression is not however conveyed by Chan Chak's account, which states unambiguously that the Triads were 'plotting to make insurrection' and that news of this had reached the Nationalist leaders even before the British made contact with them. Grim as the British predicament was, the deal struck by Zhang with Shaftain implies clearly that Zhang and his colleagues were banking on an eventual Allied victory and a restoration of British rule in Hong Kong.

46. See Chan Chak, '*Xiezhu Xianggang kangzhan*', pp. 16–17, 18, 21, and interview '*Chen Ce zongtan tuwei ji Gang zhan*', *Da Guang Bao*, 31 December 1941; Yun Yan, '*Riben qin'gong Xianggang shi zhi Zhongyi Cishanhui*', in *Zhanggu Yuekan* no. 11 July 1972, pp. 50–1. According to Yun the association had already been established on 10 December. Chan Chak apparently intended it to form part of a larger ABCD Corps (Hong Kong), ABCD referring to the new alliance of America, Britain, China and the Dutch East Indies which had been created by the Japanese lunge to the South.

47. See '*Chen Ce zongtan tuwei ji Gang zhan*', *Da Guang Bao*, 31 December 1941; Chan Chak, '*Xiezhu Xianggang kangzhan*', p. 21; Tang Hai, '*Xianggang lunxian ji*', p. 202; Sa, *Xianggang lunxian riji*, p. 44; MacDougall, 'Notes on the Siege', CO 129 590/25, p. 222; Tsang interview with MacDougall, p. 18.

48. MacDougall, 'Notes on the Siege', CO 129 590/25, pp. 221–2; Sa, *Xianggang lunxian riji*, p. 37; Ward, *Asia for the Asiatics?*, p. 32. See also Frank H. H. King, *History of the Hongkong and Shanghai Banking Corporation*, vol. III, p. 572. The Nationalist authorities in Chungking were apparently not notified of this overprinting before the fall of the colony, and reacted with 'great indignation' when they found out about it. Memorandum of G. L. Hall-Patch, British adviser Chungking, to N. E. Young at the Treasury, London, 21 October 1942, FO 371 31717.

49. MacDougall, 'Notes on the Siege', CO 129 590/25, p. 223; Ward, *Asia for the Asiatics?*, p. 36.

50. Harrop, *Hong Kong Incident*, pp. 74, 75.

51. MacDougall, 'Notes on the Siege', CO 129 590/25, pp. 222, 227.

52. Lindsay, *Going Down of the Sun*, p. 6; Morris, *Hong Kong*, p. 278; interview with the late Professor Charles Boxer, Little Gaddesden, Hertfordshire, 19 January 1994. A short Chinese biography of Chan Chak makes it clear that in fact he was busily engaged in Sun Yat-sen's service throughout the First World War, and that his leg was amputated in a Hong Kong hospital. The operation had been made necessary by a sclerosis of the blood vessels. See editors' preface to Chan Chak, 'Xiezhu Xianggang kangzhan', *Zhanggu Yuekan*, no.4, December 1971, p. 14.

53. Quoted Lindsay, *Lasting Honour*, p. 50.

54. Report of Lieutenant-Colonel L. Ride 'On the Conditions in Hong Kong', CO 129 590/25, p. 203.

55. MacDougall, 'Notes on the Siege', CO 129 590/25, p. 216.

56. Chan Chak, 'Xiezhu Xianggang kangzhan', p. 15.

57. Maltby secret cypher telegram no.1758 to War Office, 13 December 1941, FO 371 27752.

58. Tang Hai, 'Xianggang lunxian ji', p. 201; MacDougall, 'Notes on the Siege', CO 129 590/25, p. 218; Captain Freddie Guest, *Escape from the Bloodied Sun*, London, 1956, p. 39. See also Lindsay, *Lasting Honour*, p. 63. According to Tang Hai the news was released in the Hong Kong Hotel 'on the eve of the fall of Kowloon', and Lindsay similarly dates the announcement to 12 December, just before the last British troops were pulled out from the Devil's Peak peninsula on the mainland. This seems to indicate that word of the Nationalist advance had already been received (and passed on) by the British before Chan Chak's detailed information reached Maltby on 13 December.

59. *Honkon-Chosha sakusen*, p. 198.

60. Tang Hai, 'Xianggang lunxian ji', p. 211.

61. MacDougall, 'Notes on the Siege', CO 129 590/25, p. 217.

62. Ibid.; report of William Poy enclosed in letter to Colonial Office from C. K. Ledger, British Consul-General in Lourenço Marques, 31 July 1942, CO 129 590/25.

63. Gwen Priestwood, *Through Japanese Barbed Wire*, London, 1943, p. 15.

64. Diary of Regimental Sergeant-Major E. C. Ford, RA, 15 December 1941, quoted Birch and Cole, *Captive Christmas*, p. 71.

65. Harrop, *Hong Kong Incident*, p. 79.

66. I have followed here the conventional story which has been handed down in Japan and appears with slight permutations in the British secondary sources. See Lindsay, *Lasting Honour*, p. 72; Birch and Cole, *Captive Christmas*, p. 45; Wilson, *When Tigers Fight*, p. 189. According to one Japanese account the exploit was more limited: Masujima crossed the harbour by himself, in a sampan rather than swimming, and simply reconnoitred one landing site in Shaukeiwan. Nakajima, *Honkon*, pp. 131–2. Whatever the precise truth it seems clear at least that a daring reconnaissance did take place, and that Masujima was the central figure.

67. Report of William Poy, CO 129 590/25; Tang Hai, 'Xianggang lunxian ji', p. 217; Harrop, *Hong Kong Incident*, p. 81; Lindsay, *Lasting Honour*, p. 76.

68. Copy of MacDougall letter to Mrs Cathie MacDougall, 17 January 1942, p. 1, MacDougall papers, Rhodes House.

69. Searle diary, 2 September 1942.

70. Young dispatch to Secretary of State, Colonial Office, 23 December 1941, and Commodore, Hong Kong telegrams nos 737 and 741 to Admiralty, 22 and 23 December 1941, FO 371 27752; Chan Chak, 'Xiezhu Xianggang kangzhan', p. 18; Sa, *Xianggang lunxian riji*, p. 66; Endacott and Birch, *Hong Kong Eclipse*, p. 115. Chan Chak and Sa give earlier dates for the severance of the power supplies, viz. 18 and 20 December.

71. Harrop, *Hong Kong Incident*, p. 141.

72. MacDougall dispatch to Colonial Office introducing report of Lieutenant-Colonel L. Ride, 29 May 1942, CO 129 590/25, p. 193. See also *Daily Mail*, London, 12 January 1942, cutting filed in CO 129 590/23, p. 277. For a positive Chinese impression of these facilities see Chan Chak interview, 'Chen Ce zongtan tuwei ji Gang zhan', *Da Guang Bao*, 31 December 1941, and Chan Chak, 'Xiezhu Xianggang kangzhan', p. 18; Tang Hai, 'Xianggang lunxian ji', pp. 216,

220. A more critical account of the air-raid shelters is given by Sa, *Xianggang lunxian riji*, pp. 6, 26, 56.

73. Li, *Hong Kong Surgeon*, pp. 102–3. The Jesuit Fr Thomas Ryan confirms that there was 'some starvation for a few days'. Ryan, *Jesuits Under Fire*, p. 108.

74. Sa, *Xianggang lunxian riji*, p. 6.

75. Report of P. Biau, Technical Counsellor, Free French Equatorial Africa, 16 May 1942, CO 129 590/23, p. 69.

76. MacDougall, 'Notes on the Siege', CO 129 590/25, p. 225.

77. Young cable to Secretary of State for the Colonies, Most Secret, Most Immediate, 21 December 1941, FO 371 27752.

78. Winston S. Churchill, *The Second World War*, vol. III, London, 1950, p. 562.

79. For official British thinking on these lines, see letter from the Director of Military Operations to the Chief of the General Staff, London, 21 December 1941, quoted in Lindsay, *Lasting Honour*, pp. 132–3.

80. Quoted in ibid, p. 66.

81. Quoted in Selwyn-Clarke, *Footprints*, p. 65; Lindsay, *Lasting Honour* p. 203.

82. Birch and Cole, *Captive Christmas*, p. 131. It would appear however that the Governor was also issued at some point with a 'discretion' to be used 'when effective resistance was no longer possible'. See Young dispatch to Colonial Office cited in note 83 below.

83. Young dispatch to Secretary of State for the Colonies, 28 December 1941, memorized by Lieutenant-Commander Shepherd, relayed by Shepherd to the Colonial Office and enclosed with Gent report of 8 October 1942, CO 129 590/25, p. 65.

84. Interview with Tim Fortescue quoted Birch and Cole, *Captive Christmas* p. 145.

85. Internment diary of Franklin Gimson, 7 October 1943; report of Lieutenant-Colonel L. Ride, 'On the Conditions in Hong Kong', CO 129 590/25, p. 203.

86. Memoir of Gwen Priestwood quoted in Lindsay, *Lasting Honour*, p. 132; Selwyn-Clarke, *Footprints*, p. 184.

87. Quoted in MacDougall, 'Notes on the Siege', CO 129 590/25, p. 218.

88. Lindsay, *Lasting Honour* p. 93. Other students enrolled as surgeons, medical orderlies and stretcher bearers at the University Relief Hospital to replace the numerous personnel who deserted their posts in the early stages of the fighting. See Gittins, *Eastern Windows*, p. 126 and *Stanley: Behind Barbed Wire*, p. 23; L. Ride, 'The Test of War (Part 1)', Bernard Mellor, 'Strains of War and the Links Break', Gordon King, 'An Episode in the History of the University' and Guan Bee Ong, 'Dispersal and Renewal: Hong Kong University Medical and Health Services' in Matthews and Cheung (eds), *Dispersal and Renewal*, pp. 14–15, 71, 86, 390.

89. Hahn, *Hong Kong Holiday*, p. 167; Peter Hall, *In the Web*, pp. 123, 163; Clifford Matthews, 'Life Experiences: From Star Ferry to Stardust' in Matthews and Cheung (eds), *Dispersal and Renewal*, p. 232. The No.3 (Eurasian) Company, which suffered losses almost as massive, was particularly mentioned for its 'superb gallantry' in Maltby's official dispatch on the campaign. Letter from Mr Donald Malcolm, *Daily Telegraph*, London, 30 April 1990.

90. Tang Hai, 'Xianggang lunxian ji', p. 201.

91. Harrop, *Hong Kong Incident*, p. 80; see also Fan Jiping, 'Xianggang zhi zhan huiyilu', *Da Ren* no. 8, December 1970, p. 5.

92. Pennefather-Evans, Preface to War Diary of the Hong Kong Police, 29 October 1942, p. 1.

93. War Diary of the Hong Kong Police, 16 December 1941, p. 48; Mishima, 'Chizhu Youju Ji' p. 109.

94. Sa, *Xianggang lunxian riji*, p. 76; diary of Regimental Sergeant-Major E. C. Ford, RA, 23 December 1941, quoted Birch and Cole, *Captive Christmas*, p. 148. One hundred of the 250 Indian volunteers at the headquarters of the Hong Kong Volunteer Defence Corps were declared by one source to have gone to ground in the air-raid shelters for all of five days. See report of P. Biau, Technical Counsellor, Free French Equatorial Africa, 16 May 1942, CO 129 590/23, p. 70.

95. Statement of Major-General Shoji Toshishige, 18 November 1946, trial of Major-General Shoji Toshishige, WO 235/1015. One Japanese source stated that there had been a 'wholesale surrender of Indians along the Tai Hang Road', and a Japanese memoir refers to the 'Indian troops and civilians taken in by us'. See report of William Poy, CO 129 590/25, p. 78; Ishita Ichiro, '*Xianggang gonglüe zhan ji*' (Chinese translation by He Bingren) in *Xin Dong Ya*, vol. 1, no. 1, August 1942, p. 88. In addition to pan-Asiatic exhortations the Japanese leaflets also contained an offer of protection to those individuals who surrendered with them, and this will obviously have been the decisive factor for many. See specimen shown in E. Ride, *British Army Aid Group*, plate no. 4 between pp. 224 and 225.

96. Report on Operations of 2nd Motor Torpedo Boat Flotilla in Hong Kong Waters from 8 December 1941 to 26 December 1941 by Lieutenant-Commander Gandy, RN, Commanding Officer, 2nd Motor Torpedo Boat Flotilla, 8 March 1942, CO 129 590/25, pp. 172, 181.

97. Sa, *Xianggang lunxian riji*, p. 81.

98. The main source for these Nationalist activities is Chan Chak, '*Xiezhu Xianggang kangzhan*', p. 18. See also Yun, '*Zhongyi Cishanhui*', p. 51; Ward, *Asia for the Asiatics?*, p. 36; Wright-Nooth, *Prisoner of the Turnip-Heads*, p. 56.

99. See Sa, *Xianggang lunxian riji*, pp. 83, 85. Liang Shuming, who spearheaded this initiative, was a neo-Confucian philosopher and professor at Peking University who served briefly as Minister of Justice in 1918–19. In the 1930s he became involved in agrarian reform schemes as director of the Shandong Rural Reconstruction Research Institute. In 1941 he helped to organize the Democratic League, a sort of halfway house between the Nationalist and Communist parties, and subsequently became its secretary-general.

100. Letter from G. L. Hall-Patch, British adviser, Chungking, to N. E. Young at the Treasury, London, 21 October 1942, FO 371 31717, p. 69.

101. Sa, *Xianggang lunxian riji*, pp. 123–4; Wright-Nooth, *Prisoner of the Turnip-Heads*, p. 56.

102. Chan Chak, '*Xiezhu Xianggang kangzhan*', pp. 18–19. See also Commodore, Hong Kong to Admiralty, telegram no.717, 19 December 1941, FO 371 27752; Yun, '*Zhongyi Cishanhui*', p. 51. According to Yun a consignment of arms was in fact delivered by the British military authorities on 22 December to the General Headquarters of the Loyal and Righteous Charitable Association. The Political Department of the Association, who were sup-posed to take delivery of the arms, had however just moved to a new address. When the British troops in charge of the consignment learned this they refused to take the arms any further, and instead unloaded them and deposited them in the Headquarters garage.

103. Sa, *Xianggang lunxian riji*, p. 85.

104. Chan Chak, '*Xiezhu Xianggang kangzhan*', p. 18.

105. For Elsie Fairfax Cholmondeley see Hoe, *Private Life*, p. 279. I am indebted to Miss Clare Hollingworth for some further detail regarding the career of this singular lady. Following the Communist takeover on the Chinese mainland in 1949 she made her way to Peking and became one of the small community of 'foreign experts'. She spurned an offer from the British Embassy to renew her passport, and when the Embassy was sacked in the course of the Cultural Revolution is said to have distinguished herself by dancing up and down in her patent leather brogues on a portrait of Queen Elizabeth II.

106. Sa, *Xianggang lunxian riji*, p. 87.

107. Ishita, '*Xianggang gonglüe zhan ji*', pp. 88, 90; Yuan, *Xianggang shilüe*, p. 171; memoir of Sub-Lieutenant Benny Proulx, Hong Kong Royal Naval Volunteer Reserve (HKRNVR), quoted Birch and Cole, *Captive Christmas*, p. 159.

108. Letter of Lieutenant-Colonel L. Ride to British Military Attaché, Chungking, 21 November 1944, CO 129 591/4.

109. Information conveyed after the surrender by the British artillery commander, Brigadier T. MacLeod, to his Japanese counterpart Lieutenant General Kitajima. See *Honkon-Chosha sakusen*, p. 323; Lindsay, *Going Down of the Sun*, pp. 72–3. Detail confirmed in interview with Mrs Mary Goodban, Lincolnshire, 7 January 1994.

110. For this episode see confidential report of Mrs Andrew Lusk Shields to the Colonial Office, 25 November 1942, CO 129 590/25, pp. 39–41; testimony of Colonel Noma Kennosuke, Noma trial, WO 235/999, pp. 351–2.

111. Comments of A. L. Shields and Major C. M. Manners quoted by Colonel Noma Kennosuke, Noma trial, WO 235/999, p. 352.

112. Lindsay, *Lasting Honour*, p. 145; Ko and Wordie, *Ruins of War*, p. 41.

113. Ibid., pp. 148–9.

114. Young dispatch to Secretary of State for the Colonies, 28 December 1941, CO 129 590/25, p. 65.

115. Observation of Wing Commander H. T. Bennett, RAF, Liaison Officer between the British and Japanese forces, quoted in report of Gwen Priestwood based on notes by Superintendent W. P. ('Tommy') Thompson and supplemented with additional notes of her own, forwarded by Sir Horace Seymour, British ambassador Chungking, to Foreign Secretary Eden, 6 May 1942, CO 129 590/23, p. 117.

116. Observations of Sub-Lieutenant Lewis Bush, HKRNVR, quoted in Lindsay, *Lasting Honour*, p. 159, and of Wing Commander H. T. Bennett, RAF, quoted in Priestwood and Thompson report, 6 May 1942, CO 129 590/23, p. 117.

117. Chinese prone to attach superstitious significance to their own language have been struck by the fact that the first character in the name Hong Kong (*heung* in Cantonese; *xiang* in Mandarin) can be broken down into three other characters meaning 'eighteen days'. Tse, *Xianggang lunxian*, p. vi.

118. Tsang interview with MacDougall, pp. 18–19; Lindsay, *Going Down of the Sun*, pp. 6–7.

119. The scheme which the British officers had been elaborating was 'hurriedly turned into a plan of escape'. Harrop, *Hong Kong Incident*, p. 86.

120. Tsang interview with MacDougall, p. 21; Lindsay, *Going Down of the Sun*, p. 7. The precise timing of these events is a little uncertain. In this interview, granted many years later, MacDougall recalled that he and his party collected Chan Chak in the Central District at 4 p.m., and that the subsequent Japanese attack on the party's motor launch took place around 5 p.m. At 5.30, however, according to Lindsay's account, the party were still 'driving around the coast in an old Austin car'. Chan Chak states in his memoir '*Xiezhu Xianggang kangzhan*' that the party arrived in Aberdeen at 4.10 p.m., but this seems impossibly soon.

121. Lindsay, *Going Down of the Sun*, p. 7.

122. Copy of MacDougall letter to Mrs Cathie MacDougall, 17 January 1942, pp. 3–4, MacDougall papers, Rhodes House.

123. See Chan Chak remarks made in interview '*Chen Ce zongtan tuwei ji Gang zhan*', *Da Guang Bao*, 31 December 1941. Chan Chak's perspective is also illustrated by the title of his posthumously published memoir, '*Xiezhu Xianggang kangzhan*', which translates into English as 'General Report on My Help in the Hong Kong War of Resistance and *My Leading of the British Forces out of Encirclement*'.

124. Chan Chak, '*Xiezhu Xianggang kangzhan*', p. 19. For an explicit British acknowledgement of dependence on Chan Chak, see remark of F. W. Kendall, the chief of 'Z Force', to Lieutenant-Commander Gandy quoted in Lindsay, *Going Down of the Sun*, p. 7.

125. Lindsay, *Going Down of the Sun*, p. 10.

126. Tsang interview with MacDougall, p. 24.

127. Details of the advance of Yu's forces are given in the memoirs of Professor Jian Youwen, '*Chen Ce tuwei xiang ji*', of Zhang Zeshen, deputy commander of the 186th division, '*Di er ci shijie dazhan shi wo jun jiuyuan Xianggang zhi huiyi*', and of Bai Wei, '*Lüe shu Du Jiu Lü zai Huizhou kang Ri*', quoted in Tse, *Xianggang lunxian*, pp. 164–5, 166–8.

128. Tse, *Xianggang lunxian*, p. 174.

129. Maltby secret cypher telegram no. 1741 to War Office, 10 December 1941, FO 371 27752, p. 11; HKN, 10 September 1942; Woodburn Kirby, *The War Against Japan*, vol. I, p. 120.

130. *Honkon-Chosha sakusen*, pp. 546–63. See also Hsu Long-hsuen and Chang Ming-kai (eds), *History of the Sino-Japanese War (1937–1945)*, Taipei, 1971, p. 365; Wilson, *When Tigers Fight*, p. 205; Tse, *Xianggang lunxian*, pp. 172–4. Although the attack on Changsha was not

launched until Christmas Eve the troop movements undertaken in preparation for the Changsha offensive were already inhibiting the advance of Nationalist units towards Hong Kong by the middle of December.

131. See British Military Attaché in Chungking cable no. M371 to War Office, 18 December 1941 and Young message to Secretary of State for the Colonies giving text of communiqué issued 20 December 1941, FO 371 27752, pp. 49, 67; *HKN*, 31 December 1941, 10 January 1942; Tang Hai, *Xianggang lunxian ji*, p. 201; Sa, *Xianggang lunxian riji*, p. 52; Ward, *Asia for the Asiatics?*, p. 36; Tse, *Xianggang lunxian*, p. 165.

132. See Tse, *Xianggang lunxian*, pp. 165, 174. The poorly armed condition of the relief force is also remarked on in MacDougall, 'Notes on the Siege', CO 129 590/25, p. 218.

133. Memoir of Professor Jian Youwen, '*Chen Ce tuwei xiang ji*', quoted Tse, *Xianggang lunxian*, p. 165. Jian's account tallies with the advice conveyed by the British military attaché in Chungking to the Hong Kong authorities on 21 December that Yu's forces would not be ready to relieve the colony for another ten days. See p. 66 above.

134. Another possible explanation is that he was 'notoriously inefficient and careless'. See Wilson, *When Tigers Fight*, p. 132.

135. Jian Youwen, '*Chen Ce tuwei xiang ji*', quoted Tse, *Xianggang lunxian*, p. 165. Jian does not specify the source of these messages. If Chan Chak and the Nationalists were in wireless contact with Yu and consequently aware of his army's position it seems bizarre that they did not pass on this information to the British military authorities who were urgently making plans to link up with Yu's troops. See p. 70 above.

136. Secret Report on Present Political and Military Aspects of the Situation in China, November 1942, HS 1/176, p. 2. The report was apparently written by Sir George Moss, regional adviser for the Far East to the Special Operations Executive (SOE). The possibility cannot be excluded that Yu was deliberately dragging his feet. He may have hoped to ensure that by the time he reached Hong Kong the British troops still holding out there would be too weakened to prevent him assuming control. The view is still current among some Hong Kong Chinese who were alive at the period that one of the principal objects of Yu's expedition was to retake the colony for China. Conversations with Dr Steve Tsang, Oxford, 19 October 1994, and the Hon. W. S. Lau, Hong Kong, 18 April 1995.

137. See memoirs of Professor Jian Youwen, '*Chen Ce tuwei xiang ji*', and divisional commander Zhang Zeshen, '*Di er ci shijie dazhan shi wo jun jiuyuan Xianggang zhi huiyi*' quoted in Tse, *Xianggang lunxian*, pp. 166, 170.

138. Memoirs of Professor Jian Youwen, Zhang Zeshen and Bai Wei quoted in Tse, *Xianggang lunxian*, pp. 165, 167; Chan Chak, '*Xiezhu Xianggang kangzhan*', p. 20.

139. Chan Chak, '*Xiezhu Xianggang kangzhan*', p. 20. Qujiang, or Kukong in the Cantonese rendering, was the name then in use for the important city in northern Guangdong now generally known as Shaoguan.

140. Details of this second round of exploratory talks between the British and the Communists are given in Xia, '*Liao Chengzhi zai Xianggang*', p. 163. See also Xia, '*Jizhe shengya zhi huiyi*', quoted Tse, *Xianggang lunxian*, pp. 170–1. According to Xia the British authorities once again took the initiative, making contact with Liao Chengzhi through James Bertram, an Australian journalist who had interviewed Mao Zedong in Yan'an in October 1937. Xia does not suggest what precise considerations induced the British to make this overture. Nor does he explain why they should have required the mediation of Bertram, since they had been engaged in talks with the Communists in the immediate run-up to the invasion.

141. *Honkon-Chosha sakusen*, p. 188

142. Tse, *Xianggang lunxian*, p. 163. Reports from Chinese intelligence sources suggested that the Japanese had been forced to move some transport and artillery back northwards to meet the guerrilla threat. See Commodore, Hong Kong telegram no. 741 to Admiralty, 23 December 1941, FO 371 27752, p. 73. Word of the guerrilla activity got around in Hong Kong, where it appears, a little ironically, to have encouraged belief in the imminent arrival of the *Nationalist* relief force. See Tang Hai, '*Xianggang lunxian ji*', p. 201; Ward, *Asia for the Asiatics?*,

p. 36; diary of expatriate girl Barbara Redwood quoted in Lindsay, *Lasting Honour*, p. 63; Tse, *Xianggang lunxian*, pp. 163–4.

143. Report of Major Ronald Holmes, 12 July 1944, HS 1/171, p. 3. See also Gandy Report on Operations, CO 129 590/25, p. 185; Jian Shui and Li Zhaopei, '*Yingguo junguan yingjiu ji*', in Xu Yueqing (ed.), *Huoyue zai Xiangjiang*, Hong Kong, 1993, p. 42. Holmes indicates that the leader of the partisans, Leung Wing-yuen, was strictly a Communist-affiliated ex-bandit rather than a fully committed Communist. In October 1942 he broke with the East River guerrillas and even came into physical conflict with them.

144. Tsang interview with MacDougall, p. 25.

145. See H. L. Mars, letter to Churchill, 28 September 1942, CO 129 590/25, pp. 15, 16. For the corresponding episode in Kowloon, see Sa, *Xianggang lunxian riji*, p. 177. Mars claims that the fifth columnists were allowed a full three days for plunder; but the twenty-four-hour period indicated by Sa seems to accord better with the accounts given elsewhere of the movements of the Japanese troops.

146. Harrop, *Hong Kong Incident*, p. 118.

147. Sa, *Xianggang lunxian riji*, p. 140.

148. See Tang Hai, '*Xianggang lunxian ji*', p. 231; Wong Lin, '*Xin Xianggang de toushi*', in *Xin Dong Ya*, vol. 1, no. 1, August 1942, p. 66; Sa, *Xianggang lunxian riji*, p. 124. Of these three sources Wong Lin must inevitably be treated with wariness as a Japanese-sponsored propagandist; but his account of the terror in Victoria on the night of 25–26 December carries a certain conviction. For a similar mood in Kowloon see diary of Dr Isaac Newton quoted Birch and Cole, *Captive Christmas*, p. 23.

149. Testimony of Captain Ushiyama Yukio, Kempeitai commander for the Western District, trial of Major Shoji Toshishige, WO 235/1015, pp. 17, 18; report of William Poy, CO 129 590/25, p. 78. Poy claimed to have been informed after the surrender by his Japanese captors that the Imperial troops had been ordered to kill all the white soldiers but spare the Indians. For a similar Japanese policy in Malaya see Fujiwara, *F. Kikan*, pp. 40–1.

150. In the New Territories a Colonel Kuromaru arranged special protection and food for the expatriate-run Fanling Babies' Home. See *SCMP/HKT*, 9 September 1945. Mrs C. R. Lee, the wife of Governor Young's secretary who was brought across the harbour with the first Japanese 'peace mission', reported that the Imperial troops in Kowloon had behaved very well. Lindsay, *Lasting Honour*, p. 64.

151. Diary of Dr Isaac Newton, 13 and 14 December 1941, quoted in Birch and Cole, *Captive Christmas*, pp. 50, 62.

152. Quoted in Tang Hai, '*Xianggang lunxian ji*', p. 245; Di Chen, '*Huiyizhong de yi nian*', p. 72.

153. Diary of Dr Isaac Newton, 13 and 14 December 1941, quoted Birch and Cole, *Captive Christmas*, pp. 50–1.

154. See Uttley diary, 12 December 1941; Buping Shanren, *Xianggang lunxian huiyilu*, Hong Kong 1978, pp. 19–22; Tse, *Zhanshi Ri jun*, pp. 13–15.

155. Fan, '*Xianggang zhi zhan huiyilu*', p. 5.

156. *Honkon-Chosha sakusen*, p. 189. This Japanese account is confirmed in *Daily Mail*, London, 12 January 1942, cutting filed in CO 129 590/23, p. 277; report of Lieutenant-Colonel L. Ride, 'On the Conditions in Hong Kong', and MacDougall, 'Notes on the Siege', CO 129 590/25, pp. 196, 211, 214, 215; Hahn, *Hong Kong Holiday*, p. 58; Li, *Hong Kong Surgeon*, p. 103; Patrick Yu, 'Wartime Experiences in Hong Kong and China (Part 2)' in Matthews and Cheung (eds), *Dispersal and Renewal*, p. 313.

157. *Honkon-Chosha sakusen*, pp. 189–90. See also Young, telegram no. 1474 to Colonial Office, 18 December 1941, FO 371 27752, p. 45; Ward, *Asia for the Asiatics?*, p. 30.

158. Phyllis Harrop report to Foreign Secretary Eden, 7 April 1942, CO 129 590/23, p. 189; Hahn, *China to Me*, p. 273; Selwyn-Clarke, *Footprints*, p. 67. See also Lindsay, *Lasting Honour*, p. 124; Kwan, *Ri zhan shiqi de Xianggang*, p. 33. One or two Chinese sources however dissent from this lenient view: see, for example, Tang Hai, '*Xianggang lunxian ji*', pp. 211, 216–17, and Li, *Hong Kong Surgeon*, p. 97.

159. *Honkon-Chosha sakusen*, p. 187.
160. Osler Thomas, 'With the BAAG in Wartime China' in Matthews and Cheung (eds), *Dispersal and Renewal*, pp. 304–5; Harrop, *Hong Kong Incident*, p. 99; Selwyn-Clarke, *Footprints*, p. 68; Lindsay, *Lasting Honour*, pp. 87–8; Ko and Wordie, *Ruins of War*, p. 90.
161. Special Report on Conditions in Hong Kong compiled by Calcutta Censor Station, 2 April 1942, CO 129 590/24, p. 182; Harrop, *Hong Kong Incident*, p. 102. See also Endacott and Birch, *Hong Kong Eclipse*, p. 97; Birch and Cole, *Captive Christmas*, pp. 146–7.
162. Report of Sergeant Charles Hedley, 9 February 1944, CO 129 591/4, p. 24.
163. Quoted in Wright-Nooth, *Prisoner of the Turnip-Heads*, p. 143.
164. Uttley diary, 20 June 1942; Harrop, *Hong Kong Incident*, p. 97; Li, *Hong Kong Surgeon*, p. 111; Selwyn-Clarke, *Footprints*, p. 68. Selwyn-Clarke gives the number of nurses raped at Happy Valley as six.
165. Searle diary, 24 December 1942; deposition of Private H. P. Miron, Winnipeg Grenadiers, exhibit J attached to transcript of trial of Major Shoji Toshishige, WO 235/1015; Selwyn-Clarke, *Footprints*, p. 68.
166. Lindsay, *Lasting Honour*, pp. 87, 151. See also article by Martin Gilbert in the *Observer Review*, London, 20 August 1989. For the breakdown of Imperial Army discipline at the level of the regimental officers and the tendency of those officers to act as they saw fit see Hoyt, *Japan's War*, pp. 172–3.
167. Report of Lieutenant-Colonel L. Ride 'On the Conditions in Hong Kong', CO 129 590/25, p. 196.
168. Report of Gwen Priestwood based on notes by Superintendent W. P. ('Tommy') Thompson, forwarded by Ambassador Seymour to Foreign Secretary Eden, 28 May 1942, CO 129 590/23, pp. 39, 41. See also Special Report on Conditions in Hong Kong, 2 April 1942 and letter from Major D. B. D. Henchman, British Military Mission, Chungking, 8 April 1942 quoted in Further Notes on Conditions in Hong Kong from Material Gathered at the Calcutta Censor Station up to 12 May 1942, CO 129 590/24, pp. 181, 194.
169. Interview with Mrs Margaret Watson Sloss, 3 March 1994.
170. Li, *Hong Kong Surgeon*, p. 111.
171. Ibid., pp. 133–4.
172. Wright-Nooth, *Prisoner of the Turnip-Heads*, p. 64.
173. See comments of Lieutenant Joseph Hurst, quoted in *Daily Mail*, London, 29 May 1942, cutting filed in CO 129 590/23, p. 217.
174. Hahn, *China to Me*, p. 289.
175. Quoted in James B. Crowley, '*A New Asian Order?: Some Notes on Pre-War Japanese Nationalism*', in Bernard S. Silberman and Harry D. Harootunian, *Japan in Crisis: Essays on Taishi Democracy*, Princeton, NJ, 1974, p. 293. The term used for 'universal brotherhood', *hakko ichiu*, meant literally 'all eight corners of the world under one roof' – the roof being that of Imperial Japan.
176. Priestwood and Thompson report, 28 May 1942, CO 129 590/23, p. 44.
177. See Endacott and Birch, *Hong Kong Eclipse*, p. 104.
178. Tang Hai, '*Xianggang lunxian ji*', pp. 253–4. See also Sa, *Xianggang lunxian riji*, p. 113; Li, *Hong Kong Surgeon*, p. 110.
179. Sa, *Xianggang lunxian riji*, p. 131.
180. *HKN*, 5 February 1942.
181. *Honkon-Chosha sakusen*, p. 327.
182. Ibid., p. 328.
183. Sa, *Xianggang lunxian riji*, p. 190.
184. Ibid., p. 146; Tse, *San nian*, p. 159.
185. H. C. K. Woddis, 'Hong Kong and the East River Company', *Eastern World*, July 1949, p. 10. See also Zeng Hongwen, '*Chu jin Gang Jiu*', in Zeng Sheng et al., *Dong Jiang xinghuo*, Guangzhou, 1983, p. 39; David Faure, 'Sai Kung: The Making of the District and its Experience during World War II', *JHKBRAS* vol. 22, 1982, pp. 20–2. Woddis gives the total number of brigands as around 3,000.

186. See Ward, *Asia for the Asiatics?*, pp. 6, 43.
187. Forty thousand was the figure given by Allied sources a few months later for the total number of Japanese troops used in the conquest of Hong Kong. See extract from information obtained from Allied evacuees at Lourenço Marques, 28 July 1942, CO 129 590/24, p. 141. The same figure was given immediately after the British surrender by Colonel Eguchi, the 23rd Army's medical chief. Harrop, *Hong Kong Incident*, p. 92. Eguchi however appears to have been referring exclusively to the number of Japanese troops on Hong Kong Island; and it is possible that the total strength of the Japanese force in the colony may have been greater than this. Another source estimated that at the time of the British surrender there were some 60,000 to 80,000 seasoned Japanese troops in the colony as a whole. Report of B. G. Milenko, 25 May 1942, CO 129 590/23, p. 49.
188. Cable of Brigadier G. E. Grimsdale, Military Attaché Chungking, to War Office, 29 January 1942, report of B. G. Milenko, 25 May 1942, and estimate of member of Central Committee of the Chinese Nationalist Party quoted in report taken from diary of Sub-Lieutenant D. F. Davies, HKRNVR, forwarded from Chungking, 10 June 1942, CO 129 590/23, pp. 49, 111, 263; extract from information obtained from Allied evacuees at Lourenço Marques, 28 July 1942, CO 129 590/24, p. 141; Harrop, *Hong Kong Incident*, pp. 117–18.
189. Zeng, '*Chu jin Gang Jiu*', p. 39. For a similar picture see Dr J. P. Fehily conversation with Lieutenant-Colonel L. Ride, Guilin, 18 December 1942, CO 129 590/22, p. 163; Buping Shanren, *Xianggang lunxian huiyilu*, p. 57.
190. Report of Sergeant Charles Hedley, 9 February 1944, CO 129 591/4, p. 23; Searle diary, 1 September 1942. In the same way British prison officials were left in temporary charge of Stanley gaol. See Gimson diary, 2 December 1943.
191. Self-defence bodies composed of Triad vigilantes were being set up by local householders in many parts of Kowloon and Victoria while the invasion was still in progress. See Tang Hai, '*Xianggang lunxian ji*', p. 206; Cheng Jitang, '*Xianggang tuoxian ji*', p. 306; Di Chen, '*Huiyizhong de yi nian*', p. 74. For prominence of the Street Guards in the early weeks of the Japanese takeover, see *HKN*, 6, 9 and 15 January and 20 February 1942; report by Mavis Ming, an Australian Chinese lady who left Hong Kong on 4 March 1942 forwarded by Seymour to Eden, 7 May 1942, CO 129 590/23, p. 222; Wong Lin, '*Xin Xianggang de toushi*', p. 67; Sa, *Xianggang lunxian riji*, pp. 139–40, 153–4; testimony of Captain Ushiyama Yukio, Shoji trial, WO 235/1015; Ward, *Asia for the Asiatics?*, pp. 71, 74. One expert on the Triads and other Chinese secret societies has pointed out that they typically assume the role of providing basic administration in times of upheaval: absolute chaos doesn't suit them any more than anyone else. Conversation with Dr Alexei Maslov, Oxford, 21 October 1993. For specific Street Guard activities see *HKN*, 15 January 1942; Sa, *Xianggang lunxian riji*, pp. 153–4.
192. Yun, '*Zhongyi Cishanhui*', p. 51. Zhang is said to have pleaded illness and delegated the task to a younger brother.
193. Zhang, *Xianggang hei shehui*, pp. 58–9.
194. Accounts of the great epidemic of gambling are given in Tang Hai, '*Xianggang lunxian ji*', p. 249; Sa, *Xianggang lunxian riji*, pp. 105–6; memoir of Tamai Masao, '*Honkon koryaku ki*' quoted Kobayashi, '*Taiheiyo sensoka no Honkon*', p. 212; reports of Miss Thom and of B. G. Milenko CO 129 590/23, pp. 52, 90; Harrop, *Hong Kong Incident*, pp. 93–4, 96; Ward, *Asia for the Asiatics?*, pp. 75–6.
195. See E. Ride, *British Army Aid Group*, pp. 18–20, 38–41; Huang Hsing Tsung, 'Pursuing Science in Hong Kong, China and the West', in Matthews and Cheung (eds), *Dispersal and Renewal*, p. 133.
196. Letter from K. E. Mogra in Lanzhou, 12 February 1942, HS 1/349, p. 1. Mogra (also referred to in some sources as K. S. Nogra) was a British subject who had lived and traded for many years in Guilin and Canton. One informant describes him as being of 'mixed race'. He appears to have operated as an agent of the British Special Operations Executive (SOE).
197. Report of William Poy, CO 129 590/25, p. 80.
198. Harrop, *Hong Kong Incident*, p. 98.

199. Report of Professor Gordon King, 18 March 1942, CO 129 590/23, p. 135.
200. Hahn, *China to Me*, p. 285.
201. Hirano Shigeru, '*Women zai Xianggang de kezheng yu baoxing*', in Ling Ming (tr.), *Riben zhanfan huiyilu*, Hong Kong, 1971, pp. 47–8. Hirano Shigeru was a Japanese official employed in occupied Hong Kong who many years later wrote a highly penitential account of his role. According to this account he served as Deputy Governor and was responsible for drafting many of the decrees of the occupation regime. No mention can however be found either of Hirano or of the post of Deputy Governor in any contemporary source, English, Chinese or Japanese. While there is no particular reason to doubt that he served in the wartime administration in some capacity it seems likely that he was exaggerating his role; and his account must therefore be treated with caution.
202. Tang Hai, '*Xianggang lunxian ji*', p. 256. See also letter from K. E. Mogra, 12 February 1942, HS 1/349, p. 2. Mogra refers to the reported removal of over 170,000 bags of rice.
203. Harrop, *Hong Kong Incident*, p. 142.
204. Hirano, '*Kezheng yu baoxing*', p. 52. Other strategic goods said to have been picked up included the artillery which had been used by the British for the defence of the colony and large amounts of machinery from the factories. See Tang Hai, '*Xianggang lunxian ji*', p. 251; Report on Hong Kong, 31 May 1943, HS 1/171, p. 2.
205. Harrop, *Hong Kong Incident*, p. 118.
206. Sa, *Xianggang lunxian riji*, p. 184.
207. Tang Hai, '*Xianggang lunxian ji*', p. 241.
208. Harrop, *Hong Kong Incident*, pp. 130–1.
209. *Honkon-Chosha sakusen*, pp. 190, 326–7. For Navy role in the second 'peace mission' of 17 December see also Chan Chak, '*Xiezhu Xianggang kangzhan*', p. 17; Ward, *Asia for the Asiatics?*, p. 34; Birch and Cole, *Captive Christmas*, p. 91. 1st Lieutenant Goto, the Navy's representative on the mission, crossed the harbour to Queen's Pier in a separate launch from his Army counterparts.
210. Report of Miss Thom, CO 129 590/23, p. 90; Lieutenant J. D. Clague, Intelligence Summary no. 1 from Qujiang, 28 May 1942, CO 129 590/24, pp. 157–9; Sa, *Xianggang lunxian riji*, p. 166; Li, *Hong Kong Surgeon*, p. 124. See also letter from K. E. Mogra, 12 February 1942, HS 1/349. Mogra's letter appears to indicate that the Navy controlled the whole of Hong Kong Island, but this is belied by the other sources.
211. Testimony of Colonel Noma, Noma trial, WO 235/999, pp. 319, 351–2. See also *Honkon-Chosha sakusen*, p. 332; Chan Chak, '*Xiezhu Xianggang kangzhan*', p. 18.
212. Report of B. G. Milenko, CO 129 590/23, p. 53; Li, *Hong Kong Surgeon*, p. 159. Europeans tended to refer to the Kempeitai as gendarmes – a description which, while accurate from a technical point of view, none the less carries for the contemporary reader a misleadingly amiable connotation of French holidays.
213. *Honkon-Chosha sakusen*, p. 327; Kobayashi '*Taiheiyo sensoka no Honkon*', p. 216.
214. Statement of Fujita, official in the Civil Affairs Department of the Gunseicho, quoted Harrop, *Hong Kong Incident*, p. 117. For similar assessments see Mme Liang Hanzao quoted *Daily Express*, London, 4 February 1942, cutting filed in CO 129 590/23, p. 266; letter from K. E. Mogra, 12 February 1942, HS 1/349, pp. 1–2. The general sense of the Navy's rising prospects will have been reinforced by the presence of a naval squadron which was stationed in Victoria harbour immediately after the British surrender: it consisted of a 7,500-ton cruiser, three or four destroyers and some auxiliary vessels. See report of B. G. Milenko, CO 129 590/23, p. 50.
215. *Honkon-Chosha sakusen*, p. 327.
216. Accounts of the tussle within the Imperial Army over the future of Hong Kong may be found in Kobayashi, '*Taiheiyo sensoka no Honkon*', p. 216 and Kobayashi and Shibata, *Nippon gunseika no Honkon*, pp. 71, 72. See also Takagi Kenichi, Kobayashi Hideo et al., *Xianggang junpiao yu zhanhou buchang* (Chinese translation by Wu Hui), Hong Kong, 1995, p. 27. For details of the broader conflict between the China faction and the Southern faction which formed the background to this tussle I am grateful for information provided by Professor

Kobayashi Hideo of Komazawa University, Tokyo, interview, 18 July 1995. The competing priorities of the two factions are embodied in the 23rd Army Guidelines of 9 December 1941, which specify as objectives for the Japanese conquerors both the pursuit of 'political schemes' and 'the turning of Hong Kong into a military base for our forces'. See *Honkon-Chosha sakusen*, p. 327.

217. Sugiyama report to Tojo, 10 January 1942, quoted *Honkon-Chosha sakusen*, pp. 327–9.
218. For a reaction from the losers see diary of General Hata Shunroku, Commander-in-Chief of the China Expeditionary Force, 21 January 1942, quoted *Honkon-Chosha sakusen*, p. 330.
219. *HKN*, 22 January 1942; *Honkon-Chosha sakusen*, p. 329.
220. *Honkon-Chosha sakusen*, p. 331.

3. The World Turned Upside Down

1. For Yazaki background and suggested connection with Ishiwara Kanji see *Honkon-Chosha sakusen*, p. 327; Kobayashi, '*Taiheiyo sensoka no Honkon*', p. 215; Kobayashi and Shibata, *Nippon gunseika no Honkon*, pp. 58–9.
2. *Honkon-Chosha sakusen*, p. 330.
3. Tse, *San nian*, p. 34. The battle of Nomonhan (Khalkhin Gol), which helped to deter the Japanese from attacking the Soviet Union in conjunction with the Germans in 1941, remains one of the least known yet arguably most important episodes of the Second World War. For a detailed study see Alvin D. Coox, *Nomonhan: Japan Against Russia 1939* (2 vols), Stanford University Press, 1986. See also Coox, 'The Unfought War: Japan 1941–1942', Fifth University Research Lecture, San Diego State University, San Diego State University Press, 1992, and Philip Snow, 'Nomonhan: The Unknown Victory', *History Today*, July 1990.
4. Tse, *San nian*, pp. 34, 44; interviews with Professor Kobayashi Hideo, Tokyo, 18 July 1995 and Mr Oda Takeo, former head of the Foreign Affairs Department, Mount Nasu, 1 September 1995.
5. Tse, *San nian*, pp. 52–3.
6. *HKN*, 23 October 1942.
7. Tse, *San nian*, p. 52. A contrasting, Procopius-like account of a debauched Isogai is given by his self-styled 'Deputy Governor', Hirano Shigeru. But for reasons indicated earlier Hirano must be considered a somewhat suspect source. (See chapter 2, note 201.)
8. There are certain indications that Yazaki's influence may have survived the leadership change. Appointed chief of the Special Service intelligence section in Canton, Yazaki continued to make fairly frequent descents on the colony during the first few months of Governor Isogai. In July 1942, for example, we find him attending the first Canton–Hong Kong economic liaison conference, and in August he addressed the gentry on the subject of Canton–Hong Kong economic relations. On both these occasions he seems to have been promoting the China faction theme of economic integration between Hong Kong and its hinterland. See *HKN*, 4 July, 22 and 23 August 1942; Tse, *Zhanshi Ri jun*, p. 229.
9. Major-General Yazaki Kanju, '*Honkon tochi hosaku shiken*', in Kobayashi, '*Taiheiyo sensoka no Honkon*', p. 240.
10. *HKN*, 26 December 1942. For similar pronouncements from Isogai and his entourage see message issued by the Governor's Office on New Year's Day 1943, quoted in Ching, *The Li Dynasty*, p. 115; statement by Lieutenant-Colonel Yoshida, Acting Chief of the Information Bureau, quoted in *IIKN*, 29 January 1943; *HKN*, 20 February 1943.
11. For the foregoing see Yazaki, '*Honkon tochi hosaku shiken*', pp. 239, 242–3.
12. *HKN*, 21 January 1942.
13. This in turn would contribute to the larger objective of enlisting the wealth of the Overseas Chinese on behalf of Japan. See Yazaki, '*Honkon tochi hosaku shiken*', pp. 239, 242.
14. Regulations Regarding the Duties of the Governor's Office of the Conquered Territory of Hong Kong, 4 October 1944, part 1, chapter 2, section 1.8. Although only published in late

1944, these Regulations may reasonably be viewed as codifying the practice of the previous two and a half years.

15. Testimony of Colonel Noma and of Captain Yatagai Sukeo, Noma trial, WO 235/999, pp. 348, 400.

16. Report of Watanabe Takeshi of the Ministry of Finance, January 1942, quoted in Kobayashi, '*Taiheiyo sensoka no Honkon*', p. 211.

17. Observation of Fujita of the Civil Affairs Department, quoted in Harrop, *Hong Kong Incident*, p. 123.

18. Interview with the late Miss Emily Hahn, 19 January 1994.

19. Report of Ministry of Finance official, 28 April 1942, quoted in Kobayashi, '*Taiheiyo sensoka no Honkon*', p. 212; testimony of Colonel Noma, Noma trial, WO 235/999, p. 356. Noma's approximate figure for the strength of the Kempeitai is corroborated by Dr Li Shu-fan, who gives the total number of gendarmes as amounting at one point to just 176. See Li, *Hong Kong Surgeon*, p. 162.

20. Yazaki, '*Honkon tochi hosaku shiken*', p. 240.

21. Tse, *Zhanshi Ri jun*, p. 115, *San nian*, p. 59; Kobayashi, '*Taiheiyo sensoka no Honkon*', p. 215.

22. Point made by Professor Kobayashi Hideo, interview, 18 July 1995. See comments of Yazaki, '*Honkon tochi hosaku shiken*', p. 241.

23. Yazaki, '*Honkon tochi hosaku shiken*', p. 238.

24. Ibid., pp. 238, 239, 240. Much the same thinking may be detected in the 23rd Army Guidelines of 9 December 1941. The Guidelines declared that a principle had been 'decided upon of making an effort to prevent any unnecessary social change'. See *Honkon-Chosha sakusen*, p. 327.

25. Yazaki, '*Honkon tochi hosaku shiken*', p. 238.

26. *HKN*, 21 January 1942.

27. Hahn, *Hong Kong Holiday*, p. 174.

28. *HKN*, 20 February 1942. See also article by 'A Correspondent', *HKN*, 9 January 1942.

29. *HKN*, 17 February 1942.

30. Ibid.

31. *HKN*, 6 January 1942.

32. *HKN*, 23 January 1942.

33. *HKN*, 25 May 1942 and 30 July 1943; Searle diary, 23 July 1942; conversation of Dr J. P. Fehily with Lieutenant-Colonel L. Ride, Guilin, 18 December 1942, CO 129 590/22, p. 163; Gene Gleason, *Hong Kong*, London, 1964, p. 183.

34. Report of Mrs A. J. Martin, widow of British consul-general, Chungking, forwarded by British embassy, Washington, 11 September 1942, CO 129 590/24, p. 103.

35. Hahn, *China to Me*, p. 314.

36. *HKN*, 22 February and 22 July 1942; Tokyo Radio, 22 July 1942, quoted in Extracts from Far Eastern Broadcasts, 22 July 1942, CO 129 590/23, p. 31; Hong Kong Radio in Chinese, 12 November 1942, broadcast quoted in CO 129 590/24, p. 45; Wong Lin, '*Xin Xianggang de toushi*', p. 70. Forty-one Japanese district officers were said to have been appointed to 'help reform public morals'.

37. *HKN*, 20 July 1942.

38. Endacott and Birch, *Hong Kong Eclipse*, p. 137.

39. Minute of Acting Commissioner of Police, 6 April 1948, in 'War Criminals and Activities', HK RS 163 1/222, p. 22.

40. *Koa Kikan gyomu hodo* (Koa Kikan Work Report), no. 2, 10 February 1942, in Kobayashi, '*Taiheiyo sensoka no Honkon*', p. 250.

41. Ibid., p. 251.

42. Phrase quoted in Sa, *Xianggang lunxian riji*, p. 178.

43. See cable from Brigadier G. E. Grimsdale, British military attaché in Chungking, to War Office, 29 January 1942 and letter from Daniel S. K. Chang, Nationalist Foreign Ministry, to F. C. Wu, Cambridge, Massachusetts, 11 March 1942, CO 129 590/23, pp. 145, 263.

In addition to courting mainland politicians and diplomats the Koa Kikan also tried to win over a number of cultural luminaries from the mainland who had been stranded in Hong Kong. Prominent among these were the opera singer Mei Lanfang and the film star Butterfly Woo. See *HKN*, 22 January 1942; Sa, *Xianggang lunxian riji*, pp. 190–1; Ward, *Asia for the Asiatics?*, p. 49. For similar offer to another veteran mainland politician see Chen Jitang, *'Xianggang tuoxian ji'*, p. 307.

44. Tse, *San nian*, p. 45. The name of the scholar rewarded by Isogai was Jian Qinshi.
45. Ibid., pp. 48–9. Other potential mainland go-betweens approached by Isogai included Fan Guang, a former head of the Asia Department of the Nationalist Foreign Ministry; Li Genyuan, the founder of the Chinese republican movement in Yunnan province; and Xiong Lüe, an elderly general of the Guangdong provincial army. Isogai also sought the help of Toyama Mitsuru, the leader of the Black Dragon Society in Japan and doyen of the Japanese right-wing associations of the period, who had contacts with a circle of Nationalist elder statesmen.
46. *Koa Kikan gyomu hodo*, no. 2 and Koa Kikan, *Konkyo Chugoku shinshiroku*, 10 January 1942, in Kobayashi, *'Taiheiyo sensoka no Honkon'*, pp. 251, 255–9.
47. Dates given by Kobayashi, *'Taiheiyo sensoka no Honkon'*, p. 226. See also Kotewall testimony at Noma trial, WO 235/999, p. 273; Gittins, *Eastern Windows*, p. 133, and *Stanley: Behind Barbed Wire*, p. 122, 'The Lo Dynasty', *Hong Kong Inc.*, February 1990, p. 79. Gentry leaders picked up in addition to Kotewall and Lo included Tung Chung-wei, the chairman of the Hong Kong Chinese General Chamber of Commerce, on December 29, and Li Tse-fong, the manager of the Bank of East Asia, on New Year's Day 1942.
48. *Koa Kikan gyomu hodo*, no. 2, p. 254.
49. Ibid., p. 251. In a postwar submission at the trial of Colonel Noma of the Kempeitai Kotewall recalled that he and his colleagues had 'resisted the pressure for six days and six nights'. M. K. Lo similarly reported having been 'taken by the Japanese after the surrender and cross-examined for three days'. See Kotewall testimony at Noma trial, WO 235/999, p. 273; report of conversation of Dr J. P. Fehily with Lieutenant-Colonel L. Ride, Guilin, 18 December 1942, CO 129 590/22, p. 162; economic information on Far East from repatriated Americans who arrived on the *Gripsholm*, 25 August 1942, p. 4 para. 8, HS 1/171. What in fact seems to have happened in many cases is that gentry members were questioned during the daytime over a period of several days but allowed to go home overnight. This would explain the apparent discrepancy between the gentry's recollections and the Koa Kikan's own account. See Ching, *The Li Dynasty*, p. 107. For account of an interrogation see Li, *Hong Kong Surgeon*, p. 153. Li was in fact questioned by the Kempeitai rather than the Koa Kikan, but the approach adopted towards him seems to have been much the same. The offer of rewards is mentioned in Tang Hai, *'Xianggang lunxian ji'*, p. 248.
50. In the course of the first fortnight an attempt is said to have been made to cobble together some kind of a subordinate Chinese city government on the lines of a number established in Japanese-occupied parts of the mainland. The attempt was apparently instigated by the Japanese military in Shanghai. A personage named Wang Kunxi, part politician, part businessman, was flown in from Shanghai and deposited in the Hong Kong Hotel, where the Koa Kikan tried to persuade him to serve as the head of an administration composed largely of his mainland friends. See Yu Shuheng, *'Taisi fuzhong de "Xianggang shi zhengfu": ji Xianggang lunxian qizhong yi miwen'*, in *Da Hua*, no. 2, March 1966, pp. 3–4. Yu's account receives some support from the cables sent by the Chief of the East Asia Section of the Foreign Ministry, Tokyo to Canton and from Hirata in Shanghai to Vice-Consul Iwai of the Investigation Section, 31 December 1941, MAGIC Documents Reel 1; also from Sam King, *Tiger Balm King: The Life and Times of Aw Boon-haw*, Singapore, 1992, p. 328, which may indicate that Aw Boon-haw too was being fingered as a possible member of the new city government. The episode seems to illustrate both the confusion of the first days of the Japanese rule and the emphasis which was placed during that early period on promoting figures who might play a part in Japan's broader 'political schemes' without regard for the practical needs of the colony.

51. Sa, *Xianggang lunxian riji*, p. 121.

52. *HKN*, 12 January 1942; Li, *Hong Kong Surgeon*, pp. 126–7.

53. Interview, Mr Charles Sin, 29 June 1995.

54. Petitions were submitted to the Gunseicho by the Hong Kong Chinese General Chamber of Commerce on 31 December 1941 and again on 10 January 1942. See *HKN*, 13 January 1942; report of Professor Gordon King, 18 March 1942, CO 129 590/23, p. 139; Tang Hai, '*Xianggang lunxian ji*', p. 254. For report of the Gunseicho meetings see Li, *Hong Kong Surgeon*, p. 114.

55. See intercepted letter from Fok Shu Hong to Fok Yee Kworn in Johannesburg, 27 February 1942 and report taken from diary of Sub-Lieutenant D. F. Davies, HKRNVR, forwarded from Chungking, 10 June 1942, CO 129 590/23, pp. 111, 155; Tang Hai, '*Xianggang lunxian ji*', p. 254; Tao Xisheng, '*Chong di guo men*' in Ye Dewei et al. (eds), *Xianggang lunxian shi*, p. 332; Sa, *Xianggang lunxian riji*, p. 112.

56. Tse, *Zhanshi Ri jun*, p. 71; 'The Ho Tung Saga (Part 1)', *Hong Kong Inc.*, March 1990, p. 105.

57. Report of Indian businessman who left Hong Kong for India December 1942, and record of conversation of David MacDougall with Mrs Eugenie Zaitzeff, 6 December 1943, CO 129 590/22, pp. 56, 175.

58. Tse, *San nian*, p. 45.

59. Sam King, *Tiger Balm King*, pp. 328, 330. King states that Aw was detained in the Peninsula Hotel, but this may simply reflect a tendency among outsiders to think of the Peninsula as *the* hotel in Hong Kong. It seems more likely that Aw was housed in the Hong Kong Hotel along with the rest of the Koa Kikan's involuntary guests.

60. MAGIC Documents Reel II, April 1942 report of Colonel Okada in Shanghai quoted SRS 732, O841–O858, 1 October 1942. On top of his huge economic clout Aw had the added attraction of being a member of the Nationalist Party's Consultative Yuan. On 3 January 1942 proclamations carried in the Hong Kong newspapers declared that preferential treatment was to be accorded to Overseas Chinese from South-east Asia. See Sa, *Xianggang lunxian riji*, p. 116.

61. E. Ride, *British Army Aid Group*, p. 146.

62. Phrase used in Luff, *Hidden Years*, p. 170. One Chinese refugee from the colony was quoted by British sources as saying 'Indians belong No.1 people'. See Lieutenant J. D. Clague, Intelligence Summary no.1 from Qujiang, 28 May 1942 and memorandum of W. B. L. Monson, 1 October 1942, CO 129 590/24, pp. 9, 159.

63. Clark, *An End to Tears*, p. 57; E. Ride, *British Army Aid Group*, pp. 172–4.

64. *HKN*, 29 September 1942.

65. See *HKN*, 8 May 1943; testimony of Edward Sykes, former president of the Eurasian Welfare League, Noma trial, WO 235/999, p. 135.

66. Nakazawa's evangelical activities are described in Hahn, *China to Me*, pp. 345–6, and *Hong Kong Holiday*, pp. 165–8. For background of Irene Fincher and Phyllis Bliss see Peter Hall, *In the Web*, pp. 146, 150. For other propaganda directed at this minority group see editorial 'The Eurasian', *HKN*, 14 February 1942.

67. Sa, *Xianggang lunxian riji*, pp. 122–3, 127. See also post-war testimony of Major Hirao Yoshio of the Kempeitai, trial of George Wong, HK RS 2-1-1513.

68. Intercepted letter of Fok Shu Hong to Fok Yee Kworn, 27 February 1942, CO 129 590/23, p. 156.

69. *Honkon-Chosha sakusen*, pp. 188, 327; *Koa Kikan gyomu hodo*, no. 2, p. 251; Tse, *Zhanshi Ri jun*, p. 238.

70. For Kempeitai hunt for hostile elements in the aftermath of the takeover see for example Tang Hai, '*Xianggang lunxian ji*', pp. 234, 258–9; Tao, '*Chong di guo men*', pp. 325, 327–8, 329, 330, 335.

71. Endacott and Birch, *Hong Kong Eclipse*, p. 125; Sam King, *Tiger Balm King*, p. 10.

72. *Koa Kikan gyomu hodo*, no. 2, p. 251.

73. Intercepted letter from Daniel S. K. Chang of the Nationalist Foreign Ministry to his wife in Hawaii, 13 March 1942, CO 129 590/23, p. 144 and memorandum of W. B. L. Monson, 1

October 1942, CO 129 590/24, p. 10; Ward, *Asia for the Asiatics?*, pp. 96–7, 99; interview, Sir Y. K. Kan, 24 May 1995.

74. Yazaki, '*Honkon tochi hosaku shiken*', pp. 239, 241.

75. Gittins, *Stanley: Behind Barbed Wire*, p. 124; report of William Poy, CO 129 590/25, p. 80. For a similar impression see statement of Gustavo Velasco forwarded by George Ogilvie Forbes of the British Legation in Havana to Foreign Secretary Eden, 21 March 1944, CO 129 591/4, p. 37.

76. Comment of Mme Liang Hanzao quoted in *Daily Express*, London, 4 February 1942, cutting filed in CO 129 590/23, p. 266. See also letter of Yu Yuen Kee of Oriental Academy, Chungking, cited in Special Report on Notes on Conditions in Hong Kong after the Surrender taken from material gathered by Postal Censorship, Calcutta, CO 129 590/24, p. 187; Tang Hai, '*Xianggang lunxian ji*', pp. 233–4; Sa, *Xianggang lunxian riji*, p. 9.

77. *HKN*, 12 January 1942.

78. *HKN*, 13 January 1942.

79. The King's Theatre had not at this stage been renamed the Yu Lok.

80. *HKN*, 26 February 1942.

81. *HKN*, 31 March 1942. According to one contemporary speculation the Japanese were aware of pre-war rivalry between Kotewall and Chow, and wished to avoid any possible friction that might arise from having them on the same body. See Ward, *Asia for the Asiatics?*, p. 64.

82. *HKN*, 31 March 1942.

83. Translation of captured Japanese indictment of 1943, CO 129 592/6, pp. 134, 137; Tse, *San nian*, p. 62.

84. Kotewall circular letter, May 1946, in private papers of Mrs Helen Zimmern; Kotewall testimony, Noma trial WO 235/999, p. 273; interview, Mrs Helen Zimmern, 29 June 1995. See also Endacott and Birch, *Hong Kong Eclipse*, pp. 242–3; Ching, *The Li Dynasty*, p. 107. For a similar claim in the case of M. K. Lo see Gittins, *Eastern Windows*, p. 133; *Stanley: Behind Barbed Wire*, p. 122. Peter H. Sin is also said to have been authorized by the British to work with the conquerors. Interview, Mr Charles Sin, 29 June 1995. For confirmation from the British side see North remarks to Gimson quoted in Gimson internment diary, 14 April 1944; North public statement of 1 October 1945 quoted in *SCMP/HKT*, 2 October 1945. North informed Gimson that he had advised Kotewall to sign a document formalizing the imprimatur. According to Kotewall's son such a document was indeed drawn up and signed, and was verified after the war. Interview, Mr Cyril Kotewall, 26 June 1995. No trace of it however appears to survive in the archives either in London or Hong Kong.

85. Tse, *San nian*, pp. 61–2, 65.

86. Quoted in *HKN*, 17 February 1942.

87. Conversation of Dr J. P. Fehily with Lieutenant-Colonel L. Ride, Guilin, 18 December 1942, CO 129 590/22, p. 162. The remarks were addressed to a White Russian named Yashanov.

88. *HKN*, 25 April 1942.

89. Li, *Hong Kong Surgeon*, p. 139.

90. Sa, *Xianggang lunxian riji*, pp. 89, 116. The other two papers were the *Xunhuan Ribao* (Universal Circulating Herald) and the *Huayu Ribao* (China World Daily). For mainland reader's comments see autobiography of W. W. Yen, quoted in Tse, *Xianggang kang Ri*, p. 77.

91. Fehily conversation with Ride, 18 December 1942, CO 129 590/22, p. 162.

92. Ibid. See also reports of Professor Gordon King, 18 March 1942, CO 129 590/23, p. 139 and of Dr Wen Yuanning quoted in N. L. Smith minute to Monson 7 January 1944, CO 129 591/4, p. 70. One Japanese resident appears to have argued on these grounds for Lo's exclusion from the Chinese Cooperative Council: he was, however, overruled by Isogai, who professed himself anxious to secure the support of the Chinese community by 'introducing fair politics'. See *HKN*, 24 December 1944.

93. Gittins, *Stanley: Behind Barbed Wire*, p. 122; 'The Lo Dynasty', *Hong Kong Inc.*, February 1990, p. 79; minutes of the Chinese Cooperative Council sessions of 3 and 15 May, 17 June, 16 and 19 August, 25 October and 15 November 1943. Lo is listed as having been present at each of these meetings but (unlike his colleagues) is not recorded as having made a single utterance at any of them.

94. Gittins, *Stanley: Behind Barbed Wire*, pp. 122–3; 'The Lo Dynasty', *Hong Kong Inc.*, February 1990, p. 79.

95. Report by M. Heyworth of Unilever, quoted in Gent minute, 23 October 1942, CO 129 590/24, p. 4.

96. Interview, Sir Y. K. Kan, 24 May 1995. In the aftermath of the British surrender Hong Kong Island and Kowloon were completely cut off from each other, and throughout the occupation they were run as quite separate administrative areas. See report of conversation of Comte R. de Sercey, formerly of the Chinese Postal Service, with Ronald Hall, Acting British Consul-General, Chungking, 27 June 1944, CO 129 591/4, p. 15; Fan Jiping, '*Xianggang zhi zhan huiyilu*', p. 6.

97. *HKN*, 28 January and 26 February 1942.

98. Interview, Sir Y. K. Kan, 24 May 1995. After the end of the war the colony's English-language press commented on the attitude of those Hong Kong Chinese who had 'thought the British had gone for good'. See *SCMP/HKT*, 10 September 1945.

99. Interview, Mr Oda Takeo, 1 September 1995.

100. Li, *Hong Kong Surgeon*, pp. 131–2.

101. Sa, *Xianggang lunxian riji*, pp. 111, 114. Sa observed in this connection that the local merchants were keen to do business. See also *HKN*, 13 January 1942; report of Professor Gordon King, 18 March 1942, CO 129 590/23, p. 139; Sinn, *Bank of East Asia*, p. 67.

102. *HKN*, 20 January 1942.

103. *HKN*, 29 January 1942.

104. *HKN*, 1 March 1942.

105. Yazaki, '*Honkon tochi hosaku shiken*', p. 242.

106. *HKN*, 12 March 1942.

107. *HKN*, 7 April 1942.

108. *HKN*, 14 January 1942; Sa, *Xianggang lunxian riji*, p. 157.

109. *HKN*, 28 January and 19 March 1942; Ward, *Asia for the Asiatics?*, pp. 113, 153.

110. *HKN*, 16 and 23 January 1942. See also report of E. J. M. Churn, former manager of the China Provident Loan and Mortgage Co Ltd, 19 October 1942, forwarded by Seymour to Eden, 28 October 1942, CO 129 590/24, p. 63; Ward, *Asia for the Asiatics?*, p. 98; Ching, *The Li Dynasty*, p. 108. Sin remarks quoted in Hahn, *China to Me*, p. 328.

111. *HKN*, 19, 23 and 29 January and 15 February 1942. The other institutions were the Chartered Bank of India, Australia and China, the Nederlandsch Indische Handelsbank, the Chase Bank, the Mercantile Bank of India, the Banque de l'Indochine, the Netherlands Trading Society and the National City Bank of New York.

112. *HKN*, 7 February 1942; Sinn, *Bank of East Asia*, p. 66. The eight other banks were the Hong Nin Savings Bank, the Hua Chiao (Overseas Chinese) Bank, the Yien Yih Bank, the Wing On Bank, the National Commercial and Savings Bank, the Fukien Provincial Bank, the Chu Hsin Chen Bank and the Young Brothers Banking Corporation.

113. A historian of the Bank records that in consequence of the 'vital' pre-war connection, the Japanese authorities in general 'did not treat the Bank of East Asia severely'. Sinn, *Bank of East Asia*, pp. 14, 72.

114. *HKN*, 6 and 9 July 1942. See also Wong Lin, '*Xin Xianggang de toushi*', p. 69.

115. Domei news agency in English, 24 October 1942, quoted in Extract from Far Eastern Economic Notes, CO 129 590/24, pp. 28, 29; *HKN*, 20 December 1942 and 4 February 1943; Hahn, *Hong Kong Holiday*, p. 265. Encouraged by the more settled conditions, stockbrokers had apparently got together and created a kind of informal stock market. Sinn, *Bank of East Asia*, p. 72.

116. Li, *Hong Kong Surgeon*, p. 136; interview, Sir Y. K. Kan, 24 May 1995.

117. Letter from Kan Yuet Keung in Hong Kong to Mrs Nancy Eu of Palo Alto, San Francisco, California, 12 January 1943, CO 129 590/22, p. 106.

118. *HKN*, 3 and 4 February 1942.

119. *HKN*, 15 March 1942.

120. Report of Mrs A. J. Martin, 11 September 1942, CO 129 590/24, p. 95.

121. Telegram of Sir R. Campbell, British ambassador, Lisbon, to Foreign Office, 16 May 1942, CO 129 590/23, p. 131; 'The Ho Tung Saga (Part 1)', *Hong Kong Inc.*, March 1990, p. 105.

122. Account of Sir Robert Ho Tung visit given in *HKN*, 29 March 1942. See also telegram of Sir R. Campbell to Foreign Office, 16 May 1942, and minute of W. B. L. Monson, 4 June 1942, CO 129 590/23, pp. 9, 131; minute of Monson, 1 October 1942, CO 129 590/24, p. 8; Gittins, *Eastern Windows*, p. 133, and *Stanley: Behind Barbed Wire*, p. 123.

123. Telegram of Sir R. Campbell to Foreign Office, 16 May 1942, CO 129 590/23, p. 131; letter of William Wright of Dodwell and Co to G. Dodwell in Watford, 3 September 1942 and minute of Monson, 1 October 1942, CO 129 590/24, pp. 8, 132. On the basis of information from Macao dated 13 May, Sir R. Campbell reported that Sir Robert Ho Tung was currently back in the Portuguese colony 'for about ten days', while Wright's letter in early September described him as having attended a dinner in Hong Kong 'recently'. It seems clear, there-fore, that Sir Robert made at least one trip back to Hong Kong following the initial visit in March, and he may well have made a second. For the Tai Tung Publishing Company see *HKN*, 8 June 1942. *New East Asia* was produced in Chinese under the title *Xin Dong Ya*. The first issue appeared on 1 August 1942. Articles covered such topics as the history of the Indian independence movement, Australian attitudes to the war and the progress made in the reconstruction of Hong Kong over the past six months.

124. *HKN*, 12 January 1942.

125. *HKN*, 8 July 1942. On Christmas Day 1942, similarly, the two Chinese Councils declared that 'Japan and China must forget their differences', and the following month they issued a state-ment supporting the Wang Jingwei regime's declaration of war on the Allies. See *HKN*, 25 December 1942 and 11 January 1943.

126. Interview, Mr Charles Sin, 29 June 1995. Similar comments made by Mr Cyril Kotewall and Mrs Helen Zimmern, interviews 26 and 29 June 1995. Dr Li Shu-fan recalls 'command dinners' at which round robins denouncing the Nationalists and praising Japan were passed round for signature. According to Li these circulars were regarded as 'the real test of cooperation'. See Li, *Hong Kong Surgeon*, p. 167.

127. *HKN*, 28 January 1942. See also report by Professor Gordon King 18 March 1942, CO 129 590/23, p. 139.

128. Ward, *Asia for the Asiatics?*, p. 15; Hahn, *China to Me*, p. 328.

129. Sam King, *Tiger Balm King*, pp. 328–9; *HKN*, 8 June 1942. A third 'chief organiser' referred to in connection with the Tai Tung Publishing Company was Aw Boon-haw's son, Aw Hoe.

130. *HKN*, 21 August 1942; Ward, *Asia for the Asiatics?*, p. 49; Sa, *Xianggang lunxian riji*, p. 179. In a series of reports published in March 1943 the *Hong Kong News* claimed that Yen and Chen, who had previously been 'negative' or 'lukewarm' towards the Wang Jingwei govern-ment, were now 'actively participating' in it. Not a shred of evidence, however, was adduced in support of this claim. Five months later the paper appeared to retreat a step in Yen's case. An article stated that he had 'announced his readiness' to participate in the Wang Jingwei government the previous spring, and had since applied to it for permission to set up an investment company. He was still said to be 'living in retirement' in Hong Kong. *HKN*, 3, 4 and 5 March and 9 August 1943.

131. Tse, *San nian*, pp. 48–9. Similar non-cooperation is said to have been encountered from a number of other mainland figures, including the veteran politician Li Genyuan and the ex-warlord Xiong Lüe, the opera singer Mei Lanfang and the film star Butterfly Woo. See also Hirano, '*Kezheng yu baoxing*', p. 49.

132. Sa, *Xianggang lunxian riji*, pp. 146, 151.

133. Liang Yen, *The House of the Golden Dragons*, London, 1961, p. 200; Selwyn-Clarke, *Footprints*, p. 101.

134. Chen Jitang, '*Xianggang tuoxian ji*', pp. 306–7; Sa, *Xianggang lunxian riji*, p. 116; article by Mme Chiang Kai-shek in *New York Times* magazine, 19 April 1942, p. 7, cutting filed in HS 1/349.

135. Notes of Gent and other Colonial Office staff on conversation with escaped British bankers T. J. J. Fenwick and J. A. D. Morrison, 7 April 1943, CO 129 590/22, p. 168.

136. Sa, *Xianggang lunxian riji*, pp. 122–3; *HKN*, 19 January 1942; Lieutenant J. D. Clague, Intelligence Summary no.1 from Qujiang, 28 May 1942, CO 129 590/24, p. 161; report on Hong Kong, 4 June 1942, HS 1/171, p. 2.

137. *HKN*, 3 May, 31 July and 19 August 1942; Tse, *San nian*, p. 161. 'Many' new businesses were said to have started in the spring, including large numbers of restaurants and tea-houses. By the latter part of the summer over 40,000 applications are said to have been put in by business people for the continuation of trade or the establishment of new firms, and 34,000 for the reopening or establishment of shops and stalls.

138. *HKN*, 27 January 1942. Malik's background is unclear; Sehil Khan was apparently a former secretary at the Queen Mary's Hospital. See statement of Dr J. P. Fehily to India Office, 14 May 1943, CO 129 590/22, p. 119.

139. On 27 April 'over 4,000 Indians' were said to have attended an Indian Independence League rally at the King's Theatre. On 10 August 'the whole' Indian community of 'over 5,000' as well as 'some hundreds' of freed Indian POWs were reported as having attended a mass meeting at the theatre at which they were informed of the British arrest of Gandhi and Nehru, and on 7 September 'practically the whole' Indian community were said to have gathered at the Sikh Temple to pray for the success of the Indian independence cause. See *HKN*, 27 April, 10 August and 7 September 1942. The excitement among Hong Kong Indians at the apparent prospect of the overthrow of the Raj is also attested by Allied sources. See report of Miss Thom forwarded 15 May 1942, CO 129 590/23, p. 90; statement of Gustavo Velasco forwarded 29 March 1944, CO 129 591/4, p. 35. Similar Indian reactions in Malaya and Singapore are recorded in Fujiwara, *F. Kikan*, pp. 96–7, 142, 184–6, 191.

140. Report of Mrs A. J. Martin, 11 September 1942, CO 129 590/24, p. 103

141. *HKN*, 26 February 1942.

142. Intercepted letter in Gujarati apparently written by a Mr Saleh to Messrs Ebrahim Noordin and Co. of Bombay on 25 March 1942 and smuggled out of the colony, CO 129 590/23, p. 129.

143. Letter from K. E. Mogra, 12 February 1942, p. 1, HS 1/349; Pennefather-Evans, Interim Report; Harrop, *Hong Kong Incident*, p. 99; Wright-Nooth, *Prisoner of the Turnip-Heads*, p. 66.

144. Hahn, *Hong Kong Holiday*, p. 167.

145. Confidential report of Mrs Andrew Lusk Shields, 25 November 1942, CO 129 590/25, p. 39; Hahn, *China to Me*, pp. 38–9, 343–4.

146. Conflicting figures are given in the sources for the enlistment in the Indian National Army of Indian POWs taken at Hong Kong. Oliver Lindsay, for instance, gives figures of 200 and 400 at two different points in the same work. See Lindsay, *Going Down of the Sun*, pp. 102, 237. Lindsay's lower figure is followed in Wright-Nooth, *Prisoner of the Turnip-Heads*, p. 85: the higher figure however seems to receive more backing from contemporary accounts. In the early summer of 1942, for example, 'between 200 and 300' Indian troops were said to be getting infantry training at the Murray Barracks in Victoria. See p. 127 below. On 15 July an internal Japanese Foreign Ministry communication stated, 'I have just learned that about 500 Indian prisoners taken at Hong Kong were brought to Canton and, under the designation "Canton Detachment of the Indian Independence Army" received training with various units. Now we are using them as Panzer units.' MAGIC Documents, Reel 1, 18 July 1942. Even if the higher figure is accepted, however, the fact remains that a good two thirds of the Indian POWs in Hong Kong refused to change sides. The loyalty of the Indian POWs was insisted on by several Allied sources. See statement of Dr. J. P. Fehily to India Office, 14 May 1943, CO 129 590/22, pp. 118–19; report of Sergeant Charles Hedley, 9 February 1944, CO 129 591/4, p. 29; Clark, *An End to Tears*, pp. 49–57.

147. Attitude of Punjabi Muslims and Parsees described in letter from K. E. Mogra, 12 February 1942, HS 1/349; report of conversation of Dr J. P. Fehily with Lieutenant-Colonel L. Ride, Guilin, 18 December 1942, and statement of Fehily to India Office, 14 May 1943, CO 129 590/22, pp. 121, 162; Wright-Nooth, *Prisoner of the Turnip-Heads*, p. 66. Membership of the Indian Independence League was said to have climbed steadily from 500 to 1,000 and finally 1,500. The peak of 1,500 was reported on 27 April 1942. No membership figures were given

after that date. See *HKN*, 24 February and 20 and 27 April 1942. Estimate of extent of Japanese sympathies within the Indian community given by Mr. Rusy M. Shroff, interview, 30 October 1995.

148. The day before the first major Indian Independence League rally it was announced that over 4,000 Indians 'would be' attending. See *HKN*, 25 January 1942. For the League's control of rations, see notes by G. S. Kennedy-Skipton, 11 March 1943, statement of Dr. J. P. Fehily to India Office, 14 May 1943, and report of Sergeant Charles Hedley conversation with Mac-Dougall, 4 December 1943, CO 129 590/22, pp. 35, 113, 119; report of Sergeant Charles Hedley, 9 February 1944, CO 129 591/4, p. 25; White, *Turbans and Traders*, p. 45.

149. *HKN*, 4 and 5 February 1942.

150. Testimony of Maria Augusta Leigh, trial of Joseph Richards, HK RS 245-2-150. In the same spirit a Portuguese girl named Mercedes took a job with a Japanese store, the Kajima Bazaar, observing 'Mother feels that it's all right'. Hahn, *Hong Kong Holiday*, p. 202.

151. Hahn, *China to Me*, p. 360.

152. Ibid., p. 392.

153. Wilson, *Hong Kong! Hong Kong!*, p. 92.

154. Letter from Indian correspondent, *HKN*, 25 March 1943.

155. *HKN*, 9 June 1943.

156. *HKN*, 17 January 1943.

157. *SCMP/HKT*, 24 September 1945. See also *SCMP/HKT*, 4 and 12 September 1945.

158. Information Department of the Governor's Office, Hong Kong, *Gunseika no Honkon*, Hong Kong, 1944, p. 111.

159. Li, *Hong Kong Surgeon*, p. 125. Help from Hong Kong Chinese business leaders was already being sought in late January and early February, when Colonel Ikemoto, the head of the Economic Affairs Department of the Gunseicho, convened meetings of bankers and merchants to discuss with them how local business might be revived. In February Tung Chung-wei of the Hong Kong Chinese General Chamber of Commerce was appointed chairman of a new Gold and Silver Exchange. In early May Lau Tit-shing, Tung Chung-wei and Li Tse-fong were said to have held a meeting in the boardroom of the Bank of East Asia for the purpose of forming a Chinese Bank and Money-changers' Cooperative Association. See *HKN*, 23 January, 5 and 20 February and 4 May 1942; Sa, *Xianggang lunxian riji*, pp. 191, 194.

160. In mid-April the Chinese Representative Council were said to have instructed the Chinese Cooperative Council to 'consider the rent question'. See *HKN*, 14 April, 16 August and 6 September 1942. In mid-year it was reported that Li Koon-chun, M. K. Lo and other members of the Chinese Cooperative Council were to meet shortly with representatives of the local Chinese landlords and of the Hong Kong and Kowloon Tenants' Association to 'work out a fair basis for the collection of rents'. *HKN*, 1 July 1942.

161. *HKN*, 19 August 1942.

162. *HKN*, 6 January and 23 August 1942.

163. Calcutta Censor Station, Further Notes on Conditions in Hong Kong, 13 May 1942, CO 129 590/24, p. 190. 'Hong Kong Chinese' in this context should be understood to include the Eurasians and Portuguese.

164. Hahn, *Hong Kong Holiday*, p. 159. In the same way Luo Jiyi, a Chinese who had worked as a Japanese language translator for a Hong Kong newspaper, was rapidly put in charge of one of the districts in Kowloon (see below). Sa, *Xianggang lunxian riji*, p. 161.

165. *HKN*, 17 and 24 January 1942; Sa, *Xianggang lunxian riji*, pp. 194–5; Hahn, *China to Me*, p. 328; Tse, *San nian*, p. 80; interview, Mr Charles Sin, 29 June 1995. Peter H. Sin was made head of a District Administrative Liaison Office as well as of the Central District Bureau in Victoria (see following paragraph).

166. Tse, *San nian*, pp. 80–1. In March 1943 it appears that some Japanese officials were still being employed in the District Bureaux, though the intention was to eliminate this. By the summer, however, the staffs of the District Bureaux were stated to be wholly Chinese. See *HKN*, 5 March, 25 May and 27 July 1943. The Chinese heads of the various District Bureaux

are listed in a 'Scheme of the present Japanese government at Hong Kong' drawn up by the British through their Indian censorship office and circulated 25 August 1943, HS 1/171, p. 2. For the District Assemblies see *HKN*, 22 July 1942; Li, *Hong Kong Surgeon*, pp. 156–7; Tse, *San nian*, pp. 80, 82.

167. *HKN*, 24 February 1943. One street chief on Hong Kong Island was said to represent forty households, and one street chief in Kowloon ten to twenty.

168. See David Faure, 'Sai Kung: The Making of the District', pp. 122–4. I am also indebted for this paragraph to a discussion with Mr S. J. Chan, a former District Officer under the post-war British administration, on 22 September 1995 and to a lecture given by Mr Chan at the Hong Kong Museum of History on 18 October 1995. The establishment of the first rural district bureaux is reported in *HKN*, 27 March 1942.

169. *HKN*, 30 April 1942.

170. Ibid.; *HKN*, 22 May 1942.

171. Zhang, *Xianggang hei shehui*, pp. 60–1.

172. Lindsay, *Going Down of the Sun*, p. 136. See also White, *Turbans and Traders*, pp. 44–5.

173. Searle diary, 13 July 1942. One Chinese Nationalist press report of 24 July claimed that the Japanese had conscripted virtually all Indians in Hong Kong for military service. See extract from (Intelligence) Survey no. 30 of 1942 for fortnight ending 15 August 1942, CO 129 590/24, p. 136.

174. See *Koa Kikan gyomu hodo*, no. 2, p. 251. According to the Koa Kikan the Hong Kong Chinese detective force had crossed over to serve the new rulers *en masse* under the leadership of their chief, Chung Shui-nam. This defection is confirmed in Lieutenant J. D. Clague, Intelligence Summary no. 1 from Qujiang, 28 May 1942, and letter of Brigadier G. E. Grimsdale, British Military Mission, Chungking, to Director of Military Intelligence, New Delhi, 8 June 1942, CO 129 590/24, pp. 156, 161.

175. Testimony of Major Hirao Yoshio of the Kempeitai at trial of George Wong, HK RS 2-1-1513, summary, p. 5; testimony of Major Shiozawa Kunio of the Kempeitai at trial of Joseph Richards, HK RS 245-2-150; Tse, *Zhanshi ri jun*, pp. 115–16. Estimates given on different occasions for the number of Hong Kong Chinese and Indian agents employed by the Kempeitai varied from '2,000' to '1,300 to 3,000' and '1,300 to 4,000'. Small groups of the agents are said to have been attached to each Kempeitai officer. The number of agents employed by the garrison appears to have been relatively small: Hirao mentions 'about twenty'. The wartime career of George Wong is set out in testimony of William Chang, William Lee and others and defence of George Wong, Wong trial, HK RS 2-1-1513, pp. 10–46, 52–3. For activities of Call Me Howard see Searle diary, 27 and 31 December 1942, 3 January 1943; Hahn, *China to Me*, pp. 391–4, 417–18 and *Hong Kong Holiday*, pp. 225–18; Wright-Nooth, *Prisoner of the Turnip-Heads*, pp. 156–7. For employment of Millie Chun's ring see Hahn, *China to Me*, p. 349.

176. Fehily conversation with Ride, Guilin, 18 December 1942, CO 129 590/22, p. 164; letter from K. E. Mogra, 27 January 1943, p. 8, HS 1/171; testimony of Colonel Noma, Noma trial, WO 235/999, p. 322. Six hundred Chinese clerks were said to have been enrolled in the Water Police alone. See Lieutenant J. D. Clague, Intelligence Summary no. 1 from Qujiang, 28 May 1942, CO 129 590/24, p. 161. Information relating to payment for Kensa given in report of B. G. Milenko, CO 129 590/23, p. 53. Milenko's assertion is tentative and seems implausible; but the fact that this idea was current is significant in itself.

177. *HKN*, 16 and 22 April 1942. See also Endacott and Birch, *Hong Kong Eclipse*, p. 129. In the *Hong Kong News*, the Area Bureaux are often confusingly referred to as 'District Bureaux' or simply 'Bureaux': I have followed Endacott and Birch in using the term Area Bureaux to distinguish them from the District Bureaux set up to implement the rice rationing scheme of Peter H. Sin. In Chinese quite distinct terms are used, viz. *diqu shiwu suo* for the Area Bureaux and *qu zheng suo* for the District Bureaux.

178. Even here, however, Chinese staff were employed at a junior level. See, for example, *HKN*, 11, 19 and 23 June 1943.

179. *HKN*, 6 October 1942. See also Li, *Hong Kong Surgeon*, pp. 156–7.

180. See remarks of Lau Tit-shing quoted in *HKN*, 20 December 1942 and Kotewall quoted *HKN*, 29 December 1942; Tse, *San nian*, p. 81. The policing system referred to, the *baojia* or 'household guarantee' system, was first introduced in China under the Tang dynasty (AD 618–907), and from there imported into Japan. From this standpoint, its imposition in Hong Kong was a *re*introduction consistent with the conquerors' pan-Asiatic ideas.

181. *HKN*, 15 March 1942. See also statement of Dr. J. P. Fehily to India Office, 14 May 1943, CO 129 590/22, p. 118; Hahn, *China to Me*, pp. 326, 363; testimony of Colonel Noma, Noma trial, WO 235/999, p. 389. 'Pawing' by Indian women police seems to have been almost equally resented. See letter in *HKN*, 5 March 1942; Clague, Intelligence Summary no. 1, 28 May 1942, CO 129 590/24, p. 160; Liang, *House of the Golden Dragons*, pp. 204–5.

182. Accounts of the origin of the GACC are provided in Kwan Lai-hung, 'The Charitable Activities of Local Chinese Organizations during the Japanese Occupation of Hong Kong', in Faure, Hayes and Birch (eds), *From Village to City* pp. 181–2, and Tse, *San nian*, pp. 70–2. See also *HKN*, 19 August, 28 and 29 September, 25 October, 14 and 15 November 1942. According to Kwan's account Kotewall had been approached in the course of the summer by Bishop José da Costa Nunes of the Roman Catholic Church about the possibility that part of the grant which the Church received from the Vatican might be made available to help feed the starving. He apparently took the opportunity presented by this overture to seek financial help from the government for the community's overall welfare drive.

183. *HKN*, 28 September 1943. See also Kathleen J. Heasman, 'Japanese Financial and Economic Measures in Hong Kong', *Journal of the Hong Kong University Economics Society*, 1957 (first prepared by the author during internment in Stanley camp and privately circulated in July 1945), p. 86.

184. George Endacott in Endacott and Birch, *Hong Kong Eclipse*, p. 155.

185. Point about central government made by Ward, *Asia for the Asiatics?*, pp. 68–9; Lethbridge, 'Hong Kong under Japanese Occupation' p. 115; Morris, *Hong Kong*, p. 252; Ching, *The Li Dynasty*, p. 111. For local government see Endacott and Birch, *Hong Kong Eclipse*, p. 127; Kobayashi, '*Taiheiyo sensoka no Honkon*', p. 217; Tse, *San nian*, p. 80. Professor Kobayashi maintains that Hong Kong was the sole territory occupied by the Japanese during the Pacific War in which they created new local government bodies.

186. Faure, 'Sai Kung: The Making of the District', pp. 123–4.

187. Testimony of Lo Chung-ching, head of Stanley District Bureau and near-identical testimony of Kwok Hin-wang, head of Causeway Bay District Bureau and Kan Man, head of Kennedy Town District Bureau, Noma trial, WO 235/999, pp. 300, 305, 307. The British prosecutor, Major D. G. MacGregor of the Black Watch, expressed his agreement with these assertions. Ibid., Prosecutor's Opening Address, pp. 12–13.

188. Ride, 'On the Conditions in Hong Kong', CO 129 590/25, p. 198.

189. Lusk Shields report, 25 November 1942, CO 129 590/25, p. 42; memorandum of Tommy Lee to British embassy, Chungking, enclosed in dispatch from British embassy to Foreign Office, 8 July 1942, FO 371 31670, p. 2. The episode reported by Lee is undated, but it would seem to belong naturally to the early hours of the conquest when a whole series of similar incidents are recorded. Some expatriates were also put to work cleaning out filthy refugee huts with their bare hands. This systematic degradation of the British expatriates had a precedent in the treatment meted out to the European residents of Tianjin (Tientsin) after the Japanese blockaded the British and French concessions there in June 1939. See Wilson, *When Tigers Fight*, pp. 159, 161.

190. *HKN*, 5 January 1942. See also report of Mrs A. J. Martin, 11 September 1942, CO 129 590/24, pp. 84, 86; Harrop, *Hong Kong Incident*, p. 104; Wright-Nooth, *Prisoner of the Turnip-Heads*, p. 79.

191. Hahn, *China to Me*, p. 305. This motive appears to have been reinforced by a widely reported Japanese aversion to being looked down upon from above.

192. Lusk Shields report, 25 November 1942, CO 129 590/25, p. 43.

193. *Daily Express*, London, 4 February 1942, cutting filed in CO 129 590/23, p. 266.

194. Hirano, '*Kezheng yu baoxing*', p. 48.

195. This point was insisted on by a number of witnesses. See cable from Macao via Lisbon, 19 January 1942, and remarks of Bishop Ronald Hall in cutting from the *Star*, London, 2 February 1942, CO 129 590/23, pp. 268, 270; comments of Dr Selwyn Selwyn-Clarke and Professor Duncan Sloss quoted in Dr J.P. Fehily conversation with Lieutenant Colonel L. Ride, Guilin, 18 December 1942, CO 129 590/22, p. 161.

196. Lindsay, *Going Down of the Sun*, p. 56; Solomon Bard, 'Mount Davis and Sham Shui Po: A Medical Officer with the Volunteers', in Matthews and Cheung (eds), *Dispersal and Renewal*, p. 200. The benevolent sub-commandant was a Sergeant-Major Honda.

197. Selwyn-Clarke, *Footprints*, pp. 80–1; Liam Nolan, *Small Man of Nanataki*, London, 1966, pp. 31, 58–9, 101–2; Luff, *Hidden Years*, pp. 195–6. This remarkable little man became famous in internee circles.

198. Report of G. Leslie Andrew on conditions prevailing in Stanley as of 23 September 1943 compiled in Toronto 29 January 1944, HS 1/176, pp. 1, 12; E. D. Robbins, Report on Hong Kong Internment, CO 129 590/22, pp. 40, 45; report of Sergeant Charles Hedley, 9 February 1944, CO 129 591/4, p. 24. For other praise of Yamashita and Nakazawa see Searle diary, 5 and 7 November 1942; reports of MacDougall conversations with Sergeant Charles Hedley, 4 December 1943, and E. D. Robbins, 6 December 1943, CO 129 590/22, pp. 36, 42–3; Sub-Lieutenant Lewis Bush quoted in Alan Birch and Martin Cole (eds), *Captive Years*, Heinemann, 1982, p. 50.

199. Uttley diary, 6 April 1942.

200. Report of Professor Gordon King, 18 March 1942, CO 129 590/23, p. 138. See also Norman Mackenzie, 'An Academic Odyssey: A Professor in Five Continents (Part 2)' in Matthews and Cheung (eds), *Dispersal and Renewal*, p. 182; Gittins, *Stanley: Behind Barbed Wire*, p. 59.

201. Wright-Nooth, *Prisoner of the Turnip-Heads*, pp. 121, 124; Luff, *Hidden Years*, p. 181.

202. Uttley diary, 27 November 1942.

203. Uttley diary, 16 February 1942; report of Fehily conversation with Ride, Guilin, 18 December 1942, CO 129 590/22, p. 163; Luff, *Hidden Years*, p. 179.

204. Private R. J. Wright of the Middlesex Regiment, quoted in Lindsay, *Going Down of the Sun*, p. 22.

205. Gillingham, *At the Peak*, p. 167.

206. Recollection of Eric Himsworth, former internee, quoted Rafferty, *City on the Rocks*, pp. 138–9. See also Priestwood and Thompson report forwarded 6 May 1942, CO 129 590/23, p. 126; Uttley diary, 23 May 1942.

207. Searle diary, 22 May 1942.

208. Uttley diary, 28 January 1942.

209. Ibid., 24 January 1942.

210. Ibid., 26 February 1942; comment relayed to Franklin Gimson by a Mrs Dyson, Gimson diary, 22 January 1944.

211. Franklin Gimson, Internment in Hong Kong, summary, p. 10.

212. Ibid., pp. 8, 9, 10.

213. Estimates for the total number of Americans in Stanley vary considerably. One contemporary witness, Mrs Andrew Lusk Shields, gives a figure of 400, while an ex-internee, George Wright-Nooth, says the Americans totalled about 390. Oliver Lindsay in his two books on the period gives two conflicting lower figures, viz. 350 and 290. See Lusk Shields report, 25 November 1942, CO 129 590/25, p. 43; Wright-Nooth, *Prisoner of the Turnip-Heads*, p. 89; Lindsay, *Lasting Honour*, p. 167, and *Going Down of the Sun*, p. 36. I have opted for Lindsay's higher estimate as an approximately medium figure. There were also small contingents of Dutch, Belgians and other Allied nationals.

214. Searle diary, 22 May 1942.

215. Uttley diary, 4 February 1942; Wright-Nooth, *Prisoner of the Turnip-Heads*, p. 92.

216. Television documentary *Under the Rising Sun*, shown by TVB Pearl, Hong Kong, 13 December 1991. Similar derision is reported in Solomon Bard, 'Mount Davis and Sham Shui Po', Matthews and Cheung (eds), *Dispersal and Renewal*, p. 197.

217. Comment of Superintendent W. P. ('Tommy') Thompson quoted in Priestwood and Thompson report forwarded 6 May 1942, CO 129 590/23, p. 121; Priestwood and Thompson report forwarded 28 May 1942, CO 129 590/23, p. 45; minute of W. B. L. Monson, 1 October 1942, CO 129 590/24, p. 9.

218. Report of B. G. Milenko, CO 129 590/23, p. 51; Harrop, *Hong Kong Incident*, pp. 98, 103; Li, *Hong Kong Surgeon*, pp. 137, 156; Gittins, *Stanley: Behind Barbed Wire*, p. 61; G. A. Leiper, *A Yen for My Thoughts*, Hong Kong, 1982, pp. 101–3, 112, 114, 116–17, 126; Frank H. H. King, *History of the Hong Kong and Shanghai Banking Corporation*, vol. III, p. 573. The sixty bankers also included a number of Americans and Dutch.

219. On 28 December 1942, three days after the surrender, he apparently tried to induce the Japanese to accept the services of an official named Gibson as 'Petrol Controller'. See Ward, *Asia for the Asiatics?*, pp. 43–4.

220. Selwyn-Clarke, *Footprints*, p. 70.

221. Ibid. The officer concerned was a Colonel Nagakawa.

222. Hahn, *China to Me*, p. 356.

223. The allusion occurs on 2 February 1943, when Selwyn-Clarke, Sakagami and Dr A. Woo of the Medical Department are reported as having attended the fiftieth anniversary celebration of the Hospital for Babies and Home for Abandoned Children in the Canossian Convent.

224. Hahn, *China to Me*, pp. 309–10, 388; Li, *Hong Kong Surgeon*, pp. 140–1. The term 'third national' seems itself to have been vague and chaotic in its definition. Sometimes it included Portuguese and Indians, but sometimes the two latter groups were counted separately. On one occasion in early 1943, for example, there were said to be around 7,000 third nationals in Hong Kong, including 3,371 Indians, 1,203 Portuguese and 614 Eurasians: a month later, however, Hong Kong Chinese, third nationals, Indians and Portuguese were listed as four separate categories, and the term 'third nationals' apparently denoted only Eurasians and Europeans from neutral or Axis states. See *HKN*, 18 February and 14 March 1943. Fehily conversation with Ride, Guilin, 18 December 1942, CO 129 590/22, p. 161; Ward, *Asia for the Asiatics?*, p. 78.

225. Fehily conversation with Ride, Guilin, 18 December 1942, and Fehily statement to India Office, 14 May 1943, CO 129 590/22, pp. 122, 161; Ward, *Asia for the Asiatics?*, p. 41; Hahn, *Hong Kong Holiday*, pp. 153–4, 155–6; Wright-Nooth, *Prisoner of the Turnip-Heads*, p. 76.

226. For Faure's emergence as editor of *Hong Kong News* see Wright-Nooth, *Prisoner of the Turnip-Heads*, p. 98. For the 'Is Anything New?' column see, for example, *HKN*, 8 and 15 February, 26 April, 3 May, 7 and 28 June, 5 July, 23 and 30 August 1942. The presence of a few British and other Europeans as well as Eurasians and Indians on the *Hong Kong News* team is attested by Sa, *Xianggang lunxian riji*, p. 155, and Hahn, *China to Me*, p. 324.

227. Notes by G. S. Kennedy-Skipton, 11 March 1943, CO 129 590/22, p. 113. Some observers even judged that the Japanese were giving these stray Westerners better treatment than they would have been willing to accord their fellow-Asiatics. Statement of Dr J. P. Fehily to India Office, 14 May 1943, CO 129 590/22, p. 121.

228. Report of Mrs A. J. Martin, 11 September 1942, CO 129 590/24, pp. 86, 87, 110.

229. Interview with the late Miss Emily Hahn, 19 January 1994.

230. *HKN*, 1 February 1942.

231. Interview with the late Professor Charles Boxer and the late Miss Emily Hahn, 19 January 1994. For a similar assessment see statement of Dr J. P. Fehily to India Office, 14 May 1943, CO 129 590/22, p. 121.

232. Report of Mrs A. J. Martin, 11 September 1942, CO 129 590/24, p. 94.

233. Ibid., p. 107.

234. Harrop, *Hong Kong Incident*, p. 87.

235. Ibid., pp. 100, 101.

236. *SCMP/HKT*, 10 September 1945.

237. Hahn, *Hong Kong Holiday*, pp. 101–2.

238. Hahn, *China to Me*, pp. 310, 409–10, *Hong Kong Holiday*, p. 219. As an American Emily Hahn related Ah King's access of confidence particularly to the impact of Pearl Harbor. It seems reasonable, however, to assume that his attitude was influenced by the whole wave of Japanese victories over the Western powers – not least that in Hong Kong, which he had witnessed with his own eyes.

239. Diary of Phyllis Harrop, 29 January 1942, CO 129 590/23, p. 207. In the published version of the diary, which appeared a year later, this prognosis was modified to '. . . it will take us years to regain what we have lost'. See Harrop, *Hong Kong Incident*, p. 142.

240. See Tang Hai, '*Xianggang lunxian ji*', p. 202; Sa, *Xianggang lunxian riji*, pp. 18, 27, 34, 40, 52, 80, 85, 123–4; Chan Lau, *China, Britain and Hong Kong*, p. 294.

241. Mme Chiang Kai-shek article in *New York Times* magazine, 19 April 1942, p. 4, cutting filed in HS 1/349. For similar attitudes see report of P. Biau, 16 May 1942, CO 129 590/23, p. 70; Harrop, *Hong Kong Incident*, p. 150.

242. Lee is said among other things to have been a former secretary and confidant of the 'Young Marshal', Zhang Xueliang, who kidnapped Chiang Kai-shek in Xi'an in 1936.

243. Memorandum of Tommy Lee enclosed with dispatch from British embassy, Chungking to Foreign Office, 8 July 1942, FO 371 31670.

244. Summary of Notes on a Report on the China Commando Group by Erik Nyholm of the Madsen Corporation, agent of the Special Operations Executive (SOE), 9 April 1942, HS 1/349, pp. 8–9. See also statement of Duclos, Canadian Trade Commissioner in Shanghai, summer 1942, enclosed with report of William Poy CO 129 590/25, p. 82.

245. See Lane, 'Nationalist Government', pp. 97–8.

246. R. K. Law, Parliamentary Under-Secretary to the Foreign Office, 14 May 1942, quoted Chan Lau, *China, Britain and Hong Kong*, p. 298.

247. Letter from David MacDougall at British embassy, Washington, to Noel Sabine of Publicity Department, Colonial Office, 22 December 1942, p. 1, MacDougall papers, Rhodes House.

248. Quoted in Morris, *Hong Kong*, p. 114.

249. Quoted in Tsang, '*Zhengce miwen*' p. 92.

250. Quoted in and Chan Lau, 'The United States and the Question of Hong Kong', in *JHKBRAS* vol. 19, 1979, p. 7 and *China, Britain and Hong Kong*, pp. 301, 306.

251. MacDougall letter to Sabine, 30 December 1942, p. 2, MacDougall papers, Rhodes House.

252. Quoted in Chan Lau, *China, Britain and Hong Kong*, p. 316.

253. Ibid., p. 327.

254. In the summer of 1943 a British official in the Colonial Office claimed that the United States government had been ready to intervene on Britain's behalf because they were themselves having procedural difficulties with the Chinese. Professor Chan Lau Kit-ching reports similarly that the Americans indicated they 'would have been prepared to show their displeasure' with the Nationalist authorities if the latter had remained obdurate. See Monson minute, 30 June 1943, CO 825 42/15, p. 16; Chan Lau, *China, Britain and Hong Kong*, p. 308. It remains unclear, however, whether the United States would really have backed the British position to the hilt.

255. Chiang diary entry, 31 December 1942, quoted in Chen Liwen, '*Kangzhan qijian Zhongguo feichu bupingdeng tiaoyue zhi nuli*'.

256. Report of Dr K. C. Wu (Wu Guozhen), 15 January 1943, Taipei SNDC 003 2157.5999; Chan Lau, *China, Britain and Hong Kong*, p. 308; Lane, 'Nationalist Government', p. 99; Tsang, '*Zhengce miwen*', pp. 98, 101.

257. Chan Lau, *China, Britain and Hong Kong*, pp. 327–8.

4. *The Japanese Miss Their Chance*

1. *Honkon-Chosha sakusen*, pp. 11, 331; interview Professor Kobayashi Hideo, 18 July 1995.

2. Interview with Mr. Oda Takeo, former Head of the Foreign Affairs Department, 1 September 1995.

3. *HKN*, 21 February 1942.
4. Morris, *Hong Kong*, p. 251. The German presence in occupied Hong Kong wasn't entirely negligible. Germans observed during the actual course of the fighting included an officer and a civilian wearing a swastika emblem on his lapel. Both apparently made some attempt to intercede with the Japanese forces on behalf of their fellow Europeans. Shortly after the takeover, on 30 December 1941, a number of German officers with Nazi armbands are said to have watched the Allied POWs being herded into captivity. One Indian eye-witness reported, 'I have noticed many German advisers and I understand that the Germans are in charge of artillery operations.' At one point in the early months of the occupation a German Gestapo man in Hong Kong was said to have commented 'that the Japanese would never have got where they were if it had not been for the Germans'. The Defag company (Deutsche Farben Handelsgesellschaft Waibel and Co.), a subsidiary of the industrial giant I. G. Farben, was observed to have entered the colony along with the Japanese. Civilian visitors in the following year included Dr Erich Kordt, the German chargé d'affaires in Nanking. See letter from K. E. Mogra in Lanzhou, 12 February 1942, p. 2, HS 1/349; Calcutta Censor Station Further Notes on Conditions in Hong Kong, 13 May 1942, CO 129 590/24 p. 191; *HKN*, 13 April 1943; testimony and deposition of Corporal Samuel Kravinchuk and deposition of Grenadier Sidney Renton, trial of Major Shoji Toshishige, WO 235/1015 p. 66, exhibit O p. 1 and exhibit T pp. 1–2; Endacott and Birch, *Hong Kong Eclipse*, p. 165.
5. Interview with Mr Oda Takeo, 1 September 1995. Some of the civilian officials are even said to have been suspected by the military of being pro-British. See *SCMP/HKT*, 4 October 1945; Hahn, *Hong Kong Holiday*, p. 155.
6. *FEER*, 10 September 1947.
7. Ward, *Asia for the Asiatics?*, pp. 110, 121; Heasman, 'Japanese Financial and Economic Measures', p. 68. See also *HKN*, 23 January 1943. Applications had to be submitted in triplicate even for 'exports' of goods to the colony's outer islands of Lantau, Cheung Chau and Peng Chau. One copy went to the Finance Department, one to the Harbour Department and one to the Kempeitai. *HKN*, 31 March and 8 June 1943. Import permits were also required for at least some goods: see *HKN*, 18 March 1943, Hirano, '*Kezheng yu baoxing*', pp. 50–1.
8. *HKN*, 25 August 1942.
9. *HKN*, 21 January 1942.
10. Memoranda of G. L. Hall-Patch, British adviser in Chungking, to Treasury forwarded by Ambassador Seymour to Foreign Office 1 August, 1 September, 10 and 30 November 1942, Treasury letter to Hall-Patch 24 October 1942 and reports of Sir R. Campbell, British ambassador, Lisbon, to Foreign Office, 25 August and 4 September 1942, FO 371 31717, pp. 5, 27, 41, 55, 65, 73, 75; Leiper, *A Yen for My Thoughts*, pp. 137–8; Frank H. H. King, *History of the Hongkong and Shanghai Banking Corporation*, vol. III, pp. 628–9; interview, Mr Y. K. Chan, former executive of Jardine Matheson, Hong Kong, 23 March 1995. The figure of HK\$65.6m for the value of the circulated duress notes is given by King. The total estimated value of the duress notes was HK\$119m.
11. A detailed account of the Japanese tax regime is provided in Heasman, 'Japanese Financial and Economic Measures', pp. 76–8. See also *HKN*, 13 and 18 April and 20 June 1943; Tse, *San nian*, pp. 162–4. The taxes were introduced in the following order: house and property tax in early 1942, vehicle taxes in March 1942, land tax on 13 September 1942, stamp duties in November 1942, entertainment tax on 1 January 1943, business profits tax on 12 April 1943 and liquor tax on 20 April 1943.
12. *HKN*, 24 January 1943.
13. Selwyn-Clarke, *Footprints*, p. 69. The publicly stated target was slightly more modest. Asian sources in the first few weeks of the occupation report that the Japanese were intending to evacuate some 600,000 Chinese. In July 1942 Isogai declared that he thought the total population should not exceed 700,000 to 800,000. See letter from K. E. Mogra in Lanzhou, 12 February 1942, p. 2, HS 1/349; Tang Hai, '*Xianggang lunxian ji*,' p. 256; *HKN*, 30 July 1942.
14. See *Honkon-Chosha sakusen*, p. 327; Reuters report from Chungking quoted in *Evening Standard*, London, 15 October 1942, cutting filed in CO 129 590/24 p. 125; Transocean

report, 20 January 1943 and *The Times*, London 10 April 1943, cuttings filed in CO 129 590/22 pp. 170, 190; Harrop, *Hong Kong Incident*, pp. 92–3; Li Koon-chun testimony at Noma trial WO 235/999. The phrase 'rice buckets' or 'useless rice buckets' is quoted in Li, *Hong Kong Surgeon*, p. 160, and Luff, *Hidden Years*, p. 175. The 'control of population' was already specified as an objective in the 23rd Army Guidelines of 9 December 1941, and there seems no doubt that the Japanese were prepared from the outset to employ coercive measures if persuasive ones didn't work. On 28 December 1941, just after the conquest, Colonel Eguchi the 23rd Army medical chief told Phyllis Harrop, 'The trouble with Hong Kong is that there are far too many people. The Hong Kong government failed, we will not fail, we will send them back to their own country, by force if necessary.' A certain amount of compulsory evacuation may already have taken place by the summer of 1942: see Searle diary, 20 May 1942 and Uttley diary, 18 July 1942. The Japanese rationing system was also evidently used as an instrument for compelling departure through the withholding of adequate food supplies. See report of P. V. McLane, Canadian Trade Commissioner, Hong Kong, summer 1942, enclosed with report of William Poy, CO 129 590/25, p. 82. It seems clear however that persuasion was the dominant method employed until July 1943 (see below).

15. Report of Miss Thom forwarded 15 May 1942, CO 129 590/23, p. 90.
16. *HKN*, 31 March 1943.
17. No interest in handing Hong Kong back to China was shown by the Gunseicho, in spite of the fact that it was dominated by the China faction. On New Year's Day 1942, just after the Gunseicho was inaugurated, a clear statement was issued that the conquerors considered the colony to be 'new Japanese territory'. *HKN*, 1 January 1942. Even Yazaki Kanju based the recommendations made in his memorandum of February 1942 on the premise that Hong Kong had been 'made a possession of the Empire'. See Yazaki, '*Honkon tochi hosaku shiken*', p. 243. This complete disregard of the possible 'Wang Jingwei option' struck a number of observers. See comments of *The Times*, London, 10 April 1943, cutting filed in CO 129 590/22 p. 170; note of Colonial Office discussion with Dr Li Shu-fan, 10 February 1944, CO 129 591/4 p. 53.
18. *HKN*, 21 February 1942. The mass of the Chinese population however were considered subjects of the Nanking government. See Ching, *The Li Dynasty*, p. 109. This attitude of course provided a theoretical justification for the expulsion of the mainland Chinese refugees.
19. Quoted in H. L. Mars letter to Churchill, 28 September 1942, CO 129 590/25, p. 18.
20. For Cheng's allegiance see Searle diary, 13 March 1942; Wright-Nooth, *Prisoner of the Turnip-Heads*, p. 92. Most of the Chinese supervisors who were placed in Stanley during the first few weeks of the occupation were reported to be Wang Jingwei partisans.
21. See '(Draft) Steps to Accompany the Nationalist Government's Entry into the War', 15 November 1942 and 'Questions to be Studied regarding the Disposition of the Leased Territory of Kowloon', 25 November 1942, in 'Participation in the War of the Nationalist Government of the Republic of China' (1) and (2) A.7.0.0. 9–41, Diplomatic Record Office, Tokyo.
22. Yazaki, '*Honkon tochi hosaku shiken*', p. 242.
23. See *HKN*, 24 January, 28 March, 15 April, 5, 10 and 11 May 1943; *Domei* in English for Pacific Zone, 4 May 1943, CO 129 590/22, p. 125.
24. *HKN*, 13 March 1942, 29 January, 3 April and 18 June 1943; Record of Survey of Hong Kong Factories, Greater East Asia Ministry, 19 July 1943, Ministry of Finance, Tokyo; Calcutta Censor Station, Further Notes on Conditions in Hong Kong, 13 May 1942, CO 129 590/24, p. 190; MacDougall report of conversation with Mrs Eugenie Zaitzeff, 6 December 1943, CO 129 590/22, p. 55; Heasman, 'Japanese Financial and Economic Measures', pp. 70, 78; heavy industrial concerns that were taken over included the South China Iron Works at Tsuen Wan and a wolfram mine on Needle Hill.
25. Interview with Mr Sanada Iwasuke of the Asia Institute of Developing Economies, Tokyo, 7 August 1995. Information provided by Mr Sanada on this occasion was based on the

reminiscences of Mr Fujita Ichiro, a representative of Mitsui Bussan in wartime Hong Kong.

26. Hirano, '*Kezheng yu baoxing*', p. 55. A former director of Mitsui Bussan, Ishida Reisuke, was appointed economic adviser to Isogai, and the head of the Hong Kong branch of Mitsui Bussan, N. Amano, was reported as being a 'special adviser to Army Headquarters'. See *HKN*, 9 April 1942; report of Mrs A. J. Martin, 11 September 1942, CO 129 590/24, p. 110.

27. *Daily Sketch*, London, 29 October 1942, cutting filed in CO 129 590/24, p. 117.

28. See *HKN*, 17 and 29 December 1942 and 20 February 1943; Tse, *San nian*, p. 34. Tse gives the eventual size of the Japanese community as 30,000; but it seems likely that this figure includes the garrison, which had reached a level of about 20,000 by the end of the war.

29. Interview with Mr Fujita Ichiro, former representative of Mitsui Bussan in wartime Hong Kong, *Aji-ken Nyusu*, vol. 5, no. 10, October 1984, p. 24.

30. *HKN*, 19 January, 27 February, 2 March and 20 August 1942. See also Searle diary, 23 July 1942; Hahn, *Hong Kong Holiday*, p. 106; Heasman, 'Japanese Financial and Economic Measures', p. 69; Hirano, '*Kezheng yu baoxing*', p. 55. For similar annexations of the Hong Kong Hotel and the Cecil Hotel, see *HKN*, 25 and 29 May 1942. Another British department store to pass into Japanese ownership was Whiteaway Laidlaw and Co.

31. These included an iron ore mine, a manganese mine and a number of shipbuilding yards. See Report on Hong Kong, 31 May 1943 HS 1/171, p. 1; *HKN*, 18 June 1943; Ministry of Economic Warfare. Far Eastern Weekly Intelligence Summary no. 33 for week ending 13 August 1943, CO 129 590/22, p. 96.

32. Report on Hong Kong, 4 June 1942, p. 3, and report of K. E. Mogra 27 January 1943, p. 6, HS 1/171.

33. For the Hong Kong Commercial Federation, see *HKN*, 9 October 1942, 23 March and 9 October 1943; German newspaper article of summer 1943 quoted in extract from Far Eastern Weekly Intelligence Summary no. 48 for week ending 26 November 1943, CO 129 590/22, p. 63; Domei news agency report quoted in extract from Daily Digest of World Broadcasts, 25 December 1943, CO 129 591/4 p. 64; Heasman, 'Japanese Financial and Economic Measures', p. 68.

34. *HKN*, 20 February 1943; Heasman, 'Japanese Financial and Economic Measures', pp. 74, 79. In February 1943 Isogai felt obliged to deny reports that the Japanese restaurants in the colony were getting ration rice from the government. See *HKN*, 2 February 1943.

35. *HKN*, 6 April 1943.

36. Report of Sergeant Charles Hedley, 9 February 1944, and statement of Gustavo Velasco forwarded 21 March 1944, CO 129 591/4, pp. 25, 38; Li, *Hong Kong Surgeon*, p. 116. In instituting ethnically segregated brothels the Japanese were reverting to a British practice which had been the norm in Hong Kong in the late nineteenth and early twentieth centuries. See Miners, *Hong Kong under Imperial Rule*, pp. 192–4, 197–8, 203–4.

37. Hahn, *China to Me*, p. 314; Fan Jiping, '*Shengli zhi chu zai Xianggang*' in *Da Ren*, no. 16, August 1971, p. 24.

38. At the end of March 1942 it was announced that in the forthcoming renaming of all Hong Kong streets 'in all probability Japanese names will be given'. *HKN*, 30 March 1942. In practice, however, the renaming seems to have been largely confined to the principal streets, and the multitude of lesser ones were left in a confused mixture of (transliterated) English and Chinese. Prominent landmarks were generally given Japanese names: thus the Peak, for example, became Nioigamine and Repulse Bay, Midorigahama.

39. *HKN*, 1 and 2 March and 2 May 1943.

40. *HKN*, 12, 18 and 22 February 1942, 4 and 18 February, 11 March and 28 May 1943; L. Ride, 'The Test of War' (Part 1) and Anthony Sweeting, 'Controversy over the Reopening of the University of Hong Kong, 1942–48' in Matthews and Cheung (eds), *Dispersal and Renewal*, pp. 18, 397–8.

41. *HKN*, 2 February 1943.

42. These included a Hong Kong Shinto Shrine halfway up the Peak which was expected to cost at least five times as much as the war memorial; a Pagoda for the Buddha's Ashes;

a monument in memory of the Imperial Navy heroes who fell during the invasion; and an 'honorific signboard' marking the spot in Shaukeiwan where Lieutenant Masujima Zenpei carried out his reconnaissance before the Japanese landing on Hong Kong Island. See *HKN*, 1 and 8 September 1942, 2 March, 20 April, 15 August and 25 December 1943; Nakajima, *Honkon*, p. 131. In early 1943 an attempt was even made to plant Hong Kong with cherry trees, the 'symbol of the *samurai* spirit'. *HKN*, 26 February, 17 and 24 March 1943.

43. Tse, *San nian*, p. 429.

44. For this episode see *HKN*, 10 September 1942; Morris, *Hong Kong*, p. 27; Tse, *Zhanshi Ri jun*, pp. 128, 131–3. According to one source the destruction of the monument was intended in part as a deliberate swipe at the Chinese Nationalists. See Walter Schofield, Memories of the District Office South, 12 April 1961, p. 17, Schofield papers, Rhodes House.

45. *China News*, London, 20 January 1943, cutting field in CO 129 590/24, p. 16; Lindsay, *Going Down of the Sun*, p. 133; Tse, *San nian*, p. 44. Every so often we find references in the official media to the Governor's Office 'negotiating' with the Army and Kempeitai over such issues as the Chinese New Year holiday arrangements and the release of public sports grounds. See *HKN*, 17 January and 24 June 1943.

46. Memorandum of Agreement between the Governor of the Conquered Territory of Hong Kong and the Commander-in-Chief of the Second China Expeditionary Fleet regarding the Defence and Military Administration of Hong Kong, May 1942. As a further reminder of the Navy's independent status, distinguished visitors to Hong Kong had routinely to call on the naval commander as well as on Isogai. See *HKN*, 18 June and 12 November 1942, 26 April and 13 July 1943.

47. *China News*, London, 20 January 1943, cutting filed in CO 129 590/24, p. 16. For continued Army–Navy friction see also H. L. Mars, letter to Churchill, 28 September 1942, CO 129 590/25, p. 18.

48. Testimony of Colonel Noma, Noma trial and summary of examination of Colonel Noma, 3 April 1946, wo 235/999, pp. 322, 384 and exhibit K p. 4; testimony of Lieutenant-Colonel Kanazawa, Kanazawa trial WO 235/1093, p. 326. One Allied source declared flatly that the administration embodied in the Governor's Office was 'purely nominal', and that 'complete civil control was held by the Kempeitai'. Report on Hong Kong, 4 June 1942, HS 1/171, p. 2. Another European witness agreed that the 'real Governor' of Hong Kong was 'not Isogai but the gendarmerie'. Fehily conversation with Ride, Guilin, 18 December 1942, CO 129 590/22, p. 163. See also Hahn, *Hong Kong Holiday*, p. 159.

49. Report on Hong Kong, 4 June 1942, HS 1/171, p. 3.

50. Hahn, *China to Me*, p. 350. In the same way an official named Sakamoto, the head of a rice distribution centre, was said to have sold government flour and rice on the open market and pocketed the profits. Testimony of Edward Sykes, chairman of the Eurasian Welfare League, Noma trial, WO 235/999, pp. 134, 138.

51. Hahn, *China to Me*, p.350. For an account of the banishment of other Kempeitai racketeers see Fehily conversation with Ride, Guilin, 18 December 1942, CO 129 590/22, p. 161.

52. Hirano, '*Kezheng yu baoxing*', p. 55. The Hong Kong Brewery is said to have been farmed out in the same way by Isogai to a businessman from Osaka named Inouye Yahei.

53. Report by Major Y. H. Chan on Trading in Opium in Hong Kong, 3 February 1947, appended to file on Isogai trial, WO 325/135; Hirano, '*Kezheng yu baoxing*', p. 53.

54. *SCMP/HKT*, 12 September 1945.

55. Morris, *Hong Kong*, p. 250. The Navy were not angels, however. For accounts of Navy savagery to smugglers or suspected smugglers see Liang, *House of the Golden Dragons*, p. 197; Tse, *Zhanshi Ri jun*, p. 224.

56. Tse, *Zhanshi Ri jun*, pp. 75, 168–9.

57. Testimony of Captain Yatagai Sukeo of the Kempeitai, Noma trial, WO 235/999, p. 393.

58. Hahn, *China to Me*, p. 357.

59. Eyewitness account of Italian Fr Granelli relayed by Dr J. P. Fehily in conversation with Lieutenant-Colonel L. Ride, Guilin, 18 December 1942, CO 129 590/22, p. 164.

60. The Kempeitai's duties were considered to include maintaining control over a hostile civil population. Testimony of Colonel Noma, Noma trial, WO 235/999, p. 321.
61. *HKN*, 11 May 1942; Tse, *Zhanshi Ri jun*, p. 206.
62. Tse, *Zhanshi Ri jun*, p. 112. See also Fehily conversation with Ride, Guilin, 18 December 1942, CO 129 590/22, p. 163.
63. *HKN*, 5, 10 and 14 February 1942; Harrop, *Hong Kong Incident*, p. 144. This particular campaign had already been launched in the Gunseicho period.
64. See Heasman, 'Japanese Financial and Economic Measures', p. 89. Boxes are said to have been attached to the lamp-posts for the collection of dead rats.
65. Endacott and Birch, *Hong Kong Eclipse*, p. 145.
66. Hahn, *China to Me*, p. 357; Selwyn-Clarke, *Footprints*, p. 72.
67. The reduction in cases of cholera and other epidemics during the occupation was much celebrated by Japanese propagandists and their local assistants; and while their claims must inevitably be treated with caution, Allied and neutral sources seem generally to concur that an improvement was made. Gustavo Velasco, a Cuban youth who left the colony in 1943, affirmed that 'owing to the compulsory inoculations decreed by the Japanese typhoid and cholera were not, in fact, more common than before the occupation'. Kathleen Heasman, a Hong Kong University economics lecturer interned in Stanley, noted that 100 and 163 cases of cholera were reported by the Japanese for the outbreaks of June 1942 and June 1943: this compared favourably with 836 and 615 cases recorded by the British respectively for 1940 and 1941, though Heasman pointed out that there might well have been other cases which the Japanese didn't report. Emily Hahn testified that the mass inoculations yielded visible benefits. Statement of Gustavo Velasco forwarded 29 March 1944, CO 129 591/4, p. 35; Heasman, 'Japanese Financial and Economic Measures', p. 89; interview with the late Miss Emily Hahn, 19 January 1994. See also Endacott and Birch, *Hong Kong Eclipse*, p. 145. For Japanese and pro-Japanese claims see Wong Lin, '*Xin Xianggang de Toushi*', p. 68; minutes of the 134th meeting of the Chinese Cooperative Council, 16 August 1943, and the 149th meeting, 15 November 1943; Domei report of 26 September 1943; filed in CO 129 590/22, p. 81; *HKN*, 19 July 1942, 27 February and 19 October 1943, 23 October and 25 December 1944.
68. Phrase used by Sayama Yoshinobu, manager of the Hong Kong branch of the Asahi news agency, *HKN*, 24 January 1943.
69. *HKN*, 23 August, 16 September, 17 and 25 November and 17 December 1942, 17 January, 15 April, 24 June and 26 July 1943; Report on Hong Kong 4 June 1942 and reports of K. E. Mogra 27 January 1943 and F. W. Marshall 21 October 1943, HS 1/171; Heasman, 'Japanese Economic and Financial Measures' p. 70; *FEER* 3 September 1947. In 1943 a total of 65, 472 people are said to have been employed in industry in Japanese-ruled Hong Kong. See Tang Jianxun, *Zui xin Xianggang zhinan*, Hong Kong 1950, p. 10; Leeming, 'The Earlier Industrialization', p. 340 n. 8.
70. For an account of the new Japanese fish marketing system see S. Y. Lin, Brief Report on the Fisheries of Hong Kong under the Japanese Occupation, enclosed with G. A. C. Herklots report to MacDougall, CO 129 591/20, pp. 11–13. See also *HKN*, 19 October and 15 December 1942, 28 March 1943; Domei in English 2 October and 25 December 1943, cuttings filed in CO 129 590/22, p. 62; Heasman, 'Japanese Financial and Economic Measures', p. 70; Tse, *San nian*, p. 76.
71. S. Y. Lin, Brief Report, CO 129 591/20, p. 11. Some of the fishermen in the Saikung peninsula in the New Territories are said to have recalled the Japanese occupation as a time of relative prosperity. See Faure, 'Sai Kung: The Making of the District', p. 126.
72. Report of Chief of the Health Section of the Governor's Office, minutes of the 134th meeting of the Chinese Cooperative Council, 16 August 1943.
73. Ministry of Economic Warfare Far Eastern Weekly Intelligence Summary no. 33 for week ending 13 August 1943, CO 129 590/22; intercepted letter from Beth Woo to Sergeant Richard W. Foo in New York, 10 April 1944 HS 1/171.
74. Uttley diary, 15 October 1942; Samejima Moritaka, *Xianggang huixiang ji* (Chinese translation by S. S. Kong), Hong Kong, 1971, pp. 100–1; interview Sir Y. K. Kan, 24 May 1995.

Numerous other accounts testify to the occurrence of cannibalism in wartime Hong Kong. See, for example, Searle diary, 20 May and 20 August 1942; Clague, Intelligence Summary, 28 May 1942, and Martin report, 11 September 1942, CO 129 590/24, pp. 92, 157; report on Stanley from confidential source formerly of the Public Works Department, 17 February 1943, and report of MacDougall conversation with R. P. Norris, 6 December 1943, CO 129 590/22, pp. 53, 139; letter from John Braga, 24 June 1943, HS 1/171; interview of Kevin Sinclair with Mrs Wong Leung Ju-in, *SCMP*, 7 December 1991.

75. Affidavit of Emil Landau, Noma trial, WO 235/999, exhibit O.

76. Li, *Hong Kong Surgeon*, p. 161.

77. Testimony of fisherman Pang Yam-sing, Noma trial, WO 235/999, p. 293.

78. Some kind of chronology for this is provided by a daughter of Sir Robert Ho Tung, who records that 'many residents, including some of my family, had decided in less than a year after the occupation that Co-Prosperity was not for them'. Gittins, *Stanley: Behind Barbed Wire*, p. 127.

79. Endacott and Birch, *Hong Kong Eclipse*, p. 243; Li, *Hong Kong Surgeon*, p. 160.

80. See Tse, *San nian*, pp. 66–7. Further hints of disgruntlement among Wang Jingwei partisans may be detected in a letter to the *Hong Kong News* from a certain 'K.H.' complaining of the failure of the authorities to fly the flag of the Nanking government alongside the Rising Sun flag, and a report of a visit from a member of the Nanking government to 'pacify' the Chinese in Hong Kong. See *HKN*, 25 February and 10 May 1942. See also Lindsay, *Going Down of the Sun*, p. 132.

81. *HKN*, 28 April 1943. For continued procrastination on the part of the Governor's Office and resulting dissatisfaction in the business community see *HKN*, 4 and 11 May and 8 June 1943.

82. *HKN*, 12 December 1942.

83. *HKN*, 16 and 17 April 1943.

84. Li, *Hong Kong Surgeon*, pp. 136–7.

85. *HKN*, 22 November 1942.

86. Minutes of the 117th, 134th, 135th and 146th meetings of the Chinese Cooperative Council, 17 June, 16 August, 19 August and 25 October 1943.

87. Isogai comments quoted in minutes of the Chinese Cooperative Council, 17 June, 19 August and 25 October 1943. For equally negative responses from other Japanese officials to similar appeals see remarks of Colonel Noma and Captain Ishikawa of the Kempeitai quoted in minutes of the Chinese Cooperative Council, 13 May and 17 June 1943.

88. *HKN*, 27 and 28 July, 1 August and 10 September 1943.

89. MacDougall report of conversation with Mrs Eugenie Zaitzeff, 6 December 1943, CO 129 590/22, p. 57; note of Colonial Office discussion with Dr Li Shu-fan, 10 February 1944, CO 129 591/4, p. 55; Hahn, *China to Me*, p. 369; Samejima, *Xianggang huixiang ji*, p. 124; interviews with Sir Y. K. Kan, 24 May 1995 and Mr Cyril Kotewall, 26 June 1995.

90. '*Gang Ao Wan jin xun di san ji*', Nationalist intelligence report of September 1943, Nationalist Party archives Taipei 523/140.

91. Hahn, *Hong Kong Holiday*, p. 257.

92. Kotewall broadcast in Cantonese of 25 December 1943 published in *Heung Gong Yat Po*, 27 December 1943, translation filed in CO 129 591/4, pp. 50–2.

93. Speech of Aw Boon-haw, 11 December 1943 quoted Fortnightly Intelligence Reports nos 6 and 7, period ended 31 December 1943, Far Eastern Bureau of the Ministry of Information, New Delhi, CO 129 591/4, p. 61.

94. *HKN*, 25 June 1943. For suspicion of the military yen see also Report on Hong Kong 4 June 1942 and report of G. Leslie Andrew, 22 October 1943, HS 1/171, pp. 1–2, note of Colonial Office discussion with Dr Li Shu-fan, 10 February 1944, CO 129 591/4, p. 54; Hirano, '*Kezheng yu baoxing*', p. 51; Gittins, *Stanley: Behind Barbed Wire*, p. 135.

95. Heasman, 'Japanese Financial and Economic Measures', p. 68; *HKN*, 6 March 1943.

96. *HKN*, 8 May 1943. For Eurasian disgruntlement see also Hahn, *Hong Kong Holiday*, pp. 169–70. Some Eurasians are said to have complained that they were denied both rice rations (because they weren't Chinese) and flour rations (because they weren't European).

97. Hahn, *Hong Kong Holiday*, p. 257.
98. For the crisis in Japanese relations with the Indian Independence League see Fujiwara, *F. Kikan*, pp. 238–46, 247.
99. For the foregoing see Notes by G. S. Kennedy-Skipton, 11 March 1943, CO 129 590/22, pp. 112, 113; report of K. E. Mogra, 27 January 1943, HS 1/171, p. 7.
100. Report of Indian businessman who left Hong Kong for India, December 1942, CO 129 590/22, p. 186.
101. *HKN*, 16 March 1943; Uttley diary, 18 March 1943; MacDougall report of conversation with Sergeant David Fyffe, 6 December 1943, CO 129 590/22, p. 51; E. Ride, *British Army Aid Group*, p. 148.
102. Interview, Mr Y. K. Chan, 23 March 1995.
103. Quoted in article by Adam Williams, *SMP*, 19 November 1978.
104. Conversation of Dr J. P. Fehily with Lieutenant-Colonel L. Ride, Guilin, 18 December 1942, CO 129 590/22, p. 164.
105. See for example Hahn, *China to Me*, p. 395.
106. Li, *Hong Kong Surgeon*, p. 159. For assessment that the Japanese 'had a chance' in Hong Kong with their doctrine of 'Asia for the Asiatics' see Hahn, *Hong Kong Holiday*, p. 259; Tse, *Zhanshi Ri jun*, p. 11.
107. Li, *Hong Kong Surgeon*, p. 147. Something of the same impasse seems to have been reached with the English-speaking minorities. In March 1943 Major-General Suganami Ichiro, who had succeeded Arisue as Chief of Staff, made a statement conceding that English could be used to teach 'third national' children so long as Japanese was taught at the same time. See *HKN*, 9 March 1943.
108. Kwan, 'Charitable Activities', pp. 189, 263 n. 14. School attendance may possibly have risen slightly in the course of the following year. In February 1944 Kathleen Heasman recorded a figure of 7,000 given by Japanese sources for total student attendance at that time. See Heasman, 'Japanese Financial and Economic Measures', p. 86. The numbers may also be higher than those cited by either Kwan or Heasman if allowance is made for private schools as well as government-sponsored ones; in December 1943, for example, the *Hong Kong News* claimed that 8,221 students had been enrolled at a number of private schools on Hong Kong Island alone. Even if the maximum figures quoted by contemporary sources are accepted, however, school attendance was clearly still very low by comparison with pre-war days.
109. See appeal by Kotewall to factory owners and merchants quoted in *HKN*, 1 June 1942; account of Kotewall tour of local shops in *HKN*, 8 June 1942; and indications of pressure exerted by Li Tse-fong, *HKN*, 21 June 1942. A sub-committee of the Chinese Cooperative Council reported in late August 1942 that 'most' business firms had suspended work. *HKN*, 30 August 1942. One Chinese source even claims that nine out of ten shops stayed closed, though this may be an exaggeration. See Lu Ganzhi, '*Xianggang de chentong wangshi*', in *Zhanggu Yuekan* no. 6, February 1972, p. 56.
110. Conversation of Dr J. P. Fehily with Lieutenant-Colonel L. Ride, Guilin, 18 December 1942, CO 129 590/22, p. 163.
111. Testimony of Mrs Tsang Mau-ting, Noma trial, WO 235/999, p. 284.
112. Buping Shanren, *Xianggang lunxian huiyilu*, p. 52. For labour trouble in the docks see also MacDougall conversation with Mrs Eugenie Zaitzeff, 6 December 1943, CO 129 590/22, p. 56. It was apparently difficult to persuade Chinese to work in the dockyards in the first place. See Heasman, 'Japanese Economic and Financial Measures', p. 76.
113. Hahn, *China to Me*, p. 375.
114. Fan, '*Xianggang zhi zhan huiyilu*', p. 9; Nationalist Party Headquarters for Hong Kong and Macao, *Xunguo lieshi jiniance*, pp. 2, 4, 5, 6, 7, 10. See also Tse, *Zhanshi Ri jun*, p. 35.
115. Liang, *House of the Golden Dragons*, pp. 202–3, 209.
116. Memorandum of Superintendent W. P. ('Tommy') Thompson regarding the Hong Kong and Kowloon Mass Anti-Japanese Guerrillas, 14 June 1942, CO 129 590/23, pp. 27–8; report of Major Ronald Holmes, 12 July 1944, HS 1/171, p. 2; Woddis, 'Hong Kong and the East River Company', pp. 10–11; Catron, 'China and Hong Kong', pp. 28–9, 100, 308; Zeng

Hongwen, '*Chu jin Gang Jiu*', pp. 39–42; Faure, 'Sai Kung: the Making of the District', pp. 129–30.

117. Early evidence for this rural generation gap was provided in the course of the escape of Admiral Chan Chak's party to Huizhou in December 1941, when Lieutenant-Commander Gandy asked a young Chinese girl partisan who was escorting the group what her parents thought of her current activities. Her response was, 'I belong to the New China, but they do not.' See Lindsay, *Going Down of the Sun*, p. 12. For other indications, see Thompson memorandum, 14 June 1942, CO 129 590/23, p. 27; Endacott and Birch, *Hong Kong Eclipse*, p. 154.

118. Memorandum of Superintendent W. P. ('Tommy') Thompson regarding the Hong Kong and Kowloon Mass Anti-Japanese Guerrillas, 14 June 1942, CO 129 590/23, p. 27; Holmes report, 12 July 1944, HS 1/171, pp. 2–3. Phrase 'chickens with parasites' quoted in lecture given by Mr S. J. Chan at the Hong Kong Museum of History, 18 October 1995.

119. Li, *Hong Kong Surgeon* p. 169. In August word got out that the authorities were unable to collect firewood in the Saikung peninsula because the situation there was 'not very tranquil'. See report of Li Koon-chun, minutes of the 134th meeting of the Chinese Cooperative Council, 16 August 1943.

120. MacDougall dispatch to Colonial Office introducing report of Lieutenant-Colonel L. Ride, 29 May 1942, CO 129 590/25, p. 193.

121. Ride report, CO 129 590/25, p. 202.

122. A detailed account of Ride's escape from Hong Kong and foundation of the BAAG may be found in E. Ride, *British Army Aid Group*, pp. 14–63. See also Osler Thomas, 'With the BAAG in Wartime China', in Matthews and Cheung (eds), *Dispersal and Renewal*, pp. 307–9; Lindsay, *Going Down of the Sun*, pp. 28, 61–3, 90–2.

123. Selwyn-Clarke, *Footprints*, p. 77.

124. Ride report forwarded by Brigadier G. E. Grimsdale, Chungking, to MI2, War Office, 29 June 1942, CO 129 590/23, p. 79; E. Ride, *British Army Aid Group*, p. 77.

125. Wright-Nooth, *Prisoner of the Turnip-Heads*, p. 98. For subversion of *Hong Kong News*, see also MacDougall report of conversation with Sergeant David Mann and Mrs E. C. K. Mann, 4 December 1943, CO 129 590/22, p. 37; Gimson, diary, July 1943 and Hong Kong Reclaimed; Gittins, *Eastern Windows*, pp. 150–1, and *Stanley: Behind Barbed Wire*, p. 119.

126. Suggestion made by Wang Jingwei partisans to Japanese representatives in Macao, 21 February 1943. See E. Ride, *British Army Aid Group*, p. 214.

127. Frank H. H. King, *History of the Hongkong and Shanghai Banking Corporation*, vol. III, p. 615; Lu, '*Xianggang de chentong wangshi*', p. 56.

128. Quoted in E. Ride, *British Army Aid Group*, p. 213.

129. Report of F. A. Olsen 4 August 1942, HS 1/176, p. 1. For attempts by the Governor to be helpful in spite of the hostile attitude of some of his aides see Harrop, *Hong Kong Incident*, pp. 138–9.

130. Fehily conversation with Ride, Guilin, 18 December 1942, CO 129 590/22, p. 161.

131. Report of F. A. Olsen, 4 August 1942, HS 1/176, p. 2.

132. Report from British consulate in Macao cited in letter from Yumoto, Japanese intelligence officer to Joseph Richards, 21 August 1944, Richards trial documents, HK RS 245-2-150.

133. Uttley diary, 15 November 1942.

134. Frank H. H. King, *History of the Hongkong and Shanghai Banking Corporation*, vol. III, p. 574. A dentist named Ken Chaun provided similar services.

135. By the end of 1943 a total of 346 students from the University had left Hong Kong for Free China. These represented over 50 per cent of the total enrolment of the University in December 1941. Large numbers of them joined up with the BAAG. See Professor Gordon King, 'An Episode in the History of the University', and Osler Thomas, 'With the BAAG in Wartime China' in Matthews and Cheung (eds), *Dispersal and Renewal*, pp. 306–8; E. Ride, *British Army Aid Group*, pp. 85–6.

136. A history of the BAAG states that 'most' of the Chinese students who joined Ride were 'intelligent young men from well known Hong Kong families'. See E. Ride, *British Army*

Aid Group, p. 86. For divergence of views between gentry members and their children on the desirability of putting up active resistance to the Japanese see account of the disagreement between Li Koon-chun and his son Simon given in Ching, *The Li Dynasty*, p. 113. All of Li Koon-chun's sons, and most of the children of his brother Li Tse-fong, had left Hong Kong by 1944, though not necessarily to take part in resistance activities. Another patrician recruit to the British war effort in south China (though not to the BAAG) was Kitty Cheung, *née* Tse, a granddaughter of Ho Kom-tong, the chairman of the wartime Jockey Club. See Bernard Mellor, 'In India, in China and Twice in Hong Kong', in Matthews and Cheung (eds), *Dispersal and Renewal*, p. 354. The most striking instance of all of this apparent gentry generation gap would seem to be found in the family of Tung Chung-wei, the proprietor of the Dao Heng Bank and chairman of the Hong Kong Chinese General Chamber of Commerce, who took his seat on the Rehabilitation Advisory Committee set up by the Gunseicho in January 1942. Tung's eldest daughter Dong Hui was a Communist Party activist. In the pre-war years she had been one of the two agents deployed in the colony by Yan'an to coordinate the Party's different intelligence outfits. Tse, *Xianggang kang Ri*, pp. 128–9. One or two leading magnates may also have deployed their offspring strategically to ensure that thay were seen to have a stake in the Allied cause: thus the Tiger Balm King was said to have sent his son Aw Hoe to Guilin to take charge of his industrial plants in unoccupied China. Comment by British officials on Extract from Fortnightly Intelligence Report no. 13, Far Eastern Bureau, MOI, New Delhi, 1–15 July 1944, CO 129 519/4. For this pattern see Wen-hsin Yeh, Introduction and Parks M. Coble, 'Chinese capitalists and the Japanese: Collaboration and resistance in the Shanghai area, 1937–45' in Wen-hsin Yeh (ed), *Wartime Shanghai*, London and New York, 1998, pp. 20, 76, 79.

137. For details of Lee's contribution see report taken from diary of Sub-Lieutenant D. F. Davies, HKRNVR, forwarded from Chungking, 10 June 1942, CO 129 590/23, pp. 95–8; E. Ride, *British Army Aid Group*, pp. 16–18, 20–3, 31–9, 45–8, 67–8.

138. Selwyn-Clarke, *Footprints*, pp. 78–9. Selwyn-Clarke also noted the efforts of two women assistants, Dr Lai Po-chuen and Helen Ho, whom he could 'trust to carry on at any sacrifice'.

139. E. Ride, *British Army Aid Group*, p. 54.

140. Ibid., pp. 57–8. At Qujiang, which was also the headquarters of the Nationalist Seventh War Zone, Ride's path was smoothed by the fact that the general he dealt with, Zhu Laiquan, was an alumnus of Hong Kong University. The Nationalist garrison command at Huizhou were squared through the good offices of a well-known Hong Kong Chinese businessman, Dick Lee.

141. Harrop, report to Eden 7 April 1942, CO 129 590/23, pp. 188, 205 and *Hong Kong Incident*, pp. 123–4, 146–7, 152–4, 158–9. For contribution made by the Nationalists to the passage of other British resistance elements through Macao to Free China see also H. L. Mars, letter to Churchill, 28 September 1942, CO 129 590/25, p. 17.

142. For the total of British and Allied POWs who escaped under the auspices of the BAAG see E. Ride, *British Army Aid Group*, p. 328. For the guerrillas' rescue of British and Allied POWs see Thompson memorandum 14 June 1942, CO 129 590/23, p. 27; Lindsay, *Going Down of the Sun*, pp. 95–6; Zhong Zi, '*Dong Jiang Zongdui yingjiu guoji youren ji qi yingxiang*', in *Guangdong wenshi ziliao*, vol. 44, *Xianggang yi pie*, Guangzhou 1985, pp. 211–12; Jiang Shui and Li Zhaopei, '*Yingguo junguan yingjiu ji*' and '*Yuanzhu Ying Jun Fuwutuan*', in Xu Yueqing (ed.), *Huoyue zai Xiangjiang*, Hong Kong, 1993, pp. 42–8, 49. The guerrillas also helped in the rescue of over fifty Indian POWs who were brought out by the BAAG.

143. HSB 19 February 1946; Zhong Zi, '*Dong Jiang Zongdui*', p. 212. These Chinese sources state that the East River guerrillas rescued a total of eighty-nine 'international friends', including twenty British nationals, eight United States airmen, fifty-four Indians, three Danes, two Norwegians, one White Russian and one Filipino. The Chinese sources do not however distinguish clearly between POWs and civilians. Assuming that most of the British and all of the Indians rescued were POWs, the number of civilians aided by the guerrillas would seem to have been fairly small.

144. Zhong Zi, '*Dong Jiang Zongdui*', p. 212.
145. Declaration made by Ride to leaders of the East River Column in February 1946, quoted in '*Yuanzhu Ying Jun Fuwutuan*', p. 51. Decades later, in 1993, Paul Tsui acknowledged similarly that without the help and protection of the East River guerrillas the BAAG could have done nothing. Information provided by Mr S. J. Chan, lecture at the Hong Kong Museum of History, 18 October 1995.
146. Quoted E. Ride, *British Army Aid Group*, p. 49.
147. Selwyn-Clarke, *Footprints* p. 88; recollection of T. J. J. Fenwick, quoted in Frank H. H. King, *History of the Hongkong and Shanghai Banking Corporation*, vol. III, p. 574.
148. Report of J. A. D. Morrison quoted Frank H. H. King, *History of the Hongkong and Shanghai Banking Corporation*, vol. III, p. 620. For other tributes to the East River guerrillas see Grimsdale letter to DMI, MI2 and War Office introducing Thompson memorandum and Thompson memorandum, 14 June 1942 CO 129 590/23, pp. 25, 27, 29.
149. Lindsay, *Lasting Honour*, p. 183.
150. Gleason, *Hong Kong*, p. 178.
151. One example is the partnership formed between Superintendent W. P. ('Tommy') Thompson of the Hong Kong Police and his secretary Irene Fincher, *née* Gittins. Their daughter Philippa was born in 1943. See Peter Hall, *In the Web*, pp. 147, 149. Arthur Bentley, a former Government Pharmacist and part-time lecturer in pharmacy at Hong Kong University, who directed the provision of relief to escaped Hong Kong students at Qujiang till August 1942, married Man Wah Leung, an arts graduate of the University. See Bernard Mellor, 'Strains of War and The Links Break', and Professor Gordon King, 'An Episode in the History of the University', in Matthews and Cheung (eds), *Dispersal and Renewal*, pp. 81, 89–92. There is some evidence to suggest that a general weakening of the taboos against miscegenation took place at this time. In the occupied city a fair number of interracial marriages and cohabitations are recorded among the Chinese, Eurasians and Indians as well as between Asians and Europeans. See notices of the marriage of Archibald Chu and Beatrice Hutchinson and of Z. A. Abbas and Sin Kwai-yuen, *HKN*, 2 and 28 February 1943; White, *Turbans and Traders*, p. 46. Such partnerships were often contracted for pragmatic reasons; but it seems reasonable to suppose that there was also a certain sense of 'being in the same boat'.
152. For this sequence of events see Hahn, *China to Me*, pp. 386–90, 404–5; Li, *Hong Kong Surgeon*, pp. 144–5, 156; Frank H. H. King, *History of the Hongkong and Shanghai Banking Corporation*, vol. III, pp. 621–3; Selwyn-Clarke, *Footprints*, pp. 83–4. The internee who was caught with the money was Dr Harry Talbot; the banker arrested with Grayburn was E. P. Streatfield.
153. Hahn, *China to Me*, p. 394. Emily Hahn was convinced that Grayburn's death was an accident resulting from an over-enthusiastic 'investigation' by the Kempeitai. The beri-beri diagnosis seems however to have been accepted by Grayburn's fellow-internees. See Gimson and Uttley diaries, 23 August 1943; report of Sergeant Charles Hedley, 9 February 1944, CO 129 591/4, p. 27.
154. Searle and Constance Murray, diaries, 29 October 1943; Gimson diary, October 1943; Gittins, *Stanley: Behind Barbed Wire*, pp. 133–5. Constance Murray and Jean Gittins diverge from the other sources in stating that the victims were shot. The reality was apparently that all were decapitated: the last few beheadings were, however, performed so incompetently that a number of lives had to be finished off by shooting. See Lindsay, *Going Down of the Sun*, p. 119.
155. Wright-Nooth, *Prisoner of the Turnip-Heads*, p. 187.
156. Affidavit of Agnes Horton, 20 March 1946, Noma trial, WO 235/999, exhibit U, p. 2.
157. Report of Sergeant Charles Hedley, 9 February 1944, CO 129 591/4. The prosecutors at the subsequent war crimes trials stated that 1,816 Chinese were to have been imprisoned by the Japanese authorities during the occupation. See Wright-Nooth, *Prisoner of the Turnip-Heads*, p. 253. The real figure is likely to have been far higher.
158. One hundred and eighty-one Chinese were said by the post-war prosecutors to have been beheaded in the course of the occupation. Wright-Nooth, *Prisoner of the Turnip-Heads*, p.

253. Again the real figure is likely to have been vastly higher than this official total. One early British post-war source maintains that as many as 10,000 Chinese were executed, while a Chinese writer claims that 50,000 deaths may have resulted directly or indirectly from the activities of George Wong alone. See Ingrams, *Hong Kong*, p. 242; Tse, *Zhanshi Ri jun*, p. 237. It seems therefore to be not merely a safe but a somewhat conservative estimate to suggest that some hundreds of Hong Kong Chinese may have been liquidated during the purge of 1943.

159. Statement of Mrs Kaneko Bush, a Japanese lady married to a British naval officer who was coopted by the occupation authorities as an interpreter, 20 March 1946, quoted Wright-Nooth, *Prisoner of the Turnip-Heads*, p. 165.

160. Uttley, letter to Mrs Helen Uttley, undated, around 18 August 1945, Uttley papers, Rhodes House p. 191. Inmates of the POW camps observed in the same way that Hong Kong Chinese lives were being 'snuffed out with a callousness which made them believe that they were privileged in their treatment'. Birch and Cole, *Captive Years*, p. 69.

161. Noted in Searle diary, 29 October 1943. The three British POWs shot at Shek O were also executed in the company of a large number of Chinese victims. See E. Ride, *British Army Aid Group*, p. 162.

162. MacDougall report of conversation with Mrs Eugenie Zaitzeff, 6 December 1943, CO 129 590/22, pp. 57–8.

163. *HKN*, editorial, 8 May 1943.

164. Uttley diary, 21 March 1943.

165. Hahn, *Hong Kong Holiday*, p. 259.

166. Gittins, *Stanley: Behind Barbed Wire*, p. 65. Jean Gittins was, of course, a Eurasian (for Eurasian internees, see p. 200 below); but – in this context at least – she identifies herself wholeheartedly with the British cause. 'We knew', she goes on, 'that Hong Kong's faith in the British had been fully restored.'

167. Shaftain, Rough Draft, p. 14. This was probably not the first such contact: Shaftain speaks of the Triad representatives 'keeping a rendezvous'. Following their detention the Triad emissaries were tortured and shot.

168. Wright-Nooth, *Prisoner of the Turnip-Heads* p. 96. For other evidence of a change of attitude among the Indian guards in Stanley see E. D. Robbins Report on Hong Kong Internment, and MacDougall report of conversation with Sergeant Charles Hedley, 4 December 1943, CO 129 590/22, p. 35; Hedley report of 9 February 1944, CO 129 591/4, pp. 25–6.

169. MacDougall report of conversation with Sergeant David Mann, 4 December 1943, CO 129 590/22, p. 37.

170. Letter from John Braga in Macao to Viscount Samuel, 19 June 1943, HS 1/171.

171. Ingrams, *Hong Kong*, p. 267. Another Hong Kong University graduate who had been treated insensitively by an officer in British naval intelligence subsequently accepted a commission with the Nationalist Army in their Seventh War Zone. See Patrick Yu, 'Wartime Experiences in Hong Kong and China (Part 2)', in Matthews and Cheung (eds), *Dispersal and Renewal*, pp. 317–24.

172. E. Ride, *British Army Aid Group*, pp. 174, 182–3. See also 'Gang Ao Wan jin xun di san ji', September 1943, Nationalist Party archives, Taipei 523/140; Li, *Hong Kong Surgeon*, p. 191. Endo's counter-intelligence agents were thick on the ground in Guilin, where they frequented two popular night clubs called The Lido and Susie Sue's; and the founder of the OCVU, though supposedly not an agent of Endo's, was reported to have links with the Japanese in Hong Kong.

173. See report of press attaché, British embassy, Chungking, forwarded to Foreign Officer, 30 August 1943, CO 825 42/15, pp. 216–17.

174. Chiang Kai-shek, *China's Destiny* (English edition), New York, 1947, p. 154.

175. Lane, 'Nationalist Government', p. 101. One journalist did apparently raise the issue with Soong. Soong replied that if he were a member of the British government facing the House of Commons, he would say 'I must have notice of that question'. See *The Times*, London, 5 August 1943, extract filed in CO 825 42/15, p. 233. Soong is also said to have remarked infor-

mally to an official of the British Board of Trade that it was a 'foregone conclusion' the colony would be returned to China. Lindsay, *Lasting Honour*, p. 194.

176. For example at a meeting of Roosevelt and Under-Secretary of State Sumner Welles with Foreign Secretary Eden in March 1943. See Monson minute, 30 June 1943, CO 825 42/15, pp. 16–17; Chan Lau, 'The United States and the Question of Hong Kong', pp. 9–10, *China, Britain and Hong Kong*, p. 402, n. 80.

177. Report of R. K. Law, Parliamentary Under-Secretary to the Foreign Office, 20 August 1943, quoted in Chan Lau, *China, Britain and Hong Kong*, p. 310.

178. Gent minute to Thornley for attention of Secretary of State for the Colonies, 16 February 1943 and letter of China Association to Colonial Office, 27 May 1943, CO 825 42/15, pp. 9, 247–50.

179. Gent memorandum of conversation with Roberts, 6 August 1943 and Keswick letter to Gent, 17 September 1943, CO 825 42/15, pp. 226, 234–5.

180. Minute of Sir Maurice Peterson, 'A Postwar Settlement in the Far East', 1 September 1942, quoted in Chan Lau, *China, Britain and Hong Kong*, p. 303.

181. In February 1943 John Keswick wrote a paper in his capacity as chief of the Special Operations Executive's China branch (see below) emphasizing the importance of Hong Kong and insisting, 'We shall return to the East with our heads held high'. Memorandum by AD/O, 27 February 1943, p. 8, HS 1/349. See also remarks of Brigadier G. E. Grimsdale, British military attaché in Chungking 1 July 1943 quoted Aldrich, *Intelligence and the War against Japan*, p. 279.

182. See Alan Birch article in *SCMP*, 12 October 1975; Lindsay, *Lasting Honour*, p. 49; E. Ride, *British Army Aid Group*, p. 55. Z Force had been trained in Hong Kong before the invasion with a view to conducting sabotage behind the Japanese lines.

183. Memorandum of John Keswick, 13 April 1942, p. 2 and Keswick telegram from Chungking no. 679, 31 May 1943, p. 1, HS 1/349.

184. Memorandum of Lieutenant-Colonel C. M. Rait, MI9, 19 August 1944, HS 1/171.

185. 'A Plan for Sabotage Operations along the China Coast', 3 July 1943, p. 2, HS 1/171.

186. Ride to Grimsdale, August 1943, quoted in E. Ride, *British Army Aid Group*, p. 122.

187. Minute of J. J. Paskin on meeting of Far Eastern Reconstruction Committee, 2 July 1943, CO 825 35/26, pp. 8–9.

188. For the foregoing see Chan Lau, 'The United States and the Question of Hong Kong', pp. 10–11, and *China, Britain and Hong Kong*, pp. 311–12. The adviser's name was Stanley Hornbeck.

189. Chan Lau, 'The United States and the Question of Hong Kong', pp. 11–12, *China, Britain and Hong Kong*, p. 313. The outlines of the package had apparently been suggested by Roosevelt to Foreign Minister T. V. Soong on the occasion of Eden's visit to Washington in March 1943. See Lane, 'Nationalist Government', p. 100. For Churchill response to Roosevelt see E. Ride, *British Army Aid Group*, p. 117.

190. E. Ride, *British Army Aid Group*, pp. 55–6; Lindsay, *Going Down of the Sun* p. 92; Aldrich, *Intelligence and the War against Japan*, p. 281–2. The formal reason for Chiang's actions was that Z Force had ignored the directions of Nationalist commanders; but the British had no doubt that Chiang and his government were bent on forestalling British commando activities in the neighbourhood of the fallen colony.

191. E. Ride, *British Army Aid Group*, pp. 122–3; Lindsay, *Going Down of the Sun*, p. 96.

192. Report of Major Ronald Holmes, 12 July 1944, HS 1/171, pp. 4, 5; ZB 13 January 1946; Zhong Zi, '*Dong Jiang Zongdui*', p. 213.

193. Gent minute, 27 July 1943, CO 825 42/15, p. 240.

194. Chan Lau, 'The United States and the Question of Hong Kong', p. 11, and *China, Britain and Hong Kong*, p. 312.

195. MacDougall report of conversation with Sergeant David Mann and Mrs E. C. K. Mann, 4 December 1943, CO 129 590/22, p. 37.

196. Fehily conversation with Ride, Guilin, 18 December 1942 and MacDougall report of conversation with Mrs Eugenie Zaitzeff, 6 December 1943, CO 129 590/22, pp. 56, 161.

197. MacDougall report of conversations with Sergeant David Mann and Mrs E. C. K. Mann, 4 December 1943, and Mrs Eugenie Zaitzeff, 6 December 1943, CO 129 590/22, pp. 37, 56.
198. Comment on Sir Robert Ho Tung contained in letter from William Wright of Dodwell and Co. to G. Dodwell, 3 September 1942, CO 129 590/24, p. 132. For comments on Aw Boon-haw see remarks of British officials on Extract from Fortnightly Intelligence Report no. 13, Far Eastern Bureau, MOI, New Delhi, 1–15 July, cited in letter from Yumoto, Japanese intelligence officer, to Joseph Richards, 21 August 1944, Richards trial documents, HK RS 245-2-150.
199. See minute of W. B. L. Monson, 4 June 1942, CO 129 590/23, p. 10; minutes of W. B. L. Monson, 1 October 1942 and J. J. Paskin, 7 October 1942, CO 129 590/24, pp. 2–3, 8–11.
200. Monson minute, 9 February 1942, CO 129 590/23, p. 4. Opening the 'quislings' file eight months later the same official reiterated that many reports of collaboration couldn't be confirmed and that it was not currently necessary to form any definite conclusion 'except in one or two clear cases'. See Monson minute, 1 October 1942, CO 129 590/24, p. 8.
201. Monson minute, 17 February 1944, CO 129 591/14, p. 4.
202. Letter of T. M. Hazlerigg to N. L. Smith, 23 March 1945, HK RS 211-2-41.
203. N. L. Smith minute, 18 October 1943, CO 129 590/22; N. L. Smith minute to Monson, 7 January 1944, CO 129 591/4, p. 70 and minute 22 March 1945 HK RS 211-2-41.
204. N. L. Smith minute, 22 March 1945 HK RS 211-2-41.
205. Monson minute, 4 June 1942, CO 129 590/23, p. 9.
206. Calcutta Censor Station Further Notes on Conditions in Hong Kong, 13 May 1942, taken up in Monson minute, 1 October 1942, CO 129 590/24, pp. 8, 189; report of Professor Gordon King, 18 March 1942, CO 129 590/23, p. 139, taken up in Monson minutes, 4 June 1942, CO 129 590/23, p. 9, and 1 October 1942, CO 129 590/24, p. 8; observation of Dr Wen Yuanning quoted in N. L. Smith minute to Monson, 7 January 1944, CO 129 591/4, p. 70. Smith was glad to see from the various reports which had come in that Lo was 'a reluctant puppet'. Minute of 18 October 1943, CO 129 590/22.
207. E. Ride, *British Army Aid Group*, p. 182.
208. Dafydd Emrys Evans, 'A Cosy Hillside Campus' and 'The Test of War', L. Ride, 'The Test of War (Part 1)', Bernard Mellor, 'Strains of War and the Links Break', Gordon King, 'An Episode in the History of the University', Huang Hsing Tsung, 'Pursuing Science in Hong Kong, China and the West', Guan Bee Ong, 'Dispersal and Renewal: Hong Kong University Medical and Health Services', and Anthony Sweeting, 'Controversy over the Reopening of the University', in Matthews and Cheung (eds), *Dispersal and Renewal*, pp. 4, 17–18, 77–8, 87–99, 135, 390, 398; Gittins, *Eastern Windows*, p. 130; Ko and Wordie, *Ruins of War*, p. 158. These arrangements were pushed through virtually single-handed by Professor Gordon King of the University's Faculty of Medicine. By the end of 1943 243 students had been placed at mainland universities through King's intervention, and the total had risen to 357 by the end of the war. King also exerted himself to obtain recognition from the General Medical Council in Britain for the diplomas which the Hong Kong medical students had obtained at universities on the mainland.
209. Already in 1942 Dr Duncan Sloss, the Vice-Chancellor of Hong Kong University, had made a specific request that those Chinese members of the Hong Kong Volunteer Defence Corps who had been asked to go to Free China should be paid a living wage, and that their families should be cared for. Fehily conversation with Ride, Guilin, 18 December 1942, CO 129 590/22, p. 159. For subsequent measures see Paskin minute 11 March 1943 and Foreign Office telegram no. 286 to British embassy Chungking 22 March 1943, CO 825 38/6, pp. 2–4, 6; report of press attaché, British embassy Chungking, 30 August 1943, CO 825 42/15, p. 217; E. Ride, *British Army Aid Group*, pp. 118, 186; Frank H. H. King, *History of the Hongkong and Shanghai Banking Corporation*, vol. III, p. 573.
210. Comment of Fr Thomas Ryan cited in report of press attaché, British embassy, Chungking, 30 August 1943, and Monson reaction, minute of 24 September 1943, CO 825 42/15, pp. 33–4, 217.
211. See Bishop Hall memorandum, 16 January 1942, CO 825 42/15, pp. 293–7.
212. Paton, *R. O.*, p. 133. A full account of this celebrated episode may be found on pp. 125–46.

213. Caine comments on Bishop Hall memorandum, 13 February 1942, CO 825 42/15, pp. 4–5. For similar reactions see minutes of Gent, 16 January and 14 February, Jeffries, 24 January, and Cox, 30 January, in the same file, pp. 2, 3, 4, 5–6.
214. MacDougall, 'Notes on the Siege', CO 129 590/25, pp. 228–9.
215. Ibid., pp. 227–8, 229. See also MacDougall dispatch to Colonial Office introducing report of Lientenant-Colonel L. Ride, 29 May 1942, CO 129 590/25, p. 193.
216. MacDougall article, 'Britain in the Far East: The Debit Side of the Balance', in *The Times*, London, 1 August 1942, cutting filed in CO 825 42/15, p. 286; note of MacDougall on Phyllis Harrop report to Eden, 27 May 1942, CO 129 590/23.
217. MacDougall letter to Sabine, 22 December 1942, p. 5, MacDougall papers, Rhodes House.
218. Pledge to the peoples of the colonies given by the Colonial Office in July 1943. See Endacott and Birch, *Hong Kong Eclipse*, pp. 279, 318–19.
219. Caine comments on Bishop Hall memorandum, 13 February 1942 and Monson minute, 30 June 1943, CO 825 42/15, pp. 15, 290.
220. Uttley diary, 23 May 1942.
221. Ibid., 7 June 1942, 18 April 1943.
222. Comment of Mrs Mary Goodban quoted in Lindsay, *Going Down of the Sun*, p. 208.
223. Uttley diary, 28 February 1943.
224. Gittins, *Stanley: Behind Barbed Wire*, p. 66. Some resentment was also provoked by the sight of parcels which the Eurasians were getting from their relatives in town.
225. Statement of internee Pritchard quoted in Gimson diary, 26 January 1945.
226. See Pennefather-Evans, Interim Report, p. 1, 4, 5, 10, 12, 16, 18–19, 36. Background on the Police Commissioner's religious outlook is given in Wright-Nooth, *Prisoner of the Turnip-Heads*, p. 198. For Pennefather-Evans's hostility to intermarriage, see also Gimson diary, 15 and 17 November 1944.
227. Uttley diary, 6 May 1942.
228. See Gimson diary, 18, 28 and 30 August and 1 October 1943, 10 and 21 January, 12 and 28 February, 3 and 4 March, 20 April, 23 June, 8, 10, 11 and 20 July and 22 and 23 August 1944. The agitation appears to have subsided in the final year of captivity.
229. Gimson diary, 21 and 25 June 1943 and November 1943.
230. Ibid., 20 June 1943.
231. Searle diary, 2 November 1943; Wright-Nooth, *Prisoner of the Turnip-Heads*, p. 93.
232. See expressions of sympathy with Japanese administrative difficulties expressed in Gimson diary, July, 4 and 5 August, 10, 13 and 21 September 1943 and 12 and 20 January, 15 February, 27 March, 12 May, 21 August and 14 September 1944. It should however be remembered that Gimson was writing a diary which might easily be discovered and read by the Japanese, and that some of his more understanding remarks about them may have been made with this possibility in mind.
233. Gimson diary, 15 and 16 August 1943. For similar episodes see also diary entries for 31 March, 24 June, 1 and 14 July and 5 September 1944.
234. Gimson diary, 13 June 1943.
235. Gimson, Internment in Hong Kong, summary, p. 17; Gimson comment quoted in Steve Tsang, *Democracy Shelved: Great Britain, China and Attempts at Constitutional Reform in Hong Kong, 1945–1952*, Hong Kong, 1988, p. 19.
236. See Wright-Nooth, *Prisoner of the Turnip-Heads*, p. 156; Lindsay, *Going Down of the Sun*, p. 117. Four days after the meeting of the Far Eastern Reconstruction Committee held in Whitehall on 24 June 1943 to discuss for the first time the shape of a post-war administration for the colony, Gimson and his colleagues in Stanley held a 'meeting of the committee on the reform of the Hong Kong constitution'. See Gimson diary, 28 June 1943. It is difficult to believe that this was altogether a coincidence. One or two subsequent references in Gimson's diary make it clear that he did somehow manage to keep in touch with British colonial policy. On 5 January 1945, for instance, he remarks in connection with one discussion, 'I was very glad to be able to quote a statement to the effect that the policy of the British Government was the introduction into the Colonies of self-governing institutions.'

237. Gimson secret memorandum to Colonial Office, 23 July 1942, CO 129 590/24, p. 175.
238. Gimson diary, 5 May 1944.
239. Ibid., 14 June and 3 July 1944.
240. Ibid., 14 and 21 April 1944.
241. Ibid., 1 December 1943.
242. Gimson Internment in Hong Kong, summary, p. 17.
243. Gimson secret memorandum to Colonial Office, 23 July 1942, CO 129 590/24, p. 175. It seems likely that Gimson's basic policy had already been formulated as early as the spring of 1942. See Priestwood/Thompson report forwarded 6 May 1942, CO 129 590/23, p. 124.
244. Luff, *Hidden Years*, p. 184; Lindsay, *Going Down of the Sun,* pp. 43–4.
245. Gimson report forwarded from Lourenço Marques by P. V. McLane, Canadian Government Trade Commissioner, Hong Kong, to Secretary of State for the Colonies 18 July 1942, CO 129 590/24, p. 171.
246. Message from Le Rougetel, Foreign Office Counsellor evacuated from Shanghai conveying Gimson request, forwarded by British consul St Vincent to Foreign Office 2 October 1942, CO 825 42/15, p. 263; Gimson report forwarded by McLane 18 July 1942, and Gimson secret memorandum 23 July 1942, CO 129 590/24, pp. 171, 175–6.
247. Gimson diary, 14 June and 5 December 1943. For Gimson couriers see MacDougall report of conversation with Dr Greaves 6 December 1943, CO 129 590/22, p. 54. It is even possible that Gimson made use of the Triads: see Shaftain, 'Rough Draft', p. 14.
248. Gent minute 7 October 1942, CO 825 42/15, p. 262.

5. The End Game

1. Report of evacuated internee G. Leslie Andrew, 20 December 1943, p. 5 and intercepted letter from Beth Woo to Sergeant Richard W. Foo, 10 April 1944, HS 1/171, p. 3.
2. Intercepted letter from Beth Woo to Sergeant Richard W. Foo 10 April 1944, HS 1/171, p. 2.
3. *Hong Kong News* quoted Lindsay, *Lasting Honour*, p. 169. It is of course possible that this ridiculous statement was a piece of deliberate sabotage on the part of the editors of the *Hong Kong News* (see p. 179 above).
4. See comments of Tani Masayuki, Japanese ambassador to Nanking, and of Ichiki Yoshiyuki, head of the Civil Affairs Department, quoted *HKN*, 29 January and 3 February 1944.
5. Minutes of the 146th meeting of the Chinese Cooperative Council, 25 October 1943. See also Ward, *Asia for the Asiatics?*, pp. 60–1; Heasman, 'Japanese Financial and Economic Measures', pp. 66–7.
6. Testimony of Colonel Noma, Noma trial, WO 235/999, p. 339.
7. Testimony of Lieutenant-Colonel Kanazawa, Noma trial, WO 235/999, pp. 25, 27. Noma for his part admitted receiving a warning from Isogai through Kanazawa that some local policemen (Kensa) had been 'doing bad things'. See Noma testimony, p. 344.
8. Isogai quoted in *HKN*, 11 January 1944.
9. *HKN*, 6 June 1944.
10. *HKN*, 1, 2, 3 and 5 September 1944. The Japanese name of the new Trade Association was Koeki Kosha. Emphatic assurances were given to local Chinese merchants that they would be accorded the same facilities and treatment as their Japanese counterparts. See *HKN*, 3 and 8 September 1944.
11. *HKN*, 12, 16 and 17 November 1944. See also Sinn, *Bank of East Asia*, pp. 70–1.
12. Samejima, *Xianggang huixiang ji*, pp. 88, 96.
13. Ibid., p. 88. Chief of Staff Suganami seems generally to have been a moderating influence. He is described by Emily Hahn as 'a short, slight, tired man' who spoke English with a pure Oxford accent. See Hahn, *China to Me*, p. 412.
14. *HKN*, 24 December 1944.
15. Tse, *San nian*, p. 51. Information confirmed by Professor Kobayashi Hideo, interview, 18 July 1995.

16. Statement of Major-General Tomita Naosuke, former Chief of Staff, 23 March 1946, Noma trial, WO 235/999 exhibit N and Kanazawa trial, WO 235/1093 exhibit W.

17. Testimony of Lieutenant-Colonel Kanazawa at Kanazawa trial, WO 235/1093, pp. 324, 330, 359–60. See also Kanazawa guidelines for police reported *HKN*, 15 March 1945.

18. Tse, *Zhanshi Ri jun*, p. 114.

19. Heasman, 'Japanese Financial and Economic Measures', p. 73.

20. Remark of Vice Chief of Staff quoted in *HKN*, 24 April 1945. See also comments of Yamanouchi, the Secretary-General of the Governor's Office and of Tanaka himself quoted in *HKN*, 12 and 14 January 1945.

21. *HKN*, editorial, 20 February 1945. The reopening of these centres was reported in *HKN*, 3 March 1945. See also Heasman, 'Japanese Financial and Economic Measures', p. 92.

22. *HKN*, 31 March 1945.

23. See article by Alan Birch, *SCMP*, 12 September 1978. Evidence for an access of defeatism among the Japanese in Hong Kong at this early stage is provided by two other sources, both dating from January 1943. In the course of that month Bishop Hall wrote to a Church journal, *The Outpost*, from Chungking, 'In Hong Kong, they say, the Japanese admit they will be beaten, but they will go down fighting.' In late January the SOE informant K. E. Mogra reported that the Japanese in Hong Kong were planning to dig tunnels in the hills and have all their stores and particularly their planes placed there. Japanese officers and officials, he said, were pessimistic and upset by the German reverses in North Africa and on the Russian front. See Paton, *R. O.*, p. 115; report of K. E. Mogra, 27 January 1943, pp. 6, 7, HS 1/171.

24. Gimson diary, 6 and 26 July 1944; Uttley diary, 28 July 1944.

25. Samejima, *Xianggang huixiang ji*, p. 124. For defeatism of Japanese officers at this point see article by Adam Williams in *SMP*, 19 November 1978.

26. Minutes of the 146th meeting of the Chinese Cooperative Council, 25 October 1943.

27. Testimony of Captain Ushiyama Yukio, Kempeitai commander for the Western District, Noma trial, WO 235/999, p. 441. For Kashiwagi's ferocious approach to law enforcement see also *HKN*, 28 June and 29 September 1944 and 31 May 1945; Tse, *Zhanshi Ri jun*, pp. 114, 238.

28. Tse, *Zhanshi Ri jun*, p. 150.

29. Testimony of Joseph Venpin, Noma trial, WO 235/999, p. 66.

30. Heasman, 'Japanese Financial and Economic Measures', p. 70.

31. Testimony of Kan Man, Kwok Hin-wang and Li Chung-ching, heads of the District Bureaux for Kennedy Town, Causeway Bay and Stanley, Noma trial, WO 235/999, pp. 301, 307, 309.

32. On 8 June 1945 an Imperial Conference held in Tokyo observed that 'in the light of the present relations between Chungking and the United States it would now be really difficult to achieve an overall peace between Japan and China'. See Tse, *Xianggang kang Ri*, p. 168.

33. In late 1944 the proposals for the administration of Hong Kong originally drawn up by the 23rd Army in January 1942 were revised to take account of these new strategic factors. See revised document quoted in *Honkon-Chosha sakusen*, p. 328.

34. Testimony of Frederick Tyndall, Noma trial, WO 235/999, pp. 209, 217; Tse, *Zhanshi Ri jun*, pp. 213–14. Allusions to these dog attacks were often made in the official press, seemingly for the purpose of intimidating the public. See, for example, *HKN*, 2 and 19 July 1945. See also Clark, *An End to Tears*, pp. 88–9; Waters, *Faces of Hong Kong*, p. 119.

35. Quoted in *HKN*, 2 August 1945.

36. Samejima, *Xianggang huixiang ji*, p. 90. The successors were Major-Generals Uzawa, Tomita and Fukuchi. Perhaps to disguise the rapidity of the turnover no name is given by the *Hong Kong News* to the Chief of Staff from spring 1945 onwards. Press conferences are usually said to have been given by an anonymous Vice Chief of Staff.

37. *HKN*, 30 June, 21 September, 1, 4 and 15 December 1944, 18 and 22 February 1945; Samejima, *Xianggang huixiang ji*, p. 119. Officials transferred included Nakanishi, the chief of the Finance Department and his successor K. Ishii; Ichiki Yoshiyuki, chief of the Civil Affairs Department; Sato, head of the Hong Kong Island Repatriation Office; Y. Uchima, head of

the Kowloon Repatriation Office; and Yamashita, head of the Area Bureau for Hong Kong Island.

38. Article in *SCMP*, 12 February 1989; Tse, *San nian*, p. 427; Birch and Cole, *Captive Years*, p. 112. The memorial had been supposed to embody the spiritual force of Japan's samurai warriors, and the failure to complete it thus carried a powerful symbolic message. Work on the planned Shinto Shrine and the Pagoda for the Buddha's Ashes tailed off in a similar fashion.

39. *HKN*, 21 July 1945.

40. Testimonies of Lieutenant-Colonel Kanazawa and Major Shiozawa Kunio, Kanazawa trial, WO 235/1093, pp. 323, 409. The detailed breakdown of the force is said to have been: forty-five Japanese Kempei (Kempeitai members), between five and seven Japanese police officers, 1,300 Chinese and Indian police, 300 firemen, 100 Chinese and Indian trainees, 150 to 160 Indian godown guards and 300 'employees and servants'. The Japanese did of course also have the Kempeitai, now separate from the police and said by Kanazawa to have totalled around 700, viz. about 200 Japanese Kempei, 200 auxiliary Kempei, 100 'policemen' and 200 civilian 'employees and servants'. Many of these Kempei, however, were deployed on security duties in the New Territories (see p. 235 below). These figures illustrate the continuing heavy dependence of the Japanese authorities on local back-up.

41. ·*HKN*, 1 June 1945.

42. Quoted in *HKN*, 2 August 1945.

43. Isogai quoted in *HKN*, 8 February 1944.

44. Selwyn-Clarke, *Footprints*, pp. 90–1. See also *HKN*, 15 December 1943.

45. *HKN*, 3 and 25 December 1944.

46. *HKN*, 3 December 1944.

47. *HKN*, 26 December 1944. For the same resigned tone see also the farewell remarks of Ichiki Yoshiyuki, the retiring chief of the Civil Affairs Department, quoted in *HKN*, 25 and 26 November 1944.

48. *HKN*, 7 December 1943; Domei Hong Kong quoted in Daily Digest of World Broadcasts, 25 December 1943, CO 129 591/4, p. 64.

49. Quoted in *HKN*, 7 April 1944. Local merchants were also asked to help out with the import of firewood and cooking oil. See *HKN*, 4 July 1944.

50. *HKN*, 22 September 1944.

51. *HKN*, 24 February 1945.

52. Testimony of Lieutenant-Colonel Kanazawa, Kanazawa trial, WO 235/1093, pp. 325, 326. See also *HKN*, 15 and 17 March and 2 and 3 April 1945; Endacott and Birch, *Hong Kong Eclipse*, p. 136.

53. *HKN*, 12 January 1945.

54. *HKN*, 28 February 1945. Within two weeks the Bureau was said to be employing thirty 'coolies' to sweep the District's roads. *HKN*, 11 March 1945.

55. *HKN*, 24, 27 and 28 March, 7 May and 11 June 1945. See also testimony of Lieutenant-Colonel Kanazawa, Kanazawa trial, WO 235/1093, pp. 347–8. Kanazawa appears to confuse the Residents' Certificates and exit permits.

56. *HKN*, 18 July 1945. The District Bureaux were also earmarked as key sounding-boards through which the authorities might 'obtain a full knowledge of the people's opinion'. See *HKN*, 21 and 29 July and 8 August 1945; Endacott and Birch, *Hong Kong Eclipse*, p. 133.

57. Comment of Secretary-General Tomari quoted in *HKN*, 12 November 1943.

58. Tse, *San nian*, p. 296.

59. The attempt to crack down on the Triads which had marked the early months of the occupation was already being abandoned some time before Tanaka appeared on the scene. By the latter part of 1943, it appears, the authorities had begun to issue licences to the Triads for the public operation of prostitution, gambling and drug peddling joints. See Zhang Sheng, *Xianggang hei shehui*, p. 62. This process clearly ran parallel to the new assignment of responsibility to the Street Guards. It is only with Tanaka's arrival, however, that the Triads appear to have been given completely free rein.

60. Annual Report on the Hong Kong Police Force 1946–47, p. 24, 25, 35; Tse, *San nian*, pp. 296–8.

61. Quoted in Endacott and Birch, *Hong Kong Eclipse*, p. 136.

62. Interviews, Mr Cyril Kotewall and Mrs Helen Zimmern, 26 and 29 June 1995.

63. Ching, *The Li Dynasty*, pp. 116, 117

64. Ibid., pp. 120–1.

65. Tse, *San nian*, p. 75.

66. *HKN*, 14 April and 25 June 1944, 25 February and 3 August 1945.

67. Li Koon-chun testified after the war that he resigned from the Chinese Cooperative Council 'in 1943'. Contemporary sources however make it clear that he was still playing an active part on the Council in November that year. It would seem, therefore, that his resignation did not take place until the end of 1943 at earliest. See minutes of the 149th meeting of the Chinese Cooperative Council, 15 November 1943; *HKN*, 14 November 1943; Ching, *The Li Dynasty*, p. 116.

68. Ching, *The Li Dynasty*, pp. 121–2; *WKYP* (evening edition) 26 August 1945. The precise date of Tung's departure is unclear.

69. *HKN*, 12, 13, 26 and 27 December 1944; Tse, *San nian*, p. 76. Tse dates this episode incorrectly to August 1945.

70. *HKN*, 11 and 12 April 1945. It was intimated that the government would take care of Lau's family.

71. Testimony of Lieutenant-Colonel Kanazawa, Kanazawa trial, WO 235/1093, p. 353. For similar 'uneasiness' among the Chinese and Indian guards in Stanley see Wright-Nooth, *Prisoner of the Turnip-Heads,* p. 231.

72. Testimony of Joseph Carroll, Carroll trial, HK RS 245-2-208.

73. *HKN*, 2 July 1944.

74. *HKN*, 5 July 1944.

75. Testimony of Lieutenant-Colonel Kanazawa, Kanazawa trial, WO 235/1093, pp. 367, 373, 375, 376. The names of the other two Sikh ringleaders were Chanan Singh and Harbans Singh. See also *HKN*, 19 May 1945.

76. *HKN*, 15 and 27 April, 2 and 3 May 1945.

77. In June 1943, after four months in a Kempeitai cell, Faure was deposited with the rest of the British civilians in Stanley, where he spent the last two years of the war. See Gimson diary, 28 June 1943; Faure testimony, Noma trial, WO 235/999; Wright-Nooth, *Prisoner of the Turnip-Heads*, p. 98.

78. *HKN*, 1 and 12 September, 19 and 27 October 1944 and 5 April 1945.

79. Testimony of Lieutenant-Colonel Kanazawa, Kanazawa trial, WO 235/1093, p. 325.

80. Samejima, *Xianggang huixiang ji*, p. 123; Hirano, '*Kezheng yu baoxing*', p. 54; Buping Shanren, *Xianggang lunxian huiyilu*, p. 62; comments of former internee Sherry Bucks quoted by Adam Williams, article in *SMP*, 19 November 1978; interview, Sir Y. K. Kan, 24 May 1995.

81. Samejima, *Xianggang huixiang ji*, p. 124. See also testimony of Lieutenant-Colonel Kanazawa, Kanazawa trial, WO 235/1093, pp. 367, 384.

82. Quoted Tse, *San nian*, p. 427.

83. *HKN*, 27 and 30 November and 15 December 1943 and 7, 8 and 11 January 1944; Heasman, 'Japanese Financial and Economic Measures', p. 72; Ward, *Asia for the Asiatics?*, p. 109.

84. See *HKN*, 5 and 18 December 1943, 13, 18, 23 and 27 August and 15 October 1944.

85. Kwan, 'Charitable Activities', p. 185.

86. *HKN*, 26 January 1945. Kotewall also became chairman of an Association for Supporting the Emergency and First Aid Treatment Squad. See *HKN*, 25 July 1945.

87. *HKN*, 6 and 14 May 1945. See also Chow remarks quoted in *WKYP*, 19 August 1945.

88. Intercepted letter from Beth Woo to Sergeant Richard W. Foo, 10 April 1944, HS 1/171, p. 3.

89. *HKN*, 17 November 1944.

90. The *Hong Kong News* inveighed periodically against the luxurious lives still being in-dulged in by the rich. See, for example, editorials in *HKN*, 27 November 1944 and 13 February 1945.
91. Report of Comte R. de Sercey forwarded by British consul-general Chungking, 27 June 1944, co 129 591/4, p. 15.
92. Ching, *The Li Dynasty*, pp. 116, 117.
93. Heasman, 'Japanese Financial and Economic Measures', p. 72.
94. *HKN*, 25 July 1945.
95. Extract from minutes of meeting of Chinese Cooperative Council, 23 July 1945; *HKN*, 28 July 1945; testimony of Kwok Chan, Cheng Chung-wing and Kan Man, Kanazawa trial, WO 235/1093, pp. 243, 252, 261, 271. The Deputy Judge Advocate General, HQ Far Eastern Land Forces, who conducted the defence at this trial, pointed out that the Tanaka mass deporta-tion scheme was launched 'with the qualified approval of the more responsible elements of the population'. Submission to Commander, Land Forces, Hong Kong, 20 January 1948, p. 2, attached to transcript of Kanazawa trial, WO 235/1093.
96. Samejima, *Xianggang huixiang ji*, p. 99.
97. *HKN*, 22 November and 9 December 1944; Heasman, 'Japanese Financial and Economic Measures', p. 72.
98. Heasman, 'Japanese Financial and Economic Measures', p. 90; Kwan, 'Charitable Activities', pp. 185–6, 187; *HKN*, 25 August and 1 September 1944, 1 March and 18 May 1945; *SCMP/HKT*, 18 September 1945.
99. *HKN*, 15 August 1945.
100. Kwan, 'Charitable Activities', p. 190. The greater part of the funds which sustained the GACC were however provided by Yamaguchi Getsuro, a Japanese merchant who had been involved in intelligence work on the eve of the war.
101. *HKN*, 7 September 1944.
102. *HKN*, 4 July 1944; Ching, *The Li Dynasty*, pp. 119–20.
103. *HKN*, 10, 23 and 24 December 1944.
104. *HKN*, 12 December 1944.
105. *HKN*, 26 November 1944.
106. *HKN*, 28 November and 2 December 1943.
107. Statement of Gustavo Velasco forwarded 29 March 1944, CO 129 591/4, p. 34. In the first half of 1944 large numbers of candidates were reported in the same way as having applied for posts in the Harbour Office, the Area Bureau for Hong Kong Island, the Public Prosecu-tor's Office and the new Hong Kong Public Library. See *HKN*, 10 and 17 March, 7 and 9 April and 13 June 1944.
108. *HKN*, 6 and 7 October 1944.
109. *HKN*, 27 July 1944.
110. *HKN*, 17 March 1945.
111. See note of Colonial Office discussion with Dr Li Shu-fan, 10 February 1944, CO 129 591/4, p. 53.
112. Letter of Sir George Moss to John Keswick, 3 March 1944, HS 1/176, p. 1.
113. Ibid.
114. Report of the Comte de Sercey forwarded 27 June 1944, CO 129 591/4, p. 15.
115. Seymour to J. C. Sterndale-Bennett of the Foreign Office, 21 February 1945 with enclosed memorandum, CO 129 592/8, pp. 158–60. For K. C. Lee see Frank H. H. King, *History of the Hongkong and Shanghai Banking Corporation*, vol. IV, pp. 59, 61.
116. Moss memorandum, 1 May 1944, HS 1/349, pp. 2–3, 4, 7, 9, 12–13. Similar SOE views may be found in V/CD to CD, 29 March 1945, HS 1/208.
117. Gent minute on Moss memorandum, 29 May 1944, HS 1/349.
118. Minutes of Colonial Office/SOE discussion, 10 August 1944, HS 1/171, p. 2.
119. Note circulated by Colonial Office to Far Eastern Reconstruction Committee of the War Cabinet, December 1944, CO 129 592/8.

120. Gent minute 29 December 1943, CO 825 42/15, p. 37.

121. Minute of J. J. Paskin, 31 March 1945, CO 129 592/8, p. 8.

122. Gent minute on Nash paper, 7 January 1944, CO 825 42/15, p. 38.

123. Stanley to Eden, 25 May 1945 and Michael Lawford, deputy to Eden to Stanley, 13 June 1945, CO 129 592/8, pp. 116, 121–2.

124. Letter, China Association to Colonial Office, 23 November 1944, CO 825 42/15, pp. 73–5.

125. Astor questions in Commons, 6 June and 8 November 1944, cuttings filed in CO 129 592/8, pp. 79, 86, 124–6.

126. Churchill, personal minute M. 1025/4, most secret, 23 October 1944, quoted in Chan Lau, *China, Britain and Hong Kong*, p. 315.

127. Rafferty, *City on the Rocks*, pp. 139–40. Rafferty follows the account given by R. E. Sherwood in *The White House Papers of Harry L. Hopkins* (1948). Somewhat divergent descriptions of Roosevelt's position are given in A. J. P. Taylor, 'America's War', in *Europe, Grandeur and Decline*, London, 1967, pp. 317–18 and in Chan Lau, *China, Britain and Hong Kong*, p. 316. According to Taylor (following Admiral William Leahy, *I Was There*), Roosevelt expressed reluctant willingness to let Hong Kong be returned to the British if they insisted on having it to compensate for the Soviet Union gaining the Manchurian port of Dairen (Dalian). Chan Lau (following Christopher Thorne, *Allies of a Kind*) maintains Roosevelt was worried that the Soviet Union might take advantage of Britain's return to Hong Kong to press for a port of its own on the Chinese coast. Taylor's version seems to me not altogether inconsistent with Rafferty's. Chan Lau's account here appears to accord less well than either Rafferty's or Taylor's with the priority Roosevelt is known to have placed at this time on the relationship with his Soviet ally.

128. Albert C. Wedemeyer, *Wedemeyer Reports!*, New York, 1958, p. 340.

129. Steve Tsang, '*Jiang Jieshi weihe bu shouhui Xianggang*' in *Xianggang Zhanggu* vol.X, 1985, p. 115; report of G. A. Wallinger, British Minister, Chungking letter to Sterndale-Bennett 13 November 1944, enclosed with letter sent by J. Thyne-Henderson of Foreign Office on behalf of Sterndale-Bennett to Gent, 5 December 1944, CO 129 592/8, pp. 175–6.

130. W. B. L. Monson memorandum of talk with Ogden, British consul-general, Kunming, 15 March 1944, CO 825 42/15, p. 188; Professor E. R. Dodds quoted in Sweeting, 'Controversy over the Reopening of the University of Hong Kong', in *Dispersal and Renewal*, p. 407. See also Endacott and Birch, *Hong Kong Eclipse*, p. 335. Monson felt that the eagerness to recover Hong Kong was less marked among political, military and business figures; and one or two of these even appeared to be sympathetic to a British return. See comments of British embassy, Chungking regarding Dr Sun Fo, July 1945, CO 129 592/6, and of General Zheng Jiemin, head of the Nationalist International Intelligence Service (IIS) reported in Findlay Andrew, AD4 letter to CD 13 July 1945, HS 1/171, p. 2.

131. Rafferty, *City on the Rocks*, p. 140. See also Gleason, *Hong Kong*, p. 61.

132. Churchill, minute, 11 April 1945, enclosed with Stanley to Eden, 25 May 1945, CO 129 592/8, pp. 125, 147.

133. Ibid.

134. MacDougall to Gent, 18 April 1945, CO 129 592/8, p. 141; Gent to Sterndale-Bennett, 19 April 1945, FO 371 46251.

135. Extract from note for guidance to Colonial Office representative at San Francisco conference, April 1945, enclosed with Gent to Sterndale-Bennett 21 June 1945 and Sterndale-Bennett to Seymour, 13 July 1945, CO 129 592/8, p. 115.

136. Uttley diary, 5 March 1945.

137. Extract from minutes of Colonial Office/SOE discussion, 13 June 1944, HS 1/171.

138. Wedemeyer, *Wedemeyer Reports!*, pp. 320, 353, 355.

139. Extract from minutes of Colonial Office/SOE discussion, 13 June 1944, HS 1/171. See also SOE paper on British Clandestine Services in China, undated, autumn 1944, and paper on Organization of British Services in China, 23 March 1945, HS 1/208.

140. See record of Wedemeyer conversation with General Zheng Jiemin, 16 May 1945, Museum of Military History archives, Taipei 062.23/5000.4.

141. Hayes telegram to War Office (WIR) no. 0/0114, 20 July 1945, HS 1/171, p. 1. Hayes and his 'British Troops China' had just replaced Brigadier Grimsdale and the former British Military Mission. At this juncture the OSS were bribing BAAG runners to hand over to them messages they had been carrying from Hong Kong. AGAS were seeking to expand their activities in and around Canton and were also duplicating the BAAG's plans for rescuing POWs from Hainan island. E. Ride, *British Army Aid Group*, pp. 281–3.

142. BB 900, Kandy to BB 100, London, 4 August 1945, HS 1/171.

143. Weekly Intelligence Report (WIR) no. 4, 24 September 1945 and Report from Staff Officer (Intelligence) on Political Situation in Hong Kong, 1 October 1945, CO 129 592/6, pp. 126, 151.

144. Birch and Cole, *Captive Years*, p. 136.

145. Interview, Mme Cai Songying, veteran of the East River Column, 24 June 1995.

146. Woddis, 'Hong Kong and the East River Company', pp. 10–11; Yuan, *Xianggang shilüe*, p. 180.

147. *Dadui shi*, p. 116.

148. Testimony of Lieutenant-Colonel Kanazawa, Kanazawa trial, WO 235/1093; Lindsay, *Lasting Honour*, p. 194. A propaganda drive was launched simultaneously to win back the allegiance of the village elders. See *HKN*, 21 May and 3 and 7 June 1945.

149. Report of Major Ronald Holmes 12 July 1944 HS 1/171, pp. 5–6; E. Ride, *British Army Aid Group*, pp. 217–18; Osler Thomas, 'With the BAAG in Wartime China' in *Dispersal and Renewal*, p. 309. Certain tensions had already been apparent even during the period of close British–Communist cooperation in 1942–3. The Communists had been wary of the BAAG's Hong Kong Chinese employees, whom they suspected of having been planted by the Nationalists to monitor their activities. Holmes report, p. 5.

150. Report of Major Ronald Holmes 12 July 1944 HS 1/171, p. 6; *ZB*, 13 January 1946; Woddis, 'Hong Kong and the East River Company', pp. 10–11; *Dadui shi*, pp. 111–14, 116–18; E. Ride, *British Army Aid Group*, p. 220; Yuan, *Xianggang shilüe*, p. 185. Some Chinese accounts even suggest that the bulk of the guerrilla exploits in early 1944 formed part of a diversionary tactic designed to facilitate the rescue of the first downed American pilot, Lieutenant Donald W. Kerr. This sudden upsurge of helpfulness to the Americans must clearly be seen in the context of the overall blossoming of relations which took place in 1944 between the United States and the Chinese Communist Party. The Roosevelt administration had begun at that juncture to lose confidence in Chiang Kai-shek's regime and, prompted by the reports of the celebrated 'Dixie Mission' to Yan'an, was briefly contemplating the Communist leadership in Yan'an as possible alternative partners.

151. SOE India to London, 22 September 1944, HS 1/176.

152. See reports of Iwai, Japanese consul-general in Macao, MAGIC Documents Reel XIII, 8, 17 and 27 April 1945.

153. See Miss A. Ruston minute, 25 April 1945, and Gent to Sterndale-Bennett, 27 April 1945, CO 129 591/4; War Office top secret telegram to GOC British troops China, 10 July 1945, p. 1, and GOC British troops China telegram to War Office no. 0/0114, 20 July 1945, p. 2, HS 1/171; J. J. Paskin memorandum 3 August 1945 and Gent minute for Sir George Gater, 4 August 1945, CO 129 591/16, pp. 2, 94. The Colonial Office and MI9 were already making some contingency plans against a possible Communist seizure of the colony as early as August 1944: see top secret memorandum from Lieutenant-Colonel C. M. Rait of MI9, 19 August 1944, HS 1/171.

154. Wedemeyer, *Wedemeyer Reports!*, p. 332.

155. Quoted Endacott and Birch, *Hong Kong Eclipse*, p. 336.

156. Moss memorandum, 1 May 1944, HS 1/349, p. 15.

157. See top secret memorandum from BB/210 to BB/520, 'Union Jack Scheme for Hong Kong', 23 June 1944, HS 1/171, p. 1.

158. Ibid. The scheme was still under consideration in August. See minutes of Colonial Office/SOE discussion, 10 August 1944, HS 1/171, p. 2.

159. Foreign Office top secret cable to Seymour, Chungking, 28 March 1945, HS 1/349, p. 1. See also Aldrich, *Intelligence and the War against Japan*, pp. 358–9.

160. Seymour, top secret cable to Foreign Office, 30 March 1945, HS 1/349.

161. Ride to British military attaché, Chungking, 25 April 1945, FO 371 46251, pp. 142–3.

162. FIN/W to WF/435, top secret, 12 July 1945, HS 1/171.

163. Notes of inter-departmental meeting held in Colonial Office to consider general circumstances in which Hong Kong likely to be retaken, 23 July 1945, p. 2 and GOC British troops China telegram to War Office, no. 0/0114, 20 July 1945, HS 1/171, p. 2.

164. Grimsdale to Gent, 29 February 1944, CO 825 42/15, p. 187.

165. The possible need for such a Chinese piggy-back had already been foreseen as early as March 1944. In that month Ogden, the British consul-general in Kunming, remarked in connection with the suggested appointment of British liaison officers to serve with the Chinese Nationalist armies in north-east Burma that 'it would be a useful precedent for ensuring that British officers should be attached to any Chinese forces engaged in the recovery of Hong Kong from the mainland'. See Monson memorandum, 15 March 1944, CO 825 42/15, p. 188.

166. Gent minute for Gater, 4 August 1945, CO 129 591/16, p. 2.

167. Sterndale-Bennett to Foulds, 28 July 1945, quoted in Chan Lau, *China, Britain and Hong Kong*, p. 320; Gent minute for Gater, 4 August 1945, CO 129 591/16, p. 2.

168. Wedemeyer, *Wedemeyer Reports!*, p. 332. See also Commander-in-Chief, British Pacific Fleet, to Admiralty, 3 August 1945, CO 129 591/15, p. 10.

169. Gent minute for Gater, 4 August 1945, CO 129 591/16, p. 2.

170. Ibid.

171. Edward Behr, *Hirohito: Behind the Myth*, New York, 1990, pp. 300, 407.

172. For the Pacific fleet see John Winton, *The Forgotten Fleet*, Michael Joseph, London, 1969.

173. Foreign Office to Seymour, 14 August 1945, CO 129 591/16, p. 72.

174. Seymour to Foreign Office, telegram no. 857, report of meeting of British Counsellor, Chungking, with Acting Foreign Minister Dr K. C. Wu (Wu Guozhen), 16 August 1945, CO 129 591/16, p. 59.

175. Bevin to Wu, 18 August 1945, CO 129 591/16, p. 35.

176. Seymour to Foreign Office, telegram no. 857, 16 August 1945, CO 129 591/16, p. 59. See also Tsang, '*Jiang Jieshi*', pp. 119, 126–7; Yuan, *Xianggang shilüe*, p. 189; Kwan, *Ri zhan shiqi de Xianggang*, p. 159.

177. Chan Lau, 'The United States and the Question of Hong Kong', p. 15, *China, Britain and Hong Kong*, p. 321.

178. See Admiral William D. Leahy, Chief of Staff to Commander-in-Chief of the US Army and Navy, memorandum to Byrnes, 18 August 1945, USDP vol. VII, p. 505; Chan Lau, 'The United States and the Question of Hong Kong' pp. 13–15, *China, Britain and Kong Kong*, pp. 317–18, 322. The State Department's unwillingness to go all the way behind Chiang had already been indicated in April, when they submitted a paper to the State–War–Navy Sub-Committee for the Far East as part of the examination of Wedemeyer's proposed Operation Carbonado. The paper effectively recommended that the United States should adopt a hands-off policy towards the recovery of Hong Kong. It advised that United States forces should not participate in operations for the recapture of the colony unless it proved to be strictly necessary from a military point of view. If some involvement were necessary, the United States should still make no plans to take part in the interim government of Hong Kong which was to be instituted by the British in accordance with the Civil Affairs Agreement of September 1944. The State Department principle of non-involvement was reiterated in the draft report of the State-War-Navy Sub-Committee which was drawn up in mid-June.

179. Truman reply no. 6 to Attlee, 18 August 1945, CO 129 591/16, p. 33.

180. AMSSO top-secret cypher telegram to JSM, British embassy, Washington, 20 August 1945 and note from Colonial Office official to Miss Ruston, 20 August 1945, CO 129 591/16, pp. 23, 24.

181. Chan Lau, 'The United States and the Question of Hong Kong', p. 16, *China, Britain and Hong Kong*, p. 322; Lane, 'Nationalist Government', p. 101.

182. Tsang, '*Jiang Jieshi*', p. 122; Chan Lau, *China, Britain and Hong Kong*, p. 322; Lane, 'Nationalist Government', p. 101. Ambassador Seymour in Chungking alone on the British side seems to have favoured accepting this second proposal on the grounds that to do so would save Chiang's face and with luck make it possible for British forces to regain Hong Kong without a diplomatic collision with the mainland government.

183. Wedemeyer, *Wedemeyer Reports!*, p. 337.

184. See B/B 131 Kunming to A.D.1 and 0.629 Kandy, 17 August 1945, HS 1/329; B/B 131 cable 17 August 1945, HS 1/349; E. Ride, *British Army Aid Group*, p. 287; Lindsay, *Going Down of the Sun*, pp. 199–200.

185. See BAAG Kunming cable to Kandy no. 406 for General Carton de Wiart, 15 August 1945, HS 1/329; Ride top secret telegram to Cartwright, HQ British Troops China, 15 August 1945, CO 129 591/16, p. 54; Foreign Office telegram no. 924 to British embassy Chungking 18 August 1945, CO 129 591/16, p. 38.

186. Wedemeyer, *Wedemeyer Reports!*, p. 350. Wedemeyer and the United States military continued to maintain a high profile during the final days of the Hong Kong interregnum. On 20 August the planned AGAS mission to Hong Kong was launched with Ride and his colleagues in tow. The mission got as far as the White Cloud airport in Canton, where they received an unfriendly reception from the local Japanese forces. The American and British contingents clashed sharply, the British favouring withdrawal to Kunming while the Americans wished to stay in the hope of being allowed to go further. The AGAS mission leader, a Lieutenant Fenn, eventually came round to the British view; but not before the British had been reminded that they were guests in the party and could have no voice in the decisions that had to be made. Throughout these final days United States Air Force planes dropped leaflets into the Hong Kong POW and internment camps with a message from Wedemeyer instructing the inmates to stay where they were, and on 29 August they dropped a consignment of food, medical supplies and cigarettes. See E. Ride, *British Army Aid Group*, pp. 292–8; Lindsay, *Lasting Honour*, p. 196 and *Going Down of the Sun*, p. 207; Selwyn-Clarke, *Footprints*, p. 98; Uttley diary, 29 August 1945. None of this American activity now had any political significance. But it did have some impact on the POWs and internees, many of whom still assumed (not surprisingly) that the Americans rather than the British would be liberating them. See note 211 below.

187. Quoted in *WKYP*, 28 and 29 August 1945; Lane, 'Nationalist Government', p. 102. See also E. Ride, *British Army Aid Group*, pp. 302–3; Tsang, '*Jiang Jieshi*', p. 122; Chan Lau, 'The United States and the Question of Hong Kong', p. 15, *China, Britain and Hong Kong*, p. 321.

188. Seymour to Bevin, 10 September 1945, CO 129 592/8, p. 43.

189. General Zhang Fakui preface to account of liberation of Guangdong province, '*Guangdong shoujiang jishu*', 15 June 1946, Nationalist party archives, Taipei, 532/157. For apparent British reaction to this step see Seymour to Foreign Office telegrams no. 857, 16 August 1945 and no. 865, 17 August 1945, CO 129 591/16, pp. 57, 59.

190. Zhang Fakui preface to '*Guangdong shoujiang jishu*'. As early as 21 August Japanese officials in Canton had reported the infiltration of various Nationalist units into the Canton area. MAGIC Documents Reel xiv, 26 August 1945. See also Yuan, *Xianggang shilüe*, p. 188; Tse, *San nian*, p. 400.

191. *Dadui shi*, pp. 181–2.

192. The Japanese soldiers responded to the Communist advance by slaughtering 500 inhabitants of four local villages in a Hong Kong equivalent of Oradour-sur-Glane. It was the final Japanese atrocity of the occupation. See Buping Shanren, *Xianggang lunxian huiyilu*, p. 92; Endacott and Birch, *Hong Kong Eclipse*, p. 248; Tse, *Zhanshi Ri jun*, pp. 219–20.

193. *Dadui shi*, p. 183; Woddis, 'Hong Kong and the East River Company', pp. 10–11; Endacott and Birch, *Hong Kong Eclipse*, pp. 331–2.

194. Fan, '*Shengli zhi chu zai Xianggang*', p. 23; Tsang, '*Jiang Jieshi*', p. 127; Ye Dewei, '*Xianggang chongguang*', in Ye (ed.), *Xianggang lunxian shi*, p. 160; Yuan, *Xianggang shilüe*, pp. 187, 188. Chiang was also engaged in a bid to restore China's prestige by taking the Japanese surrender in a number of outlying places which had been detached from the Chinese sphere of influence

in the course of the previous sixty-odd years. These included northern Vietnam, Taiwan and Korea. See Supreme National Defence Council, Problems Relating to Acceptance of Japan's Surrender by the Four Powers, Nationalist Party archives, Taipei 004.0131.0406. No allusion to Hong Kong was made in this document; and it seems unlikely that the British colony can have loomed very large in the minds of the Nationalist leadership by comparison with these major objectives.

195. Information conveyed by a 'spy' to Iwai, Japanese consul-general in Macao, MAGIC Documents Reel XIII, 13 April 1945. The military chief entrusted with this assignment was said to be none other than General Yu Hanmou, commander of the Seventh War Zone, who had led the abortive Nationalist relief expedition towards Hong Kong in December 1941.

196. Report by H. G. W. Woodhead, CBE in *Shanghai Evening Post and Mercury*, 31 August 1945, cutting filed in CO 129 592/8, p. 65; Hayes to Ismay, 30 August 1945 CO 129 591/19, p. 52.

197. On 8 June 1945 consul-general Iwai in Macao forwarded to Tokyo reports emanating from a number of different Japanese intelligence posts on a conference that had recently been held by the Communist forces in south China. The conference had decided that when the Communists launched their planned 'general offensive' in south China, Canton was to be occupied in a 'swift anticipatory stroke'. A number of Communist units in the Canton area were currently being reorganized with this plan in mind. Further Communist activity near Canton was reported on 22 June. See MAGIC Documents Reel XIV, 22 June 1945.

198. Report of Major Ronald Holmes, 12 July 1944, HS 1/171, p. 3. For the role of the East River band in impeding a possible Nationalist advance see also E. Ride, *British Army Aid Group*, pp. 270–1.

199. *Dadui shi*, p. 184.

200. *SCMP/HKT*, 8 September 1945.

201. For Zhang Fakui's competence as a general, see Grantham, *Via Ports*, p. 127. His soldiers, like those of Oliver Cromwell, were known as the Ironsides for their doughty performance in the campaigns of the late 1920s.

202. This relatively slow pace is suggested by the point, still quite far from Hong Kong, which the troops had apparently reached at the end of August. See note 260 below. See also Steve Tsang, *Hong Kong: An Appointment with China*, I. B. Tauris, London, 1997, p. 46.

203. Quoted Clark, *An End to Tears*, pp. 58, 61.

204. Gittins, *Stanley: Behind Barbed Wire*, p. 153.

205. Endacott and Birch, *Hong Kong Eclipse*, p. 336; Foreign Office to Seymour, telegram no. 879, 13 August 1945, CO 129 591/16, p. 81.

206. Seymour to Foreign Office, telegram no. 831, 14 August 1945, CO 129 591/16, p. 80; telegram no. 831 from G. A. Wallinger, British Minister in Chungking to Foreign Office, 14 August 1945, HS 1/171.

207. Gimson, Hong Kong Reclaimed, p. 5.

208. Ibid, p. 6. There was also some concern as to whether a formal assumption of authority on Gimson's part might not deter the Japanese from giving the internees the cooperation they needed (see p. 251 below).

209. Ibid., pp. 7–8.

210. Birch and Cole, *Captive Years*, p. 152; Tsang, '*Jiang Jieshi*', p. 25.

211. Gimson, Hong Kong Reclaimed, p. 8; Selwyn-Clarke, *Footprints*, pp. 98–9. General Maltby, who had commanded the garrison during the invasion of December 1941, and thirteen other senior British officers had been removed to Taiwan on 4 August 1943 as a punishment for the successful escape of some of their fellow POWs. See Lindsay, *Lasting Honour*, p. 108. Gimson's concern over the possible effect of installing a military government is likely to have been intensified by the initial hesitancy of Lieutenant-Colonel White. White had apparently been convinced by the leaflets dropped from American planes that the arrival of United States forces was imminent. He was inclined consequently to obey the orders of the American military authorities, and in particular the instructions conveyed in the leaflets to all POWs and internees to remain in their camps. He is said to begin with to have taken 'a distinctly dubious

view' of the proposed installation of a British civilian government. See Selwyn-Clarke, *Footprints*, p. 98.

212. Gimson, Hong Kong Reclaimed, p. 9. Gimson was deliberately ignoring the instructions to stay in camp which were issued to the internees in the leaflets dropped by United States planes.

213. Luff, *Hidden Years*, p. 226.

214. Gimson telegram to Secretary of State, Colonial Office, 23 August 1945, in Documents concerning the Wartime Activities in Hong Kong and Macao of Y. C. Liang, CBE, HK MS 30.

215. Gimson telegram to Secretary of State, Colonial Office, 27 August 1945, in Y.C. Liang Documents, HK MS 30.

216. Alan Birch article in *SCMP*, 14 October 1973; Endacott and Birch, *Hong Kong Eclipse*, p. 230; Morris, *Hong Kong*, p. 258; Kwan, *Ri zhan shiqi de Xianggang*, p. 160. For comments of Tokunaga and Makimura see Gimson, Hong Kong Reclaimed, p. 7; Tsang, '*Jiang Jieshi*', p. 124. Tsang suggests that the two Japanese officials were aware of the Nationalist advance on Hong Kong; but this seems unlikely, particularly as detailed orders for the advance were only issued on 21 August.

217. *SCMP/HKT*, 5 September 1945; Selwyn-Clarke, *Footprints*, pp. 97–8; Endacott and Birch, *Hong Kong Eclipse*, p. 231. The precise length of time the flag remained up seems uncertain: Selwyn-Clarke states that it flew for just two hours, but Endacott and Birch maintain that it stayed up for four and a half, from 9 a.m. to about 1.30 p.m.

218. See Gimson diary, 10 and 11 August, 10 September and 17 November 1944, 23 January and 14 March 1945.

219. The likely attitude of the East River guerrillas to any capitulating Japanese was demonstrated on 29 August when a plane carrying Makimura with a number of British escorts to rendezvous with Harcourt's approaching fleet had to make an unscheduled landing in Communist territory. The guerrillas were only dissuaded with some difficulty from cutting Makimura's throat. See Gimson, Hong Kong Reclaimed, pp. 11–12; Lindsay, *Going Down of the Sun*, pp. 203–4.

220. Draft Japanese surrender document shown (in translation) to Rear Admiral Harcourt on 21 September 1945. See Alan Birch article in *SCMP*, 12 September 1978; Rear Admiral Cecil Harcourt lecture on the British Military Administration of Hong Kong to the Royal Central Asian Society, London, 13 November 1946, published in *Journal of the Royal Central Asian Society*, vol. 34, 1947, pp. 7–18; Clark, *An End to Tears*, p. 147.

221. Tse, *San nian*, p. 399.

222. Gimson, Hong Kong Reclaimed, p. 10.

223. Gimson, Hong Kong Reclaimed, pp. 9, 10. See also Endacott and Birch, *Hong Kong Eclipse*, p. 230; Tse, *San nian*, p. 399. In his broadcast on 28 August Gimson acknowledged that he had established his office in the French Mission building 'with the concurrence of the Japanese'.

224. Gimson to Secretary of State, Colonial Office, 23 August 1945, and 27 August 1945, in Y. C. Liang Documents, HK MS 30.

225. Luff, *Hidden Years*, p. 227.

226. Endacott and Birch, *Hong Kong Eclipse*, p. 233.

227. Uttley, letter to Mrs Helen Uttley, undated, around 18 August 1945, Uttley papers, Rhodes House, p. 191. The doctor went on, 'Hate and vindictiveness will get us nowhere. The Japanese . . . will need a lot of careful handling and downright kindness showing to them in order to get them back on the right and sensible path of national development.' Ibid., pp. 191–2. The Japanese also dispensed extra rations to the camps, where many of the British had been told to remain for want of any other accommodation. They regaled the former POWs with jam and 11,000 packets of cigarettes, and glutted Stanley with more meat than the internees could possibly get down. See Uttley diary, 28 August 1945; Lindsay, *Lasting Honour*, p. 196; Wright-Nooth, *Prisoner of the Turnip-Heads*, p. 248. No doubt this contributed in some measure to the appreciative British reaction.

228. For accounts of this phenomenon, see Patrick Davis, 'Troubled Loyalties: Marginal Experiences in Bangkok, Saigon and Batavia, 1945–46' in *International Studies*, 1991 no. III, pp. 58–64, 69, 71, Suntory-Toyota International Centre for Economics and Related Disciplines, London School of Economics; Aldrich, *Intelligence and the War against Japan*, pp. 347, 355.

229. Gimson, Hong Kong Reclaimed, p. 10. The original charge was made in a report by Lieutenant-Colonel Owen Hughes of the British Military Administration, 9 October 1945. See Sweeting, 'Controversy over the Reopening of the University', pp. 402, 420 n. 11.

230. Gimson, Hong Kong Reclaimed, p. 7.

231. Clark, *An End to Tears*, p. 223.

232. See WIR no. 4, 24 September 1945 and Report from Staff Officer (Intelligence) on Political Situation in Hong Kong, 1 October 1945, CO 129 592/6, pp. 126, 151; Allen, *End of the War in Asia*, pp. 253–4.

233. Endacott and Birch, *Hong Kong Eclipse*, p. 230 n. 1; article by Alan Birch in *SCMP*, 5 February 1978.

234. *WKYP*, 17 and 18 August 1945.

235. Ibid.

236. *WKYP*, 19 August 1945.

237. *WKYP*, 26 August 1945.

238. *WKYP*, 20 and 29 August 1945 (evening editions). The reported presence of Tanaka at these functions constitutes a real puzzle. Other sources give the impression that the Governor was away in Canton throughout this transitional fortnight; and he was certainly there at the time Harcourt's squadron arrived in Hong Kong on 30 August. See Clark, *An End to Tears,* pp. 19–20; Lindsay, *Going Down of the Sun*, p. 203; Yuan, *Xianggang shilüe*, p. 188; Tse, *San nian*, p. 51. One British account, however, appears to confirm that Tanaka was in Hong Kong at least on the date of the first banquet on 20 August. See E. Ride, *British Army Aid Group*, p. 295. The most likely conclusion would seem to be that Tanaka was in fact in the colony for some of the time during these two weeks, or made one or two short trips there. Alternatively it may be that the newspaper reports are inaccurate, and that Tanaka was represented at these two functions by some deputy, e.g. the Chief of Staff, Major-General Fukuchi. The main point here, however, is not the identity of the top Japanese present but the gentry leaders' effort to maintain a smooth formal relationship with the occupation authorities right up to the end.

239. Interview, Mr Cyril Kotewall, 26 June 1995; *SCMP/HKT*, 6 September 1945.

240. *HKN*, 16 August 1945.

241. See *WKYP*, 29 August 1945.

242. *WKYP*, 17 August 1945.

243. *WKYP*, 19, 20, 21, 24 and 26 August 1945. The proclamation of Zhang Fakui's appointment was however offset by a reference to the statement of Premier Attlee which had been reported on the previous day (see p. 257 below).

244. *WKYP*, 19 August 1945.

245. Ibid.

246. *WKYP*, 25 August 1945.

247. *WKYP*, 27 August 1945.

248. *WKYP*, 29 August 1945. The editors were clearly thinking of Bismarck, not Metternich.

249. Ibid.

250. Ibid.

251. Harcourt radio signal quoted *SCMP/HKT* Extra, 30 August 1945.

252. Enclosure to Commander, Task Force, 21 August 1945, Papers Relating to Naval Agreement for the Reoccupation of Hong Kong 1944–5, HK MS 74–6.

253. Landing Force Administrative Order, 29 August 1945, Papers Relating to Naval Agreement, HK MS 74–6.

254. Enclosure to Commander, Task Force, 21 August 1945; Landing Force Administrative Order, 29 August 1945; Landing Force Commander, *Swiftsure* to *Euryalus* and *Prince Robert*, 30 August 1945, Papers Relating to Naval Agreement, HK MS 74–6.

255. Harcourt lecture to Royal Central Asian Society; Allen, *End of the War in Asia*, p. 254; Lindsay, *Going Down of the Sun*, p. 211; Ko and Wordie, *Ruins of War*, p. 182. The British had apparently received reports of 'almost a hundred small wooden Japanese suicide boats'. According to Harcourt the 'suicide boats' were manned by Japanese Army rather than Navy men: the Navy were 'terrified' of their Army opposite numbers and asked him to round them up. The old Army-Navy friction went on to the last.

256. Clark, *An End to Tears*, pp. 27–9.

257. MacDougall to Gent, 7 November 1945, CO 129 591/20, p. 32. See also Harcourt to A.V. Alexander, First Lord of the Admiralty, 7 November 1945, CO 129 592/6, p. 25; Harcourt lecture to Royal Central Asian Society; Tsang interview with MacDougall, p. 50; Lindsay, *Going Down of the Sun*, p. 211.

258. Lindsay, *Lasting Honour*, p. 195; Tse, *San nian*, p. 400; Tsang, *Democracy Shelved*, p. 26; Morris, *Hong Kong*, p. 261. Most of these flags had apparently been distributed by agents of Chiang Kai-shek and Wedemeyer earlier in the year. See p. 236, above. For local Chinese ambivalence towards the British return see remarks of 'Mr X' quoted by Adam Williams, article in *SMP*, 19 November 1978.

259. *SCMP/HKT*, 31 August 1945. See also Luff, *Hidden Years*, p. 231.

260. Zhang Fakui, preface to '*Guangdong shoujiang jishu*'. The 13th Army are known to have started off near Wuzhou, a city rather under 300 miles to the north-west of Hong Kong; but the question of how far they then got remains obscure. Zhang Fakui gives a date for the turn-around of 3 September, but mentions no places. Chinese authorities consulted by me in recent years suggest variously that the army advanced to a place about 200 miles to the north-west of the colony; to a point 'two days away'; and to the northern part of the New Territories. The latter suggestion seems impossible, since a Nationalist advance into the New Territories could hardly fail to have been recorded and would in all likelihood have resulted in fighting with the East River guerrillas. One old British Hong Kong hand however maintains that the volume of hearsay which has accumulated about the proximity of the Nationalist troops is simply too great to warrant placing automatic reliance on the very conservative suggestion that they never got nearer than 200 miles from the colony. In the absence of any clear evidence I have preferred to opt for the middling suggestion of 'two days away'. This would place Shi's forces still some distance from the border but a fair bit closer than 200 miles. Conversations with Mr Y. K. Chan, 23 March 1995, with Mr S. J. Chan, 19 June 1995, and with Mr Dan Waters, 18 October 1995; article by Yu-ming Shaw, 'An ROC View of the Hong Kong Issue', in Jürgen Domes and Yu-ming Shaw (eds), *Hong Kong: A Chinese and International Concern*, Boulder and London, 1988, p. 100; Tsang, *Appointment with China*, p. 45.

261. Zhang Fakui, preface to '*Guangdong shoujiang jishu*'.

6. A Frail Restoration

1. MacDougall quoted in Lindsay, *Going Down of the Sun*, p. 216. For description of Harcourt see also Tsang interview with MacDougall, p. 53.

2. Tsang interview with MacDougall, p. 42.

3. *SCMP/HKT*, 1 September 1945. The press report explicitly noted the resemblance to the Gunseicho's round-up of Allied civilians in January 1942.

4. Hong Kong Joint Intelligence Committee Weekly Intelligence Summary (WIS) no. 5, 25 October 1945, CO 129 592/6, p. 69.

5. Notes of G. A. Wallinger, British Minister in Chungking, on visit to Hong Kong, 26 September to 3 October 1945, letter from Harcourt to Alexander, 7 November 1945 and WIS no. 8, 13 November 1945, CO 129 592/6, pp. 25, 32, 108. The element of poetic justice was underlined by Wallinger, who noted, 'It was refreshing to see Japanese POWs hard at work on the airfield unloading drums of petrol from a lighter under robust commando guards.'

6. Under the arrangements agreed on at the end of the war an International Military Tribunal for the Far East was set up in Tokyo by the United Nations to try 'major' or Class A war

criminals. Individual Allied countries had the right at the same time to conduct their own trials of 'minor' or Class B and C war criminals. In Britain's case a decision was made that Japanese war crimes suspects should be tried by military courts under the general supervision of the War Office. The South-east Asia Command (SEAC) under Lord Louis Mountbatten and the Allied Land Forces in South-east Asia (ALFSEA) were given responsibility for convening the courts and conducting the trials. The two courts set up in Hong Kong formed part of a series established in a total of twenty-five cities: others were located in Burma, Malaya, Singapore and North Borneo. As well as investigating atrocities perpetrated in Hong Kong itself the Hong Kong courts were intended to try a number of cases relating to war crimes committed in Japan, Taiwan, on the Chinese mainland and on the high seas. See article 'British War Crimes Trials of Japanese', in Kanto Gakuin University, *Nature-People-Society: Science and the Humanities*, no. 31, July 2001.

7. Harcourt to Alexander, 7 November 1945, CO 129 592/6, p. 26. Harcourt's opinion was shared by G. A. Wallinger, the British Minister in Chungking, who felt that the Japanese had put the building into 'excellent shape', and by John Stericker, an assistant to Gimson, who commented that 'the Japanese had rebuilt Government House and rebuilt it very well'. One dissenter was the aesthetic MacDougall, who found the rebuilding hideous. 'Entering it is somehow like meeting a hitherto reputable old lady turned painted and wanton with too much rouge and too obviously a lifted face.' See Notes of G. A. Wallinger, CO 129 592/6, p. 108; John Stericker, quoted in Birch and Cole, *Captive Years*, p. 177; MacDougall quoted Lindsay, *Going Down of the Sun*, p. 215.

8. Endacott and Birch, *Hong Kong Eclipse*, p. 153; Faure, 'Sai Kung: The Making of the District', p. 203.

9. MacDougall quoted in Lindsay, *Going Down of the Sun*, p. 216. A Japanese journalist, Onoe Etsuzo, who visited the colony in 1960, observed that 'a large number of Hong Kong Chinese speak Japanese'. Onoe maintained that many of these Japanese speakers were people who had studied in Japan or graduated from Japanese language schools in Manchuria, while a number were Overseas Chinese from South-east Asia; but he also observed that people with a smattering of Japanese 'could be found everywhere in the city'. See Onoe Etsuzo, '*Honkon no chu no Nihon*', in *Ajia Keizai* vol. 1, no. 3, September 1960.

10. ZB, 23 January 1946.

11. Judgement of George Endacott, Endacott and Birch, *Hong Kong Eclipse*, p. 317.

12. Harcourt cables to War Office, 2 October 1945 CO 129 591/10, p. 71 and Colonial Office, 2 October 1945, CO 129 592/6, pp. 145, 156.

13. Harcourt letters to Alexander 7 November 1945 and G. H. Hall, Secretary of State for the Colonies, 11 November 1945 CO 129 592/6, pp. 22, 25. See also Harcourt lecture to Royal Central Asian Society.

14. Compliments were beginning to flow as early as October. See Seymour to Bevin quoting Brigadier O. M. Kay, Canadian military attaché in Chungking, 5 October 1945, CO 129 592/6, p. 106. In November Miss R. Clifford of the Ministry of Information thanked Alice Ruston of the Colonial Office in general terms for details of 'the good job of reconstruction being done by Britain in the Far East'. Clifford to Ruston, 9 November 1945, CO 129 592/6, p. 121. See also Gleason, *Hong Kong*, p. 38. For speed of the postwar rehabilitation in Hong Kong see Morris, *Hong Kong*, p. 259; Tsang, *Appointment with China*, p. 53.

15. Ingrams, *Hong Kong*, p. 243. Scarce foreign currency was used by the Hongkong and Shanghai Bank to finance the import of race horses.

16. Clark, *An End to Tears*, p. 42.

17. Quoted in Lindsay, *Lasting Honour*, p. 195.

18. Report from Staff Officer (Intelligence) Hong Kong on Political Situation in Hong Kong 1 October 1945, CO 129 592/6, pp. 150–1; Annual Report on the Hong Kong Police Force 1946–47, p. 24. See also Clark, *An End to Tears*, p. 44; Lindsay, *Going Down of the Sun*, p. 217.

19. Lindsay, *Going Down of the Sun*, p. 217.

20. Lieutenant-Colonel R.E.O.C.M.E. 93 Kunming to HQ Force 136 (G) 16 September 1945, HS 1/329, p. 1. See also Harcourt Report on the Occupation of Hong Kong, HK RS 411/573, para. 30; Clark, *An End to Tears*, p. 100; Yuan, *Xianggang shilüe*, p. 190.

21. BMA Proclamation no. 1, 1 September 1945, published in Hong Kong (BMA) Gazette, vol. 1 no. 1 p. 2, CO 132 89.

22. *SCMP/HKT*, 4 September 1945.

23. See WIR no. 4, 24 September 1945, and Report from Staff Officer (Intelligence) Hong Kong on Political Situation in Hong Kong, 1 October 1945, CO 129 592/6, pp. 126, 150–1. See also Lindsay, *Going Down of the Sun*, p. 218. According to one report, the Gambling House Gang were given a pay-off of M¥5m. It seems unlikely, however, that the two gangs would have been offered conspicuously different sums, or indeed that either would have been offered military yen at a time when the bogus Japanese currency had fallen so sharply in value. A reasonable guess would be that both gangs were offered HK$5m from money raised by the SOE out of their black marketeering operations.

24. *SCMP/HKT*, 4 September 1945; Appreciation of the Police Organization, 10 October 1945, CO 129 591/20, p. 62; Miners, 'Localization of the Hong Kong Police Force', p. 311.

25. George Endacott in Endacott and Birch, *Hong Kong Eclipse*, p. 232.

26. See *SCMP/HKT*, 19 September and 11 October 1945; ZB 5 May 1946; *Dadui shi*, pp. 184–5; Yuan, *Xianggang shilüe*, pp. 190–2.

27. On 1 September Harcourt had actually appointed Gimson Lieutenant Governor, only to be informed by London that the appointment was inconsistent with a military administration and had to be cancelled. See *SCMP/HKT*, 1 September 1945; Lindsay, *Going Down of the Sun*, p. 214; Gittins, *Stanley: Behind Barbed Wire*, p. 154; Tsang, *Appointment with China*, p. 52. For mental state of the ex-internees see Clark, *An End to Tears*, p. 23. There appears in addition to have been a certain amount of friction between Gimson's 'skeleton government' and MacDougall's incoming Civil Affairs team. 'I'm afraid', MacDougall later wrote of Gimson and his colleagues, 'that deep down our arrival was interpreted as a vote of no confidence in themselves'. See Lindsay, *Going Down of the Sun*, p. 215; Kwan, *Ri zhan shiqi de Xianggang*, p. 162; Frank Welsh, *A History of Hong Kong*, London, 1997, p. 432. Similar though their outlooks were on most major issues, it is perhaps difficult to imagine that Gimson and MacDougall could have worked very comfortably together. Gimson disappeared from Hong Kong for ever having spent virtually his entire term of office there in Japanese captivity. He was, however, rewarded for his solitary labours with a knighthood and the governorship of Singapore.

28. See C. Delamain, Report on General Administrative Branch, 12 October 1945, Appreciation of the Police Organization, 10 October 1945, Colonel H. S. Rouse, Works Branch, Progress Report up to 27 October 1945, report of Colonel Thomson, Imports and Exports Department, 1 November 1945 and Central Executive Branch Progress Report no. 2, 1 November 1945, CO 129 591/20, pp. 49, 51, 54, 62–3, 65, 74.

29. Appreciation of the Police Organization, 10 October 1945 and report of Colonel Thomson, Imports and Exports Department, 1 November 1945, CO 129 591/20, pp. 63, 74.

30. *SCMP/HKT*, 4 September 1945. They were said to be 'not very well trained'.

31. Central Executive Branch Progress Report no. 2, 1 November 1945 and Appreciation of the Police Organization, 10 October 1945, CO 129 591/20, pp. 49, 63.

32. Harcourt to War Office, 22 September 1945, CO 129 591/10, p. 89.

33. Harcourt to War Office, 6 October 1945, CO 129 591/10, p. 59.

34. See Harcourt lecture to Royal Central Asian Society. Macao was of course still under Portuguese rule; but that little enclave had been tacitly conceded to Portugal at a much earlier period.

35. Tsang, *Appointment with China*, p. 62.

36. In a letter written in mid-October Alice Ruston of the Colonial Office had indeed observed that the new airport would be still deeper inside the New Territories than Kai Tak, and that this would 'show still further how closely the New Territories and the rest of the colony are

connected'. Ruston to W. W. McVittie of Cabinet Office Far Eastern Planning Unit, 18 October 1945, CO 129 592/8, p. 54.

37. Foreign Ministry, Chungking, report of 26 November 1945 interview with British chargé d'affaires and Wang Shijie memorandum to Chiang, 29 November 1945, Museum of Military History, Taipei 062.23/5000.4.

38. Wang Shijie memorandum to Chiang, 12 January 1946, Museum of Military History, 062.23/5000.4.

39. Foreign Ministry, Chungking, correspondence with President's Office, January 1946, Museum of Military History, 062.23/5000.4. The name of the warship was the *Black Swan*. In March 1946 the Foreign Ministry further proposed that from now on British warships shouldn't be allowed to enter Chinese territorial waters without permission, and that any British warships currently in China should leave it. In June a British warship entered the Bocca Tigris (Humen) on the Pearl River on the orders of the Naval Commander in Hong Kong to take soundings for mines laid by United States aircraft in the final stages of the war. The ship's progress met with obstruction when it was discovered that the commander didn't have the necessary Nationalist government documents giving permission to do this. Foreign Ministry paper 31 March 1946 and Chief of Staff Chen Cheng submission to General Zhang Fakui, 8 June 1946, Museum of Military History, 062.23/5000.4. See also Harcourt lecture to Royal Central Asian Society.

40. For example in January 1946 over the Pingshan airport issue. See *HSB*, 29 January 1946; *FEER*, 2 August 1951.

41. Zhang Fakui to President's Office, 29 October 1945, Museum of Military History, 062.23/5000.4.

42. Harcourt cable to Colonial Office, 25 October 1945, and WIS no. 6, 1 November 1945, CO 129 592/6, pp. 62, 146; MacDougall, General Report, 2 November 1945, CO 129 591/20, p. 29. See also Lindsay, *Going Down of the Sun*, p. 219.

43. WIR no. 4, 24 September 1945, WIS, no. 4, 18 October 1945, no. 5, 25 October 1945 and no. 6, 1 November 1945, CO 129 592/6, pp. 57, 71, 80, 81, 125.

44. WIS no. 5, 25 October 1945, CO 129 592/6, p. 71.

45. WIS no. 7, 6 November 1945, CO 129 592/6, p. 50. The colonel professed to his British interlocutors to be a 'non-party man', 'speaking for himself'; but his claims shouldn't necessarily be taken at face value. The other reasons he offered for Britain returning the colony (that Hong Kong was the only part of China which hadn't reverted to Chinese sovereignty, that Hong Kong's existence depended on trade with China which could easily be denied) amounted to a breakdown of current Nationalist thinking on the subject. For a growing consensus that Hong Kong was no longer defensible see also H. G. W. Woodhead article in *Shanghai Evening Post and Mercury*, 31 August 1945, cutting filed in CO 129 592/8, p. 66; Clark, *An End to Tears*, p. 168.

46. Chan Lau, *China, Britain and Hong Kong*, pp. 322–3.

47. WIS no. 5, 25 October 1945, CO 129 592/6, p. 71. Fourteen vessels of the US Navy arrived in Hong Kong on 7 October. See ZB, 1 January 1946.

48. Notes of G. A. Wallinger, CO 129 592/6, p. 116.

49. Paskin minute on draft memorandum prepared by G. V. Kitson of Foreign Office for Foreign Secretary Bevin, 9 September 1945 and Ruston report, 2 October 1945, CO 129 592/8, pp. 26, 28.

50. Kitson memorandum of late February 1946 quoted Tsang, *Appointment with China*, p. 59.

51. General policy document drawn up by the Far Eastern Planning Unit of the Cabinet Office in October 1945. The portion of the document dealing with Hong Kong was based mainly on a Colonial Office paper on Hong Kong's future. Tsang, *Appointment with China*, p. 57. References to the possible return of Hong Kong to the Nationalists continued to be made by British officials right up to the end of 1946. See Sweeting, 'Controversy over the Reopening of the University', pp. 408, 413, 414, 421 n. 26.

52. BMA Proclamation no. 7, 13 September 1945, published in Hong Kong (BMA) Gazette, vol. 1, no. 1, pp. 8–9, CO 132 89.

53. MacDougall to Gent, 7 November 1945, CO 129 591/20, p. 33. Five days earlier MacDougall had described Hong Kong as being 'at the mercy' of neighbouring areas of the mainland 'in the matter of several essential supplies'. See MacDougall, General Report, 2 November 1945, CO 129 591/20, p. 28.

54. Notes of G. A. Wallinger, CO 129 592/6, p. 116.

55. Harcourt to Admiralty, 9 September 1945, CO 129 591/18, p. 53.

56. WIS no. 1, 29 September 1945, CO 129 592/6, p. 98.

57. Tsang interview with MacDougall, p. 59; MacDougall to Gent, 19 October 1945, CO 129 592/6, p. 105.

58. Tsang interview with MacDougall, pp. 92–3. See also Harcourt telegram to War Office, 15 November 1945, CO 129 592/6, p. 103. MacDougall's reference to 'food they haven't got' should be compared with his deeply apprehensive remarks some days earlier about Hong Kong's dependence on the mainland for essential supplies. See note 53.

59. Harcourt press conference in Chungking 9 January 1946, Museum of Military History, 062.23/5000.4.

60. BMA announcement, 2 April 1946. See *ZB*, 13 April 1946; Foreign Ministry, Nanking report to President's Office, 10 May 1946, Museum of Military History, 062.23/5000.4; *FEER*, 2 August 1951.

61. See Shaftain, Rough Draft, p. 14; Clark, *An End to Tears*, pp. 92–3; Birch and Cole, *Captive Christmas*, p. 62; Wright-Nooth, *Prisoner of the Turnip-Heads*, p. 49.

62. Tsang, *Democracy Shelved*, p. 29. Thought had already been given during the war to the eventual unbanning of the Party both in Hong Kong and elsewhere in the Far East. See draft letter from the SOE to the Colonial Office regarding the Chinese community in Malaya 10 August 1944, HS 1/171. Following the Allied victory the ban on the Party was lifted not only in Hong Kong but also in Malaya and a number of other places.

63. WIS no. 7, 6 November 1945, and no. 8, 13 November 1945, CO 129 592/6, pp. 34, 48.

64. *DGB*, 27 October 1945, cutting filed in CO 129 592/8, p. 40; MacDougall, General Report, 2 November 1945, CO 129 591/20, p. 29; *ZB*, 23 January 1946; Catron, 'China and Hong Kong', p. 38.

65. Tsang, *Democracy Shelved*, p. 28. The appointment of a Chinese consul in Hong Kong had been agreed on in late 1941 as part of the belated closing of ranks between British and Nationalists which took place at that time; but the Japanese invasion had supervened before any steps could be taken to implement the agreement.

66. WIS no. 8, 13 November 1945, CO 129 592/6, p. 34. He subsequently did just that, becoming a prominent figure in the colony's banking and insurance circles. See Wright-Nooth, *Prisoner of the Turnip-Heads*, p. 258.

67. MacDougall, General Report, 2 November 1945, CO 129 591/20, p. 29; Harcourt to Hall, 11 November 1945, CO 129 592/6, p. 23.

68. Harcourt to Alexander, 7 November 1945, CO 129 592/6, p. 26.

69. Harcourt to Hall, 11 November 1945, CO 129 592/6, p. 23. An attempt to conciliate Zhang was eventually made in April 1947, when Governor Young paid a visit to Canton. Zhang was presented on that occasion with a CBE in recognition of services he was supposed to have rendered during the war to the BAAG and the other British forces in south China. The attempt appears to have been successful: Zhang was said subsequently to be 'on especially good terms with the British elite in Hong Kong', and he retired there in due course to live (rumour had it) off investments he had made in the 1930s. See E. Ride, *British Army Aid Group*, p. 259; Lane, 'Nationalist Government' p. 103; Catron, 'China and Hong Kong', p. 23.

70. Tsang interview with MacDougall, p. 59.

71. Harcourt lecture to Royal Central Asian Society.

72. WIS no. 1, 29 September 1945, no. 4, 18 October 1945, and no. 6, 1 November 1945, CO 129 592/6, pp. 57, 81, 98.

73. MacDougall, General Report, 2 November 1945 and MacDougall to Gent, 7 November 1945, CO 129 591/20, pp. 29, 32.

74. Tsang interview with MacDougall, p. 87.

75. Ibid., p. 85.
76. See *SCMP/HKT*, 6, 8 and 27 September 1945; *ZB*, 1 January 1946. The new body was also referred to as the Hong Kong Reconstruction Advisory Committee, a name ironically reminiscent of the Rehabilitation Advisory Committee set up by the Gunseicho. It was formally established on 10 September 1945.
77. T. M. Hazlerigg memorandum to Gent, 31 December 1945, CO 129 594/9, p. 151. See also WIS no. 7, 6 November 1945, CO 129 592/6, p. 51; Wright-Nooth, *Prisoner of the Turnip-Heads*, p. 254.
78. *SCMP/HKT*, 4, 21 and 30 September 1945.
79. Hazlerigg memorandum to Gent 31 December 1945, CO 129 594/9, p. 153.
80. *SCMP/HKT*, 12 September 1945.
81. Letter from Dr Harry Talbot, *SCMP/HKT* 14 September 1945; *SCMP/HKT*, 17 September 1945.
82. Letter from 'A Yenless Chinese', *SCMP/HKT*, 16 September 1945. See also letters from 'Chatter-box' and 'Pro Bono Publico', *SCMP/HKT*, 10 and 12 September 1945. A local surgeon was reported to be among a number of Hong Kong Chinese complaining about the presence at British functions of leading local personages who had been equally prominent at Japanese ones. See WIS no. 7, 6 November 1945, CO 129 592/6, p. 51; Lindsay, *Going Down of the Sun*, p. 240.
83. MacDougall, General Report, 2 November 1945, CO 129 591/20, p. 30.
84. MacDougall to Gent, 7 November 1945, CO 129 591/20, pp. 32–3.
85. MacDougall letter to Ronald Holmes, Acting Secretary for Chinese Affairs, 13 July 1969, in private papers of Mrs Helen Zimmern; Tsang interview with MacDougall, p. 64.
86. MacDougall, General Report, 2 November 1945, CO 129 591/20, p. 28. Harcourt commented similarly on the large quantities of rice which had been distributed by the local charities. See Harcourt to Alexander, 7 November 1945, CO 129 592/6, p. 25; Harcourt lecture to Royal Central Asian Society.
87. *SCMP/HKT* editorial, 14 September 1945.
88. MacDougall to Gent, 7 November 1945, CO 129 591/20, p. 32. MacDougall went on to explain more concretely, if less picturesquely: 'Locally the most serious (and from the point of view of our pre-war system, the most damning) factor is that there seem to be no new Chinese of the younger generation anxious to shoulder the responsibility of public affairs. I have been unable to find candidates anxious to dispute local leadership with the established order.' See also extracts from MacDougall letter to T. I. K. Lloyd, Gent's successor as the Hong Kong overseer at the Colonial Office, 16 February 1946, CO 129 594/9, p. 143; Lethbridge, 'Hong Kong under Japanese Occupation', p. 118; Lindsay, *Going Down of the Sun*, p. 240.
89. Daniel Lee in *DGB*, 17 September 1945, article forwarded by Seymour to Foreign Office, 27 September 1945, CO 129 592/8, p. 53.
90. *SCMP/HKT*, 7 October 1945.
91. In 1946 the Hong Kong authorities were actually obliged by Chinese pressure to introduce a Chinese Collaborators (Surrender) Bill providing for the deportation to the mainland of Chinese nationals who had worked with the Japanese between 1937 and 1945. Lethbridge, 'Hong Kong under Japanese Occupation' pp. 117–18. This did not of course affect members of the gentry holding British passports.
92. As early as July 1944 Gimson had fretted in Stanley over the risk that the Nationalists might attempt to try Kotewall and his colleagues at the end of the war. It was, he judged, 'imperative' that the post-war Chinese government 'should not be allowed to interfere in any matter which might concern the [Hong Kong] Government and the people of Chinese race who were considered to be the responsibility of that Government'. Gimson diary, 3 July 1944. On 15 November 1945, Colonel G. Strickland, of the BMA's Legal Department, wrote in the same spirit to MacDougall, 'If any resident Chinese are to be treated as war criminals we cannot be indifferent'. HK RS 163 1/222A, p. 1.

93. A British need for Chinese 'loyal to the concept of a separate status for Hong Kong' is referred to in Lethbridge, 'Hong Kong under Japanese Occupation', p. 117.

94. An oblique effort to calm the expatriates was made as early as 16 September, in a farewell radio broadcast delivered by Gimson on the eve of his departure from Hong Kong. In it Gimson drew attention to those 'others in the colony to whom some expression of the gratitude which we who were interned feel towards them is long overdue'. He was referring, he explained, 'to some of our fellow-nationals of the Chinese, Portuguese and Indian communities, who were left behind to bear the brunt of the Japanese oppression in Hong Kong and who in spite of persecutions and privations – in some cases taking the extreme forms of torture and imprisonment – refused to do anything which would injure the cause of the United Nations, but rather did their best to promote it by any means in their power. Since their release the faithful cooperation of these loyal people has contributed materially to the smooth resumption of normal life here. It is my earnest hope that all who have behaved so nobly will regain their former livelihood and reestablish themselves, either in their private businesses or in the public service, on a sound basis of prosperity, and that the Government will do its utmost to assist in the restoration of such people to their rightful places in the life of the community.' Gimson, 'Hong Kong Reclaimed'. While not an explicit defence of the gentry, these remarks were clearly designed to counter the howls of treason in the press.

95. See *SCMP/HKT* and *China Mail*, 2 October 1945.

96. Tsang interview with MacDougall, p. 65.

97. *SCMP/HKT*, 2 October 1945; Notes of G. A. Wallinger and WIS no. 2, 4 October 1945, CO 129 592/6, pp. 96, 114; Endacott and Birch, *Hong Kong Eclipse*, pp. 244–5. The draft directive issued by the Colonial Office in this connection had however spelt out from the start the desirability of a lenient approach. 'In order', it advised, 'to dissipate as speedily as possible whatever pro-Japanese sentiments still exist in the Far Eastern territories and to promote the conditions in which those territories can resume their position in the Empire on a basis of goodwill, it will repay us if our treatment of those who have collaborated with the enemy during the years of Japanese occupation is founded on a generous and tolerant view of their conduct. Experience has already shown that only by so doing can we secure the services of the men of education, ability, initiative and authority on whom we must necessarily depend, but who, by virtue of their position, have been employed by the Japanese'. Colonial Office Draft Directive on Treatment of Renegades and Quislings, March 1945, pp. 2–3, HK RS 211-2-41. For Harcourt's refusal to have Kotewall tried see Alice Ruston minute, 4 February 1946, CO 129 594/9, p. 3. In another report written three days earlier a colleague of Ruston's observed that the Kotewall question 'appears to have been dealt with as a Hong Kong political matter'. Note to Ruston of 1 February 1946, CO 129 594/9, p. 3.

98. Lethbridge, 'Hong Kong under Japanese Occupation', p. 118.

99. Hazlerigg memorandum to Gent, 31 December 1945, CO 129 594/9, p. 152; Tsang interview with MacDougall, p. 65.

100. Hazlerigg memorandum to Gent, 31 December 1945, CO 129 594/9, p. 152.

101. Lindsay, *Going Down of the Sun*, p. 241.

102. Ruston minutes, 12 and 16 March 1946, Ruston letter to MacDougall, 18 March 1946, Ruston minute, 19 March 1946, and Young telegram to Arthur Creech-Jones, Secretary of State for the Colonies, 8 May 1946, CO 129 594/9, pp. 8, 11, 12, 107, 127; Tsang interview with MacDougall, p. 72. See also Lethbridge, 'Hong Kong under Japanese Occupation', p. 118.

103. Circular distributed by Sir Robert Kotewall, May 1946. Copy supplied to me by Mrs Helen Zimmern.

104. Lethbridge, 'Hong Kong under Japanese Occupation', p. 119; interviews, Sir Y. K. Kan, 24 May 1995 and Mr Charles Sin, 29 June 1995.

105. *FEER*, 5 February 1947; Lethbridge, 'Hong Kong under Japanese Occupation', p. 119; Ching, *The Li Dynasty*, pp. 125–6.

106. See Hong Kong (BMA) Gazette, vol. 2, no. 1, CO 132 89, p. 10.

107. 'The Ho Tung Saga (Part 1)', p. 105.

108. The change of title, which took place in October 1945, was apparently accompanied by a fairly drastic purge of the newspaper's wartime staff. The placid reappearance of the paper none the less caused a certain amount of indignation among ordinary Chinese residents. See Fan, '*Xianggang zhi zhan huiyilu*', p. 10 and '*Shengli zhi chu zai Xianggang*', p. 24; Buping Shanren, *Xianggang lunxian huiyilu*, p. 45.
109. Notes of G. A. Wallinger, CO 129 592/6, p. 114.
110. Harcourt telegram to Creech-Jones, 20 April 1946, Ruston memorandum, 16 May 1946 and Lloyd to Gater, 20 May 1946, CO 129 594/9, pp. 17, 18, 108.
111. MacDougall report of 4 October 1945 quoted in attachment to Lloyd letter to Young, 6 March 1946, CO 129 594/9, p. 140. See also Ruston minute of 16 May 1946 and Lloyd minute to Gater, 20 May 1946, same file, pp. 17, 18.
112. Harcourt to Creech-Jones, 12 April 1946 and Ruston to Young, 13 April 1946, CO 129 594/9, pp. 118, 119.
113. Gittins, *Eastern Windows*, p. 216 and *Stanley: Behind Barbed Wire*, p. 123; E. Ride, *British Army Aid Group*, p. 190 n. 4; 'The Lo Dynasty' p. 80; Waters, *Faces of Hong Kong*, p. 141.
114. Three days before Harcourt's arrival Gimson had reported to the Colonial Office, 'Uncertainty as to future of Colony reflected in currency speculation, speculators gambling on conversion as against repudiation of [military] yen. Speculators also hold millions of old Hong Kong currency obtained at favourable rates [in] Macao, Indochina and elsewhere.' Gimson cable to Secretary of State for the Colonies, 27 August 1945, Y. C. Liang Documents, HK MS 30. Some at least of the 'old Hong Kong currency' will have consisted of duress notes. For other evidence of speculation in duress notes and military yen see *SCMP/HKT*, 31 August 1945; *ZB*, 16 November 1945; Clark, *An End to Tears*, p. 41; Frank H. H. King, *History of the Hongkong and Shanghai Banking Corporation*, vol. IV, pp. 129–30; Morris, *Hong Kong*, pp. 259–60.
115. Wilson, *Hong Kong! Hong Kong!*, p. 11.
116. Harcourt to Hall, 11 November 1945, CO 129 592/6, p. 22. Although this report bears Harcourt's signature, the literary flavour of the language strongly suggests that the original author was MacDougall. Other passages in the report are almost identical to portions of a dispatch which was written by MacDougall to Gent four days earlier.
117. *ZB*, 9 April 1946; *FEER*, 12 March 1947; King, *History of the Hongkong and Shanghai Banking Corparation*, vol. IV, pp. 124, 126, 128, 131; Yuan, *Xianggang shilüe*, pp. 196, 200; letter from Mr Adam Williams OBE, 6 June 1994; interview, Mr Y. K. Chan, 23 March 1995. The choice of April Fool's Day for the Bank's announcement was presumably a coincidence.
118. *FEER*, 12 March 1947. Information confirmed by the late Professor Leonard Rayner, 16 July 1991.
119. Tsang interview with MacDougall, p. 54. For assistance given by Dick Lee to the BAAG, see chapter 4, note 140.
120. Li, *Hong Kong Surgeon*, pp. 206, 210. Local gentry who had invested in Hong Kong dollars during the final years of the war were now said to be 'the happiest of all people'. *SCMP/HKT*, 27 September 1945.
121. *ZB*, 19 April 1946. The official recognition of the duress notes is said to have been the foundation of several fortunes. See Morris, *Hong Kong*, pp. 259–60; Wilson, *Hong Kong! Hong Kong!*, p. 11.
122. Interview, Sir Y. K. Kan, 24 May 1995.
123. Tsang interview with MacDougall, pp. 54–5.
124. Report of Henry Bough of Reuters, Hong Kong, undated, March 1946, p. 3, MacDougall papers, Rhodes House.
125. *FEER*, 12 March and 20 August 1947; Lethbridge, 'Hong Kong under Japanese Occupation', pp. 84–5, n. 2; Irene Cheng, *Clara Ho Tung: A Hong Kong Lady, Her Family and Her Times*, Hong Kong, 1976, pp. 15, 147; 'The Ho Tung Saga (Part 1)', p. 105; L. Ride, 'The Test of War (Part 1)' and Mellor, 'A New Start', in Matthews and Cheung (eds), *Dispersal and Renewal*, pp. 298, 434.
126. Quoted in Lethbridge, 'Hong Kong under Japanese Occupation', p. 123.

127. *SCMP/HKT*, 16 September 1945. Three days later the paper editorialized, 'The seeming neglect of the Chinese population for the first fortnight of our freedom revived some dying bitterness, and the queer contradictions and changes in the evacuation system for Stanley internees has added to it.' The editorial quoted one correspondent as saying, 'We are getting back to the old Hong Kong all right.' *SCMP/HKT*, 19 September 1945.

128. BMA Proclamation no. 14, 28 September 1945 published in Hong Kong (BMA) Gazette vol. 1 no. 1 pp. 19–20, CO 132 89; Lethbridge, 'Hong Kong under Japanese Occupation', p. 124 n. 1.

129. Tse, *San nian*, p. 74.

130. Tsang interview with MacDougall, p. 51.

131. Comments of a 'Hong Kong Chinese lady teacher' and a 'well known and respected banker' cited in WIS no. 5, 25 October 1945 and comments of a 'Chinese lady graduate of the University of Hong Kong' cited in WIS no. 6, 1 November 1945, CO 129 592/6, pp. 61, 74–5; comment of a young university-educated Chinese with a Eurasian wife quoted Clark, *An End to Tears*, p. 165.

132. Comments of a Chinese lady formerly employed as a clerk by Jardine Matheson and of a Chinese employed by the Hong Kong government cited in WIS no. 5, 25 October 1945 and WIS no. 7, 6 November 1945, CO 129 592/6, pp. 50, 74; letter from J. Lee, *SCMP/HKT*, 9 September 1945.

133. Letters from J. Lee and 'Res Publica', *SCMP/HKT*, 9 and 18 September 1945.

134. Harcourt lecture to Royal Central Asian Society.

135. Ibid. See also Tsang, *Democracy Shelved*, p. 26; Welsh, *History of Hong Kong*, p. 434.

136. *FEER*, 11 December 1946.

137. Tsang interview with MacDougall, p. 68.

138. Quoted in Lindsay, *Going Down of the Sun*, pp. 241–2.

139. *SCMP/HKT*, 9 September 1945.

140. Uttley diary, 20 August 1945.

141. MacDougall to Gent, 19 October, 1945, CO 129 592/6, p. 104.

142. Tsang, *Democracy Shelved*, p. 27, and *Appointment with China*, p. 59. G. A. Wallinger, the British Minister in Chungking, in the same way judged it 'important that Hong Kong be presented to the outside world in general and to China in particular as a progressive place'. Notes of G. A. Wallinger, CO 129 592/6, p. 117.

143. *SCMP/HKT*, 9 September 1945.

144. Lethbridge, 'Hong Kong under Japanese Occupation', p. 124 n. 1. In 1950 the constitution of the Hong Kong Defence Force, the successor body to the Hong Kong Volunteer Defence Corps, was said a little defensively to 'provide for complete equality of treatment of all members and the complete mixing up of all racial elements'. Ingrams, *Hong Kong*, p. 247.

145. Tsang interview with MacDougall, p. 115.

146. Ibid.; Hong Kong (BMA) Gazette, vol. 1, no. 1, p. 40 and vol. 1, no. 2, CO 132 89, p. 33.

147. MacDougall, General Report, 2 November 1945, CO 129 591/20, p. 30. See also Harcourt lecture to Royal Central Asian Society. The Eurasian Deputy Director was K. J. Attwell, formerly of the 2nd Battery of the Hong Kong Volunteer Defence Corps. In the course of the autumn an Oxford graduate named Yu Wan and a Hong Kong University graduate named Y. P. Law were both appointed senior inspectors in the Education Department. See Colonel J. R. Rowell, Central Executive Branch Progress Report no. 1, 5 October 1945, CO 129 591/20, p. 36; Mellor, 'In India, in China and twice in Hong Kong' in Matthews and Cheung (eds), *Dispersal and Renewal*, p. 366.

148. See Annual Report on the Hong Kong Police Force 1946–47, pp. 9–10; Miners, 'Localisation of the Hong Kong Police Force', pp. 311–12. A contingent of British police from the former Shanghai Municipal Police Force were brought to Hong Kong in 1945–46, mostly in the capacity of sub-inspectors. This move was however a temporary one, presumably intended to tighten the British grip in the first precarious months after Harcourt's arrival, and doesn't seem to have held back the drive towards localization which took place under Young.

149. Young to Creech-Jones telegram no. 84, 10 May 1946, CO 129 594/9, p. 104; Tsang, *Democracy Shelved*, p. 47. Several officials, including both Gent in London and MacDougall in Hong Kong, had argued in favour of strengthening the Chinese presence on the Legislative Council as well. MacDougall had urged that at least three seats on the Legislative Council should be occupied by Chinese, and had recommended that as few Europeans as possible should be appointed to the Council. Young however maintained more cautiously that there should be at least three Europeans on the Council to balance the Chinese; and other influential figures, notably the special adviser Hazlerigg, were opposed to making drastic changes in either the Executive or Legislative Councils at a time when the altogether novel Municipal Council was being introduced.

150. Quoted in Endacott and Birch, *Hong Kong Eclipse*, p. 280; Tsang, *Democracy Shelved*, p. 32 and *Appointment with China*, p. 54. See also Lethbridge, 'Hong Kong under Japanese Occupation', p. 123. A move of this kind was seen as all the more desirable in view of the 'tainted' character of the pre-war Chinese leadership. See Hazlerigg memorandum to Gent, 31 December 1945, CO 129 594/9, pp. 153–4.

151. Lethbridge, 'Hong Kong under Japanese Occupation' p. 120. Part of the reason for this experiment is said to have been the persistence in rural areas of the wartime generation gap between the village elders who had acquiesced in the Japanese occupation and the younger people who had joined the resistance. Rancour and recrimination had persisted in the villages considerably longer than in urban Hong Kong. Under these circumstances popular election was judged to be the sole available way to choose rural committees which could be regarded as representative and on whose authority the government could rely. The British decision was also influenced by the continuing presence in some places of village committees set up by the Japanese: see p. 303 below.

152. Ingrams, *Hong Kong*, p. 243.

153. Endacott and Birch, *Hong Kong Eclipse*, p. 320.

154. Maggie Keswick, *The Thistle and The Jade: A Celebration of 150 Years of Jardine Matheson & Co.*, London, 1982, p. 98; Peter Hall, *In the Web*, p. 113.

155. Quoted in 'The Lo Dynasty', p. 79; Lethbridge, 'Hong Kong under Japanese Occupation', p. 123.

156. Minutes of the Executive Council, 2 August 1946, CO 131 116, p. 67; Lethbridge, 'Hong Kong under Japanese Occupation', p. 123.

157. Quoted in Lethbridge, 'Hong Kong under Japanese Occupation', p. 91.

158. Li, *Hong Kong Surgeon*, pp. viii, 222–3. The site had been used five years earlier as General Maltby's headquarters because of its commanding position above Victoria.

159. Quoted Clark, *An End to Tears*, p. 165. Another Chinese witness recalled thirty years later, 'It was only when the navy came and started helping out that the English became popular again'. Reminiscences of 'Mr X' quoted by Adam Williams, *SMP*, 19 November 1978.

160. Wilson, *Hong Kong! Hong Kong!*, p. 111.

161. *FEER*, 26 November 1947. For increased post-war use of Western names in a leading gentry clan, see genealogy of the Li family given in Ching, *The Li Dynasty*, pp. 268–9.

162. Clark, *An End to Tears*, p. 167.

163. See Lethbridge, 'The Best of Both Worlds?', p. 129; Fisher, 'Eurasians in Hong Kong', p. 179. Although no comparable figures appear to have been kept in the pre-war years, this total is thought to represent a marked increase on the number of intermarriages (as opposed to lower class cohabitations) which took place at that time. Another decade and a half would, however, elapse before the figure had crept up to the total of 112 reported by Dr Lethbridge for 1962.

164. Lethbridge, 'Hong Kong under Japanese Occupation', p. 125.

165. *FEER*, 23 April 1947.

166. Grantham, *Via Ports*, p. 104.

167. Ching, *The Li Dynasty*, pp. 126–7.

168. Gittins, *Eastern Windows*, p. 21. See also Irene Cheng, *Clara Ho Tung*, p. 30; 'The Ho Tung Saga (Part 1)', p. 105; Robin Hutcheon, preface to Peter Hall, *In the Web*, p. xii.

169. Waters, *Faces of Hong Kong*, p. 143. See also Gillingham, *At the Peak*, p. 125; Miners, *Hong Kong under Imperial Rule*, p. 190.
170. Grantham, *Via Ports*, p. 126; Hoe, *Private Life*, p. ix. One of the first women JPs was a Portuguese lady, Clotilde Barreto d'Almada e Castro. See d'Almada e Castro, 'Some Notes', p. 275.
171. Interview, Mrs Margaret Watson Sloss, 3 March 1994.
172. See Waters, *Faces of Hong Kong*, p. 143, Tse, *Zhanshi Ri jun*, p. 238 and *San nian*, p. 431.
173. *ZB*, 11 and 15 May 1946; Annual Report on the Hong Kong Police Force 1946–47, p. 26; Luff, *Hidden Years*, p. 213; Lethbridge, 'Hong Kong under Japanese Occupation' p. 116. A large-scale rape and lynching of Chinese girls said to have slept with the Japanese is reported by one source to have taken place in mid-September. See diary of Lieutenant John Guyther, 14 September 1945, quoted *SCMP*, 28 April 1974. On 1 October Ma Yui-ting, a village elder in Taipo known to have worked with the Japanese, was murdered by two unknown Chinese assailants. WIS no. 3, 10 October 1945, CO 129 592/6, p. 90.
174. *SCMP/HKT*, 4 September and 9, 10 and 11 October 1945.
175. Clark, *An End to Tears*, p. 168. This speculation was only increased by the advent of the Nationalist armies *en route* for Manchuria. The troops are said to have fostered a rumour that Hong Kong was to be returned to the mainland. See WIS no. 5, 25 October 1945, CO 129 592/6, p. 69; Lindsay, *Going Down of the Sun*, p. 219.
176. WIS no. 3, 10 October 1945, CO 129 592/6, p. 87. See also Tsang, *Democracy Shelved*, p. 26; Welsh, *History of Hong Kong*, p. 432. Anger was also said to have been aroused by another drunken serviceman who had thrown a citizen into the sea from a pier.
177. WIS no. 6, 1 November 1945 and no. 7, 6 November 1945, CO 129 592/6, pp. 48, 62. See also cable of Deng Songnian et al. to Chiang Kai-shek January 1946 and Foreign Ministry, Nanking report, 26 March 1946, Museum of Military History, 062.23/5000.4.
178. Clark, *An End to Tears*, p. 178.
179. MacDougall, General Report, 2 November 1945, CO 129 591/20, p. 26. See also Tsang, *Democracy Shelved*, p. 25; Kwan, *Ri zhan shiqi de Xianggang*, p. 162.
180. Comments of comprador employed by the Hong Kong branch of a leading British trading firm, quoted in WIS no. 5, 25 October 1945, CO 129 592/6, p. 74. See also Buping Shanren, *Xianggang lunxian huiyilu*, p. 92. At one point in September a deputation of educated Chinese residents were said to have informed a European clergyman that the plight of the masses was now 'worse than under the Japanese'. Clark, *An End to Tears*, p. 134. In October the public were reported to be 'as apprehensive now about the safety of their lives and property as they were during the Japanese occupation'. WIS no. 6, 1 November 1945, CO 129 592/6, p. 61.
181. Letters from J. Lee and 'Res Publica' in *SCMP/HKT*, 9 and 18 September 1945; comment of Chinese lady formerly employed as a clerk by Jardine Matheson and comment of Chinese schoolmaster quoted WIS no. 5, 25 October 1945 and no. 8, 13 November 1945, CO 129 592/6, pp. 36, 74. See also Tsang, *Democracy Shelved*, p. 27.
182. MacDougall, General Report, 2 November 1945, CO 129 591/20, pp. 28, 31.
183. MacDougall to Gent, 7 November 1945, CO 129 591/20, p. 32.
184. MacDougall, General Report, 2 November 1945, CO 129 591/20, p. 28. MacDougall went on to observe that the labour situation was 'potentially one of the most serious facing the colony'. Every effort was being made with 'the exiguous staff available' to 'keep watch for the first signs of unrest'. For a similar expression of anxiety see Harcourt to Hall, 11 November 1945, CO 129 592/6, p. 23. Harcourt observed in the same letter that care had had to be taken not to employ Japanese POWs in such a way as might expose the British to accusations of taking the rice out of the mouths of local working people. Any misstep in this area might of course have fused the disgruntlement at perceived British softness to the Japanese and the unhappiness caused by material hardships in an explosive combination.
185. Appreciation of the Police Organization, 10 October 1945, CO 129 591/20, p. 63; WIS no. 5, 25 October 1945, CO 129 592/6, p. 71; Miners, 'Localisation of the Hong Kong Police Force', pp. 311–12; White, *Turbans and Traders*, p. 58; Wright-Nooth, *Prisoner of the Turnip-Heads*,

p. 37. The purging of the Indians was complicated by the delicate political situation which prevailed in the immediate post-war period in India itself. The British authorities in India were unwilling to take back Indians who had served the Japanese in Hong Kong on the grounds that they would constitute a 'military security menace'. Of the Indian police 185 were eventually returned to the Raj, of whom one third were Sikhs; but a fair number of these (including the Sikhs) were later allowed back to Hong Kong to finish their contracts. No fresh Sikhs however were recruited, and the last Sikh policeman had disappeared from the Hong Kong force by the end of 1952.

186. Endacott and Birch, *Hong Kong Eclipse*, pp. 245–6. According to this account thirty-one local citizens had been brought before the military courts on charges of collaboration by the end of the BMA period. A further twenty-nine appeared before the Supreme Court in the year following the restoration of civil government under Sir Mark Young. Of these sixty persons however only twenty-eight are said by Endacott and Birch to have been found guilty, viz. fifteen Chinese, seven Europeans or Eurasians and six Indians – plus one Japanese, the vicious interpreter Inouye Kanao, who had ended up getting tried for treason rather than war crimes on the grounds that he held Canadian citizenship. Oliver Lindsay declares on the basis of 'newspaper reports' that fifty-four citizens were found guilty. See Lindsay, *Going Down of the Sun*, p. 241. It seems possible however that Lindsay may be confusing the number of arraignments with the number of guilty verdicts. In any event I find the detailed breakdown of sentences given by Endacott and Birch more convincing than Lindsay's general figure.

187. For reasons connected (once again) with the extreme political tension in the postwar Raj the British appear to have been particularly reluctant to prosecute local Indians who had been active in the Indian Independence League. In a letter of early 1946, for example, Lloyd of the Colonial Office referred to the question of whether action should be taken against a specific member of the League 'in view of the Indian aspect'. Lloyd to MacDougall 23 January 1946, CO 129 594/9. See also Lethbridge, 'Hong Kong under Japanese Occupation', pp. 121–2.

188. Harcourt lecture to Royal Central Asian Society. The wisdom of this judgement was confirmed by an incident which took place on 26 October 1946, a fortnight before Harcourt gave his retrospective lecture in London. Violent disturbances erupted that day after a Chinese peanut hawker was shot dead by a Sikh policeman during a raid on unlicensed premises in Kowloon. See minutes of the Executive Council, 11 December 1946, CO 131 116, pp. 170–1; Ye Dewei, '*Zhanhou de huifu gongzuo*', in Ye (ed.), *Xianggang lunxian shi*, p. 166; Tsang, *Democracy Shelved*, p. 26.

189. See Harcourt cable to Colonial Office, 25 October 1945 and letter to Alexander, 7 November 1945, CO 129 592/6, pp. 25, 147; MacDougall, General Report, 2 November 1945, CO 129 591/20, pp. 26–8; Tsang interview with MacDougall, p. 43.

190. MacDougall to Gent, 19 October 1945, CO 129 592/6, p. 105.

191. Minutes of the Executive Council, 2 August, 4 September, 30 October and 18 December 1946, CO 131 116. Selwyn-Clarke had been active in the colony during the first month of the British return, when he reports having helped to push through the increase in the daily labour rate and the HK$1 daily rehabilitation allowance in the teeth of resistance from 'the commercial lobby of the taipans'. He set off home on rehabilitation leave on 20 October 1945, returning in July 1946. He recorded that Young always gave 'sympathetic consideration' to his proposals for improving the health and welfare of the public. See Selwyn-Clarke, *Footprints*, pp. 103–5.

192. *FEER*, 26 March 1947; Ingrams, *Hong Kong*, pp. 276–7. Such a tax had already been brought in as an emergency measure on the outbreak of war in Europe in 1939. See Miners, *Hong Kong under Imperial Rule*, p. 124. The question now at issue was whether it should be reintroduced on a permanent basis.

193. WIS no. 4, 18 October 1945, CO 129 592/6, p. 81.

194. See Harcourt cable to Colonial Office, 25 October 1945, CO 129 592/6, p. 147; MacDougall, General Report, 2 November 1945, CO 129 591/20, p. 28; Harcourt lecture to Royal Central

Asian Society. MacDougall also observed that his measures to keep down rents had had 'a more favourable reception by the public of Hong Kong than any I can remember'.

195. Gittins, *Eastern Windows*, p. 196.
196. Ward, *Asia for the Asiatics?* p. 10. In September 1943 Emily Hahn predicted similarly, 'We'll win, but we'll still be up against the colour bar and all the resentment it stirs up.' The Japanese, she noted, had got a 'head start' in this respect. See Hahn, *Hong Kong Holiday*, p. 259.
197. Chinese schoolmaster quoted in WIS no. 8, 13 November 1945, CO 129 592/6, p. 36.
198. Letter from 'Res Publica', *SCMP/HKT*, 18 September 1945. Two other suggestions thrown up in the correspondence columns of the newspapers may possibly show the impact of wartime arrangements. The vision of Chinese members of the Executive and Legislative Councils whose task would be 'to coordinate public opinion and the Government' may reflect memories of the wartime Cooperative Council whose function was precisely to act as a sounding board. And the call for free schooling may indicate a desire to maintain the innovative if limited experiment with a scholarship system which the gentry had pioneered through the General Relief Association between 1942 and 1945. In both of these cases, however, the links are unprovable.
199. See S. Y. Lin, Brief Report on Fisheries of Hong Kong under the Japanese Occupation, enclosed with G. A. C. Herklots report to MacDougall on Fisheries Organization, 18 October 1945, CO 129 591/20, pp. 11–13. The fact that the writer's name is given as Lin rather than the Cantonese equivalent Lam would seem to suggest that he was of northern rather than local origin.
200. G. A. C. Herklots note on Lin Brief Report enclosed with Herklots report to MacDougall on Fisheries Organization, 18 October 1945, CO 129 591/20 p. 13. See also Tse, *San nian*, p. 76.
201. Hayes, 'The Nature of Village Life', p. 60.
202. Ibid., See also Faure, 'Sai Kung: The Making of the District', pp. 202–3.

Epilogue

1. Tse, *Zhanshi Ri jun*, pp. xi, 239–42.
2. See Shi Meiyu, '*Shenpan zhanfan huiyilu*', Nationalist Party archives 537/197; War Office to Allied Land Forces South-east Asia (ALFSEA) 7 August 1946, 21 November 1946 and 16 December 1946, British Embassy, Nanking, to ALFSEA 10 October 1946 and 23 November 1946 and ALFSEA to War Office October 1946, WO 325/135. A report on the Tanaka trial was sent by Ronald Hall, the British consul-general in Canton, to the British ambassador in Nanking on 18 October 1946. See HK RS 163 1/222A. For British representation at Isogai trial see War Crimes Investigation Team, Hong Kong to Machin, British military attaché, Nanking, 17 July 1947 and report of Captain F. V. Collison, 7 August 1947, WO 325/135.
3. Report by Major Y. H. Chan on Trading in Opium in Hong Kong, 3 February 1947, War Crimes Investigation Unit, Hong Kong, to Colonel 'A', War Crimes Section, General Headquarters, ALFSEA, Singapore, 4 February 1947 and Colonel 'A', War Crimes Section, to War Crimes Investigation Unit, 3 March 1947, WO 325/135.
4. See letters from Colonel, Legal Staff, for Deputy Judge Advocate General, ALFSEA, to Coordination Section, 17 August 1946 and to Colonel 'A', War Crimes Section, 22 August 1946, and memoranda from Machin, Nanking, to ALFSEA, 29 November 1946 and from ALFSEA to Machin, 22 December 1946, WO 325/135. Some grounds for the British concern about reciprocity may be found in a letter sent by T. W. Kwok, the Nationalist Special Commissioner in Hong Kong to Consul-General Hall in Canton on 19 October 1946. Kwok suggested that the extradition of nineteen Japanese war criminals sought by the British on the mainland 'should be made conditional upon the handing over of the Chinese collaborators hiding in Hong Kong'. HK RS 163 1/222A, p. 69.1.
5. Testimony of Colonel Noma, Noma trial, WO 235/999, p. 326.

6. Testimony of Lieutenant-Colonel Kanazawa, Kanazawa trial, WO 235/1093, pp. 324–5, 359–63.
7. Clark, *An End to Tears*, p. 97.
8. Samejima, *Xianggang huixiang ji*, p. 174; Tse *Zhanshi Ri jun*, p. 235.
9. See *SCMP/HKT*, 15 October 1945; WIS, no. 6, 1 November 1945, CO 129 592/6, p. 56; correspondence relating to the arrest of Kiichi Fukutomi, 11 and 13 February 1946, HK RS 163 1/222A, pp. 20–1; reminiscences of 'Mr X', interviewed by Adam Williams, *SMP*, 19 November 1978.
10. *SCMP*, 20 June 1995.
11. Li, *Hong Kong Surgeon*, pp. 121–2; Tse, *Zhanshi Ri jun*, pp. 41, 44–5; Gittins, *Stanley: Behind Barbed Wire*, p. 124.
12. See Tse, *San nian*, p. 64.
13. Interview, Mrs Helen Zimmern, 29 June 1995.
14. Lethbridge, 'Hong Kong under Japanese Occupation', p. 119.
15. Letters from Ronald Holmes, Secretary for Chinese Affairs to former Colonial Secretary MacDougall 11 June 1969 and MacDougall to Holmes 13 July 1969 regarding forthcoming history by G. B. Endacott, in private papers of Mrs Helen Zimmern; letter from MacDougall to Frank Ching quoted in Ching, *The Li Dynasty*, p. 125; Tsang interview with MacDougall, p. 73.
16. For application of this phrase to Chow in his final years, see, for example, Ingrams, *Hong Kong*, pp. 111, 194, and Cheng, 'Unofficial Members', p. 21.
17. Grantham, *Via Ports*, p. 127.
18. Gittins, *Eastern Windows*, p. 11 and *Stanley: Behind Barbed Wire*, p. 10; 'The Ho Tung Saga (Part 1)', p. 108; Frank H. H. King, *History of the Hongkong and Shanghai Banking Corporation*, vol. IV, p. 309.
19. Ingrams, *Hong Kong*, p. 86.
20. Report of the Commissioner of Police for 1947–8.
21. Grantham, *Via Ports*, p. 110; Peter Hall, *In the Web*, p. 112.
22. Lethbridge, 'Hong Kong under Japanese Occupation', p. 121. As early as March 1946 MacDougall was expressing the view that 'the issue of collaboration was almost dead in Hong Kong'. Ruston minute, 12 March 1946, CO 129 594/9, p. 8.
23. Ingrams, *Hong Kong*, p. 242. Already in 1947 an expatriate journal was talking of 'the few' Hong Kong merchants who had carried on business under the Japanese. See *FEER*, 26 March 1947.
24. Foreign Ministry, Nanking, report, 7 March 1946, Museum of Military History, 062.23/5000.4.
25. Tsang, *Appointment with China*, pp. 64–5, 232. The two officials were Vice President Sun Ke and General Luo Zhuoying, Governor of Guangdong province.
26. *FEER*, 23 April 1947. This was one of a series of minor border incidents. In December 1946 and August 1948 Nationalist passions were inflamed after news was received of the shooting of individual Chinese on the border by, respectively, a British soldier and a Hong Kong Chinese policeman. See *GMRB*, 4 December 1946; Foreign Ministry, Nanking, report of 20 September 1948, Museum of Military History, 062.23/5000.4; Catron, 'China and Hong Kong' p. 39.
27. Intercepted report of Thomas Clayton Davis, Canadian ambassador in Nanking, to Ministry of External Affairs, Ottawa, 15 March 1948, Museum of Military History, Taipei, 062.24 0028. A few days after this conversation took place T. V. Soong, the newly appointed Governor of Guangdong Province, announced in Canton that US$60m of the relief funds which had been made available by the United States to the Nationalist government should be used to build a port at the mouth of the Pearl River. The Canadian ambassador saw this as further evidence that the United States might be joining forces with the Nationalists to prise Britain out of Hong Kong. Clark is also said to have suggested to the British ambassador in Nanking, Sir Ralph Stevenson, that the British government should 'take into consideration whether the best interests of Britain lay in continuing the irritant [of its presence in Hong Kong] or

removing it at some appropriate time'. In 1947 the United States ambassador in London had advised similarly that Britain could avoid further trouble over Hong Kong by 'graciously and generously' returning it to China 'at a given date'. Welsh, *History of Hong Kong*, p. 438.

28. Quoted in Grantham, *Via Ports*, p. 138; Yuan, *Xianggang shilüe*, p. 205.

29. Soong cables to Chiang, 15 and 16 January 1948, Museum of Military History, 062.24 0028. Most observers believed that the attack on the British consulate was the work of the hard-line Nationalist C. C. Clique, whose objectives included discrediting Soong. Soong's use of the term 'bandits' (Nationalist-speak for the Chinese Communist Party) suggests however that a decision had been made to pin the blame on the Communists. On the same day the incident took place Wu Tiecheng, the Secretary-General of the Central Executive Committee of the Nationalist Party and Vice-Chairman of the Legislative Yuan, told the Central News Agency, 'We want to wipe out the Chinese Communist Party, who have seized the opportunity to get in the way [sc. of harmonious Sino-British relations].' See intercepted cable from Sir Ralph Stevenson, British ambassador, Nanking, to Hong Kong government, 18 January 1948, Museum of Military History, 062.24 0028; Grantham, *Via Ports*, pp. 131–2; Tsang interview with MacDougall, pp. 90–1.

30. Kwok to MacDougall, 26 January 1948 p. 1, MacDougall papers, Rhodes House. See Tsang, *Democracy Shelved*, plate no. 8 between pp. 110 and 111. MacDougall later recalled that Kwok 'tried to smooth the affair over' and 'made it easy for us'. Tsang interview with MacDougall, pp. 90–1.

31. Lane, 'Nationalist Government', p. 107.

32. Gordon Harmon interview with Mao, December 1946, quoted in Tsang, *Appointment with China*, p. 69.

33. *HSB*, 1 May 1946.

34. *HSB*, 29 January 1946, 25 July 1947 and 13 January 1948; Catron, 'China and Hong Kong', p. 56. A succession of Nationalist intelligence reports claimed that the Communists had effectively joined forces with the British in the aftermath of the Walled City crisis. According to one source the Communist groups in the colony offered to exchange information with the Hong Kong government to help the government deal with any ensuing labour unrest. The *quid pro quo* was that the British should give them an increased measure of protection from their Nationalist enemies. A second informant reported that Qiao Guanhua and his colleagues had held a meeting at which the decision was taken to use the Walled City incident to foment discord between the British and Nationalist authorities. A third claimed the British were counting on Communist technicians to keep the colony's factories and utilities going in the event that the Nationalist government stirred up the Hong Kong Chinese workers to express their resentment at the Walled City evictions through a sympathy strike. See intelligence reports from the Nationalist Chief of Military Police in Canton, 27 January 1948, from the Nationalist Bureau of Investigation and Statistics in Hong Kong, 30 January 1948 and from Su Bicheng in Shanghai, 24 February 1948, Museum of Military History, 062.24 0028.

35. Catron, 'China and Hong Kong', p. 94; Tsang, *Democracy Shelved*, pp. 85–6.

36. Intercepted report of Ambassador Davis to Ministry of External Affairs, Ottawa, 27 January 1948, Museum of Military History, Taipei 062.24 0028.

37. Tsang interview with MacDougall, p. 75.

38. *FEER*, 23 July 1947.

39. Foreign Ministry, Nanking submissions to President's Office, 25 October and 28 November 1946, Museum of Military History, 062.23/5000.4; *FEER*, 16 October 1946; Tsang, *Appointment with China*, p. 62.

40. Grantham, *Via Ports*, p. 131.

41. Annual Report of the Hong Kong Government 1948, p. 1; Catron, 'China and Hong Kong', p. 60.

42. Tsang interview with MacDougall, p. 101.

43. Quoted in Tsang, *Democracy Shelved*, p. 56. See also Tsang interview with MacDougall, p. 101.

44. Interview, Mrs Margaret Watson Sloss, 3 March 1994.

45. Sermon of 21 August 1949 quoted Paton, *R.O.*, pp. 252–5.
46. Letter from Trafford Smith, Colonial Office to Lieutenant-Colonel P. R. M. Waterfield, MBE, 19 November 1948, CO 537/4163, p. 2; Governor Grantham secret telegram no. 884 to Secretary of State for the Colonies, 24 August 1949, pp. 1–2 and Ministry of Defence minute, 6 February 1950, DEFE 7/599, p. 1. A general 'lack of discipline' was anticipated among Asiatic personnel.
47. Tsang, *Appointment with China*, p. 71. The phrase 'ventilation shaft' for Hong Kong was apparently widespread among Chinese in the early 1950s.
48. Wilson, *Hong Kong! Hong Kong!*, pp. 195–6; Cottrell, *The End of Hong Kong*, p. 27. This information is said to have been conveyed in the course of Governor Grantham's visit to Peking in October 1955.
49. Ingrams, *Hong Kong*, pp. 179–80.
50. Ibid., p. 66.
51. Grantham, *Via Ports*, p. 139.
52. Ibid., p. 106; Catron, 'China and Hong Kong' p. 169; Morris, *Hong Kong*, p. 278; Cottrell, *The End of Hong Kong*, pp. 27, 226 n.11. See also Paton, *R.O.*, p. 235.
53. *FEER*, 23 July 1947.
54. Interview, Mrs Margaret Watson Sloss, 3 March 1994. Selwyn-Clarke went on to agitate the European planters in the Seychelles with his 'socialist' outlook before winding up his career in a more conventional fashion as Principal Medical Officer to the Ministry of Health. He died in 1975. See Selwyn-Clarke, *Footprints*, pp. 112–16, 123; Gittins: *Stanley: Behind Barbed Wire*, pp. 145–6.
55. Letter from Stewart Gray, editor of the *Hong Kong Telegraph* to MacDougall, 3 February 1949, MacDougall papers, Rhodes House. Gray's indignation was echoed in the local Chinese community by the *Wah Kiu Yat Po*, which on 18 March published an editorial entitled 'We Want Colonial Secretary MacDougall to Remain'. The editorial noted that MacDougall had been 'closely connected with the Chinese of Hong Kong', and that he had helped to rehabilitate Hong Kong into a 'happy land where millions of Chinese have been living and carrying on trade in peace while the world was in turmoil'. Precis of translated *WKYP* editorial 18 March 1949, MacDougall papers, Rhodes House. In spite of his signal achievements in the early post-war period the colony was content to forget MacDougall's existence. The streets of Hong Kong have preserved the names of large numbers of Governors and other leading officials, but his is not among them.
56. Paton, *R.O.*, pp. 183–4, 188, 234–6. Zhou Enlai had originally met the Bishop in the days when he served as the Chinese Communist Party's representative in wartime Chungking.
57. Gleason, *Hong Kong*, p. 179.
58. Tsang interview with MacDougall, pp. 80, 106, 110.
59. Report of the Commissioner of Police for 1948–9, p. 10; Miners, 'Localization of the Hong Kong Police Force', p. 312; Morris, *Hong Kong*, pp. 225–6. The increased Chinese presence in the rank and file of the police force, however, proved permanent. By 1947 85 per cent of the rank and file were local Chinese, and by 1950 it was noticeable that 'under almost every peaked cap was a Chinese face'. Ingrams, *Hong Kong*, p. 236.
60. Grantham, *Via Ports*, p. 120.
61. Morris, *Hong Kong*, p. 228. The rules prescribing political censorship of films were only lifted in 1965.
62. *FEER*, 5 March 1947.
63. Grantham, *Via Ports*, p. 112; Tsang, *Democracy Shelved*, pp. 157–8, 161–5; Welsh, *History of Hong Kong*, pp. 440–1.
64. Address of summer 1952 quoted in Paton, *R.O.*, p. 308.
65. Grantham, *Via Ports*, p. 128.
66. Ibid.; Lethbridge, 'Hong Kong under Japanese Occupation', p. 94 n. 3; Grantham, *Via Ports*, p. 128. One Chinese lawyer recalls an occasion in these years when he was bathing with a friend in Repulse Bay. An expatriate woman in their vicinity made a swishing motion in the water to drive them off. Interview, Mr Charles Sin, 29 June 1995.

67. Frank H. H. King, *History of the Hongkong and Shanghai Banking Corporation*, vol. IV, pp. 307–8; Waters, *Faces of Hong Kong*, pp. 142, 145.
68. Morris, *Hong Kong*, p. 67.
69. Grantham, *Via Ports*, p. 122.
70. Ching, *The Li Dynasty*, p. 151.
71. Quoted in Waters, *Faces of Hong Kong*, p. 144.
72. Ingrams, *Hong Kong*, pp. 252–3.
73. Pope-Hennessy, *Half-Crown Colony*, pp. 48–9.
74. Wilson, *Hong Kong! Hong Kong!*, p. 88; Waters, *Faces of Hong Kong*, p. 145. See also Peter Hall, *In the Web*, p. 138.
75. Grantham, *Via Ports*, p. 128.
76. Waters, *Faces of Hong Kong*, p. 144.
77. Ibid.; interview, Mrs Mary Goodban, 7 January 1994.
78. Grantham, *Via Ports*, p. 140.
79. Patrick Yu, *A Seventh Child and the Law*, Hong Kong, 1998, pp. 126–7; Ching, *The Li Dynasty*, p. 151. In 1948 a Chinese writer contributed an essay on European racism in Hong Kong in the early twentieth century to a belated centenary history of the colony. The writer noted regretfully, 'Right up till now it still hasn't been possible to eradicate this kind of attitude.' See Pan Kongyan, '*Zhongzu qishi de bianlun*' in Li Jinwei (ed.) *Xianggang bai nian shi*, p. 53.
80. Ingrams, *Hong Kong*, pp. 113–14, 116. Ingrams summarized that 'the Period of the Peak has not yet entirely passed'.
81. Waters, *Faces of Hong Kong*, pp. 143–4.
82. Han Suyin, *Love is a Many-Splendoured Thing*, London, 1952, p. 174.
83. 'The Lee Empire', *Hong Kong Inc.*, January 1990, p. 81. Another gentry figure to distance himself from the British at this time was F. S. Li, a son of Li Koon-chun, the wartime gentry leader, who was currently serving as a member of both the Executive and Legislative Councils. In July 1967 Li cooperated with the British in helping to head off a strike threatened by the Hong Kong Tramway Workers Union – a stance which brought down on him anger and even a death threat from the leftist camp. Over the following months he seems to have been staking out a position opposed to the Hong Kong government on various issues. In June 1968 he was denied reappointment to the Executive Council 'in view of his stated unhappiness with the government and his frequent threats to resign'; and the following month he resigned from the Legislative Council of his own accord. See Ching, *The Li Dynasty*, pp. 143–8.
84. Ian Scott, *Political Change and the Crisis of Legitimacy in Hong Kong*, London, 1989, pp. 106–10; Ching, *The Li Dynasty*, p. 146. The establishment of these officers recalled in some measure the wartime attempts of the Japanese to extend their control at the local government level. When the system was expanded in 1982 through the creation of District Boards eighteen districts were demarcated in the urban areas for the first time since the war. This demarcation was observed to be 'conceptually modelled' on the precedent of the wartime District Bureaux. Caption in Second World War exhibition at the Hong Kong Museum of History, September 1995. Information confirmed by Mr S. J. Chan, former Hong Kong government officer, 22 September 1995.
85. Article by Mark Roberti, *SCMP*, 4 February 1995. Roberti comments that this document 'clearly laid the foundations for Hong Kong's progress during the 1970s'.
86. Ibid.
87. Comment of Dr Ming Chan, quoted *SCMP*, 20 February 1997.
88. Jason Wordie, *Streets: Exploring Hong Kong Island*, Hong Kong, 2002, p. 32. The cricket ground had been stubbornly 'kept British' during the BMA period when so much else was being altered, because the Navy had insisted that 'Hong Kong was a British colony and cricket a British game'. Ingrams, *Hong Kong*, p. 243.
89. Lethbridge, 'The Best of Both Worlds?', p. 129.
90. Miners, 'Localization of the Hong Kong Police Force', p. 312; Morris, *Hong Kong*, p. 101.
91. *FEER*, 6 August 1982; interview with the late Mr Andrew Choa, 24 June 1995.

92. One young American scholar who arrived in the colony after a stay of some months in Shanghai in 1993 noted, 'I still sense Hong Kong is a racist place.' Waters, *Faces of Hong Kong*, p. 146.

93. Address by Lieutenant-Colonel Owen Hughes to the Hong Kong General Chamber of Commerce in the Gloucester Hotel quoted *SCMP/HKT*, 22 September 1945.

94. *FEER*, 22 January 1947.

95. Harcourt lecture to Royal Central Asian Society. MacDougall in the same way attributed the economic recovery of 1945–7 primarily to the efforts of the local Chinese. 'It's that absolutely invincible . . . this refusal to do nothing, whatever happened.' Tsang interview with MacDougall, p. 77.

96. *SCMP/HKT* editorial, 26 September 1945.

97. See Hong Kong (BMA) Gazette, vol. 2, no. 7, CO 132 89, pp. 98–9.

98. Report of Henry Bough of Reuters, Hong Kong, undated, March 1946, p. 3, MacDougall papers, Rhodes House.

99. Yuan, *Xianggang shilüe*, p. 194. Forty per cent of the machinery in the factories was said to have been looted or destroyed by the Japanese. *HSB*, 5 January 1946.

100. *FEER*, 19 February, 12 March, 16 April and 24 September 1947. A total of 100 rubber footwear factories were said to be in operation of which six were relatively large. Prominent among these were the Fung Keong Rubber Manufacturing Company and the Wah Keong Rubber Company.

101. *FEER*, 3 September 1947. See also Gleason, *Hong Kong*, p. 93. For the potential shown by the textile, rubber footwear and other light industries in the immediate aftermath of the British return see also *SCMP/HKT*, 5 September 1945; Colonel A. Burgess, Department of Supplies, Transport and Industry Report no. 1 to London, 10 October 1945, CO 129 591/20, p. 57; ZB, 27 March 1946.

102. WIS no. 7, 6 November 1945, CO 129 592/6, p. 52.

103. Endacott and Birch, *Hong Kong Eclipse*, p. 319.

104. *FEER*, 11 December 1946; Wong, *Emigrant Entrepreneurs*, pp. 16, 18.

105. Hong Kong General Chamber of Commerce Report for the Year 1947, p. 45.

106. Ingrams, *Hong Kong*, p. 116.

107. See Wong, *Emigrant Entrepreneurs*, pp. 53–4; King, *History of the Hongkong and Shanghai Banking Corporation*, vol. iv, p. 352. Shanghainese dash is proverbial. A Hong Kong saying has it that a Cantonese in possession of HK$100 will commit HK$50 to a venture and save up the rest; a Shanghainese in the same position will commit HK$10,000! Interview, Mr Y. K. Chan, 23 March 1995.

108. Wong, *Emigrant Entrepreneurs*, p. 128. Professor Wong draws attention to the illuminating contrast between a Legislative Council debate in 1948, when T. N. Chau still delivered his remarks in a forelock-tugging way 'on behalf of the Chinese community', and a second debate in 1965, when P. Y. Tang, another Shanghainese textile magnate, spoke out confidently 'on behalf of industry'. Ibid., p. 131.

109. Notes of G. A. Wallinger, CO 129 592/6, p. 116.

110. WIS no. 5, 25 October 1945, CO 129 592/6, p. 74.

111. MacDougall, General Report, 2 November 1945, CO 129 591/20, p. 28.

112. Intercepted report of Thomas Clayton Davis, Canadian ambassador in Nanking, to Ministry of External Affairs, Ottawa, 15 March 1948, Museum of Military History, 062.24 0028.

113. Ingrams, *Hong Kong*, p. 32.

114. Ibid., p. 122.

115. 'The Ho Tung Saga (Part 2)', *Hong Kong Inc.*, April 1990, pp. 93, 95; Ching, *The Li Dynasty*, pp. 189, 212; 'The Lee Empire', p. 86. Dick Lee's nephew is said to have been sent to the United States rather than Britain 'as a sign of changing times and loyalties'.

116. Sweeting, 'Controversy over the Reopening of the University', pp. 412, 418. The dismayed Conservative was Walter Fletcher, a rubber merchant and mastermind of the SOE's wartime black-marketeering operation, who had subsequently become MP for Bury.

117. *FEER Yearbook*, 1972, p. 178.

118. Morris, *Hong Kong*, p. 113.
119. *FEER*, 16 October 1946.
120. *FEER*, 5 February 1947.
121. *FEER*, 22 September 1948. The three firms were Sugano Trading Ltd. (dealers in textile fabrics and cotton yarn), Toyo Bussan Kaisha Ltd. (dealers in general merchandise, building materials and porcelain), and Mainami Trading Co. Ltd. (dealers in tinned food, tinned fish and agar-agar).
122. See interview with Mr Fujita Ichiro, former representative of Mitsui Bussan in Hong Kong, *Aji-ken Nyusu*, vol. 5, no. 10, October 1984, p. 18. During the first few years after the defeat of Japan Mitsui Bussan was known as Dai-Ichi Bussan, in deference to the American occupation policy of breaking up Mitsui and the other great Japanese conglomerates.
123. Article in the *Hong Kong Standard* forwarded by the Bank of England, enclosed with letter from A. J. Phelps of Treasury to I. Watt of Colonial Office, 19 October 1951, CO 129 623/7, p. 10.
124. Record of Fujita Ichiro talk to Japanese business colloquium in Hong Kong, 27 January 1989 in *A Twenty-Year History of the Hong Kong Japanese Chamber of Commence and Industry*, p. 114. See also Gittins, *Eastern Windows*, p. 223 and *Stanley: Behind Barbed Wire*, p. 146.
125. *FEER*, 30 November 1952; Fujita interview, p. 18; Ogawa Heishiro, 'My Hong Kong Connection', talk to students at Robert Black College, University of Hong Kong, in Tam Yue-him (ed.), *Hong Kong and Japan: Growing Cultural and Economic Interactions*, p. 481.
126. *FEER*, 6 August 1947. It is sometimes unclear whether the *Far Eastern Economic Review* is referring to British or Chinese merchants or both. One article of September 1947 lists ten companies which have received approval from London for the resumption of trade with Japan. Only one of these (Wang Kee and Co.) is self-evidently a Chinese firm. This may simply imply that the *Review* was more in contact with the expatriate than with the Chinese business community: it could however also suggest that the continued aversion to trading with Japan was stronger among the Chinese than among their British counterparts. See *FEER*, 3 September 1947.
127. *FEER*, 10 November 1948.
128. Article in the *Hong Kong Standard* enclosed with letter from A. J. Phelps of Treasury to I. Watt of Colonial Office, 19 October 1951, CO 129 623/7, p. 10. See also *FEER*, 2 August 1951.
129. *FEER*, 2 June 1948.
130. Record of Fujita talk to Japanese business colloquium, 27 January 1989, p. 114.
131. *FEER*, 14 May 1953.
132. Fujita interview, p. 18; Ogawa Heishiro, 'My Hong Kong Connection', p. 482; interview, Sir Y. K. Kan, 24 May 1995. The Kans also helped the Bank of Tokyo set up the first postwar office of a Japanese bank in Hong Kong (see p. 336), and responded helpfully to similar approaches which were made to them by a number of other Japanese firms including Mitsubishi and Sumitomo. In later years Sir Y. K. Kan was successively presented by the Japanese government with the Order of Merit, Grade 3, and the Order of Merit, Grade 2, for his 'services to Hong Kong-Japanese friendship'. Major role of the Kans in facilitating the postwar return of Japanese business to Hong Kong confirmed by Mr Okada Akira, former Japanese consul-general in Hong Kong and chairman of the Japan-Hong Kong Society, interview, Tokyo, 6 September 1995.
133. Interview with Sir Y. K. Kan, 24 May 1995. The question was put by Ogawa Heishiro, a diplomat who came to Hong Kong to help Itagaki with the reopening of the Japanese consulate in 1952 and in 1960 was sent back there to serve as consul himself.
134. Conversation with Mr Komari Yasuo, former General Manager of Mitsui Bussan (Hong Kong), Tokyo, 29 July 1995.
135. Fujita interview, p. 25. Kenneth Fung Ping-fan was a son-in-law of Kan Tong-po and a brother-in-law of Sir Y. K. Kan. He served in the Bank of East Asia during and after the war years and became a chief manager of the Bank in 1963. He was a prominent member of the Executive and Legislative Councils and was knighted by the British. In the 1960s and 1970s he played a major role in the Japanese return to Hong Kong. He sat on the board of a

number of Hong Kong-Chinese Japanese joint ventures such as Aiwa Dransfield and Co Ltd. In 1967–68 he provided 'a great deal of assistance' with the establishment of a new Japanese School in the colony, and in 1975–80 he served as the third president of the Japan Society of Hong Kong. Appreciated as a 'pro-Japanese personage', Sir Kenneth Fung was presented by the Japanese government with the Order of Merit, Grade 3.

136. *FEER*, 30 April 1964.
137. *FEER*, 10 November 1960.
138. Tse, *San nian*, p. 54.
139. Interview, Mr Y. Yanagisawa, Executive Vice President of Nishimatsu, Hong Kong, 9 May 1995.
140. *FEER*, 30 April 1964.
141. Onoe, '*Honkon no chu no Nihon*'. For hostile Hong Kong Chinese attitudes to Japan at this period see also Zhou Pinjing et al., '*Cong Xianggang baozhang kan shuibianzhong de Riben xingxiang*' in Tam Yue-him (ed.), *Hong Kong and Japan: Growing Cultural and Economic Interactions*, p. 242.
142. Article by David Bonavia, *FEER*, 3 February 1966.
143. Figures given in Gerald Segal draft paper, 'The Fate of Hong Kong', 1991; Nakajima Mineo, 'The Hong Kong Agreement and its Impact on the International Position of Japan' in Domes and Shaw (eds), *Hong Kong: A Chinese and International Concern*, p. 201. As the century wore on it would seem that even some of the older generation who did remember the past were succumbing to the attractions of postwar Japan. By the early 1990s veterans who had fought with the Hong Kong Volunteer Defence Corps fifty years earlier were reported to be buying Toyota cars, patronizing sushi bars and karaoke joints and spending their holidays on the ski slopes of Sapporo. See article by Alan Boyd in *SMP*, 8 December 1991.
144. *FEER Yearbook*, 1972, p. 155; Zhou Pinjing et al., '*Riben xingxiang*', pp. 231, 235, 238, 239, 242, 243; Wilson, *Hong Kong! Hong Kong!*, p, 47; article by Vivian Chiu, *SCMP*, 7 December 1991; *SCMP*, 27 September 1996.
145. Conversation with the late Professor Leonard Rayner, 16 July 1991. For attitude of holders of military yen in the immediate postwar period see *FEER*, 12 March 1947.
146. For this interpretation see Wilson, *Hong Kong! Hong Kong!*, pp. 46–7.
147. See Rafferty, *City on the Rocks*, p. 226; Kevin Hamlin, Special Report for *The Independent*, London, 26 September 1990; Miron Mushkat, *The Economic Future of Hong Kong*, Hong Kong, 1990, p. 150, n. 5; Gerald Segal draft paper, 'The Fate of Hong Kong', 1991.
148. *FEER Yearbook*, 1972, p. 178; Segal, 'The Fate of Hong Kong'. By 1994 Japan and the United States were said to be level-pegging in their overall share of foreign investment in the colony, with total investments of around US$10bn each. Information provided by Mr Hamamoto Ryoichi of the Hong Kong office of *Yomiuri Shimbun*, 27 March 1995.
149. Zhou Pinjing et al., '*Riben xingxiang*', p. 243.
150. Frank H. H. King, *History of the Hongkong and Shanghai Banking Corporation*, vol. IV, p. 434.
151. Zhou Pinjing et al., '*Riben xingxiang*', p. 243; Jane Lam Hui Kong-wai, 'The Japan Society of Hong Kong – A Historical Account 1962–1987', in Tam Yue-him (ed.), *Hong Kong and Japan: Growing Cultural and Economic Interactions*, pp. 81, 85.
152. Morris, *Hong Kong*, p. 286. See also Rafferty, *City on the Rocks*, pp. 73–4.
153. Nakajima, 'The Hong Kong Agreement', pp. 199, 201; Segal, 'The Fate of Hong Kong'; Morris, *Hong Kong*, p. 108. The community was of course back to its wartime level in absolute rather than relative terms. The Japanese now represented a very much smaller proportion of the vastly increased Hong Kong population.
154. Welsh, *History of Hong Kong*, p. 472. Zhou Enlai at the same time told a British journalist that he expected the Hong Kong question to be settled through negotiations. See Tsang, *Appointment with China*, p. 72.
155. *SCMP*, 9 and 10 February 1995; *The Economist*, London, 28 October 1995.
156. Like their Japanese counterparts these mainland Chinese businesses were wading vigorously into the Hong Kong property market. By 1987 mainland holdings in Hong Kong property were valued at roughly HK$1bn.

157. Wilson, *Hong Kong! Hong Kong!*, p. 229; information provided by Mr Hamamoto Ryoichi of the Hong Kong office of *Yomiuri Shimbun*, 27 March 1995.
158. See Cottrell, *The End of Hong Kong*, pp. 116, 128, 157–8.
159. *SCMP*, 10 December 1996.
160. *SCMP*, 25 September, 2, 24 and 28 October 1996.
161. *SCMP*, 4 June 1996. Following his selection as Chief Executive Tung proclaimed, 'Now at last we are masters in our own house'. *SCMP*, 11 December 1996.
162. Quoted in *The Economist*, London, 13 April 1996.
163. See letters printed in *SCMP*, 8 August 1996 and 10 January 1997.
164. Lee had been a prominent supporter of the 1989 democracy movement on the mainland, and had indeed been arrested while attempting to deliver cash to the student demonstrators in Peking. See Wilson, *Hong Kong! Hong Kong!*, p. 222.
165. *SCMP*, 20 February 1997.
166. Chiefs of Staff Planning Committee Joint Planning Staff Report 'Hong Kong Policy in War', 16 December 1949, pp. 1–2 and Memorandum of the Commanders in Chief Committee, Far East, 'Defence Policy for Hong Kong in a War with Russia', CO 537/6316, pp. 3, 7; Chiefs of Staff Planning Committee Confidential Annex to C.O.S. (51) 9th Meeting held on 11 January 1951, circulated by Ministry of Defence 13 January 1951, FO 371 92299.
167. Minutes of discussion regarding defence of Hong Kong at Chiefs of Staff Planning Committee (51) 51st meeting, 21 March 1951 and General Headquarters Far Eastern Land Forces to Ministry of Defence, London, 11 April 1951, FO 371 92299, p. 1.
168. Tsang, *Appointment with China*, p. 77.
169. Gleason, *Hong Kong*, p. 69.
170. Grantham, *Via Ports*, pp. 193–4; Welsh, *History of Hong Kong*, p. 453. The phrase 'Gibraltar of the Far East' was originally used by Harold Macmillan in the House of Commons on 5 May 1949. Ironically it was a government headed by Macmillan that closed the dockyard nine years later.
171. *SCMP*, 24 and 28 March 1995.
172. Minute of Sir John Paskin, 11 March 1950, quoted in Tsang, *Appointment with China*, p. 77.
173. Colonial Office and Foreign Office Joint Memorandum on the Future of Hong Kong submitted to Colonel V. W. Street, Chiefs of Staff Secretariat, Ministry of Defence, 16 February 1951, FO 371 92299. See also letter from Paskin to R. H. Scott of Foreign Office, 9 February 1951 in same file.
174. Free port issue raised at Cabinet meeting of 29 August 1950. Notion rejected in paper, 'International Control of Hong Kong', annex to Colonial Office and Foreign Office Joint Memorandum on the Future of Hong Kong, 16 February 1951, FO 371 92299. For Plan Cinderella see R. H. Scott of Foreign Office letter to Paskin, 23 August 1951, letters from Paskin and J. B. Sidebotham of Colonial Office to Secretary, Chiefs of Staff Committee 23 August and 10 September 1951 and letter from Secretary, Chiefs of Staff Committee to Sidebotham, 14 September 1951, DEFE 11/380.
175. Catron, 'China and Hong Kong', p. 350, n. 1.
176. Cottrell, *The End of Hong Kong*, p. 127.
177. Welsh, *History of Hong Kong*, p. 496. See also Nakajima, 'The Hong Kong Agreement', p. 199. General trend confirmed by the Honourable W. S. Lau, interview, 8 June 1995.
178. As one eminent Hong Kong Chinese public servant remarked, how else could they have come?

Select Bibliography

Primary sources

1. Archives

Public Record Office, Kew, London

Colonial Office

CO 129   Original Correspondence, Hong Kong

535/3	572/11	590/24	591/19
536/6	582/12	590/25	591/20
555/10	589/18	591/4	592/6
556/17	590/13	591/10	592/8
559/10	590/18	591/15	594/9
562/23	590/22	591/16	623/7
572/6	590/23	591/18	

CO 131   Minutes of Executive Council, Hong Kong
          116

CO 132   Hong Kong Government Gazettes
          89

CO 537   Original Correspondence, Hong Kong, supplementary
          4163
          6316

CO 825   Original Correspondence, Eastern
          35/26
          38/6
          42/15

Foreign Office

FO 371   Far Eastern Department General Political Files

22153	27719	31717
23516	27752	46251
27621	31670	92299
27622		

War Office

WO 235   Judge Advocate General's Office: War Crimes Case Files, Second World War
          235/999
          235/1015
          235/1093

WO 325   General Headquarters, Allied Land Forces South-east Asia War Crimes Group: Investigation
          Files
          325/135

Ministry of Defence

DEFE 7   Registered Files: General Series
          599

DEFE 11 Chiefs of Staff Committee: Registered Files
          380

Special Operations Executive

HS 1 Special Operations Executive Records, Far East
       171   329
       176   349
       208

Minutes of the Chinese Cooperative Council, Hong Kong, 1943, filed with transcript of trial of Colonel Noma Kennosuke, WO 235/999

Public Record Office, Hong Kong

Hong Kong Record Series
          2-1-1513   211-2-41
          163-1-222A   245-2-150
          170-1-573   245-2-208

Hong Kong Manuscript Series
          30
          74–76

Chinese Nationalist Party archives, Yangmingshan, Taipei

          523/137   532/157
          523/140   532/197

Supreme National Defence Council papers
          003. 2157. 5999
          004. 0131. 0406

Museum of Military History, Taipei

          062. 23/5000.4
          062. 24/0028

Diplomatic Record Office, Tokyo

          A. 7. 0. 0. 9. – 41
          A. 7. 0. 0. 9 – 41–2

Ministry of Finance, Tokyo

Akimoto archive
          144. 2   145. 38
          144. 4   145. 39

Record of Survey of Hong Kong Factories, Greater East Asia Ministry, 19 July 1943

2. Published collections of documents

Foreign Relations of the United States, Diplomatic Papers, 1945, vol. VII, The Far East; China, US Government Printing Office, Washington, 1969

The MAGIC Documents: Summaries and Transcripts of the Top Secret Communications of Japan, 1938–45, University Publications of America, Washington, 1980

Zhonghua Minguo shiliao chu bian, dui Ri kangzhan shiqi di san bian, zhanshi waijiao, vol. 2, Party History Committee, Central Committee of the Chinese Nationalist Party, Taipei, 1981.

3. Newspapers and journals

pre-1950

Hong Kong
China Mail
Far Eastern Economic Review
Gong Shang Ribao
Guomin Ribao
Hong Kong News
Hong Kong Telegraph
Hua Shang Bao
South China Morning Post
Wah Kiu Yat Po (Huaqiao Ribao)
Xin Dong Ya
Zheng Bao

Nationalist China
Da Gong Bao, Chungking
Shijie Zhanwang, Hankou

Other
Eastern World, London
The Egyptian Gazette, Cairo

post-1950

Hong Kong
Da Hua
Da Ren
Far Eastern Economic Review
Far Eastern Economic Review Yearbook
Hong Kong Inc.
South China Morning Post
Sunday Morning Post
Zhanggu Yuekan

London
Daily Telegraph
The Economist
Independent
Observer

Tokyo
Ajia Keizai
Aji-ken Nyusu (newsletter of the Ajia Keizai Kenkyujo)

4. Correspondence and diaries

Clarabut, Cecil (ed.), *Some Letters of Stella Benson 1928–1933*, Libra Press, Hong Kong, 1978.
Correspondence of David MacDougall, MacDougall papers, Rhodes House.
Correspondence relating to Sir Robert Kotewall, in the private papers of Mrs Helen Zimmern, Hong Kong.
Diary of Constance Murray, Rhodes House, Oxford.
Internment diary of Franklin Gimson, Rhodes House.
Internment diary of Dr Kenneth Uttley, Rhodes House.
Internment diary of Assistant Superintendent Lance Searle, Rhodes House.
Letter of Dr Kenneth Uttley to Mrs Helen Uttley, undated, around 18 August 1945, Uttley papers, Rhodes House.
War Diary of the Hong Kong Police, compiled by Superintendent L. H. C. Calthrop and with a preface by Police Commissioner John Pennefather-Evans, 29 October 1942, Hong Kong Police Archives, Police Training School, Wong Chuk Hang, Hong Kong

5. Reports

Hong Kong Government Administration Reports: Secretariat for Chinese Affairs, 1934–39.

Reports of the Inspector-General of Police for 1930–36.

Reports of the Commissioner of Police for 1937–39.

Report by Assistant Superintendent Lance Searle, Commander, Sub-Area no. 4, on Police Action during period covering from 0200 hours on 8 December 1941 to 0200 hours on 12 December 1941, 29 August 1942, Searle papers, Rhodes House.

Interim Report on the Hong Kong Police by Police Commissioner John Pennefather-Evans, 1 October 1943, Hong Kong Police Archives.

Annual Report on the Hong Kong Police Force, 1946–47.

Reports of the Commissioner of Police for 1947–49.

Annual Reports of the Registrar-General's Department, 1963 to 1979.

Annual Report of the Hong Kong Government, 1948.

Hong Kong General Chamber of Commerce Report for the Year 1947.

Koa Kikan, *Konkyo Chugoku shinshiroku*, 10 January 1942, in Kobayashi Hideo, '*Taiheiyo sensoka no Honkon: Honkon gunsei no tenkai*', published in Komazawa University, Tokyo Economic Association *Keizaigaku Ronshu*, no. 3, December 1994, pp. 255–9.

Koa Kikan gyomu hodo (Koa Kikan Work Report), no. 2, 10 February 1942, in Kobayashi, '*Taiheiyo sensoka no Honkon*', pp. 250–5.

Major-General Yazaki Kanju, '*Honkon tochi hosaku shiken*', February 1942, in Kobayashi, '*Taiheiyo sensoka no Honkon*', pp. 236–49.

6. Memoirs

Bard, Solomon, 'Mount Davis and Sham Shui Po: A Medical Officer with the Volunteers', in Clifford Matthews and Oswald Cheung (eds) *Dispersal and Renewal: Hong Kong University during the War Years*, Hong Kong University Press, 1998, pp. 193–202.

Bentley, Man Wah Leung, 'Remembrances of Times Past: the University and Chungking', in Matthews and Cheung (eds), *Dispersal and Renewal*, pp. 105–7.

Buping Shanren ('Unquiet Hermit'), *Xianggang lunxian huiyilu*, Xiangjiang Publishing House, Hong Kong, 1978.

Chan Chak, '*Xiezhu Xianggang kangzhan ji shuai Ying jun tuwei zong baogao*', in *Zhanggu Yuekan*, no. 4, December 1971, pp. 14–21.

Chen Jitang, '*Xianggang tuoxian ji*', in Ye Dewei et al. (eds), *Xianggang lunxian shi*, Wide Angle Press, Hong Kong, 1984, pp. 301–15.

Chen, Percy, *China Called Me: My Life inside the Chinese Revolution*, Little, Brown & Co., Boston and Toronto, 1979.

Cheng, Irene, *Clara Ho Tung: A Hong Kong Lady, Her Family and Her Times*, Chinese University of Hong Kong, 1976.

Davis, Patrick, 'Troubled Loyalties: Marginal Experiences in Bangkok, Saigon and Batavia, 1945–46' in *International Studies*, 1991, no. III, pp. 53–75, Suntory-Toyota Centre for Economics and Related Disciplines, London School of Economics.

Di Chen, '*Huiyizhong de yi nian*', in *Xin Dong Ya*, vol. 1, no. 5, December 1942, pp. 69–76.

Evans, Dafydd Emrys, 'Prologue: A Cosy Hillside Campus', in Matthews and Cheung (eds), *Dispersal and Renewal*, pp. 1–5.

———, 'The Test of War', in Matthews and Cheung (eds), *Dispersal and Renewal*, pp. 169–75.

Fan Jiping, '*Xianggang zhi zhan huiyilu*', in *Da Ren*, no. 8, December 1970, pp. 2–10.

———, '*Shengli zhi chu zai Xianggang*', in *Da Ren*, no. 16, August 1971, pp. 23–4.

Fujii Kingo, '*Xianggang bianjing chongpo ji*' (Chinese translation by Lu Yu), in *Xin Dong Ya*, vol. 1, no. 1, August 1942, p. 85.

Fujiwara Iwaichi, Lieutenant-General, *F. Kikan: Japanese Army Intelligence Operations in South-east Asia during World War II*, translated by Akashi Yoji, Heinemann Asia, Hong Kong, Kuala Lumpur and Singapore, 1983.

Gimson, Franklin, Internment in Hong Kong, summary, Gimson papers, Rhodes House.

———, Hong Kong Reclaimed, Gimson papers, Rhodes House.

Gittins, Jean, *Eastern Windows, Western Skies*, South China Morning Post Ltd., Hong Kong, 1969.

———, *Stanley: Behind Barbed Wire*, Hong Kong University Press, 1982.

Grantham, Alexander, *Via Ports: From Hong Kong to Hong Kong*, Hong Kong University Press, 1965.

Guan Bee Ong, 'Dispersal and Renewal: Hong Kong University Medical and Health Services', in Matthews and Cheung (eds), *Dispersal and Renewal*, pp. 389–95.

Guest, Captain Freddie, *Escape from the Bloodied Sun*, Jarrolds, London, 1956.

Hahn, Emily, *China to Me*, Blakiston, Philadelphia, 1944.

———, *Hong Kong Holiday*, Doubleday, New York, 1946.

Harcourt, Rear Admiral Cecil, lecture on the British Military Administration of Hong Kong to the Royal Central Asian Society, London, 13 November 1946, published in *Journal of the Royal Central Asian Society*, vol. 34, 1947, pp. 7–18.

Harrop, Phyllis, *Hong Kong Incident*, Eyre & Spottiswoode, London, 1943.

Hirano Shigeru, 'Women zai Xianggang de kezheng yu baoxing', in Ling Ming (trans.), *Riben zhanfan huiyilu*, Four Seas Publishing House, Hong Kong, 1971, pp. 47–58.

Huang Hsing Tsung, 'Pursuing Science in Hong Kong, China and the West', in Matthews and Cheung (eds), *Dispersal and Renewal*, pp. 127–42.

Huang, Rayson, 'Full Circle: University Life in Hong Kong and Beyond', in Matthews and Cheung (eds), *Dispersal and Renewal*, pp. 115–25.

Ishita Ichiro, 'Xianggang gonglüe zhan ji' (Chinese translation by He Bingren), in *Xin Dong Ya*, vol. 1, no. 1, August 1942, pp. 86–90.

Jiang Shui and Li Zhaopei, 'Yingguo junguan yingjiu ji', in Xu Yueqing (ed.), *Huoyue zai Xiangjiang*, Joint Publishing Co., Hong Kong, 1993, pp. 42–8.

King, Gordon, 'An Episode in the History of the University', in Matthews and Cheung (eds), *Dispersal and Renewal*, pp. 85–103.

Kipling, Rudyard, *From Sea to Sea*, Scribner's, New York, 1906.

Lee Kuan Yew, *The Singapore Story*, Times Editions, Singapore, 1998.

Leiper, G. A., *A Yen for My Thoughts*, South China Morning Post Ltd., Hong Kong, 1982.

Li Shu-fan, *Hong Kong Surgeon*, Gollancz, London, 1964.

Liang Yen, *The House of the Golden Dragons*, Souvenir Press, London, 1961.

Lu Ganzhi, 'Xianggang de chentong wangshi', in *Zhanggu Yuekan*, no. 6, February 1972, pp. 56–7.

Mackenzie, Norman, 'An Academic Odyssey: A Professor in Five Continents (Part 2)', in Matthews and Cheung (eds), *Dispersal and Renewal*, pp. 179–91.

Matthews, Clifford, 'Life Experiences: From Star Ferry to Stardust', in Matthews and Cheung (eds), *Dispersal and Renewal*, pp. 227–46.

Mellor, Bernard, 'A New Start', in Matthews and Cheung (eds), *Dispersal and Renewal*, pp. 425–40.

———, 'In India, in China and Twice in Hong Kong', in Matthews and Cheung (eds), *Dispersal and Renewal*, pp. 345–73.

———, 'Strains of War and The Links Break', in Matthews and Cheung (eds), *Dispersal and Renewal*, pp. 61–81.

Mishima Bunpei, 'Chizhu youju ji' (Chinese translation by Shen Yixu), in *Xin Dong Ya*, vol. 1, no. 1, August 1942, pp. 93–4, 109.

Nationalist Party Headquarters in Hong Kong and Macao, *Gang Ao xunguo lieshi jiniance*, 1946.

Ozawa Seiichi, 'Diedu Xianggang zhi xing' (Chinese translation by Lü Fang), in *Shijie Zhanwang*, no. 1, Hankou, March 1938.

Priestwood, Gwen, *Through Japanese Barbed Wire*, D. Appleton-Century Company, New York and London, 1943.

Ride, Lindsay, 'The Test of War (Part 1)', in Matthews and Cheung (eds), *Dispersal and Renewal*, pp. 9–23.

Ryan, Fr. Thomas, SJ, *Jesuits under Fire in the Siege of Hong Kong, 1941*, Burns, Oates & Washbourne Ltd, London and Dublin, 1944.

Sa Kongliao, *Xianggang lunxian riji*, Beijing, 1985 (first edition Hong Kong, 1946).

Samejima Moritaka, *Xianggang huixiang ji* (Chinese translation by S. S. Kong), Chinese Christian Literature Council, Hong Kong, 1971.

Schofield, Walter, papers, Rhodes House.

Selwyn-Clarke, Sir Selwyn, *Footprints*, Sino-American Publishing Co., Hong Kong, 1975.

Shaftain, F. W., Rough Draft for Proposed Articles, Hong Kong Police Archives, G56 (4).

Tang Hai, 'Xianggang lunxian ji', in Ye Dewei et al. (eds) *Xianggang lunxian shi*, pp. 173–259.

Tao Xisheng, 'Chong di guo men', in Ye Dewei et al. (eds), *Xianggang lunxian shi*, pp. 317–38.

Thomas, Osler, 'With the BAAG in Wartime China', in Matthews and Cheung (eds), *Dispersal and Renewal*, pp. 313–34.

Waters, Dan, *Faces of Hong Kong*, Prentice Hall, London and New York, 1995.

Wedemeyer, Albert C., *Wedemeyer Reports!*, Henry Holt & Co., New York, 1958.

Wright-Nooth, George, *Prisoner of the Turnip-Heads: The Fall of Hong Kong and Imprisonment by the Japanese*, Leo Cooper, London, 1994.

Xia Yan, '*Liao Chengzhi zai Xianggang*', in Lu Yan et al. (eds), *Xianggang Zhanggu*, vol. VII, Wide Angle Press, Hong Kong, 1984, pp. 154–64.

Yu, Patrick, *A Seventh Child and the Law*, Hong Kong University Press, 1998.

———, 'Wartime Experiences in Hong Kong and China (Part 2)', in Matthews and Cheung (eds), *Dispersal and Renewal*, pp. 313–34.

Yu Shuheng, '*Taisi fuzhong de "Xianggang shi zhengfu": ji Xianggang lunxian qizhong yi miwen*', in *Da Hua*, no. 2, March 1966, pp. 3–4.

Zeng Hongwen, '*Chu jin Gang Jiu*', in Zeng Sheng et al., *Dong Jiang xinghuo*, Guangdong People's Publishing House, Guangzhou, 1983, pp. 37–43.

7. Interviews

Interviews conducted by author

Mr Okada Akira, Tokyo, 6 September 1995
Professor Charles Boxer, Little Gaddesden, Hertfordshire, 19 January 1994
Mme Cai Songying, veteran of the East River Column, Hong Kong, 24 June 1995
Mr Y. K. Chan, Hong Kong, 23 March 1995
Mr Andrew Choa, Hong Kong, 24 June 1995
Mr Jack Edwards, Hong Kong, 18 March 1998
Mrs Mary Goodban, Lincolnshire, 7 January 1994
Miss Emily Hahn, Little Gaddesden, Hertfordshire, 19 January 1994
Dr Stanley Ho Hung-sun, Hong Kong, 27 September 1995
Sir Y. K. Kan, Hong Kong, 24 May 1995
Professor Kobayashi Hideo, Tokyo, 18 July 1995
Mr Komari Yasuo, Tokyo, 29 July 1995
Mr Cyril Kotewall, Hong Kong, 26 June 1995
The Hon. W. S. Lau, Hong Kong, 8 June 1995
Mr Oda Takeo, Mount Nasu, 1 September 1995
Mr Sanada Iwasuke, Tokyo, 7 August 1995
Mr Rusy M. Shroff, Hong Kong, 30 October 1995
Mr Charles Sin, Hong Kong, 29 June 1995
Mrs Margaret Watson Sloss, Oxford, 3 March 1994
Mr Y. Yanagisawa, Hong Kong, 9 May 1995
Mrs Helen Zimmern, Hong Kong, 29 June 1995

Other interviews

Record of interview given by Fujita Ichiro in *Aji-ken Nyusu*, vol. 5, no. 10, October 1984, pp. 18–27.

Record of talk given by Fujita Ichiro to Japanese business colloquium in Hong Kong, 27 January 1989 in 'A Twenty-Year History of the Hong Kong Japanese Chamber of Commerce and Industry', pp. 113–122.

Transcript of interview conducted by Dr Steve Tsang with David MacDougall, 26 February 1987, Rhodes House.

Record of talk, 'My Hong Kong Connection', given by Ogawa Heishiro to students at Robert Black College, University of Hong Kong, in Tam Yue-him (ed.), *Hong Kong and Japan: Growing Cultural and Economic Interactions, 1845–1987*, 25th Anniversary Commemorative Volume of the Japan Society of Hong Kong, Hong Kong, 1988.

8. Other

Gunseika no Honkon, published by Toyo Keizaisha under the supervision of the Information Department of the Governor's Office, Hong Kong, 1944.

Regulations regarding the Duties of the Governor's Office of the Conquered Territory of Hong Kong, 4 October 1944.

Chiang Kai-shek, *China's Destiny*, (English edition), Roy Publishers, New York, 1947.

Secondary sources

Works of a secondary character which appeared at the time of the main events described in this book

d'Almada e Castro, Leo, 'Some Notes on the Portuguese in Hong Kong', *Instituto Portugues de Hong Kong, Boletim* no. 2, September 1949, pp. 265–76.

Bough, Henry, Reuters correspondent, Hong Kong, undated report, March 1946, in MacDougall papers, Rhodes House.

Churchill, Winston S., *The Second World War*, vol. III, *The Grand Alliance*, Cassell, London, 1950.

Clark, Russell S., *An End to Tears*, Peter Huston, Sydney, 1946.

Crow, Carl, *Handbook for China*, South China Morning Post Ltd, Shanghai, 1925.

Eitel, E. J., *Europe in China*, Oxford University Press, Hong Kong, 1983 (first edition 1895).

Heasman, Kathleen J., 'Japanese Financial and Economic Measures in Hong Kong (25 December 1941–June 1945)', in *Journal of the Hong Kong University Students' Union Economics Society*, 1957, pp. 65–92 (first prepared by the author during internment in Stanley camp and circulated privately in July 1945).

Ho, Stanley Dzu-fang, 'A Hundred Years of Hong Kong', unpublished PhD thesis, Princeton, 1946.

Ingrams, Harold, *Hong Kong*, HMSO, London, 1952.

Li Jinwei (ed.), *Xianggang bai nian shi*, South China Translation and Editing House, Hong Kong, 1948.

Pan Kongyan, '*Zhongzu qishi de bianlun*', in Li Jinwei (ed.), *Xianggang bai nian shi*, p. 53.

Sayer, G. R., *Hong Kong, 1862–1919: Years of Discretion*, Hong Kong University Press, 1975 (MS completed in 1939).

Tang Jianxun, *Zui xin Xianggang zhinan*, Man Wah Publishing House, Hong Kong, 1950.

Wang Tieya, '*Jiulong zujiedi wenti*', in Li Jinwei (ed.), *Xianggang bai nian shi*, p. 102.

Ward, Robert S., *Asia for the Asiatics? The Techniques of Japanese Occupation*, University of Chicago Press, 1945.

Woddis, H. C. K., 'Hong Kong and the East River Company', in *Eastern World*, vol. 3, no. 8, August 1949, pp. 10–11.

Wong Lin, '*Xin Xianggang de toushi*', in *Xin Dong Ya*, vol. 1, no. 1, August 1942, pp. 64–70.

Woo Sing-lim, Professor, *The Prominent Chinese in Hong Kong*, The Five Continents Book Co., Hong Kong, 1937.

Wood, Winifred, *A Brief History of Hong Kong*, South China Morning Post Ltd, Hong Kong, 1940.

Subsequent works

1. Books

Airlie, Shiona, *Thistle and Bamboo: The Life and Times of Sir James Stewart Lockhart*, Oxford University Press, Hong Kong, 1989.

Aldrich, Richard J., *Intelligence and the War against Japan: Britain, America and the Politics of Secret Service*, Cambridge University Press, 2000.

Allen, Louis, *The End of the War in Asia*, Hart-Davis, MacGibbon, London, 1976.

Baker, Carlos, *Ernest Hemingway: A Life Story*, Scribner's, New York, 1969.

Behr, Edward, *Hirohito: Behind the Myth*, Vintage Books, New York, 1990.

Bennett, J. W., Hobart, W. A. and Spitzer, J. P. (eds), *Intelligence and Cryptanalytic Activities of the Japanese during World War II*, Aegean Park Press, Laguna Hills, California, 1986.

Birch, Alan and Cole, Martin (eds), *Captive Christmas*, Heinemann Asia, 1979.

———, *Captive Years*, Heinemann Asia, 1982.

Blake, Robert, *Jardine Matheson: Traders of the Far East*, Weidenfeld and Nicolson, London, 1999.

Boeicho Boei Kenshusho (eds), *Senshi sosho, Honkon-Chosha sakusen*, Tokyo, 1971.

Bruce, Phillip, *Second to None: The Story of the Hong Kong Volunteers*, Oxford University Press, Hong Kong, 1991.

Carew, Tim, *The Fall of Hong Kong*, Anthony Blond, London, 1960.

Chan Lau Kit-ching, *China, Britain and Hong Kong*, Chinese University Press, Chinese University of Hong Kong, 1990.

Chang, Iris, *The Rape of Nanking: The Forgotten Holocaust of World War II*, Penguin, London, 1998.

Chang Jung with Halliday, Jon, *Mme Sun Yat-sen*, Penguin, London, 1986.

Ching, Frank, *The Li Dynasty: Hong Kong Aristocrats*, Oxford University Press, Hong Kong, 1999.

Cohen, Paul A., *Between Tradition and Modernity: Wang Tao and Reform in Late Ch'ing China*, Harvard University Press, Cambridge, Mass., 1974.

Coox, Alvin D., *Nomonhan: Japan against Russia, 1939* (2 vols.), Stanford University Press, 1986.

Cottrell, Robert, *The End of Hong Kong: The Secret Diplomacy of Imperial Retreat*, John Murray, London, 1993.

Elphick, Peter, *Singapore: The Pregnable Fortress, A Study in Deception, Discord and Desertion*, Hodder & Stoughton, London, 1995.

Endacott, G. B., *Hong Kong Eclipse*, edited with additional material by Alan Birch, Oxford University Press, Hong Kong, 1978.

Endacott, G. B. and Hinton, A., *Fragrant Harbour: A Short History of Hong Kong*, Oxford University Press, Hong Kong, 1962.

Faure, David, Hayes, James and Birch, Alan (eds), *From Village to City: Studies in the Traditional Roots of Hong Kong Society*, Hong Kong University Press, 1984.

Faure, David (ed.), *History of Hong Kong 1842–1984*, Tamarind Books, Hong Kong and London, 1995.

Gang Jiu Duli Dadui shi Editorial and Writing Group, *Gang Jiu Duli Dadui shi*, Guangdong People's Publishing House, Guangzhou, 1989.

Gildea, Robert, *Marianne in Chains: In Search of the German Occupation, 1940–45*, Macmillan, London, 2002.

Gillingham, Paul, *At the Peak: Hong Kong between the Wars*, Macmillan, London, 1983.

Gleason, Gene, *Hong Kong*, Robert Hale, London, 1964.

Grant, Joy, *Stella Benson – A Biography*, Macmillan, London, 1987.

Hall, Peter, *In the Web*, privately published by author, Heswall, 1992.

Hayashi Saburo in collaboration with Alvin D. Coox, *Kogun: The Japanese Army in the Pacific War*, US Marine Corps Association, Quantico, Virginia, 1989 (first edition 1959).

Hoe, Susanna, *The Private Life of Old Hong Kong: Western Women in the British Colony, 1841–1941*, Oxford University Press, Hong Kong, 1991.

Hoyt, Edwin P., *Japan's War: The Great Pacific Conflict*, Da Capo Press, New York, 1986.

Hsu Long-hsuen and Chang Ming-kai (eds), *History of the Sino-Japanese War (1937–1945)*, Chung Wu Publishing Co., Taipei, 1971.

Keswick, Maggie, *The Thistle and the Jade: A Celebration of 150 Years of Jardine Matheson & Co.*, Octopus Books, London, 1982.

King, Frank H. H., *The History of the Hongkong and Shanghai Banking Corporation*, vol. III, *The Hongkong Bank between the Wars and the Bank Interned, 1919–45 – Retreat from Grandeur*, Cambridge University Press, 1988.

———, *The History of the Hongkong and Shanghai Banking Corporation*, vol. IV, *The Hongkong Bank in the Period of Development and Nationalism, 1941–84: From Regional Bank to Multinational Group*, Cambridge University Press, 1991.

King, Sam, *Tiger Balm King: The Life and Times of Aw Boon Haw*, Times Books International, Singapore, 1992.

Ko Tim Keung and Wordie, Jason, *Ruins of War: A Guide to Hong Kong's Battlefields and Wartime Sites*, Joint Publishing (HK) Co., Hong Kong, 1996.

Kobayashi Hideo and Shibata Yoshimasa, *Nippon gunseika no Honkon*, Shakai Hyoronsha, Tokyo, 1996.

Kwan Lai-hung, *Ri zhan shiqi de Xianggang*, Joint Publishing (HK) Co., Hong Kong, 1993.

Lindsay, Oliver, *The Lasting Honour*, Hamish Hamilton, London, 1978.

———, *At the Going Down of the Sun*, Hamish Hamilton, London, 1981.

Luff, John, *The Hidden Years*, South China Morning Post Ltd, Hong Kong, 1967.

Martin, Brian G., *The Shanghai Green Gang: Politics and Organized Crime, 1919–1937*, University of California Press, Berkeley, 1996.

Matthews, Clifford and Cheung, Oswald (eds), *Dispersal and Renewal: Hong Kong University during the War Years*, Hong Kong University Press, 1998.

Miners, Norman, *Hong Kong under Imperial Rule, 1912–1941*, Oxford University Press, Hong Kong, 1987.

Morris, Jan, *Hong Kong: Epilogue to an Empire*, Penguin, London, 1993 (first edition 1989).

Mushkat, Miron, *The Economic Future of Hong Kong*, Lynne Riener Publishers, Boulder and London/Hong Kong University Press, 1990.

Nakajima Mineo, *Honkon: utsuriyuku toshi kokka*, Jiji Tsushinsha, Tokyo, 1985.

Nolan, Liam, *Small Man of Nanataki*, Peter Davies, London, 1966.

Pan, Lynn, *Sons of the Yellow Emperor: The Story of the Overseas Chinese*, Secker & Warburg, London, 1990.

Paton, David, *R. O.: The Life and Times of Bishop Ronald Hall of Hong Kong*, The Diocese of Hong Kong and Macao and the Hong Kong Diocesan Association, 1985.

Patrikeeff, Felix, *Mouldering Pearl: Hong Kong at the Crossroads*, Hodder & Stoughton, London, 1990 (first edition 1989).

Peattie, Mark R., *Ishiwara Kanji and Japan's Confrontation with the West*, Princeton University Press, 1975.

Pope-Hennessy, James, *Half-Crown Colony: A Hong Kong Notebook*, Jonathan Cape, London, 1969.

Rafferty, Kevin, *City on the Rocks: Hong Kong's Uncertain Future*, Viking, London, 1989.

Rees, Laurence, *Horror in the East*, BBC, 2001.

Ride, Edwin, *British Army Aid Group: Hong Kong Resistance 1942–1945*, Oxford University Press, Hong Kong, 1981.
Scott, Ian, *Political Change and the Crisis of Legitimacy in Hong Kong*, Hurst & Co., London, 1989.
Seagrave, Sterling, *The Soong Dynasty*, Corgi Books, London, 1996 (first edition 1985).
Sinn, Elizabeth, *Power and Charity: The Early History of the Tung Wah Hospital, Hong Kong*, Oxford University Press, Hong Kong, 1989.
———, *Growing with Hong Kong: The Bank of East Asia 1919–1994*, The Bank of East Asia Ltd, Hong Kong, 1994.
Spurr, Russell, *Excellency*, FormAsia, Hong Kong, 1995.
Takagi Kenichi, Kobayashi Hideo et al., *Xianggang junpiao yu zhanhou buchang* (Chinese translation by Wu Hui), Ming Pao, Hong Kong, 1995.
Tam Yue-him (ed.), *Hong Kong and Japan: Growing Cultural and Economic Interactions, 1845–1987*, 25th Anniversary Commemorative Volume of the Japan Society of Hong Kong, 1988.
Taylor, A. J. P., *Europe, Grandeur and Decline*, Pelican Books, London, 1967.
Tsang, Steve Yui-sang, *Democracy Shelved: Great Britain, China and Attempts at Constitutional Reform in Hong Kong, 1945–1952*, Oxford University Press, Hong Kong, 1988.
———, *Hong Kong: An Appointment with China*, I. B. Tauris, London, 1997.
Tse Wing-kwong, *Zhanshi Ri jun zai Xianggang baoxing*, Ming Pao, Hong Kong, 1991.
———, *San nian ling bage yue de kunnan*, Ming Pao, Hong Kong, 1994.
———, *Xianggang kang Ri fengyun lu*, Cosmos Books, Hong Kong, 1995.
———, *Xianggang lunxian*, Commercial Press, Hong Kong, 1995.
Wasserstein, Bernard, *Secret War in Shanghai: Treachery, Subversion and Collaboration in the Second World War*, Profile Books, London, 1998.
Welsh, Frank, *A History of Hong Kong*, HarperCollins, London, 1997 (first edition 1993).
White, Barbara-Sue, *Turbans and Traders: Hong Kong's Indian Communities*, Oxford University Press, Hong Kong, 1994.
Wilson, Dick, *When Tigers Fight: The Story of the Sino-Japanese War 1937–45*, Hutchinson, London, 1982.
———, *Hong Kong! Hong Kong!*, Unwin Hyman, London, 1990.
Wong Siu-lun, *Emigrant Entrepreneurs – Shanghai Industrialists in Hong Kong*, Oxford University Press, Hong Kong, 1988.
Woodburn Kirby, S., *The War Against Japan*, vol. I, *The Loss of Singapore*, HMSO, London, 1957.
———, *The War Against Japan*, vol. V, *The Surrender of Japan*, HMSO, London, 1969.
Wordie, Jason, *Streets: Exploring Hong Kong Island*, Hong Kong University Press, 2002.
Xu Yueqing (ed.) *Huoyue zai Xiangjiang*, Joint Publishing (HK) Co., Hong Kong, 1993.
Ye Dewei et al. (eds), *Xianggang lunxian shi*, Wide Angle Press, Hong Kong, 1984.
Yeh Wen-hsin (ed.), *Wartime Shanghai*, Routledge, London and New York, 1998.
Yuan Bangjian, *Xianggang shilüe*, Zhongliu Publishing House, Hong Kong, 1988.
Zhang Sheng, *Xianggang hei shehui huodong zhen xiang*, Cosmos Books, Hong Kong, 1979.
Zhang Zhongli, Chen Zengnian and Yao Xinrong, *The Swire Group in Old China*, Shanghai People's Publishing House, Shanghai, 1991.

2. Unpublished dissertations

Catron, Gary Wayne, 'China and Hong Kong, 1945–1967', unpublished PhD thesis, Harvard, 1971.
Fisher, Stephen Frederick, 'Eurasians in Hong Kong: A Sociological Study of a Marginal Group', unpublished MPhil. thesis, University of Hong Kong, 1975.

3. Articles and chapters

Chan Lau Kit-ching, 'The Hong Kong Question during the Pacific War', *Journal of Imperial and Commonwealth History*, vol. II, 1973–4, pp. 56–78.
———, 'The United States and the Question of Hong Kong', *Journal of the Hong Kong Branch of the Royal Asiatic Society*, vol. 19, 1979, pp. 1–20.
Chen Liwen, '*Kangzhan qijian Zhongguo feichu bupingdeng tiaoyue zhi nuli*', paper contributed to '*Kangzhan jianguo ji Taiwan guangfu*', ROC Third Historical Seminar, Taipei, 19–21 October 1995.
Cheng, T. C., 'Chinese Unofficial Members of the Legislative and Executive Councils in Hong Kong up to 1941', *Journal of the Hong Kong Branch of the Royal Asiatic Society*, vol. 9, 1969, pp. 7–30.
Crowley, James B., 'A New Asian Order: Some Notes on Pre-War Japanese Nationalism', in Bernard S. Silberman and Harry D. Harootunian, *Japan in Crisis: Essays on Taisho Democracy*, Princeton, NJ, 1974, pp. 270–98.
Faure, David, 'Sai Kung: The Making of the District and its Experience during World War II', *Journal of the Hong Kong Branch of the Royal Asiatic Society*, vol. 22, 1982, pp. 161–216.

Fujii Hiroaki, 'Japan and Hong Kong in Historical Perspective', in Tam Yue-him (ed.), *Hong Kong and Japan: Growing Cultural and Economic Interactions*, pp. 103–6.

Hayes, James, 'The Nature of Village Life', in Faure, Hayes and Birch (eds) *From Village to City*, pp. 55–72.

'The Ho Tung Saga (Part 1)', *Hong Kong Inc.*, March 1990, pp. 96–109.

'The Ho Tung Saga (Part 2)', *Hong Kong Inc.*, April 1990, pp. 86–101.

Kanto Gakuin University, *Nature-People-Society: Science and the Humanities*, no. 31, July 2001, article on 'British War Crimes Trials of Japanese'.

Katsumi Usui, 'The Politics of War', in James William Morley (ed.), *The China Quagmire: Japan's Expansion on the Asian Continent 1933–1941*, Columbia University Press, New York, 1983, pp. 309–435.

Kobayashi Hideo, '*Taiheiyo sensoka no Honkon: Honkon gunsei no tenkai*', published in Komazawa University, Tokyo, Economic Association, *Keizaigaku Ronshu*, vol. 26, no. 3, December 1994, pp. 209–81.

Kwan Lai-hung, 'The Charitable Activities of Local Chinese Organizations during the Japanese Occupation of Hong Kong, December 1941–August 1945', in Faure, Hayes and Birch (eds), *From Village to City*, pp. 178–90.

Lam Hui Kong-wai, Jane, 'The Japan Society of Hong Kong, A Historical Account 1962–1987', in Tam Yue-him (ed.) *Hong Kong and Japan: Growing Cultural and Economic Interactions*, pp. 81–7.

Lane, Kevin P., 'The Nationalist Government and the Struggle for Hong Kong's Return', in David Faure (ed.), *History of Hong Kong 1842–1984*, pp. 93–110.

'The Lee Empire', *Hong Kong Inc.*, January 1990, pp. 74–89.

Leeming, Frank, 'The Earlier Industrialization of Hong Kong', *Modern Asian Studies*, vol. 9, 3, 1975, pp. 337–42.

Lethbridge, Henry J., 'The Best of Both Worlds?', *FEER*, 10 October 1968, pp. 128–30.

———, 'Hong Kong under Japanese Occupation: Changes in Social Structure', in I. C. Jarvie and Joseph Agassi (eds), *Hong Kong: A Society in Transition*, Routledge & Kegan Paul, London 1969, pp. 77–127.

———, 'The District Watch Committee: "The Chinese Executive Council of Hong Kong"', *Journal of the Hong Kong Branch of the Royal Asiatic Society*, vol. 11, 1971, pp. 116–41.

———, 'Caste, Class and Race in Hong Kong before the Japanese Occupation', in Henry J. Lethbridge (ed.), *Hong Kong: Stability and Change*, Oxford University Press, Hong Kong, 1978, pp. 163–88.

'The Lo Dynasty', *Hong Kong Inc.*, February 1990, pp. 74–84.

Miners, Norman, 'The Attempt to Assassinate the Governor in 1912', *Journal of the Hong Kong Branch of the Royal Asiatic Society*, vol. 22, 1982, pp. 279–84.

———, 'The Localization of the Hong Kong Police Force, 1842–1947', *Journal of Imperial and Commonwealth History*, vol. XVIII, no. 3, October 1990, pp. 296–315.

Nakajima Mineo, 'The Hong Kong Agreement and its Impact on the International Position of Japan', in Jürgen Domes and Yu-ming Shaw (eds), *Hong Kong: A Chinese and International Concern*, Westview Press, Boulder and London, 1988, pp. 196–202.

Onoe Etsuzo, '*Honkon no chu no Nihon*', in *Ajia Keizai*, vol. 1, no. 3, September 1960, pp. 104–7.

Peattie, Mark R., '*Nanshin*: The "Southward Advance" 1931–1941 as a Prelude to the Japanese Occupation of South-east Asia', in Peter Duus, Ramon H. Myers and Mark R. Peattie (eds), *The Japanese Wartime Empire*, Princeton University Press, 1996, pp. 189–242.

Pritchard, R. John, 'The Nature and Significance of British Post-War Trials of Japanese War Criminals', *Proceedings of the British Association for Japanese Studies*, vol. 2, 1977, pp. 189–219.

Ren Wenzheng, '*Shijiu shiji Gang Ri jiaotong wanglai shulüe*', in Tam Yue-him (ed.), *Hong Kong and Japan: Growing Cultural and Economic Interactions*, pp. 107–13.

Segal, Gerald, draft paper, 'The Fate of Hong Kong', 1991.

Shaw Yu-ming, 'An ROC View of the Hong Kong Issue', in Domes and Shaw (eds), *Hong Kong: A Chinese and International Concern*, pp. 95–109.

Snow, Philip, 'Nomonhan: The Unknown Victory', *History Today*, July 1990.

Sweeting, Anthony, 'Controversy over the Reopening of the University of Hong Kong, 1942–48', in Matthews and Cheung (eds), *Dispersal and Renewal*, pp. 397–424.

Tam Yue-him, '*Xianggang Riben guanxi da shi nianbiao chu gao (1845–1945)*', in Tam Yue-him (ed.) *Hong Kong and Japan: Growing Cultural and Economic Interactions*, pp. 165–6.

Tsang, Steve Yui-sang, '*Taipingyang zhanzheng qijian Yingguo dui Xianggang zhengce miwen*', in *Xianggang Zhanggu*, vol. IX, Wide Angle Press, Hong Kong, 1985, pp. 90–102.

———, '*Jiang Jieshi weihe bu shouhui Xianggang*', in *Xianggang Zhanggu*, vol. X, Wide Angle Press, Hong Kong, 1985, pp. 113–27.

Wong Siu-lun, 'The Migration of Shanghainese Entrepreneurs to Hong Kong', in Faure, Hayes and Birch (eds), *From Village to City*, pp. 206–27.

Ye Dewei, '*Xianggang chongguang*', in Ye Dewei et al. (eds), *Xianggang lunxian shi*, pp. 160–1.

——, '*Zhanhou de huifu gongzuo*', in Ye Dewei et al. (eds), *Xianggang lunxian shi*, pp. 162–71.

'*Yuanzhu Ying Jun Fuwutuan*', extract from *Gang Jiu Duli Dadui shi*, chapter 7, in Xu Yueqing (ed.), *Huoyue zai Xiangjiang*, Joint Publishing (HK) Co., Hong Kong 1993, pp. 49–51.

Zhong Zi, '*Dong Jiang Zongdui yingjiu guoji youren ji qi yingxiang*', in *Guangdong wenshi ziliao*, vol. 44, *Xianggang yi pie*, Guangdong People's Publishing House, Guangzhou, 1985, pp. 211–18.

Zhou Pinjing et al., '*Cong Xianggang baozhang kan shuibianzhong de Riben xingxiang*', in Tam Yue-him (ed.), *Hong Kong and Japan: Growing Cultural and Economic Interactions*, pp. 226–44.

4. Other

Lecture given by Professor Ian Nish, London School of Economics to Pacific War Conference held at the Imperial War Museum, London, 5 December 1991.

Coox, Alvin D. 'The Unfought War: Japan 1941–1942', Fifth University Research Lecture, San Diego State University, San Diego State University Press, 1992.

Lecture given by Mr S. J. Chan at the Hong Kong Museum of History, 18 October 1995.

Under the Rising Sun, television documentary shown on TVB Pearl, Hong Kong, 13 December 1991.

Index